Religion • *Art and Beauty* • *Morality*
Truth and Illusion • *Music* • *The Germans*
Famous Men • *History* • *Psychology*
The Greeks • *The Spirit of Modernity*
Aristocratic Radicalism • *Autobiography*

The selections in this anthology cover a
vast range. In this book the reader will
find contradiction, ambivalence, ambiguity. But he will also find the insight, the brilliant prose style, the often
mordant wit, the impassioned attempt
to create human values in a post-
Christian world which have made
Nietzsche one of the most relevant of
philosophers for contemporary man. He
represents an intellectual force we must
seek to understand in order to comprehend not only the age in which we live,
but our very selves as well.

The Philosophy of
NIETZSCHE

Edited and with an Introduction by
GEOFFREY CLIVE

A MERIDIAN CLASSIC
NEW AMERICAN LIBRARY

NEW YORK AND SCARBOROUGH, ONTARIO

Introduction Copyright © 1965 by Geoffrey Clive

Library of Congress Catalog Card Number: 84-60054

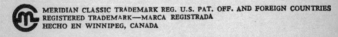 MERIDIAN CLASSIC TRADEMARK REG. U.S. PAT. OFF. AND FOREIGN COUNTRIES
REGISTERED TRADEMARK—MARCA REGISTRADA
HECHO EN WINNIPEG, CANADA

SIGNET, SIGNET CLASSIC, MENTOR, PLUME, MERIDIAN AND NAL
BOOKS *are published by New American Library,*
1633 Broadway, New York, New York 10019

FIRST MERIDIAN CLASSIC PRINTING, 1984

1 2 3 4 5 6 7 8 9

PRINTED IN CANADA

For *John Clive*

CONTENTS

CONTENTS

Introduction

Nietzsche belongs among the most ambiguous and ambivalent thinkers of modern times. The objects of his hostility offer the best clue to his major concerns just as, conversely, his intense affinities almost invariably suggest those opposites which enthralled his imagination. Whether it be his religious preoccupation with the eclipse of God, his preposterous assessment of Bizet's *Carmen* as the greatest opera ever written, or his transcendence as a visionary and poet of the very Enlightenment mechanism he seems to have espoused as a critic of traditional metaphysics, again and again the advocate of the Superman uses his strident voice to describe the suffering of finite human beings. His dazzling psychological insights and his devastating destruction of cant are in constant tension with his aim to overcome nihilism and to save the modern soul not only from the idolatry of false prophets but also from the tyranny of absolute cognition yielding a meaningless universe in which to be alive. As an Apollonian, Nietzsche may be compared with Voltaire's shredding the errors of his day, but he was also a highly self-conscious Dionysian in accord with Kierkegaard's injunction that "truth is subjectivity." There is no simple Nietzsche in any single tradition except for those who cannot bear to face, as Nietzsche did, the terrors of existence in their awesome concreteness.

THE AMBIVALENT NIETZSCHE

Throughout his life Nietzsche was subject to migraine headaches and diverse psychosomatic disorders which in his forty-fifth year culminated in an irreversible breakdown. But Nietzsche's writings contain numerous passages conveying an almost vindictive contempt for the weak and their need for help, a need his own letters dramatize on many occasions. A similar ambivalence marks his attitude toward the Jews. On the one hand, he singles them out for their intelligence; on the other, insofar as they helped set the stage for the Christian "slave morality," he blames them for promoting a distorted egalitarianism. Particularly his attitude toward his fellow Germans remained ambivalent. At times his contempt is a clear case of projected self-hatred. What Nietzsche had done was to translate his disgust with German middle-class philistinism and chauvinism into a series of statements, many of which were meant to give offense rather than to depict the facts. Thus, he would have liked to pass himself off as a Pole, he praises the Italian and French schools of composition to the sky, and, in typical German fashion, he idealizes "the land where the lemon trees bloom" and an artist's life in Paris. No derogation of his penetrating critique of things German is intended in pointing out that this incorrigible enthusiast for *Tristan und Isolde* embraced extremes with an abandon that Carmen herself would have been hard put to comprehend.

Another *bête noire* of his was socialism. It was his faith in the moral inequality of man and in the inferiority of woman which prevented him from finding an echo for his echoless voice among the left-wing European intelligentsia. They were ready as he was to battle for a "transvaluation of values" which would constitute a clean break with established traditions. Nietzsche's radicalism, however, was too individualistic to fit any theory of society. His celebrated declaration of "God's death" was more Dostoyevskian than Voltairean. Like the Russian novelist he realized that enlightened man, too, cannot live without faith or hope. His particular problem as an atheist was the justification of a set of illusions compatible with the shifting claims of scientific knowledge. He never saw antitheism in itself as offering adequate grounds for human liberation and rejoicing, though admittedly his rejection of Christianity went far beyond Kierkegaard's crucial distinction between nineteenth-century Christendom—which Nietzsche also despised—and the pristine faith of Jesus and His disciples. The point to note is that for Nietzsche the "death of God" was at one and the same time a cultural disaster and a philosophical blessing. His reflections on religion disclose a religious passion which his most intense diatribes only tend to enhance. Nietzsche was divided, finally, between a Faustian antipathy to close scholarship as usurping the "greenness of life" and an admiration for the exact sciences as emancipating mankind from its history of ignorance and partial truth. Side by side in his works can be found the sharpest strictures against Socrates for being the first great Athenian to divest man of some of his most cherished and necessary illusions combined with the highest regard for the spirit of *Wissenschaft* and ceaseless inquiry. When immediately after his collapse he wrote Jacob Burckhardt that perhaps it would have been better had he become a historian, he placed his principle of *amor fati* (the love of fate or eternal return) in its proper dialectical setting—Nietzsche's openness to an authentic future which some day would represent a truly new order.

All undialectical interpretations of Nietzsche break down as a result of their failure to see him in his love-hate relationship to himself. It was his special genius to write most perceptively about what he knew firsthand: the waverings of the modern soul. Herein also lay his exceptional courage. He did not spare himself (as Goethe had done deliberately) in exposing the antinomies of "man the rebel" against each and every authority handed down from the past. With zeal amounting to recklessness Nietzsche sought out the *Hintergedanken*—the disturbing forces concealed, so to speak, behind our ostensible explanations masquerading as justifications. He knew that honesty and truthfulness were not enough unless anchored in some ideals beyond the reach of analytic dissection. But how was the critical intelligence to light upon such ends unaided? His glorification of action, force, and vitality is no less vulnerable to scepticism than Christ's advocacy of faith, hope, and compassion. The poet manqué of *Thus Spake Zarathustra* is as suspect a witness to the "genealogy of morals" as the narrator of *The Gospel According to John,* who can be relied upon to give a faithful account of Christ's existential actions and choices. Not only did Nietzsche change his mind about many things but all too often he was of two minds about the same thing. Nor did he hesitate to state in an apothegm what appeared inconsistent with his wider view. He was more honest than most philosophers in sharing with his readers shadow reflections as they intruded on his overt formulations. He spoke in many voices, but in all of them he emerges as a modern foe of modernity. His idealization of the pre-Socratics (subsequently taken up by Heidegger) is no less romantic than his longing for a high civilization freed from civilization's discontents (Freud).

As an Apollonian champion of Dionysos, a philosopher in a rage with the history of western philosophy, or as a classical philologist disillusioned by some of the best scholarship of his day, Nietzsche's lot was to argue against himself, to turn himself inside out much as Freud was to do when he embarked on his self-analysis. To put it another way, Nietzsche could not accept the idea of fulfillment. His chronic dissatisfaction with the way things had gotten to be is characteristic of the very consciousness he set out to annihilate: the modern consciousness self-referentially ironic even in its moments of supreme illumination. Whether Nietzsche in fact achieved such transcendence is doubtful. But that he enjoyed moments of surpassing intellectual illumination would appear to be beyond dispute.

NIETZSCHE AND THE TRADITION

If philosophizing in a tradition confined to highly selected writings from Aristotle, Thomas Aquinas, David Hume, Kant, and J. S. Mill be a necessary condition for doing contemporary analytic philosophy, Nietzsche was not an "analyst," though he too broke with Platonic-Christian-Idealist metaphysics in order to see things hardheadedly. He, however, in addition to being a prophet of disaster in the twentieth century, steeped himself in the history of philosophy as affording him significant points of departure for the development of his own distinctive perspective. Furthermore, as a philosopher of culture and a genuine "outsider" to boot, he addressed himself to the kind of substantive issues with which the major thinkers have always grappled, wrongheadedly or otherwise. He read widely and fondly in the French moralists. Pascal's psychological genius captivated him, while his Jansenism repelled him. What drew him to Socrates was his irony. On the other hand, he protested against the Socratic intellectualization of life and held Socrates largely responsible for the destruction of the tragic sense in the Platonic and Aristotelian systems. His mechanism closely resembles that of Thomas Hobbes, especially in its commitment to struggle as the natural state of the human condition. With Spinoza he shares a commitment to ateleology, free thought, and the denial of free will. The refined hedonism of Epicurus had a considerable impact on his celebration of life and joy, while his *amor fati* reflects not a little his attachment to the Greek tragedians. Clearly, Nietzsche picked and chose among the Greeks (and elsewhere) not to reduce the history of philosophy to a few trivial if presumably perennial problems nor as an antiquarian in the interest of completeness but rather to single out critical turning points in the making of the modern mind—his overriding concern as a creative thinker.

Coming closer to his own times, he was much taken by Stendhal's demythologization of the human soul to animal spiritedness and found himself agreeing with the Marquis de Sade that the problems of mankind are basically physiological. Though he never grew weary of castigating the nineteenth century for its fashionable pessimism, his affinities for Heine and Schopenhauer were not unrelated to their gloomy prognoses of the future. Once again we are confronted by one of Nietzsche's agonizing love-hate relationships. His rejection of the idea of moral progress in history is part of the nineteenth-century reaction against the *philosophes*. So far as he was concerned, the desirable rejection of Christian transcendentalism did not vindicate Helvétius' vision of many Shakespeares walking the streets of Paris by virtue of public education. As a young man he was literally swept off his feet by Schopenhauer's unconventional paradoxes describing an Irrational Will ultimately bent on overcoming its own irrationality for the sake of tranquillity.* After Kant, Schelling, Hegel, and Fichte, this idea had the force of a revelation. Dionysos had reappeared outside German academic philosophy but within German thought. Together with Wagner's romantic notions and music dramas these were the two seminal influences on Nietzsche's thought. Yet some critics would like to interpret Nietzsche as a "western" as against a German thinker, an untenable hypostatization in light of the facts. It would be truer to say that he strove to combine the critical philosophy of the Enlightenment with the enhanced historical and psychological sophistication of the best in German romanticism. Thus, his reason led him to question the universality of Reason as normative for grasping the diverse structures of human destiny. At the same time he had lost all traditional faith, religious or philosophical, in furnishing a system of existence.

Nietzsche's admiration for Goethe should not obscure the profound differences between them. To be sure, both understood themselves as good Europeans first and Germans second; both were anticlerical and foes of orthodox theism; and both, Faust-like, preferred wandering through the Alps

---

* For Schopenhauer, in sharp contrast to Hegel and the whole school of German idealism (with the possible exception of the late Schelling), the world is basically arbitrary and at the mercy of non-directed passion. It follows that thought, art, law, and order—in fact, all of civilization is epiphenomenal.

toward Italy to sitting in dreary studies. But it is hard to visualize Nietzsche's sighing for the Eternal Feminine or, more seriously, settling down in Weimar to a bourgeois existence. Goethe learned how to cope with life by retreating into neoclassicism and assuming the role of oracle for a curious world. Nietzsche, on the other hand, destroyed himself by not ceasing to ask embarrassing questions to which his contemporaries paid virtually no attention, thus reducing him to an unbearable condition of loneliness and isolation. Nietzsche's restlessness knew no bounds. Goethe's was self-protectively concealed behind an Olympian mask which was deceptive but also decisive in determining the limits of his genius.*

NIETZSCHE AND KIERKEGAARD

What among other considerations helps make intellectual history exciting is the emergence within three generations of two independent but commonly exceptional thinkers of such towering rank as Kierkegaard and Nietzsche. A year before his breakdown Nietzsche wrote to the Danish critic Georg Brandes that he planned to read Kierkegaard in the course of a projected trip to Copenhagen, but sickness intervened and nothing came of his intention to do so. Brandes, a literary critic rather than a professional philosopher, was incidentally among the first to give a course of lectures on Nietzsche just as he became instrumental in calling serious attention to the works of Kierkegaard.

Nietzsche was eleven years old when Kierkegaard died at the age of forty-two. A few years later he wrote a youthful essay on the Kierkegaardian theme: the daemonic in music. Both Nietzsche and Kierkegaard were passionately fond of music, with Kierkegaard being inspired to write *Either* of *Either/Or* by Mozart's operas, particularly *Don Giovanni*, and with Nietzsche's *Birth of Tragedy* echoing his enthusiasm for the revolutionary music dramas of Richard Wagner. Curiously enough, each seemed to break with his respective

---

* For confirmation of my view of Goethe see esp. Goethe's *Autobiography: Poetry and Truth from My Own Life*, trans. by R. O. Moon (Washington, D.C., Public Affairs Press, 1949), pp. 692–694, as quoted in *History as Art and as Science* by Henry Stuart Hughes (New York, Harper & Row Publishers, 1964), pp. 66–67. Professor Hughes quotes Goethe on the Daemonic: ". . . I sought to save myself before this fearful principle, by fleeing as was my custom, behind an image. . . ."

idol without actually doing so. As a Christian author Kierkegaard confronts us with a dilemmatic choice between the aesthetic mode of existence (which includes the genius of Mozart) and the ethical-religious mode of existence (which can demand the martyrdom of a St. Sebastian). Nietzsche in later life becomes an anti-Wagnerite in order to guard his intellectual integrity. In either case, however, it would be a mistake to construe the development in question literally. What Nietzsche came to find intolerable was not the music of Richard Wagner but the ideological proposals which Wagner himself and many of his disciples were pushing on behalf of his art. With his uncanny instinct of what was to be the case, Nietzsche turned against the tabernacle of Bayreuth as embodying some of the worst features of the new Bismarckian Germany. But, as he tells us in his correspondence, his love and admiration for *Die Meistersinger* and *Tristan und Isolde* remained undimmed. Analogously, what Kierkegaard objected to was *not* Mozart's musical genius but, as he chose to see it in *Either/Or*, the embodiment of the erotic as a first principle of human conduct in such uncommitted characters as Cherubino and Papageno or in the daemonic appeal of Don Giovanni. The very significance Kierkegaard and Nietzsche attached to the nonpropositional language of music as revelatory of "human being in the world," or *Dasein*, comprises a striking correspondence between them.

Like Kierkegaard, Nietzsche collapsed in his forties. Throughout their lives both thinkers were subject to excessively ill health. The one could not shake off his fits of depression nor the other his migraine headaches and stomach disorders. Their philosophizing is directly autobiographical, not only in the sense of Kierkegaard's *Journals* and Nietzsche's *Ecce Homo* giving an account of themselves but in the less obvious way in which a significant portion of their thought is rooted in transformed personal experience—for example, Kierkegaard's broken engagement to Regina Olsen in *Repetition* or Nietzsche's disillusionment with German Academe in his essay *Schopenhauer Als Erzieher (Schopenhauer as Educator)*. Moreover, Nietzsche is far from sparing in his use of the first person singular and the first person plural. Kierkegaard's appearance in print in the garb of pseudonymous authors of his own invention fooled few in Copenhagen even during his lifetime. In any case, both Kierkegaard and Nietzsche preferred to embody their ideas in persons lest perhaps the truth of what a Socrates had to say should ever become separable fom the example of his life. Nietzsche remarked frequently that only like-minded readers would be able to grasp his true meaning while Kierkegaard took great pains to show that the transition from one "stage on life's way" to the next can become intelligible solely to those who have been initiated in the experiences corresponding to the phenomena under discussion. The comprehension of philosophical truth, Kierkegaard and Nietzsche often suggest, presupposes certain "elective affinities" for its reception on the part of the student—a Socratic notion which European philosophers since Descartes had almost totally overlooked.

Both showed themselves ingenious in psychological analysis. Kierkegaard's distinction between fear and anxiety (the fear of an objective threat and the "fears of things" in general) is no less a pre-Freudian revelation than Nietzsche's treatment of the concept of equality in terms of the resentment of the have-nots against the haves. A further point of resemblance is their antimoralism: Kierkegaard with his "teleological suspension of the ethical," and Nietzsche with his notion of "beyond good and evil," were less interested in moralizing about what ought to be done than in illuminating possibilities of human action and choice. To be sure, both Kierkegaard and Nietzsche wanted their thought to change the world, but not by virtue of crusades or philosophical salesmanship. Like Ludwig Wittgenstein they spurned disciples. Neither had much use for the pale abstractions of academic philosophy. Whereas Kierkegaard emphasized the existential duplication of ideas under the aspect of time and personal judgment, Nietzsche exposed the "enduring questions of philosophy" as rooted in ever-changing historical conditions: in short, the life-span of a philosophical problem does not exceed the peculiar factors which gave rise to it. Although each in this sense was committed to philosophical radicalism, Nietzsche and Kierkegaard remained political conservatives whose joint lack of adequate social theory can easily play into the hands of reactionaries. They cherished the concept of inequality, with Nietzsche envisaging an aristocracy of Supermen to guide the befuddled masses and Kierkegaard in *The Present Age* bemoaning the "leveling process" as a symptom of democratic degeneration. Their preference for the inequality of excellence among men, be it conceived as spiritual or physiological, is antithetical to the dominant trends of modern sociology, which never gives up hope of transforming clay into gold by some form of environmental manipulation. Although Nietzsche was an anti-Christian, his estimate of human nature in general was certainly no higher than Kierkegaard's sin-centered perspective would allow.

Both Kierkegaard and Nietzsche turned their backs on their respective Establishments, Nietzsche by resigning his professorship at the University of Basel (because of poor health) and Kierkegaard by refusing to pursue a promising career in the Church of Denmark. Instead, each launched an uncompromising attack on the ethos of the middle class. In his *Attack Upon Christendom* Kierkegaard singled out for vivisection the dishonesty of false believers dissembling respectability. Nietzsche concentrated his ire on the philistinism and chauvinism of the Germans, who, as he correctly surmised, were succumbing to daemonic nationalism. Kierkegaard still hoped to salvage Christianity from Christendom, in contrast to Nietzsche, who was dead set against the Christian faith itself. Both, however, were primarily motivated to make their protests in the name of "honesty," being less concerned to "do good" than to arouse their contemporaries to a gnawing sense of their intellectual hypocrisy.

Only in the wake of World War I did a true appreciation of their writings set in. With respect to Nietzsche it is no more accurate to claim him for existentialism than to classify him as a positivist, but Karl Jaspers is certainly right in stressing Nietzsche's unwitting kinship with Kierkegaard as an exceptional witness to the catastrophes of recent history and as an iconoclast in the history of thought. To remark that Nietzsche has more in common with Kierkegaard than with Goethe is an understatement, their conflicting attitudes toward Christianity notwithstanding. Perhaps it should not be too paradoxical that two of the three greatest students of suffering in the nineteenth century agreed on so many fundamentals. After all, Nietzsche also held in highest esteem the Christian author of *Notes from Underground* and *The Brothers Karamazov.*

NIETZSCHE TODAY

When Nietzsche's health collapsed in 1889, he was virtually unknown, except to a few close friends, including the previously deceased Richard Wagner and the eminent historian, Jacob Burckhardt. Significantly enough, no professor of philosophy knew him. In fact, he had gone out of his way to alienate the entire academic Establishment of his day by repeatedly charging it with the betrayal of its calling and, what must have been even harder to take, with guilt incurred by excessive dullness and pedantry. Having while only in his twenties become a brilliant professor himself, his charges could not be dismissed as originating from a non-peer, and so they cut very deep. All this makes it doubly remarkable that by the time of his death in 1900 Niezsche's writings were not only popular but had even gained a certain institutional respectability—alas, at a price.

With Nietzsche no longer able to speak for himself, German secondary-school teachers and their overwrought students seized upon those aspects of his thought which reinforced their frustrations and grievances. Toward the end of the nineteenth century there emerged a widespread feeling, particularly among the young, that life was passing them by, that the two-facedness of bourgeois (Victorian) morality with its ludicrous show of constraints was intolerable to bear, and that for the sake of general revitalization new horizons needed to be explored in every area of endeavor. In literature one thinks in this connection of such different expressions of the same as Henry James's invocation to "life" in *The Ambassadors* and Goncharov's dissection of torpidity and apathy in his masterpiece, *Oblomov*. Clearly, there are Nietzschean ideas in rapport with this state of mind, enhanced for the general reader by Nietzsche's visionary power and mastery of language. Had Nietzsche not been a stylist of genius as well as a persuasive pleader of causes, it is extremely doubtful whether his appropriation by the *avant garde* in the first decade of the twentieth century would ever have been as complete as it turned out to be.

Nietzsche's first great wave of popularity was broadly based on his abhorrence of academic drabness and on his paradoxically Romantic repudiation of Romantic decadence. Thus, to cite but a single example, artists welcomed his rejection of moral norms for evaluating works of art, enthusiastically embracing his contention that the only lesson works of art are required to teach is their autonomous realization of symbolic forms. Thomas Mann's *Death in Venice* remains the outstanding kaleidoscope of such Nietzschean themes as the unity of beauty and ugliness, the irony of thought in conflict with life, and the fascination of art inexorably intertwined with the pain of sickness, delirium, and death. Mann's hero, Gustav von Aschenbach, symbolizes the death of the old Europe but also points to alternative manifestations of beauty yet to be thoroughly explored.

Admittedly, Nietzsche could also seem to provide the in-

tellectual framework for American teen-agers to commit
gratuitous murder just as he had helped inspire the German
Wandervoegel—German youths who started by taking hikes
together and singing songs around campfires as a protest
against their stuffy parents, and ended dying in World Wars
I and II, not always as disillusioned nationalists. Nietzsche
would have been appalled by the systematic distortion of his
views on the part of such people, yet it would be equally
misleading to assert that he must not bear considerable responsibility for these developments. Moderation in self-ex-
pression was not one of his virtues, and his often impetuous
or preposterous reflections (referring to J. S. Mill as "pig-
headed," to mention one of the worst examples) appeared to
be made to dazzle and confuse. Of course, he was not the
philosopher of national socialism. Virtually all he stood for—
cosmopolitanism, intellectual excellence, beauty for beauty's
sake—was anathema to the leaders of that political movement. At the same time, it is a matter of historical record that
numerous self-elected Nietzscheans, among them his own sister who went so far as to falsify some of his papers and
letters, chose to identify Nietzsche's philosophy with the politics of racism and virulent German nationalism. Why this
should have occurred calls for a detailed study. Suffice it to
remark here that Nietzsche's profound dissatisfaction with
the modern world and his "philosophizing with the hammer"
appealed to many who lacked his rigorous habits of mind
and who remained insensitive to his *Hintergedanken*. Disciples like Yeats, Stefan George, and D'Annunzio were simply
unable to weigh Nietzsche's ambiguities.

Today Nietzschean studies and Nietzsche's reputation are
quite changed. Two world wars and the threat of atomic war
have placed his dire prophecies in a perspective largely
freed from the excess of the late nineteenth-century vitalism
and racism. Scholars have related Nietzsche to every conceivable movement of thought and, irony of ironies, placed
this incorruptible iconoclast in the "great tradition."* No
educated German or Frenchman is wholly ignorant of his
impact on symbolist poetry, existential philosophy, expres-
sionist drama, and the emergence of Freudian psychoanalysis.
Even the theologians have caught up, as David Hume pre-
dicted they always would, by brooding endlessly, and it
would appear not too unhappily, on the "death of God." In

---

* Heidegger's attempt to make a metaphysician out of the rebellious
Nietzsche [see Martin Heidegger, *Nietzsche* (Verlag Günther Neske
Pfullingem, 1961)] confirms Kierkegaard's fears of exceptional thinkers
becoming the property of professors of philosophy.

sum, Nietzsche's influence is already beyond reckoning. Our image of what has become of us in the West is largely determined by his diagnosis of our condition. All the fashionable books on the crisis in western civilization, from Spengler's *Decline* to *The Lonely Crowd*, would be unthinkable apart from Nietzsche's pioneer analyses.

Seen as a school philosopher, however, his current fortunes are considerably less spectacular. His vogue in Anglo-Saxon thought was chiefly connected with the rise of Bernard Shaw and defunct controversies over Social Darwinism.* Nietzsche's often unjust hatred of British philosophers has been duly reciprocated with indifference. (He regarded the utilitarians as utterly devoid of spirituality.) His provocative fusion of descriptive and hortatory discourse simply cannot satisfy the strict requirements of current linguistic analysis. Consequently, most English and American students of philosophy remain ignorant of his thought unless they encounter him in political science or comparative literature courses. But for philosophers anywhere to ignore Nietzsche because he failed to identify cognitive significance with verifiability or philosophy as a whole with a particular type of argument seems as unsound as it is unworthy of learned men.

Why should anyone read Nietzsche today, especially if he has to read him in translation? First, because twentieth-century continental thought and literature are incomprehensible without a knowledge of his writings. Second, because he ranks as one of the outstanding critics of traditional philosophy who challenges us to rethink the very categories of thinking philosophically. Third, because he is an excellent corrective of the shallow rationalism of those liberals who persist in interpreting Voltaire's mockery of priests as the beginning of the kingdom of heaven on earth. No thinker has been more antitraditionalist than Nietzsche, but at the same time he preserved a "tragic sense of life" which eludes the typical spokesmen of the Enlightenment and their disciples. Fourth, even though he failed in this himself, Nietzsche's thought contains many valuable clues for a possible future reconciliation between the respective claims of knowledge and wisdom. For the post-Christian generations yet to be born the urgency of this task scarcely needs any underscoring.

---

* For one of the best recent discussions of Nietzsche's influence on the modern drama, see Robert Brustein's *The Theatre of Revolt* (Boston, Little, Brown & Company, 1964), especially Chapters I–III.

THE PRESENT ANTHOLOGY

The originality of this anthology of Nietzsche's philosophy in English consists in the topical presentation of his thought and in being based on the new German edition of his works edited by Karl Schlechta.*

The topics have been chosen with a view of conveying the best possible idea of Nietzsche's extraordinary range of interests. Previous anthologists have concentrated on the anti-Christ or the Dionysian theme, inevitably at the expense of seeing Nietzsche as a whole. For, in addition to being a revolutionary "transvaluator of values" and a negative theologian in the guise of Mephistopheles, Nietzsche was a poet —in the tradition of Blake's "Marriage of Heaven and Hell" —and a caustic man of letters—not unlike Schopenhauer in this regard—who took great delight in making outrageous comments on a vast array of topics. Even when provocatively wrongheaded, Nietzsche's aphorisms rarely fail to be stimulating and arresting. He had a great deal of value to say about the ancient Greeks and the modern Germans, about history and music, about famous men of all ages, and particularly about himself. In addition to being of intrinsic interest, it casts considerable new light on Nietzsche's position as a transitional figure in the history of thought between the death of Hegel and the birth of Heidegger—the decline of the last genuine system of philosophy in the modern west on the one hand and the advent of formal *Existenzphilosophie* on the other.

Schlechta's understanding of Nietzsche's bibliographical history as set forth in the long appendix to his edition, while unavoidably controversial, strikes me as convincing and basically sound. The following, I take it, are Schlechta's major contentions: First, Nietzsche's sister falsified some of his letters and manuscripts in order to show him in a light partial to her particular likes and dislikes. (Her husband was a virulent anti-Semite and German nationalist. She herself was anything but free from these biases which Nietz-

---

* Karl Schlechta, ed., *Friedrich Nietzsche: Werke in Drei Bänden* (Munich, Carl Hanser Verlag, 1954–56). Also see Karl Schlechta, *Der Fall Nietzsche* (Munich, Carl Hanser Verlag, 1958). For an interesting though polemical summary of "Nietzsche in the light of His Suppressed Manuscripts" see Walter Kaufmann's article by that title in the *Journal of the History of Philosophy*, Vol. II, No. 2, (Oct., 1964), pp. 205–225.

sche abhorred. Moreover, her abiding affection for the
Wagner Circle and her jealous antipathy to some of Nietzsche's friends, notably Lou Salome who had turned down
his proposal of marriage, motivated her to twist the image
of her brother in accord with her own often diametrically
opposed predilections. Owing to Nietzsche's breakdown and
her subsequent overbearing control of his manuscripts, she
succeeded with considerable skill and cunning in creating a
Nietzsche legend.) Schlechta has exposed the forgeries and
offers us a clean text of Nietzsche's writings and letters.

Second, Schlechta argues persuasively (it seems to me) that
the core of Nietzsche's thought is to be found in his middle-
period works and that, as any reader can confirm for himself,
he returned to the same themes again and again without
adding anything substantially new at the end. *The Will to
Power*, Nietzsche's unfinished last work, is regarded by
Schlechta as a collection of disorganized fragments, which,
apart from not having been prepared by him for publication, add little of significance to the Nietzsche canon. Had
Nietzsche written nothing else of the kind, they would, much
like Pascal's *Pensées*, be the legitimate cause of extraordinarily difficult explication and interpretation. Since, however, this is fortunately not the case, they should only be
read with great caution as an inchoate *Nachlass*. They are
omitted from this anthology.

Finally, Schlechta holds that as Nietzsche approached
his last crisis, his ways of saying things, most of which he
had said many times before, were adversely affected. In
general, subtlety tended to give way to hysterical desperation, analogous to Kierkegaard's sacrifice of "indirect communication" in his last book, *Attack Upon Christendom*,
which is a powerful instance of "theologizing with a hammer," in sharp contrast to the scalpel approach of the earlier
writings. This anthology follows Schlechta in drawing heavily
on Nietzsche's early and middle-period writings.

I. Autobiographical Writings

The major events in Nietzsche's life were the following:
the subsequently ironic fact that his father had been a Protestant pastor; his father's death when he was still a young
boy; his school days at Pforta, a celebrated German board-
ing school emphasizing the classics; his student years at
Bonn and Leipzig where he took up classical philology, soon

gaining the special attention of the famous teacher, Professor Ritschl, who recommended the brilliant young (then twenty-four years old) Nietzsche for a professorship that had opened up at the University of Basel; his meeting in Basel with Jacob Burckhardt and the unforgettable days in Triebschen with the Wagners; Nietzsche's resignation from his professorship in 1879 because of ill health; his lonely wanderings through Italy and Switzerland in quest of tolerable health; his failure to marry and his trying dependence on his sister with whom he may conceivably have had incestuous relations; the neglect of his writings in German academic circles during the better part of his lifetime.

His terrible loneliness, of which he speaks again and again in his letters, is characteristic of the great European autobiographers since the Renaissance. Rousseau in particular comes immediately to mind. But in Nietzsche's life there were the compensations of his remarkable high-spiritedness, his capacity to bounce back from misfortune, his tumultuous gaiety, and his courage in the face of circumstances which most mortals could not bear. His refusal to make any compromise with his philosophical mission is indeed a noble chapter in the all too often sad story of modern intellectuals being tested by the exigencies of life.

II. The Prefaces

Nietzsche himself thought very highly of the prefaces to his major works (a collection of which was published during his lifetime). They are presented here in chronological order, with the exception of the prologue to *Thus Spake Zarathustra* which is included among selections from that singular work. These prefaces touch on each of Nietzsche's favorite themes.

III. The Greeks

As a heretical classical philologist Nietzsche came to revolutionize our understanding of Greek civilization (it is apposite to remark in this connection that Goethe, with whom, according to some authorities, Nietzsche had so much in common, seems to have been virtually insensitive to the irrational elements in Greek thought. This is hardly a surprising fact when one considers that his attitudes toward the ancient world were primarily shaped by his reading of Winckelmann whose *Schoengeistlerei*—the idyllic Apollonian view of Greece—Nietzsche shredded.) In daring opposition to the entrenched interpretation since the Enlightenment, Nietzsche stressed the Dionysian facets of the Greek genius as against the Apollonian—preferring Heraclitus to Plato, the tragedies of Aeschylus to those of Euripides, and the historical sense of Thucydides to the uncommon sense of Socrates. For Nietzsche the elaborate systems of Plato and Aristotle with their fantastic abstractions already marked a decline from the the semimystical directness of earlier speculation. He was among the first to see the destructive potency of Reason when divorced from the soil of ritual and passion which had helped give birth to it. Plato's proposed exclusion of the poets from his ideal state validates Nietzsche's view of the tyranny of the discursive intellect over flesh-and-blood human beings. His suggestion that the Greek dramatists and historians give us a truer picture of their superior civilization than its systematic philosophers remains a radical challenge to the hold of the classical tradition as conventionally conceived. What is perhaps a lopsided emphasis on the Greeks and the irrational on his part still serves as a salutary corrective to all the idealistic nonsense which had been disseminated in the name of a diluted humanism. Nietzsche's Greeks are not Kantian transcendental egos worshipping at the shrine of *Reine Vernunft* under the aspect of an unclouded sky but agents caught up in the tragedy of life which their finest philosophers could not banish from consciousness. The contemporary student of Greek culture could not even begin his investigations without taking Nietzsche's view into serious account. The Greeks have not been the same since he wrote.

IV. *The Germans*

Nietzsche's admiration for the Greeks, particularly before their so-called "golden age," was only matched by his contempt for the Germans after theirs. It is worth noting how often he addressed himself to what has become one of the most fashionable intellectual preoccupations of our day: the analysis of the mysterious German soul.* Like Heine, he did

---

* Someone should make a study of why German and Russian souls have been thought to be more mysterious than other souls.

not trust its manic-depressive oscillations, especially in the light of Bismarck's military triumphs. (He himself had served as a medical orderly in the Prussian Army at the height of its spectacular successes, retaining only too vivid memories of its vaunted efficiency, so frightening and stupid at the same time.) Nietzsche regarded the unification of Germany by force of arms as a national disaster as well as a potential European tragedy. (Scarcely any of his contemporaries could guess how right he was.) He was appalled by the insane national pride which seized the German middle classes in the throes of military victory, much as Flaubert in *Madame Bovary* (1857) satirized French chauvinism and provincialism. Most frightening of all he found the decline of German culture and learning after the death of Hegel. On the surface, German universities were flourishing throughout the nineteenth century and attracting students from all over the world, not least in the natural sciences, but Nietzsche realized that the humanistic ideal which had made their greatness possible in the first place had long since been shattered and unreplaced by any alternative unifying principle. The result was pedantry and narrow overspecialization devoid of contemporaneity. Nietzsche's prophecies of the German catastrophe are required reading not only for all Germans and students of history but also for skeptics who deny that there can be such a thing as national character unless it remains shrouded in mystery.

V. History

Nietzsche's attitude toward history was characteristically ambivalent. His notion of the Eternal Return (according to which no event is unique) is pagan, cyclical, and basically ahistorical. On the other hand, he expressed the deepest respect for history insofar as it helps man better to understand "the present of things to come" through insights into "the present of things past." Like Kierkegaard, Nietzsche opposed "antiquarian history"—by which he meant the study of the past solely for its own sake. Instead, he champions what he calls "authentic history"—the study of the past in order to learn from its mistakes, or history as it bears on existential problems of the specious present.

VI. Music

Already in his youth Nietzsche was a passionate lover of music. Moreover, this love remained far from being merely passive. He learned to play the piano and to compose music of his own which, if still in existence, might be interesting to hear performed. He corresponded with the famous conductor Hans von Bülow, and one of his closest friends was the composer Peter Gast. But, of course, what he is rightly most celebrated for in matters musical is his tempestuous friendship with Richard Wagner. (Nietzsche and Wagner like Nietzsche and Burckhardt or Nietzsche and Venice is one of those *Innenbegriffe*—coupling of internal ideas—which help define the sensibility of twentieth-century educated Central Europeans.) His writings on this subject speak quite clearly for themselves—from his youthful infatuation to his disappointment and the embarrassing break. Nietzsche, as it were, never lost his admiration for Wagner's musical genius. He simply could no longer tolerate his showmanship and what he took to be his subordination of musical values to the extramusical demands of the music drama. No doubt Nietzsche would have welcomed the symphonic suites that have been arranged for orchestra alone and on which, ironically enough, Wagner's popularity with most musical audiences of today seems to rest. Nietzsche's early insistence on the more conventional aspects of Wagner's genius is a further instance of his prescience in reading the signs of the times.

Apart from Wagner, Nietzsche commented at considerable length on music in general. He was disturbed by the German intoxication with German music, surely knowing of its dangers first hand. His glorification of Bizet's *Carmen* is a classical case of overcompensation. In *Buddenbrooks* Thomas Mann has immortalized the two chief loves of Nietzsche's early intellectual development by placing them in contrapuntal juxtaposition to one another: the philosophy of Schopenhauer and the ravishing freshness of *Tristan und Isolde*. Perhaps Nietzsche was the last great philosopher to seek salvation as a professional.

VII. Famous Men

Nietzsche's elitism is most engagingly exhibited in his sketches of famous individuals that occur throughout his writings. Note how he can illuminate the character of an entire era by giving us the portrait of a single outstanding contemporary.

VIII. The Spirit of Modernity

The appeal of Nietzsche's writings, especially in the years immediately preceding World War I, lay not a little in his trenchant analysis of "l'âme moderne"—the modern soul, for which he had much abuse. In this rejection he was scarcely alone. One has only to consider three independently conceived late nineteenth-century novels to get a sense of decadence similar to his conception of it: *Madame Bovary, Anna Karenina,* and Theodore Fontane's *Effie Briest.* He deplored western civilization's growing addiction to creature comforts, its overrefinement at the expense of spontaneity, its feminism, and its self-indulgence. He strongly felt an overall waning of energy reminiscent of Kierkegaard's complaint in *The Present Age* that the nineteenth century was devoid of passion. His glorification of war, although inexcusable in the light of twentieth-century history, can in part be explained as a reaction against the phenomenon of devitalization. Anticipating Freud's argument in *Civilization and Its Discontents,* Nietzsche was prepared to suggest a return to the instinctive as a necessary condition for overcoming nihilism. This dangerous idea presumably was among the considerations which elicited Heidegger's initial support of national socialism. Nietzsche must be given credit for having been among the first to diagnose the syndrome of post-Christian meaninglessness. The inadequacy of his answer should not detract from the keenness of his questioning.

IX. Aristocratic Radicalism

The chief tenets of Nietzsche's "aristocratic radicalism" can be summarized as follows:
1. Man is essentially animal.
2. His behavior should be biologically explained.
3. Men are unequal: Each generation has its "herd" and its superior members, the latter constituting a more or less constant minority throughout history.
4. The values men live by are necessarily in accord with

their inclinations. No "slave" can ever take Nietzsche's thought seriously and, conversely, all "true aristocrats" will remain invulnerable to the intentions of those not on a par with them.

5. The "superior man" is richly endowed with vigor, gaiety, the will to affirm himself in action, and the willingness to fight for his mode of life and thought. At the same time, he spurns pettiness, all resentment rooted in jealousy, envy or touchiness, and all gratuitous cruelty. Instead, he shows himself open-minded, magnamimous, and never falsely modest.

6. Above all, he is wary of pity and self-pity.

Christianity for Nietzsche is the embodiment par excellence of the "slave morality" with its emphasis on the equality of sinners before God, its counsels of indiscriminate compassion, and its elevation of the last to be first. Nietzsche's indictment of Christendom, on the other hand, was based on his preference for free thought, his total rejection of ecclesiastical authority, and his abhorrence of hypocrisy. Insofar as Christianity maintains that man is essentially spiritual and insofar as Christendom betrays this false claim through its disingenuous politics, both stand condemned for Nietzsche as aberrations of the human condition. For Christ Nietzsche had a grudging respect, nevertheless. For Christendom he had nothing but contempt.

X. Truth and Illusion

While Nietzsche condemned traditional religion as a bundle of man-made illusions, he himself remained of two minds as to the value of knowledge. On the one hand, he acknowledges the need of illusion (the right kind) to reconcile men to the terrors of life. Herein according to Nietzsche lies the justification of art. But, on the other hand, he advocates a rigorous quest for the way things are, irrespective of the consequences for human comfort. Time and again, Nietzsche will designate "cognition" as the supreme value, only to turn around and attack as pedants those researchers who in their single-minded pursuit of fact (complete "demythologization") would rob man of all his reasons for living. Nietzsche, in short, never could quite decide whether the "death of God" was an unmixed blessing or a curse. Probably he meant to say both.

This dilemma, the roots of which go back to Kant's regulative principles of the practical reason, characterizes a recurring conflict in modern thought between our allegiance to scientific data and the demands of human existence. If pure knowledge is our supreme value, we should be prepared to follow, for example, wherever experiments with atomic energy would take us. Obviously, this is madness. If pure knowledge is not our supreme value, we must subordinate the validation of scientific hypotheses to alternative concerns of greater importance for us. These questions then arise: What are these concerns of greater importance? How do we reach agreement on them? And how do we distinguish legitimate from false illusions? Like Faust, Nietzsche wanted to know everything while knowing that such knowledge, if obtainable, would destroy the human race. Thus, Karl Jaspers, a close student of Nietzsche, rejects demythologization in theology as suicidal, arguing that man will always have recourse to myths of one sort or another. Myths may change, but the need for them remains the same. The central ambiguity in Nietzsche's philosophy revolves around his intellectual passion for the naked truth divided from his emotive love for the illusions of art.

XI. Art and Beauty

Nietzsche was among the first to acknowledge art as a substitute religion for post-Christian western man. In taking this position he was deeply influenced by Schopenhauer, who had seen in the contemplation of great works of art a temporary escape from the threat of chaos. Inasmuch as man for Nietzsche cannot live without illusions, art provides his mind and senses with surrogates for the bitter truth of his condition. Modern science explains to us the workings of a world which is meaningless with regard to human values and ideals. Thus, the task of the artist becomes the creation of other worlds within which man can find himself at home again, if only for or under a spell. Consistent with this view, Nietzsche proclaimed the total autonomy of art, insisting on its purification from all heterodox elements such as being the veritable embodiment of moral principles (as in the medieval miracle play, for example) or the vehicle of political propaganda (as in totalitarian states). Nietzsche's insistence on art for art's sake is consistently anti-Platonic. With Baudelaire, a kindred spirit, he discovered the trinity of modern art: the abnormal, the ugly, and the exaggerated. As is well known, much of the shocking quality of modern art and literature derives from its exploration of what earlier generations dismissed as disgusting and certainly would not have regarded as suitable material for the expression of aesthetic feeling. Anticipating such writers as Kafka, Joyce, and Beckett, Nietzsche provided the theoretical foundations for the profound treatment of the trivial and the repugnant. Jean Paul Sartre's recent glorification of the criminal-genius, Jean Genet, is typically Nietzschean in its outrageousness. And yet Nietzsche's personal favorites in literature were the classical tragedies of Greece, the neoclassical writings of Goethe, and Adalbert Stifter's novel, *Nachsommer*, as innocuous and conventional a piece of prose fiction as was ever conceived by the mind of a writer. This again is perfectly consistent with Nietzsche's enmity to the modern soul. The irony is that he knew it so well.

XII. Philosophy and Philosophers

Throughout his writings Nietzsche commented frequently on philosophy and philosophers. As must be apparent by now, his views were rather unorthodox, particularly for his day when G. E. Moore had yet to challenge F. H. Bradley. His rejection of much of academic philosophy is, however, in the best Faustian and Schopenhauerian tradition. Considerably more subtle is his emphasis on what William James was to call "the sentiment of rationality." His conception of philosophy as disguised autobiography (being true to one's inner experience) clashed with the scientific temper of the age. For Nietzsche the very act of philosophical reflection signifies a diminution of vitality. Those who really enjoy life, he often seems to be saying, do not brood excessively on their observations. Yet Nietzsche himself was one of the unfortunate few who relished less than they thought. Although never pretentious, his self-exaltation, especially in the last few years, often led him to suppose that he was the greatest philosopher of all. His oracular voice in *Thus Spake Zarathustra* is the most grating in his impressive armory of persuasive instruments. His own favorite philosophers were Socrates, Pascal, Spinoza, and Schopenhauer. Needless to remark at this juncture, with the possible exception of Spinoza, he loved and hated each of them at once. Interestingly enough, all these thinkers were primarily concerned with the cure of sick souls. Wittgenstein's lectures on philosophical psychology with his understanding of philosophical dilemmas as illnesses would have pleased Nietzsche, for whom a genuine philosopher was essentially a physician of the interior self, subject to the most intense cramps conceivable.

XIII. Psychology

Nietzsche's dazzling insights as a psychologist are best left to dazzle for themselves. In the illustrious company of St. Augustine, Pascal, Kierkegaard, Stendhal, and Dostoyevsky, Nietzsche had an uncanny knack for seeing through the intricate disguises of human dissimulation. It is worth repeating in this context that Freud regarded Nietzsche and Dostoyevsky as his most influential guides on the road to the theory of psychoanalysis.

XIV. Random Reflections

Space does not permit an adequate sampling of Nietzsche's opinions on almost every conceivable subject. His low opinion of women is legendary. Also of particular interest are his dietary ruminations. However wrongheaded he may have been at times, he can never be accused of dullness. Nietzsche was a master of the well-turned phrase, and his aphorisms on life, like Schopenhauer's, are reliably refreshing as well as amusing.

Prefatory Note

I hope that before too long someone will be able to undertake the monumental task of translating Professor Schlechta's definitive edition of Nietzsche into English. Until that time comes, the Oscar Levy edition will continue to remain as helpful as any, especially in view of its editorial and terminological consistency. All translations in this anthology have been taken from the Levy edition. Titles and volume numbers referred to in excerpt headings and footnotes refer to the titles and volume numbers of the Oscar Levy edition. Following is a list of the titles in the Levy edition and their translators:

   I. *The Birth of Tragedy*, trans. by William A. Haussmann.
  II. *Early Greek Philosophy and Other Essays*, trans. by M. A. Mügge.
 III. *The Future of Our Educational Institutions*, trans. by J. M. Kennedy.
  IV. *Thoughts Out of Season*, Vol. I, trans. by A. M. Ludovici.
   V. *Thoughts Out of Season*, Vol. II, trans. by Adrian Collins.
  VI. *Human, All Too Human*, Vol. I, trans. by Helen Zimmern.
 VII. *Human, All Too Human*, Vol. II, trans. by Paul V. Cohn.
VIII. *The Case of Wagner*, trans. by A. M. Ludovici.
  IX. *The Dawn of Day*, trans. by J. M. Kennedy.

I am indebted to my students in seminars in German philosophy at Washington University, St. Louis, and at Vanderbilt University, Nashville, for numerous suggestive comments and insights pertaining to Nietzsche's thought and its interpretations. Of particular help to me in formulating my ideas has been Professor Egon Schwarz of the German Department at Washington University. Above all, I should like to thank Robert Meister, editor of the *Journal of Existentialism,* without whose constant support and concrete help this book would not have come into existence.

G. C.

I am indebted to my students in sémenirs and seminar
fellowships at Vanderbilt University, St. Louis, and
Vanderbilt University, Nashville, for numerous suggestive
criticisms and interest-relating to Nietzsche's thought, and
for encouragement of persistent help to me in formulating
the same. I am indebted to Miss Susan of the German
Department of Washington University. Above all, I should
like to thank Robert Stuart, editor of the Journal of
Philosophy, without whose patient encouragement the
work would not have been done sooner.

I. Autobiographical Writings

FROM LETTER TO GEORG BRANDES,
APRIL 10, 1888*

Vita

I was born on the 15th of October, 1844, on the battle-field of Lützen. The first name I remember was that of Gustavus Adolphus. My ancestors were Poles belonging to the aristocracy (Niëzky). The type seems to be well preserved, in spite of three German mothers. Abroad I am generally taken for a Pole. In the visitors' list at Nice only this winter I was entered as a Pole. They tell me that my head is familiar in Matejko's † pictures. My grandmother mixed in the Schiller-Goethe circles of Weimar; her brother succeeded Herder in the post of Weimar's General-Superintendent. It was my good fortune to be a pupil at the celebrated and historic Pforta School, where so many (Klopstock, Fichte, Schlegel, Ranke, etc.) who have added luster to German literature preceded me. We had teachers who would have been (or have been) creditable to every university. I next studied in Bonn, later on at Leipzig, where the venerable Ritschl, at that time the premier philologist of Germany, singled me out for distinction from the first. At twenty-two years of age I was a contributor to the *Litterarisches Centralblatt* (edited by Zarncke). The founding of the Philologi-

* From *Selected Letters of Friedrich Nietzsche*, Oscar Levy, ed. (London, William Heinemann, 1921).
† Famous Polish painter (1838–93).—Translator.

cal Society of Leipzig, which still exists, originated with me. In the winter of 1868–69 the University of Basel offered me a professorial chair, before I had even been made doctor. Whereupon the Leipzig University did me the extraordinary honor of conferring on me the degree of Doctor without any examination or dissertation being required.

I stayed at Basel from 1869 till 1879. It became necessary for me to give up my rights as a German subject, owing to the fact that as an officer in the Horse Artillery I was too often called out and disturbed in my academic duties.

Nevertheless, I understand the use at least of two weapons, saber and cannon, and perhaps I know something about a third. All went smoothly at Basel. It often happened at promotion examinations for the Doctorate that the examiner was younger than the examinee! A great advantage I enjoyed there was the genial relations existing between Jakob Burckhardt and myself; something quite unusual on the part of that hermitlike thinker, who lived a very retired life.

Another still more incalculable advantage was that from the beginning of my residence in Basel a quite unusual intimacy sprang up between me and Richard and Cosima Wagner, who at that time were living on their country estate, Triebschen, on the lake of Lucerne, as much cut off from all their earlier connections as if they were on a desert island. For several years we shared every joy and sorrow; a friendship of unbounded confidence. You will find that in Wagner's collected works, Vol. VII, there is printed an epistle to me apropos of the *Birth of Tragedy*. My relations with them brought me in contact with a large circle of interesting men and women, in fact, the best society that moves between St. Petersburg and Paris. Toward 1876 my health began to decline. I spent a winter in Sorrento with my old friend Baroness Meysenbug (author of *Memoiren einer Idealistin*) and Dr. Reé, with whom I was then in sympathy. It did me no good. An exceedingly painful and stubborn form of headache set in that exhausted all my strength. As years went on, it increased, and reached such a climax of habitual suffering that the year contained for me at that time two hundred days of torture. The cause of the malady must have been entirely local, as any kind of neuropathological grounds for it were absent. I never had the least sign of mental disturbance, no fever, no fainting. My pulse was the whole time as slow as the first Napoleon's (60). My speciality was to endure excruciating pain and *cru et vert* with an absolutely clear brain for two or three days on end, vomiting bile the whole time. A report got wind that I was in an asylum (indeed, that I had died there). Nothing could have been further from the truth. My mind did not really mature until this frightful time. Evidence of it is *The Dawn of Day,* which I wrote in 1881 during a winter of unspeakable wretchedness in Genoa, beyond reach of doctors, friends, and relations. I composed the book with a minimum of health and strength, so it stands for a kind of *Dynamometer* of my powers. From 1882 onward I progressed, even if slowly, toward recovery. The crisis was overcome (my father died young, at exactly the same age at which I myself was at death's door). Even today I have to be extremely careful; certain conditions, climatic and meteorological, are indispensable. It is not choice, but compulsion, which takes me every summer to the Upper Engadine and every winter to the Riviera.

Finally, this illness has been of the very greatest help to me; it has set me free; it has restored me the courage to be myself. My instincts are those of a brave, even of a military, beast. The prolonged struggle has slightly exasperated my pride of spirit. After all, am I a philosopher? But what does it matter?

FROM ECCE HOMO

How One Becomes What One Is

WHY I AM SO WISE

1

THE happiness of my existence, its unique character perhaps, consists in its fatefulness: To speak in a riddle, as my own father I am already dead, as my own mother I still live and grow old. This double origin, taken as it were from the highest and lowest rungs of the ladder of life, at once a decadent and a beginning, this, if anything, explains that neutrality, that freedom from partisanship in regard to the general problem of existence, which perhaps distinguishes me. To the first indications of ascending or of descending life my nostrils are more sensitive than those of any man that has yet lived. In this domain I am a master to my backbone—I know both sides, for I am both sides. My father died in his six-and-thirtieth year: he was delicate, lovable, and morbid, like one who is preordained to pay simply a flying visit—a gracious reminder of life rather than life itself. In the same year that his life declined, mine also declined: in my six-and-thirtieth year I reached the lowest point in my vitality—I still lived, but my eyes could distinguish nothing that lay three paces away from me. At that time—it was the year 1879—I resigned my professorship at Basel, lived through the summer like a shadow in St. Moritz, and spent the following winter, the most sunless of my life, like a shadow in Naumburg. This was my lowest ebb. During this period I wrote *The Wanderer and His Shadow*. Without a doubt I was conversant with shadows then. The winter that followed, my first winter in Genoa, brought forth that sweetness and spirituality which is almost inseparable from extreme poverty of blood and muscle, in the shape of *The Dawn of Day*. The perfect lucidity and cheerfulness, the intellectual exuberance even, that this work reflects coincides, in my case, not only with the most profound physiological weakness but also with an excess of suffering. In the midst of the agony of a headache which lasted three days, accompanied by violent nausea, I was possessed of most singular dialectical clearness, and in absolutely cold blood I then thought out things, for which, in my more healthy moments, I am not enough of a climber, not sufficiently subtle, not sufficiently cold. My readers perhaps know to what extent I consider dialectic a symptom of decadence, as, for instance, in the most famous of all cases—the case of Socrates. All the morbid disturbances of the intellect, even that semistupor which accompanies fever, have, unto this day, remained completely unknown to me; and for my first information concerning their nature and frequency, I was obliged to have recourse to the learned works which have been compiled on the subject. My circulation is slow. No one has ever been able to detect fever in me. A doctor who treated me for some time as a nerve patient finally declared: "No! There is nothing wrong with your nerves; it is simply I who am nervous." It has been absolutely impossible to ascertain any local degeneration in me, nor any organic stomach trouble, however much I may have suffered from profound weakness of the gastric system as the result of general exhaustion. Even my eye trouble, which sometimes approached so parlously near to blindness, was only an effect and not a cause; for, whenever my general vital condition improved, my power of vision

also increased. Having admitted all this, do I need to say
that I am experienced in questions of decadence? I know
them inside and out. Even that filigree art of prehension and
comprehension in general, that feeling for delicate shades of
difference, that psychology of "seeing through brick walls,"
and whatever else I may be able to do, was first learnt then,
and is the specific gift of that period during which everything
in me was subtilized—observation itself, together with all
the organs of observation. To look upon healthier concepts
and values from the standpoint of the sick, and conversely to
look down upon the secret work of the instincts of decadence
from the standpoint of him who is laden and self-reliant
with the richness of life—this has been my longest exercise,
my principal experience. If in anything at all, it was in this
that I became a master. Today my hand knows the trick; I
now have the knack of reversing perspectives: the first reason
perhaps why a *Transvaluation of All Values* has been possible to me alone.

2

For, apart from the fact that I am a decadent, I am also
the reverse of such a creature. Among other things my proof
of this is that I always instinctively select the proper remedy
when my spiritual or bodily health is low; whereas the decadent, as such, invariably chooses those remedies which are
bad for him. As a whole I was sound, but in certain details
I was a decadent. That energy with which I sentenced myself
to absolute solitude, and to a severance from all those conditions in life to which I had grown accustomed; my discipline
of myself, and my refusal to allow myself to be pampered, to
be tended hand and foot, and to be doctored—all this betrays the absolute certainty of my instincts respecting what
at that time was most needful to me. I placed myself in my
own hands, I restored myself to health: the first condition
of success in such an undertaking, as every physiologist will
admit, is that at bottom a man should be sound. An intrinsically morbid nature cannot become healthy. On the
other hand, to an intrinsically sound nature, illness may even
constitute a powerful stimulus to life, to a surplus of life. It
is in this light that I now regard the long period of illness
that I endured: It seemed as if I had discovered life afresh,
my own self included. I tasted all good things and even
trifles in a way in which it was not easy for others to taste

them—out of my Will to Health and to Life I made my philosophy. . . . For this should be thoroughly understood; it was during those years in which my vitality reached its lowest point that I ceased from being a pessimist: the instinct of self-recovery forbade my holding to a philosophy of poverty and desperation. Now, by what signs are Nature's lucky strokes recognized among men? They are recognized by the fact that any such lucky stroke gladdens our senses; that he is carved from one integral block, which is hard, sweet, and fragrant as well. He enjoys that only which is good for him; his pleasure, his desire, ceases when the limits of that which is good for him are overstepped. He divines remedies for injuries; he knows how to turn serious accidents to his own advantage; that which does not kill him makes him stronger. He instinctively gathers his material from all he sees, hears, and experiences. He is a selective principle; he rejects much. He is always in his own company, whether his intercourse be with books, with men, or with natural scenery; he honors the things he chooses, the things he acknowledges, the things he trusts. He reacts slowly to all kinds of stimuli, with that tardiness which long caution and deliberate pride have bred in him—he tests the approaching stimulus; he would not dream of meeting it halfway. He believes neither in "ill luck" nor "guilt"; he can digest himself and others; he knows how to forget—he is strong enough to make everything turn to his own advantage.

Lo then! I am the very reverse of a decadent, for he whom I have just described is none other than myself.

3

This double thread of experiences, this means of access to two worlds that seem so far asunder, finds in every detail its counterpart in my own nature—I am my own complement: I have a "second" sight, as well as a first. And perhaps I also have a third sight. By the very nature of my origin I was allowed an outlook beyond all merely local, merely national and limited horizons; it required no effort on my part to be a "good European." On the other hand, I am perhaps more German than modern Germans—mere Imperial Germans—can hope to be—I, the last antipolitical German. Be this as it may, my ancestors were Polish noblemen: it is owing to them that I have so much race instinct in my blood—who knows? perhaps even the *liberum veto*.* When I think of the number of times in my travels that I have been accosted as a Pole, even by Poles themselves, and how seldom I have been taken for a German, it seems to me as if I belonged to those only who have a sprinkling of German in them. But my mother, Franziska Oehler, is at any rate something very German; as is also my paternal grandmother, Erdmuthe Krause. The latter spent the whole of her youth in good old Weimar, not without coming into contact with Goethe's circle. Her brother, Krause, the Professor of Theology in Königsberg, was called to the post of General Superintendent at Weimar after Herder's death. It is not unlikely that her mother, my great-grandmother, is mentioned in young Goethe's diary under the name of "Muthgen." She married twice, and her second husband was Superintendent Nietzsche of Eilenburg. In 1813, the year of the great war, when Napoleon with his general staff entered Eilenburg on the 10th of October, she gave birth to a son. As a daughter of Saxony she was a great admirer of Napoleon, and maybe I am so still. My father, born in 1813, died in 1849. Previous to taking over the pastorship of the parish of Röcken, not far from Lützen, he lived for some years at the Castle of Altenburg, where he had charge of the education of the four princesses. His pupils are the Queen of Hanover, the Grand Duchess Constantine, the Grand Duchess of Oldenburg, and the Princess Theresa of Saxe-Altenburg. He was full of loyal respect for the Prussian King, Frederick William the Fourth, from whom he obtained his living at Röcken; the events of 1848 saddened him extremely. As I was born on the 15th of October, the birthday of the king above mentioned, I naturally received the Hohenzollern names of Frederick William. There was at all events one advantage in the choice of this day: My birthday throughout the whole of my childhood was a day of public rejoicing. I regard it as a great privilege to have had such a father; it even seems to me that this embraces all that I can claim in the matter of privileges—life, the great yea to life, excepted. What I owe to him above all is this, that I do not need any special intention, but merely a little patience, in order involuntarily to enter a world of higher and more delicate things. There I am at home, there alone does my inmost passion become free. The fact that I had to pay for this privilege almost

* The right which every Polish deputy, whether a great or an inferior nobleman, possessed of forbidding the passing of any measure by the Diet, was called in Poland the *liberum veto* (in Polish *nie pozwalam*), and brought all legislation to a standstill.—Tᴿ.

with my life certainly does not make it a bad bargain. In order to understand even a little of my *Zarathustra*, perhaps a man must be situated and constituted very much as I am myself—with one foot beyond the realm of the living.

4

I have never understood the art of arousing ill feeling against myself—this is also something for which I have to thank my incomparable father—even when it seemed to me highly desirable to do so. However un-Christian it may seem, I do not even bear any ill-feeling toward myself. Turn my life about as you may, you will find but seldom—perhaps indeed only once—any trace of someone's having shown me ill will. You might perhaps discover, however, too many traces of *good* will. . . . My experiences even with those on whom every other man has burnt his fingers speak without exception in their favor; I tame every bear, I can make even clowns behave decently. During the seven years in which I taught Greek to the sixth form of the College at Basel, I never had occasion to administer a punishment; the laziest youths were diligent in my class. The unexpected has always found me equal to it; I must be unprepared in order to keep my self-command. Whatever the instrument was, even if it were as out of tune as the instrument "man" can possibly be, it was only when I was ill that I could not succeed in making it express something that was worth hearing. And how often have I not been told by the "instruments" themselves that they had never before heard their voices express such beautiful things. . . . This was said to me most delightfully perhaps by that young fellow Heinrich von Stein, who died at such an unpardonably early age, and who, after having considerately asked leave to do so, once appeared in Sils-Maria for a three days' sojourn, telling everybody there that it was *not* for the Engadine that he had come. This excellent person, who with all the impetuous simplicity of a young Prussian nobleman, had waded deep into the swamp of Wagnerism (and into that of Dühringism * into the bargain!), seemed almost transformed during these three days by a hurricane of freedom, like one who has been suddenly raised to his full height and given wings. Again and again I said to him that this was all owing to the splendid air; ev-

---

* Eugen Dühring was a philosopher and political economist whose general doctrine might be characterized as a sort of abstract Materialism with an optimistic coloring.—TR.

erybody felt the same—one could not stand 6,000 feet above Bayreuth for nothing—but he would not believe me. . . . Be this as it may, if I have been the victim of many a small or even great offense, it was not "will," and least of all *ill* will that actuated the offenders; but rather, as I have already suggested, it was good will, the cause of no small amount of mischief in my life, about which I had to complain. My experience gave me a right to feel suspicious in regard to all so-called "unselfish" instincts, in regard to the whole of "neighborly love" which is ever ready and waiting with deeds or with advice. To me it seems that these instincts are a sign of weakness, they are an example of the inability to withstand a stimulus—it is only among decadents that this *pity* is called a virtue. What I reproach the pitiful with is that they are too ready to forget shame, reverence, and the delicacy of feeling which knows how to keep at a distance; they do not remember that this gushing pity stinks of the mob, and that it is next of kin to bad manners—that pitiful hands may be thrust with results fatally destructive into a great destiny, into a lonely and wounded retirement, and into the privileges with which great guilt endows one. The overcoming of pity I reckon among the noble virtues. In the "Temptation of Zarathustra" I have imagined a case in which a great cry of distress reaches his ears, in which pity swoops down upon him like a last sin, and would make him break faith with himself. To remain one's own master in such circumstances, to keep the sublimity of one's mission pure in such cases—pure from the many ignoble and more shortsighted impulses which come into play in so-called unselfish actions—this is the rub, the last test perhaps which a Zarathustra has to undergo—the actual proof of his power.

5

In yet another respect I am no more than my father over again, and as it were the continuation of his life after an all-too-early death. Like every man who has never been able to meet his equal, and unto whom the concept "retaliation" is just as incomprehensible as the notion of "equal rights," I have forbidden myself the use of any sort of measure of security or protection—and also, of course, of defense and "justification"—in all cases in which I have been made the victim either of trifling or even *very great* foolishness. My form of retaliation consists in this: as soon as possible to set a piece of cleverness at the heels of an act of stupidity;

by this means perhaps it may still be possible to overtake it.
To speak in a parable: I dispatch a pot of jam in order to
get rid of a bitter experience. . . . Let anybody only give
me offense, I shall "retaliate," he can be quite sure of that.
Before long I discover an opportunity of expressing my
thanks to the "offender" (among other things even for the
offense)—or of *asking* him for something, which can be more
courteous even than giving. It also seems to me that the
rudest word, the rudest letter, is more good-natured, more
straightforward, than silence. Those who keep silent are almost always lacking in subtlety and refinement of heart; silence is an objection, to swallow a grievance must necessarily
produce a bad temper—it even upsets the stomach. All silent
people are dyspeptic. You perceive that I should not like to
see rudeness undervalued; it is by far the most *humane* form
of contradiction, and, in the midst of modern effeminacy, it
is one of our first virtues. If one is sufficiently rich for it, it
may even be a joy to be wrong. If a god were to descend to
this earth, he would have to do nothing but wrong—to take
guilt, not punishment, on one's shoulders is the first proof of
divinity.

6

Freedom from resentment and the understanding of the
nature of resentment—who knows how very much after all
I am indebted to my long illness for these two things? The
problem is not exactly simple; a man must have experienced both through his strength and through his weakness. If
illness and weakness are to be charged with anything at all,
it is with the fact that when they prevail, the very instinct of
recovery, which is the instinct of defense and of war in man,
becomes decayed. He knows not how to get rid of anything,
how to come to terms with anything, and how to cast anything behind him. Everything wounds him. People and things
draw importunately near, all experiences strike deep, memory is a gathering wound. To be ill is a sort of resentment
in itself. Against this resentment the invalid has only one
great remedy—I call it *Russian fatalism*, that fatalism which
is free from revolt, and with which the Russian soldier, to
whom a campaign proves unbearable, ultimately lays himself down in the snow. To accept nothing more, to undertake nothing more, to absorb nothing more—to cease entirely from reacting. . . . The tremendous sagacity of this
fatalism, which does not always imply merely the courage for

death, but which in the most dangerous cases may actually constitute a self-preservative measure, amounts to a reduction of activity in the vital functions, the slackening down of which is like a sort of will to hibernate. A few steps farther in this direction we find the fakir, who will sleep for weeks in a tomb. . . . Owing to the fact that one would be used up too quickly if one reacted, one no longer reacts at all; this is the principle. And nothing on earth consumes a man more quickly than the passion of resentment. Mortification, morbid susceptibility, the inability to wreak revenge, the desire and thirst for revenge, the concoction of every sort of poison—this is surely the most injurious manner of reacting which could possibly be conceived by exhausted men. It involves a rapid wasting away of nervous energy, an abnormal increase of detrimental secretions, as, for instance, that of bile into the stomach. To the sick man resentment ought to be more strictly forbidden than anything else—it is *his* special danger; unfortunately, however, it is also his most natural propensity. This was fully grasped by that profound physiologist Buddha. His "religion," which it would be better to call a system of hygiene in order to avoid confounding it with a creed so wretched as Christianity, depended for its effect upon the triumph over resentment; to make the soul free therefrom was considered the first step toward recovery. "Not through hostility is hostility put to flight; through friendship does hostility end." This stands at the beginning of Buddha's teaching—this is not a precept of morality, but of physiology. Resentment born of weakness is not more deleterious to anybody than it is to the weak man himself—conversely, in the case of that man whose nature is fundamentally a rich one, resentment is a superfluous feeling, a feeling to remain master of which is almost a proof of riches. Those of my readers who know the earnestness with which my philosophy wages war against the feelings of revenge and rancor, even to the extent of attacking the doctrine of "free will" (my conflict with Christianity is only a particular instance of it), will understand why I wish to focus attention upon my own personal attitude and the certainty of my practical instincts precisely in this matter. In my moments of decadence I forbade myself the indulgence of the above feelings because they were harmful; as soon as my life recovered enough riches and pride, however, I regarded them again as forbidden, but this time because they were *beneath* me. That "Russian fatalism" of which I have spoken manifested itself in me in such a way that for years I held tenaciously to almost insufferable conditions, places,

habitations, and companions, once chance had placed them
on my path—it was better than changing them, than feeling
that they could be changed, than revolting against them.
. . . He who stirred me from this fatalism, he who violently
tried to shake me into consciousness, seemed to me then a
mortal enemy—in point of fact, there was danger of death
each time this was done. To regard one's self as a destiny,
not to wish one's self "different"—this, in such circumstances, is sagacity itself.

7

War, on the other hand, is something different. At heart I
am a warrior. Attacking belongs to my instincts. To *be able
to be* an enemy, to *be* an enemy—maybe these things
presuppose a strong nature; in any case all strong natures involve these things. Such natures need resistance; consequently they go in search of obstacles. The pathos of ag-
gression belongs of necessity to strength as much as the
feelings of revenge and of rancor belong to weakness.
Woman, for instance, is revengeful; her weakness involves
this passion, just as it involves her susceptibility in the presence of other people's suffering. The strength of the ag-
gressor can be measured by the opposition which he needs;
every increase of growth betrays itself by a seeking out of
more formidable opponents—or problems; for a philosopher
who is combative challenges even problems to a duel. The
task is not to overcome opponents in general, but only those
opponents against whom one has to summon all one's strength,
one's skill, and one's swordsmanship—in fact, opponents who
are one's equals. . . . To be one's enemy's equal—this is the
first condition of an honorable duel. Where one despises, one
cannot wage war. Where one commands, where one sees
something *beneath* one, one *ought* not to wage war. My war
tactics can be reduced to four principles: First, I attack only
things that are triumphant—if necessary I wait until they
become triumphant. Secondly, I attack only those things
against which I find no allies, against which I stand alone—
against which I compromise nobody but myself. . . . I have
not yet taken one single step before the public eye which did
not compromise me; that is *my* criterion of a proper mode
of action. Thirdly, I never make personal attacks—I use a
personality merely as a magnifying glass, by means of
which I render a general, but elusive and scarcely noticeable, evil more apparent. In this way I attacked David Strauss,

or rather the success given to a senile book by the cultured classes of Germany—by this means I caught German culture red-handed. In this way I attacked Wagner, or rather the falsity or mongrel instincts of our "culture" which confounds the super-refined with the strong, and the effete with the great. Fourthly, I attack only those things from which all personal differences are excluded, in which any such thing as a background of disagreeable experiences is lacking. On the contrary, attacking is to me a proof of good will and, in certain circumstances, of gratitude. By means of it, I do honor to a thing, I distinguish a thing; whether I associate my name with that of an institution or a person, by being *against* or *for* either, is all the same to me. If I wage war against Christianity, I feel justified in doing so, because in that quarter I have met with no fatal experiences and difficulties—the most earnest Christians have always been kindly disposed to me. I, personally, the most essential opponent of Christianity, am far from holding the individual responsible for what is the fatality of long ages.

8

May I be allowed to hazard a suggestion concerning one last trait in my character which in my intercourse with other men has led me into some difficulties? I am gifted with a sense of cleanliness the keenness of which is phenomenal; so much so, that I can ascertain physiologically—that is to say, smell—the proximity, nay, the inmost core, the "entrails" of every human soul. . . . This sensitiveness of mine is furnished with psychological antennæ, wherewith I feel and grasp every secret. The quality of concealed filth lying at the base of many a human character which may be the inevitable outcome of base blood, and which education may have veneered, is revealed to me at the first glance. If my observation has been correct, such people, whom my sense of cleanliness rejects, also become conscious, on their part, of the cautiousness to which my loathing prompts me; and this does not make them any more fragrant. . . . In keeping with a custom which I have long observed—pure habits and honesty toward myself are among the first conditions of my existence; I would die in unclean surroundings—I swim, bathe, and splash about, as it were, incessantly in water, in any kind of perfectly transparent and shining element. That is why my relations with my fellows try my patience to no small extent; my humanity does not consist in the fact that I understand the feelings of my fellows, but that I can endure to understand. . . . My humanity is a perpetual process of self-mastery. But I need solitude—that is to say, recovery, return to myself, the breathing of free, crisp, bracing air. . . . The whole of my *Zarathustra* is a dithyramb in honor of solitude, or, if I have been understood, in honor of purity. Thank Heaven, it is not in honor of "pure foolery"! * He who has an eye for color will call him a diamond. The loathing of mankind, of the rabble, was always my greatest danger. . . . Would you hearken to the words spoken by Zarathustra concerning deliverance from loathing?

"What forsooth hath come unto me? How did I deliver myself from loathing? Who hath made mine eye younger? How did I soar to the height, where there are no more rabble sitting about the well?

"Did my very loathing forge me wings and the strength to scent fountains afar off? Verily to the loftiest heights did I need to fly, to find once more the spring of joyfulness.

"Oh, I found it, my brethren! Up here, on the loftiest height, the spring of joyfulness gusheth forth for me. And there is a life at the well of which no rabble can drink with you.

"Almost too fiercely dost thou rush, for me, thou spring of joyfulness! And ofttimes dost thou empty the pitcher again in trying to fill it.

"And yet must I learn to draw near thee more humbly. Far too eagerly doth my heart jump to meet thee.

"My heart, whereon my summer burneth, my short, hot, melancholy, over-blessed summer; how my summer heart yearneth for thy coolness!

"Farewell, the lingering affliction of my spring! Past is the wickedness of my snowflakes in June! Summer have I become entirely, and summer noontide!

"A summer in the loftiest heights, with cold springs and blessed stillness: Oh come, my friends, that the stillness may wax even more blessed!

"For this is our height and our home. Too high and steep is our dwelling for all the unclean and their appetites.

"Do but cast your pure eyes into the well of my joyfulness, my friends! How could it thus become muddy! It will laugh back at you with its purity.

"On the tree called Future do we build our nest; eagles shall bring food in their beaks unto us lonely ones!

* This, of course, is a reference to Wagner's *Parsifal*. See my note on p. 96 of *The Will to Power*, Vol. I—Tr.

"Verily not the food whereof the unclean might partake. They would think they ate fire and would burn their mouths!

"Verily, no abodes for the unclean do we here hold in readiness! To their bodies our happiness would seem an ice cavern, and to their spirits also!

"And like strong winds will we live above them, neighbors to the eagles, companions of the snow, and playmates of the sun. Thus do strong winds live.

"And like a wind shall I one day blow amidst them, and take away their soul's breath with my spirit. Thus my future willeth it.

"Verily, a strong wind is Zarathustra to all low lands; and this is his counsel to his foes and to all those who spit and spew: 'Beware of spitting against the wind!' "

WHY I AM SO CLEVER

1

WHY do I know more things than other people? Why, in fact, am I so clever? I have never pondered over questions that are not questions. I have never squandered my strength. Of actual religious difficulties, for instance, I have no experience. I have never known what it is to feel "sinful." In the same way I completely lack any reliable criterion for ascertaining what constitutes a prick of conscience. From all accounts a prick of conscience does not seem to be a very estimable thing. . . . Once it was done I should hate to leave an action of mine in the lurch; I should prefer completely to omit the evil outcome, the consequences, from the problem concerning the value of an action. In the face of evil consequences one is too ready to lose the proper standpoint from which one's deed ought to be considered. A prick of conscience strikes me as a sort of "evil eye." Something that has failed should be honored all the more jealously, precisely because it has failed—this is much more in keeping with my morality. "God," "the immortality of the soul," "salvation," a "beyond"—to all these notions, even as a child, I never paid any attention whatsoever, nor did I waste any time upon them—maybe I was never naïve enough for that? I am quite unacquainted with atheism as a result, and still less as an event in my life; in me it is inborn, instinctive

I am too inquisitive, too incredulous, too high-spirited, to be satisfied with such a palpably clumsy solution of things. God is a too palpably clumsy solution of things, a solution which shows a lack of delicacy toward us thinkers—at bottom He is really no more than a coarse and rude *prohibition* of us: ye shall not think! . . . I am much more interested in another question, a question upon which the "salvation of humanity" depends to a far greater degree than it does upon any piece of theological curiosity. I refer to nutrition. For ordinary purposes, it may be formulated as follows: "How precisely must *thou* feed thyself in order to attain to thy maximum of power, or *virtù* in the Renaissance style—of virtue free from moralic acid?" My experiences in regard to this matter have been as bad as they possibly could be; I am surprised that I set myself this question so late in life, and that it took me so long to draw "rational" conclusions from my experiences. Only the absolute worthlessness of German culture—its "idealism"—can to some extent explain how it was that precisely in this matter I was so backward that my ignorance was almost saintly. This "culture," which from first to last teaches one to lose sight of actual things and to hunt after thoroughly problematic and so-called ideal aims, as, for instance, "classical culture"—as if it were not hopeless from the start to try to unite "classical" and "German" in one concept. It is even a little comical—try and imagine a "classically cultured" citizen of Leipzig! Indeed, I can say that up to a very mature age, my food was entirely bad—expressed morally, it was "impersonal," "selfless," "altruistic," to the glory of cooks and all other fellow-Christians. It was through the cooking in vogue at Leipzig, for instance, together with my first study of Schopenhauer (1865), that I earnestly renounced my "Will to Live." To spoil one's stomach by absorbing insufficient nourishment—this problem seemed to my mind solved with admirable felicity by the above-mentioned cookery. (It is said that in the year 1866 changes were introduced into this department.) But as to German cookery in general—what has it not got on its conscience! Soup *before* the meal (still called *alla tedesca* in the Venetian cookery books of the sixteenth century); meat boiled to shreds; vegetables cooked with fat and flour; the degeneration of pastries into paperweights! And, if you add thereto the absolutely bestial postprandial drinking habits of the *ancients,* and not alone of the ancient Germans, you will understand where German intellect took its origin—that is to say, in sadly disordered intestines. . . . German intellect is indigestion; it can assimilate nothing. But even English diet, which in comparison with German, and indeed with French alimentation, seems to me to constitute a "return to Nature"—that is to say, to cannibalism—is profoundly opposed to my own instincts. It seems to me to give the intellect heavy feet, in fact, Englishwomen's feet. . . . The best cooking is that of Piedmont. Alcoholic drinks do not agree with me; a single glass of wine or beer a day is amply sufficient to turn life into a valley of tears for me; in Munich live my antipodes. Although I admit that this knowledge came to me somewhat late, it already formed part of my experience even as a child. As a boy I believed that the drinking of wine and the smoking of tobacco were at first but the vanities of youths, and later merely bad habits. Maybe the poor wine of Naumburg was partly responsible for this poor opinion of wine in general. In order to believe that wine was exhilarating, I should have had to be a Christian—in other words, I should have had to believe in what, to my mind, is an absurdity. Strange to say, whereas small quantities of alcohol, taken with plenty of water, succeeded in making me feel out of sorts, large quantities turn me almost into a rollicking tar. Even as a boy I showed my bravado in this respect. To compose a long Latin essay in one night, to revise and recopy it, to aspire with my pen to emulating the exactitude and the terseness of my model, Sallust, and to pour a few very strong grogs over it all—this mode of procedure, while I was a pupil at the venerable old school of Pforta, was not in the least out of keeping with my physiology, nor perhaps with that of Sallust, however much it may have been alien to dignified Pforta. Later on, toward the middle of my life, I grew more and more opposed to alcoholic drinks: I, an opponent of vegetarianism, who have experienced what vegetarianism is—just as Wagner, who converted me back to meat, experienced it—cannot with sufficient earnestness advise all more *spiritual* natures to abstain absolutely from alcohol. Water answers the purpose. . . . I have a predilection in favor of those places where in all directions one has opportunities of drinking from running brooks (Nice, Turin, Sils). *In vino veritas:* it seems that here once more I am at variance with the rest of the world about the concept "Truth"—with me spirit moves on the face of the waters. . . . Here are a few more indications as to my morality. A heavy meal is digested more easily than an inadequate one. The first principle of a good digestion is that the stomach should become active as a whole. A man ought, therefore, to know the size of his stomach. For the same reasons all those

interminable meals, which I call interrupted sacrificial feasts,
and which are to be had at any table d'hôte, are strongly
to be deprecated. Nothing should be eaten between meals,
coffee should be given up—coffee makes one gloomy. Tea is
beneficial only in the morning. It should be taken in small
quantities, but very strong. It may be very harmful, and
indispose you for the whole day, if it be taken the least bit
too weak. Everybody has his own standard in this matter,
often between the narrowest and most delicate limits. In an
enervating climate tea is not a good beverage with which to
start the day; an hour before taking it an excellent thing is
to drink a cup of thick cocoa, freed from oil. Remain seated
as little as possible, put no trust in any thought that is not
born in the open to the accompaniment of free bodily motion—nor in one in which even the muscles do not celebrate
a feast. All prejudices take their origin in the intestines. A
sedentary life, as I have already said elsewhere, is the real
sin against the Holy Spirit.

2

To the question of nutrition, that of locality and climate is
next of kin. Nobody is so constituted as to be able to live
everywhere and anywhere; and he who has great duties to
perform, which lay claim to all his strength, has, in this
respect, a very limited choice. The influence of climate upon
the bodily functions, affecting their acceleration or retardation, extends so far that a blunder in the choice of locality
and climate is able not only to alienate a man from his
actual duty but also to withhold it from him altogether, so
that he never even comes face to face with it. Animal vigor
never acquires enough strength in him in order to reach
that pitch of artistic freedom which makes his own soul
whisper to him: I, alone, can do that. . . . Ever so slight a
tendency to laziness in the intestines, once it has become a
habit, is quite sufficient to make something mediocre, something "German" out of a genius; the climate of Germany,
alone, is enough to discourage the strongest and most he-
roically disposed intestines. The tempo of the body's functions is closely bound up with the agility or the clumsiness
of the spirit's feet; spirit itself is indeed only a form of
these organic functions. Let anybody make a list of the
places in which men of great intellect have been found, and
are still found; where wit, subtlety, and malice constitute
happiness; where genius is almost necessarily at home: all

of them rejoice in exceptionally dry air. Paris, Provence, Florence, Jerusalem, Athens—these names prove something, namely, that genius is conditioned by dry air, by a pure sky—that is to say, by rapid organic functions, by the constant and ever present possibility of procuring for one's self great and even enormous quantities of strength. I have a certain case in mind in which a man of remarkable intellect and independent spirit became a narrow, craven specialist and a grumpy old crank, simply owing to a lack of subtlety in his instinct for climate. And I myself might have been an example of the same thing if illness had not compelled me to reason, and to reflect upon reason realistically. Now that I have learnt through long practice to read the effects of climatic and meteorological influences from my own body, as though from a very delicate and reliable instrument, and that I am able to calculate the change in degrees of atmospheric moisture by means of physiological observations upon myself, even on so short a journey as that from Turin to Milan, I think with horror of the ghastly fact that my whole life, until the last ten years—the most perilous years—has always been spent in the wrong, and what to me ought to have been the most forbidden, places. Naumburg, Pforta, Thuringia in general, Leipzig, Basel, Venice—so many ill-starred places for a constitution like mine. If I cannot recall one single happy reminiscence of my childhood and youth, it is nonsense to suppose that so-called "moral" causes could account for this—as, for instance, the incontestable fact that I lacked companions that could have satisfied me; for this fact is the same today as it ever was, and it does not prevent me from being cheerful and brave. But it was ignorance in physiological matters—that confounded "Idealism"—that was the real curse of my life. This was the superfluous and foolish element in my existence; something from which nothing could spring, and for which there can be no settlement and no compensation. As the outcome of this "Idealism" I regard all the blunders, the great aberrations of instinct, and the "modest specializations" which drew me aside from the task of my life, as, for instance, the fact that I became a philologist—why not at least a medical man or anything else which might have opened my eyes? My days at Basel, the whole of my intellectual routine, including my daily time-table, was an absolutely senseless abuse of extraordinary powers, without the slightest compensation for the strength that I spent, without even a thought of what I was squandering and how its place might be filled. I lacked all subtlety in egoism, all the fostering care of an imperative instinct; I

was in a state in which one is ready to regard one's self as
anybody's equal, a state of "disinterestedness," a forgetting
of one's distance from others—something, in short, for which
I can never forgive myself. When I had well-nigh reached
the end of my tether, simply because I had almost reached
my end, I began to reflect upon the fundamental absurdity of
my life—"Idealism." It was *illness* that first brought me to
reason.

3

After the choice of nutrition, the choice of climate and
locality, the third matter concerning which one must not on
any account make a blunder, is the choice of the manner in
which one *recuperates one's strength*. Here, again, according
to the extent to which a spirit is *sui generis*, the limits of
that which he can allow himself—in other words, the limits
of that which is beneficial to him—become more and more
confined. As far as I in particular am concerned, *reading* in
general belongs to my means of recuperation; consequently
it belongs to that which rids me of myself, to that which
enables me to wander in strange sciences and strange souls
—to that, in fact, about which I am no longer in earnest.
Indeed, it is while reading that I recover from *my* earnestness. During the time that I am deeply absorbed in my work,
no books are found within my reach; it would never occur to
me to allow anyone to speak or even to think in my presence. For that is what reading would mean. . . . Has anyone
ever actually noticed that during the period of profound
tension to which the state of pregnancy condemns not only
the mind but also, at bottom, the whole organism accident
and every kind of external stimulus acts too acutely and
strikes too deep? Accident and external stimuli must, as far as
possible, be avoided; a sort of walling-of-one's-self-in is one
of the primary instinctive precautions of spiritual pregnancy.
Shall I allow a strange thought to steal secretly over the
wall? For that is what reading would mean. . . . The periods of work and fruitfulness are followed by periods of recuperation; come hither, ye delightful, intellectual, intelligent books! Shall I read German books? . . . I must go
back six months to catch myself with a book in my hand.
What was it? An excellent study by Victor Brochard upon
the Greek sceptics, in which my Laertiana* was used to

---

* Nietzsche, as is well known, devoted much time when a student at
Leipzig to the study of three Greek philosophers, Theognis, Diogenes

advantage. The sceptics!—the only *honorable* types among that double-faced and sometimes quintuple-faced throng, the philosophers! . . . Otherwise I almost always take refuge in the same books. Altogether their number is small; they are books which are precisely my proper fare. It is not perhaps in my nature to read much, and of all sorts; a library makes me ill. Neither is it my nature to love much or many kinds of things. Suspicion or even hostility toward new books is much more akin to my instinctive feeling than "toleration," *largeur de cœur*, and other forms of "neighbor-love." . . . It is to a small number of old French authors that I always return again and again; I believe only in French culture, and regard everything else in Europe which calls itself "culture" as a misunderstanding. I do not even take the German kind into consideration. . . . The few instances of higher culture with which I have met in Germany were all French in their original. The most striking example of this was Madame Cosima Wagner, by far the most decisive voice in matters of taste that I have ever heard. If I do not read, but literally love Pascal, as the most instinctive sacrifice to Christianity, killing himself inch by inch, first bodily, then spiritually, according to the terrible consistency of this most appalling form of inhuman cruelty; if I have something of Montaigne's mischievousness in my soul, and—who knows?—perhaps also in my body; if my artist's taste endeavors to defend the names of Molière, Corneille, and Racine, and not without bitterness, against such a wild genius as Shakespeare—all this does not prevent me from regarding even the latter-day Frenchmen also as charming companions. I can think of absolutely no century in history, in which a netful of more inquisitive and at the same time more subtle psychologists could be drawn up together than in the Paris of the present day. Let me mention a few at random—for their number is by no means small—Paul Bourget, Pierre Loti, Gyp, Meilhac, Anatole France, Jules Lemaître or, to point to one of strong race, a genuine Latin, of whom I am particularly fond, Guy de Maupassant. Between ourselves, I prefer this generation, even to its masters, all of whom were corrupted

---

Laertius, and Democritus. This study first bore fruit in the case of a paper, *Zur Geschichte der Theognideischen Spruchsammlung*, which was subsequently published by the most influential journal of classical philology in Germany. Later, however, it enabled Nietzsche to enter for the prize offered by the University of Leipzig for an essay, *De fontibus Diogenis Laertii*. He was successful in gaining the prize, and the treatise was afterward published in the *Rheinisches Museum*, and is still quoted as an authority. It is to this essay, written when he was twenty-three years of age, that he here refers.—Tr.

by German philosophy (Taine, for instance, by Hegel, whom he has to thank for his misunderstanding of great men and great periods). Wherever Germany extends her sway, she *ruins* culture. It was the war which first saved the spirit of France. . . . Stendhal is one of the happiest accidents of my life—for everything that marks an epoch in it has been brought to me by accident and never by means of a recommendation. He is quite priceless, with his psychologist's eye, quick at forestalling and anticipating; with his grasp of facts, which is reminiscent of the same art in the greatest of all masters of facts (*ex ungue Napoleonem*); and, last but not least, as an honest atheist—a specimen which is both rare and difficult to discover in France—all honor to Prosper Mérimée! . . . Maybe that I am even envious of Stendhal? He robbed me of the best atheistic joke which I of all people could have perpetrated: "God's only excuse is that He does not exist." . . . I myself have said somewhere: What has been the greatest objection to Life hitherto?— God. . . .

4

It was Heinrich Heine who gave me the most perfect idea of what a lyrical poet could be. In vain do I search through all the kingdoms of antiquity or of modern times for anything to resemble his sweet and passionate music. He possessed that divine wickedness without which perfection itself becomes unthinkable to me—I estimate the value of men, of races, according to the extent to which they are unable to conceive of a god who has not a dash of the satyr in him. And with what mastery he wields his native tongue! One day it will be said of Heine and me that we were by far the greatest artists of the German language that have ever existed, and that we left all the efforts that mere Germans made in this language an incalculable distance behind us. I must be profoundly related to Byron's *Manfred*; of all the dark abysses in this work I found the counterparts in my own soul—at the age of thirteen I was ripe for this book. Words fail me, I have only a look, for those who dare to utter the name of *Faust* in the presence of *Manfred*. The Germans are *incapable* of conceiving anything sublime; for a proof of this, look at Schumann! Out of anger for this mawkish Saxon, I once deliberately composed a counteroverture to *Manfred*; of which Hans von Bülow declared he had never seen the like before on paper; such compositions amounted to a violation of Euterpe. When I cast about me for my highest formula of Shakespeare, I find invariably but this one: that he conceived the type of Caesar. Such things a man cannot guess—he either is the thing, or he is not. The great poet draws his creations only from out of his own reality. This is so to such an extent that often after a lapse of time he can no longer endure his own work. . . . After casting a glance between the pages of my *Zarathustra,* I pace my room to and fro for half an hour at a time, unable to overcome an insufferable fit of tears. I know of no more heartrending reading than Shakespeare: how a man must have suffered to be so much in need of playing the clown! Is Hamlet *understood?* It is not doubt but certitude that drives one mad. . . . But in order to feel this, one must be profound, one must be an abyss, a philosopher. . . . We all fear the truth. . . . And, to make a confession, I feel instinctively certain and convinced that Lord Bacon is the originator, the self-torturer, of this most sinister kind of literature: what do I care about the miserable gabble of American muddlers and blockheads? But the power for the greatest realism in vision is not only compatible with the greatest realism in deeds, with the monstrous in deeds, with crime—*it actually presupposes the latter.* . . . We do not know half enough about Lord Bacon—the first realist in all the highest acceptation of this word—to be sure of everything he did, everything he willed, and everything he experienced in his inmost soul. . . . Let the critics go to hell! Suppose I had christened my *Zarathustra* with a name not my own—let us say with Richard Wagner's name—the acumen of two thousand years would not have sufficed to guess that the author of *Human, All Too Human* was the visionary of *Zarathustra.*

5

As I am speaking here of the recreations of my life, I feel I must express a word or two of gratitude for that which has refreshed me by far the most heartily and most profoundly. This, without the slightest doubt, was my intimate relationship with Richard Wagner. All my other relationships with men I treat quite lightly; but I would not have the days I spent at Triebschen—those days of confidence, of cheerfulness, of sublime flashes, and of profound moments—blotted from my life at any price. I know not what Wagner may have been for others; but no cloud ever darkened *our* sky. And this brings me back again to France—I have no argu-

ments against Wagnerites, and *hoc genus omne,* who believe
that they do honor to Wagner by believing him to be like
themselves; for such people I have only a contemptuous curl
of my lip. With a nature like mine, which is so strange to
everything Teutonic that even the presence of a German re-
tards my digestion, my first meeting with Wagner was the first
moment in my life in which I breathed freely: I felt him, I
honored him, as a foreigner, as the opposite and the incarnate contradiction of all "German virtues." We who as
children breathed the marshy atmosphere of the fifties, are
necessarily pessimists in regard to the concept "German"; we
cannot be anything else than revolutionaries—we can assent
to no state of affairs which allows the canting bigot to be at
the top. I care not a jot whether this canting bigot acts in
different colors today, whether he dresses in scarlet or dons
the uniform of a hussar.* Very well, then! Wagner was a
revolutionary—he fled from the Germans. . . . As an artist,
a man has no home in Europe save in Paris; that subtlety of
all the five senses which Wagner's art presupposes, those
fingers that can detect slight gradations, psychological mor-
bidity—all these things can be found only in Paris. Nowhere
else can you meet with this passion for questions of form,
this earnestness in matters of *mise-en-scène,* which is the
Parisian earnestness *par excellence.* In Germany no one has
any idea of the tremendous ambition that fills the heart of a
Parisian artist. The German is a good fellow. Wagner was
by no means a good fellow. . . . But I have already said quite
enough on the subject of Wagner's real nature (see *Beyond
Good and Evil,* Aphorism 269), and about those to whom
he is most closely related. He is one of the late French romanticists, that high-soaring and heaven-aspiring band of
artists, like Delacroix and Berlioz, who in their inmost natures are sick and incurable, and who are all fanatics of
expression, and virtuosos through and through. . . . Who, in
sooth, was the first intelligent follower of Wagner? Charles
Baudelaire, the very man who first understood Delacroix
—that typical decadent, in whom a whole generation of
artists saw their reflection; he was perhaps the last of
them too. . . . What is it that I have never forgiven Wagner?
The fact that he condescended to the Germans—that he became a German Imperialist. . . . Wherever Germany spreads,
she *ruins* culture.

* The favorite uniform of the Geman Emperor, William II.—TR.

6

Taking everything into consideration, I could never have survived my youth without Wagnerian music. For I was condemned to the society of Germans. If a man wishes to get rid of a feeling of insufferable oppression, he has to take to hashish. Well, I had to take to Wagner. Wagner is the counterpoison to everything essentially German—the fact that he is a poison, too, I do not deny. From the moment that *Tristan* was arranged for the piano—all honor to you, Herr von Bülow!—I was a Wagnerite. Wagner's previous works seemed beneath me—they were too commonplace, too "German." . . . But to this day I am still seeking for a work which would be a match to *Tristan* in dangerous fascination, and possess the same gruesome and dulcet quality of infinity; I seek among all the arts in vain. All the quaint features of Leonardo da Vinci's work lose their charm at the sound of the first bar in *Tristan*. This work is without question Wagner's *non plus ultra*; after its creation, the composition of *Die Meistersinger* and of the *Ring* was a relaxation to him. To become more healthy—this in a nature like Wagner's amounts to going backward. The curiosity of the psychologist is so great in me that I regard it as quite a special privilege to have lived at the right time, and to have lived precisely among Germans, in order to be ripe for this work. The world must indeed be empty for him who has never been unhealthy enough for this "infernal voluptuousness"; it is allowable, it is even imperative, to employ a mystic formula for this purpose. I suppose I know better than anyone the prodigious feats of which Wagner was capable, the fifty worlds of strange ecstasies to which no one else had wings to soar; and as I am alive today and strong enough to turn even the most suspicious and most dangerous things to my own advantage, and thus to grow stronger, I declare Wagner to have been the greatest benefactor of my life. The bond which unites us is the fact that we have suffered greater agony, even at each other's hands, than most men are able to bear nowadays, and this will always keep our names associated in the minds of men. For, just as Wagner is merely a misunderstanding among Germans, so, in truth, am I, and ever will be. Ye lack two centuries of psychological and artistic discipline, my dear countrymen! . . . But ye can never recover the time lost.

7

To the most exceptional of my readers I should like to say just one word about what I really exact from music. It must be cheerful and yet profound, like an October afternoon. It must be original, exuberant, and tender, and like a dainty, soft woman in roguishness and grace. . . . I shall never admit that a German *can* understand what music is. Those musicians who are called German, the greatest and most famous foremost, are all foreigners, either Slavs, Croats, Italians, Dutchmen—or Jews; or else, like Heinrich Schütz, Bach, and Handel, they are Germans of a strong race which is now extinct. For my own part, I have still enough of the Pole left in me to let all other music go, if only I can keep Chopin. For three reasons I would except Wagner's *Siegfried Idyll*, and perhaps also one or two things of Liszt, who excelled all other musicians in the noble tone of his orchestration; and finally everything that has been produced beyond the Alps—*this side* of the Alps.* I could not possibly dispense with Rossini, and still less with my Southern soul in music, the work of my Venetian maestro, Pietro Gasti. And when I say beyond the Alps, all I really mean is Venice. If I try to find a new word for music, I can never find any other than Venice. I know not how to draw any distinction between tears and music. I do not know how to think either of joy, or of the south, without a shudder of fear.

> On the bridge I stood
> Lately, in gloomy night.
> Came a distant song:
> In golden drops it rolled
> Over the glittering rim away.
> Music, gondolas, lights—
> Drunk, swam far forth in the gloom. . . .
>
> A stringed instrument, my soul,
> Sang, imperceptibly moved,
> A gondola song by stealth,
> Gleaming for gaudy blessedness.
> —Hearkened any thereto?

* In the latter years of his life, Nietzsche practically made Italy his home.—Tr.

8

In all these things—in the choice of food, place, climate, and recreation—the instinct of self-preservation is dominant, and this instinct manifests itself with least ambiguity when it acts as an instinct of defense. To close one's eyes to much, to seal one's ears to much, to keep certain things at a distance —this is the first principle of prudence, the first proof of the fact that a man is not an accident but a necessity. The popular word for this instinct of defense is *taste*. A man's imperative command is not only to say "no" in cases where "yes" would be a sign of "disinterestedness" but also to say "no" *as seldom as possible*. One must part with all that which compels one to repeat "no" with ever greater frequency. The rationale of this principle is that all discharges of defensive forces, however slight they may be, involve enormous and absolutely superfluous losses when they become regular and habitual. Our greatest expenditure of strength is made up of those small and most frequent discharges of it. The act of keeping things off, of holding them at a distance, amounts to a discharge of strength—do not deceive yourselves on this point!—and an expenditure of energy directed at purely negative ends. Simply by being compelled to keep constantly on his guard, a man may grow so weak as to be unable any longer to defend himself. Suppose I were to step out of my house, and, instead of the quiet and aristocratic city of Turin, I were to find a German provincial town, my instinct would have to brace itself together in order to repel all that which would pour in upon it from this crushed-down and cowardly world. Or suppose I were to find a large German city—that structure of vice in which nothing grows, but where every single thing, whether good or bad, is squeezed in from outside. In such circumstances should I not be compelled to become a hedgehog? But to have prickles amounts to a squandering of strength; they even constitute a twofold luxury, when, if we only chose to do so, we could dispense with them and open our hands instead. . . .

Another form of prudence and self-defense consists in trying to react as seldom as possible, and to keep one's self aloof from those circumstances and conditions wherein one would be condemned, as it were, to suspend one's "liberty" and one's initiative, and become a mere reacting medium. As an example of this I point to the intercourse with books. The scholar who, in sooth, does little else than handle books

—with the philologist of average attainments their number
may amount to two hundred a day—ultimately forgets entirely and completely the capacity of thinking for himself.
When he has not a book between his fingers, he cannot think.
When he thinks, he responds to a stimulus (a thought he
has read)—finally all he does is to react. The scholar exhausts
his whole strength in saying either "yes" or "no" to matter
which has already been thought out, or in criticizing it—he
is no longer capable of thought on his own account. . . .
In him the instinct of self-defense has decayed, otherwise
he would defend himself against books. The scholar is a
decadent. With my own eyes I have seen gifted, richly endowed, and free-spirited natures already "read to ruins" at
thirty, and mere wax vestas that have to be rubbed before
they can give off any sparks—or "thoughts." To set to early
in the morning, at the break of day, in all the fullness and
dawn of one's strength, and to read a book—this I call
positively vicious!

9

At this point I can no longer evade a direct answer to
the question, *how one becomes what one is*. And in giving it,
I shall have to touch upon that masterpiece in the art of self-
preservation, which is *selfishness*. . . . Granting that one's life
task—the determination and the fate of one's life task—
greatly exceeds the average measure of such things, nothing
more dangerous could be conceived than to come face to
face with one's self by the side of this life task. The fact that
one becomes what one is presupposes that one has not the
remotest suspicion of what one is. From this standpoint even
the blunders of one's life have their own meaning and value,
the temporary deviations and aberrations, the moments of
hesitation and of modesty, the earnestness wasted upon duties which lie outside the actual life task. In these matters
great wisdom, perhaps even the highest wisdom, comes into
activity; in these circumstances, in which *nosce teipsum*
would be the sure road to ruin, forgetting one's self, misunderstanding one's self, belittling one's self, narrowing one's
self, and making one's self mediocre amount to reason itself. Expressed morally, to love one's neighbor and to live
for others and for other things *may* be the means of protection employed to maintain the hardest kind of egoism. This
is the exceptional case in which I, contrary to my principle
and conviction, take the side of the altruistic instincts; for

here they are concerned in subserving selfishness and self-discipline. The whole surface of consciousness—for consciousness *is* a surface—must be kept free from any one of the great imperatives. Beware even of every striking word, of every striking attitude! They are all so many risks which the instinct runs of "understanding itself" too soon. Meanwhile the organizing "idea," which is destined to become master, grows and continues to grow into the depths—it begins to command, it leads you slowly back from your deviations and aberrations, it prepares individual qualities and capacities, which one day will make themselves felt as indispensable to the whole of your task—step by step it cultivates all the serviceable faculties before it ever whispers a word concerning the dominant task, the "goal," the "object," and the "meaning" of it all. Looked at from this standpoint my life is simply amazing. For the task of *transvaluing values,* more capacities were needful perhaps than could well be found side by side in one individual; and above all, antagonistic capacities which had to be free from the mutual strife and destruction which they involve. An order of rank among capacities; distance; the art of separating without creating hostility; to refrain from confounding things; to keep from reconciling things; to possess enormous multifariousness and yet to be the reverse of chaos—all this was the first condition, the long secret work, and the artistic mastery of my instinct. Its superior guardianship manifested itself with such exceeding strength that not once did I ever dream of what was growing within me—until suddenly all my capacities were ripe, and one day burst forth in all the perfection of their highest bloom. I cannot remember ever having exerted myself, I can point to no trace of *struggle* in my life; I am the reverse of a heroic nature. To "will" something, to "strive" after something, to have an "aim" or a "desire" in my mind—I know none of these things from experience. Even at this moment I look out upon my future—a *broad* future!—as upon a calm sea; no sigh of longing makes a ripple on its surface. I have not the slightest wish that anything should be otherwise than it is: I myself would not be otherwise. . . . But in this matter I have always been the same. I have never had a desire. A man who, after his four-and-fortieth year, can say that he has never bothered himself about *honors, women,* or *money!*—not that they did not come his way. . . . It was thus that I became one day a university professor—I had never had the remotest idea of such a thing, for I was scarcely four-and-twenty years of age. In the same way, two years previously, I had one day become a philologist, in the sense that my *first* philological work, my start in every way, was expressly obtained by my master Ritschl for publication in his *Rheinisches Museum*. (Ritschl—and I say it in all reverence—was the only genial scholar that I have ever met. He possessed that pleasant kind of depravity which distinguishes us Thuringians, and which makes even a German sympathetic—even in the pursuit of truth we prefer to avail ourselves of roundabout ways. In saying this I do not mean to underestimate in any way my Thuringian brother, the intelligent Leopold von Ranke. . . .)

10

You may be wondering why I should actually have related all these trivial and, according to traditional accounts, insignificant details to you; such action can but tell against me, more particularly if I am fated to figure in great causes. To this I reply that these trivial matters—diet, locality, climate, and one's mode of recreation, the whole casuistry of self-love—are inconceivably more important than all that which has hitherto been held in high esteem. It is precisely in this quarter that we must begin to learn afresh. All those things which mankind has valued with such earnestness heretofore are not even real; they are mere creations of fancy, or, more strictly speaking, *lies* born of the evil instincts of diseased and, in the deepest sense, noxious natures—all the concepts, "God," "soul," "virtue," "sin," "Beyond," "truth," "eternal life." . . . But the greatness of human nature, its "divinity," was sought for in them. . . . All questions of politics, of social order, of education, have been falsified, root and branch, owing to the fact that the most noxious men have been taken for great men, and that people were taught to despise the small things, or rather the fundamental things, of life. If I now choose to compare myself with those creatures who have hitherto been honored as the first among men, the difference becomes obvious. I do not reckon the so-called "first" men even as human beings—for me they are the excrements of mankind, the products of disease and of the instinct of revenge; they are so many monsters laden with rottenness, so many hopeless incurables, who avenge themselves on life. . . . I wish to be the opposite of these people; it is my privilege to have the very sharpest discernment for every sign of healthy instincts. There is no such thing as a morbid trait in me; even in times of serious illness I have never grown morbid, and you might seek in vain for a trace of fanaticism in my nature. No one can point to any moment of my life in which I have assumed either an arrogant or a pathetic attitude. Pathetic attitudes are not in keeping with greatness; he who needs attitudes is false. . . . Beware of all picturesque men! Life was easy—in fact easiest —to me in those periods when it exacted the heaviest duties from me. Whoever could have seen me during the seventy days of this autumn, when, without interruption, I did a host of things of the highest rank—things that no man can do nowadays—with a sense of responsibility for all the ages yet to come, would have noticed no sign of tension in my condition, but rather a state of overflowing freshness and good cheer. Never have I eaten with more pleasant sensations, never has my sleep been better. I know of no other manner of dealing with great tasks than as *play;* this, as a sign of greatness, is an essential prerequisite. The slightest constraint, a somber mien, any hard accent in the voice—all these things are objections to a man, but how much more to his work! . . . One must not have nerves. . . . Even to *suffer* from solitude is an objection—the only thing I have always suffered from is "multitude." * At an absurdly tender age, in fact when I was seven years old, I already knew that no human speech would ever reach me. Did anyone ever see me sad on that account? At present I still possess the same affability toward everybody, I am even full of consideration for the lowest; in all this there is not an atom of haughtiness or of secret contempt. He whom I despise soon guesses that he is despised by me; the very fact of my existence is enough to rouse indignation in all those who have polluted blood in their veins. My formula for greatness in man is *amor fati:* the fact that a man wishes nothing to be different, either in front of him or behind him, or for all eternity. Not only must the necessary be borne, and on no account concealed— all idealism is falsehood in the face of necessity—but it must also be *loved*. . . .

* The German words are *Einsamkeit* and *Vielsamkeit.* The latter was coined by Nietzsche. The English word "multitude" should, therefore, be understood as signifying multifarious instincts and gifts, which in Nietzsche strove for ascendancy and caused him more suffering than any solitude. Complexity of this sort, held in check by a dominant instinct, as in Nietzsche's case, is of course the only possible basis of an artistic nature.—Tr.

FROM NIETZSCHE CONTRA WAGNER*

We Antipodes

Perhaps a few people, or at least my friends, will remember that I made my first plunge into life armed with some errors and some exaggerations, but that, in any case, I began with *hope* in my heart. In the philosophical pessimism of the nineteenth century, I recognized—who knows by what by-paths of personal experience—the symptom of a higher power of thought, a more triumphant plenitude of life, than had manifested itself hitherto in the philosophies of Hume, Kant and Hegel!—I regarded *tragic* knowledge as the most beautiful luxury of our culture, as its most precious, most noble, most dangerous kind of prodigality; but, nevertheless, in view of its overflowing wealth, as a justifiable *luxury*. In the same way, I began by interpreting Wagner's music as the expression of a Dionysian powerfulness of soul. In it I thought I heard the earthquake by means of which a primeval life-force, which had been constrained for ages, was seeking at last to burst its bonds, quite indifferent to how much of that which nowadays calls itself culture, would thereby be shaken to ruins. You see how I misinterpreted, you see also, what I *bestowed* upon Wagner and Schopenhauer—myself. . . . Every art and every philosophy may be regarded either as a cure or as a stimulant to ascending or declining life: they always presuppose suffering and sufferers. But there are two kinds of sufferers: those that suffer from *overflowing vitality*, who need Dionysian art and require a tragic insight into, and a tragic outlook upon, the phenomenon life—and there are those who suffer from *reduced* vitality, and who crave for repose, quietness, calm seas, or else the intoxication, the spasm, the bewilderment which art and philosophy provide. Revenge upon life itself—this is the most voluptuous form of intoxication for such indigent souls! . . . Now Wagner responds quite as well as Schopenhauer to the twofold cravings of these people—they both deny life; they both slander it, but precisely on this account they are my antipodes. The richest creature, brimming over with vitality, the Dionysian

* From *The Case of Wagner*.

God and man, may not only allow himself to gaze upon the horrible and the questionable; but he can also lend his hand to the terrible deed, and can indulge in all the luxury of destruction, disaggregation, and negation—in him evil, purposelessness, and ugliness seem just as allowable as they are in nature—because of his bursting plenitude of creative and rejuvenating powers, which are able to convert every desert into a luxurious land of plenty. Conversely, it is the greatest sufferer and pauper in vitality who is most in need of mildness, peace, and goodness—that which today is called humaneness—in thought as well as in action, and possibly of a God whose speciality is to be a God of the sick, a Saviour, and also of logic or the abstract intelligibility of existence even for idiots (the typical "free spirits," like the idealists, and "beautiful souls," are *decadents*); in short, of a warm, danger-tight, and narrow confinement, between optimistic horizons which would allow of stultification. . . . And thus very gradually, I began to understand Epicurus, the opposite of a Dionysian Greek, and also the Christian who in fact is only a kind of Epicurean, and who, with his belief that "faith saves," carries the principle of Hedonism *as far as possible*—far beyond all intellectual honesty. . . . If I am ahead of all other psychologists in anything, it is in this fact that my eyes are more keen for tracing those most difficult and most captious of all deductions, in which the largest number of mistakes have been made—the deduction which makes one infer something concerning the author from his work, something concerning the doer from his deed, something concerning the idealist from the need which produced this ideal, and something concerning the imperious *craving* which stands at the back of all thinking and valuing. In regard to all artists of what kind soever, I shall now avail myself of this radical distinction: Does the creative power in this case arise from a loathing of life, or from an excessive *plenitude* of life? In Goethe, for instance, an overflow of vitality was creative, in Flaubert—hate: Flaubert, a new edition of Pascal, but as an artist with this instinctive belief at heart: *"Flaubert est toujours haïssable, l'homme n'est rien, l'œuvre est tout."* . . . He tortured himself when he wrote, just as Pascal tortured himself when he thought—the feelings of both were inclined to be "nonegoistic." . . . "Disinterestedness"—principle of decadence, the will to nonentity in art as well as in morality.

FROM THE JOYFUL WISDOM

377

WE HOMELESS ONES.—Among the Europeans of today there are not lacking those who may call themselves homeless ones in a way which is at once a distinction and an honor; it is by them that my secret wisdom and *gaya scienza* is expressly to be laid to heart. For their lot is hard, their hope uncertain; it is a clever feat to devise consolation for them. But what good does it do! We children of the future, how *could* we be at home in the present? We are unfavorable to all ideals which could make us feel at home in this frail, broken-down, transition period; and as regards the "realities" thereof, we do not believe in their *endurance*. The ice which still carries us has become very thin; the thawing wind blows; we ourselves, the homeless ones, are an influence that breaks the ice, and the other all too thin "realities." . . . We "preserve" nothing, nor would we return to any past age; we are not at all "liberal," we do not labor for "progress," we do not need first to stop our ears to the song of the market place and the sirens of the future—their song of "equal rights," "free society," "no longer either lords or slaves" does not allure us! We do not by any means think it desirable that the kingdom of righteousness and peace should be established on earth (because under any circumstances it would be the kingdom of the profoundest mediocrity and Chinaism); we rejoice in all men, who, like ourselves, love danger, war, and adventure, who do not make compromises, nor let themselves be captured, conciliated and stunted; we count ourselves among the conquerors; we ponder over the need of a new order of things, even of a new slavery—for every strengthening and elevation of the type "man" also involves a new form of slavery. Is it not obvious that with all this we must feel ill at ease in an age which claims the honor of being the most humane, gentle, and just that the sun has ever seen? What a pity that at the mere mention of these fine words, the thoughts at the back of our minds are all the most unpleasant, that we see therein only the expression—or the masquerade—of profound weakening, exhaustion, age, and declining power! What can it matter to us with what kind of tinsel an invalid decks out his weakness? He may parade it as his *virtue;* there is no doubt whatever that weakness makes people gentle, alas, so gentle, so just, so inoffensive, so "humane"! The "religion of pity," to which people would like to persuade us—yes, we know sufficiently well the hysterical little men and women who need this religion at present as a cloak and adornment! We are no humanitarians; we should not dare to speak of our "love of mankind"; for that, a person of our stamp is not enough of an actor! Or not sufficiently Saint-Simonist, not sufficiently French. A person must have been affected with a *Gallic* excess of erotic susceptibility and amorous impatience even to approach mankind honorably with his lewdness. . . . Mankind! Was there ever a more hideous old woman among all old women (unless perhaps it were "the Truth": a question for philosophers)? No, we do not love Mankind! On the other hand, however, we are not nearly "German" enough (in the sense in which the word "German" is current at present) to advocate nationalism and race-hatred, or take delight in the national heart-itch and blood poisoning, on account of which the nations of Europe are at present bounded off and secluded from one another as if by quarantines. We are too unprejudiced for that, too perverse, too fastidious, also too well-informed, and too much "traveled." We prefer much rather to live on mountains, apart and "out of season," in past or coming centuries, in order merely to spare ourselves the silent rage to which we know we should be condemned as witnesses of a system of politics which makes the German nation barren by making it vain, and which is a *petty* system besides. Will it not be necessary for this system to plant itself between two mortal hatreds, lest its own creation should immediately collapse? Will it not *be obliged* to desire the perpetuation of the petty-state system of Europe? . . . We homeless ones are too diverse and mixed in race and descent as "modern men," and are consequently little tempted to participate in the falsified racial self-admiration and lewdness which at present display themselves in Germany, as signs of German sentiment, and which strike one as doubly false and unbecoming in the people with the "historical sense." We are, in a word—and it shall be our word of honor!—*good Europeans,* the heirs of Europe, the rich, overwealthy heirs, also the too deeply pledged heirs of millenniums of European thought. As such, we have also outgrown Christianity, and are disinclined to it—and just because we have grown *out of* it, because our forefathers were Christians uncompromising in their Christian integrity, who willingly sacrificed possessions and positions, blood and country, for the sake of their belief. We—do the same. For what, then? For our unbelief? For all sorts of unbelief? Nay, you know better than that, my friends! The hidden *Yea* in you is stronger than all the Nays and Perhapses, of which you and your age are sick; and when you are obliged to put out to sea, you emigrants, it is—once more a *faith* which urges you thereto! . . .

378

"AND ONCE MORE GROW CLEAR."—We, the generous and rich in spirit, who stand at the sides of the streets like open fountains and would hinder no one from drinking from us, we do not know, alas! how to defend ourselves when we should like to do so; we have no means of preventing ourselves being made *turbid* and dark—we have no means of preventing the age in which we live casting its "up-to-date rubbish" into us, nor of hindering filthy birds throwing their excrement, the boys their trash, and fatigued resting travelers their misery, great and small, into us. But we do as we have always done; we take whatever is cast into us down into our depths—for we are deep, we do not forget—*and once more grow clear*. . . .

379

THE FOOL'S INTERRUPTION.—It is not a misanthrope who has written this book; the hatred of men costs too dear today. To hate as they formerly hated *man*, in the fashion of Timon, completely, without qualification, with all the heart, from the pure *love* of hatred—for that purpose one would have to renounce contempt—and how much refined pleasure, how much patience, how much benevolence even, do we owe to contempt! Moreover we are thereby the "elect of God"; refined contempt is our taste and privilege, our art, our virtue perhaps, we, the most modern amongst the moderns! . . . Hatred, on the contrary, makes equal, it puts men face to face, in hatred there is honor; finally, in hatred there is *fear*, quite a large amount of fear. We fearless ones, however, we, the most intellectual men of the period, know our advantage well enough to live without fear as the most intellectual persons of this age. People will not easily behead us, shut us up, or banish us; they will not even ban or burn our books. The age loves intellect, it loves us, and needs us, even when we have to give it to understand that we are artists in despising; that all intercourse with men is something of a horror to us; that with all our gentleness, patience, humanity and courteousness, we cannot persuade our nose to abandon its prejudice against the proximity of man; that we love nature the more, the less humanly things are done by her, and that we love art *when* it is the flight of the artist from man, or the raillery of the artist at man, or the raillery of the artist at himself. . . .

380

"THE WANDERER" SPEAKS.—In order for one to get a glimpse of our European morality from a distance, in order to compare it with other earlier or future moralities, one must do as the traveler who wants to know the height of the towers of a city; for that purpose he *leaves* the city. "Thoughts concerning moral prejudices," if they are not to be prejudices concerning prejudices, presuppose a position *outside of* morality, some sort of world beyond good and evil, to which one must ascend, climb, or fly—and in the given case at any rate, a position beyond *our* good and evil, an emancipation from all "Europe," understood as a sum of inviolable valuations which have become part and parcel of our flesh and blood. That one *wants* in fact to get outside, or aloft, is perhaps a sort of madness, a peculiarly unreasonable "thou must"—for even we thinkers have our idiosyncrasies of "unfree will"—; the question is whether one *can* really get there. That may depend on manifold conditions; in the main it is a question of how light or how heavy we are, the problem of our "specific gravity." One must be *very light* in order to impel one's will to knowledge to such a distance, and as it were beyond one's age, in order to create eyes for oneself for the survey of millenniums, and a pure heaven in these eyes besides! One must have freed oneself from many things by which we Europeans of today are oppressed, hindered, held down, and made heavy. The man of such a "Beyond," who wants to get even in sight of the highest standards of worth of his age, must first of all "surmount" this age in himself—it is the test of his power—and consequently not only his age, but also his past aversion and opposition *to* his age, his suffering *caused by* his age, his unseasonableness, his Romanticism. . . .

FROM THE TWILIGHT OF THE IDOLS

2

I am not indebted to the Greeks for anything like such strong impressions; and, to speak frankly, they cannot be to us what the Romans are. One cannot *learn* from the Greeks —their style is too strange, it is also too fluid, to be imperative or to have the effect of a classic. Who would ever have learnt writing from a Greek! Who would ever have learned it without the Romans! . . . Do not let anyone suggest Plato to me. In regard to Plato I am a thorough sceptic, and have never been able to agree to the admiration of Plato the *artist*, which is traditional among scholars. And after all, in this matter, the most refined judges of taste in antiquity are on my side. In my opinion Plato bundles all the forms of style pell-mell together; in this respect he is one of the first decadents of style. He has something similar on his conscience to that which the Cynics had who invented the *satura Menippea*. For the Platonic dialogue—this revoltingly self-complacent and childish kind of dialectics—to exercise any charm over you, you must never have read any good French authors—Fontenelle for instance. Plato is boring. In reality my distrust of Plato is fundamental. I find him so very much astray from all the deepest instincts of the Hellenes, so steeped in moral prejudices, so pre-existently Christian—the concept "good" is already the highest value with him—that rather than use any other expression I would prefer to designate the whole phenomenon Plato with the hard word "superior swindle," or, if you would like it better, "idealism." Humanity has had to pay dearly for this Athenian having gone to school among the Egyptians (or among the Jews in Egypt? . . .). In the great fatality of Christianity, Plato is that double-faced fascination called the "ideal," which made it possible for the more noble natures of antiquity to misunderstand themselves and to tread the *bridge* which led to the "cross." And what an amount of Plato is still to be found in the concept "church," and in the construction, the system and the practice of the church! My recreation, my predilection, my cure, after all Platonism, has always been Thucydides. Thucydides and perhaps Machiavelli's *Principe* are most closely related to me owing to the absolute determination which they show of refusing to deceive themselves and of seeing reason in *reality*—not in "rationality," and still less in "morality." There is no more radical cure than Thucydides for the lamentably rose-colored idealization of the Greeks which the "classically cultured" stripling bears with him into life, as a reward for his public school training. His writings must be carefully studied line by line, and his unuttered thoughts must be read as distinctly as what he actually says. There are few thinkers so rich in unuttered thoughts. In him the culture "of the Sophists"— that is to say, the culture of realism, receives its most perfect expression: this inestimable movement in the midst of the moral and idealistic knavery of the Socratic schools which was then breaking out in all directions. Greek philosophy is the decadence of the Greek instinct: Thucydides is the great summing up, the final manifestation of that strong, severe positivism which lay in the instincts of the ancient Hellene. After all, it is courage in the face of reality that distinguishes such natures as Thucydides from Plato: Plato is a coward in the face of reality—consequently he takes refuge in the ideal: Thucydides is master of himself—consequently he is able to master life.

3

To rout up cases of "beautiful souls," "golden means" and other perfections among the Greeks, to admire, say, their calm grandeur, their ideal attitude of mind, their exalted simplicity—from this "exalted simplicity," which after all is a piece of *niaiserie allemande,* I was preserved by the psychologist within me. I saw their strongest instinct, the Will to Power, I saw them quivering with the fierce violence of this instinct—I saw all their institutions grow out of measures of security calculated to preserve each member of their society from the inner *explosive material* that lay in his neighbor's breast. This enormous internal tension thus discharged itself in terrible and reckless hostility outside the state; the various states mutually tore each other to bits in order that each individual state could remain at peace with itself. It was then necessary to be strong; for danger lay close at hand—it lurked in ambush everywhere. The superb suppleness of their bodies, the daring realism and immorality which is peculiar to the Hellenes, was a necessity not an inherent quality. It was a result, it had not been there from

the beginning. Even their festivals and their arts where but
means in producing a feeling of superiority, and of showing
it; they are measures of self-glorification, and in certain circumstances of making one's self terrible. . . . Fancy judging
the Greeks in the German style, from their philosophers;
fancy using the suburban respectability of the Socratic schools
as a key to what is fundamentally Hellenic! . . . The philosophers are of course the decadents of Hellas, the counter-
movement directed against the old and noble taste (—against
the agonal instinct, against the *Polis*, against the value of
the race, against the authority of tradition). Socratic virtues were preached to the Greeks, *because* the Greeks had
lost virtue. Irritable, cowardly, unsteady, and all turned to
play actors, they had more than sufficient reason to submit to having morality preached to them. Not that it helped
them in any way, but great words and attitudes are so becoming to decadents.

4

I was the first who, in order to understand the ancient, still
rich and even superabundant Hellenic instinct, took that
marvelous phenomenon which bears the name of Dionysus
seriously. It can be explained only as a manifestation of
excessive energy. Whoever had studied the Greeks, as that
most profound of modern connoisseurs of their culture,
Jakob Burckhardt of Basel, had done, knew at once that
something had been achieved by means of this interpretation.
And in his *Cultur der Griechen*, Burckhardt inserted a special chapter on the phenomenon in question. If you would
like a glimpse of the other side, you have only to refer
to the almost laughable poverty of instinct among German
philologists when they approach the Dionysian question. The
celebrated Lobeck, especially, who with the venerable assurance of a worm dried up between books, crawled into this
world of mysterious states, succeeded in convincing himself
that he was scientific, whereas he was simply revoltingly
superficial and childish—Lobeck, with all the pomp of profound erudition, gave us to understand that, as a matter of
fact, there was nothing at all in all these curiosities. Truth
to tell, the priests may well have communicated not a few
things of value to the participators in such orgies; for instance, the fact that wine provokes desire, that man in certain
circumstances lives on fruit, that plants bloom in the spring
and fade in the autumn. As regards the astounding wealth

of rites, symbols, and myths which take their origin in the orgy, and with which the world of antiquity is literally smothered, Lobeck finds that it prompts him to a feat of even greater ingenuity than the foregoing phenomenon did. "The Greeks," he says, (*Aglaophamus*, I, p. 672), "when they had nothing better to do, laughed, sprang and romped about, or, inasmuch as men also like a change at times, they would sit down, weep and bewail their lot. Others then came up who tried to discover some reason for this strange behavior; and thus, as an explanation of these habits, there arose an incalculable number of festivals, legends, and myths. On the other hand it was believed that the *ludicrous performances* which then perchance began to take place on festival days, necessarily formed part of the celebrations, and they were retained as an indispensable part of the ritual." This is contemptible nonsense, and no one will take a man like Lobeck seriously for a moment. We are very differently affected when we examine the notion "Hellenic," as Winckelmann and Goethe conceived it, and find it incompatible with that element out of which Dionysian art springs—I speak of orgiasm. In reality I do not doubt that Goethe would have completely excluded any such thing from the potentialities of the Greek soul. *Consequently Goethe did not understand the Greeks.* For it is only in the Dionysian mysteries, in the psychology of the Dionysian state, that the *fundamental fact* of the Hellenic instinct—its "will to life"—is expressed. What did the Hellene secure himself with these mysteries? *Eternal* life, the eternal recurrence of life; the future promised and hallowed in the past; the triumphant Yea to life despite death and change; real life conceived as the collective prolongation of life through procreation, through the mysteries of sexuality. To the Greeks, the symbol of sex was the most venerated of symbols, the really deep significance of all the piety of antiquity. All the details of the act of procreation, pregnancy, and birth gave rise to the loftiest and most solemn feelings. In the doctrine of mysteries, *pain* was pronounced holy; the "pains of childbirth" sanctify pain in general—all becoming and all growth, everything that guarantees the future *involves* pain. . . . In order that there may be eternal joy in creating, in order that the will to life may say Yea to itself in all eternity, the "pains of childbirth" must also be eternal. All this is what the word Dionysus signifies: I know of no higher symbolism than this Greek symbolism, this symbolism of the Dionysian phenomenon. In it the profoundest instinct of life, the instinct that guarantees the future of life and life eternal, is understood religiously—the road to life itself, procreation, is pronounced *holy*. . . . It was only Christianity which, with its fundamental resentment against life, made something impure out of sexuality; it flung *filth* at the very basis, the very first condition of our life.

LETTER TO
FREIHERR KARL VON GERSDORFF*

Naumburg, April 7, 1866.

DEAR FRIEND:

Now and again one enjoys hours of peaceful reflection when, with mingled gladness and sorrow, one seems to hover over one's life just as those lovely summer days, so exquisitely described by Emerson, seem to lie stretched out at ease above the hilltops. It is then, as he says, that Nature is perfect, and we feel the same; then we are free from the spell of the ever-vigilant will; then we are nothing but a pure, contemplative and dispassionate eye.† It is in a mood such as this—a mood desirable above all others—that I take up my pen to reply to your kind and thoughtful letter. The interests we share have become welded together to the smallest particle; once again we have realized that mere strokes of the pen—in fact, even the most unexpected whims in the past of a few individuals—determine the history of countless numbers of others; and we readily leave it to the pious to thank their God for these accidents. We may perhaps laugh at this thought when we meet again in Leipzig.

I had already made myself familiar with the thought of being a soldier. I often wished that I might be snatched from my monotonous labors; I yearned for the opposite extreme to my excitement, to the tempestuous stress of my life and to the raptures of my enthusiasm. For, despite all my efforts, it has been brought home to me more clearly every day that it is impossible to shuffle such work out of one's coat sleeve. During the holidays I have learnt, relatively speaking, a good deal, and now they are at an end. My Theognis finds itself at least one term further forward. I have, moreover, made many illuminating discoveries which will considerably enrich my *quaestiones Theognideae*.‡

---

* The letters quoted are from *Selected Letters of Friedrich Nietzsche*, Oscar Levy, ed. (London, William Heinemann, 1921).
† This remark reveals Schopenhauerian influence.—Translator.
‡ Theognis, the aristocratic poet of Megara, awoke Nietzsche's interest even when he was still at Pforta.—Translator.

For recreation I turn to three things, and a wonderful recreation they provide!—my Schopenhauer, Schumann's music, and, finally, solitary walks. Yesterday a heavy storm hung in the sky, and I hastened up a neighboring hill, called Leusch (perhaps you can explain the word to me?). On the summit I found a hut and a man killing two kids, with his son looking on. The storm broke with a mighty crash, discharging thunder and hail, and I felt inexpressibly well and full of zest, and realized with singular clearness that to understand Nature one must go to her as I had just done, as a refuge from all worries and oppressions. What did man with his restless will matter to me then? What did I care for the eternal "Thou shalt" and "Thou shalt not?" How different are lightning, storm and hail—free powers without ethics! How happy, how strong they are—pure will untrammeled by the muddling influence of the intellect!

For have I not seen examples enough of how muddling a man's intellect frequently is? Not long ago I had occasion to speak to a man who was on the point of going out to India as a missionary. I put a few questions to him and learned that he had not read a single Indian work, knew nothing about the Upanishads—not even their name—and had resolved to have nothing to do with the Brahmans because they had philosophical training. Holy Ganges!

Today I listened to a profoundly clever sermon of ——'s on Christianity—the Faith that has conquered the world. It was intolerably haughty in its attitude toward all nations that were not Christian, and yet it was exceedingly ingenious. For instance, every now and then he would describe as Christian something else, which always gave an appropriate sense even according to our lights. If the sentence, "Christianity has conquered the world," be changed to "the feeling of sin," or briefly "a metaphysical need has conquered the world," we can raise no reasonable objection; but then one ought to be consistent and say, "All true Hindus are Christians," and also "All true Christians are Hindus." As a matter of fact, however, the interchange of such words and concepts as these, which have a fixed meaning, is not altogether honest; it lands the poor in spirit in total confusion. If by Christianity is meant "Faith in an historical event, or in an historical personage," I have nothing to do with it. If, however, it is said to signify briefly a craving for salvation or redemption, then I can set a high value upon it, and do not even object to its endeavoring to discipline the philosophers. For how very few these are compared to the vast masses of men who are in need of salvation! How many of them are not actually made of the same stuff as these masses! If only all those who dabble in philosophy were followers of Schopenhauer! But only too often behind the mask of philosopher stands the exalted majesty of the "Will," which is trying to achieve its own self-glorification. If the philosophers ruled τὸ πλῆθος* would be lost; were the masses to prevail, as they do at present, the philosophers *rari in gurgite vasto*† would still be able, like Aeschylus, δίχα ἄλλων φρονέειν.‡

Apart from this, it is certainly extremely irksome to restrain our Schopenhauerian ideas, still so young, vigorous and half expressed, and to have weighing forever upon our hearts this unfortunate disparity between theory and practice. And for this I can think of no consolation; on the contrary, I am in need of it myself.

And now farewell, old man! Remember me to all your family. Mine wish to be remembered to you; let us leave it at that. When we meet again we shall probably smile, and rightly too!

Yours,

FRIEDRICH NIETZSCHE.

LETTER TO ROHDE

Leipzig, November 9, 1868.

MY DEAR FRIEND:

Today I intend to relate a whole host of sprightly experiences, to look merrily into the future and to conduct myself in such idyllic and easy fashion that your sinister guest —that feline fever—will arch its back and retire spitting and swearing. And in order that all discordant notes may be avoided I shall discuss the famous *res severa* § which is responsible for your second letter on a special sheet of paper, so that you will be able to read it when you are in the right mood and place for it.

The acts of my comedy are: (1) A Club-night or the Assistant Professor; (2) The Ejected Tailor; (3) A Rendezvous

---

* The masses.

† "Few survivors in the unmeasured seas." From the famous verse in Virgil's *Aeneid*, I, 118.—Translator.

‡ "To differ from the opinions of others." See Aeschylus, *Agamemnon* 757.—Translator.

§ "Serious thing."—Transalator.

with X. Some old women take part in the performance. . . .

At home I found two letters, yours and an invitation from Curtius, whom I am glad to get to know better. When two friends like us write letters to each other, it is well known that the angels rejoice. And they rejoiced as I read your letter—aye, they even giggled. . . .

When I reached home yesterday, I found a card addressed to me with this note upon it: "If you would like to meet Richard Wagner, come to the Theatre Café at a quarter to four. Windisch."

Forgive me, but this news so turned my head that I quite forgot what I was doing before it came, and was thoroughly bewildered.

I naturally ran there and found our loyal friend, who gave me a lot of fresh information. Wagner was staying in Leipzig with his relations in the strictest incognito. The press had no inkling of his visit and all Brockhaus's servants were as dumb as graves in livery. Now Wagner's sister, Frau Brockhaus, that determined and clever woman, had introduced her friend Frau Ritschl to her brother, and on this occasion was able proudly to boast of the friend to the brother and of the brother to the friend, the lucky creature! Wagner played the *Meisterlied*, which you must know, in Frau Ritschl's presence, and this good lady told him that she already knew the song very well, *mea opera*.* Imagine Wagner's joy and surprise! And with the utmost readiness in the world he graciously declared his willingness to meet me incognito. I was to be invited on Friday evening. Windisch, however, pointed out that I should be prevented from coming by my official post and duties; Saturday afternoon was accordingly proposed. On that day Windisch and I ran to the Brockhaus's, found the Professor's family but no Wagner. He had just gone out with an enormous hat on his huge head. It was thus that I made the acquaintance of the excellent family and received a kind invitation for Sunday evening.

On these days I felt as though I was living in a novel, and you must allow that in view of the inaccessibility of the exceptional man, the circumstances leading up to this acquaintance were somewhat romantic.

As I was under the impression that a large company of guests had been invited, I decided to dress very ceremoniously, and was glad that my tailor had promised to deliver a new dress suit for this very evening. It was a horrid day

---

* "Through my offices."—Translator.

with constant showers of rain and snow. One shuddered at the thought of leaving the house, and I was therefore very pleased when little Roscher paid me a visit in the afternoon to tell me something about the Eleatics and about God in philosophy—for, as *candidandus* he is working up the material collected by Ahrens in his *Development of the Idea of God up to the Time of Aristotle*, while Romundt is trying for the prize essay of the University, the subject of which is "On the Will." It was getting dark, the tailor did not turn up, and Roscher left me. I accompanied him, called on the tailor myself, and found his minions busily engaged on my clothes, which they promised to send round in three-quarters of an hour.

I went on my way in a jolly mood, looked in at Kintschy's, read the *Kladderadatsch*, and was amused to find a paragraph saying that Wagner was in Switzerland and that a fine house was being built for him in Munich, while I knew all the time that I was going to see him that evening and that the day before he had received a letter from the little monarch * addressed to "The Great German Tone Poet, Richard Wagner."

But at home there was no tailor awaiting me, so I sat down and read the treatise on the Eudokia at my ease, but was constantly disturbed by the sound of a shrill bell that seemed to be ringing some distance away. At last I felt certain that someone was standing at the old iron gate; it was shut, as was also the door of the house. I shouted across the garden to the man to enter the house, but it was impossible to make oneself understood through the pouring rain. The whole house was disturbed, the door was ultimately opened, and a little old man bearing a parcel came up to me. It was half past 6, time for me to dress and get ready, as I lived a long way off. It was all right, the man had my things. I tried them on and they fitted. But what was this suspicious development? He actually presented me with a bill. I took it politely, but he declared he must be paid on delivery. I was surprised, and explained that I had nothing to do with him as the servant of my tailor, but that my dealings were with his master to whom I had given the order. The man grew more pressing, as did also the time. I snatched at the things and began to put them on. He snatched them too and did all he could to prevent me from dressing. What with violence on my part and violence on his, there was soon

* Ludwig II of Bavaria.

a scene, and all the time I was fighting in my shirt, as I wished to get the new trousers.

At last, after a display of dignity, solemn threats, the utterance of curses on my tailor and his accomplice, and vows of vengeance, the little man vanished with my clothes. End of the First Act. I sat on my sofa and meditated while I examined a black coat and wondered whether it was good enough for Richard.

Outside the rain continued to pour.

It was a quarter past 7. I had promised to meet Windisch at half past 7 at the Theatre Café. I plunged into the dark and rainy night, also a little man in black and without evening dress, yet in a beatific mood, for chance was in my favor—even the scene with the tailor's man had something tremendously unusual about it.

At last we entered Frau Brockhaus's exceedingly comfortable drawing room. There was nobody there except the most intimate members of the family, Richard, and us two. I was introduced to Wagner and muttered a few respectful words to him. He questioned me closely as to how I had become so well acquainted with his music, complained bitterly about the way his operas were produced with the exception of the famous Munich performances, and made great fun of the conductors who tried to encourage their orchestra in friendly tones as follows: "Now, gentlemen, let's have some passion! My good people, still a little more passion if you please!" Wagner enjoys imitating the Leipzig dialect.

Now let me give you a brief account of all that happened that evening. Really the joys were of such a rare and stimulating kind that even today I am not back in the old groove, but can think of nothing better to do than come to you, my dear friend, to tell you these wonderful tidings. Wagner played to us before and after supper, and went through every one of the more important passages of the *Meistersinger*. He imitated all the voices and was in very high spirits. He is, by the bye, an extraordinarily energetic and fiery man. He speaks very quickly and wittily, and can keep a private company of the sort assembled on that evening very jolly. I managed to have quite a long talk with him about Schopenhauer. Oh, and you can imagine what joy it was for me to hear him speak with such indescribable warmth of our master—what a lot we owed to him, how he was the only philosopher who had understood the essence of music! Then he inquired as to how the professors were disposed toward him; laughed a good deal about the Philosophers' Congress at Prague, and spoke of them as philosophical footmen. Later on he read me a piece out of the autobiography he is now writing, a thoroughly amusing scene from his Leipzig student days which I still cannot recall without a laugh. He writes extraordinarily cleverly and intellectually. At the close of the evening, when we were both ready to go, he shook my hand very warmly and kindly asked me to come and see him so that we might have some music and philosophy together. He also entrusted me with the task of making his music known to his sister and his relations, a duty which I undertook very solemnly to fulfill. You will hear more about it when I have succeeded in looking at this evening more objectively and from a greater distance. For the time being a hearty farewell and best wishes for your health from yours,   F. N.

LETTER TO
FREIHERR KARL VON GERSDORFF

Naumburg, April 11, 1869.

MY DEAR FRIEND:

My hour has come and this is the last evening I shall spend at home for some time. Early tomorrow morning I go out into the wide, wide world, to enter a new and untried profession, in an atmosphere heavy and oppressive with duty and work. Once more I must take leave of everything, the golden time of free and unconstrained activity, in which every instant is sovereign, in which the joys of art and the world are spread out before us as a mere spectacle in which we scarcely participate. This time is now forever in the past for me. Now the inexorable goddess "Daily Duty" rules supreme. *"Bemooster Bursche zieh' ich aus!"* * [As a moss-grown student I go out into the world.] But you know that touching student song of course! *"Muss selber nun Philister sein!"*† [I too must be a Philistine now.] In one way or another this line always comes true. One cannot take up posts and honors with impunity—the only question is, are the fetters of iron or of thread? For I have the pluck which will one day perhaps enable me to burst my bonds and venture into this precarious life from a different direction and in a different way. As yet I see no sign of the inevitable humpback of the

* A song sung by German students on leaving the University.—Translator.

† Another line of the same song.—Translator.

professor. May Zeus and all the Muses preserve me from
ever becoming a Philistine, an ἄνθρωπος ἄμουσος*, a man
of the herd. But I do not know how I could become one,
seeing that I am not one. It is true I stand a little nearer
to another kind of Philistine—the Philistine of the "specialist"
species; for it is only natural that the daily task, and the
unremitting concentration of the mind upon certain specified
subjects and problems, should tend to abate the free
receptivity of the mind and undermine the philosophic sense.
But I flatter myself that I shall be able to meet this danger
with more calm and assurance than the majority of
philologists. Philosophical seriousness is already too deeply
rooted in me; the true and essential problems of life and
thought have been too clearly revealed to me by that great
mystagogue, Schopenhauer, to allow of my ever being
obliged to dread such a disgraceful defection from the "Idea."
To infuse this new blood into my science, to communicate to
my pupils that Schopenhauerian earnestness which is stamped
on the brow of the sublime man—such is my desire, such is
my undaunted hope. I should like to be something more than
a mere trainer of efficient philologists. The present generation of teachers, the care of the coming generation—all this is
in my mind. If we must live our lives out to the bitter end
let us at least do so in such wise that others may bless our
life as a priceless treasure, once we have been happily released from its tolls.

As for you, old man, with whom I agree on such a number of vital and fundamental questions, I wish you the luck
you deserve and myself your old and tried friendship. Fare
thee well!

FRIEDRICH NIETZSCHE, DR.

TO MADAME LOUISE O.

Basel, September, 1876.

DEAR, KIND FRIEND:

In the first place I was unable to write, for I underwent an
eye-cure, and now I ought not to write for a long long
time to come! Nevertheless I read your two letters again and
again; I almost believe I read them too often. But this new

* A man who takes no interest in the Muses or Arts.—Translator.

friendship is like new wine—very agreeable though perhaps
a trifle dangerous.

At least for me.

But for you also, especially when I think of the sort of
free spirit you have lighted upon!—a man who longs for
nothing more than daily to be rid of some comforting belief, and who seeks and finds his happiness in this daily increase in the emancipation of his spirit. It is possible I *wish*
to become more of a free spirit than I am *capable* of becoming.

So what is to be done? An "Abduction from the Harem" *
of Faith, without Mozart's music?

Do you know Fräulein von Meysenbug's autobiography
published under the title of "Memoirs of an Idealist"?

What is poor little Marcel doing with his little teeth? We
all have to suffer before we really learn to bite, physically
and morally—biting in order to nourish ourselves, of course,
not simply for the sake of biting!

Is there no good portrait in existence of a certain blond
and beautiful woman?

Sunday week I shall go to Italy for a long stay. You
will hear from me when I get there. In any case a letter
sent to my address in Basel (45 Schützengraben) will reach
me.

> In brotherly affection,
> Yours
> DR. FRIEDR. NIETZSCHE.

NIETZSCHE TO PETER GAST

Address, St. Moriz-Dorf, Poste Restante.

September 11, 1879.

DEAR, DEAR FRIEND:

When you read these lines my MS. will already have reached
you; it may deliver its own request to you; I have not the
courage to do so. But you must share a few of the moments of joy that I now feel over my completed work. I am
at the end of my thirty-fifth year—"the middle of life,"
as people for a century and a half used to say of this age.

* "Die Entführung aus dem Sérail," first performed in Vienna July
10th, 1782.—Translator.

It was at this age that Dante had his vision, and in the opening lines of his poem he mentions the fact. Now I am in the middle of life and so "encircled by death" that at any minute it can lay hold of me. From the nature of my sufferings I must reckon upon a *sudden* death through convulsions (although I should prefer a hundred times a slow, lucid death, before which I should be able to converse with my friends, even if it were more painful). In this way I feel like the oldest of men, even from the standpoint of having completed my life task. I have poured out a salutary drop of *oil;* this I know, and I shall not be forgotten for it. At bottom I have already undergone the test of my own view of life; many more will have to undergo it after me. Up to the present my spirit has not been depressed by the unremitting suffering that my ailments have caused me; at times I even feel more cheerful and more benevolent than I ever felt in my life before; to what do I owe this invigorating and ameliorating effect? Certainly not to my fellow men; for, with but few exceptions, they have all during the last few years shown themselves "offended" by me; * nor have they shrunk from letting me know it. Just read this last MS. through, my dear friend, and ask yourself whether there are any traces of suffering or depression to be found in it. *I don't believe there are,* and this very belief is a sign that there must be *powers* concealed in these views, and not the proofs of impotence and lassitude after which my enemies will seek.

Now I shall not rest until I have sent those pages, transcribed by my self-sacrificing friend and revised by me, to my printers in Chemnitz. I shall not come to you myself—however urgently the Overbecks and my sister may press me to do so; there are states in which it seems to me more fitting to return to the neighborhood of one's mother, one's home, and the memories of one's childhood. But do not take all this as final and irrevocable. According as his hopes rise or fall, an invalid should be allowed to make or unmake his plans. My program for the summer is complete: three weeks at a moderate altitude (in Wiesen), three months in the Engadine, and the last month in taking the real St. Moritz drink-cure, the best effect of which is not supposed to be felt before the winter. This *working out* of a program was a pleasure to me, but it was not *easy!* Self-denial in everything (I had no friends, no company; I could read no books; all art was far removed from me; a small bedroom with a bed, the food of an ascetic—which BY THE BYE suited

* See Matthew XXVI. 28.

me excellently, for I have had no indigestion the whole of the summer)—this self-denial was complete except for one point—I gave myself up to my thoughts—what else could I do! Of course, this was the *very worst thing* for my head, but I still do not see how I could have *avoided it*. But enough; this winter my program will be to *recover* from myself, to rest myself away from my thoughts—for years I have not had this experience. Perhaps in Naumburg I shall be able so to arrange my day as to profit by this repose. But first of all the "sequel"—*The Wanderer and his Shadow!*

Your last letter full of ideas pleased Overbeck and me so much that I allowed him to take it with him to Zurich to read to his womenfolk there. Forgive me for having done this. And forgive me for more important things!

Your friend,
N.

NIETZSCHE TO BURCKHARDT

Sils-Maria, Oberengadine, September 22, 1886.

MY VERY DEAR PROFESSOR: *

I am truly pained at not having seen you or spoken to you for so long! With whom would I fain speak, forsooth, if I may no longer speak to you! The *"silentium"* about me increases daily.

Meanwhile I trust C. G. Naumann has done his duty and sent you my last book. Please read it (although it says the same things as my *Zarathustra*, but differently, very differently). I can think of no one who has a greater number of first principles in common with me than you have. It seems to me that you have faced the same problems as I have—that you are working upon the same problems in a similar way, perhaps even in a more powerful and more profound way than I, because you are more silent. But then it should be remembered that I am the younger man. . . . The terrible conditions that determine every advance in culture, the extremely ticklish relation between what is called the "improvement" of mankind (or rather "humanization") and the *"enhancement"* of the type man; above all the conflict of every moral concept with every scientific notion of *life*—

---

* This letter accompanied *Beyond Good and Evil*.—Translator.

but enough, enough! Here is a problem which fortunately, it seems to me, we may have in common with very few of our contemporaries or predecessors. To give expression to it is perhaps the greatest feat of daring on earth, and that not so much on the part of him who dares it, as of those whom he addresses. My consolation is that, in the first place, the ears for apprehending my prodigious novelties are lacking —your ears excepted, my dear and honored friend. But to you, on the other hand, they will not be "novelties"!

Your devoted friend,
DR. FRIEDRICH NIETZSCHE.

Address *Genova, ferma in posta.*

TO SEYDLITZ

Nice, Thursday, February 24, 1887.
Rue des Ponchettes 29. 1st floor.

DEAR FRIEND:

Fortunately your letter, as far as your own case is concerned, did not by any means prove *quod erat demonstrandum;* otherwise, however, I admit all you say, the disastrous effects of a gray sky, the prolonged damp cold, the proximity of Bavarians and of Bavarian beer—I admire every artist who turns to face these foes—not to speak of German politics, which are only another form of permanent winter and bad weather. It seems to me that Germany for the last fifteen years has become a regular school of besotment. Water, rubbish and filth, far and wide—that is what it looks like from a distance. I beg a thousand pardons if I have hurt your more noble feelings in speaking in this way, but for present-day Germany, however much it may bristle, hedgehoglike, with arms, I no longer have any respect. It represents the stupidest, most depraved and most mendacious form of the German spirit that has ever existed—and what absurdities has not this spirit dared to perpetrate! I forgive no one for compromising with it in any way, even if his name be Richard Wagner, particularly when this compromise is effected in the shamefully equivocal and cautious manner in which this shrewd, all-too-shrewd glorifier of *"reine Thorheit"* * has effected it in the latter years of his life.

---

* "Pure foolishness." This is a reference to Wagner's *Parsifal.* See my note on the "Pure Fool," page 96, of *The Will to Power,* Vol. I.—Translator.

Here in our land of sunshine what different things we have in mind! Only a moment ago Nice was in the middle of her long international carnival (incidentally with a preponderance of Spanish women) and immediately after it was over, six hours after the last Girandola, there followed some more new and rarely tasted charms of existence. For we are all living in the interesting expectation of being swallowed up—thanks to a well-meaning earthquake, which caused howling far and wide not only among dogs. You can imagine what fun it is to hear the houses rattling over one's head like coffee mills, to watch the inkstands beginning to show signs of free will, while the streets fill with horrified half-dressed figures and unhinged nervous systems. This morning, from about two to three o'clock, like the *gaillard* I am, I made a round of inspection in the various quarters of the town, in order to ascertain where the fear was greatest. For the inhabitants camp out in the open night and day, and it looks delightfully martial. In the hotels where there is much damage, panic of course reigns supreme. I found all my friends, male and female, lying pitifully beneath the green trees, well swathed in flannels, for it was very cold, and, at the slightest sign of a vibration, thinking gloomily of the end. I should not be surprised if this brought the season to a sudden conclusion. Everyone is thinking of leaving (provided of course they can get away and the railways are not all torn up). Already yesterday evening the visitors at the hotel where I board could not be induced to partake of their table d'hôte inside the house, but ate and drank in the open, and but for an exceedingly pious old woman who is convinced that the Almighty has absolutely no right to injure her, I was "the only cheerful being among a host of masks." *

I have just got hold of a newspaper containing a description of this awful night, which is far more picturesque than the one your humble friend has been able to give you. I am enclosing it in this letter. Please read it to your dear wife, and bear me in mind.

Your devoted
NIETZSCHE.

* "Unter Larven die einzige Fühlende Brust." These words are a quotation from a well-known poem of Schiller's conveying the idea of a jolly fellow being alone amongst a lot of wooden creatures.— Translator.

NIETZSCHE TO MALVIDA VON MEYSENBUG

[May 12, 1887]

Address: Chur (Schweiz) Rosenhügel

Until June 10

afterward: Celerina, Oberengadine.

DEAREST FRÄULEIN:

How strange it is! With regard to what you so kindly said to me at the last moment, I wonder whether it might not prove both refreshing and fruitful for us both once more to join our two solitudes in closest and heartiest proximity! I have frequently thought about this of late, and asked myself searching questions about it. To spend one more winter with you and to be looked after and waited upon perhaps by Trina * herself—that is indeed an extremely alluring prospect for which I cannot thank you sufficiently! I should prefer above all to return to Sorrento once more (δὶς καὶ τρὶς τὸ καλόν say the Greeks: "All good things twice or thrice!") Or to Capri—where I shall play the piano to you again but better than I did before! Or to Amalfi or Castellamare. Finally even to Rome (although my suspicion of the Roman climate and of large towns in general is based on good reasons and is not to be overthrown so easily). Solitude in the midst of solitary nature has hitherto been my chief refreshment, my means of recovery; such cities of modern traffic as Nice or even Zurich (which I have just left) in the end always make me feel irritable, sad, uncertain, desperate, unproductive, and ill. I have retained a sort of longing and superstition with regard to that peaceful sojourn *down there,* as if there I had breathed more deeply, if only for a few moments, than anywhere else in my life. For instance, on the occasion of that very first drive we took together in Naples when we went to Posilippo.

Taking everything into consideration, you are the only person on earth about whom I could cherish such a wish; besides, I feel that I am *condemned* to my solitude and my citadel. There is no longer any alternative. That which bids

* The chambermaid of Frl. v. Meysenbug.—Translator.

me live, my exceptional and weighty task, bids me also keep out of the way of men and no longer attach myself to anyone. Perhaps it is the pure element in which this task has placed me that explains why it is that I have gradually grown unable even to bear the smell of men and least of all "young men," with whom I am not infrequently afflicted (—oh, how obtrusively clumsy they are, just like puppies!) In the old days, in our solitude in Sorrento, B. and R. were too much for me; I fancy that at that time I was very reticent with you—even about things of which there is no one I should have spoken to more readily than yourself.

On my table there lies the new edition (in two volumes) of *Human, All Too Human*, the first part of which I worked out then—how strange! Strange that it should have been in your respected neighborhood. In the long "address" which I found a necessary preface for the new edition of my complete works there are a number of curious things about myself which are quite *uncompromising* in their honesty. By this means I shall hold "the many" once and for all at arm's length; for nothing annoys men more than to show them some of the severity and hardness with which, under the discipline of one's own ideal, one deals and has dealt out to *oneself*. That is why I have cast my line out for "the few," and this after all I did without impatience, for it is in the nature of the indescribable strangeness and dangerousness of my thoughts that ears should not be opened for them until very late—certainly *not* before 1901.

You ask me to come to Versailles—oh, if only it were possible! For I esteem the circle of men that you meet there (a curious admission for a German, but in present-day Europe I feel related only to the most intellectual among the French and Russians, and in no way whatever to my countrymen who judge all things on the principle of "Germany, Germany above all"). But I *must* return to the cold air of the Engadine; spring attacks me unconsciously; I dare not tell you into what abysses of despair I sink under its influence. My body (and my philosophy, too, for that matter) feels the *cold* to be its appointed preservative element—that sounds paradoxical and negative, but it is the most thoroughly demonstrated fact of my life.

This is by no means a sign of a "cold nature"; but you, of course, understand that, my most dear and faithful friend!

Always your affectionate and grateful friend,

NIETZSCHE.

P. S.—Fräulein Salome has also informed me of her engagement, but I did not answer her either, however much happiness and prosperity I may honestly wish her. One must keep out of the way of the kind of creature who does not understand awe and respect.

NIETZSCHE TO HANS VON BÜLOW

[Venice, October 22, 1887.]

MY DEAR SIR:

Once upon a time I sent you a piece of my music and you passed sentence of death upon it in the most justifiable manner possible *in rebus musicis et musicantibus*. And now, in spite of all that, I dare to send you something else—a Hymn to Life, to which I attach all the more the hope that it will be *allowed to live*. One day either in the near or the remote future, it will be sung to my memory, to the memory of a philosopher who had no contemporaries, and who did not even wish to have them. Does he *deserve* it? . . .

Be this as it may, it is quite possible that *I* may have learnt something during the last ten years, even as a musician.

Always as of old, your devoted friend,

DR. F. NIETZSCHE.

TO SEYDLITZ

Nice, Pension de Genève.

February 12, 1888.

DEAR FRIEND:

It has not been a "proud silence" that has sealed my lips to everyone all this time, but rather the humble silence of a sufferer who was ashamed of betraying the extent of his pain. When an animal is ill it crawls into its cave—so does *la bête philosophe*. So seldom does a friendly voice come my way. I am now alone, absurdly alone, and in my unrelenting subterranean war against all that mankind has hitherto honored and loved (—my formula for this is "the Transvaluation of all Values") I myself seem unwittingly to have become something of a cave, something concealed that can no longer be found even when it is a definite object of search. *But no one goes in search of it.* Between us three, it is not beyond the limits of possibility that I am the leading philosopher of the age—aye, maybe a little more than that, something decisive and fateful that stands between two epochs. But a man is *constantly* paying for holding such an isolated position by an isolation which becomes every day more complete, more icy, and more cutting. And look at our dear Germans! . . . Although I am in my forty-fifth year and have published about fifteen books (—among them that *non plus ultra* "Zarathustra") no one in Germany has yet succeeded in producing even a moderately good review of a single one of my works. They are now getting out of the difficulty with such words as "eccentric," "pathological," "psychiatric." There have been evil and slanderous hints enough about me, and in the papers both scholarly and unscholarly, the prevailing attitude is one of ungoverned animosity; but how is it that no one protests against this? How is it that no one feels insulted when I am abused? And all these years no comfort, no drop of human sympathy, not a breath of love.

In these circumstances one has to live at Nice. This season it is again full of idlers, *grecs,* and other philosophers—it is full of my like. And, with his own peculiar cynicism, God allows his sun to shine more brightly on us than on the more respectable Europe of Herr von Bismarck (—which with feverish virtue is working at its armaments, and looks for all the world like a heroic hedgehog). The days seem to dawn here with unblushing beauty; never have we had a more beautiful winter. How I should like to send you some of the coloring of Nice! It is all besprinkled with a glittering silver gray; intellectual, highly intellectual coloring; free from every vestige of the brutal ground tone. The advantage of this small stretch of coast between Alassio and Nice is the suggestion of Africa in the coloring, the vegetation, and the dryness of the air. This is not to be found in other parts of Europe.

Oh, how gladly would I not sit with you and your dear wife beneath some Homeric Phaeacian sky! But I must not go further south (—my eyes will soon drive me to more northern and more stupid landscapes). Please let me know when you will be in Munich again and forgive this gloomy letter.

Your devoted friend,

NIETZSCHE.

NIETZSCHE TO BRANDES

Nice, February 19, 1988.

DEAR SIR:

You have put me in your debt in the most agreeable way possible with your treatise on the idea of "modernity." For during this very winter I am circling round the question which stands in the first rank as one worthy of consideration. I am trying, to the best of my ability, in as unmodern a way as can be, to take a very cursory bird's-eye, retrospective survey of things modern. I admire—let me confess it—your toleration in criticism and your reticence in judgment. How you "suffer the little ones to come unto you," even Heyse.*

I intend on my next journey into Germany to tackle Kierkegaard's psychological problems, and to renew my acquaintance with your older literature. That will be of use to me in the best sense of the word, and will serve to cajole my own critical harshness and arrogance into a good temper. Yesterday my publisher telegraphed to me that he had sent off the books. I will spare you and myself the explanation of why this has come to pass so late in the day. Make the best of a bad business, my dear Sir. I mean of this Nietzschean literature.

For my part I rather fancy that I have given these "New Germans" the richest, most vital, and independent books that they possess, and at the same time I claim that my personality stands for a supreme event at the present crisis in our estimating of values. But this may be an error, and, what is more, a piece of crass stupidity. I don't want to be forced to believe in myself.

A few remarks now relating to my first-born work ("Juvenilia and Juvenalia"). The pamphlet against Strauss, a malicious "making merry" on the part of an extreme freethinker at the expense of one who imagined himself to be a freethinker, stirred up a tremendous scandal. At that time I was already *Professor ordinarius,* despite my tender age of twenty-seven years, and in consequence a kind of authority, something recognized, as it were.

The most ingenuous account of this controversy in which every notability took part for or against me, and over which

* Paul Heyse, a veteran German dramatist, writer of "Novelen," popular in the last century.—Translator.

an enormous quantity of ink was spilled, is in the second volume of Karl Hillebrand's *Zeiten, Völker und Menschen*. The head and front of my offending was not so much that I held up to ridicule the exploded machinery of an amazing method of criticism, but that I should catch our German taste in a flagrant and compromising lack of taste. Teutonic taste had, in spite of all religious and party differences, been unanimous in admiration of Strauss's "Old and New Faith," pronouncing it a masterpiece of acuteness and freedom of thought, and even of style. My pamphlet was the first attack on German culture, that culture which it was boasted had conquered France. A phrase of mine, "Culture philistine," survived the thrusts of violent polemical controversy, and has taken root in the language. The two essays on Schopenhauer and Richard Wagner represent, it appears to me today, more self-confessions, above all, more avowals of self, than any real psychology of those masters who were both related to me as intimately as they were antagonistically. I was the first to distil, as it were, out of them both, a kind of unity. At present this superstition is very much in the foreground of German culture. All Wagnerites are disciples of Schopenhauer. It was quite the other way when I was young. In those days it was the last of the Hegelians who rallied round Wagner. And "Wagner and Hegel" was the battle cry of the fifties.

Between *Thoughts Out of Season* and *Human, All Too Human*, there lies a crisis and a skin-casting. Moreover, I lay physically for years at the gates of death. This was, positively, a great piece of good fortune. I forgot myself, lived myself down. And I have accomplished the same feat a second time. Thus it comes about that you and I have exchanged courtesies. I think we are a pair of wanderers in the wilderness who are glad to have met each other.

With true regards, I remain,

Yours,

NIETZSCHE.

NIETZSCHE TO BURCKHARDT

Sils-Maria, Autumn, 1888.

MY DEAR PROFESSOR: *

Herewith I take the liberty of sending you a small aesthetic

---

* This letter accompanied "The Case of Wagner."

treatise which, however much it may have been intended as a respite amid the serious preoccupations of my life task, is nevertheless in its way a serious work. You must not let yourself be led astray for one instant by its tone of levity and irony. Perhaps I have a right to speak *clearly* for once about this "Case of Wagner"—maybe it is even my duty to do so. The movement is now at the zenith of its glory. Three-quarters of the musicians of Europe are now wholly or partly convinced, from St. Petersburg to Paris, Bologna, and Montevideo, the theaters are living on this art, and only yesterday, even the young German Kaiser characterized the whole of the Wagner movement as a national affair of the *first magnitude*, and placed himself at the head of it. These are sufficient reasons for *allowing me* to enter the lists. I admit that in view of the international European character of the problem, the essay should not have been written in German but in French. Up to a certain point it is written in French, and at all events it might prove an easier task to translate it into French than into German. . . .

It is no secret to me that not long ago, on a certain day, a whole city, with reverential gratitude, piously showed its recognition of its first teacher and benefactor. With all due modesty I ventured to add my own personal feelings to those of that city. With deep love and respect,

Yours,
DR. FRIEDRICH NIETZSCHE.

(My address till the middle of November will be Torino, *poste restante*. One word from you would make me happy.)

NIETZSCHE TO BRANDES

Torino, via Carlo Alberta 6,
November 20th, 1888.

Forgive me, dear Sir, for answering you on the spot. Curious things are passing at this crisis in my life, things which have never had their like. The day before yesterday, again today. Ah! if you could only know what I had been writing when your letter reached me! With a cynicism which will become part of the world's history I have now related "myself." The book is called *Ecce Homo*, and is an onslaught on the Crucified without the ghost of a scruple; it ends with thunderclaps and lightning flashes, that deafen and blind, against everything that is Christian or tainted with Christianity. I am, in short, the first psychologist of Christianity, and, old artilleryman that I am, can fire heavier cannon than any opponent of Christianity has ever before dreamed the existence of. The whole is the prelude of "The Transvaluation of all Values," the work which lies ready before me. I vow to you that in two years we shall have the whole inhabited globe in convulsions. I am a Destiny.

Guess who comes off the worst in *Ecce Homo.* Messieurs the Germans! I have told them awful things. For instance, the Germans have it on their conscience that they ruined the conception of the last great epoch of history, the Renaissance, at a moment when Christian values, the decadence values, were humiliated, when these instincts in even princes of the Church were yielding to the instincts diametrically opposed thereto, the instincts of life.

It meant simply the restoration of Christianity to attack the Church. Caesar Borgia as Pope, that was the conception of the Renaissance, its genuine symbol.

You must not be angry, either, that in a decisive passage of the book you crop up. I wrote it as an indictment of the conduct of my friends, their leaving me completely in the lurch, both with regard to reputation and philosophy. At this juncture you come on the scene with a halo of glory round your head.

What you say of Dostoyevsky is just what I think. On the other hand, I estimate him as the most valuable psychological material I know. I am grateful to him in a quite remarkable fashion, however much he may stand in contradiction to my deepest-lying instincts. As for my attitude to Pascal, I almost love him, because he has taught me an infinite amount. He is the one logical Christian.

The day before yesterday I read and was charmed with *Les Mariés,* by August Strindberg, and I found myself at home in his pages. The only detriment to my sincere admiration was the feeling that I was at the same time admiring myself!

Turin is still my residence.

> Your NIETZSCHE.
> (Now a "Monster".)

Where shall I address the *Twilight of the Idols?* Should you be in Copenhagen for the next fortnight, no answer is necessary.

II. The Prefaces

FROM HUMAN, ALL TOO HUMAN, VOL. I

Preface

1

I HAVE been told frequently, and always with great surprise, that there is something common and distinctive in all my writings, from the *Birth of Tragedy* to the latest published *Prelude to a Philosophy of the Future*. They all contain, I have been told, snares and nets for unwary birds, and an almost perpetual unconscious demand for the inversion of customary valuations and valued customs. What? *Everything* only—human—all too human? People lay down my writings with this sigh, not without a certain dread and distrust of morality itself, indeed almost tempted and encouraged to become advocates of the *worst* things: as being perhaps only the *best* disparaged? My writings have been called a school of suspicion and especially of disdain, more happily, also, a school of courage and even of audacity. Indeed, I myself do not think that anyone has ever looked at the world with such a profound suspicion; and not only as occasional Devil's Advocate, but equally also, to speak theologically, as enemy and impeacher of God; and he who realizes something of the consequences involved, in every profound suspicion, something of the chills and anxieties of loneliness to which every uncompromising *difference of outlook* condemns him who is affected therewith, will also understand how often I sought shelter in some kind of reverence or hostility, or scientifical-ity or levity or stupidity, in order to recover from myself, and, as it were, to obtain temporary self-forgetfulness; also why, when I did not find what I *needed*, I was obliged to manufacture it, to counterfeit and to imagine it in a suitable manner (and what else have poets ever done? And for what purpose has all the art in the world existed?). What I always required most, however, for my cure and self-recovery, was the belief that I was *not* isolated in such circumstances, that I did not *see* in an isolated manner—a magic suspicion of relationship and similarity to others in outlook and desire, a repose in the confidence of friendship, a blindness in both parties without suspicion or note of interrogation, an enjoyment of foregrounds, and surfaces of the near and the nearest, of all that has color, epidermis, and outside appearance. Perhaps I might be reproached in this respect for much "art" and fine false coinage; for instance, for voluntarily and knowingly shutting my eyes to Schopenhauer's blind will to morality at a time when I had become sufficiently clear-sighted about morality; also for deceiving myself about Richard Wagner's incurable romanticism, as if it were a beginning and not an end; also about the Greeks, also about the Germans and their future—and there would still probably be quite a long list of such alsos? Supposing however, that this were all true and that I were reproached with good reason, what do *you* know, what *could* you know as to how much artifice of self-preservation, how much rationality and higher protection there is in such self-deception—and how much falseness I still *require* in order to allow myself again and again the luxury of *my* sincerity? . . . In short, I still live; and life, in spite of ourselves, is not devised by morality; it *demands* illusion, it *lives* by illusion . . . but—— There! I am already beginning again and doing what I have always done, old immoralist and bird catcher that I am—I am talking unmorally, ultramorally, "beyond good and evil"? . . .

2

Thus then, when I found it necessary, I *invented* once on a time the "free spirits," to whom this discouragingly encouraging book with the title, *Human, All Too Human,* is dedicated. There are no such "free spirits" nor have there been such, but, as already said, I then required them for company to keep me cheerful in the midst of evils (sickness, loneliness, foreignness—*acedia,* inactivity) as brave companions and ghosts with whom I could laugh and gossip when so inclined and send to the devil when they became bores—as compensation for the lack of friends. That such free spirits *will be possible* some day, that our Europe *will* have such bold and cheerful wights amongst her sons of tomorrow and the day after tomorrow, actually and bodily, and not merely, as in my case, as the shadows of a hermit's phantasmagoria —*I* should be the last to doubt thereof. Already I see them *coming*, slowly, slowly; and perhaps I am doing something to hasten their coming when I describe in advance under what auspices I *see* them originate, and upon what paths I *see* them come.

3

One may suppose that a spirit in which the type "free spirit" is to become fully mature and sweet has had its decisive event in a *great emancipation*, and that it was all the more fettered previously and apparently bound forever to its corner and pillar. What is it that binds most strongly? What cords are almost unrendable? In men of a lofty and select type it will be their duties; the reverence which is suitable to youth, respect, and tenderness for all that is time-honored and worthy, gratitude to the land which bore them, to the hand which led them, to the sanctuary where they learnt to adore—their most exalted moments themselves will bind them most effectively, will lay upon them the most enduring obligations. For those who are thus bound the great emancipation comes suddenly, like an earthquake; the young soul is all at once convulsed, unloosened and extricated—it does not itself know what is happening. An impulsion and compulsion sway and overmaster it like a command; a will and a wish awaken, to go forth on their course, anywhere, at any cost; a violent, dangerous curiosity about an undiscovered world flames and flares in every sense. "Better to die than live *here*"—says the imperious voice and seduction, and this "here," this "at home" is all that the soul has hitherto loved! A sudden fear and suspicion of that which it loved, a flash of disdain for what was called its "duty," a rebellious, arbitrary, volcanically throbbing longing for travel, foreignness, estrangement, coldness, disenchantment, glaciation, a hatred of love, perhaps a sacrilegious clutch and look *backward*, to where it hitherto adored and loved, perhaps a glow of shame at what it was just doing, and at the same time a rejoicing *that* it was doing it, an intoxicated, internal, exulting thrill which betrays a triumph—a triumph?

Over what? Over whom? An enigmatical, questionable, doubtful triumph, but the *first* triumph nevertheless; such evil and painful incidents belong to the history of the great emancipation. It is, at the same time, a disease which may destroy the man, this first outbreak of power and will to self-decision, self-valuation, this will to *free* will; and how much disease is manifested in the wild attempts and eccentricities by which the liberated and emancipated one now seeks to demonstrate his mastery over things! He roves about raging with unsatisfied longing; whatever he captures has to suffer for the dangerous tension of his pride; he tears to pieces whatever attracts him. With a malicious laugh he twirls round whatever he finds veiled or guarded by a sense of shame; he tries how these things look when turned upside down. It is a matter of abitrariness with him, and pleasure in arbitrariness, if he now perhaps bestow his favor on what had hitherto a bad repute—if he inquisitively and temptingly haunt what is specially forbidden. In the background of his activities and wanderings—for he is restless and aimless in his course as in a desert—stands the note of interrogation of an increasingly dangerous curiosity. "Cannot *all* valuations be reversed? And is good perhaps evil? And God only an invention and artifice of the devil? Is everything, perhaps, radically false? And if we are the deceived, are we not thereby also deceivers? *Must* we not also be deceivers?"— Such thoughts lead and mislead him more and more, onward and away. Solitude encircles and engirdles him, always more threatening, more throttling, more heart-oppressing, that terrible goddess and *mater saeva cupidinum*—but who knows nowadays what *solitude* is? . . .

4

From this morbid solitariness, from the desert of such years of experiment, it is still a long way to the copious, overflowing safety and soundness which does not care to dispense with disease itself as an instrument and anglinghook of knowledge; to that *mature* freedom of spirit which is equally self-control and discipline of the heart, and gives access to many and opposed modes of thought; to that inward comprehensiveness and daintiness of superabundance, which excludes any danger of the spirit's becoming enamored and lost in its own paths, and lying intoxicated in some corner or other; to that excess of plastic, healing, formative, and restorative powers, which is exactly the sign of *splendid* health, that excess which gives the free spirit the dangerous prerogative of being entitled to live by *experiments* and offer itself to adventure; the free spirit's prerogative of mastership! Long years of convalescence may lie in-between, years full of many-colored, painfully enchanting magical transformations, curbed and led by a tough *will to health,* which often dares to dress and disguise itself as actual health. There is a middle condition therein, which a man of such a fate never calls to mind later on without emotion; a pale, delicate light and a sunshine-happiness are peculiar to him, a feeling of birdlike freedom, prospect, and haughtiness, a *tertium quid* in which curiosity and gentle disdain are combined. A "free spirit"—this cool expression does good in every condition, it almost warms. One no longer lives, in the fetters of love and hatred, without Yea, without Nay, voluntarily near, voluntarily distant, preferring to escape, to turn aside, to flutter forth, to fly up and away; one is fastidious like every one who has once seen an immense variety *beneath* him—and one has become the opposite to those who trouble themselves about things which do not concern them. In fact, it is nothing but things which now concern the free spirit—and how many things!—which no longer *trouble* him!

5

A step further toward recovery, and the free spirit again draws near to life; slowly, it is true, and almost stubbornly, almost distrustfully. Again it grows warmer around him, and, as it were, yellower; feeling and sympathy gain depth, thawing winds of every kind pass lightly over him. He almost feels as if his eyes were now first opened to what is *near.* He marvels and is still; where has he been? The near and nearest things, how changed they appear to him! What a bloom and magic they have acquired meanwhile! He looks back gratefully—grateful to his wandering, his austerity and self-estrangement, his farsightedness and his birdlike flights in cold heights. What a good thing that he did not always stay "at home," "by himself," like a sensitive, stupid tenderling. He has been *beside himself,* there is no doubt. He now sees himself for the first time—and what surprises he feels thereby! What thrills unexperienced hitherto! What joy even in the weariness, in the old illness, in the relapses of the convalescent! How he likes to sit still and suffer, to practice patience, to lie in the sun! Who is as familiar as he with the joy of winter, with the patch of sunshine upon the wall! They are the most grateful animals in the world, and also the most unassuming, these lizards of convalescents with their faces half-turned toward life once more: there are those amongst them who never let a day pass without hanging a little hymn of praise on its trailing fringe. And, speaking seriously, it is a radical *cure* for all pessimism (the well-known disease of old idealists and falsehood-mongers) to become ill after the manner of these free spirits, to remain ill a good while, and then grow well (I mean "better") for a still longer period. It is wisdom, practical wisdom, to prescribe even health for one's self for a long time only in small doses.

6

About this time it may at last happen, under the sudden illuminations of still disturbed and changing health, that the enigma of that great emancipation begins to reveal itself to the free, and ever freer, spirit—that enigma which had hitherto lain obscure, questionable, and almost intangible, in his memory. If for a long time he scarcely dared to ask himself, "Why so apart? So alone? Denying everything that I revered? Denying reverence itself? Why this hatred, this suspicion, this severity toward my own virtues?"—he now dares and asks the questions aloud, and already hears something like an answer to them—"Thou shouldst become master over thyself and master also of thine own virtues. Formerly *they* were thy masters; but they are only entitled to be thy tools amongst other tools. Thou shouldst obtain power over the pro and contra, and learn how to put them forth and withdraw them again in accordance with thy higher purpose. Thou shouldst learn how to take the proper perspective of every valuation—the shifting, distortion, and apparent teleology of the horizons and everything that belongs to perspective; also the amount of stupidity which opposite values involve, and all the intellectual loss with which every pro and every contra has to be paid for. Thou shouldst learn how much *necessary* injustice there is in every for and against, injustice as inseparable from life, and life itself as *conditioned* by the perspective and its injustice. Above all thou shouldst see clearly where the injustice is always greatest: namely, where life has developed most punily, restrictedly, necessitously, and incipiently, and yet cannot help regarding *itself* as the purpose and standard of things, and for the sake of self-preservation, secretly, basely, and continuously wasting away and calling in question the higher, greater, and

richer—thou shouldst see clearly the problem of gradation of
rank, and how power and right and amplitude of perspective
grow up together. Thou shouldst——" But enough; the free
spirit *knows* henceforth which "thou shalt" he has obeyed,
and also what he *can* now *do*, what he only now—*may do.* . . .

7

Thus doth the free spirit answer himself with regard to the
riddle of emancipation, and ends therewith, while he generalizes his case, in order thus to decide with regard to his
experience. "As it has happened to *me*," he says to himself,
"so must it happen to every one in whom a *mission* seeks to
embody itself and to 'come into the world.' " The secret
power and necessity of this mission will operate in and upon
the destined individuals like an unconscious pregnancy—long
before they have had the mission itself in view and have
known its name. Our destiny rules over us, even when we are
not yet aware of it; it is the future that makes laws for our
today. Granted that it is *the problem of the gradations of
rank*, of which we may say that it is *our* problem, we free
spirits; now only in the midday of our life do we first understand what preparations, detours, tests, experiments, and disguises the problem needed, before it *was permitted* to rise
before us, and how we had first to experience the most manifold and opposing conditions of distress and happiness in soul
and body, as adventurers and circumnavigators of the inner
world called "man," as surveyors of all the "higher" and the
"one-above-another," also called "man"—penetrating everywhere, almost without fear, rejecting nothing, losing nothing, tasting everything, cleansing everything from all that is
accidental, and, as it were, sifting it out—until at last we
could say, we free spirits, "Here—a *new* problem! Here a
long ladder, the rungs of which we ourselves have sat upon
and mounted—which we ourselves at some time have *been*!
Here a higher place, a lower place, an under-us, an immeasurably long order, a hierarchy which we *see*; here—*our*
problem!"

8

No psychologist or augur will be in doubt for a moment
as to what stage of the development just described the following book belongs (or is assigned to). But where are these

psychologists nowadays? In France, certainly; perhaps in Russia; assuredly not in Germany. Reasons are not lacking why the present-day Germans could still even count this as an honor to them—bad enough, surely, for one who in this respect is un-German in disposition and constitution! This *German* book, which has been able to find readers in a wide circle of countries and nations—it has been about ten years going its rounds—and must understand some sort of music and piping art, by means of which even coy foreign ears are seduced into listening—it is precisely in Germany that this book has been most negligently read, and worst *listened to*; what is the reason? "It demands too much," I have been told. "It appeals to men free from the pressure of coarse duties, it wants refined and fastidious senses, it needs superfluity—superfluity of time, of clearness of sky and heart, of *otium* in the boldest sense of the term: purely good things, which we Germans of today do not possess and therefore cannot give." After such a polite answer my philosophy advises me to be silent and not to question further; besides, in certain cases, as the proverb points out, one only *remains* a philosopher by being—silent.*

NICE, *Spring*, 1886.

FROM HUMAN, ALL TOO HUMAN, II

Preface

1

ONE should only speak where one cannot remain silent, and only speak of what one has *conquered*—the rest is all chatter, "literature," bad breeding. My writings speak only of my conquests. "I" am in them, with all that is hostile to me, *ego ipsissimus*, or, if a more haughty expression be permitted, *ego ipsissimum*. It may be guessed that I have many below me. . . . But first I always needed time, convalescence, distance, separation, before I felt the stirrings of a desire to flay, despoil, lay bare, "represent" (or whatever one likes to call it) for the additional knowledge of the world, some-

---

* An allusion to the medieval Latin distich:

O si tacuisses,
Philosophus mansisses.

thing that I had lived through and outlived, something done or suffered. Hence all my writings—with one exception, important, it is true—must be *antedated*—they always tell of a "behind-me." Some even, like the first three *Thoughts out of Season*, must be thrown back before the period of creation and experience of a previously published book (*The Birth of Tragedy* in the case cited, as anyone with subtle powers of observation and comparison could not fail to perceive). That wrathful outburst against the Germanism, smugness, and raggedness of speech of old David Strauss, the contents of the first *Thought out of Season*, gave a vent to feelings that had inspired me long before, as a student, in the midst of German culture and cultured Philistinism (I claim the paternity of the now much used and misused phrase "cultured Philistinism"). What I said against the "historical disease" I said as one who had slowly and laboriously recovered from that disease, and who was not at all disposed to renounce "history" in the future because he had suffered from her in the past. When in the third *Thought out of Season* I gave expression to my reverence for my first and only teacher, the *great* Arthur Schopenhauer—I should now give it a far more personal and emphatic voice—I was for my part already in the throes of moral scepticism and dissolution, that is, as much concerned with the criticism as with the study of all pessimism down to the present day. I already did not believe in "a blessed thing," as the people say, not even in Schopenhauer. It was at this very period that an unpublished essay of mine, "On Truth and Falsehood in an Extramoral Sense," came into being. Even my ceremonial oration in honor of Richard Wagner, on the occasion of his triumphal celebration at Bayreuth in 1876—Bayreuth signifies the greatest triumph that an artist has ever won—a work that bears the strongest stamp of "individuality," was in the background an act of homage and gratitude to a bit of the past in me, to the fairest and most perilous calm of my sea voyage . . . and as a matter of fact a severance and a farewell. (Was Richard Wagner mistaken on this point? I do not think so. So long as we still love, we do not paint such pictures, we do not yet "examine," we do not place ourselves so far away as is essential for one who "examines." "Examining needs at least a secret antagonism, that of an opposite point of view," it is said on page 46 of the above-named work itself, with an insidious, melancholy application that was perhaps understood by few.) The composure that gave me the *power* to speak after many intervening years of solitude and abstinence first came with the book,

Human, All Too Human, to which this second preface and apologia * is dedicated. As a book for "free spirits" it shows some trace of that almost cheerful and inquisitive coldness of the psychologist, who has *behind* him many painful things that he keeps *under* him, and moreover establishes them for himself and fixes them firmly as with a needle-point. Is it to be wondered at that at such sharp, ticklish work blood flows now and again, that indeed the psychologist has blood on his fingers and not *only* on his fingers?

2

The *Miscellaneous Maxims and Opinions* were in the first place, like *The Wanderer and His Shadow,* published separately as continuations and appendices to the above-mentioned human, all too human *Book for Free Spirits:* and at the same time, as a continuation and confirmation of an intellectual cure, consisting in a course of antiromantic self-treatment, such as my instinct, which had always remained healthy, had itself discovered and prescribed against a temporary attack of the most dangerous form of romantics. After a convalescence of six years I may well be permitted to collect these same writings and publish them as a second volume of *Human, All Too Human.* Perhaps, if surveyed together, they will more clearly and effectively teach their lesson—a lesson of health that may be recommended as a *disciplina voluntatis* to the more intellectual natures of the rising generation. Here speaks a pessimist who has often leaped out of his skin but has always returned into it, thus, a pessimist with good will toward pessimism—at all events a romanticist no longer. And has not a pessimist, who possesses this serpentine knack of changing his skin, the right to read a lecture to our pessimists of today, who are one and all still in the toils of romanticism? Or at least to show them how it is—done?

3

It was then, in fact, high time to bid farewell, and I soon received proof. Richard Wagner, who seemed all-conquering, but was in reality only a decayed and despairing romantic,

* Foreword" and "forword" would be the literal rendering of the play on words.—TR.

suddenly collapsed, helpless and broken, before the Christian Cross. . . . Was there not a single German with eyes in his head and sympathy in his heart for this appalling spectacle? In any case, the unexpected event illumined for me in one lightning flash the place that I had abandoned, and also the horror that is felt by everyone who is unconscious of a great danger until he has passed through it. As I went forward alone, I shuddered, and not long afterward I was ill, or rather more than ill—weary: weary from my ceaseless disappointment about all that remained to make us modern men enthusiastic, at the thought of the power, work, hope, youth, love, flung to all the winds: weary from disgust at the effeminacy and undisciplined rhapsody of this romanticism, at the whole tissue of idealistic lies and softening of conscience, which here again have won the day over one of the bravest of men: last, and not least, weary from the bitterness of an inexorable suspicion—that after this disappointment I was doomed to mistrust more thoroughly, to despise more thoroughly, to be alone more thoroughly than ever before. My task—whither had it flown? Did it not look now as if my task were retreating from me and as if I should for a long future period have no more right to it? What was I to do to endure this most terrible privation? I began by entirely forbidding myself all romantic music, that ambiguous, pompous, stifling art, which robs the mind of its sternness and its joyousness and provide a fertile soil for every kind of vague yearning and spongy sensuality. "Cave musicam" is even today my advice to all who are enough of men to cling to purity in matters of the intellect. Such music enervates, softens, feminizes, its "eternal feminine" draws us—*down!* * My first suspicions, my most immediate precaution, was directed against romantic music. If I hoped for anything at all from music, it was in the expectation of the coming of a musician bold, subtle, malignant, southern, healthy enough to take an immortal revenge upon that other music.

4

Lonely now and miserably self-distrustful, I took sides, not without resentment, *against* myself and *for* everything that hurt me and was hard to me. Thus I once more found the way to that courageous pessimism that is the antithesis of all

---

* The allusion is to the ending of the Second Part of Goethe's *Faust* —"das Ewig Weibliche Zieht uns *hinan!*"—"The Eternal Feminine Draweth us *on!*"—Tr.

romantic fraud, and, as it seems to me today, the way to
"myself," to my task. That hidden masterful Something, for
which we long have no name until at last it shows itself as
our task—that tyrant in us exacts a terrible price for every
attempt that we make to escape him or give him the slip, for
every premature act of self-constraint, for every reconciliation with those to whom we do not belong, for every activity,
however reputable, which turns us aside from our main purpose, yes, even for every virtue that would fain protect us
from the cruelty of our most individual responsibility. "Disease" is always the answer when we wish to have doubts of
our rights to our own task, when we begin to make it easier
for ourselves in any way. How strange and how terrible! It is
our very alleviations for which we have to make the severest
atonement! And if we want to return to health, we have no
choice left—we must load ourselves *more heavily* than we
were ever laden before.

5

It was then that I learned the hermitical habit of speech
acquired only by the most silent and suffering. I spoke without witnesses, or rather indifferent to the presence of witnesses, so as not to suffer from silence, I spoke of various
things that did not concern me in a style that gave the impression that they did. Then, too, I learnt the art of showing myself cheerful, objective, inquisitive in the presence of all that
is healthy and evil—is this, in an invalid, as it seems to me,
his "good taste"? Nevertheless, a more subtle eye and sympathy will not miss what perhaps gives a charm to these
writings—the fact that here speaks one who has suffered
and abstained in such a way as if he had never suffered or
abstained. Here equipoise, composure, even gratitude toward
life *shall* be maintained, here rules a stern, proud, ever
vigilant, ever susceptible will, which has undertaken the task
of defending life against pain and snapping off all conclusions
that are wont to grow like poisonous fungi from pain, disappointment, satiety, isolation and other morasses. Perhaps
this gives our pessimists a hint of self-examination? For it
was then that I hit upon the aphorism, "a sufferer has as
yet no right to pessimism," and that I engaged in a tedious,
patient campaign against the unscientific first principles of all
romantic pessimism, which seeks to magnify and interpret individual, personal experiences into "general judgments," universal condemnations—it was then, in short, that I sighted a

new world. Optimism for the sake of restitution, in order at some time to have the right to become a pessimist—do you understand that? Just as a physician transfers his patient to totally strange surroundings, in order to displace him from his entire "past," his troubles, friends, letters, duties, stupid mistakes and painful memories, and teaches him to stretch out hands and senses toward new nourishment, a new sun, a new future: so I, as physician and invalid in one, forced myself into an utterly different and untried zone of the soul, and particularly into an absorbing journey to a strange land, a strange atmosphere, into a curiosity for all that was strange. A long process of roaming, seeking, changing followed, a distaste for fixity of any kind—a dislike for clumsy affirmation and negation: and at the same time a dietary and discipline which aimed at making it as easy as possible for the soul to fly high, and above all constantly to fly away. In fact a minimum of life, an unfettering from all coarser forms of sensuality, an independence in the midst of all marks of outward disfavor, together with the pride in being able to live in the midst of all this disfavor: a little cynicism perhaps, a little of the "tub of Diogenes," a good deal of whimsical happiness, whimsical gaiety, much calm, light, subtle folly, hidden enthusiasm—all this produced in the end a great spiritual strengthening, a growing joy and exuberance of health. Life itself rewards us for our tenacious will to life, for such a long war as I waged against the pessimistic weariness of life, even for every observant glance of our gratitude, glances that do not miss the smallest, most delicate, most fugitive gifts. . . . In the end we receive Life's great gifts, perhaps the greatest it can bestow—we regain *our* task.

6

Should my experience—the history of an illness and a convalescence, for it resulted in a convalescence—be only my personal experience? and merely just my *Human, All Too Human?* Today I would fain believe the reverse, for I am becoming more and more confident that my books of travel were not penned for my sole benefit, as appeared for a time to be the case. May I, after six years of growing assurance, send them once more on a journey for an experiment? May I commend them particularly to the ears and hearts of those who are afflicted with some sort of a "past," and have enough intellect left to suffer even intellectually from their past? But above all would I commend them to you whose burden is heaviest, you choice spirits, most encompassed with perils, most intellectual, most courageous, who must be the *conscience* of the modern soul and as such be versed in its *science*: * in whom is concentrated all of disease, poison or danger that can exist today: whose lot decrees that you must be more sick than any individual because you are not "mere individuals": whose consolation it is to know and, ah! to walk the path to a new health, a health of tomorrow and the day after: you men of destiny, triumphant, conquerors of time, the healthiest and the strongest, you *good Europeans*!

7

To express finally in a single formula my opposition to the romantic pessimism of the abstinent, the unfortunate, the conquered: there is a will to the tragic and to pessimism, which is a sign as much of the severity as of the strength of the intellect (taste, emotion, conscience). With this will in our hearts we do not fear, but we investigate ourselves the terrible and the problematical elements characteristic of all existence. Behind such a will stand courage and pride and the desire for a really great enemy. That was *my* pessimistic outlook from the first—a new outlook, methinks, an outlook that even at this day is new and strange? To this moment I hold to it firmly and (if it will be believed) not only *for* myself but occasionally *against* myself. . . . You would prefer to have that proved first? Well, what else does all this long preface—prove?

SILS-MARIA, UPPER ENGADINE,
        September, 1886.

FROM THE DAWN OF DAY

Preface

1

IN this book we find a "subterrestrial" at work, digging, mining, undermining. You can see him, always provided that

---

* It has been attempted to render the play on "Gewissen" and "Wissen."—TR.

you have eyes for such deep work—how he makes his way slowly, cautiously, gently but surely, without showing signs of the weariness that usually accompanies a long privation of light and air. He might even be called happy, despite his labors in the dark. Does it not seem as if some faith were leading him on, some solace recompensing him for his toil? Or that he himself desires a long period of darkness, an unintelligible, hidden, enigmatic something, knowing as he does that he will in time have his own morning, his own redemption, his own rosy dawn? Yea, verily he will return. Ask him not what he seeketh in the depths; for he himself will tell you, this apparent Trophonius and subterrestrial, whensoever he once again becomes man. One easily unlearns how to hold one's tongue when one has for so long been a mole, and all alone, like him.

2

Indeed, my indulgent friends, I will tell you—here, in this late preface, * which might easily have become an obituary or a funeral oration—what I sought in the depths below; for I have come back, and—I have escaped. Think not that I will urge you to run the same perilous risk or that I will urge you on even to the same solitude! For whoever proceeds on his own path needs nobody: this is the feature of one's "own path." No one comes to help him in his task: he must face everything quite alone—danger, bad luck, wickedness, foul weather. He goes his own way; and, as is only right, meets with bitterness and occasional irritation because he pursues this "own way" of his: for instance, the knowledge that not even his friends can guess who he is and whither he is going, and that they ask themselves now and then, "Well? Is he really moving at all? Has he still . . . a path before him?" At that time I had undertaken something which could not have been done by everybody: I went down into the deepest depths; I tunneled to the very bottom; I started to investigate and unearth an old *faith* which for thousands of years we philosophers used to build on as the safest of all foundations —which we built on again and again although every previous structure fell in: I began to undermine our *faith in morals*. But ye do not understand me?

* The book was first published in 1881, the preface being added to the second edition, 1886.—Tr.

3

So far it is on Good and Evil that we have meditated least profoundly; this was always too dangerous a subject. Conscience, a good reputation, hell, and at times even the police, have not allowed and do not allow of impartiality; in the presence of morality, as before all authority, we *must* not even think, much less speak: here we must obey! Ever since the beginning of the world, no authority has permitted itself to be made the subject of criticism; and to criticize morals—to look upon morality as a problem, as problematic—what! was that not—*is* that not—immoral? But morality has at its disposal not only every means of intimidation wherewith to keep itself free from critical hands and instruments of torture: its security lies rather in a certain art of enchantment, in which it is a past master—it knows how to "enrapture." It can often paralyze the critical will with a single look, or even seduce it to itself. Yea, there are even cases where morality can turn the critical will against itself; so that then, like the scorpion, it thrusts the sting into its own body. Morality has for ages been an expert in all kinds of devilry in the art of convincing; even at the present day there is no orator who would not turn to it for assistance (only hearken to our anarchists, for instance: how morally they speak when they would fain convince! In the end they even call themselves "the good and the just"). Morality has shown herself to be the greatest mistress of seduction ever since men began to discourse and persuade on earth—and, what concerns us philosophers even more, she is the veritable *Circe of philosophers*. For, to what is it due that, from Plato onward, all the philosophic architects in Europe have built in vain? That everything which they themselves honestly believed to be *aere perennius* threatens to subside or is already laid in ruins? Oh, how wrong is the answer which, even in our own day, rolls glibly off the tongue when this question is asked: "Because they have all neglected the prerequisite, the examination of the foundation, a critique of all reason"—that fatal answer made by Kant, who has certainly not thereby attracted us modern philosophers to firmer and less treacherous ground! (And, one may ask apropos of this, was it not rather strange to demand that an instrument should criticize its own value and effectiveness? That the intellect itself should "recognize" its own worth, power, and limits? Was it not even just a little ridiculous?) The right answer would rather have been, that all philosophers, including Kant himself, were building under the seductive influence of morality—that they aimed at certainty and "truth" only in appearance; but that in reality their attention was directed toward *"majestic moral edifices,"* to use once more Kant's innocent mode of expression, who deems it his "less brilliant, but not undeserving" task and work "to level the ground and prepare a solid foundation for the erection of those majestic moral edifices" (*Critique of Pure Reason,* ii. 257). Alas! He did not succeed in his aim, quite the contrary—as we must acknowledge today. With his exalted aim, Kant was merely a true son of his century, which more than any other may justly be called the century of exaltation; and this he fortunately continued to be in respect to the more valuable side of this century (with that solid piece of sensuality, for example, which he introduced into his theory of knowledge). He, too, had been bitten by the moral tarantula, Rousseau; he, too, felt weighing on his soul that moral fanaticism of which another disciple of Rousseau's, Robespierre, felt and proclaimed himself to be the executor: *de fonder sur la terre l'empire de la sagesse, de la justice, et de la vertu* (speech of June 4th, 1794). On the other hand, with such a French fanaticism in his heart, no one could have cultivated it in a less French, more deep, more thorough and more German manner—if the word German is still permissible in this sense—than Kant did: in order to make room for *his* "moral kingdom," he found himself compelled to add to it an indemonstrable world, a logical "beyond"—that was why he required his critique of pure reason! In other words, *he would not have wanted it* if he had not deemed one thing to be more important than all the others: to render his moral kingdom unassailable by—or, better still, invisible to, reason—for he felt too strongly the vulnerability of a moral order of things in the face of reason. For, when confronted with nature and history, when confronted with the ingrained *immorality* of nature and history, Kant was, like all good Germans from the earliest times, a pessimist. He believed in morality, not because it is demonstrated through nature and history, but despite its being steadily contradicted by them. To understand this "despite," we should perhaps recall a somewhat similar trait in Luther, that other great pessimist, who once urged it upon his friends with true Lutheran audacity: "If we could conceive by reason alone how that God who shows so much wrath and malignity could be merciful and just, what use should we have for faith?" For, from the earliest times, nothing has ever made a deeper impression upon the German soul, nothing has ever "tempted" it more, than that deduction, the most dangerous of all, which for every true Latin is a sin against the intellect: *credo quia absurdum est.* With it German logic enters for the first time into the history of Christian dogma; but even today, a thousand years later, we Germans of the present, late Germans in every way, catch the scent of truth, a *possibility* of truth, at the back of the famous fundamental principle of dialectics with which Hegel secured the victory of the German spirit over Europe —"contradiction moves the world; all things contradict themselves." We are pessimists—even in logic.

4

But logical judgments are not the deepest and most fundamental to which the daring of our suspicion descends: the confidence in reason which is inseparable from the validity of these judgments, is, as confidence, a *moral* phenomenon . . . perhaps German pessimism has yet to take its last step? Perhaps it has once more to draw up its "credo" opposite its "absurdum" in a terrible manner? And if this book is pessimistic even in regard to morals, even above the confidence in morals—should it not be a German book for that very reason? For, in fact, it represents a contradiction, and one which it does not fear: in it confidence in morals is retracted—but why? Out of *morality!* Or how shall we call that which takes place in it—in *us*? for our taste inclines to the employment of more modest phrases. But there is no doubt that to us likewise there speaketh a "thou shalt"; we likewise obey a strict law which is set above us—and this is the last cry of morals which is still audible to us, which we too must *live*: here, if anywhere, are we still *men of conscience*, because, to put the matter in plain words, we will not return to that which we look upon as decayed, outlived, and superseded; we will not return to something "unworthy of belief," whether it be called God, virtue, truth, justice, love of one's neighbor, or what not; we will not permit ourselves to open up a lying path to old ideals; we are thoroughly and unalterably opposed to anything that would intercede and mingle with us; opposed to all forms of present-day faith and Christianity; opposed to the lukewarmness of all romanticism and fatherlandism; opposed also to the artistic sense of enjoyment and lack of principle which would fain make us worship where we no longer believe—for we are artists—opposed, in short, to all this European feminism (or idealism, if this term be thought preferable) which everlastingly "draws upward," and which in consequence everlastingly "lowers" and "degrades." Yet, being men of *this* conscience, we feel that we are related to that German uprightness and piety which dates back thousands of years, although we immoralists and atheists may be the late and uncertain offspring of these virtues—yea, we even consider ourselves, in a certain respect, as their heirs, the executors of their inmost will: a pessimistic will, as I have already pointed out, which is not afraid to deny itself, because it denies itself with *joy!* In us is consummated, if you desire a formula—*the autosuppression of morals.*

5

But, after all, why must we proclaim so loudly and with such intensity what we are, what we want, and what we do not want? Let us look at this more calmly and wisely, from a higher and more distant point of view. Let us proclaim it, as if among ourselves, in so low a tone that all the world fails to hear it and *us!* Above all, however, let us say it *slowly.* . . . This preface comes late, but not too late: what, after all, do five or six years matter? Such a book, and such a problem, are in no hurry; besides, we are friends of the *lento,* I and my book. I have not been a philologist in vain—perhaps I am one yet: a teacher of slow reading. I even come to write slowly. At present it is not only my habit but even my taste—a perverted taste, maybe—to write nothing but what will drive to despair everyone who is "in a hurry." For philology is that venerable art which exacts from its followers one thing above all—to step to one side, to leave themselves spare moments, to grow silent, to become slow—the leisurely art of the goldsmith applied to language: an art which must carry out slow, fine work, and attains nothing if not *lento.* For this very reason philology is now more desirable than ever before; for this very reason it is the highest attraction and incitement in an age of "work": that is to say, of haste, of unseemly and immoderate hurry-skurry, which is intent upon "getting things done" at once, even every book, whether old or new. Philology itself, perhaps, will not "get things done" so hurriedly: it teaches how to read *well,* i.e., slowly, profoundly, attentively, prudently, with inner thoughts, with the mental doors ajar, with delicate fingers and eyes . . . my patient friends, this book appeals only to perfect readers and philologists; *learn* to read me well!

RUTA, NEAR GENOA,
Autumn, 1886.

FROM THE JOYFUL WISDOM

Preface to the Second Edition

1

PERHAPS more than one preface would be necessary for this book; and after all it might still be doubtful whether anyone could be brought nearer to the *experiences* in it by means of prefaces, without having himself experienced something similar. It seems to be written in the language of the thawing wind: there is wantonness, restlessness, contradiction and April weather in it; so that one is as constantly reminded of the proximity of winter as of the *victory* over it: the victory which is coming, which must come, which has perhaps already come. . . . Gratitude continually flows forth, as if the most unexpected thing had happened, the gratitude of a convalescent—for *convalescence* was this most unexpected thing. "Joyful Wisdom": that implies the Saturnalia of a spirit which has patiently withstood a long, frightful pressure—patiently, strenuously, impassionately, without submitting, but without hope—and which is now suddenly o'erpowered with hope, the hope of health, the *intoxication* of convalescence. What wonder that much that is unreasonable and foolish thereby comes to light: much wanton tenderness expended even on problems which have a prickly hide, and are not therefore fit to be fondled and allured. The whole book is really nothing but a revel after long privation and impotence: the frolicking of returning energy, of newly awakened belief in a tomorrow and after-tomorrow; of sudden sentience and prescience of a future, of near adventures, of seas open once more, and aims once more permitted and believed in. And what was now all behind me! This track of desert, exhaustion, unbelief, and frigidity in the midst of youth, this advent of gray hairs at the wrong time, this tyranny of pain, surpassed, however, by the tyranny of pride which repudiated the *consequences* of pain—and consequences are comforts—this radical isolation, as defense against the contempt of mankind become morbidly clairvoyant, this restriction upon principle to all that is bitter, sharp, and painful in knowledge, as prescribed by the *disgust* which had gradually resulted from imprudent spiritual diet and pampering—it is called romanticism—oh, who could realize all those feelings of mine! He, however, who could do so would certainly forgive me everything, and more than a little folly, boisterousness and "Joyful Wisdom"—for example, the handful of songs which are given along with the book on this occasion—songs in which a poet makes merry over all poets in a way not easily pardoned. Alas, it is not only on the poets and their fine "lyrical sentiments" that this reconvalescent must vent his malignity: who knows what kind of victim he seeks, what kind of monster of material for parody will allure him ere long? *Incipit tragaedia*, it is said at the conclusion of this seriously frivolous book; let people be on their guard! Something or other extraordinarily bad and wicked announces itself: *incipit parodia*, there is no doubt. . . .

2

But let us leave Herr Nietzsche; what does it matter to people that Herr Nietzsche has got well again? . . . A psychologist knows few questions so attractive as those concerning the relations of health to philosophy, and in the case when he himself falls sick, he carries with him all his scientific curiosity into his sickness. For, granting that one is a person, one has necessarily also the philosophy of one's personality, there is, however, an important distinction here. With the one it is his defects which philosophize, with the other it is his riches and powers. The former *requires* his philosophy, whether it be as support, sedative, or medicine, as salvation, elevation, or self-alienation; with the latter it is merely a fine luxury, at best the voluptuousness of a triumphant gratitude, which must inscribe itself ultimately in cosmic capitals on the heaven of ideas. In the other more usual case, however, when states of distress occupy themselves with philosophy (as is the case with all sickly thinkers—and perhaps the sickly thinkers preponderate in the history of philosophy), what will happen to the thought itself which is brought under the *pressure* of sickness? This is the important question for psychologists: and here experiment is possible. We philosophers do just like a traveler who resolves to awake at a given hour, and then quietly yields himself to sleep: we surrender ourselves temporarily, body and soul, to the sickness, supposing we become ill—we shut, as it were, our eyes on ourselves. And as the traveler knows that something *does not* sleep, that something counts the hours and will awake him, we also know that the critical moment will find us awake—that then something will spring forward and surprise the spirit *in the very act*, I mean in weakness, or reversion, or submission, or obduracy, or obscurity, or whatever the morbid conditions are called, which in times of good health have the *pride* of the spirit opposed to them (for it is as in the old rhyme: "The spirit proud, peacock and horse are the three proudest things of earthly source"). After such self-questioning and self-testing, one learns to look with a sharper eye at all that has hitherto been philosophized; one divines better than before the arbitrary byways, side streets, resting places, and *sunny* places of thought to which suffering thinkers, precisely as sufferers, are led and misled. One knows now in what direction the sickly *body* and its requirements unconsciously press, push, and allure the spirit—toward the sun, stillness, gentleness, patience, medicine, refreshment in any sense whatever. Every philosophy which puts peace higher than war, every ethic with a negative grasp of the idea of happiness, every metaphysic and physic that knows a finale, an ultimate condition of any kind whatever, every predominating aesthetic or religious longing for an aside, a beyond, an outside, an above—all these permit one to ask whether sickness has not been the motive which inspired the philosopher. The unconscious disguising of physiological requirements under the cloak of the objective, the ideal, the purely spiritual, is carried on to an alarming extent, and I have often enough asked myself, whether, on the whole, philosophy hitherto has not generally been merely an interpretation of the body, and a *misunderstanding of the body*. Behind the loftiest estimates of value by which the history of thought has hitherto been governed, misunderstandings of the bodily constitution, either of individuals, classes, or entire races are concealed. One may always primarily consider these audacious freaks of metaphysics, and especially its answers to the question of the *worth* of existence, as symptoms of certain bodily constitutions; and if, on the whole, when scientifically determined, not a particle of significance attaches to such affirmations and denials of the world, they nevertheless furnish the historian and psychologist with hints so much the more valuable (as we have said) as symptoms of the bodily constitution, its good or bad condition, its fullness, powerfulness, and sovereignty in history; or else of its obstructions, exhaustions and impoverishments, its premonition of the end, its will to the end. I still expect that a philosophical *physician*, in the exceptional sense of the word—one who applies himself to the problem of the collective health of peoples, periods, races, and mankind generally—will some day have the courage to follow out my suspicion to its ultimate conclusions, and to venture on the judgment that in all philosophizing it has not hitherto been a question of "truth" at all, but of something else—namely, of health, futurity, growth, power, life. . . .

3

It will be surmised that I should not like to take leave ungratefully of that period of severe sickness, the advantage of which is not even yet exhausted in me; for I am sufficiently conscious of what I have in advance of the spiritually robust generally, in my changeful state of health. A philosopher who has made the tour of many states of health, and always makes it anew, has also gone through just as many philosophies; he really *cannot* do otherwise than transform his condition on every occasion into the more ingenious posture and position—this art of transfiguration *is* just philosophy. We philosophers are not at liberty to separate soul and body, as the people separate them; and we are still less at liberty to separate soul and spirit. We are not thinking frogs, we are not objectifying and registering apparatuses with cold entrails —our thoughts must be continually born to us out of our pain and we must, motherlike, share with them all that we have in us of blood, heart, ardor, joy, passion, pang, conscience, fate and fatality. Life—that means for us to transform constantly into light and flame all that we are, and also all that we meet with; we *cannot* possibly do otherwise. And as regards sickness, should we not be almost tempted to ask whether we could in general dispense with it? It is great pain only which is the ultimate emancipator of the spirit; for it is the teacher of the *strong suspicion* which makes an X out of every U,* a true, correct X, i.e., the antepenultimate

---

* This means literally to put the numeral X instead of the numeral V (formerly U); hence it means to double a number unfairly, to exaggerate, humbug, cheat.—TR.

letter. . . . It is great pain only, the long slow pain which takes time, by which we are burned as it were with green wood, that compels us philosophers to descend into our ultimate depths, and divest ourselves of all trust, all goodnature, veiling, gentleness, and averageness, wherein we have perhaps formerly installed our humanity. I doubt whether such pain "improves" us, but I know that it *deepens* us. Be it that we learn to confront it with our pride, our scorn, our strength of will, doing like the Indian who, however sorely tortured, revenges himself on his tormentor with his bitter tongue; be it that we withdraw from the pain into the oriental nothingness—it is called Nirvana—into mute, benumbed, deaf self-surrender, self-forgetfulness, and self-effacement. One emerges from such long, dangerous exercises in self-mastery as another being, with several additional notes of interrogation, and above all, with the *will* to question more than ever, more profoundly, more strictly, more sternly, more wickedly, more quietly than has ever been questioned hitherto. Confidence in life is gone; life itself has become a *problem*. Let it not be imagined that one has necessarily become a hypochondriac thereby! Even love of life is still possible—only one loves differently. It is the love of a woman of whom one is doubtful. . . . The charm, however, of all that is problematic, the delight in the X, is too great in those more spiritual and more spiritualized men, not to spread itself again and again like a clear glow over all the trouble of the problematic, over all the danger of uncertainty, and even over the jealousy of the lover. We know a new happiness. . . .

4

Finally (that the most essential may not remain unsaid), one comes back out of such abysses, out of such severe sickness, and out of the sickness of strong suspicion—*newborn*, with the skin cast; more sensitive, more wicked, with a finer taste for joy, with a more delicate tongue for all good things, with a merrier disposition, with a second and more dangerous innocence in joy; more childish at the same time, and a hundred times more refined than ever before. Oh, how repugnant to us now is pleasure, coarse, dull, drab pleasure, as the pleasure seekers, our "cultured" classes, our rich and ruling classes, usually understand it! How malignantly we now listen to the great holiday hubbub with which "cultured people" and city men at present allow themselves to be forced to "spiritual enjoyment" by art, books, and music, with the help of spirituous liquors! How the theatrical cry of passion now pains our ear, how strange to our taste has all the romantic riot and sensuous bustle which the cultured populace love become (together with their aspirations after the exalted, the elevated, and the intricate)! No, if we convalescents need an art at all, it is another art—a mocking, light, volatile, divinely serene, divinely ingenious art, which blazes up like a clear flame, into a cloudless heaven! Above all, an art for artists, only for artists! We at last know better what is first of all necessary *for it*—namely, cheerfulness, *every* kind of cheerfulness, my friends! also as artists: I should like to prove it. We now know something too well, we men of knowledge: oh, how well we are now learning to forget and *not* know, as artists! And as to our future, we are not likely to be found again in the tracks of those Egyptian youths who at night make the temples unsafe, embrace statues, and would fain unveil, uncover, and put in clear light, everything which for good reasons is kept concealed.* No, we have got disgusted with this bad taste, this will to truth, to "truth at all costs," this youthful madness in the love of truth; we are now too experienced, too serious, too joyful, too singed, too profound for that. . . . We no longer believe that truth remains truth when the veil is withdrawn from it: we have lived long enough to believe this. At present we regard it as a matter of propriety not to be anxious either to see everything naked, or to be present at everything, or to understand and "know" everything. "Is it true that the good God is everywhere present?" asked a little girl of her mother; "I think that is indecent": a hint to philosophers! One should have more reverence for the *shamefacedness* with which nature has concealed herself behind enigmas and motley uncertainties. Perhaps truth is a woman who has reasons for not showing her reasons? Perhaps her name is Baubo, to speak in Greek? . . . Oh, those Greeks! They knew how to *live:* for that purpose it is necessary to keep bravely to the surface, the fold, and the skin; to worship appearance, to believe in forms, tones, and words, in the whole Olympus of appearance! Those Greeks were superficial—*from profundity!* And are we not coming back precisely to this point, we daredevils of the spirit, who have scaled the highest and most dangerous peak of contemporary thought, and have looked around us from it, have *looked down* from it? Are we

---

* An allusion to Schiller's poem, "The Veiled Image of Sais."—Tr.

not precisely in this respect—Greeks? Worshippers of forms, of tones and of words? And precisely on that account— artists?

RUTA, near GENOA,
    Autumn, 1886.

FROM BEYOND GOOD AND EVIL

Preface

SUPPOSING that Truth is a woman—what then? Is there not ground for suspecting that all philosophers, in so far as they have been dogmatists, have failed to understand women— that the terrible seriousness and clumsy importunity with which they have usually paid their addresses to Truth have been unskilled and unseemly methods for winning a woman? Certainly she has never allowed herself to be won; and at present every kind of dogma stands with sad and discouraged mien—*if*, indeed, it stands at all! For there are scoffers who maintain that it has fallen, that all dogma lies on the ground —nay more, that it is at its last gasp. But to speak seriously, there are good grounds for hoping that all dogmatizing in philosophy, whatever solemn, whatever conclusive and de- cided airs it has assumed, may have been only a noble pueril- ism and tyronism; and probably the time is at hand when it will be once and again understood *what* has actually sufficed for the basis of such imposing and absolute philosophical edifices as the dogmatists have hitherto reared: perhaps some popular superstition of immemorial time (such as the soul- superstition, which, in the form of subject- and ego-super- stition, has not yet ceased doing mischief); perhaps some play upon words, a deception on the part of grammar, or an audacious generalization of very restricted, very personal, very human—all too human facts. The philosophy of the dog- matists, it is to be hoped, was only a promise for thousands of years afterward, as was astrology in still earlier times, in the service of which probably more labor, gold, acuteness, and pa- tience have been spent than on any actual science hitherto: we owe to it, and to its "superterrestrial" pretensions in Asia and Egypt, the grand style of architecture. It seems that in order to inscribe themselves upon the heart of humanity with everlasting claims, all great things have first to wander about the earth as enormous and awe-inspiring caricatures: dogmatic philosophy has been a caricature of this kind—for instance, the Vedanta doctrine in Asia, and Platonism in Europe. Let us not be ungrateful to it, although it must certainly be confessed that the worst, the most tiresome, and the most dangerous of errors hitherto has been a dogmatist error—namely, Plato's invention of Pure Spirit and the Good in Itself. But now when it has been surmounted, when Europe, rid of this nightmare, can again draw breath freely and at least enjoy a healthier—sleep, we, *whose duty is wakefulness itself,* are the heirs of all the strength which the struggle against this error has fostered. It amounted to the very inversion of truth, and the denial of the *perspective*—the fundamental condition—of life, to speak of Spirit and the Good as Plato spoke of them, indeed one might ask, as a physician: "How did such a malady attack that finest product of antiquity, Plato? Had the wicked Socrates really corrupted him? Was Socrates after all a corrupter of youths, and deserved his hemlock?" But the struggle against Plato, or—to speak plainer, and for the "people"— the struggle against the ecclesiastical oppression of millenniums of Christianity (for Christianity is Platonism for the "people"), produced in Europe a magnificent tension of soul, such as had not existed anywhere previously; with such a tensely strained bow one can now aim at the furthest goals. As a matter of fact, the European feels this tension as a state of distress, and twice attempts have been made in grand style to unbend the bow: once by means of Jesuitism, and the second time by means of democratic enlightenment—which, with the aid of liberty of the press and newspaper reading, might, in fact, bring it about that the spirit would not so easily find itself in "distress"! (The Germans invented gunpowder— all credit to them! but they again made things square—they invented printing.) But we, who are neither Jesuits, nor democrats, nor even sufficiently Germans, we *good Europeans,* and free, *very* free spirits—we have it still, all the distress of spirit and all the tension of its bow! And perhaps also the arrow, the duty, and, who knows? *the goal to aim at. . . .*

Sils-Maria, Upper Engadine,
    June, 1885.

FROM THE GENEALOGY OF MORALS

Preface

1

WE are unknown, we knowers, ourselves to ourselves; this has its own good reason. We have never searched for ourselves—how should it then come to pass that we should ever *find* ourselves? Rightly has it been said: "Where your treasure is, there will your heart be also." *Our* treasure is there, where stand the hives of our knowledge. It is to those hives that we are always striving; as born creatures of flight, and as the honey gatherers of the spirit, we care really in our hearts only for one thing—to bring something "home to the hive!"

As far as the rest of life with its so-called "experiences" is concerned, which of us has even sufficient serious interest? Or sufficient time? In our dealings with such points of life, we are, I fear, never properly to the point; to be precise, our heart is not there, and certainly not our ear. Rather like one who, delighting in a divine distraction, or sunken in the seas of his own soul, in whose ear the clock has just thundered with all its force its twelve strokes of noon, suddenly wakes up, and asks himself, "What has in point of fact just struck?" so do we at times rub afterward, as it were, our puzzled ears, and ask in complete astonishment and complete embarrassment, "Through what have we in point of fact just lived?" further, "Who are we in point of fact?" and count, *after they have struck,* as I have explained, all the twelve throbbing beats of the clock of our experience, of our life, of our being—ah!—and count wrong in the endeavor. Of necessity we remain strangers to ourselves, we understand ourselves not, in ourselves we are bound to be mistaken, for of us holds good to all eternity the motto, "Each one is the farthest away from himself"—as far as ourselves are concerned we are not "knowers."

2

My thoughts concerning the *genealogy* of our moral prejudices—for they constitute the issue in this polemic—have their first, bald, and provisional expression in that collection of aphorisms entitled *Human, All Too Human, a Book for Free Minds*, the writing of which was begun in Sorrento, during a winter which allowed me to gaze over the broad and dangerous territory through which my mind had up to that time wandered. This took place in the winter of 1876–77; the thoughts themselves are older.

They were in their substance already the same thoughts which I take up again in the following treatises—we hope that they have derived benefit from the long interval, that they have grown riper, clearer, stronger, more complete. The fact, however, that I still cling to them even now, that in the meanwhile they have always held faster by each other, have, in fact, grown out of their original shape and into each other, all this strengthens in my mind the joyous confidence that they must have been originally neither separate disconnected capricious nor sporadic phenomena, but have sprung from a common root, from a fundamental *fiat* of knowledge, whose empire reached to the soul's depth, and that ever grew more definite in its voice, and more definite in its demands. That is the only state of affairs that is proper in the case of a philosopher.

We have no right to be "disconnected"; we must neither err "disconnectedly" nor strike the truth "disconnectedly." Rather with the necessity with which a tree bears its fruit, so do our thoughts, our values, our Yes's and No's and If's and Whether's, grow connected and interrelated, mutual witnesses of *one* will, *one* health, *one* kingdom, *one* sun—as to whether they are to *your* taste, these fruits of ours? But what matters that to the trees? What matters that to us, the philosophers?

3

Owing to a scrupulosity peculiar to myself, which I confess reluctantly—it concerns indeed *morality*—a scrupulosity which manifests itself in my life at such an early period, with so much spontaneity, with so chronic a persistence and so keen an opposition to environment, epoch, precedent, and ancestry that I should have been almost entitled to style it my "a priori"—my curiosity and my suspicion felt themselves betimes bound to halt at the question, of what in point of actual fact was the *origin* of our "Good" and of our "Evil." Indeed, at the boyish age of thirteen the problem of the origin of Evil already haunted me; at an age "when games and God divide one's heart," I devoted to that problem my first childish attempt at the literary game, my first philosophic essay—and as regards my infantile solution of the problem, well, I gave quite properly the honor to God, and made him the *father* of evil. Did my own a priori demand that precise solution from me? That new, immoral, or at least "amoral" a priori and that "categorical imperative" which was its voice (but oh! how hostile to the Kantian article, and how pregnant with problems!), to which since then I have given more and more attention, and indeed what is more than attention. Fortunately I soon learned to separate theological from moral prejudices, and I gave up looking for a *supernatural* origin of evil. A certain amount of historical and philological education, to say nothing of an innate faculty of psychological discrimination par excellence succeeded in transforming almost immediately my original problem into the following one: Under what conditions did Man invent for himself those judgments of values, "Good" and "Evil"? *And what intrinsic value do they possess in themselves?* Have they up to the present hindered or advanced human well-being? Are they a symptom of the distress, impoverishment, and degeneration of Human Life? Or, conversely, is it in them that is manifested the fullness, the strength, and the will of Life, its courage, its self-confidence, its future? On this point I found and hazarded in my mind the most diverse answers; I established distinctions in periods, peoples, and castes; I became a specialist in my problem, and from my answers grew new questions, new investigations, new conjectures, new probabilities; until at last I had a land of my own and a soil of my own, a whole secret world growing and flowering, like hidden gardens of whose existence no one could have an inkling—oh, how happy are we, we finders of knowledge, provided that we know how to keep silent sufficiently long.

4

My first impulse to publish some of my hypotheses concerning the origin of morality I owe to a clear, well-written, and even precocious little book, in which a perverse and vicious kind of moral philosophy (your real *English* kind) was definitely presented to me for the first time; and this attracted me—with that magnetic attraction, inherent in that which is diametrically opposed and antithetical to one's own ideas. The title of the book was *The Origin of the Moral Emotions*; its author, Dr. Paul Rée; the year of its appearance, 1877. I may almost say that I have never read anything

in which every single dogma and conclusion has called forth
from me so emphatic a negation as did that book; albeit a
negation untainted by either pique or intolerance. I referred
accordingly both in season and out of season in the previous
works, at which I was then working, to the arguments of that
book, not to refute them—for what have I got to do with
mere refutations—but substituting, as is natural to a positive
mind, for an improbable theory one which is more probable,
and occasionally no doubt for one philosophic error another.
In that early period I gave, as I have said, the first public expression to those theories of origin to which these essays are
devoted, but with a clumsiness which I was the last to conceal from myself, for I was as yet cramped, being still without a special language for these special subjects, still frequently liable to relapse and to vacillation. To go into details,
compare what I say in *Human, All Too Human,* part i, about
the parallel early history of Good and Evil, Aph. 45 (namely,
their origin from the castes of the aristocrats and the slaves);
similarly, Aph. 136 et seq., concerning the birth and value of
ascetic morality; similarly, Aphs. 96, 99, vol. ii, Aph. 89,
concerning the Morality of Custom, that far older and more
original kind of morality which is *toto caelo* different from
the altruistic ethics (in which Dr. Rée, like all the English
moral philosophers, sees the ethical "Thing-in-itself"); finally,
Aph. 92. Similarly, Aph. 26 in *Human, All Too Human,*
part ii, and Aph. 112, the *Dawn of Day,* concerning the origin
of Justice as a balance between persons of approximately
equal power (equilibrium as the hypothesis of all contract,
consequently of all law); similarly, concerning the origin of
Punishment, *Human, All Too Human,* part ii, Aphs. 22, 23,
in regard to which the deterrent object is neither essential nor
original (as Dr. Rée thinks—rather is it that this object is
only imported, under certain definite conditions, and always
as something extra and additional).

5

In reality I had set my heart at that time on something
much more important than the nature of the theories of myself or others concerning the origin of morality (or, more
precisely, the real function from my view of these theories
was to point an end to which they were one among many
means). The issue for me was the value of morality, and on
that subject I had to place myself in a state of abstraction, in
which I was almost alone with my great teacher Schopen-

hauer, to whom that book, with all its passion and inherent
contradiction (for that book also was a polemic), turned for
present help as though he were still alive. The issue was,
strangely enough, the value of the "unegoistic" instincts, the
instincts of pity, self-denial, and self-sacrifice which Schopenhauer had so persistently painted in golden colors, deified and
etherealized, that eventually they appeared to him, as it were,
high and dry, as "intrinsic values in themselves," on the
strength of which he uttered both to Life and to himself his
own negation. But against *these very* instincts there voiced itself in my soul a more and more fundamental mistrust, a
scepticism that dug ever deeper and deeper; and in this very
instinct I saw the *great* danger of mankind, its most sublime
temptation and seduction—seduction to what? to nothingness?—in these very instincts I saw the beginning of the end,
stability, the exhaustion that gazes backward, the will turning
against Life, the last illness announcing itself with its own
mincing melancholy: I realized that the morality of pity which
spread wider and wider, and whose grip infected even philosophers with its disease, was the most sinister symptom to our
modern European civilization; I realized that it was the route
along which that civilization slid on its way to—a new Buddhism?—a European Buddhism?—*Nihilism?* This exaggerated
estimation in which modern philosophers have held pity, is
quite a new phenomenon; up to that time philosophers were
absolutely unanimous as to the *worthlessness* of pity. I need
only mention Plato, Spinoza, La Rochefoucauld, and Kant
—four minds as mutually different as is possible, but united
on one point: their contempt of pity.

6

This problem of the value of pity and of the pity-morality
(I am an opponent of the modern infamous emasculation of
our emotions) seems at the first blush a mere isolated problem, a note of interrogation for itself; he, however, who
once halts at this problem, and learns how to put questions,
will experience what I experienced: a new and immense vista
unfolds itself before him, a sense of potentiality seizes him
like a vertigo, every species of doubt, mistrust, and fear
springs up, the belief in morality, nay, in all morality, totters
—finally a new demand voices itself. Let us speak out this
new demand; we need a *critique* of moral values, *the value of
these values* is for the first time to be called into question—
and for this purpose a knowledge is necessary of the condi-

tions and circumstances out of which these values grew, and under which they experienced their evolution and their distortion (morality as a result, as a symptom, as a mask, as Tartuffism, as disease, as a misunderstanding; but also morality as a cause, as a remedy, as a stimulant, as a fetter, as a drug), especially as such a knowledge has neither existed up to the present time nor is even now generally desired. The value of these "values" was taken for granted as an indisputable fact, which was beyond all question. No one has, up to the present, exhibited the faintest doubt or hesitation in judging the "good man" to be of a higher value than the "evil man," of a higher value with regard specifically to human progress, utility, and prosperity generally, not forgetting the future. What? Suppose the converse were the truth! What? Suppose there lurked in the "good man" a symptom of retrogression, such as a danger, a temptation, a poison, a *narcotic*, by means of which the present *battened on the future*! More comfortable and less risky perhaps than its opposite, but also pettier, meaner! So that morality would really be saddled with the guilt, if the *maximum potentiality of the power and splendor* of the human species were never to be attained? So that really morality would be the danger of dangers?

7

Enough, that after this vista had disclosed itself to me, I myself had reason to search for learned, bold, and industrious colleagues (I am doing it even to this very day). It means traversing with new clamorous questions, and at the same time with new eyes, the immense, distant, and completely unexplored land of morality—of a morality which has actually existed and been actually lived! And is this not practically equivalent to first *discovering* that land? If, in this context, I thought, amongst others, of the aforesaid Dr. Rée, I did so because I had no doubt that from the very nature of his questions he would be compelled to have recourse to a truer method, in order to obtain his answers. Have I deceived myself on that score? I wished at all events to give a better direction of vision to an eye of such keenness, and such impartiality. I wished to direct him to the real *history of morality*, and to warn him, while there was yet time, against a world of English theories that culminated *in the blue vacuum of heaven*. Other colors, of course, rise immediately to one's mind as being a hundred times more potent than

blue for a genealogy of morals—for instance, *gray*, by which
I mean authentic facts capable of definite proof and having
actually existed, or, to put it shortly, the whole of that long
hieroglyphic script (which is so hard to decipher) about the
past history of human morals. This script was unknown to
Dr. Rée; but he had read Darwin—and so in his philosophy
the Darwinian beast and that pink of modernity, the demure
weakling and dilettante, who "bites no longer," shake hands
politely in a fashion that is at least instructive, the latter
exhibiting a certain facial expression of refined and good-
humored indolence, tinged with a touch of pessimism and
exhaustion; as if it really did not pay to take all these
things—I mean moral problems—so seriously. I, on the other
hand, think that there are no subjects which *pay* better for
being taken seriously; part of this payment is, that perhaps
eventually they admit of being taken *gaily*. This gaiety indeed, or, to use my own language, this *joyful wisdom*, is
a payment; a payment for a protracted, brave, laborious, and
burrowing seriousness, which, it goes without saying, is
the attribute of but a few. But on that day on which we say
from the fullness of our hearts, "Forward! our old morality
too is fit material *for Comedy*," we shall have discovered a
new plot, and a new possibility for the Dionysian drama entitled *The Soul's Fate*—and he will speedily utilize it, one
can wager safely, he, the great ancient eternal dramatist of
the comedy of our existence.

8

If this writing be obscure to any individual, and jar on his
ears, I do not think that it is necessarily I who am to blame.
It is clear enough, on the hypothesis which I presuppose,
namely, that the reader has first read my previous writings
and has not grudged them a certain amount of trouble: it is
not, indeed, a simple matter to get really at their essence.
Take, for instance, my *Zarathustra*; I allow no one to pass
muster as knowing that book, unless every single word therein
has at some time wrought in him a profound wound, and
at some time exercised on him a profound enchantment.
Then and not till then can he enjoy the privilege of partici-
pating reverently in the halcyon element, from which that
work is born, in its sunny brilliance, its distance, its spa-
ciousness, its certainty. In other cases the aphoristic form
produces difficulty, but this is only because this form is
treated *too casually*. An aphorism properly coined and cast

into its final mold is far from being "deciphered" as soon as it has been read; on the contrary, it is then that it first requires *to be expounded*—of course for that purpose an art of exposition is necessary. The third essay in this book provides an example of what is offered, of what in such cases I call exposition; an aphorism is prefixed to that essay, the essay itself is its commentary. Certainly one *quality* which nowadays has been best forgotten—and that is why it will take some time yet for my writings to become readable—is essential in order to practice reading as an art—a quality for the exercise of which it is necessary to be a cow, and under *no circumstances* a modern man!—*rumination.*

SILS-MARIA, UPPER ENGADINE,
  July, 1887.

FROM THE CASE OF WAGNER

Preface

I AM writing this to relieve my mind. It is not malice alone which makes me praise Bizet at the expense of Wagner in this essay. Amid a good deal of jesting I wish to make one point clear which does not admit of levity. To turn my back on Wagner was for me a piece of fate; to get to like anything else whatever afterward was for me a triumph. Nobody, perhaps, had ever been more dangerously involved in Wagnerism, nobody had defended himself more obstinately against it, nobody had ever been so overjoyed at ridding himself of it. A long history!—Shall I give it a name?—If I were a moralist, who knows what I might not call it! Perhaps a piece of *self-mastery.* But the philosopher does not like the moralist, neither does he like highfalutin words. . . .

What is the first and last thing that a philosopher demands of himself? To overcome his age in himself, to become "timeless." With what then does the philosopher have the greatest fight? With all that in him which makes him the child of his time. Very well then! I am just as much a child of my age as Wagner—i.e., I am a decadent. The only difference is that I recognized the fact, that I struggled against it. The philosopher in me struggled against it.

My greatest preoccupation hitherto has been the problem of *decadence,* and I had reasons for this. "Good and evil" form only a playful subdivision of this problem. If one has trained one's eye to detect the symptoms of decline, one also understands morality—one understands what lies concealed beneath its holiest names and tables of values, e.g., *impoverished* life, the will to nonentity, great exhaustion. Morality *denies* life. . . . In order to undertake such a mission I was obliged to exercise self-discipline: I had to side against all that was morbid in myself, including Wagner, including Schopenhauer, including the whole of modern *humanity*. A profound estrangement, coldness, and soberness toward all that belongs to my age, all that was contemporary: and as the highest wish, Zarathustra's eye, an eye which surveys the whole phenomenon—mankind—from an enormous distance—which looks down upon it. For such a goal —what sacrifice would not have been worth while? What "self-mastery"! What "self-denial"!

The greatest event of my life took the form of a *recovery*. Wagner belongs only to my diseases.

Not that I wish to appear ungrateful to this disease. If in this essay I support the proposition that Wagner is *harmful*, I nonetheless wish to point out unto whom, in spite of all, he is indispensable—to the philosopher. Anyone else may perhaps be able to get on without Wagner; but the philosopher is not free to pass him by. The philosopher must be the evil conscience of his age—but to this end he must be possessed of its best knowledge. And what better guide, or more thoroughly efficient revealer of the soul, could be found for the labyrinth of the modern spirit than Wagner? Through Wagner modernity speaks her most intimate language: It conceals neither its good nor its evil; it has thrown off all shame. And, conversely, one has almost calculated the whole of the value of modernity once one is clear concerning what is good and evil in Wagner. I can perfectly well understand a musician of today who says: "I hate Wagner but I can endure no other music." But I should also understand a philosopher who said: "Wagner is modernity in concentrated form." There is no help for it, we must first be Wagnerites. . . .

FROM NIETZSCHE CONTRA WAGNER*

Preface

THE following chapters have been selected from past works of mine, and not without care. Some of them date back as far as 1877. Here and there, of course, they will be found to have been made a little more intelligible, but above all, more brief. Read consecutively, they can leave no one in any doubt, either concerning myself, or concerning Wagner: we are antipodes. The reader will come to other conclusions, too, in his perusal of these pages; for instance, that this is an essay for psychologists and *not* for Germans. . . . I have my readers everywhere, in Vienna, St. Petersburg, Copenhagen, Stockholm, Paris, and New York—but *I have none* in Europe's Flatland—Germany. . . . And I might even have something to say to Italians whom I love just as much as I . . . *Quousque tandem, Crispi* . . . Triple alliance: a people can only conclude a *mésalliance* with the "Empire." . . .

FRIEDRICH NIETZSCHE.

TURIN, *Christmas,* 1888

FROM ECCE HOMO

Preface

1

As it is my intention within a very short time to confront my fellowmen with the very greatest demand that has ever yet been made upon them, it seems to me above all necessary to declare here who and what I am. As a matter of fact, this ought to be pretty well known already, for I have not "held my tongue" about myself. But the disparity which obtains between the greatness of my task and the smallness of my

* From *The Case of Wagner.*

contemporaries is revealed by the fact that people have neither heard me nor yet seen me. I live on my own self-made credit, and it is probably only a prejudice to suppose that I am alive at all. I do but require to speak to any one of the scholars who come to the Ober-Engadine in the summer in order to convince myself that I am *not* alive. . . . Under these circumstances, it is a duty—and one against which my customary reserve, and to a still greater degree the pride of my instincts, rebel—to say: *Listen! for I am such and such a person. For Heaven's sake do not confound me with anyone else!*

2

I am, for instance, in no wise a bogeyman, or moral monster. On the contrary, I am the very opposite in nature to the kind of man that has been honored hitherto as virtuous. Between ourselves, it seems to me that this is precisely a matter on which I may feel proud. I am a disciple of the philosopher Dionysus, and I would prefer to be even a satyr than a saint. But just read this book! Maybe I have here succeeded in expressing this contrast in a cheerful and at the same time sympathetic manner—maybe this is the only purpose of the present work.

The very last thing I should promise to accomplish would be to "improve" mankind. I do not set up any new idols; may old idols only learn what it costs to have legs of clay. To overthrow idols (idols is the name I give to all ideals) is much more like my business. In proportion as an ideal world has been falsely assumed, reality has been robbed of its value, its meaning, and its truthfulness. . . . The "true world" and the "apparent world"—in plain English, the fictitious world and reality. . . . Hitherto the *lie* of the ideal has been the curse of reality; by means of it the very source of mankind's instinct has become mendacious and false; so much so that those values have come to be worshipped which are the exact *opposite* of the ones which would ensure man's prosperity, his future, and his great right to a future.

3

He who knows how to breathe in the air of my writings is conscious that it is the air of the heights, that it is bracing. A man must be built for it, otherwise the chances are that it will chill him. The ice is near, the loneliness is terrible—but how serenely everything lies in the sunshine! How freely one can breathe! How much, one feels, lies beneath one! Philosophy, as I have understood it hitherto, is a voluntary retirement into regions of ice and mountain peaks—the seeking-out of everything strange and questionable in existence, everything upon which, hitherto, morality has set its ban. Through long experience, derived from such wanderings in forbidden country, I acquired an opinion very different from that which may seem generally desirable, of the causes which hitherto have led to men's moralizing and idealizing. The secret history of philosophers, the psychology of their great names, was revealed to me. How much truth can a certain mind endure; how much truth can it dare?—these questions became for me ever more and more the actual test of values. Error (the belief in the ideal) is not blindness; error is cowardice. . . . Every conquest, every step forward in knowledge, is the outcome of courage, of hardness toward one's self, of cleanliness toward one's self. I do not refute ideals; all I do is to draw on my gloves in their presence. . . . *Nitimur in vetitum:* with this device my philosophy will one day be victorious; for that which has hitherto been most stringently forbidden is, without exception, Truth.

4

In my lifework, my *Zarathustra* holds a place apart. With it, I gave my fellow men the greatest gift that has ever been bestowed upon them. This book, the voice of which speaks out across the ages, is not only the loftiest book on earth, literally the book of mountain air—the whole phenomenon, mankind, lies at an incalculable distance beneath it—but it is also the deepest book, born of the inmost abundance of truth; an inexhaustible well, into which no pitcher can be lowered without coming up again laden with gold and with goodness. Here it is not a "prophet" who speaks, one of those gruesome hybrids of sickness and Will to Power, whom men call founders of religions. If a man would not do a sad wrong to his wisdom, he must above all give proper heed to the tones—the halcyonic tones—that fall from the lips of Zarathustra:

"The most silent words are harbingers of the storm; thoughts that come on dove's feet lead the world.

"The figs fall from the trees; they are good and sweet, and, when they fall, their red skins are rent.

"A north wind am I unto ripe figs.

"Thus, like figs, do these precepts drop down to you, my friends; now drink their juice and their sweet pulp.

"It is autumn all around, and clear sky, and afternoon."

No fanatic speaks to you here; this is not a "sermon"; no faith is demanded in these pages. From out an infinite treasure of light and well of joy, drop by drop, my words fall out—a slow and gentle gait is the cadence of these discourses. Such things can reach only the most elect; it is a rare privilege to be a listener here; not every one who likes can have ears to hear Zarathustra. Is not Zarathustra, because of these things, a *seducer*? . . . But what, indeed, does he himself say, when for the first time he goes back to his solitude? Just the reverse of that which any "Sage," "Saint," "Saviour of the world," and other decadent would say. . . . Not only his words but he himself is other than they.

"Alone do I now go, my disciples! Get ye also hence, and alone! Thus would I have it.

"Verily, I beseech you: take your leave of me and arm yourselves against Zarathustra! And better still, be ashamed of him! Maybe he hath deceived you.

"The knight of knowledge must be able not only to love his enemies but also to hate his friends.

"The man who remaineth a pupil requiteth his teacher but ill. And why would ye not pluck at my wreath?

"Ye honor me; but what if your reverence should one day break down? Take heed, lest a statue crush you.

"Ye say ye believe in Zarathustra? But of what account is Zarathustra? Ye are my believers: but of what account are all believers?

"Ye had not yet sought yourselves when ye found me. Thus do all believers; therefore is all believing worth so little.

"Now I bid you lose me and find yourselves; and only when ye have all denied me will I come back unto you."

FRIEDRICH NIETZSCHE.

FROM THE ANTICHRIST*

Preface

THIS book belongs to the very few. Maybe not one of them is yet alive; unless he be of those who understand my Zarathus-

* From *The Twilight of the Idols*.

tra. How *can* I confound myself with those for whom ears
are already growing today?—Only the day after tomorrow
belongs to me. Some are born posthumously.

I am only too well aware of the conditions under which a
man understands me, and then *necessarily* understands. He
must be intellectually upright to the point of hardness, in
order even to endure my seriousness and my passion. He
must be used to living on mountaintops—and to feeling the
wretched gabble of politics and national egotism *beneath*
him. He must have become indifferent; he must never inquire
whether truth is profitable or whether it may prove fatal. . . .
Possessing from strength a predilection for questions to
which no one has enough courage nowadays; the courage for
the *forbidden*; his predestination must be the labyrinth. The
experience of seven solitudes. New ears for new music. New
eyes for the most remote things. A new conscience for truths
which hitherto have remained dumb. And the will to economy
on a large scale: to husband his strength and his enthusiasm.
. . . He must honor himself, he must love himself; he must
be absolutely free with regard to himself. . . . Very well
then! Such men alone are my readers, my proper readers, my
preordained readers: of what account are the rest?—the rest
are simply—humanity. One must be superior to humanity in
power, in loftiness of soul—in contempt.

FRIEDRICH NIETZSCHE.

FROM FIVE PREFACES TO
UNWRITTEN WORKS

On Schopenhauer and German Culture

IN dear vile Germany culture now lies so decayed in the
streets, jealousy of all that is great rules so shamelessly, and
the general tumult of those who race for "Fortune" resounds so deafeningly, that one must have a strong faith, almost in the sense of *credo quia absurdum est*, in order to
hope still for a growing Culture, and above all—in opposition to the press with her "public opinion"—to be able to
work by public teaching. With violence must those, in whose
hearts lies the immortal care for the people, free themselves

from all the inrushing impressions of that which is just now
actual and valid, and evoke the appearance of reckoning them
indifferent things. They must appear so, because they want to
think, and because a loathsome sight and a confused noise,
perhaps even mixed with the trumpet flourishes of war-
glory, disturb their thinking, and above all, because they
want to *believe* in the German character and because with
this faith they would lose their strength. Do not find fault
with these believers if they look from their distant aloofness
and from the heights toward their Promised Land! They fear
those experiences to which the kindly disposed foreigner sur-
renders himself when he lives among the Germans, and must
be surprised how little German life corresponds to those
great individuals, works, and actions, which, in his kind disposition he has learned to revere as the true German character. Where the German cannot lift himself into the sublime
he makes an impression less than the mediocre. Even the celebrated German scholarship, in which a number of the most
useful domestic and homely virtues such as faithfulness, self-
restriction, industry, moderation, cleanliness appear trans-
posed into a purer atmosphere and, as it were, transfigured,
is by no means the result of these virtues; looked at closely,
the motive urging to unlimited knowledge appears in Germany much more like a defect, a gap, than an abundance of
forces; it looks almost like the consequence of a needy, formless atrophied life and even like a flight from the moral nar-
row-mindedness and malice to which the German without
such diversions is subjected, and which also in spite of that
scholarship, yea still within scholarship itself, often break
forth. As the true virtuosi of philistinism, the Germans are
at home in narrowness of life, discerning, and judging; if
anyone will carry them above themselves into the sublime,
then they make themselves heavy as lead, and as such lead
weights they hang to their truly great men, in order to pull
them down out of the ether to the level of their own necessi-
tous indigence. Perhaps this Philistine homeliness may be
only the degeneration of a genuine German virtue—a profound submersion into the detail, the minute, the nearest and
into the mysteries of the individual—but this virtue grown
moldy is now worse than the most open vice, especially
since one has now become conscious, with gladness of the
heart, of this quality, even to literary self-glorification. Now
the "Educated" among the proverbially so cultured Germans
and the "Philistines" among the, as everybody knows, so
uncultured Germans shake hands in public and agree with
one another concerning the way in which henceforth one will

have to write, compose poetry, paint, make music, and even philosophize, yea—rule, so as neither to stand too much aloof from the culture of the one, nor to give offense to the "homeliness" of the other. This they call now "The German Culture of our times." Well, it is only necessary to inquire after the characteristic by which that "educated" person is to be recognized; now that we know that his foster brother, the German Philistine, makes himself known as such to all the world, without bashfulness, as it were, after innocence is lost.

The educated person nowadays is educated above all "historically," by his historic consciousness he saves himself from the sublime in which the Philistine succeeds by his "homeliness." No longer that enthusiasm which history inspires—as Goethe was allowed to suppose—but just the blunting of all enthusiasm is now the goal of these admirers of the *nil admirari*, when they try to conceive everything historically; to them however we should exclaim: Ye are the fools of all centuries! History will make to you only those confessions which you are worthy to receive. The world has been at all times full of trivialities and nonentities; to your historic hankering just these and only these unveil themselves. By your thousands you may pounce upon an epoch—you will afterward hunger as before and be allowed to boast of your sort of starved soundness. *Illam ipsam quam iactant sanitatem non firmitate sed ieiunio consequuntur. (Dialogus de oratoribus, cap. 25.)* History has not thought fit to tell you anything that is essential, but scorning and invisible she stood by your side, slipping into this one's hand some state proceedings, into that one's an ambassadorial report, into another's a date or an etymology or a pragmatic cobweb. Do you really believe yourself able to reckon up history like an addition sum, and do you consider your common intellect and your mathematical education good enough for that? How it must vex you to hear that others narrate things, out of the best-known periods, which you will never conceive, never!

If now to this "education," calling itself historic but destitute of enthusiasm, and to the hostile Philistine activity, foaming with rage against all that is great, is added that third brutal and excited company of those who race after "Fortune"—then that in *summa* results in such a confused shrieking and such a limb-dislocating turmoil that the thinker with stopped-up ears and blindfolded eyes flees into the most solitary wilderness—where he may see what those never will see, where he must hear sounds which rise to him out of all the depths of nature and come down to him from the stars. Here he confers with the great problems floating toward him, whose voices of course sound just as comfortless-awful, as unhistoric-eternal. The feeble person flees back from their cold breath, and the calculating one runs right through them without perceiving them. They deal worst, however, with the "educated man" who at times bestows great pains upon them. To him these phantoms transform themselves into conceptual cobwebs and hollow sound figures. Grasping after them he imagines he has philosophy; in order to search for them he climbs about in the so-called history of philosophy—and when at last he has collected and piled up quite a cloud of such abstractions and stereotyped patterns, then it may happen to him that a real thinker crosses his path and—puffs them away. What a desperate annoyance indeed to meddle with philosophy as an—"educated person"! From time to time it is true it appears to him as if the impossible connection of philosophy with that which nowadays gives itself airs as "German Culture" has become possible; some mongrel dallies and ogles between the two spheres and confuses fantasy on this side and on the other. Meanwhile, however, *one* piece of advice is to be given to the Germans, if they do not wish to let themselves be confused. They may put to themselves the question about everything that they now call Culture: Is *this* the hoped-for German Culture, so serious and creative, so redeeming for the German mind, so purifying for the German virtues that their only philosopher in this century, Arthur *Schopenhauer*, should have to espouse its cause?

Here you have the philosopher—now search for the Culture proper to him! And if you are able to divine what kind of culture that would have to be, which would correspond to such a philosopher, then you have, in this divination, already *passed sentence* on all your culture and on yourselves!

FROM PHILOSOPHY IN THE
TRAGIC AGE OF THE GREEKS*

Preface

(Probably 1874)

IF we know the aims of men who are strangers to us, it is sufficient for us to approve of or condemn them as wholes.

* From *Early Greek Philosophy and Other Essays.*

Those who stand nearer to us we judge according to the means by which they further their aims; we often disapprove of their aims, but love them for the sake of their means and the style of their volition. Now philosophical systems are absolutely true only to their founders, to all later philosophers they are usually *one* big mistake, and to feebler minds a sum of mistakes and truths; at any rate if regarded as highest aim they are an error, and in so far reprehensible. Therefore many disapprove of every philosopher, because his aim is not theirs; they are those whom I called "strangers to us." Whoever on the contrary finds any pleasure at all in great men finds pleasure also in such systems, be they ever so erroneous, for they all have in them one point which is irrefutable, a personal touch, and color; one can use them in order to form a picture of the philosopher, just as from a plant growing in a certain place one can form conclusions as to the soil. *That* mode of life, of viewing human affairs at any rate, has existed once and is therefore possible; the "system" is the growth in this soil or at least a part of this system. . . .

I narrate the history of those philosophers simplified; I shall bring into relief only *that* point in every system which is a little bit of *personality*, and belongs to that which is irrefutable, and indiscussable, which history has to preserve: it is a first attempt to regain and recreate those natures by comparison, and to let the polyphony of Greek nature at least resound once again. The task is, to bring to light that which we must *always love and revere* and of which no later knowledge can rob us: the great man.

Later Preface

(Toward the end of 1879)

THIS attempt to relate the history of the earlier Greek philosophers distinguishes itself from similar attempts by its brevity. This has been accomplished by mentioning but a small number of the doctrines of every philosopher, i.e., by incompleteness. Those doctrines, however, have been selected in which the personal element of the philosopher re-echoes most strongly; whereas a complete enumeration of all possible propositions handed down to us—as is the custom in textbooks—merely brings about one thing, the absolute silencing

of the personal element. It is through this that those records
become so tedious; for in systems which have been refuted it
is only this personal element that can still interest us, for this
alone is eternally irrefutable. It is possible to shape the picture of a man out of three anecdotes. I endeavor to bring into
relief three anecdotes out of every system and abandon the
remainder.

FROM THE BIRTH OF TRAGEDY

An Attempt at Self-Criticism

1

WHATEVER may lie at the bottom of this doubtful book must
be a question of the first rank and attractiveness, moreover
a deeply personal question—in proof thereof observe the time
in which it originated, *in spite* of which it originated, the
exciting period of the Franco-German war of 1870–71. While
the thunder of the battle of Wörth rolled over Europe, the
ruminator and riddle-lover, who had to be the parent of this
book, sat somewhere in a nook of the Alps, lost in riddles and
ruminations, consequently very much concerned and uncon-
cerned at the same time, and wrote down his meditations on
the *Greeks*—the kernel of the curious and almost inaccessible
book, to which this belated prologue (or epilogue) is to be
devoted. A few weeks later: and he found himself under the
walls of Metz, still wrestling with the notes of interrogation
he had set down concerning the alleged "cheerfulness" of the
Greeks and of Greek art; till at last, in that month of deep
suspense, when peace was debated at Versailles, he too attained to peace with himself, and, slowly recovering from a
disease brought home from the field, made up his mind
definitely regarding the "Birth of Tragedy from the Spirit of
Music."—From music? Music and Tragedy? Greeks and tragic
music? Greeks and the Artwork of pessimism? A race of men,
well-fashioned, beautiful, envied, life-inspiring, like no other
race hitherto, the Greeks—indeed? The Greeks were *in need*
of tragedy? Yes—of art? Wherefore—Greek art? . . .
    We can thus guess where the great note of interrogation
concerning the value of existence had been set. Is pessimism
necessarily the sign of decline, of decay, of failure, of exhausted and weakened instincts?—as was the case with the

Indians, as is, to all appearance, the case with us "modern" men and Europeans? Is there a pessimism of *strength?* An intellectual predilection for what is hard, awful, evil, problematical in existence, owing to well-being, to exuberant health, to *fullness* of existence? Is there perhaps suffering in overfullness itself? A seductive fortitude with the keenest of glances, which *yearns* for the terrible, as for the enemy, the worthy enemy, with whom it may try its strength? From whom it is willing to learn what "fear" is? What means *tragic* myth to the Greeks of the best, strongest, bravest era? And the prodigious phenomenon of the Dionysian? And that which was born thereof, tragedy? And again: that of which tragedy died, the Socratism of morality, the dialectics, contentedness, and cheerfulness of the theoretical man—indeed? Might not this very Socratism be a sign of decline, of weariness, of disease, of anarchically disintegrating instincts? And the "Hellenic cheerfulness" of the later Hellenism merely a glowing sunset? The Epicurean will *counter* to pessimism merely a precaution of the sufferer? And science itself, our science—ay, viewed as a symptom of life, what really signifies all science? Whither, worse still, *whence*—all science? Well? Is scientism perhaps only fear and evasion of pessimism? A subtle defense against—*truth?* Morally speaking, something like falsehood and cowardice? And, unmorally speaking, an artifice? O Socrates, Socrates, was this perhaps *thy* secret? Oh mysterious ironist, was this perhaps thine—irony? . . .

2

What I then laid hands on, something terrible and dangerous, a problem with horns, not necessarily a bull itself, but at all events a *new* problem: I should say today it was the *problem of science* itself—science conceived for the first time as problematic, as questionable. But the book, in which my youthful ardor and suspicion then discharged themselves—what an *impossible* book must needs grow out of a task so disagreeable to youth. Constructed of nought but precocious, unripened self-experiences, all of which lay close to the threshold of the communicable, based on the groundwork of *art* —for the problem of science cannot be discerned on the groundwork of science—a book perhaps for artists, with collateral analytical and retrospective aptitudes (that is, an exceptional kind of artists, for whom one must seek and does not even care to seek . . .), full of psychological innovations and artists' secrets, with an artist's metaphysics in the background, a work of youth, full of youth's mettle and youth's melancholy, independent, defiantly self-sufficient even when it seems to bow to some authority and self-veneration; in short, a firstling-work, even in every absence of the term; in spite of its senile problem, affected with every fault of youth, above all with youth's prolixity and youth's "storm and stress": on the other hand, in view of the success it had (especially with the great artist to whom it addressed itself, as it were, in a duologue, Richard Wagner) a *demonstrated* book, I mean a book which, at any rate, sufficed "for the best of its time." On this account, if for no other reason, it should be treated with some consideration and reserve; yet I shall not altogether conceal how disagreeable it now appears to me, how after sixteen years it stands a total stranger before me—before an eye which is more mature, and a hundred times more fastidious, but which has by no means grown colder nor lost any of its interest in that selfsame task essayed for the first time by this daring book—*to view science through the optics of the artist, and art moreover through the optics of life.* . . .

3

I say again, today it is an impossible book to me—I call it badly written, heavy, painful, image-angling and image-entangling, maudlin, sugared at times even to femininism, uneven in tempo, void of the will to logical cleanliness, very convinced and therefore rising above the necessity of demonstration, distrustful even of the *propriety* of demonstration, as being a book for initiates, as "music" for those who are baptized with the name of Music, who are united from the beginning of things by common ties of rare experiences in art, as a countersign for blood relations *in artibus*—a haughty and fantastic book, which from the very first withdraws even more from the *profanum vulgus* of the "cultured" than from the "people," but which also, as its effect has shown and still shows, knows very well how to seek fellow enthusiasts and lure them to new byways and dancing grounds. Here, at any rate—thus much was acknowledged with curiosity as well as with aversion—a *strange* voice spoke, the disciple of a still "unknown God," who for the time being had hidden himself under the hood of the scholar, under the German's gravity and disinclination for dialectics, even under the bad manners of the Wagnerian; here was a spirit with strange and still nameless needs, a memory bristling with questions, experiences and obscurities, beside which stood the name Dionysos like one more note of interrogation; here spoke—people said to themselves with misgivings—something like a mystic and almost maenadic soul, which, undecided whether it should disclose or conceal itself, stammers with an effort and capriciously as in a strange tongue. It should have *sung,* this "new soul"—and not spoken! What a pity, that I did not dare to say what I then had to say, as a poet: I could have done so perhaps! Or at least as a philologist—for even at the present day well-nigh everything in this domain remains to be discovered and disinterred by the philologist! Above all the problem, *that* here there *is* a problem before us—and that, so long as we have no answer to the question "what is Dionysian?" the Greeks are now as ever wholly unknown and inconceivable . . .

4

Ay, what is Dionysian? In this book may be found an answer—a "knowing one" speaks here, the votary and disciple of his god. Perhaps I should now speak more guardedly and less eloquently of a psychological question so difficult as the origin of tragedy among the Greeks. A fundamental question is the relation of the Greek to pain, his degree of sensibility —did this relation remain constant? or did it veer about?— the question, whether his ever-increasing *longing for beauty,* for festivals, gaieties, new cults, did really grow out of want, privation, melancholy, pain? For suppose even this to be true —and Pericles (or Thucydides) intimates as much in the great Funeral Speech: whence then the opposite longing, which appeared first in the order of time, the *longing for the ugly,* the good, resolute desire of the Old Hellene for pessimism, for tragic myth, for the picture of all that is terrible, evil, enigmatical, destructive, fatal at the basis of existence—whence then must tragedy have sprung? Perhaps from *joy,* from strength, from exuberant health, from overfullness. And what then, physiologically speaking, is the meaning of that madness, out of which comic as well as tragic art has grown, the Dionysian madness? What? Perhaps madness is not necessarily the symptom of degeneration, of decline, of belated culture? Perhaps there are—a question for alienists—neuroses of *health*? of folk-youth and -youthfulness? What does that synthesis of god and goat in the Satyr point to? What self-experience, what "stress," made the Greek think of the Dionysian reveler and primitive man as a satyr? And as regards the origin of the tragic chorus: perhaps there were endemic ecstasies in the eras when the Greek body bloomed and the Greek soul brimmed over with life? Visions and hallucinations, which took hold of entire communities, entire cult-assemblies? What if the Greeks in the very wealth of their youth had the will *to be* tragic and were pessimists? What if it was madness itself, to use a word of Plato's, which brought the *greatest* blessings upon Hellas? And what if, on the other hand and conversely, at the very time of their dissolution and weakness, the Greeks became always more optimistic, more superficial, more histrionic, also more ardent for logic and the logicizing of the world—consequently at the same time more "cheerful" and more "scientific"? Ay, despite all "modern ideas" and prejudices of the democratic taste, may not the triumph of *optimism*, the *common sense* that has gained the upper hand, the practical and theoretical *utilitarianism*, like democracy itself, with which it is synchronous—be symptomatic of declining vigor, of approaching age, of physiological weariness? And *not* at all—pessimism? Was Epicurus an optimist—because a *sufferer*? . . . We see it is a whole bundle of weighty questions which this book has taken upon itself—let us not fail to add its weightiest question! Viewed through the optics of *life*, what is the meaning of —morality? . . .

5

Already in the foreword to Richard Wagner, art—and *not* morality—is set down as the properly *metaphysical* activity of man; in the book itself the piquant proposition recurs time and again, that the existence of the world is *justified* only as an aesthetic phenomenon. Indeed, the entire book recognizes only an artist-thought and artist-afterthought behind all occurrences—a "God," if you will, but certainly only an altogether thoughtless and unmoral artist-God, who, in construction as in destruction, in good as in evil, desires to become conscious of his own equable joy and sovereign glory; who, in creating worlds, frees himself from the *anguish* of fullness and *overfullness*, from the *suffering* of the contradictions concentrated within him. The world, that is, the redemption of God *attained* at every moment, as the perpetually changing, perpetually new vision of the most suffering, most antithetical, most contradictory being, who contrives to redeem himself only in *appearance*: this entire artist-metaphysics, call it arbitrary, idle, fantastic, if you will—the point is, that it already betrays a spirit, which is determined some day, at all hazards, to make a stand against the *moral* interpretation and significance of life. Here, perhaps for the first time, a pessimism "Beyond Good and Evil" announces itself, here that "perverseness of disposition" obtains expression and formulation, against which Schopenhauer never grew tired of hurling beforehand his angriest imprecations and thunderbolts—a philosophy which dares to put, derogatorily put, morality itself in the world of phenomena, and not only among "phenomena" (in the sense of the idealistic *terminus technicus*), but among the "illusions," as appearance, semblance, error, interpretation, accommodation, art. Perhaps the depth of this *antimoral* tendency may be best estimated from the guarded and hostile silence with which Christianity is treated throughout this book—Christianity, as being the most extravagant burlesque of the moral theme to which mankind has hitherto been obliged to listen. In fact, to the purely aesthetic world-interpretation and justification taught in this book, there is no greater antithesis than the Christian dogma, which is *only* and will be only moral, and which, with its absolute standards, for instance, its truthfulness of God, relegates—that is, disowns, convicts, condemns—art, *all* art, to the realm of *falsehood*. Behind such a mode of thought and valuation, which, if at all genuine, must be hostile to art, I always experienced what was *hostile to life,* the wrathful, vindictive counterwill to life itself; for all life rests on appearance, art, illusion, optics, necessity of perspective and error. From the very first Christianity was, essentially and thoroughly, the nausea and surfeit of Life for Life, which only disguised, concealed, and decked itself out under the belief in "another" or "better" life. The hatred of the "world," the curse on the affections, the fear of beauty and sensuality, another world, invented for the purpose of slandering this world the more, at bottom a longing for Nothingness, for the end, for rest, for the "Sabbath of Sabbaths"—all this, as also the unconditional will of Christianity to recognize *only* moral values, has always appeared to me as the most dangerous and ominous of all possible forms of a "will to perish"; at the least, as the symptom of a most fatal disease, of profoundest weariness, despondency, exhaustion, impoverishment of life —for before the tribunal of morality (especially Christian, that is, unconditional morality) life *must* constantly and inevitably be the loser, because life *is* something essentially unmoral—indeed, oppressed with the weight of contempt and the everlasting No, life *must* finally be regarded as unworthy of desire, as in itself unworthy. Morality itself what?—may not morality be a "will to disown life," a secret instinct for annihilation, a principle of decay, of depreciation, of slander, a beginning of the end? And, consequently, the danger of dangers? . . . It was *against* morality, therefore, that my instinct, as an intercessory instinct for life, turned in this questionable book, inventing for itself a fundamental counter-dogma and countervaluation of life, purely artistic, purely *anti-Christian*. What should I call it? As a philologist and man of words I baptized it, not without some liberty—for who could be sure of the proper name of the Antichrist?—with the name of a Greek god: I called it Dionysian.

6

You see which problem I ventured to touch upon in this early work? . . . How I now regret that I had not then the courage (or immodesty?) to allow myself, in all respects, the use of an *individual language* for such *individual* contemplations and ventures in the field of thought—that I labored to express, in Kantian and Schopenhauerian formulas, strange and new valuations, which ran fundamentally counter to the spirit of Kant and Schopenhauer, as well as to their taste! What, forsooth, were Schopenhauer's views on tragedy? "What gives"—he says in *Welt als Wille und Vorstellung*, II. 495—"to all tragedy that singular swing towards elevation, is the awakening of the knowledge that the world, that life, cannot satisfy us thoroughly, and consequently is *not worthy* of our attachment. In this consists the tragic spirit: it therefore leads to *resignation*." Oh, how differently Dionysos spoke to me! Oh how far from me then was just this entire resignationism! But there is something far worse in this book, which I now regret even more than having obscured and spoiled Dionysian anticipations with Schopenhauerian formulas: to wit, that, in general, I *spoiled* the grand *Hellenic problem,* as it had opened up before me, by the admixture of the most modern things! That I entertained hopes, where nothing was to be hoped for, where everything pointed all too clearly to an approaching end! That, on the basis of our latter-day German music, I began to fable about the "spirit of Teutonism," as if it were on the point of discovering and returning to itself—ay, at the very time that the German spirit which not so very long before had had the will to the lordship over Europe, the strength to lead and govern Europe, testamentarily and conclusively *resigned* and, under the pompous, pretense of empire-founding, effected its transition to mediocritization, democracy, and "modern ideas." In very fact, I have since learned to regard this "spirit of Teutonism" as something to be despaired of and unsparingly treated, as also our present *German music,* which is romanticism through and through and the most un-Grecian of all possible forms of art: and moreover a first-rate nerve-destroyer, doubly dangerous for a people given to drinking and revering the unclear as a virtue, namely, in its twofold capacity of an intoxicating and stupefying narcotic. Of course, apart from all precipitate hopes and faulty applications to matters specially modern, with which I then spoiled my first book, the great Dionysian note of interrogation, as set down therein, continues standing on and on, even with reference to music: how must we conceive of a music, which is no longer of romantic origin, like the German, but of *Dionysian?* . . .

7

But, my dear Sir, if *your* book is not romanticism, what in the world is? Can the deep hatred of the present, of "reality" and "modern ideas" be pushed farther than has been done in your artist-metaphysics?—which would rather believe in Nothing, or in the devil, than in the "Now"? Does not a radical bass of wrath and annihilative pleasure growl on beneath all your contrapuntal vocal art and aural seduction, a mad determination to oppose all that "now" is, a will which is not so very far removed from practical nihilism and which seems to say: "Rather let nothing be true, than that *you* should be in the right, than that *your* truth should prevail!" Hear, yourself, my dear Sir Pessimist and art-deifier, with ever so unlocked ears, a single select passage of your own book, that not ineloquent dragon-slayer passage, which may sound insidiously rat-charming to young ears and hearts. What? Is not that the true blue romanticist-confession of 1830 under the mask of the pessimism of 1850? After which, of course, the usual romanticist finale at once strikes up—rupture, collapse, return, and prostration before an old belief, before *the* old God. . . . What? Is not your pessimist book itself a piece of anti-Hellenism and romanticism, something "equally intoxicating and befogging," a narcotic at all events, ay, a piece of music, of *German* music? But listen:

Let us imagine a rising generation with this undauntedness of vision, with this heroic impulse toward the prodigious, let us imagine the bold step of these dragonslayers, the proud daring with which they turn their backs on all the effeminate doctrines of optimism, in order "to live resolutely" in the Whole and in the Full: *would it not be necessary* for the tragic man of this culture, with his self-discipline to earnestness and terror, to desire a new art, *the art of metaphysical comfort*, tragedy as the Helena belonging to him, and that he should exclaim with Faust:

"Und sollt ich nicht, sehnsüchtigster Gewalt,
In's Leben ziehn die einzigste Gestalt?" *

"Would it not be *necessary?*" . . . No, thrice no! ye young romanticists: it would *not* be necessary! But it is very probable that things may *end* thus, that ye may end thus, namely "comforted," as it is written, in spite of all self-discipline to earnestness and terror; metaphysically comforted, in short, as romanticists are wont to end, as *Christians*. . . . No! ye should first of all learn the art of earthly comfort, ye should learn to *laugh*, my young friends, if ye are at all determined to remain pessimists: if so, you will perhaps, as laughing ones, eventually send all metaphysical comfortism to the devil—and metaphysics first of all! Or, to say it in the language of that Dionysian ogre, called *Zarathustra*:

"Lift up your hearts, my brethren, high, higher! And do not forget your legs! Lift up also your legs, ye good dancers—and better still if ye stand also on your heads!

"This crown of the laughter, this rose-garland crown —I myself have put on this crown; I myself have consecrated my laughter. No one else have I found today strong enough for this.

"Zarathustra the dancer, Zarathustra the light one, who beckoneth with his pinions, one ready for flight, beckoning unto all birds, ready and prepared, a blissfully light-spirited one:

"Zarathustra the soothsayer, Zarathustra the soothlaugher, no impatient one, no absolute one, one who loveth leaps and side-leaps: I myself have put on this crown!

"This crown of the laughter, this rose-garland crown

---

* And shall not I, by mightiest desire,
In living shape that sole fair form acquire?
SWANWICK, trans. of *Faust*.

—to you my brethren do I cast this crown! Laughing have I consecrated: ye higher men, *learn*, I pray you—to laugh!"

Thus Spake Zarathustra, lxxii 17, 18, and 20.

Sils-Maria, Oberengadin,
August, 1886.

III. The Greeks

FROM PHILOSOPHY IN THE TRAGIC AGE OF THE GREEKS*

1

There are opponents of philosophy, and one does well to listen to them, especially if they dissuade the distempered heads of Germans from metaphysics and on the other hand preach to them purification through the Physis, as Goethe did, or healing through Music, as Wagner. The physicians of the people condemn philosophy; he, therefore, who wants to justify it must show to what purpose healthy nations use and have used philosophy. If he can show that, perhaps even the sick people will benefit by learning why philosophy is harmful just to them. There are indeed good instances of a health which can exist without any philosophy or with quite a moderate, almost a toying use of it; thus the Romans at their best period lived without philosophy. But where is to be found the instance of a nation becoming diseased whom philosophy had restored to health? Whenever philosophy showed itself helping, saving, prophylactic, it was with healthy people; it made sick people still more ill. If ever a nation was disintegrated and but loosely connected with the individuals, never has philosophy bound these individuals closer to the whole. If ever an individual was willing to stand aside and plant around himself the hedge of self-sufficiency, philosophy was always ready

* From *Early Greek Philosophy and Other Essays*.

to isolate him still more and to destroy him through isolation. She is dangerous where she is not in her full right, and it is only the health of a nation but not that of every nation which gives her this right.

Let us now look around for the highest authority as to what constitutes the health of a nation. The Greeks, as *the* truly healthy nation, have *justified* philosophy once for all by having philosophized; and that indeed more than all other nations. They could not even stop at the right time, for still in their withered age they comported themselves as heated votaries of philosophy, although they understood by it only the pious sophistries and the sacrosanct hairsplittings of Christian dogmatics. They themselves have much lessened their merit for barbarian posterity by not being able to stop at the right time, because that posterity in its uninstructed and impetuous youth necessarily became entangled in those artfully woven nets and ropes.

On the contrary, the Greeks knew how to begin at the right time, and this lesson, when one ought to begin philosophizing, they teach more distinctly than any other nation. For it should not be begun when trouble comes as perhaps some presume who derive philosophy from moroseness; no, but in good fortune, in mature manhood, out of the midst of the fervent serenity of a brave and victorious man's estate. The fact that the Greeks philosophized at that time throws light on the nature of philosophy and her task as well as on the nature of the Greeks themselves. Had they at that time been such commonsense and precocious experts and gayards as the learned Philistine of our days perhaps imagines, or had their life been only a state of voluptuous soaring, chiming, breathing, and feeling, as the unlearned visionary is pleased to assume, then the spring of philosophy would not have come to light among them. At the best there would have come forth a brook soon trickling away in the sand or evaporating into fogs, but never that broad river flowing forth with the proud beat of its waves, the river which we know as Greek Philosophy.

True, it has been eagerly pointed out how much the Greeks could find and learn abroad, in the Orient, and how many different things they may easily have brought from there. Of course an odd spectacle resulted when certain scholars brought together the alleged masters from the Orient and the possible disciples from Greece, and exhibited Zarathustra near Heraclitus, the Hindus near the Eleates, the Egyptians near Empedocles, or even Anaxagoras among the Jews and Pythagoras among the Chinese. In detail little has been determined; but we should in no way object to the general idea, if people did not burden us with the conclusion that therefore Philosophy had only been imported into Greece and was not indigenous to the soil, yea, that she, as something foreign, had possible ruined rather than improved the Greek. Nothing is more foolish than to swear by the fact that the Greeks had an aboriginal culture; no, they rather absorbed all the culture flourishing among other nations, and they advanced so far, just because they understood how to hurl the spear further from the very spot where another nation had let it rest. They were admirable in the art of learning productively, and so, like them, we *ought* to learn from our neighbors, with a view to Life not to pedantic knowledge, using everything learnt as a foothold whence to leap high and still higher than our neighbor. The questions as to the beginning of philosophy are quite negligible, for everywhere in the beginning there is the crude, the unformed, the empty and the ugly; and in all things only the higher stages come into consideration. He who in the place of Greek philosophy prefers to concern himself with that of Egypt and Persia, because the latter are perhaps more "original" and certainly older, proceeds just as ill-advisedly as those who cannot be at ease before they have traced back the Greek mythology, so grand and profound, to such physical trivialities as sun, lightning, weather, and fog, as its prime origins, and who fondly imagine they have rediscovered for instance in the restricted worship of the one celestial vault among the other Indo-Germans a purer form of religion than the polytheistic worship of the Greek had been. The road toward the beginning always leads into barbarism, and he who is concerned with the Greeks ought always to keep in mind the fact that the unsubdued thirst for knowledge in itself always barbarizes just as much as the hatred of knowledge, and that the Greeks have subdued their inherently insatiable thirst for knowledge by their regard for Life, by an ideal need of Life—since they wished to live immediately that which they learnt. The Greeks also philosophized as men of culture and with the aims of culture, and therefore saved themselves the trouble of inventing once again the elements of philosophy and knowledge out of some autochthonous conceit, and with a will they at once set themselves to fill out, enhance, raise, and purify these elements they had taken over in such a way, that only now in a higher sense and in a purer sphere they became inventors. For they discovered the *typical philosopher's genius*, and the inventions of all posterity have added nothing essential.

Every nation is put to shame if one points out such a wonderfully idealized company of philosophers as that of the early Greek masters, Thales, Anaximander, Heraclitus, Parmenides, Anaxagoras, Empedocles, Democritus, and Socrates. All those men are integral, entire and self-contained,* and hewn out of one stone. Severe necessity exists between their thinking and their character. They are not bound by any convention, because at that time no professional class of philosophers and scholars existed. They all stand before us in magnificent solitude as the only ones who then devoted their life exclusively to knowledge. They all possess the virtuous energy of the Ancients, whereby they excel all the later philosophers in finding their own form and in perfecting it by metamorphosis in its most minute details and general aspect. For they were met by no helpful and facilitating fashion. Thus together they form what Schopenhauer, in opposition to the Republic of Scholars, has called a Republic of Geniuses; one giant calls to another across the arid intervals of ages, and, undisturbed by a wanton, noisy race of dwarfs, creeping about beneath them, the sublime intercourse of spirits continues.

Of this sublime intercourse of spirits I have resolved to relate those items which our modern hardness of hearing might perhaps hear and understand; that means certainly the least of all. It seems to me that those old sages from Thales to Socrates have discussed in that intercourse, although in its most general aspect, everything that constitutes for our contemplation the peculiarly Hellenic. In their intercourse, as already in their personalities, they express distinctly the great features of Greek genius of which the whole of Greek history is a shadowy impression, a hazy copy, which consequently speaks less clearly. If we could rightly interpret the total life of the Greek nation, we should ever find reflected only that picture which in her highest geniuses shines with more resplendent colors. Even the first experience of philosophy on Greek soil, the sanction of the Seven Sages, is a distinct and unforgettable line in the picture of the Hellenic. Other nations have their Saints, the Greeks have Sages. Rightly it has been said that a nation is characterized not only by her great men but rather by the manner in which she recognizes and honors them. In other ages the philosopher is an accidental solitary wanderer in the most hostile environment, either slinking through or pushing himself through with clenched fists. With the Greek, however, the philosopher is not accidental; when in the sixth and fifth centuries amidst the most frightful dangers and seductions of secularization he appears

* Cf. Napoleon's word about Goethe: "Voilà un homme!"—Tr.

and as it were steps forth from the cave of Trophonios into the
very midst of luxuriance, the discoverers' happiness, the
wealth, and the sensuousness of the Greek colonies, then we
divine that he comes as a noble warner for the same purpose
for which in those centuries Tragedy was born and which the
Orphic mysteries in their grotesque hieroglyphics give us to
understand. The opinion of those philosophers on Life and
Existence altogether means so much more than a modern
opinion because they had before themselves Life in a luxuriant perfection, and because with them, unlike us, the sense
of the thinker was not muddled by the disunion engendered
by the wish for freedom, beauty, fullness of life and the love
for truth that only asks: What is the good of Life at all? The
mission which the philosopher has to discharge within a real
Culture, fashioned in a homogeneous style, cannot be clearly
conjectured out of our circumstances and experiences for the
simple reason that we have no such culture. No, it is only a
Culture like the Greek which can answer the question as to
that task of the philosopher, only such a Culture can, as I
said before, justify philosophy at all; because such a Culture
alone knows and can demonstrate why and how the philosopher is *not* an accidental, chance wanderer driven now hither,
now thither. There is a steely necessity which fetters the
philosopher to a true Culture; but what if this Culture does not
exist? Then the philosopher is an incalculable and therefore
terror-inspiring comet, whereas in the favorable case, he
shines as the central star in the solar system of culture. It is
for this reason that the Greeks justify the philosopher, because with them he is no comet.

2

After such contemplations it will be accepted without offense if I speak of the pre-Platonic philosophers as of a
homogeneous company, and devote this paper to them exclusively. Something quite new begins with Plato; or it might
be said with equal justice that in comparison with that
Republic of Geniuses from Thales to Socrates, the philosophers since Plato lack something essential.

Whoever wants to express himself unfavorably about those
older masters may call them one-sided, and their epigones,
with Plato as head, many-sided. Yet it would be more just and
unbiased to conceive of the latter as philosophic hybrid characters, of the former as the pure types. Plato himself is the
first magnificent hybrid character, and as such finds expres-

sion as well in his philosophy as in his personality. In his ideology are united Socratian, Pythagorean, and Heraclitean elements, and for this reason it is no typically pure phenomenon. As man, too, Plato mingles the features of the royally secluded, all-sufficing Heraclitus, of the melancholy, compassionate, and legislatory Pythagoras and of the psychoexpert dialectician Socrates. All later philosophers are such hybrid characters; wherever something one-sided does come into prominence with them as in the case of the Cynics, it is not type but caricature. Much more important, however, is the fact that they are founders of sects and that the sects founded by them are all institutions in direct opposition to the Hellenic culture and the unity of its style prevailing up to that time. In their way they seek a redemption, but only for the individuals or at the best for groups of friends and disciples closely connected with them. The activity of the older philosophers tends, although they were unconscious of it, toward a cure and purification on a large scale; the mighty course of Greek culture is not to be stopped; awful dangers are to be removed out of the way of its current; the philosopher protects and defends his native country. Now, since Plato, he is in exile and conspires against his fatherland.

It is a real misfortune that so very little of those older philosophic masters has come down to us and that all complete works of theirs are withheld from us. Involuntarily, on account of that loss, we measure them according to wrong standards and allow ourselves to be influenced unfavorably toward them by the mere accidental fact that Plato and Aristotle never lacked appreciators and copyists. Some people presuppose a special providence for books, a *fatum librorum;* such a providence, however, would at any rate be a very malicious one if it deemed it wise to withhold from us the works of Heraclitus, Empedocles' wonderful poem, and the writings of Democritus, whom the ancients put on a par with Plato, whom he even excels as far as ingenuity goes, and as a substitute put into our hand Stoics, Epicureans, and Cicero. Probably the most sublime part of Greek thought and its expression in words is lost to us; a fate which will not surprise the man who remembers the misfortunes of Scotus Erigena or of Pascal, and who considers that even in this enlightened century the first edition of Schopenhauer's *The World as Will and Idea* became wastepaper. If somebody will presuppose a special fatalistic power with respect to such things he may do so and say with Goethe: "Let no one complain about and grumble at things vile and mean, they *are* the real rulers—however much this be gainsaid!" In particular they are more powerful than the power of truth. Mankind very rarely produces a good book in which with daring freedom is intonated the battle song of truth, the song of philosophic heroism; and yet whether it is to live a century longer or to crumble and molder into dust and ashes depends on the most miserable accidents, on the sudden mental eclipse of men's heads, on superstitious convulsions and antipathies, finally on fingers not too fond of writing, or even on eroding bookworms and rainy weather. But we will not lament but rather take the advice of the reproving and consolatory words which Hamann addresses to scholars who lament over lost works. "Would not the artist who succeeded in throwing a lentil through the eye of a needle have sufficient, with a bushel of lentils, to practice his acquired skill? One would like to put this question to all scholars who do not know how to use the works of the Ancients any better than that man used his lentils." It might be added in our case that not one more word, anecdote, or date needed to be transmitted to us than has been transmitted, indeed that even much less might have been preserved for us and yet we should have been able to establish the general doctrine that the Greeks justify philosophy.

A time which suffers from the so-called "general education" but has no culture and no unity of style in her life hardly knows what to do with philosophy, even if the latter were proclaimed by the very Genius of Truth in the streets and market places. She rather remains at such a time the learned monologue of the solitary rambler, the accidental booty of the individual, the hidden closet-secret or the innocuous chatter between academic senility and childhood. Nobody dare venture to fulfill in himself the law of philosophy, nobody lives philosophically, with that simple manly faith which compelled an Ancient, wherever he was, whatever he did, to deport himself as a Stoic, when he had once pledged his faith to the Stoa. All modern philosophizing is limited politically and regulated by the police to learned semblance. Thanks to governments, churches, academies, customs, fashions, and the cowardice of man, it never gets beyond the sigh: "If only! . . ." or beyond the knowledge: "Once upon a time there was . . ." Philosophy is without rights; therefore modern man, if he were at all courageous and conscientious, ought to condemn her and perhaps banish her with words similar to those by which Plato banished the tragic poets from his State. Of course there would be left a reply for her, as there remained to those poets against Plato. If one once compelled her to speak out she might say perhaps: "Miserable

Nation! Is it my fault if among you I am on the tramp, like a fortuneteller through the land, and must hide and disguise myself, as if I were a great sinner and ye my judges? Just look at my sister, Art! It is with her as with me; we have been cast adrift among the Barbarians and no longer know how to save ourselves. Here we are lacking, it is true, every good right; but the judges before whom we find justice judge you also and will tell you: first acquire a culture; then you shall experience what Philosophy can and will do."

3

Greek philosophy seems to begin with a preposterous fancy, with the proposition that *water* is the origin and mother-womb of all things. Is it really necessary to stop there and become serious? Yes, and for three reasons: firstly, because the proposition does enunciate something about the origin of things; secondly, because it does so without figure and fable; thirdly and lastly, because in it is contained, although only in the chrysalis state, the idea: everything is one. The first mentioned reason leaves Thales still in the company of religious and superstitious people, the second, however, takes him out of this company and shows him to us as a natural philosopher, but by virtue of the third, Thales becomes the first Greek philosopher. If he had said: "Out of water earth is evolved," we should only have a scientific hypothesis; a false one, though nevertheless difficult to refute. But he went beyond the scientific. In his presentation of this concept of unity through the hypothesis of water, Thales has not surmounted the low level of the physical discernments of his time, but at the best overleapt them. The deficient and unorganized observations of an empiric nature which Thales had made as to the occurrence and transformations of water, or to be more exact, of the Moist, would not in the least have made possible or even suggested such an immense generalization. That which drove him to this generalization was a metaphysical dogma, which had its origin in a mystic intuition and which together with the ever renewed endeavors to express it better, we find in all philosophies—the proposition: *everything is one!*

How despotically such a faith deals with all empiricism is worthy of note; with Thales especially one can learn how Philosophy has behaved at all times, when she wanted to get beyond the hedges of experience to her magically attracting goal. On light supports she leaps in advance; hope and divination wing her feet. Calculating reason, too, clumsily pants after her and seeks better supports in its attempt to reach that alluring goal, at which its divine companion has already arrived. One sees in imagination two wanderers by a wild forest stream which carries with it rolling stones; the one, light-footed, leaps over it using the stones and swinging himself upon them ever further and further, though they precipitously sink into the depths behind him. The other stands helpless there most of the time; he has first to build a pathway which will bear his heavy, weary step; sometimes that cannot be done and then no god will help him across the stream. What therefore carries philosophical thinking so quickly to its goal? Does it distinguish itself from calculating and measuring thought only by its more rapid flight through large spaces? No, for a strange illogical power wings the foot of philosophical thinking; and this power is Fancy. Lifted by the latter philosophical thinking leaps from possibility to possibility, and these for the time being are taken as certainties; and now and then even whilst on the wing it gets hold of certainties. An ingenious presentiment shows them to the flier; demonstrable certainties are divined at a distance to be at this point. Especially powerful is the strength of Fancy in the lightning-like seizing and illuminating of similarities; afterward reflection applies its standards and models and seeks to substitute the similarities by equalities, that which was seen side by side by causalities. But though this should never be possible, even in the case of Thales the indemonstrable philosophizing has yet its value; although all supports are broken when Logic and the rigidity of Empiricism want to get across to the proposition: everything is water; yet still there is always, after the demolition of the scientific edifice, a remainder, and in this very remainder lies a moving force and as it were the hope of future fertility.

Of course I do not mean that the thought in any restriction or attenuation, or as allegory, still retains some kind of "truth"; as if, for instance, one might imagine the creating artist standing near a waterfall, and seeing in the forms which leap toward him, an artistically prefiguring game of the water with human and animal bodies, masks, plants, rocks, nymphs, griffins, and with all existing types in general, so that to him the proposition, everything is water, is confirmed. The thought of Thales has rather its value—even after the perception of its indemonstrableness—in the very fact that it was meant unmythically and unallegorically. The Greeks among whom Thales became so suddenly conspicuous were the antitype of all realists by only believing essentially in the reality of men and gods, and by contemplating the whole of nature as if it were only a disguise, masquerade, and metamorphosis of these god-men. Man was to them the truth and essence of things; everything else mere phenomenon and deceiving play. For that very reason they experienced incredible difficulty in conceiving of ideas as ideas. Whilst with the moderns the most personal item sublimates itself into abstractions, with them the most abstract notions became personified. Thales, however, said, "Not man but water is the reality of things"; he began to believe in nature, in so far that he at least believed in water. As a mathematician and astronomer he had grown cold toward everything mythical and allegorical, and even if he did not succeed in becoming disillusioned as to the pure abstraction, Everything is one, and although he left off at a physical expression he was nevertheless among the Greeks of his time a surprising rarity. Perhaps the exceedingly conspicuous *Orpheans* possessed in a still higher degree than he the faculty of conceiving abstractions and of thinking unplastically; only they did not succeed in expressing these abstractions except in the form of the allegory. Also Pherecydes of Syros, who is a contemporary of Thales and akin to him in many physical conceptions, hovers with the expression of the latter in that middle region where Allegory is wedded to Mythos, so that he dares, for example, to compare the earth with a winged oak which hangs in the air with spread pinions and which Zeus bedecks, after the defeat of Cronus, with a magnificent robe of honor, into which with his own hands Zeus embroiders lands, water, and rivers. In contrast with such gloomy allegorical philosophizing scarcely to be translated into the realm of the comprehensible, Thales' are the works of a creative master who began to look into Nature's depths without fantastic fabling. If as it is true he used Science and the demonstrable but soon outleapt them, then this likewise is a typical characteristic of the philosophical genius. The Greek word which designates the Sage belongs etymologically to *sapio*, I taste, *sapiens*, the tasting one, *sisyphos*, the man of the most delicate taste; the peculiar art of the philosopher therefore consists, according to the opinion of the people, in a delicate selective judgment by taste, by discernment, by significant differentiation. He is not prudent, if one calls *him* prudent, who in his own affairs finds out the good; Aristotle rightly says: "That which Thales and Anaxagoras know, people will call unusual, astounding, difficult, divine but—useless, since human possessions were of no concern to those two." Through thus selecting and precipitating the unusual, astounding, difficult, and divine, Philosophy marks the boundary lines dividing her from Science in the same way as she does it from Prudence by the emphasizing of the useless. Science without thus selecting, without such delicate taste, pounces upon everything knowable, in the blind covetousness to know all at any price; philosophical thinking, however, is always on the track of the things worth knowing, on the track of the great and most important discernments. Now the idea of greatness is changeable, as well in the moral as in the aesthetic realm, thus Philosophy begins with a legislation with respect to greatness, she becomes a Nomenclator. "That is great," she says, and therewith she raises man above the blind, untamed covetousness of his thirst for knowledge. By the idea of greatness she assuages this thirst: and it is chiefly by this that she contemplates the greatest discernment, that of the essence and kernel of things, as attainable and attained. When Thales says, "Everything is water," man is startled up out of his wormlike mauling of and crawling about among the individual sciences; he divines the last solution of things and masters through this divination the common perplexity of the lower grades of knowledge. The philosopher tries to make the total-chord of the universe re-echo within himself and then to project it into ideas outside himself: whilst he is contemplative like the creating artist, sympathetic like the religionist, looking out for ends and causalities like the scientific man, whilst he feels himself swell up to the macrocosm, he still retains the circumspection to contemplate himself coldly as the reflex of the world; he retains that coolheadedness, which the dramatic artist possesses, when he transforms himself into other bodies, speaks out of them, and yet knows how to project this transformation outside himself into written verses. What the verse is to the poet, dialectic thinking is to the philosopher; he snatches at it in order to hold fast his enchantment, in order to petrify it. And just as words and verse to the dramatist are only stammerings in a foreign language, to tell in it what he lived, what he saw, and what he can directly promulgate by gesture and music only, thus the expression of every deep philosophical intuition by means of dialectics and scientific reflection is, it is true, on the one hand the only means to communicate what has been seen, but on the other hand it is a paltry means, and at the bottom a metaphorical, absolutely inexact translation into a different sphere and language. Thus Thales saw the Unity of the "Existent," and when he wanted to communicate this idea he talked of water.

4

Whilst the general type of the philosopher in the picture of Thales is set off rather hazily, the picture of his great successor already speaks much more distinctly to us. *Anaximander* of Milet, the first philosophical author of the Ancients, writes in the very way that the typical philosopher will always write as long as he is not alienated from ingenuousness and naïveté by odd claims: in a grand lapidarian style of writing, sentence for sentence . . . a witness of a new inspiration, and an expression of the sojourning in sublime contemplations. The thought and its form are milestones on the path toward the highest wisdom. With such a lapidarian emphasis Anaximander once said: "Whence things originated, thither, according to necessity, they must return and perish; for they must pay penalty and be judged for their injustices according to the order of time." Enigmatical utterance of a true pessimist, oracular inscription on the boundary stone of Greek philosophy, how shall we explain thee?

The only serious moralist of our century in the Parergis (Vol. II, chap. 12, "Additional Remarks on The Doctrine about the Suffering in the World, Appendix of Corresponding Passages") urges on us a similar contemplation: "The right standard by which to judge every human being is that he really is a being who ought not to exist at all, but who is expiating his existence by manifold forms of suffering and death:—What can one expect from such a being? Are we not all sinners condemned to death? We expiate our birth firstly by our life and secondly by our death." He who in the physiognomy of our universal human lot reads this doctrine and already recognizes the fundamental bad quality of every human life, in the fact that none can stand a very close and careful contemplation—although our time, accustomed to the biographical epidemic, seems to think otherwise and more loftily about the dignity of man; he who, like Schopenhauer, on "the heights of the Indian breezes" has heard the sacred word about the moral value of existence, will be kept with difficulty from making an extremely anthropomorphic metaphor and from generalizing that melancholy doctrine—at first only limited to human life—and applying it by transmission to the general character of all existence. It may not be very logical; it is, however, at any rate very human and moreover quite in harmony with the philosophical leaping described above, now with Anaximander to consider all Becoming as a punishable emancipation from eternal "Being," as a wrong that is to be atoned for by destruction. Everything that has once come into existence also perishes, whether we think of human life or of water or of heat and cold; everywhere where definite qualities are to be noticed, we are allowed to prophesy the extinction of these qualities—according to the all-embracing proof of experience. Thus a being that possesses definite qualities and consists of them can never be the origin and principle of things; the veritable *ens*, the "Existent," Anaximander concluded, cannot possess any definite qualities, otherwise, like all other things, it would necessarily have originated and perished. In order that Becoming may not cease, the Primordial-being must be indefinite. The immortality and eternity of the Primordial-being lies not in an infiniteness and inexhaustibility—as usually the expounders of Anaximander presuppose—but in this, that it lacks the definite qualities which lead to destruction, for which reason it bears also its name: The Indefinite. The thus labeled Primordial-being is superior to all Becoming and for this very reason it guarantees the eternity and unimpeded course of Becoming. This last unity in that Indefinite, the mother-womb of all things, can, it is true, be designated only negatively by man, as something to which no predicate out of the existing world of Becoming can be allotted, and might be considered a peer to the Kantian "Thing-in-itself."

Of course he who is able to wrangle persistently with others as to what kind of thing that primordial substance really was, whether perhaps an intermediate thing between air and water, or perhaps between air and fire, has not understood our philosopher at all; this is likewise to be said about those who seriously ask themselves whether Anaximander had thought of his primordial substance as a mixture of all existing substances. Rather we must direct our gaze to the place where we can learn that Anaximander no longer treated the question of the origin of the world as purely physical; we must direct our gaze toward that first stated lapidarian proposition. When on the contrary he saw a sum of wrongs to be expiated in the plurality of things that have become, then he, as the first Greek, with daring grasp caught up the tangle of the most profound ethical problem. How can anything perish that has a right to exist? Whence that restless Becoming and giving-birth, whence that expression of painful distortion on the face of Nature, whence the never-ending dirge in all realms of existence? Out of this world of injustice, of audacious apostasy from the primordial unity of things, Anaximander flees into a metaphysical castle, leaning out of which he turns his gaze far and wide in order at last, after a pensive silence, to address to all beings this question: "What is your existence worth? And if it is worth nothing why are you there? By your guilt, I observe, you sojourn in this world. You will have to expiate it by death. Look how your earth fades; the seas decrease and dry up, the marine shell on the mountain shows you how much already they have dried up; fire destroys your world even now, finally it will end in smoke and ashes. But again and again such a world of transitoriness will ever build itself up; who shall redeem you from the curse of Becoming?"

Not every kind of life may have been welcome to a man who put such questions, whose upward-soaring thinking continually broke the empiric ropes, in order to take at once to the highest, superlunary flight. Willingly we believe tradition, that he walked along in especially dignified attire and showed a truly tragic hauteur in his gestures and habits of life. He lived as he wrote; he spoke as solemnly as he dressed himself, he raised his hand and placed his foot as if this existence was a tragedy, and he had been born in order to co-operate in that tragedy by playing the role of hero. In all that he was the great model of Empedocles. His fellow citizens elected him the leader of an emigrating colony—perhaps they were pleased at being able to honor him and at the same time to get rid of him. His thought emigrated and founded colonies; in Ephesus and in Elea they could not get rid of him; and if they could not resolve upon staying at the spot where he stood, they nevertheless knew that they had been led there by him, whence they now prepared to proceed without him.

Thales shows the need of simplifying the empire of plurality, and of reducing it to a mere expansion or disguise of the *one single* existing quality, water. Anaximander goes beyond him with two steps. Firstly he puts the question to himself: how, if there exists an eternal Unity at all, is that Plurality possible? And he takes the answer out of the contradictory, self-devouring, and denying character of this Plurality. The existence of this Plurality becomes a moral phenomenon to him; it is not justified, it expiates itself continually through destruction. But then the questions occur to him: yet why has not everything that has become perished long ago, since, indeed, quite an eternity of time has already gone by? Whence the ceaseless current of the River of Becoming? He can save himself from these questions only by mystic possibilities: the eternal Becoming can have its origin only in the eternal "Being," the conditions for that apostasy from the eternal

"Being" to a Becoming in injustice are ever the same, the constellation of things cannot help itself being thus fashioned, that no end is to be seen of that stepping forth of the individual being out of the lap of the "Indefinite." At this Anaximander stayed; that is, he remained within the deep shadows which like gigantic specters were lying on the mountain range of such a world-perception. The more one wanted to approach the problem of solving how out of the Indefinite the Definite, out of the Eternal the Temporal, out of the Just the Unjust could by secession ever originate, the darker the night became.

5

Toward the mist of this mystic night, in which Anaximander's problem of the Becoming was wrapped up, Heraclitus of Ephesus approached and illuminated it by a divine flash of lightning. "I contemplate the Becoming," he exclaimed,—"and nobody has so attentively watched this eternal wave-surging and rhythm of things. And what do I behold? Lawfulness, infallible certainty, ever equal paths of justice, condemning Erinyes behind all transgressions of the laws, the whole world the spectacle of a governing justice and of demoniacally omnipresent natural forces subject to justice's sway. I do not behold the punishment of that which has become, but the justification of Becoming. When has sacrilege, when has apostasy manifested itself in inviolable forms, in laws esteemed sacred? Where injustice sways, there is caprice, disorder, irregularity, contradiction; where, however, Law and Zeus' daughter, Dike, rule alone, as in this world, how could the sphere of guilt, of expiation, of judgment, and, as it were, the place of execution of all condemned ones be there?"

From this intuition Heraclitus took two coherent negations, which are put into the right light only by a comparison with the propositions of his predecessor. Firstly, he denied the duality of two quite diverse worlds, into the assumption of which Anaximander had been pushed; he no longer distinguished a physical world from a metaphysical, a realm of definite qualities from a realm of indefinable indefiniteness. Now after the first step he could neither be kept back any longer from a still greater audacity of denying: he denied "Being" altogether. For this one world which was left to him —shielded all round by eternal, unwritten laws, flowing up and down in the brazen beat of rhythm—shows nowhere persistence, indestructibility, a bulwark in the stream. Louder than Anaximander, Heraclitus exclaimed: "I see nothing but Becoming. Be not deceived! It is the fault of your limited outlook and not the fault of the essence of things if you believe that you see firm land anywhere in the ocean of Becoming and Passing. You need names for things, just as if they had a rigid permanence, but the very river in which you bathe a second time is no longer the same one which you entered before."

Heraclitus has as his royal property the highest power of intuitive conception, whereas toward the other mode of conception which is consummated by ideas and logical combinations, that is toward reason, he shows himself cool, apathetic, even hostile, and he seems to derive a pleasure when he is able to contradict reason by means of a truth gained intuitively, and this he does in such propositions as: "Everything has always its opposite within itself," so fearlessly that Aristotle before the tribunal of Reason accuses him of the highest crime, of having sinned against the law of opposition. Intuitive representation, however, embraces two things: firstly, the present, motley, changing world, pressing on us in all experiences; secondly, the conditions by means of which alone any experience of this world becomes possible: time and space. For these are able to be intuitively apprehended, purely in themselves and independent of any experience, i.e., they can be perceived, although they are without definite contents. If now Heraclitus considered time in this fashion, dissociated from all experiences, he had in it the most instructive monogram of all that which falls within the realm of intuitive conception. Just as he conceived of time, so also for instance did Schopenhauer, who repeatedly says of it that in it every instant exists only in so far as it has annihilated the preceding one, its father, in order to be itself effaced equally quickly; that past and future are as unreal as any dream; that the present is only the dimensionless and unstable boundary between the two; that, however, like time, so space, and again like the latter, so also everything that is simultaneously in space and time, has only a relative existence, only through and for the sake of a something else, of the same kind as itself, i.e., existing only under the same limitations. This truth is in the highest degree self-evident, accessible to everyone, and just for that very reason, abstractly and rationally, it is only attained with great difficulty. Whoever has this truth before his eyes must, however, also proceed at once to the next Heraclitean consequence and say that the whole essence of actuality is in fact activity, and that for actuality there is no other kind of existence and reality, as Schopenhauer has likewise expounded (*The World as Will and Idea*, Vol. I, Bk. I, sec. 4): "Only as active does it fill space and time: its action upon the immediate object determines the perception in which alone it exists: the effect of the action of any material object upon any other is known only in so far as the latter acts upon the immediate object in a different way from that in which it acted before; it consists in this alone. Cause and effect thus constitute the whole nature of matter; its true being *is* its action. The totality of everything material is therefore very appropriately called in German *Wirklichkeit* [actuality]—a word which is far more expressive than *Realität* [reality].* That upon which actuality acts is always matter; actuality's whole 'Being' and essence therefore consist only in the orderly change, which *one* part of it causes in another, and is therefore wholly relative, according to a relation which is valid only within the boundary of actuality, as in the case of time and space."

The eternal and exclusive Becoming, the total instability of all reality and actuality, which continually works and becomes and never *is*, as Heraclitus teaches—is an awful and appalling conception, and in its effects most nearly related to that sensation by which during an earthquake one loses confidence in the firmly grounded earth. It required an astonishing strength to translate this effect into its opposite, into the sublime, into happy astonishment. Heraclitus accomplished this through an observation of the proper course of all Becoming and Passing, which he conceived of under the form of polarity, as the divergence of a force into two qualitatively different, opposite actions, striving after reunion. A quality is set continually at variance with itself and separates itself into its opposites: these opposites continually strive again one toward another. The common people, of course, think to recognize something rigid, completed, consistent; but the fact of the matter is that at any instant, bright and dark, sour and sweet are side by side and attached to one another like two wrestlers of whom sometimes the one succeeds, sometimes the other. According to Heraclitus honey is at the same time sweet and bitter, and the world itself an amphora whose contents constantly need stirring up. Out of the war of the opposites all Becoming originates; the definite and to us seemingly persistent qualities express only the momentary predominance of the one fighter, but with that the war is not at

---

* Mira in quibusdam rebus verborum proprietas est, et consuetudo sermonis antiqui quaedam efficacissimis notis signat (Seneca, Epist. 81).—TR.

an end; the wrestling continues to all eternity. Everything happens according to this struggle, and this very struggle manifests eternal justice. It is a wonderful conception, drawn from the purest source of Hellenism, which considers the struggle as the continual sway of a homogeneous, severe justice bound by eternal laws. Only a Greek was able to consider this conception as the fundament of a *Cosmodicy;* it is Hesiod's good Eris transfigured into the cosmic principle, it is the idea of a contest, an idea held by individual Greeks and by their State, and translated out of the gymnasiums and palaestra, out of the artistic agonistics, out of the struggle of the political parties and of the towns into the most general principle, so that the machinery of the universe is regulated by it. Just as every Greek fought as though he alone were in the right, and as though an absolutely sure standard of judicial opinion could at any instant decide whither victory is inclining, thus the qualities wrestle one with another, according to inviolable laws and standards which are inherent in the struggle. The Things themselves in the permanency of which the limited intellect of man and animal believes do not "exist" at all; they are as the fierce flashing and fiery sparkling of drawn swords, as the stars of Victory rising with a radiant resplendence in the battle of the opposite qualities.

That struggle which is peculiar to all Becoming, that eternal interchange of victory is again described by Schopenhauer (*The World as Will and Idea,* Vol. I, Bk. 2, sec. 27): "The permanent matter must constantly change its form; for under the guidance of causality, mechanical, physical, chemical, and organic phenomena, eagerly striving to appear, wrest the matter from each other, for each desires to reveal its own Idea. This strife may be followed up through the whole of nature; indeed nature exists only through it." The following pages give the most noteworthy illustrations of this struggle, only that the prevailing tone of this description ever remains other than that of Heraclitus in so far as to Schopenhauer the struggle is a proof of the Will to Life falling out with itself; it is to him a feasting on itself on the part of this dismal, dull impulse, as a phenomenon on the whole horrible and not at all making for happiness. The arena and the object of this struggle is Matter—which some natural forces alternately endeavor to disintegrate and build up again at the expense of other natural forces—as also Space and Time, the union of which through causality *is* this very matter.

6

Whilst the imagination of Heraclitus measured the rest-
lessly moving universe, the "actuality" (*Wirklichkeit*), with
the eye of the happy spectator, who sees innumerable pairs
wrestling in joyous combat entrusted to the superintendence
of severe umpires, a still higher presentiment seized him, he
no longer could contemplate the wrestling pairs and the umpires, separated one from another; the very umpires seemed
to fight, and the fighters seemed to be their own judges—yea,
since at the bottom he conceived only of the one Justice
eternally swaying, he dared to exclaim: "The contest of The
Many is itself pure justice. And after all: The One is The
Many. For what are all those qualities according to their
nature? Are they immortal gods? Are they separate beings
working for themselves from the beginning and without end?
And if the world which we see knows only Becoming and
Passing but no Permanence, should perhaps those qualities
constitute a differently fashioned metaphysical world, true,
not a world of unity as Anaximander sought behind the
fluttering veil of plurality, but a world of eternal and essential pluralities?" Is it possible that however violently he had
denied such duality, Heraclitus has after all by a roundabout way accidentally got into the dual cosmic order, an
order with an Olympus of numerous immortal gods and
demons—viz., *many* realities—and with a human world,
which sees only the dustcloud of the Olympic struggle and
the flashing of divine spears—i.e., only a Becoming? Anaximander had fled just from these definite qualities into the
lap of the metaphysical "Indefinite"; because the former *became* and passed, he had denied them a true and essential
existence; however, should it not seem now as if the Becoming is only the looming-into-view of a struggle of eternal
qualities? When we speak of the Becoming, should not the
original cause of this be sought in the peculiar feebleness of
human cognition—whereas in the nature of things there is
perhaps no Becoming, but only a coexisting of many true
increate indestructible realities?

These are Heraclitean loopholes and labyrinths; he exclaims
once again: "The 'One' is the 'Many.' " The many perceptible
qualities are neither eternal entities, nor phantasmata of our
senses (Anaxagoras conceives them later on as the former,
Permenides as the latter), they are neither rigid, sovereign
"Being" nor fleeting Appearance hovering in human minds.

The third possibility which alone was left to Heraclitus nobody will be able to divine with dialectic sagacity and, as it were, by calculation, for what he invented here is a rarity even in the realm of mystic incredibilities and unexpected cosmic metaphors.—The world is the *game* of Zeus, or expressed more physically, the game of fire with itself, the "One" is only in this sense at the same time the "Many."—

In order to elucidate in the first place the introduction of fire as a world-shaping force, I recall how Anaximander had further developed the theory of water as the origin of things. Placing confidence in the essential part of Thales' theory, and strengthening and adding to the latter's observations, Anaximander, however, was not to be convinced that before the water and, as it were, after the water there was no further stage of quality: no, to him out of the Warm and the Cold the Moist seemed to form itself, and the Warm and the Cold therefore were supposed to be the preliminary stages, the still more original qualities. With their issuing forth from the primordial existence of the "Indefinite," Becoming begins. Heraclitus, who as physicist subordinated himself to the importance of Anaximander, explains to himself this Anaximandrian "Warm" as the respiration, the warm breath, the dry vapors, in short as the fiery element: about this fire he now enunciates the same as Thales and Anaximander had enunciated about the water: that in innumerable metamorphoses it was passing along the path of Becoming, especially in the three chief aggregate stages as something Warm, Moist, and Firm. For water in descending is transformed into earth, in ascending into fire: or as Heraclitus appears to have expressed himself more exactly: from the sea ascend only the pure vapors which serve as food to the divine fire of the stars, from the earth only the dark, foggy ones, from which the Moist derives its nourishment. The pure vapors are the transitional stage in the passing of sea into fire, the impure the transitional stage in the passing of earth into water. Thus the two paths of metamorphosis of the fire run continuously side by side, upward and downward, to and fro, from fire to water, from water to earth, from earth back again to water, from water to fire. Whereas Heraclitus is a follower of Anaximander in the most important of these conceptions, e.g., that the fire is kept up by the evaporations, or herein, that out of the water is dissolved partly earth, partly fire; he is on the other hand quite independent and in opposition to Anaximander in excluding the "Cold" from the physical process, whilst Anaximander had put it side by side with the "Warm" as having the same rights, so as to let the "Moist" originate out of both. To do so was, of course, a necessity to Heraclitus, for if everything is to be fire, then, however many possibilities of its transformation might be assumed, nothing can exist that would be the absolute antithesis to fire; he has, therefore, probably interpreted only as a degree of the "Warm" that which is called the "Cold," and he could justify this interpretation without difficulty. Much more important than this deviation from the doctrine of Anaximander is a further agreement; he, like the latter, believes in an end of the world periodically repeating itself and in an ever-renewed emerging of another world out of the all-destroying world-fire. The period during which the world hastens toward that world-fire and the dissolution into pure fire is characterized by him most strikingly as a demand and a need; the state of being completely swallowed up by the fire as satiety; and now to us remains the question as to how he understood and named the newly awakening impulse for world-creation, the pouring-out-of-itself into the forms of plurality. The Greek proverb seems to come to our assistance with the thought that "satiety gives birth to crime" (the Hybris) and one may indeed ask oneself for a minute whether perhaps Heraclitus has derived that return to plurality out of the Hybris. Let us just take this thought seriously; in its light the face of Heraclitus changes before our eyes, the proud gleam of his eyes dies out, a wrinkled expression of painful resignation, of impotence, becomes distinct, it seems that we know why later antiquity called him the "weeping philosopher." Is not the whole world-process now an act of punishment of the Hybris? The plurality the result of a crime? The transformation of the pure into the impure, the consequence of injustice? Is not the guilt now shifted into the essence of the things and indeed, the world of Becoming and of individuals accordingly exonerated from guilt; yet at the same time are they not condemned forever and ever to bear the consequences of guilt?

7

That dangerous word, Hybris, is indeed the touchstone for every Heraclitean; here he may show whether he has understood or mistaken his master. Is there in this world guilt, injustice, contradiction, suffering?

Yes, exclaims Heraclitus, but only for the limited human being, who sees divergently and not convergently, not for the contuitive god; to him everything opposing converges into one harmony, invisible it is true to the common human eye, yet comprehensible to him who like Heraclitus resembles the contemplative god. Before his fiery eye no drop of injustice is left in the world poured out around him, and even that cardinal obstacle—how pure fire can take up its quarters in forms so impure—he masters by means of a sublime simile. A Becoming and Passing, a building and destroying, without any moral bias, in perpetual innocence is in this world only the play of the artist and of the child. And similarly, just as the child and the artist play, the eternally living fire plays, builds up, and destroys, in innocence—and this game the Aeon plays with himself. Transforming himself into water and earth, like a child he piles heaps of sand by the sea, piles up and demolishes; from time to time he recommences the game. A moment of satiety, then again desire seizes him, as desire compels the artist to create. Not wantonness but the ever newly awakening impulse to play calls into life other worlds. The child throws away his toys, but soon he starts again in an innocent frame of mind. As soon, however, as the child builds, he connects, joins, and forms lawfully and according to an innate sense of order.

Thus only is the world contemplated by the aesthetic man, who has learned from the artist and the genesis of the latter's work, how the struggle of plurality can yet bear within itself law and justice, how the artist stands contemplative above, and working within the work of art, how necessity and play, antagonism and harmony must pair themselves for the procreation of the work of art.

Who now will still demand from such a philosophy a system of Ethics with the necessary imperatives—Thou Shalt —or even reproach Heraclitus with such a deficiency. Man down to his last fiber is Necessity and absolutely "unfree" —if by freedom one understands the foolish claim to be able to change at will one's *essentia* like a garment, a claim, which up to the present every serious philosophy has rejected with due scorn. That so few human beings live with consciousness in the Logos and in accordance with the all-overlooking artist's eye originates from their souls being wet and from the fact that men's eyes and ears, their intellect in general is a bad witness when "moist ooze fills their souls." Why that is so is not questioned any more than why fire becomes water and earth. Heraclitus is not *compelled* to prove (as Leibnitz was) that this world was even the best of all; it was sufficient for him that the world is the beautiful, innocent play of the Aeon. Man on the whole is to him even an irrational being, with which the fact that in all his essence the law of all-ruling reason is fulfilled does not clash. He does not occupy a specially favored position in nature, whose highest phenomenon is not simple-minded man, but fire, for instance, as stars. In so far as man has through necessity received a share of fire, he is a little more rational; as far as he consists of earth and water it stands badly with his reason. He is not compelled to take cognizance of the Logos simply because he is a human being. Why is there water, why earth? This to Heraclitus is a much more serious problem than to ask why men are so stupid and bad. In the highest and the most perverted men the same inherent lawfulness and justice manifest themselves. If, however, one would ask Heraclitus the question: "Why is fire not always fire, why is it now water, now earth?" then he would only just answer: "It is a game, don't take it too pathetically and still less, morally." Heraclitus describes only the existing world and has the same contemplative pleasure in it which the artist experiences when looking at his growing work. Only those who have cause to be discontented with his natural history of man find him gloomy, melancholy, tearful, somber, atrabilarious, pessimistic, and altogether hateful. He however would take these discontented people, together with their antipathies and sympathies, their hatred and their love, as negligible and perhaps answer them with some such comment as: "Dogs bark at anything they do not know," or, "To the ass chaff is preferable to gold."

With such discontented persons also originate the numerous complaints as to the obscurity of the Heraclitean style; probably no man has ever written clearer and more illuminatingly; of course, very abruptly, and therefore naturally obscure to the racing readers. But why a philosopher should intentionally write obscurely—a thing habitually said about Heraclitus—is absolutely inexplicable; unless he has some cause to hide his thoughts or is sufficiently a rogue to conceal his thoughtlessness underneath words. One is, as Schopenhauer says, indeed compelled by lucid expression to prevent misunderstandings even in affairs of practical everyday life, how then should one be allowed to express oneself indistinctly, indeed puzzlingly in the most difficult, most abstruse, scarcely attainable object of thinking, the tasks of philosophy? With respect to brevity, however, Jean Paul gives a good precept: "On the whole it is right that everything great—of deep meaning to a rare mind—should be uttered with brevity and (therefore) obscurely so that the paltry mind would rather proclaim it to be nonsense than translate it into the realm of his empty-headedness. For common minds have an ugly ability to perceive in the deepest and richest

saying nothing but their own everyday opinion." Moreover
and in spite of it Heraclitus has not escaped the "paltry
minds"; already the Stoics have "re-expounded" him into the
shallow and dragged down his aesthetic fundamental-percep-
tion as to the play of the world to the miserable level of
the common regard for the practical ends of the world and
more explicitly for the advantages of man, so that out of his
Physics has arisen in those heads a crude optimism, with the
continual invitation to Dick, Tom, and Harry, *"Plaudite
amici!"*

8

Heraclitus was proud; and if it comes to pride with a philosopher then it is a great pride. His work never refers him
to a "public," the applause of the masses, and the hailing
chorus of contemporaries. To wander lonely along his path
belongs to the nature of the philosopher. His talents are the
most rare, in a certain sense the most unnatural and at the
same time exclusive and hostile even toward kindred talents.
The wall of his self-sufficiency must be of diamond, if it is
not to be demolished and broken, for everything is in motion
against him. His journey to immortality is more cumbersome
and impeded than any other and yet nobody can believe more
firmly than the philosopher that he will attain the goal by that
journey—because he does not know where he is to stand if
not on the widely spread wings of all time; for the disregard
of everything present and momentary lies in the essence
of the great philosophic nature. He has truth; the wheel of
time may roll whither it pleases, never can it escape from
truth. It is important to hear that such men have lived.
Never, for example, would one be able to imagine the pride of
Heraclitus as an idle possibility. In itself every endeavor
after knowledge seems by its nature to be eternally unsatisfied and unsatisfactory. Therefore nobody unless instructed by
history will like to believe in such a royal self-esteem and
conviction of being the only wooer of truth. Such men live in
their own solar system—one has to look for them there. A
Pythagoras, an Empedocles treated themselves too with a
superhuman esteem, yea, with almost religious awe; but the
tie of sympathy united with the great conviction of the
metempsychosis and the unity of everything living led them
back to other men, for their welfare and salvation. Of that
feeling of solitude, however, which permeated the Ephesian
recluse of the Artemis Temple, one can only divine some-

thing, when growing benumbed in the wildest mountain desert. No paramount feeling of compassionate agitation, no desire to help, heal, and save emanates from him. He is a star without an atmosphere. His eye, directed blazingly inward, looks outward, for appearance's sake only, extinct and icy. All around him, immediately upon the citadel of his pride beat the waves of folly and perversity; with loathing he turns away from them. But men with a feeling heart would also shun such a Gorgon monster as cast out of brass; within an out-of-the-way sanctuary, among the statues of gods, by the side of cold composedly-sublime architecture such a being may appear more comprehensible. As man among men Heraclitus was incredible; and though he was seen paying attention to the play of noisy children, even then he was reflecting upon what never man thought of on such an occasion: the play of the great world-child, Zeus. He had no need of men, not even for his discernments. He was not interested in all that which one might perhaps ascertain from them, and in what the other sages before him had been endeavoring to ascertain. He spoke with disdain of such questioning, collecting, in short, "historic" men. "I sought and investigated myself," he said, with a word by which one designates the investigation of an oracle; as if he and no one else were the true fulfiller and achiever of the Delphic precept: "Know thyself."

What he learned from this oracle, he deemed immortal wisdom, and eternally worthy of explanation, of unlimited effect even in the distance, after the model of the prophetic speeches of the Sibyl. It is sufficient for the latest mankind: let the latter have that expounded to her, as oracular sayings, which he like the Delphic god "neither enunciates nor conceals." Although it is proclaimed by him, "without smiles, finery, and the scent of ointments," but rather as with "foaming mouth," it *must* force its way through the millenniums of the future. For the world needs truth eternally, therefore she needs also Heraclitus eternally; although he has no need of her. What does his fame matter to *him?*—fame with "mortals ever flowing on!" as he exclaims scornfully. His fame is of concern to man, not to himself; the immortality of mankind needs him, not he the immortality of the man Heraclitus. That which he beheld, *the doctrine of the Law in the Becoming, and of the Play in the Necessity,* must henceforth be beheld eternally; he has raised the curtain of this greatest stage play.

9

Whereas in every word of Heraclitus are expressed the pride and the majesty of truth, but of truth caught by intuitions, not scaled by the rope ladder of Logic, whereas in sublime ecstasy he beholds but does not espy, discerns but does not reckon, he is contrasted with his contemporary *Parmenides*, a man likewise with the type of a prophet of truth, but formed, as it were, out of ice and not out of fire, and shedding around himself cold, piercing light.

Parmenides once had, probably in his later years, a moment of the very purest abstraction, undimmed by any reality, perfectly lifeless; this moment—un-Greek, like no other in the two centuries of the Tragic Age—the product of which is the doctrine of "Being," became a boundary stone for his own life, which divided it into two periods; at the same time, however, the same moment divides the pre-Socratic thinking into two halves, of which the first might be called the Anaximandrian, the second the Parmenidean. The first period in Parmenides' own philosophizing bears still the signature of Anaximander; this period produced a detailed philosophic-physical system as answer to Anaximander's questions. When later that icy abstraction-horror caught him, and the simplest proposition treating of "Being" and "Not-Being" was advanced by him, then among the many older doctrines thrown by him upon the scrap heap was also his own system. However, he does not appear to have lost all paternal piety toward the strong and well-shapen child of his youth, and he saved himself therefore by saying: "It is true there is only one right way; if one, however, wants at any time to betake oneself to another, then my earlier opinion according to its purity and consequence alone is right." Sheltering himself with this phrase he has allowed his former physical system a worthy and extensive space in his great poem on Nature, which really was to proclaim the new discernment as the only signpost to truth. This fatherly regard, even though an error should have crept in through it, is a remainder of human feeling, in a nature quite petrified by logical rigidity and almost changed into a thinking machine.

Parmenides, whose personal intercourse with Anaximander does not seem incredible to me, and whose starting from Anaximander's doctrine is not only credible but evident, had the same distrust for the complete separation of a world which only is, and a world which only becomes, as had also caught

Heraclitus and led to a denying of "Being" altogether. Both
sought a way out from that contrast and divergence of a dual
order of the world. That leap into the Indefinite, Indefinable,
by which once for all Anaximander had escaped from the
realm of Becoming and from the empirically given qualities
of such realm, that leap did not become an easy matter to
minds so independently fashioned as those of Heraclitus and
Parmenides; first they endeavored to walk as far as they
could and reserved to themselves the leap for that place
where the foot finds no more hold and one has to leap, in
order not to fall. Both looked repeatedly at that very world
which Anaximander had condemned in so melancholy a way
and declared to be the place of wanton crime and at the same
time the penitentiary cell for the injustice of Becoming. Contemplating this world, Heraclitus, as we know already, had
discovered what a wonderful order, regularity, and security
manifest themselves in every Becoming; from that he concluded that the Becoming could not be anything evil and
unjust. Quite a different outlook had Parmenides; he compared the qualities one with another, and believed that they
were not all of the same kind, but ought to be classified under
two headings. If, for example, he compared bright and dark,
then the second quality was obviously only the *negation* of the
first; and thus he distinguished positive and negative qualities,
seriously endeavoring to rediscover and register that fundamental antithesis in the whole realm of Nature. His method
was the following: he took a few antitheses, e.g., light and
heavy, rare and dense, active and passive, and compared them
with that typical antithesis of bright and dark: that which
corresponded with the bright was the positive, that which
corresponded with the dark the negative quality. If he took
perhaps the heavy and light, the light fell to the side of the
bright, the heavy to the side of the dark; and thus "heavy" was
to him only the negation of "light," but the "light" a positive
quality. This method alone shows that he had a defiant aptitude for abstract logical procedure, closed against the sug-
gestions of the senses. The "heavy" seems indeed to offer
itself very forcibly to the senses as a positive quality; that did
not keep Parmenides from stamping it as a negation. Similarly he placed the earth in opposition to the fire, the "cold"
in opposition to the "warm," the "dense" in opposition to the
"rare," the "female" in opposition to the "male," the "passive"
in opposition to the "active," merely as negations: so that
before his gaze our empiric world divided itself into two
separate spheres, into that of the positive qualities—with a
bright, fiery, warm, light, rare, active-masculine character—

and into that of the negative qualities. The latter express really only the lack, the absence of the others, the positive ones. He therefore described the sphere in which the positive qualities are absent as dark, earthy, cold, heavy, dense and altogether as of feminine-passive character. Instead of the expressions "positive" and "negative" he used the standing term "existent" and "nonexistent" and had arrived with this at the proposition, that, in contradiction to Anaximander, this our world itself contains something "existent," and of course something "nonexistent." One is not to seek that "existent" outside the world and, as it were, above our horizon; but before us, and everywhere in every Becoming, something "existent" and active is contained.

With that, however, still remained to him the task of giving the more exact answer to the question: what is the Becoming? And here was the moment where he had to leap, in order not to fall, although perhaps to such natures as that of Parmenides, even any leaping means a falling. Enough! We get into fog, into the mysticism of *qualitates occultae*, and even a little into mythology. Parmenides, like Heraclitus, looks at the general Becoming and Not-remaining and explains to himself a Passing only thus, that the "Nonexistent" bore the guilt. For how should the "Existent" bear the guilt of Passing? Likewise, however, the Originating, i.e., the Becoming, must come about through the assistance of the "Nonexistent"; for the "Existent" is always there and could not of itself first originate and it could not explain any Originating, any Becoming. Therefore the Originating, the Becoming as well as the Passing and Perishing have been brought about by the negative qualities. But that the originating "thing" has a content, and the passing "thing" loses a content, presupposes that the positive qualities —and that just means that very content—participate likewise in both processes. In short the proposition results: "For the Becoming the 'Existent' as well as the 'Nonexistent' is necessary; when they co-operate then a Becoming results." But how come the "positive" and the "negative" to one another? Should they not on the contrary eternally flee one another as antitheses and thereby make every Becoming impossible? Here Parmenides appeals to a *qualitas occulta*, to a mystic tendency of the antithetical pairs to approach and attract one another, and he allegorizes that peculiar contrariety by the name of Aphrodite, and by the empirically known relation of the male and female principle. It is the power of Aphrodite which plays the matchmaker between the antithetical pair, the "Existent" and the "Nonexistent." Passion brings together the antagonistic and antipathetic elements: the result is a

Becoming. When Desire has become satiated, Hatred and the innate antagonism again drive asunder the "Existent" and the "Nonexistent"—then man says: the thing perishes, passes.

10

But no one with impunity lays his profane hands on such awful abstractions as the "Existent" and the "Nonexistent"; the blood freezes slowly as one touches them. There was a day upon which an odd idea suddenly occurred to Parmenides, an idea which seemed to take all value away from his former combinations, so that he felt inclined to throw them aside, like a money bag with old worn-out coins. It is commonly believed that an external impression, in addition to the centrifugal consequence of such ideas as "existent" and "nonexistent," has also been coactive in the invention of that day; this impression was an acquaintance with the theology of the old roamer and rhapsodist, the singer of a mystic deification of Nature, the Kolophonian *Xenophanes*. Throughout an extraordinary life Xenophanes lived as a wandering poet and became through his travels a well-informed and most instructive man who knew how to question and how to narrate, for which reason Heraclitus reckoned him amongst the polyhistorians and above all amongst the "historic" natures, in the sense mentioned. Whence and when came to him the mystic bent into the One and the eternally Resting, nobody will be able to compute; perhaps it is only the conception of the finally settled old man, to whom, after the agitation of his erratic wanderings, and after the restless learning and searching for truth, the vision of a divine rest, the permanence of all things within a pantheistic primal peace appears as *the* highest and greatest ideal. After all, it seems to me quite accidental that in the same place in Elea two men lived together for a time, each of whom carried in his head a conception of unity; they formed no school and had nothing in common which perhaps the one might have learned from the other and then might have handed on. For, in the case of these two men, the origin of that conception of unity is quite different, yea opposite; and if either of them has become at all acquainted with the doctrine of the other then, in order to understand it at all, he had to translate it first into his own language. With this translation, however, the very specific element of the other doctrine was lost. Whereas Parmenides arrived at the unity of the "Existent" purely through an alleged logical consequence and whereas he spun that

unity out of the ideas "Being" and "Not-Being," Xenophanes
was a religious mystic and belonged, with that mystic unity,
very properly to the sixth century. Although he was no such
revolutionizing personality as Pythagoras, he had nevertheless in his wanderings the same bent and impulse to improve,
purify, and cure men. He was the ethical teacher, but still in
the stage of the rhapsodist; in a later time he would have
been a sophist. In the daring disapproval of the existing customs and valuations he had not his equal in Greece; moreover he did not, like Heraclitus and Plato, retire into solitude but placed himself before the very public whose exulting admiration of Homer, whose passionate propensity for
the honors of the gymnastic festivals, whose adoration of
stones in human shape he criticized severely with wrath and
scorn, yet not as a brawling Thersites. The freedom of the
individual was with him on its zenith; and by this almost
limitless stepping free from all conventions he was more
closely related to Parmenides than by that last divine unity,
which once he had beheld, in a visionary state worthy of
that century. His unity scarcely had expression and word in
common with the one "Being" of Parmenides, and certainly
had not the same origin.

It was rather an opposite state of mind in which Parmenides found his doctrine of "Being." On that day and in
that state he examined his two co-operating antitheses, the
"Existent" and the "Nonexistent," the positive and the negative qualities, of which Desire and Hatred constitute the
world and the Becoming. He was suddenly caught up, mis-
trusting, by the idea of negative quality, of the "Nonexistent." For can something which does not exist be a
quality? Or to put the question in a broader sense: can anything indeed which does not exist, exist? The only form of
knowledge in which we at once put unconditional trust and
the disapproval of which amounts to madness is the tautology
$A = A$. But this very tautological knowledge called inexorably
to him: what does not exist, exists not! What is, is! Suddenly he feels upon his life the load of an enormous
logical sin; for had he not always without hesitation assumed that *there were existing* negative qualities, in short a
"Nonexistent," that therefore, to express it by a formula,
$A = $ Not-A, which indeed could only be advanced by the most
out-and-out perversity of thinking. It is true, as he recollected,
the whole great mass of men judge with the same perversity;
he himself has only participated in the general crime against
logic. But the same moment which charges him with this
crime surrounds him with the light of the glory of an in-

vention; he has found, apart from all human illusion, a principle, the key to the world-secret; he now descends into the abyss of things, guided by the firm and fearful hand of the tautological truth as to "Being."

On the way thither he meets Heraclitus—an unfortunate encounter! Just now Heraclitus' play with antinomies was bound to be very hateful to him, who placed the utmost importance upon the severest separation of "Being" and "Not-Being"; propositions like this: "We are and at the same time we are not"—" 'Being' and 'Not-Being' is at the same time the same thing and again not the same thing," propositions through which all that he had just elucidated and disentangled became again dim and inextricable, incited him to wrath. "Away with the men," he exclaimed, "who seem to have two heads and yet know nothing! With them truly everything is in flux, even their thinking! They stare at things stupidly, but they must be deaf as well as blind so to mix up the opposites"! The want of judgment on the part of the masses, glorified by playful antinomies and praised as the acme of all knowledge was to him a painful and incomprehensible experience.

Now he dived into the cold bath of his awful abstractions. That which is true must exist in eternal presence; about it cannot be said "it was," "it will be." The "Existent" cannot have become; for out of what should it have become? Out of the "Nonexistent"? But that does not exist and can produce nothing. Out of the "Existent"? This would not produce anything but itself. The same applies to the Passing; it is just as impossible as the Becoming, as any change, any increase, any decrease. On the whole the proposition is valid: everything about which it can be said: "it has been" or "it will be" does not exist; about the "Existent," however, it can never be said "it does not exist." The "Existent" is indivisible, for where is the second power, which should divide it? It is immovable, for whither should it move itself? It cannot be infinitely great nor infinitely small, for it is perfect and a perfectly given infinitude is a contradiction. Thus the "Existent" is suspended, delimited, perfect, immovable, everywhere equally balanced and such equilibrium equally perfect at any point, like a globe, but not in a space, for otherwise this space would be a second "Existent." But there cannot exist several "Existents," for in order to separate them, something would have to exist which was not existing, an assumption which neutralizes itself. Thus there exists only the eternal Unity.

If now, however, Parmenides turned back his gaze to the

world of Becoming, the existence of which he had formerly tried to understand by such ingenious conjectures, he was wroth at his eye seeing the Becoming at all, his ear hearing it. "Do not follow the dim-sighted eyes," now his command runs, "not the resounding ear nor the tongue, but examine only by the power of the thought." Therewith he accomplished the extremely important first critique of the apparatus of knowledge, although this critique was still inadequate and proved disastrous in its consequences. By tearing entirely asunder the senses and the ability to think in abstractions, i.e., reason, just as if they were two thoroughly separate capacities, he demolished the intellect itself, and incited people to that wholly erroneous separation of "mind" and "body" which, especially since Plato, lies like a curse on philosophy. All sense perceptions, Parmenides judges, cause only illusions, and their chief illusion is their deluding us to believe that even the "Nonexistent" exists, that even the Becoming has a "Being." All that plurality, diversity, and variety of the empirically known world, the change of its qualities, the order in its ups and downs, is thrown aside mercilessly as mere appearance and delusion; from there nothing is to be learnt, therefore all labor is wasted which one bestows upon this false, through-and-through futile world, the conception of which has been obtained by being humbugged by the senses. He who judges in such generalizations as Parmenides did ceases therewith to be an investigator of natural philosophy in detail; his interest in phenomena withers away; there develops even a hatred of being unable to get rid of this eternal fraud of the senses. Truth is now to dwell only in the most faded, most abstract generalities, in the empty husks of the most indefinite words, as in a maze of cobwebs; and by such a "truth" now the philosopher sits, bloodless as an abstraction and surrounded by a web of formulas. The spider undoubtedly wants the blood of its victims, but the Parmenidean philosopher hates the very blood of his victims, the blood of Empiricism sacrificed by him.

FROM HUMAN, ALL TOO HUMAN, VOL. II

140 *

DANCING IN CHAINS. In the case of every Greek artist, poet, or writer we must ask: what is the new constraint

* From *The Wanderer and His Shadow*.

which he imposes upon himself and makes attractive to his contemporaries, so as to find imitators? For the thing called "invention" (in meter, for example) is always a self-imposed fetter of this kind. "Dancing in chains"—to make that hard for themselves and then to spread a false notion that it is easy—that is the trick that they wish to show us. Even in Homer we may perceive a wealth of inherited formulas and laws of epic narration, within the circle of which he had to dance, and he himself created new conventions for them that came after. This was the discipline of the Greek poets: first to impose upon themselves a manifold constraint by means of the earlier poets; then to invent in addition a new constraint, to impose it upon themselves and cheerfully to overcome it, so that constraint and victory are perceived and admired.

FROM THE JOYFUL WISDOM

80

ART AND NATURE. The Greeks (or at least the Athenians) liked to hear good talking: indeed they had an eager inclination for it, which distinguished them more than anything else from non-Greeks. And so they required good talking even from passion on the stage, and submitted to the unnaturalness of dramatic verse with delight—in nature, forsooth, passion is so sparing of words! so dumb and confused! Or if it finds words, so embarrassed and irrational and a shame to itself! We have now, all of us, thanks to the Greeks, accustomed ourselves to this unnaturalness on the stage, as we endure that other unnaturalness, the *singing* passion, and willingly endure it, thanks to the Italians. It has become a necessity to us, which we cannot satisfy out of the resources of actuality, to hear men talk well and in full detail in the most trying situations; it enraptures us at present when the tragic hero still finds words, reasons, eloquent gestures, and on the whole a bright spirituality, where life approaches the abysses, and where the actual man mostly loses his head, and certainly his fine language. This kind of *deviation from nature* is perhaps the most agreeable repast for man's pride; he loves art generally on account of it, as the expression of high, heroic unnaturalness and convention. One rightly objects to the dramatic poet when he does not transform everything into reason and speech, but always retains a remnant of *silence*—just as one is dissatisfied with an operatic musician who cannot find a melody for the highest emotion, but only an emotional, "natural" stammering and crying. Here nature *has to* be contradicted! Here the common charm of illusion *has to* give place to a higher charm! The Greeks go far, far in this direction— frightfully far! As they constructed the stage as narrow as possible and dispensed with all the effect of deep backgrounds, as they made pantomime and easy motion impossible to the actor, and transformed him into a solemn, stiff, masked bogy, so they have also deprived passion itself of its deep background, and have dictated to it a law of fine talk; indeed, they have really done everything to counteract the elementary effect of representations that inspire pity and terror. *They did not want pity and terror*—with due deference, with the highest deference to Aristotle! But he certainly did not hit the nail, to say nothing of the head of the nail, when he spoke about the final aim of Greek tragedy! Let us but look at the Grecian tragic poets with respect to *what* most excited their diligence, their inventiveness, and their emulation—certainly it was not the intention of subjugating the spectators by emotion! The Athenian went to the theatre *to hear fine talking!* And fine talking was arrived at by Sophocles!—Pardon me this heresy!—It is very different with *serious opera*; all its masters make it their business to prevent their personages being understood. "An occasional word picked up may come to the assistance of the inattentive listener; but on the whole the situation must be self-explanatory—the *talking* is of no account!"—so they all think, and so they have all made fun of the words. Perhaps they have only lacked courage to express fully their extreme contempt for words: a little additional insolence in Rossini, and he would have allowed la-la-la-la to be sung throughout —and it might have been the rational course! The personages of the opera are *not* meant to be believed "in their words," but in their tones! That is the difference, that is the fine *unnaturalness* on account of which people go to the opera! Even the *recitative secco* is not really intended to be heard as words and text; this kind of half-music is meant rather in the first place to give the musical ear a little repose (the repose from *melody*, as from the sublimest, and on that account the most straining enjoyment of this art)—but very soon something different results, namely, an increasing impatience, an increasing resistance, a new longing for *entire* music, for melody. How is it with the art of Richard Wagner as seen from this standpoint? Is it perhaps the same? Perhaps otherwise? It would often seem to me as if one needed to have learned by heart both the words *and* the music of his creations before the performances; for without that—so it seemed to me—one *may hear* neither the words, nor even the music.

FROM THE TWILIGHT OF THE IDOLS

The Problem of Socrates

1

IN all ages the wisest have always agreed in their judgment of life: *it is no good*. At all times and places the same words have been on their lips—words full of doubt, full of melancholy, full of weariness of life, full of hostility to life. Even Socrates' dying words were: "To live—means to be ill a long while: I owe a cock to the god Aesculapius." Even Socrates had had enough of it. What does that prove? What does it point to? Formerly people would have said (—oh, it has been said, and loudly enough too; by our Pessimists loudest of all!): "In any case there must be some truth in this! The *consensus sapientium* is a proof of truth." Shall we say the same today? *May* we do so? "In any case there must be some sickness here," we make reply. These great sages of all periods should first be examined more closely! It is possible that they were, every one of them, a little shaky on their legs, effete, rocky, decadent? Does wisdom perhaps appear on earth after the manner of a crow attracted by a slight smell of carrion?

2

This irreverent belief that the great sages were decadent types first occurred to me precisely in regard to that case concerning which both learned and vulgar prejudice was most opposed to my view. I recognized Socrates and Plato as symptoms of decline, as instruments in the disintegration of Hellas, as pseudo-Greek, as anti-Greek (*The Birth of Tragedy*, 1872). That *consensus sapientium*, as I perceived ever more and more clearly, did not in the least prove that they were right in the matter on which they agreed. It proved rather that these sages themselves must have been alike in some physiological particular, in order to assume the same negative attitude toward life—in order to be bound to assume that attitude. After all, judgments and valuations of life, whether for or against, cannot be true: their only value lies in the fact that they are symptoms; they can be considered only as symptoms—*per se* such judgments are nonsense. You must therefore endeavor by all means to reach out and try to grasp this astonishingly subtle axiom, *that the value of life cannot be estimated*. A living man cannot do so, because he is a contending party, or rather the very object in the dispute, and not a judge; nor can a dead man estimate it—for other reasons. For a philosopher to see a problem in the value of life is almost an objection against him, a note of interrogation set against his wisdom—a lack of wisdom. What? Is it possible that all these great sages were not only decadents, but that they were not even wise? Let me, however, return to the problem of Socrates.

3

To judge from his origin, Socrates belonged to the lowest of the low: Socrates was mob. You know, and you can still see it for yourself, how ugly he was. But ugliness, which in itself is an objection, was almost a refutation among the Greeks. Was Socrates really a Greek? Ugliness is not infrequently the expression of thwarted development, or of development arrested by crossing. In other cases it appears as a decadent development. The anthropologists among the criminal specialists declare that the typical criminal is ugly: *monstrum in fronte, monstrum in animo*. But the criminal is a decadent.* Was Socrates a typical criminal? At all events this would not clash with that famous physiognomist's judgment which was so repugnant to Socrates. While on his way through Athens a certain foreigner, who was no fool at

---

* It should be borne in mind that Nietzsche recognized two types of criminals—the criminal from strength, and the criminal from weakness. This passage alludes to the latter; Aphorism 45, alludes to the former.—Tr.

judging by looks, told Socrates to his face that he was a
monster, that his body harbored all the worst vices and passions. And Socrates replied simply: "You know me, sir!"

4

Not only are the acknowledged wildness and anarchy of
Socrates' instincts indicative of decadence, but also that preponderance of the logical faculties and that malignity of the
misshapen which was his special characteristic. Neither should
we forget those aural delusions which were religiously interpreted as "the demon of Socrates." Everything in him is
exaggerated, *buffo*, caricature; his nature is also full of concealment, of ulterior motives, and of underground currents.
I try to understand the idiosyncrasy from which the Socratic
equation, Reason = Virtue = Happiness, could have arisen:
the weirdest equation ever seen, and one which was essentially
opposed to all the instincts of the older Hellenes.

5

With Socrates Greek taste veers round in favor of dialectics: what actually occurs? In the first place a noble taste is
vanquished: with dialectics the mob comes to the top. Before
Socrates' time, dialectical manners were avoided in good society; they were regarded as bad manners, they were compromising. Young men were cautioned against them. All such
proffering of one's reasons was looked upon with suspicion.
Honest things like honest men do not carry their reasons on
their sleeve in such fashion. It is not good form to make a
show of everything. That which needs to be proved cannot be
worth much. Wherever authority still belongs to good usage,
wherever men do not prove but command, the dialectician
is regarded as a sort of clown. People laugh at him, they do
not take him seriously. Socrates was a clown who succeeded
in making men take him seriously: what then was the matter?

6

A man resorts to dialectics only when he has no other
means to hand. People know that they excite suspicion with
it and that it is not very convincing. Nothing is more easily
dispelled than a dialectical effect; this is proved by the

experience of every gathering in which discussions are held. It can be only the last defense of those who have no other weapons. One must require to extort one's right, otherwise one makes no use of it. That is why the Jews were dialecticians. Reynard the Fox was a dialectician: what?—and was Socrates one as well?

7

Is the Socratic irony an expression of revolt, of mob resentment? Does Socrates, as a creature suffering under oppression, enjoy his innate ferocity in the knife thrusts of the syllogism? Does he wreak his revenge on the noblemen he fascinates? As a dialectician a man has a merciless instrument to wield; he can play the tyrant with it: he compromises when he conquers with it. The dialectician leaves it to his opponent to prove that he is no idiot; he infuriates, he likewise paralyzes. The dialectician cripples the intellect of his opponent. Can it be that dialectics was only a form of revenge in Socrates?

8

I have given you to understand in what way Socrates was able to repel; now it is all the more necessary to explain how he fascinated. One reason is that he discovered a new kind of Agon, and that he was the first fencing master in the best circles in Athens. He fascinated by appealing to the combative instinct of the Greeks—he introduced a variation into the contests between men and youths. Socrates was also a great erotic.

9

But Socrates divined still more. He saw right through his noble Athenians; he perceived that his case, his peculiar case, was no exception even in his time. The same kind of degeneracy was silently preparing itself everywhere: ancient Athens was dying out. And Socrates understood that the whole world needed him—his means, his remedy, his special artifice for self-preservation. Everywhere the instincts were in a state of anarchy; everywhere people were within an ace of excess: the *monstrum in animo* was the general danger.

"The instincts would play the tyrant; we must discover a countertyrant who is stronger than they." On the occasion when the physiognomist had unmasked Socrates, and had told him what he was, a crater full of evil desires, the great Master of Irony let fall one or two words more, which provide the key to his nature. "This is true," he said, "but I overcame them all." How did Socrates succeed in mastering himself? His case was at bottom only the extreme and most apparent example of a state of distress which was beginning to be general: that state in which no one was able to master himself and in which the instincts turned one against the other. As the extreme example of this state, he fascinated—his terrifying ugliness made him conspicuous to every eye: it is quite obvious that he fascinated still more as a reply, as a solution, as an apparent cure of this case.

10

When a man finds it necessary, as Socrates did, to create a tyrant out of reason, there is no small danger that something else wishes to play the tyrant. Reason was then discovered as a saviour; neither Socrates nor his "patients" were at liberty to be rational or not, as they pleased; at that time it was *de rigueur*, it had become a last shift. The fanaticism with which the whole of Greek thought plunges into reason betrays a critical condition of things: men were in danger; there were only two alternatives: either perish or else be absurdly rational. The moral bias of Greek philosophy from Plato onward is the outcome of a pathological condition, as is also its appreciation of dialectics. Reason = Virtue = Happiness simply means: we must imitate Socrates, and confront the dark passions permanently with the light of day—the light of reason. We must at all costs be clever, precise, clear: all yielding to the instincts, to the unconscious, leads downwards.

11

I have now explained how Socrates fascinated: he seemed to be a doctor, a Saviour. Is it necessary to expose the errors which lay in his faith in "reason at any price"? It is a piece of self-deception on the part of philosophers and moralists to suppose that they can extricate themselves from degeneration by merely waging war upon it. They cannot thus extricate themselves: that which they choose as a means, as the road to salvation, is in itself again only an expression of degeneration—they only modify its mode of manifesting itself: they do not abolish it. Socrates was a misunderstanding. *The whole of the morality of amelioration—that of Christianity as well—was a misunderstanding.* The most blinding light of day: reason at any price; life made clear, cold, cautious, conscious, without instincts, opposed to the instincts, was in itself only a disease, another kind of disease—and by no means a return to "virtue," to "health," and to happiness. To be obliged to fight the instincts—this is the formula of degeneration: as long as life is in the ascending line, happiness is the same as instinct.

12

Did he understand this himself, this most intelligent of self-deceivers? Did he confess this to himself in the end, in the wisdom of his courage before death. Socrates wished to die. Not Athens, but his own hand gave him the draught of hemlock; he drove Athens to the poisoned cup. "Socrates is not a doctor," he whispered to himself, "death alone can be a doctor here. . . . Socrates himself has only been ill a long while."

IV. The Germans

FROM HUMAN, ALL TOO HUMAN, II

216*

"GERMAN VIRTUE." There is no denying that from the end of the eighteenth century a current of moral awakening flowed through Europe. Then only Virtue found again the power of speech. She learnt to discover the unrestrained gestures of exaltation and emotion, she was no longer ashamed of herself, and she created philosophies and poems for her own glorifications. If we look for the sources of this current, we come upon Rousseau, but the mythical Rousseau, the phantom formed from the impression left by his writings (one might almost say again, his mythically interpreted writings) and by the indications that he provided himself. He and his public constantly worked at the fashioning of this ideal figure. The other origin lies in the resurrection of the Stoical side of Rome's greatness, whereby the French so nobly carried on the task of the Renaissance. With striking success they proceeded from the reproduction of antique forms to the reproduction of antique characters. Thus they may always claim a title to the highest honors, as the nation which has hitherto given the modern world its best books and its best men. How this twofold archetype, the mythical Rousseau and the resurrected spirit of Rome, affected France's weaker neighbors is particularly noticeable in Germany, which, in consequence of her novel and quite

* From *The Wanderer and His Shadow*.

unwonted impulse to seriousness and loftiness in will and self-control, finally came to feel astonishment at her own new-found virtue, and launched into the world the concept "German virtue," as if this were the most original and hereditary of her possessions. The first great men who transfused into their own blood that French impulse toward greatness and consciousness of the moral will were more honest, and more grateful. Whence comes the moralism of Kant? He is continually reminding us: from Rousseau and the revival of Stoic Rome. The moralism of Schiller has the same source and the same glorification of the source. The moralism of Beethoven in notes is a continual song in praise of Rousseau, the antique French, and Schiller. "Young Germany" was the first to forget its gratitude, because in the meantime people had listened to the preachers of hatred of the French. The "young German" came to the fore with more consciousness than is generally allowed to youths. When he investigated his paternity, he might well think of the proximity of Schiller, Schleiermacher, and Fichte. But he should have looked for his grandfathers in Paris and Geneva, and it was very shortsighted of him to believe what he believed: that virtue was not more than thirty years old. People became used to demanding that the word "German" should connote "virtue," and this process has not been wholly forgotten to this day. Be it observed further that this moral awakening, as may almost be guessed, has resulted only in drawbacks and obstacles to the *recognition* of moral phenomena. What is the entire German philosophy, starting from Kant, with all its French, English, and Italian offshoots and by-products? A semitheological attack upon Helvétius, a rejection of the slowly and laboriously acquired views and signposts of the right road, which in the end he collected and expressed so well. To this day Helvétius is the best-abused of all good moralists and good men in Germany.

FROM THE DAWN OF DAY

167

UNCONDITIONAL HOMAGE. When I think of the most read German philosopher, the most popular German musician, and the most distinguished German statesman, I cannot but acknowledge that life is now rendered unusually arduous for these Germans, this nation of unconditional sentiments, and that, too, by their own great men. We see three magnificent spectacles spread out before us: on each occasion there is a river rushing along in the bed which it has made for itself, and even so agitated that one thinks at times it intends to flow uphill. And yet, however we might admire Schopenhauer, who would not, all things considered, like to have other opinions than his. Who in all greater and smaller things would now share the opinions of Richard Wagner, although there may be truth in the view expressed by some one, viz., that wherever Wagner gave or took offense some problem lay hidden—which, however, he did not unearth for us. And, finally, how many are there who would be willing and eager to agree with Bismarck, if only he could always agree with himself, or were even to show some signs of doing so for the future! It is true that it is by no means astonishing to find statesmen without principles, but with dominant instincts; a versatile mind, actuated by these dominant and violent instincts, and hence without principles —these qualities are looked upon as reasonable and natural in a statesman. But, alas, this has up to the present been so un-German; as un-German as the fuss made about music and the discord and bad temper excited around the person of the musician; or as un-German as the new and extraordinary position taken up by Schopenhauer: he did not feel himself to be either above things or on his knees before them— one or other of these alternatives might still have been German—but he assumed an attitude against things! How incredible and disagreeable! To range one's self with things and nevertheless be their adversary, and finally the adversary of one's self—what can the unconditional admirer do with such an example? And what, again, can he do with three such examples who cannot keep the peace toward one another! Here we see Schopenhauer as the antagonist of Wagner's music, Wagner attacking Bismarck's politics, and Bismarck attacking Wagnerism and Schopenhauerism. What remains for us to do? Where shall we flee with our thirst for wholesale hero worship! Would it not be possible to choose from the music of the musician a few hundred bars of good music which appealed to the heart, and which we should like to take to heart because they are inspired by the heart—could we not stand aside with this small piece of plunder, and forget the rest? And could we not make a similar compromise as regards the philosopher and the statesman—select, take to heart, and in particular forget the rest?

Yes, if only forgetfulness were not so difficult! There was

once a very proud man who would never on any account accept anything, good or evil, from others—from anyone, indeed, but himself. When he wanted to forget, however, he could not bestow this gift upon himself, and was three times compelled to conjure up the spirits. They came, listened to his desire, and said at last, "This is the only thing it is not in our power to give!" Could not the Germans take warning by this experience of Manfred? Why, then, should the spirits be conjured up? It is useless. We never forget what we endeavor to forget. And how great would be the "balance" which we should have to forget if we wished henceforth to continue wholesale admirers of these three great men! It would therefore be far more advisable to profit by the excellent opportunity offered us to try something new, i.e., to advance in the spirit of honesty toward ourselves and become, instead of a nation of credulous repetition and of bitter and blind animosity, a people of conditional assent and benevolent opposition. We must come to learn in the first place, however, that unconditional homage to people is something rather ridiculous, that a change of view on this point would not discredit even Germans, and that there is a profound and memorable saying: "Ce qui importe, ce ne sont point les personnes: mais les choses." This saying is like the man who uttered it—great, honest, simple, and silent—just like Carnot, the soldier and Republican. But may I at the present time speak thus to Germans of a Frenchman, and a Republican into the bargain? Perhaps not: perhaps I must not even recall what Niebuhr in his time dared to say to the Germans: that no one had made such an impression of true greatness upon him as Carnot.

190

FORMER GERMAN CULTURE. When the Germans began to interest other European nations, which is not so very long ago, it was owing to a culture which they no longer possess today, and which they have indeed shaken off with a blind ardor, as if it had been some disease; and yet they have not been able to replace it by anything better than political and national lunacy. They have in this way succeeded in becoming even more interesting to other nations than they were formerly through their culture: and may that satisfy them! It is nevertheless undeniable that this German culture has fooled Europeans, and that it did not deserve the interest shown in it, and much less the imitation and emulation displayed by other nations in trying to rival it.

Let us look back for a moment upon Schiller, Wilhelm von Humboldt, Schleiermacher, Hegel, and Schelling; let us read their correspondence and mingle for a time with the large circle of their followers. What have they in common, what characteristics have they, that fill us, as we are now, partly with a feeling of nausea and partly with pitiful and touching emotions? First and foremost, the passion for appearing at all costs to be morally exalted, and then the desire for giving utterance to brilliant, feeble, and inconsequential remarks, together with their fixed purpose of looking upon everything (characters, passions, times, customs) as beautiful—"beautiful," alas, in accordance with a bad and vague taste, which nevertheless pretended to be of Hellenic origin. We behold in these people a weak, good-natured, and glistening idealism, which, above all, wished to exhibit noble attitudes and noble voices, something at once presumptuous and inoffensive, and animated by a cordial aversion to "cold" or "dry" reality—as also to anatomy, complete passions, and every kind of philosophical continence and scepticism, but especially toward the knowledge of nature in so far as it was impossible to use it as religious symbolism.

Goethe, in his own characteristic fashion, observed from afar these movements of German culture: placing himself beyond their influence, gently remonstrating, silent, more and more confirmed in his own better course. A little later, and Schopenhauer also was an observer of these movements—a great deal of the world and devilry of the world had again been revealed to him, and he spoke of it both roughly and enthusiastically, for there is a certain beauty in this devilry! And what was it, then, that really seduced the foreigners and prevented them from viewing this movement as did Goethe and Schopenhauer, or, better, from ignoring it altogether? It was that faint luster, that inexplicable starlight which formed a mysterious halo around this culture. The foreigners said to themselves: "This is all very, very remote from us; our sight, hearing, understanding, enjoyment, and powers of valuations are lost here, but in spite of that there may be some stars! There may be something in it! Is it possible that the Germans have quietly discovered some corner of heaven and settled there? We must try to come nearer to these Germans." So they did begin to come nearer to the Germans, while not so very long afterward the Germans put themselves to some trouble to get rid of this starlight halo: they knew only too well that they had not been in heaven, but only in a cloud!

193

ESPRIT AND MORALS. The German, who possesses the secret of knowing how to be tedious in spite of wit, knowledge, and feeling, and who has habituated himself to consider tediousness as moral, is in dread in the presence of French *esprit* lest it should tear out the eyes of morality—but a dread mingled with "fascination," like that experienced by the little bird in the presence of the rattlesnake.

Amongst all the celebrated Germans none possessed more *esprit* than Hegel, but he also had that great German dread of it which brought about his peculiar and defective style. For the nature of this style resembles a kernel, which is wrapped up so many times in an outer covering that it can scarcely peep through, now and then glancing forth bashfully and inquisitively, like "young women peeping through their veils," to use the words of that old woman-hater, Aeschylus. This kernel, however, is a witty though often impertinent joke on intellectual subjects, a subtle and daring combination of words, such as is necessary in a society of thinkers as gilding for a scientific pill—but, enveloped as it is in an almost impenetrable cover, it exhibits itself as the most abstruse science, and likewise as the worst possible moral tediousness. Here the Germans had a permissible form of *esprit* and they reveled in it with such boundless delight that even Schopenhauer's unusually fine understanding could not grasp it—during the whole of his life he thundered against the spectacle that the Germans offered to him, but he could never explain it.

197

ENMITY OF THE GERMANS TOWARD ENLIGHTENMENT. Let us consider the contributions which in the first half of this century the Germans made to general culture by their intellectual work. In the first place, let us take the German philosophers: they went back to the first and oldest stage of speculation, for they were content with conceptions instead of explanations, like the thinkers of dreamy epochs—a prescientific type of philosophy was thus revived by them. Secondly, we have the German historians and romanticists: their efforts on the whole aimed at restoring to the place of honor certain old and primitive sentiments, especially Christianity, the "soul of the people," folklore, folk speech, medievalism, Oriental asceticism, and Hinduism. In the third place, there are the natural philosophers who fought against the spirit of Newton and Voltaire, and, like Goethe and Schopenhauer, endeavored to re-establish the idea of a deified or diabolized nature, and of its absolute ethical and symbolical meaning. The main general tendency of the Germans was directed against enlightenment and against those social revolutions which were stupidly mistaken for the consequences of enlightenment: the piety toward everything that existed tried to become piety toward everything that had ever existed, only in order that heart and mind might be permitted to fill themselves and gush forth again, thus leaving no space for future and novel aims. The cult of feeling took the place of the cult of reason, and the German musicians, as the best exponents of all that is invisible, enthusiastic, legendary, and passionate, showed themselves more successful in building up the new temple than all the other artists in words and thoughts.

If, in considering these details, we have taken into account the fact that many good things were said and investigated, and that many things have since then been more fairly judged than on any previous occasion, there yet remains to be said of the whole that it was a general danger, and one by no means small, to set knowledge altogether below feeling under the appearance of an entire and definitive acquaintance with the past—and, to use that expression of Kant, who thus defined his own particular task—"To make way again for belief by fixing the limits of knowledge." Let us once more breathe freely, the hour of this danger is past! And yet, strange to say, the very spirits which these Germans conjured up with such eloquence have at length become the most dangerous for the intentions of those who did conjure them up: history, the comprehension of origin and development, sympathy with the past, the new passion for feeling and knowledge, after they had been for a long time at the service of this obscure exalted and retrograde spirit, have once more assumed another nature, and are now soaring with outstretched wings above the heads of those who once upon a time conjured them forth, as new and stronger genii of that very enlightenment to combat which they had been resuscitated. It is this enlightenment which we have now to carry forward—caring nothing for the fact that there has been and still is "a great revolution," and again a great "reaction" against it: these are but playful

crests of foam when compared with the truly great current
on which we float, and want to float.

207

THE ATTITUDE OF THE GERMANS TO MORALITY.
A German is capable of great things, but he is unlikely to
accomplish them, for he obeys whenever he can, as suits a
naturally lazy intellect. If he is ever in the dangerous situation of having to stand alone and cast aside his sloth, when
he finds it no longer possible to disappear like a cipher in a
number (in which respect he is far inferior to a Frenchman
or an Englishman), he shows his true strength: then he becomes dangerous, evil, deep, and audacious, and exhibits to
the light of day that wealth of latent energy which he had
previously carried hidden in himself, and in which no one,
not even himself, had ever believed. When in such a case a
German obeys himself—it is very exceptional for him to do
so—he does so with the same heaviness, inflexibility, and endurance with which he obeys his prince and performs his official duties; so that, as I have said, he is then capable of
great things which bear no relation to the "weak disposition"
he attributes to himself.

As a rule, however, he is afraid of depending upon himself alone, he is afraid of taking the initiative; that is why
Germany uses up so many officials and so much ink. Light-
heartedness is a stranger to the German; he is too timid for
it; but in entirely new situations which rouse him from his
torpor he exhibits an almost frivolous spirit—he then de-
lights in the novelty of his new position as if it were some
intoxicating drink, and he is, as we know, quite a connoisseur
in intoxication. It thus happens that the German of the present day is almost always frivolous in politics, though even
here he has the advantage and prejudice of thoroughness
and seriousness; and, although he may take full advantage of
these qualities in negotiations with other political powers, he
nevertheless rejoices inwardly at being able for once in his
life to feel enthusiastic and capricious, to show his fondness
for innovations, and to change persons, parties, and hopes
as if they were masks. Those learned German scholars who
hitherto have been considered as the most German of Germans were and perhaps still are as good as the German
soldiers on account of their profound and almost childish
inclination to obey in all external things, and on account of
being often compelled to stand alone in science and to an-

swer for many things; if they can only preserve their proud, simple, and patient disposition and their freedom from political madness at those times when the wind changes, we may yet expect great things from them—such as they are or such as they were, they are the embryonic stage of something higher.

So far the advantages and disadvantages of the Germans, including even their learned men, have been that they were more given to superstition and showed greater eagerness to believe than any of the other nations; their vices are, and always have been, their drunkenness and suicidal inclinations (the latter a proof of the clumsiness of their intellect, which is easily tempted to throw away the reins). Their danger is to be sought in everything that binds down the faculties of reason and unchains the passions (as, for example, the excessive use of music and spirits), for the German passion acts contrarily to its own advantage, and is as self-destructive as the passions of the drunkard. Indeed, German enthusiasm is worth less than that of other nations, for it is barren. When a German ever did anything great it was done at a time of danger, or when his courage was high, with his teeth firmly set and his prudence on the alert, and often enough in a fit of generosity. Intercourse with these Germans is indeed advisable, for almost every one of them has something to give, if we can only understand how to make him find it, or rather recover it (for he is very untidy in storing away his knowledge).

Well: when people of this type occupy themselves with morals, what precisely will be the morality that will satisfy them? In the first place, they will wish to see idealized in their morals their sincere instinct for obedience. "Man must have something which he can implicitly obey"—this is a German sentiment, a German deduction; it is the basis of all German moral teaching. How different is the impression, however, when we compare this with the entire morality of the ancient world! All those Greek thinkers, however varied they may appear to us, seem to resemble, as moralists, the gymnastic teacher who encourages his pupils by saying, "Come, follow me! Submit to my discipline! Then perhaps you may carry off the prize from all the other Greeks." Personal distinction: such was the virtue of antiquity. Submission, obedience, whether public or private: such is German virtue. Long before Kant set forth his doctrine of the Categorical Imperative, Luther, actuated by the same impulse, said that there surely must be a being in whom man could trust implicitly—it was his proof of the existence of God; it was his wish, coarser and more popular than that of Kant, that people should implicitly obey a person and not an idea, and Kant also finally took his roundabout route through morals merely that he might secure obedience for the person. This is indeed the worship of the German, the more so as there is now less worship left in his religion.

The Greeks and Romans had other opinions on these matters, and would have laughed at such "there must be a being": it is part of the boldness of their Southern nature to take up a stand against "implicit belief," and to retain in their inmost heart a trace of scepticism against all and everyone, whether God, man, or idea. The thinker of antiquity went even further, and said *nil admirari:* in this phrase he saw reflected all philosophy. A German, Schopenhauer, goes so far in the contrary direction as to say: *admirari id est philosophari.* But what if, as happens now and then, the German should attain to that state of mind which would enable him to perform great things? if the hour of exception comes, the hour of disobedience? I do not think Schopenhauer is right in saying that the single advantage the Germans have over other nations is that there are more atheists among them than elsewhere; but I do know this: whenever the German reaches the state in which he is capable of great things, he invariably raises himself above morals! And why should he not? Now he has something new to do, viz., to command—either himself or others! But this German morality of his has not taught him how to command! Commanding has been forgotten in it.

481

TWO GERMANS. If we compare Kant and Schopenhauer with Plato, Spinoza, Pascal, Rousseau, and Goethe, with reference to their souls and not their intellects, we shall see that the two first-named thinkers are at a disadvantage: their thoughts do not constitute a passionate history of their souls—we are not led to expect in them romance, crises, catastrophies, or death struggles. Their thinking is not at the same time the involuntary biography of a soul, but in the case of Kant merely of a head; and in the case of Schopenhauer again merely the description and reflection of a character ("the invariable") and the pleasure which this reflection causes, that is to say, the pleasure of meeting with an intellect of the first order.

Kant, when he shimmers through his thoughts, appears to

us as an honest and honorable man in the best sense of the
words, but likewise as an insignificant one: he is wanting in
breadth and power; he had not come through many experiences, and his method of working did not allow him sufficient time to undergo experiences. Of course, in speaking
of experiences, I do not refer to the ordinary external events
of life, but to those fatalities and convulsions which occur
in the course of the most solitary and quiet life which has
some leisure and glows with the passion for thinking. Schopenhauer has at all events one advantage over him, for he
at least was distinguished by a certain fierce ugliness of
disposition, which showed itself in hatred, desire, vanity, and
suspicion; he was of a rather more ferocious disposition, and
had both time and leisure to indulge this ferocity. But he
lacked "development," which was also wanting in his range
of thought: he had no "history."

FROM THE JOYFUL WISDOM

146

GERMAN HOPES. Do not let us forget that the names
of peoples are generally names of reproach. The Tartars, for
example, according to their name, are "the dogs"; they were
so christened by the Chinese. *Deutschen* (Germans) means
originally "heathen"; it is thus that the Goths after their
conversion named the great mass of their unbaptized fellow
tribes, according to the indication in their translation of the
Septuagint, in which the heathen are designated by the word
which in Greek signifies "the nations." (See Ulfilas.) It might
still be possible for the Germans to make an honorable name
ultimately out of their old name of reproach, by becoming
the first *non-Christian* nation of Europe; for which purpose
Schopenhauer, to their honor, regarded them as highly qualified. The work of *Luther* would thus be consummated—he
who taught them to be anti-Roman and to say: "Here *I*
stand! *I* cannot do otherwise!"

357

THE OLD PROBLEM: "WHAT IS GERMAN?"—Let us
count up apart the real acquisitions of philosophical thought

for which we have to thank German intellects. Are they in any allowable sense to be counted also to the credit of the whole race? Can we say that they are at the same time the work of the "German soul," or at least a symptom of it, in the sense in which we are accustomed to think, for example, of Plato's ideomania, his almost religious madness for form, as an event and an evidence of the "Greek soul"? Or would the reverse perhaps be true? Were they so individual, so much an exception to the spirit of the race, as was, for example, Goethe's Paganism with a good conscience? Or as Bismarck's Machiavellism was with a good conscience, his so-called "practical politics" in Germany? Did our philosophers perhaps even go counter to the *need* of the "German soul"? In short, were the German philosophers really philosophical *Germans?* I call to mind three cases. Firstly, *Leibnitz's* incomparable insight—with which he obtained the advantage not only over Descartes but over all who had philosophized up to his time—that consciousness is only an accident of mental representation and *not* its necessary and essential attribute; that consequently what we call consciousness only constitutes a state of our spiritual and psychical world (perhaps a morbid state), and is *far from being that world itself*—is there anything German in this thought, the profundity of which has not as yet been exhausted? Is there reason to think that a person of the Latin race would not readily have stumbled on this reversal of the apparent?—for it is a reversal. Let us call to mind secondly the immense note of interrogation which *Kant* wrote after the notion of causality. Not that he at all doubted its legitimacy, like Hume; on the contrary, he began cautiously to define the domain within which this notion has significance generally (we have not even yet got finished with the marking out of these limits). Let us take thirdly the astonishing hit of *Hegel*, who stuck at no logical usage or fastidiousness when he ventured to teach that the conceptions of kinds develop *out of one another*, with which theory the thinkers in Europe were prepared for the last great scientific movement, for Darwinism—for without Hegel there would have been no Darwin. Is there anything German in this Hegelian innovation which first introduced the decisive conception of evolution into science? Yes, without doubt we feel that there is something of ourselves "discovered" and divined in all three cases; we are thankful for it, and at the same time surprised; each of these three principles is a thoughtful piece of German self-confession, self-understanding, and self-knowledge. We feel with Leibnitz that "our inner world is far richer, ampler, and more concealed"; as Germans we are doubtful, like Kant, about the ultimate validity of scientific knowledge of nature, and in general about whatever *can* be known *causaliter:* the *knowable* as such now appears to us of *less* worth. We Germans should still have been Hegelians, even though there had never been a Hegel, inasmuch as we (in contradistinction to all Latin peoples) instinctively attribute to becoming, to evolution, a profounder significance and higher value than to that which "is"—we hardly believe at all in the validity of the concept "being." This is all the more the case because we are not inclined to concede to our human logic that it is logic in itself, that it is the only kind of logic (we should rather like, on the contrary, to convince ourselves that it is only a special case, and perhaps one of the strangest and most stupid). A fourth question would be whether also *Schopenhauer* with his Pessimism, that is to say the problem of *the worth of existence,* had to be a German. I think not. The event *after* which this problem was to be expected with certainty, so that an astronomer of the soul could have calculated the day and the hour for it—namely, the decay of the belief in the Christian God, the victory of scientific atheism —is a universal European event, in which all races are to have their share of service and honor. On the contrary, it has to be ascribed precisely to the Germans—those with whom Schopenhauer was contemporary—that they delayed this victory of atheism longest, and endangered it most. Hegel especially was its retarder par excellence, in virtue of the grandiose attempt which he made to persuade us of the divinity of existence, with the help at the very last of our sixth sense, "the historical sense." As philosopher, Schopenhauer was the *first* avowed and inflexible atheist we Germans have had: his hostility to Hegel had here its background. The nondivinity of existence was regarded by him as something understood, palpable, indisputable; he always lost his philosophical composure and got into a passion when he saw anyone hesitate and beat about the bush here. It is at this point that his thorough uprightness of character comes in: unconditional, honest atheism is precisely the *preliminary condition* for his raising the problem, as a final and hard-won victory of the European conscience, as the most prolific act of two thousand years' discipline to truth, which in the end no longer tolerates the *lie* of the belief in a God. . . . One sees what has really gained the victory over the Christian God—Christian morality itself, the conception of veracity, taken ever more strictly, the confessional subtlety of the Christian conscience, translated and sublimated to the scientific conscience, to intellectual purity at any price. To look upon nature as if it were a proof of the goodness and care of a God; to interpret history in honor of a divine reason, as a constant testimony to a moral order in the world and a moral final purpose; to explain personal experiences as pious men have long enough explained them, as if everything were a dispensation or intimation of Providence, something planned and sent on behalf of the salvation of the soul: all that is now *past*, it has conscience *against* it, it is regarded by all the more acute consciences as disreputable and dishonorable, as mendaciousness, femininism, weakness, and cowardice—by virtue of this severity, if by anything, we are *good* Europeans, the heirs of Europe's longest and bravest self-conquest. When we thus reject the Christian interpretation, and condemn its "significance" as a forgery, we are immediately confronted in a striking manner with the *Schopenhauerian* question: *Has existence then a significance at all?*—the question which will require a couple of centuries even to be completely heard in all its profundity. Schopenhauer's own answer to this question was—if I may be forgiven for saying so—a premature, juvenile reply, a mere compromise, a stoppage and sticking in the very same Christian-ascetic, moral perspectives, *the belief in which had got notice to quit* along with the belief in God. . . . But he *raised* the question—as a good European, as we have said, and *not* as a German. Or did the Germans prove at least by the way in which they seized on the Schopenhauerian question their inner connection and relationship to him, their preparation for his problem, and their *need* of it? That there has been thinking and printing even in Germany since Schopenhauer's time on the problem raised by him—it was late enough!—does not at all suffice to enable us to decide in favor of this closer relationship; one could, on the contrary, lay great stress on the peculiar *awkwardness* of their post-Schopenhauerian Pessimism—Germans evidently do not behave themselves there as in their element. I do not at all allude here to Eduard von Hartmann; on the contrary, my old suspicion is not vanished even at present that he is *too clever* for us; I mean to say that as arrant rogue from the very first, he did not perhaps make merry solely over German Pessimism—and that in the end he might probably "bequeathe" to them the truth as to how far a person could bamboozle the Germans themselves in the age of bubble companies. But further, are we perhaps to reckon to the honor of Germans, the old humming-top, Bahnsen, who all his life spun about with the greatest pleasure around his

realistically dialectic misery and "personal ill luck"—was
that German? (In passing I recommend his writings for the
purpose for which I myself have used them, as antipessimistic
fare, especially on account of his *elegantia psychologica,*
which, it seems to me, could alleviate even the most con-
stipated body and soul.) Or would it be proper to count such
dilettanti and old maids as the mawkish apostle of virginity,
Mainländer, among the genuine Germans? After all he was
probably a Jew (all Jews become mawkish when they
moralize). Neither Bahnsen, nor Mainländer, nor even
Eduard von Hartmann, gives us a reliable grasp of the question whether the pessimism of Schopenhauer (his frightened
glance into an undeified world, which has become stupid,
blind, deranged, and problematic, his *honorable* fright) was
not only an exceptional case among Germans but a *German*
event; while everything else which stands in the foreground,
like our valiant politics and our joyful Jingoism (which decidedly enough regards everything with reference to a principle sufficiently unphilosophical: *"Deutschland, Deutschland,
über Alles,"* * consequently *sub specie speciei,* namely, the
German *species*), testifies very plainly to the contrary. No!
The Germans of today are *not* pessimists! And Schopenhauer was a pessimist, I repeat it once more, as a good
European, and *not* as a German.

FROM BEYOND GOOD AND EVIL

240

I HEARD, once again for the first time, Richard Wagner's overture to *Die Meistersinger*: it is a piece of magnificent, gor-
geous, heavy, latter-day art, which has the pride to presuppose two centuries of music as still living, in order that it
may be understood—it is an honor to Germans that such a
pride did not miscalculate! What flavors and forces, what
seasons and climes do we not find mingled in it! It impresses us at one time as ancient, at another time as foreign,
bitter, and too modern; it is as arbitrary as it is pompously
traditional; it is not infrequently roguish, still oftener rough
and coarse—it has fire and courage, and at the same time

---

* "Germany, Germany, above all": the first line of the German national song.—TR.

the loose, dun-colored skin of fruits which ripen too late.
It flows broad and full; and suddenly there is a moment of
inexplicable hesitation, like a gap that opens between cause
and effect, an oppression that makes us dream, almost a
nightmare; but already it broadens and widens anew, the
old stream of delight—the most manifold delight—of
old and new happiness, including *especially* the joy of the
artist in himself, which he refuses to conceal, his astonished, happy cognizance of his mastery of the expedition
here employed, the new, newly acquired, imperfectly tested
expedients of art which he apparently betrays to us. All in
all, however, no beauty, no South, nothing of the delicate
southern clearness of the sky, nothing of grace, no dance,
hardly a will to logic; a certain clumsiness even, which is
also emphasized, as though the artist wished to say to us:
"It is part of my intention"; a cumbersome drapery, something arbitrarily barbaric and ceremonious, a flirring of
learned and venerable conceits and witticisms; something
German in the best and worst sense of the word, something in the German style, manifold, formless, and inexhaustible; a certain German potency and superplenitude of
soul, which is not afraid to hide itself under the *raffine-
ments* of decadence—which, perhaps, feels itself most at
ease there; a real, genuine token of the German soul, which
is at the same time young and aged, too ripe and yet still
too rich in futurity. This kind of music expresses best what
I think of the Germans: they belong to the day before yesterday and the day after tomorrow—*they have as yet no
today*.

244

There was a time when it was customary to call Germans
"deep," by way of distinction; but now that the most successful type of new Germanism is covetous of quite other
honors, and perhaps misses "smartness" in all that has depth,
it is almost opportune and patriotic to doubt whether we did
not formerly deceive ourselves with that commendation: in
short, whether German depth is not at bottom something
different and worse—and something from which, thank God,
we are on the point of successfully ridding ourselves. Let
us try, then, to relearn with regard to German depth; the
only thing necessary for the purpose is a little vivisection of
the German soul. The German soul is above all manifold,
varied in its source, aggregated and superimposed, rather

than actually built; this is owing to its origin. A German who would embolden himself to assert: "Two souls, alas, dwell in my breast," would make a bad guess at the truth, or, more correctly, he would come far short of the truth about the number of souls. As a people made up of the most extraordinary mixing and mingling of races, perhaps even with a preponderance of the pre-Aryan element, as the "people of the center" in every sense of the term, the Germans are more intangible, more ample, more contradictory, more unknown, more incalculable, more surprising, and even more terrifying than other peoples are to themselves—they escape *definition*, and are thereby alone the despair of the French. It is characteristic of the Germans that the question: "What is German?" never dies out among them. Kotzebue certainly knew his Germans well enough: "we are known," they cried jubilantly to him—but Sand also thought he knew them. Jean Paul knew what he was doing when he declared himself incensed at Fichte's lying but patriotic flatteries and exaggerations—but it is probable that Goethe thought differently about Germans from Jean Paul, even though he acknowledged him to be right with regard to Fichte. It is a question what Goethe really thought about the Germans, but about many things around him he never spoke explicitly, and all his life he knew how to keep an astute silence—probably he had good reason for it. It is certain that it was not the "Wars of Independence" that made him look up more joyfully, any more than it was the French Revolution —the event on account of which he *reconstructed* his "Faust," and indeed the whole problem of "man," was the appearance of Napoleon. There are words of Goethe in which he condemns with impatient severity, as from a foreign land, that which Germans take a pride in; he once defined the famous German turn of mind as "indulgence toward its own and others' weaknesses." Was he wrong? It is characteristic of Germans that one is seldom entirely wrong about them. The German soul has passages and galleries in it, there are caves, hiding places, and dungeons therein; its disorder has much of the charm of the mysterious; the German is well acquainted with the bypaths to chaos. And as everything loves its symbol, so the German loves the clouds and all that is obscure, evolving, crepuscular, damp, and shrouded; it seems to him that everything uncertain, undeveloped, self-displacing, and growing is "deep." The German himself does not *exist;* he is *becoming,* he is "developing himself." "Development" is therefore the essentially German discovery and hit in the great domain of philosophical formulas—a ruling idea, which, together with German beer and German music, is laboring to Germanize all Europe. Foreigners are astonished and attracted by the riddles which the conflicting nature at the basis of the German soul propounds to them (riddles which Hegel systematized and Richard Wagner has in the end set to music). "Good-natured and spiteful"—Such a juxtaposition, preposterous in the case of every other people, is unfortunately only too often justified in Germany: one has only to live for a while among Swabians to know this! The clumsiness of the German scholar and his social distastefulness agree alarmingly well with his psychical ropedancing and nimble boldness, of which all the gods have learnt to be afraid. If anyone wishes to see the "German soul" demonstrated *ad oculos,* let him only look at German taste, at German arts and manners; what boorish indifference to "taste"! How the noblest and the commonest stand there in juxtaposition! How disorderly and how rich is the whole constitution of this soul! The German *drags* at his soul, he drags at everything he experiences. He digests his events badly; he never gets "done" with them; and German depth is often only a difficult, hesitating "digestion." And just as all chronic invalids, all dyspeptics, like what is convenient, so the German loves "frankness" and "honesty"; it is so *convenient* to be frank and honest!—This confidingness, this complaisance, this showing-the-cards of German *honesty,* is probably the most dangerous and most successful disguise which the German is up to nowadays: it is his proper Mephistophelean art; with this he can "still achieve much"! The German lets himself go, and thereby gazes with faithful, blue, empty German eyes—and other countries immediately confound him with his dressing gown!—I meant to say that, let "German depth" be what it will—among ourselves alone we perhaps take the liberty to laugh at it—we shall do well to continue henceforth to honor its appearance and good name, and not barter away too cheaply our old reputation as a people of depth for Prussian "smartness," and Berlin wit and sand. It is wise for a people to pose, and *let* itself be regarded, as profound, clumsy, good-natured, honest, and foolish: it might even be —profound to do so! Finally, we should do honor to our name—we are not called the *tiusche Volk* (deceptive people) for nothing. . . .

251

It must be taken into the bargain, if various clouds and disturbances—in short, slight attacks of stupidity—pass over the spirit of a people that suffers and *wants* to suffer from national nervous fever and political ambition; for instance, among present-day Germans there is alternately the anti-French folly, the anti-Semitic folly, the anti-Polish folly, the Christian-romantic folly, the Wagnerian folly, the Teutonic folly, the Prussian folly (just look at those poor historians, the Sybels and Treitschkes, and their closely bandaged heads), and whatever else these little obscurations of the German spirit and conscience may be called. May it be forgiven me that I, too, when on a short daring sojourn on very infected ground, did not remain wholly exempt from the disease, but like everyone else began to entertain thoughts about matters which did not concern me—the first symptom of political infection. About the Jews, for instance, listen to the following: I have never yet met a German who was favorably inclined to the Jews; and however decided the repudiation of actual anti-Semitism may be on the part of all prudent and political men, this prudence and policy is not perhaps directed against the nature of the sentiment itself, but only against its dangerous excess, and especially against the distasteful and infamous expression of this excess of sentiment—on this point we must not deceive ourselves. That Germany has amply *sufficient* Jews, that the German stomach, the German blood, has difficulty (and will long have difficulty) in disposing only of this quantity of "Jew"—as the Italian, the Frenchman, and the Englishman have done by means of a stronger digestion—that is the unmistakable declaration and language of a general instinct, to which one must listen and according to which one must act. "Let no more Jews come in! And shut the doors, especially toward the East (also toward Austria)!"—thus commands the instinct of a people whose nature is still feeble and uncertain, so that it could be easily wiped out, easily extinguished, by a stronger race. The Jews, however, are beyond all doubt the strongest, toughest, and purest race at present living in Europe; they know how to succeed even under the worst conditions (in fact better than under favorable ones) by means of virtues of some sort, which one would like nowadays to label as vices—owing above all to a resolute faith which does not need to be ashamed before "modern ideas"; they alter only, *when* they do alter, in the same way that the Russian Empire makes its conquest—as an empire that has plenty of time and is not of yesterday —namely, according to the principle, "as slowly as possible"! A thinker who has the future of Europe at heart will, in all his perspectives concerning the future, calculate upon the Jews, as he will calculate upon the Russians, as above all the surest and likeliest factors in the great play and battle of forces. That which is at present called a "nation" in Europe, and is really rather a *res facta* than *nata* (indeed, sometimes confusingly similar to a *res ficta et picta*), is in every case something evolving, young, easily displaced, and not yet a race, much less such a race *aere perennius*, as the Jews are: such "nations" should most carefully avoid all hotheaded rivalry and hostility! It is certain that the Jews, if they desired—or if they were driven to it, as the anti-Semites seem to wish—*could* now have the ascendancy, nay, literally the supremacy, over Europe; that they are *not* working and planning for that end is equally certain. Meanwhile, they rather wish and desire, even somewhat importunately, to be insorbed and absorbed by Europe; they long to be finally settled, authorized, and respected somewhere, and wish to put an end to the nomadic life, to the "wandering Jew";—and one should certainly take account of this impulse and tendency, and *make advances* to it (it possibly betokens a mitigation of the Jewish instincts): for which purpose it would perhaps be useful and fair to banish the anti-Semitic bawlers out of the country. One should make advances with all prudence, and with selection, pretty much as the English nobility do. It stands to reason that the more powerful and strongly marked types of new Germanism could enter into relation with the Jews with the least hesitation, for instance, the nobleman officer from the Prussian border; it would be interesting in many ways to see whether the genius for money and patience (and especially some intellect and intellectuality—sadly lacking in the place referred to) could not in addition be annexed and trained to the hereditary art of commanding and obeying—for both of which the country in question has now a classic reputation. But here it is expedient to break off my festal discourse and my sprightly Teutonomania; for I have already reached my *serious topic*, the "European problem," as I understand it, the rearing of a new ruling caste for Europe.

FROM THE TWILIGHT OF THE IDOLS

33

What trifles constitute happiness! The sound of a bag-pipe. Without music life would be a mistake. The German imagines even God as a songster.

Things the Germans Lack

1

AMONG Germans at the present day it does not suffice to have intellect; one is actually forced to appropriate it, to lay claim to it.

Maybe I know the Germans, perhaps I may tell them a few home truths. Modern Germany represents such an enormous store of inherited and acquired capacity that for some time it might spend this accumulated treasure even with some prodigality. It is no superior culture that has ultimately become prevalent with this modern tendency, nor is it by any means delicate taste, or noble beauty of the instincts; but rather a number of virtues more manly than any that other European countries can show. An amount of good spirits and self-respect, plenty of firmness in human relations and in the reciprocity of duties; much industry and much perseverance—and a certain inherited soberness which is much more in need of a spur than of a brake. Let me add that in this country people still obey without feeling that obedience humiliates. And no one despises his opponent.

You observe that it is my desire to be fair to the Germans, and in this respect I should not like to be untrue to my-self—I must therefore also state my objections to them. It costs a good deal to attain to a position of power; for power *stultifies*. The Germans—they were once called a peo-ple of thinkers: do they really think at all at present? Now-adays the Germans are bored by intellect, they mistrust in-tellect; politics have swallowed up all earnestness for really

intellectual things—"Germany, Germany above all." * I fear
this was the deathblow to German philosophy. "Are there
any German philosophers? Are there any German poets?
Are there any good German books?" people ask me abroad.
I blush; but with that pluck which is peculiar to me, even in
moments of desperation, I reply: "Yes, Bismarck!"—Could I
have dared to confess what books *are* read today? Cursed
instinct of mediocrity!

4

Let us examine another aspect of the question: it is not
only obvious that German culture is declining, but adequate
reasons for this decline are not lacking. After all, nobody
can spend more than he has—this is true of individuals,
it is also true of nations. If you spend your strength in
acquiring power, or in politics on a large scale; or in
economy, or in universal commerce, or in parliamentarism,
or in military interests—if you dissipate the modicum of reason, of earnestness, of will, and of self-control that constitutes your nature in one particular fashion, you cannot
dissipate it in another. Culture and the state—let no one
be deceived on this point—are antagonists: a "culture-state" †
is merely a modern idea. The one lives upon the other,
the one flourishes at the expense of the other. All great
periods of culture have been periods of political decline;
that which is great from the standpoint of culture was always unpolitical—even antipolitical. Goethe's heart opened
at the coming of Napoleon—it closed at the thought of the
"Wars of Liberation." At the very moment when Germany
arose as a great power in the world of politics, France won
new importance as a force in the world of culture. Even at
this moment a large amount of fresh intellectual earnestness and passion has emigrated to Paris; the question of
pessimism, for instance, and the question of Wagner; in France
almost all psychological and artistic questions are considered
with incomparably more subtlety and thoroughness than
they are in Germany—the Germans are even incapable of
this kind of earnestness. In the history of European culture the rise of the Empire signifies, above all, a displace-

---

* The German national hymn: *"Deutschland, Deutschland über alles."*
—Tr.

† The word *Kultur-Staat*, "culture-state," has become a standard expression in the German language, and is applied to the leading European states.—Tr.

ment of the center of gravity. Everywhere people are already aware of this: in things that really matter—and these after all constitute culture—the Germans are no longer worth considering. I ask you, can you show me one single man of brains who could be mentioned in the same breath with other European thinkers, like your Goethe, your Hegel, your Heinrich Heine, and your Schopenhauer?—The fact that there is no longer a single German philosopher worth mentioning is an increasing wonder.

5

Everything that matters has been lost sight of by the whole of the higher educational system of Germany: the end quite as much as the means to that end. People forget that education, the process of cultivation itself, is the end— and not "the Empire"—they forget that the *educator* is required for this end—and not the public-school teacher and university scholar. Educators are needed who are themselves educated, superior and noble intellects, who can prove that they are thus qualified, that they are ripe and mellow products of culture at every moment of their lives, in word and in gesture—not the learned louts who, like "superior wet nurses," are now thrust upon the youth of the land by public schools and universities. With but rare exceptions, that which is lacking in Germany is the first prerequisite of education—that is to say, the educators; hence the decline of German culture. One of those rarest exceptions is my highly respected friend Jakob Burckhardt of Basel: to him above all is Basel indebted for its foremost position in human culture. What the higher schools of Germany really do accomplish is this, they brutally train a vast crowd of young men, in the smallest amount of time possible, to become useful and exploitable servants of the state. "Higher education" and a vast crowd—these terms contradict each other from the start. All superior education can only concern the exception: a man must be privileged in order to have a right to such a great privilege. All great and beautiful things cannot be a common possession: *pulchrum est paucorum hominum.* What is it that brings about the decline of German culture? The fact that "higher education" is no longer a special privilege—the democracy of a process of cultivation that has become "general," *common.* Nor must it be forgotten that the privileges of the military profession by urging many too many to attend the higher schools involve the downfall of the latter. In modern Germany nobody is at liberty to give his children a noble education; in regard to their teachers, their curriculums, and their educational aims, our higher schools are one and all established upon a fundamentally doubtful mediocre basis. Everywhere, too, a hastiness which is unbecoming rules supreme; just as if something would be forfeited if the young man were not "finished" at the age of twenty-three, or did not know how to reply to the most essential question, "which calling to choose?"—The superior kind of man, if you please, does not like "callings," precisely because he knows himself to be called. He has time, he takes time, he cannot possibly think of becoming "finished"—in the matter of higher culture, a man of thirty years is a beginner, a child. Our overcrowded public schools, our accumulation of foolishly manufactured public-school masters, are a scandal; maybe there are very serious *motives* for defending this state of affairs, as was shown quite recently by the professors of Heidelberg, but there can be no reasons for doing so.

FROM THE ANTICHRIST*

61

Here it is necessary to revive a memory which will be a hundred times more painful to Germans. The Germans have destroyed the last great harvest of culture which was to be garnered for Europe—it destroyed the *Renaissance*. Does anybody at last understand, *will* anybody understand what the Renaissance was? *The transvaluation of Christian values,* the attempt undertaken with all means, all instincts and all genius to make the *opposite* values, the *noble* values triumph. . . . Hitherto there has been only *this* great war: there has never yet been a more decisive question than the Renaissance—*my* question is the question of the Renaissance: there has never been a more fundamental, a more direct and a more severe *attack*, delivered with a whole front upon the center of the foe. To attack at the decisive quarter, at the very seat of Christianity, and there to place *noble* values on the throne, that is to say, to *introduce* them into the in-

* From *The Twilight of the Idols.*

stincts, into the most fundamental needs and desires of those sitting there. . . . I see before me a possibility perfectly magic in its charm and glorious coloring—it seems to me to scintillate with all the quivering grandeur of refined beauty, that there is an art at work within it which is so divine, so infernally divine, that one might seek through millenniums in vain for another such possibility; I see a spectacle so rich in meaning and so wonderfully paradoxical to boot, that it would be enough to make all the gods of Olympus rock with immortal laughter—*Caesar Borgia as Pope*. . . . Do you understand me? . . . Very well then, this would have been the triumph which *I* alone am longing for today; this would have *swept* Christianity *away!* What happened? A German monk, Luther, came to Rome. This monk, with all the vindictive instincts of an abortive priest in his body, foamed with rage over the Renaissance in Rome. . . . Instead of, with the profoundest gratitude, understanding the vast miracle that had taken place, the overcoming of Christianity at its *headquarters*, the fire of his hate knew only how to draw fresh fuel from this spectacle. A religious man thinks only of himself. Luther saw the corruption of the Papacy when the very reverse stared him in the face: the old corruption, the *peccatum originale*, Christianity *no* longer sat upon the Papal chair! But Life! The triumph of Life! The great yea to all lofty, beautiful, and daring things! . . . And Luther reinstated the Church; he attacked it. The Renaissance thus became an event without meaning, a great *in vain!*—Ah these Germans, what have they not cost us already! In vain—this has always been the achievement of the Germans.—The Reformation, Leibnitz, Kant and so-called German philosophy, the Wars of Liberation, the Empire—in each case and in vain for something which had already existed, for something which *cannot be recovered.* . . . I confess it, these Germans are my enemies: I despise every sort of uncleanliness in concepts and valuations in them, every kind of cowardice in the face of every honest yea or nay. For almost one thousand years now, they have tangled and confused everything they have laid their hands on; they have on their conscience all the half measures, all the three-eighth measures of which Europe is sick; they also have the most unclean, the most incurable, and the most irrefutable kind of Christianity—Protestantism—on their conscience. . . . If we shall never be able to get rid of Christianity, the *Germans* will be to blame.

V. History

FROM THOUGHTS OUT OF SEASON, VOL. II

Preface

"I HATE everything that merely instructs me without increasing or directly quickening my activity." These words of Goethe, like a sincere *ceterum censeo*, may well stand at the head of my thoughts on the worth and the worthlessness of history. I will show in them why instruction that does not "quicken," knowledge that slackens the rein of activity, why in fact history, in Goethe's phrase, must be seriously "hated," as a costly and superfluous luxury of the understanding; for we are still in want of the necessaries of life, and the superfluous is an enemy to the necessary. We do need history, but quite differently from the jaded idlers in the garden of knowledge, however grandly they may look down on our rude and unpicturesque requirements. In other words, we need it for life and action, not as a convenient way to avoid life and action, or to excuse a selfish life and a cowardly or base action. We would serve history only so far as it serves life; but to value its study beyond a certain point mutilates and degrades life, and this is a fact that certain marked symptoms of our time make it as necessary as it may be painful to bring to the test of experience.

I have tried to describe a feeling that has often troubled me: I revenge myself on it by giving it publicity. This may lead someone to explain to me that he has also had the feeling, but that I do not feel it purely and elementally enough, and cannot express it with the ripe certainty of experience. A few may say so; but most people will tell me that it is a perverted, unnatural, horrible, and altogether unlawful feeling to have, and that I show myself unworthy of the great historical movement which is especially strong among the German people for the last two generations.

I am at all costs going to venture on a description of my feelings, which will be decidedly in the interests of propriety, as I shall give plenty of opportunity for paying compliments to such a "movement." And I gain an advantage for myself that is more valuable to me than propriety—the attainment of a correct point of view, through my critics, with regard to our age.

These thoughts are "out of season," because I am trying to represent something of which the age is rightly proud— its historical culture—as a fault and a defect in our time, believing as I do that we are all suffering from a malignant historical fever and should at least recognize the fact. But even if it be a virtue, Goethe may be right in asserting that we cannot help developing our faults at the same time as our virtues; and an excess of virtue can obviously bring a nation to ruin, as well as an excess of vice. In any case I may be allowed my say. But I will first relieve my mind by the confession that the experiences which produced those disturbing feelings were mostly drawn from myself—and from other sources only for the sake of comparison, and that I have only reached such "unseasonable" experience, so far as I am the nursling of older ages like the Greek, and less a child of this age. I must admit so much in virtue of my profession as a classical scholar; for I do not know what meaning classical scholarship may have for our time except in its being "unseasonable," that is, contrary to our time, and yet with an influence on it for the benefit, it may be hoped, of a future time.

The Use and Abuse of History

I

CONSIDER the herds that are feeding yonder; they know not the meaning of yesterday or today; they graze and ruminate, move or rest, from morning to night, from day to day, taken up with their little loves and hates, at the mercy of the moment, feeling neither melancholy nor satiety. Man cannot see them without regret, for even in the pride of his humanity he looks enviously on the beast's happiness. He wishes simply to live without satiety or pain, like the beast; yet it is all in vain, for he will not change places with it. He may ask the beast—"Why do you look at me and not speak to me of your happiness?" The beast wants to answer—"Because I always forget what I wished to say": but he forgets this answer too, and is silent; and the man is left to wonder.

He wonders also about himself, that he cannot learn to forget, but hangs on the past; however far or fast he run, that chain runs with him. It is matter for wonder: the moment, that is here and gone, that was nothing before and nothing after, returns like a specter to trouble the quiet of a later moment. A leaf is continually dropping out of the volume of time and fluttering away—and suddenly it flutters back into the man's lap. Then he says, "I remember . . . ," and envies the beast that forgets at once, and sees every moment really die, sink into night and mist, extinguished forever. The beast lives *unhistorically;* for it "goes into" the present, like a number, without leaving any curious remainder. It cannot dissimulate, it conceals nothing; at every moment it seems what it actually is, and thus can be nothing that is not honest. But man is always resisting the great and continually increasing weight of the past; it presses him down, and bows his shoulders; he travels with a dark invisible burden that he can plausibly disown, and is only too glad to disown in converse with his fellows—in order to excite their envy. And so it hurts him, like the thought of a lost Paradise, to see a herd grazing, or, nearer still, a child, that has nothing yet of the past to disown, and plays in a happy blindness between the walls of the past and the future. And yet its play must be disturbed, and only too soon will it be summoned from its little kingdom of oblivion. Then it learns to understand the words "once upon a time," the "open sesame" that lets in battle, suffering, and weariness on mankind, and reminds them what their existence really is, an imperfect tense that never becomes a present. And when death brings at last the desired forgetfulness, it abolishes life and being together, and sets the seal on the knowledge that "being" is merely a continual "has been," a thing that lives by denying and destroying and contradicting itself.

If happiness and the chase for new happiness keep alive in any sense the will to live, no philosophy has perhaps more truth than the cynic's; for the beast's happiness, like that of the perfect cynic, is the visible proof of the truth of cynicism. The smallest pleasure, if it be only continuous and make one happy, is incomparably a greater happiness than the more intense pleasure that comes as an episode, a wild freak, a mad interval between ennui, desire, and privation. But in the smallest and greatest happiness there is always one thing that makes it happiness: the power of forgetting, or, in more learned phrase, the capacity of feeling "unhistorically" throughout its duration. One who cannot leave himself behind on the threshold of the moment and forget the past, who cannot stand on a single point, like a goddess of victory, without fear or giddiness, will never know what happiness is; and, worse still, will never do anything to make others happy. The extreme case would be the man without any power to forget, who is condemned to see "becoming" everywhere. Such a man believes no more in himself or his own existence, he sees everything fly past in an eternal succession, and loses himself in the stream of becoming. At last, like the logical disciple of Heraclitus, he will hardly dare to raise his finger. Forgetfulness is a property of all action; just as not only light but darkness is bound up with the life of every organism. One who wished to feel everything historically would be like a man forcing himself to refrain from sleep, or a beast who had to live by chewing a continual cud. Thus even a happy life is possible with remembrance, as the beast shows, but life in any true sense is absolutely impossible without forgetfulness. Or, to put my conclusion better, there is a degree of sleeplessness, of rumination, of "historical sense," that injures and finally destroys the living thing, be it a man or a people or a system of culture.

To fix this degree and the limits to the memory of the past, if it is not to become the gravedigger of the present, we must see clearly how great is the "plastic power" of a man or a community or a culture; I mean the power of specifically growing out of one's self, of making the past and the strange one body with the near and the present, of healing wounds, replacing what is lost, repairing broken molds. There are men who have this power so slightly that a single sharp experience, a single pain, often a little injustice, will lacerate their souls like the scratch of a poisoned knife. There are others who are so little injured by the worst misfortunes, and even by their own spiteful actions, as to feel tolerably comfortable, with a fairly quiet conscience, in the midst of them—or at any rate shortly afterward. The deeper the roots of a man's inner nature, the better will he take the past into himself; and the greatest

and most powerful nature would be known by the absence
of limits for the historical sense to overgrow and work
harm. It would assimilate and digest the past, however foreign, and turn it to sap. Such a nature can forget what it
cannot subdue; there is no break in the horizon and nothing
to remind it that there are still men, passions, theories, and
aims on the other side. This is a universal law; a living
thing can only be healthy, strong, and productive within a
certain horizon: if it be incapable of drawing one round itself, or too selfish to lose its own view in another's, it will
come to an untimely end. Cheerfulness, a good conscience,
belief in the future, the joyful deed, all depend, in the individual as well as the nation, on there being a line that
divides the visible and clear from the vague and shadowy:
we must know the right time to forget as well as the right
time to remember, and instinctively see when it is necessary
to feel historically, and when unhistorically. This is the point
that the reader is asked to consider; that the unhistorical
and the historical are equally necessary to the health of an
individual, a community, and a system of culture.

Everyone has noticed that a man's historical knowledge
and range of feeling may be very limited, his horizon as
narrow as that of an Alpine valley, his judgments incorrect
and his experience falsely supposed original, and yet in spite
of all the incorrectness and falsity he may stand forth in
unconquerable health and vigor, to the joy of all who see
him; whereas another man with far more judgment and learning will fail in comparison, because the lines of his horizon
are continually changing and shifting, and he cannot shake
himself free from the delicate network of his truth and
righteousness for a downright act of will or desire. We saw
that the beast, absolutely "unhistorical," with the narrowest
of horizons, has yet a certain happiness, and lives at least
without hypocrisy or ennui; and so we may hold the capacity of feeling (to a certain extent) unhistorically, to be the
more important and elemental, as providing the foundation
of every sound and real growth, everything that is truly
great and human. The unhistorical is like the surrounding
atmosphere that can alone create life, and in whose annihilation life itself disappears. It is true that man can only become man by first suppressing this unhistorical element in
his thoughts, comparisons, distinctions, and conclusions,
letting a clear sudden light break through these misty clouds
by his power of turning the past to the uses of the present.
But an excess of history makes him flag again, while without
the veil of the unhistorical he would never have the courage

to begin. What deeds could man ever have done if he had not been enveloped in the dust cloud of the unhistorical? Or, to leave metaphors and take a concrete example, imagine a man swayed and driven by a strong passion, whether for a woman or a theory. His world is quite altered. He is blind to everything behind him, new sounds are muffled and meaningless, though his perceptions were never so intimately felt in all their color, light, and music, and he seems to grasp them with his five senses together. All his judgments of value are changed for the worse; there is much he can no longer value, as he can scarcely feel it; he wonders that he has so long been the sport of strange words and opinions, that his recollections have run round in one unwearying circle and are yet too weak and weary to make a single step away from it. His whole case is most indefensible; it is narrow, ungrateful to the past, blind to danger, deaf to warnings, a small living eddy in a dead sea of night and forgetfulness. And yet this condition, unhistorical and antihistorical throughout, is the cradle not only of unjust action but of every just and justifiable action in the world. No artist will paint his picture, no general win his victory, no nation gain its freedom, without having striven and yearned for it under those very "unhistorical" conditions. If the man of action, in Goethe's phrase, is without conscience, he is also without knowledge: he forgets most things in order to do one, he is unjust to what is behind him, and only recognizes one law, the law of that which is to be. So he loves his work infinitely more than it deserves to be loved; and the best works are produced in such an ecstasy of love that they must always be unworthy of it, however great their worth otherwise.

Should anyone be able to dissilve the unhistorical atmosphere in which every great event happens, and breathe afterward, he might be capable of rising to the "superhistorical" standpoint of consciousness that Niebuhr has described as the possible result of historical research. "History," he says, "is useful for one purpose, if studied in detail: that men may know, as the greatest and best spirits of our generation do not know, the accidental nature of the forms in which they see and insist on others seeing—insist, I say, because their consciousness of them is exceptionally intense. Anyone who has not grasped this idea in its different applications will fall under the spell of a more powerful spirit who reads a deeper emotion into the given form." Such a standpoint might be called "superhistorical," as one who took it could feel no impulse from history to any further life or work, for he would have recognized the blindness and injustice in the soul of the doer as a condition of every deed; he would be cured henceforth of taking history too seriously, and have learnt to answer the question how and why life should be lived—for all men and all circumstances, Greeks or Turks, the first century or the nineteenth. Whoever asks his friends whether they would live the last ten or twenty years over again will easily see which of them is born for the "superhistorical standpoint": they will all answer no, but will give different reasons for their answer. Some will say they have the consolation that the next twenty will be better; they are the men referred to satirically by David Hume:

> "And from the dregs of life hope to receive,
> What the first sprightly running could not give."

We will call them the "historical men." Their vision of the past turns them toward the future, encourages them to persevere with life, and kindles the hope that justice will yet come and happiness is behind the mountain they are climbing. They believe that the meaning of existence will become ever clearer in the course of its evolution; they only look backward at the process to understand the present and stimulate their longing for the future. They do not know how unhistorical their thoughts and actions are in spite of all their history, and how their preoccupation with it is for the sake of life rather than mere science.

But that question to which we have heard the first answer is capable of another; also a "no," but on different grounds. It is the "no" of the "superhistorical" man who sees no salvation in evolution, for whom the world is complete and fulfills its aim in every single moment. How could the next ten years teach what the past ten were not able to teach?

Whether the aim of the teaching be happiness or resignation, virtue or penance, these superhistorical men are not agreed; but as against all merely historical ways of viewing the past, they are unanimous in the theory that the past and the present are one and the same, typically alike in all their diversity, and forming together a picture of eternally present imperishable types of unchangeable value and significance. Just as the hundreds of different languages correspond to the same constant and elemental needs of mankind, and one who understood the needs could learn nothing new from the languages; so the "superhistorical" philosopher sees all the history of nations and individuals from within. He has a divine insight into the original meaning of the hieroglyphs, and comes even to be weary of the letters that are continually unrolled before him. How should the endless rush of events not bring satiety, surfeit, loathing? So the boldest of us is ready perhaps at last to say from his heart with Giacomo Leopardi: "Nothing lives that were worth thy pains, and the earth deserves not a sigh. Our being is pain and weariness, and the world is mud—nothing else. Be calm."

But we will leave the superhistorical men to their loathings and their wisdom: we wish rather today to be joyful in our unwisdom and have a pleasant life as active men who go forward, and respect the course of the world. The value we put on the historical may be merely a Western prejudice; let us at least go forward within this prejudice and not stand still. If we could only learn better to study history as a means to life! We would gladly grant the superhistorical people their superior wisdom, so long as we are sure of having more life than they; for in that case our unwisdom would have a greater future before it than their wisdom. To make my opposition between life and wisdom clear, I will take the usual road of the short summary.

A historical phenomenon, completely understood and reduced to an item of knowledge, is, in relation to the man who knows it, dead; for he has found out its madness, its injustice, its blind passion, and especially the earthly and darkened horizon that was the source of its power for history. This power has now become, for him who has recognized it, powerless; not yet, perhaps, for him who is alive.

History regarded as pure knowledge and allowed to sway the intellect would mean for men the final balancing of the ledger of life. Historical study is only fruitful for the future if it follows a powerful life-giving influence, for example, a new system of culture; only, therefore, if it is guided and dominated by a higher force, and does not itself guide and dominate.

History, so far as it serves life, serves an unhistorical power, and thus will never become a pure science like mathematics. The question how far life needs such a service is one of the most serious questions affecting the well-being of a man, a people, and a culture. For by excess of history, life becomes maimed and degenerate, and is followed by the degeneration of history as well.

II

The fact that life does need the service of history must be as clearly grasped as that an excess of history hurts it; this will be proved later. History is necessary to the living man in three ways: in relation to his action and struggle, his conservatism and reverence, his suffering and his desire for deliverance. These three relations answer to the three kinds of history—so far as they can be distinguished—the *monumental,* the *antiquarian,* and the *critical.*

History is necessary above all to the man of action and power who fights a great fight and needs examples, teachers, and comforters; he cannot find them among his contemporaries. It was necessary in this sense to Schiller; for our time is so evil, Goethe says, that the poet meets no nature that will profit him, among living men. Polybius is thinking of the active man when he calls political history the true preparation for governing a state; it is the great teacher that shows us how to bear steadfastly the reverses of fortune, by reminding us of what others have suffered. Whoever has learned to recognize this meaning in history must hate to see curious tourists and laborious beetle-hunters climbing up the great pyramids of antiquity. He does not wish to meet the idler who is rushing through the picture galleries of the past for a new distraction or sensation, where he himself is looking for example and encouragement. To avoid being troubled by the weak and hopeless idlers, and those whose apparent activity is merely neurotic, he looks behind him and stays his course toward the goal in order to breathe. His goal is happiness, not perhaps his own, but often the nation's, or humanity's at large; he avoids quietism, and uses history as a weapon against it. For the most part he has no hope of reward except fame, which means the expectation of a niche in the temple of history, where he in his turn may be the consoler and counsellor of posterity. For his orders are that what has once been able to extend the conception "man" and give it a fairer content must ever exist for the same office. The great moments in the individual battle form a chain, a high road for humanity through the ages, and the highest points of those vanished moments are yet great and living for men; and this is the fundamental idea of the belief in humanity that finds a voice in the demand for a "monumental" history.

But the fiercest battle is fought round the demand for

greatness to be eternal. Every other living thing cries no.
"Away with the monuments," is the watchword. Dull custom fills all the chambers of the world with its meanness,
and rises in thick vapor round anything that is great, barring
its way to immortality, blinding and stifling it. And the way
passes through mortal brains! Through the brains of sick
and short-lived beasts that ever rise to the surface to breathe,
and painfully keep off annihilation for a little space. For
they wish but one thing: to live at any cost. Who would
ever dream of any "monumental history" among them, the
hard torch race that alone gives life to greatness? And yet
there are always men awakening, who are strengthened and
made happy by gazing on past greatness, as though man's
life were a lordly thing, and the fairest fruit of this bitter
tree were the knowledge that there was once a man who
walked sternly and proudly through this world, another who
had pity and loving-kindness, another who lived in contemplation—but all leaving one truth behind them, that his life is
the fairest who thinks least about life. The common man
snatches greedily at this little span, with tragic earnestness,
but they, on their way to monumental history and immortality, knew how to greet it with Olympic laughter, or at
least with a lofty scorn; and they went down to their graves
in irony—for what had they to bury? Only what they had
always treated as dross, refuse, and vanity, and which now
falls into its true home of oblivion, after being so long
the sport of their contempt. One thing will live, the sign
manual of their inmost being, the rare flash of light, the
deed, the creation; because posterity cannot do without it.
In this spiritualized form fame is something more than the
sweetest morsel for our egoism, in Schopenhauer's phrase:
it is the belief in the oneness and continuity of the great in
every age, and a protest against the change and decay of
generations.

What is the use to the modern man of this "monumental"
contemplation of the past, this preoccupation with the rare
and classic? It is the knowledge that the great thing existed
and was therefore possible, and so may be possible again.
He is heartened on his way; for his doubt in weaker moments, whether his desire be not for the impossible, is struck
aside. Suppose one believes that no more than a hundred
men, brought up in the new spirit, efficient and productive,
were needed to give the deathblow to the present fashion of
education in Germany; he will gather strength from the
remembrance that the culture of the Renaissance was raised
on the shoulders of such another band of a hundred men.

And yet if we really wish to learn something from an example, how vague and elusive do we find the comparison! If it is to give us strength, many of the differences must be neglected, the individuality of the past forced into a general formula and all the sharp angles broken off for the sake of correspondence. Ultimately, of course, what was once possible can only become possible a second time on the Pythagorean theory, that when the heavenly bodies are in the same position again, the events on earth are reproduced to the smallest detail; so when the stars have a certain relation, a Stoic and an Epicurean will form a conspiracy to murder Caesar, and a different conjunction will show another Columbus discovering America. Only if the earth always began its drama again after the fifth act, and it were certain that the same interaction of motives, the same *deus ex machina,* the same catastrophe would occur at particular intervals, could the man of action venture to look for the whole archetypic truth in monumental history, to see each fact fully set out in its uniqueness: it would not probably be before the astronomers became astrologers again. Till then monumental history will never be able to have complete truth; it will always bring together things that are incompatible and generalize them into compatibility, will always weaken the differences of motive and occasion. Its object is to depict effects at the expense of the causes—"monumentally," that is, as examples for imitation; it turns aside, as far as it may, from reasons, and might be called with far less exaggeration a collection of "effects in themselves," than of events that will have an effect on all ages. The events of war or religion cherished in our popular celebrations are such "effects in themselves"; it is these that will not let ambition sleep, and lie like amulets on the bolder hearts—not the real historical nexus of cause and effect, which, rightly understood, would only prove that nothing quite similar could ever be cast again from the diceboxes of fate and the future.

As long as the soul of history is found in the great impulse that it gives to a powerful spirit, as long as the past is principally used as a model for imitation, it is always in danger of being a little altered and touched up, and brought nearer to fiction. Sometimes there is no possible distinction between a "monumental" past and a mythical romance, as the same motives for action can be gathered from the one world as the other. If this monumental method of surveying the past dominates the others—the antiquarian and the critical—the past itself suffers wrong. Whole tracts of it are forgotten and despised; they flow away like a dark unbroken river, with only a few gaily colored islands of fact rising above it. There is something beyond nature in the rare figures that become visible, like the golden hips that his disciples attributed to Pythagoras. Monumental history lives by false analogy; it entices the brave to rashness, and the enthusiastic to fanaticism by its tempting comparisons. Imagine this history in the hands—and the head—of a gifted egoist or an inspired scoundrel; kingdoms will be overthrown, princes murdered, war and revolution let loose, and the number of "effects in themselves"—in other words, effects without sufficient cause—increased. So much for the harm done by monumental history to the powerful men of action, be they good or bad; but what if the weak and the inactive take it as their servant—or their master!

Consider the simplest and commonest example, the inartistic or half-artistic natures whom a monumental history provides with sword and buckler. They will use the weapons against their hereditary enemies, the great artistic spirits, who alone can learn from that history the one real lesson, how to live, and embody what they have learnt in noble action. Their way is obstructed, their free air darkened by the idolatrous—and conscientious—dance round the half-understood monument of a great past. "See, that is the true and real art," we seem to hear. "Of what use are these aspiring little people of today?" The dancing crowd has apparently the monopoly of "good taste," for the creator is always at a disadvantage compared with the mere looker-on, who never put a hand to the work; just as the armchair politician has ever had more wisdom and foresight than the actual statesman. But if the custom of democratic suffrage and numerical majorities be transferred to the realm of art, and the artist put on his defense before the court of aesthetic dilettanti, you may take your oath on his condemnation; although, or rather because, his judges had proclaimed solemnly the canon of "monumental art," the art that has "had an effect on all ages," according to the official definition. In their eyes no need nor inclination nor historical authority is in favor of the art which is not yet "monumental" because it is contemporary. Their instinct tells them that art can be slain by art: the monumental will never be reproduced, and the weight of its authority is invoked from the past to make it sure. They are connoisseurs of art, primarily because they wish to kill art; they pretend to be physicians, when their real idea is to dabble in poisons. They develop their tastes to a point of perversion, that they may be able to show a reason for continually rejecting all the nourishing artistic fare that is offered them. For they do not want greatness to arise: their method is to say, "See, the great thing is already here!" In reality they care as little about the great thing that is already here, as that which is about to arise; their lives are evidence of that. Monumental history is the cloak under which their hatred of present power and greatness masquerades as an extreme admiration of the past; the real meaning of this way of viewing history is disguised as its opposite; whether they wish it or no, they are acting as though their motto were, "Let the dead bury the—living."

Each of the three kinds of history will only flourish in one ground and climate; otherwise it grows to a noxious weed. If the man who will produce something great have need of the past, he makes himself its master by means of monumental history; the man who can rest content with the traditional and venerable uses the past as an "antiquarian historian"; and only he whose heart is oppressed by an instant need, and who will cast the burden off at any price, feels the want of "critical history," the history that judges and condemns. There is much harm wrought by wrong and thoughtless planting: the critic without the need, the antiquary without piety, the knower of the great deed who cannot be the doer of it, are plants that have grown to weeds; they are torn from their native soil and therefore degenerate.

III

Secondly, history is necessary to the man of conservative and reverent nature who looks back to the origins of his existence with love and trust; through it, he gives thanks for life. He is careful to preserve what survives from ancient days, and will reproduce the conditions of his own upbringing for those who come after him; thus he does life a service. The possession of his ancestors' furniture changes its meaning in his soul, for his soul is rather possessed by it. All that is small and limited, moldy and obsolete, gains a worth and inviolability of its own from the conservative and reverent soul of the antiquary migrating into it, and building a secret nest there. The history of his town becomes the history of himself; he looks on the walls, the turreted gate, the town council, the fair, as an illustrated diary of his youth, and sees himself in it all—his strength, industry, desire, reason, faults, and follies. "Here one could live," he says, "as one can live here now—and will go on living; for we are tough folk, and will not be uprooted in the night." And so, with his "we," he surveys the marvelous individual life of the past and identifies himself with the spirit of the house, the family, and the city. He greets the soul of his people from afar as his own, across the dim and troubled centuries; his gifts and his virtues lie in such power of feeling and divination, his scent of a half-vanished trail, his instinctive correctness in reading the scribbled past, and understanding at once its palimpsests—nay, its polypsests. Goethe stood with such thoughts before the monument of Erwin von Steinbach: the storm of his feeling rent the historical cloud veil that hung between them, and he saw the German work for the first time "coming from the stern, rough, German soul." This was the road that the Italians of the Renaissance traveled, the spirit that reawakened the ancient Italic genius in their poets to "a wondrous echo of the immemorial lyre," as Jakob Burckhardt says. But the greatest value of this antiquarian spirit of reverence lies in the simple emotions of pleasure and content that it lends to the drab, rough, even painful circumstances of a nation's or individual's life: Niebuhr confesses that he could live happily on a moor among free peasants with a history, and would never feel the want of art. How could history serve life better than by anchoring the less gifted races and peoples to the homes and customs of their ancestors, and keeping them from ranging far afield in search of better, to find only struggle and competition? The influence that ties men down to the same companions and circumstances, to the daily round of toil, to their bare mountainside, seems to be selfish and unreasonable; but it is a healthy unreason and of profit to the community, as everyone knows who has clearly realized the terrible consequences of mere desire for migration and adventure— perhaps in whole peoples—or who watches the destiny of a nation that has lost confidence in its earlier days, and is given up to a restless cosmopolitanism and an unceasing desire for novelty. The feeling of the tree that clings to its roots, the happiness of knowing one's growth to be not merely arbitrary and fortuitous but the inheritance, the fruit and blossom of a past that does not merely justify but crown the present—this is what we nowadays prefer to call the real historical sense.

These are not the conditions most favorable to reducing the past to pure science; and we see here, too, as we saw in the case of monumental history, that the past itself suffers when history serves life and is directed by its end. To vary the metaphor, the tree feels its roots better than it can see

them: the greatness of the feeling is measured by the greatness and strength of the visible branches. The tree may
be wrong here; how far more wrong will it be in regard to
the whole forest, which it only knows and feels so far as it
is hindered or helped by it, and not otherwise! The antiquarian sense of a man, a city, or a nation has always a
very limited field. Many things are not noticed at all; the
others are seen in isolation, as through a microscope. There
is no measure: equal importance is given to everything, and
therefore too much to anything. For the things of the past
are never viewed in their true perspective or receive their
just value, but value and perspective change with that individual or the nation that is looking back on its past.

There is always the danger here that everything ancient will
be regarded as equally venerable, and everything without this
respect for antiquity, like a new spirit, rejected as an enemy.
The Greeks themselves admitted the archaic style of plastic
art by the side of the freer and greater style, and later
did not merely tolerate the pointed nose and the cold
mouth, but made them even a canon of taste. If the judgment
of a people hardens in this way, and history's service to the
past life be to undermine a further and higher life; if the
historical sense no longer preserves life, but mummifies it;
then the tree dies, unnaturally, from the top downward,
and at last the roots themselves wither. Antiquarian history
degenerates from the moment that it no longer gives a soul
and inspiration to the fresh life of the present. The spring of
piety is dried up, but the learned habit persists without it and
revolves complaisantly round its own center. The horrid
spectacle is seen of the mad collector raking over all the
dust heaps of the past. He breathes a moldy air; the antiquarian habit may degrade a considerable talent, a real
spiritual need in him, to a mere insatiable curiosity for
everything old: he often sinks so low as to be satisfied with
any food, and greedily devours all the scraps that fall from
the bibliographical table.

Even if this degeneration does not take place, and the
foundation be not withered on which antiquarian history
can alone take root with profit to life, yet there are dangers
enough, if it becomes too powerful and invades the ter-
ritories of the other methods. It only understands how to preserve life, not to create it; and thus always undervalues
the present growth, having, unlike monumental history, no
certain instinct for it. Thus it hinders the mighty impulse to
a new deed and paralyzes the doer, who must always, as
doer, be grazing some piety or other. The fact that has grown

old carries with it a demand for its own immortality. For when one considers the life history of such an ancient fact, the amount of reverence paid to it for generations—whether it be a custom, a religious creed, or a political principle—it seems presumptuous, even impious, to replace it by a new fact, and the ancient congregation of pieties by a new piety.

Here we see clearly how necessary a third way of looking at the past is to man, beside the other two. This is the "critical" way, which is also in the service of life. Man must have the strength to break up the past and apply it, too, in order to live. He must bring the past to the bar of judgment, interrogate it remorselessly, and finally condemn it. Every past is worth condemning: this is the rule in mortal affairs, which always contain a large measure of human power and human weakness. It is not justice that sits in judgment here, nor mercy that proclaims the verdict; but only life, the dim, driving force that insatiably desires—itself. Its sentence is always unmerciful, always unjust, as it never flows from a pure fountain of knowledge: though it would generally turn out the same, if Justice herself delivered it. "For everything that is born is *worthy* of being destroyed: better were it then that nothing should be born." It requires great strength to be able to live and forget how far life and injustice are one. Luther himself once said that the world only arose by an oversight of God; if he had ever dreamed of heavy ordnance, he would never have created it. The same life that needs forgetfulness needs sometimes its destruction; for should the injustice of something ever become obvious—a monopoly, a caste, a dynasty, for example—the thing deserves to fall. Its past is critically examined, the knife put to its roots, and all the "pieties" are grimly trodden underfoot. The process is always dangerous, even for life; and the men or the times that serve life in this way, by judging and annihilating the past, are always dangerous to themselves and others. For as we are merely the resultant of previous generations, we are also the resultant of their errors, passions, and crimes; it is impossible to shake off this chain. Though we condemn the errors and think we have escaped them, we cannot escape the fact that we spring from them. At best, it comes to a conflict between our innate, inherited nature and our knowledge, between a stern, new discipline and an ancient tradition; and we plant a new way of life, a new instinct, a second nature, that withers the first. It is an attempt to gain a past a posteriori from which we might spring, as against that from which we do spring; always a dangerous attempt, as it is difficult to find a limit to the denial of the past, and the second natures are generally weaker than the first. We stop too often at knowing the good without doing it, because we also know the better but cannot do it. Here and there the victory is won, which gives a strange consolation to the fighters, to those who use critical history for the sake of life. The consolation is the knowledge that this "first nature" was once a second, and that every conquering "second nature" becomes a first.

IV

This is how history can serve life. Every man and nation needs a certain knowledge of the past, whether it be through monumental, antiquarian, or critical history, according to his objects, powers, and necessities. The need is not that of the mere thinkers who only look on at life, or the few who desire knowledge and can only be satisfied with knowledge; but it has always a reference to the end of life, and is under its absolute rule and direction. This is the natural relation of an age, a culture, and a people to history; hunger is its source, necessity its norm, the inner plastic power assigns its limits. The knowledge of the past is only desired for the service of the future and the present, not to weaken the present or undermine a living future. All this is as simple as truth itself, and quite convincing to anyone who is not in the toils of "historical deduction."

And now to take a quick glance at our time! We fly back in astonishment. The clearness, naturalness, and purity of the connection between life and history has vanished; and in what a maze of exaggeration and contradiction do we now see the problem! Is the guilt ours who see it, or have life and history really altered their conjunction and an inauspicious star risen between them? Others may prove we have seen falsely; I am merely saying what we believe we see. There is such a star, a bright and lordly star, and the conjunction is really altered—by science, and the demand for history to be a science. Life is no more dominant, and knowledge of the past no longer its thrall: boundary marks are overthrown and everything bursts its limits. The perspective of events is blurred, and the blur extends through their whole immeasurable course. No generation has seen such a panoramic comedy as is shown by the "science of universal evolution," history; that shows it with the dangerous audacity of its motto—"Fiat veritas, pereat vita."

Let me give a picture of the spiritual events in the soul

of the modern man. Historical knowledge streams on him from sources that are inexhaustible, strange incoherencies come together, memory opens all its gates and yet is never open wide enough, nature busies herself to receive all the foreign guests, to honor them and put them in their places. But they are at war with each other: violent measures seem necessary in order to escape destruction one's self. It becomes second nature to grow gradually accustomed to this irregular and stormy home life, though this second nature is unquestionably weaker, more restless, more radically unsound than the first. The modern man carries inside him an enormous heap of indigestible knowledge stones that occasionally rattle together in his body, as the fairy tale has it. And the rattle reveals the most striking characteristic of these modern men, the opposition of something inside them to which nothing external corresponds; and the reverse. The ancient nations knew nothing of this. Knowledge, taken in excess without hunger, even contrary to desire, has no more the effect of transforming the external life; and remains hidden in a chaotic inner world that the modern man has a curious pride in calling his "real personality." He has the substance, he says, and only wants the form; but this is quite an unreal opposition in a living thing. Our modern culture is for that reason not a living one, because it cannot be understood without that opposition. In other words, it is not a real culture but a kind of knowledge about culture, a complex of various thoughts and feelings about it, from which no decision as to its direction can come. Its real motive force that issues in visible action is often no more than a mere convention, a wretched imitation, or even a shameless caricature. The man probably feels like the snake that has swallowed a rabbit whole and lies still in the sun, avoiding all movement not absolutely necessary. The "inner life" is now the only thing that matters to education, and all who see it hope that the education may not fail by being too indigestible. Imagine a Greek meeting it; he would observe that for modern men "education" and "historical education" seem to mean the same thing, with the difference that the one phrase is longer. And if he spoke of his own theory, that a man can be very well educated without any history at all, people would shake their heads and think they had not heard aright. The Greeks, the famous people of a past still near to us, had the "unhistorical sense" strongly developed in the period of their greatest power. If a typical child of his age were transported to that world by some enchantment, he would probably find the Greeks very "uneducated." And that discovery would betray the closely guarded secret of modern culture to the laughter of the world. For we moderns have nothing of our own. We only become worth notice by filling ourselves to overflowing with foreign customs, arts, philosophies, religions, and sciences: we are wandering encyclopedias, as an ancient Greek who had strayed into our time would probably call us. But the only value of an encyclopedia lies in the inside, in the contents, not in what is written outside, in the binding or the wrapper. And so the whole of modern culture is essentially internal; the bookbinder prints something like this on the cover: "Manual of internal culture for external barbarians." The opposition of inner and outer makes the outer side still more barbarous, as it would naturally be, when the outward growth of a rude people merely developed its primitive inner needs. For what means has nature of repressing too great a luxuriance from without? Only one—to be affected by it as little as possible, to set it aside and stamp it out at the first opportunity. And so we have the custom of no longer taking real things seriously, we get the feeble personality on which the real and the permanent make so little impression. Men become at last more careless and accommodating in external matters, and the considerable cleft between substance and form is widened, until they have no longer any feeling for barbarism, if only their memories be kept continually titillated, and there flows a constant stream of new things to be known that can be neatly packed up in the cupboards of their memory. The culture of a people as against this barbarism can be, I think, described with justice as the "unity of artistic style in every outward expression of the people's life." This must not be misunderstood, as though it were merely a question of the opposition between barbarism and "fine style." The people that can be called cultured must be in a real sense a living unity, and not be miserably cleft asunder into form and substance. If one wishes to promote a people's culture, let him try to promote this higher unity first, and work for the destruction of the modern educative system for the sake of a true education. Let him dare to consider how the health of a people that has been destroyed by history may be restored, and how it may recover its instincts with its honor.

I am only speaking, directly, about the Germans of the present day, who have had to suffer more than other people from the feebleness of personality and the opposition of substance and form. "Form" generally implies for us some convention, disguise, or hypocrisy, and if not hated is at any rate not loved. We have an extraordinary fear of both the word convention and the thing. This fear drove the German from the French school, for he wished to become more natural, and therefore more German. But he seems to have come to a false conclusion with his "therefore." First he ran away from his school of convention, and went by any road he liked; he has come ultimately to imitate voluntarily in a slovenly fashion what he imitated painfully and often successfully before. So now the lazy fellow lives under French conventions that are actually incorrect; his manner of walking shows it, his conversation and dress, his general way of life. In the belief that he was returning to Nature, he merely followed caprice and comfort, with the smallest possible amount of self-control. Go through any German town; you will see conventions that are nothing but the negative aspect of the national characteristics of foreign states. Everything is colorless, worn-out, shoddy, and ill-copied. Everyone acts at his own sweet will—which is not a strong or serious will—on laws dictated by the universal rush and the general desire for comfort. A dress that made no head ache in its inventing and wasted no time in the making, borrowed from foreign models and imperfectly copied, is regarded as an important contribution to German fashion. The sense of form is ironically disclaimed by the people—for they have the "sense of substance": they are famous for their cult of "inwardness."

But there is also a famous danger in their "inwardness": the internal substance cannot be seen from the outside, and so may one day take the opportunity of vanishing, and no one notice its absence, any more than its presence before. One may think the German people to be very far from this danger; yet the foreigner will have some warrant for his reproach that our inward life is too weak and ill-organized to provide a form and external expression for itself. It may in rare cases show itself finely receptive, earnest, and powerful, richer perhaps than the inward life of other peoples; but, taken as a whole, it remains weak, as all its fine threads are not tied together in one strong knot. The visible action is not the self-manifestation of the inward life but only a weak and crude attempt of a single thread to make a show of representing the whole. And thus the German is not to be judged on any one action, for the individual may be as completely obscure after it as before. He must obviously be measured by his thoughts and feelings, which are now expressed in his books; if only the books did not, more than ever, raise the doubt whether the famous inward life is still really sitting in its inaccessible shrine. It might one day vanish and leave behind it only the external life—with its vulgar pride and vain servility—to mark the German. Fearful thought!—as fearful as if the inward life still sat there, painted and rouged and disguised, become a play-actress or something worse; as his theatrical experience seems to have taught the quiet observer Grillparzer, standing aside as he did from the main press. "We feel by theory," he says. "We hardly know any more how our contemporaries give expression to their feelings: we make them use gestures that are impossible nowadays. Shakespeare has spoilt us moderns."

This is a single example, its general application perhaps too hastily assumed. But how terrible it would be were that generalization justified before our eyes! There would be then a note of despair in the phrase, "We Germans feel by theory, we are all spoilt by history"—a phrase that would cut at the roots of any hope for a future national culture. For every hope of that kind grows from the belief in the genuineness and immediacy of German feeling, from the belief in an untarnished inward life. Where is our hope or belief, when its spring is muddied, and the inward quality has learned gestures and dances and the use of cosmetics, has learned to express itself "with due reflection in abstract terms," and gradually to lose itself? And how should a great productive spirit exist among a nation that is not sure of its inward unity and is divided into educated men whose inner life has been drawn from the true path of education, and uneducated men whose inner life cannot be approached at all? How should it exist, I say, when the people has lost its own unity of feeling, and knows that the feeling of the part calling itself the educated part and claiming the right of controlling the artistic spirit of the nation is false and hypocritical? Here and there the judgment and taste of individuals may be higher and finer than the rest, but that is no compensation; it tortures a man to have to speak only to one section and be no longer in sympathy with his people. He would rather bury his treasure now, in disgust at the vulgar patronage of a class, though his heart be filled with tenderness for all. The instinct of the people can no longer meet him halfway; it is useless for them to stretch their arms out to him in yearning. What remains but to turn his quickened hatred against the ban, strike at the barrier raised by the so-called culture, and condemn as judge what blasted and degraded him as a living man and a source of life? He takes a profound insight into fate in exchange for the godlike desire of creation and help, and ends his days as a lonely philosopher, with the wisdom of disillusion. It is the painfulest comedy; he who sees it will feel a sacred obligation on him, and say to himself, "Help must come: the higher unity in the nature and soul of a people must be brought back, the cleft between inner and outer must again disappear under the hammer of necessity." But to what means can he look? What remains to him now but his knowledge? He hopes to plant the feeling of a need, by speaking from the breadth of that knowledge, giving it freely with both hands. From the strong need the strong action may one day arise. And to leave no doubt of the instance I am taking of the need and the knowledge, my testimony shall stand, that it is German unity in its highest sense which is the goal of our endeavor, far more than political union: it is the unity of the German spirit and life after the annihilation of the antagonism between form and substance, inward life and convention.

FROM HUMAN, ALL TOO HUMAN, I

224

ENNOBLEMENT THROUGH DEGENERATION. History teaches that a race of people is best preserved where the greater number hold one common spirit in consequence of the similarity of their accustomed and indisputable principles: in consequence, therefore, of their common faith. Thus strength is afforded by good and thorough customs, thus is learnt the subjection of the individual, and strenuousness of character becomes a birth gift and afterward is fostered as a habit. The danger to these communities founded on individuals of strong and similar character is that gradually increasing stupidity through transmission, which follows all stability like its shadow. It is on the more unrestricted, more uncertain and morally weaker individuals that depends the *intellectual progress* of such communities; it is they who attempt all that is new and manifold. Numbers of these perish on account of their weakness, without having achieved any specially visible effect; but generally, particularly when they have descendants, they flare up and from time to time inflict a wound on the stable element of the community. Precisely in this sore and weakened place the community is *inoculated* with something new, but its general strength must be great enough to absorb and assimilate this new thing into its blood. Deviating natures are of the utmost importance wherever there is to be progress. Every wholesale progress must be preceded by a partial weakening. The strongest natures *retain* the type, the weaker ones help it to *develop*. Something similar happens in the case of individuals; a deterioration, a mutilation, even a vice and, above all, a physical or moral loss is seldom without its advantage. For instance, a sickly man in the midst of a warlike and restless race will perhaps have more chance of being alone and thereby growing quieter and wiser, the one-eyed man will possess a stronger eye, the blind man will have a deeper inward sight and will certainly have a keener sense of hearing. In so far it appears to me that the famous Struggle for Existence is not the only point of view from which an explanation can be given of the progress or strengthening of an individual or a race. Rather must two different things converge: firstly, the multiplying of stable strength through mental binding in faith and common feeling; secondly, the possibility of attaining to higher aims, through the fact that there are deviating natures and, in consequence, partial weakening and wounding of the stable strength; it is precisely the weaker nature, as the more delicate and free, that makes all progress at all possible. A people that is crumbling and weak in any one part, but as a whole still strong and healthy, is able to absorb the infection of what is new and incorporate it to its advantage. The task of education in a single individual is this: to plant him so firmly and surely that, as a whole, he can no longer be diverted from his path. Then, however, the educator must wound him, or else make use of the wounds which fate inflicts, and when pain and need have thus arisen, something new and noble can be inoculated into the wounded places. With regard to the state, Machiavelli says that, "the form of Government is of very small importance, although half-educated people think otherwise. The great aim of statecraft should be duration, which outweighs all else, inasmuch as it is more valuable than liberty." It is only with securely founded and guaranteed duration that continual development and ennobling inoculation are at all possible. As a rule, however, authority, the dangerous companion of all duration, will rise in opposition to this.

THE VOICE OF HISTORY. In general, history *appears*

to teach the following about the production of genius: it ill-treats and torments mankind—calls to the passions of envy, hatred, and rivalry—drives them to desperation, people against people, throughout whole centuries! Then, perhaps, like a stray spark from the terrible energy thereby aroused, there flames up suddenly the light of genius; the will, like a horse maddened by the rider's spur, thereupon breaks out and leaps over into another domain. He who could attain to a comprehension of the production of genius, and desires to carry out practically the manner in which Nature usually goes to work, would have to be just as evil and regardless as Nature itself. But perhaps we have not heard rightly.

237

RENAISSANCE AND REFORMATION. The Italian Renaissance contained within itself all the positive forces to which we owe modern culture. Such were the liberation of thought, the disregard of authorities, the triumph of education over the darkness of tradition, enthusiasm for science and the scientific past of mankind, the unfettering of the Individual, an ardor for truthfulness and a dislike of delusion and mere effect (which ardor blazed forth in an entire company of artistic characters, who with the greatest moral purity required from themselves perfection in their works, and nothing but perfection); yes, the Renaissance had positive forces, which have, *as yet*, never become so mighty again in our modern culture. It was the Golden Age of the last thousand years, in spite of all its blemishes and vices. On the other hand, the German Reformation stands out as an energetic protest of antiquated spirits, who were by no means tired of medieval views of life, and who received the signs of its dissolution, the extraordinary flatness and alienation of the religious life, with deep dejection instead of with the rejoicing that would have been seemly. With their northern strength and stiff-neckedness they threw mankind back again, brought about the Counter Reformation, that is, a Catholic Christianity of self-defense, with all the violences of a state of siege, and delayed for two or three centuries the complete awakening and mastery of the sciences; just as they probably made forever impossible the complete intergrowth of the antique and the modern spirit. The great task of the Renaissance could not be brought to a termination; this was prevented by the protest of the contemporary backward German spirit (which, for its salvation, had had sufficient sense in the Middle Ages to cross the Alps again and again). It was the chance of an extraordinary constellation of politics that Luther was preserved, and that his protest gained strength, for the Emperor protected him in order to employ him as a weapon against the Pope, and in the same way he was secretly favored by the Pope in order to use the Protestant princes as a counterweight against the Emperor. Without this curious counterplay of intentions, Luther would have been burnt like Huss —and the morning sun of enlightenment would probably have risen somewhat earlier, and with a splendor more beauteous than we can now imagine.

261

THE TYRANTS OF THE MIND. It is only where the ray of myth falls that the life of the Greeks shines; otherwise it is gloomy. The Greek philosophers are now robbing themselves of this myth; is it not as if they wished to quit the sunshine for shadow and gloom? Yet no plant avoids the light; and, as a matter of fact, those philosophers were only seeking a *brighter* sun; the myth was not pure enough, not shining enough for them. They found this light in their knowledge, in that which each of them called his "truth." But in those times knowledge shone with a greater glory; it was still young and knew but little of all the difficulties and dangers of its path; it could still hope to reach in one single bound the central point of all being, and from thence to solve the riddle of the world. These philosophers had a firm belief in themselves and their "truth," and with it they overthrew all their neighbors and predecessors; each one was a warlike, violent *tyrant*. The happiness in believing themselves the possessors of truth was perhaps never greater in the world, but neither were the hardness, the arrogance, and the tyranny and evil of such a belief. They were tyrants, they were that, therefore, which every Greek wanted to be, and which everyone was if he *was able*. Perhaps Solon alone is an exception; he tells in his poems how he disdained personal tyranny. But he did it for love of his works, of his lawgiving; and to be a lawgiver is a sublimated form of tyranny. Parmenides also made laws. Pythagoras and Empedocles probably did the same; Anaximander founded a city. Plato was the incarnate wish to become the greatest philosophic lawgiver and founder of states; he appears to have suffered terribly over the non-fulfillment of his nature, and toward his end his soul was filled with the bitterest gall. The more the Greek philosophers lost in power the more they suffered inwardly from this bitterness and malice; when the various sects fought for their truths in the street, then first were the souls of these wooers of truth completely clogged through envy and spleen; the tyrannical element then raged like poison within their bodies. These many petty tyrants would have liked to devour each other; there survived not a single spark of love and very little joy in their own knowledge. The saying that tyrants are generally murdered and that their descendants are short-lived is true also of the tyrants of the mind. Their history is short and violent, and their aftereffects break off suddenly. It may be said of almost all great Hellenes that they appear to have come too late: it was thus with Aeschylus, with Pindar, with Demosthenes, with Thucydides: one generation—and then it is passed forever. That is the stormy and dismal element in Greek history. We now, it is true, admire the gospel of the tortoises. To think historically is almost the same thing now as if in all ages history had been made according to the theory "The smallest possible amount in the longest possible time!" Oh! how quickly Greek history runs on! Since then life has never been so extravagant—so unbounded. I cannot persuade myself that the history of the Greeks followed that *natural* course for which it is so celebrated. They were much too variously gifted to be *gradual* in the orderly manner of the tortoise when running a race with Achilles, and that is called natural development. The Greeks went rapidly forward, but equally rapidly downward; the movement of the whole machine is so intensified that a single stone thrown amid its wheels was sufficient to break it. Such a stone, for instance, was Socrates; the hitherto so wonderfully regular, although certainly too rapid, development of the philosophical science was destroyed in one night. It is no idle question whether Plato, had he remained free from the Socratic charm, would not have discovered a still higher type of the philosophic man, which type is forever lost to us. We look into the ages before him as into a sculptor's workshop of such types. The fifth and sixth centuries B.C. seemed to promise something more and higher even than they produced; they stopped short at promising and announcing. And yet there is hardly a greater loss than the loss of a type, of a new, hitherto undiscovered highest *possibility of the philosophic life*. Even of the older type the greater number are badly transmitted; it seems to me that all philosophers, from Thales to Democritus, are remarkably difficult to recognize, but whoever succeeds in imitating these figures walks amongst specimens of the mightiest and purest type. This ability is certainly rare; it was even absent in those later Greeks who occupied themselves with the knowledge of the older philosophy; Aristotle, especially, hardly seems to have had eyes in his head when he stands before these great ones. And thus it appears as if these splendid philosophers had lived in vain, or as if they had only been intended to prepare the quarrelsome and talkative followers of the Socratic schools. As I have said, here is a gap, a break in development; some great misfortune must have happened, and the only statue which might have revealed the meaning and purpose of that great artistic training was either broken or unsuccessful; what actually happened has remained forever a secret of the workshop.

That which happened amongst the Greeks—namely, that every great thinker who believed himself to be in possession of the absolute truth became a tyrant, so that even the mental history of the Greeks acquired that violent, hasty, and dangerous character shown by their political history—this type of event was not therewith exhausted; much that is similar has happened even in more modern times, although gradually becoming rarer and now but seldom showing the pure, naïve conscience of the Greek philosophers. For on the whole, opposition doctrines and scepticism now speak too powerfully, too loudly. The period of mental tyranny is past. It is true that in the spheres of higher culture there must always be a supremacy, but henceforth this supremacy lies in the hands of the *oligarchs of the mind*. In spite of local and political separation they form a cohesive society, whose members *recognize and acknowledge* each other, whatever public opinion and the verdicts of review and newspaper writers who influence the masses may circulate in favor of or against them. Mental superiority, which formerly divided and embittered, nowadays generally *unites*; how could the separate individuals assert themselves and swim through life on their own course, against all currents, if they did not see others like them living here and there under similar conditions, and grasp their hands, in the struggle as much against the ochlocratic character of the half mind and half culture as against the occasional attempts to establish a tyranny with the help of the masses? Oligarchs are necessary to each other, they are each other's best joy, they understand their signs, but each is nevertheless free, he fights and conquers in *his* place and perishes rather than submit.

630

Conviction is belief in the possession of absolute truth on any matter of knowledge. This belief takes it for granted, therefore, that there are absolute truths; also, that perfect methods have been found for attaining to them; and finally, that everyone who has convictions makes use of these perfect methods. All three notions show at once that the man of convictions is not the man of scientific thought; he seems to us still in the age of theoretical innocence, and is practically a child, however grown-up he may be. Whole centuries, however, have been lived under the influence of those childlike presuppositions, and out of them have flowed the mightiest sources of human strength. The countless numbers who sacrificed themselves for their convictions believed they were doing it for the sake of absolute truth. They were all wrong, however; probably no one has ever sacrificed himself for Truth; at least, the dogmatic expression of the faith of any such person has been unscientific or only partly scientific. But really, people wanted to carry their point because they believed that they *must be* in the right. To allow their belief to be wrested from them probably meant calling in question their eternal salvation. In an affair of such extreme importance the "will" was too audibly the prompter of the intellect. The presupposition of every believer of every shade of belief has been that he *could not* be confuted; if the counterarguments happened to be very strong, it always remained for him to decry intellect generally, and, perhaps, even to set up the *credo quia absurdum est* as the standard of extreme fanaticism. It is not the struggle of opinions that has made history so turbulent but the struggle of belief in opinions, that is to say, of convictions. If all those who thought so highly of their convictions, who made sacrifices of all kinds for them, and spared neither honor, body, nor life in their service, had only devoted half of their energy to examining their right to adhere to this or that conviction and by what road they arrived at it, how peaceable would the history of mankind now appear! How much more knowledge would there be! All the cruel scenes in connection with the persecution of heretics of all kinds would have been avoided, for two reasons: firstly, because the inquisitors would above all have inquired of themselves, and would have recognized the presumption of defending absolute truth; and secondly, because the heretics themselves would, after examination, have taken no more interest in such badly established doctrines as those of all religious sectarians and "orthodox" believers.

FROM HUMAN, ALL TOO HUMAN, II

17*

THE HAPPINESS OF THE HISTORIAN. "When we hear the hairsplitting metaphysicians and prophets of the afterworld speak, we others feel indeed that we are the 'poor in spirit,' but that ours is the heavenly kingdom of change, with spring and autumn, summer and winter, and theirs the afterworld, with its gray, everlasting frosts and shadows." Thus soliloquized a man as he walked in the morning sunshine, a man who in his pursuit of history has constantly changed not only his mind but his heart. In contrast to the metaphysicians, he is happy to harbor in himself not an "immortal soul" but many *mortal* souls.

22

HISTORIA IN NUCE. The most serious parody I ever heard was this: "In the beginning was the nonsense, and the nonsense was with God, and the nonsense was God." †

97

OF THE FUTURE OF CHRISTIANITY. We may be allowed to form a conjecture as to the disappearance of Christianity and as to the places where it will be the slowest to retreat, if we consider where and for what reasons Protestantism spread with such startling rapidity. As is well known, Protestantism promised to do far more cheaply all that the old Church did, without costly masses, pilgrimages, and priestly pomp and circumstance. It spread particularly among the northern nations, which were not so deeply rooted as those of the south in the old Church's symbolism and love of ritual. In the south the more powerful pagan religion survived in Christianity, whereas in the north Christianity

---

* From *Miscellaneous Maxims and Opinions.*
† Cf. John i.i.—TR.

meant an opposition to and a break with the old-time creed, and hence was from the first more thoughtful and less sensual, but for that very reason, in times of peril, more fanatical and more obstinate. If from the standpoint of *thought* we succeed in uprooting Christianity, we can at once know the point where it will begin to disappear—the very point at which it will be most stubborn in defense. In other places it will bend but not break, lose its leaves but burst into leaf afresh, because the senses, and not thought, have gone over to its side. But it is the senses that maintain the belief that with all its expensive outlay the Church is more cheaply and conveniently managed than under the stern conditions of work and wages. Yet what does one hold leisure (or semi-idleness) to be worth, when once one has become accustomed to it? The senses plead against a dechristianized world, saying that there would be too much work to do in it and an insufficient supply of leisure. They take the part of magic—that is, they let God work himself (*oremus nos, Deus laboret*).

223

WHITHER WE MUST TRAVEL. Immediate self-observation is not enough, by a long way, to enable us to learn to know ourselves. We need history, for the past continues to flow through us in a hundred channels. We ourselves are, after all, nothing but our own sensation at every moment of this continued flow. Even here, when we wish to step down into the stream of our apparently most peculiar and personal development, Heraclitus' aphorism, "You cannot step twice into the same river," holds good. This is a piece of wisdom which has, indeed, gradually become trite, but nevertheless has remained as strong and true as it ever was. It is the same with the saying that, in order to understand history, we must scrutinize the living remains of historical periods; that we must travel, as old Herodotus traveled, to other nations, especially to those so-called savage or half-savage races in regions where man has doffed or not yet donned European garb. For they are ancient and firmly established steps of culture on which we can stand. There is, however, a more subtle art and aim in traveling, which does not always necessitate our passing from place to place and going thousands of miles away. Very probably the last three centuries, in all their colorings and refractions of culture, survive even in our vicinity, only they have to be discovered. In some families, or even in individuals, the strata are still superimposed on each other, beautifully and perceptibly; in other places there are dispersions and displacements of the structure which are harder to understand. Certainly in remote districts, in less known mountain valleys, circumscribed communities have been able more easily to maintain an admirable pattern of a far older sentiment, a pattern that must here be investigated. On the other hand, it is improbable that such discoveries will be made in Berlin, where man comes into the world washed-out and sapless. He who after long practice of this art of travel has become a hundred-eyed Argus will accompany his Io—I mean his ego—everywhere, and in Egypt and Greece, Byzantium and Rome, France and Germany, in the age of wandering or settled races in Renaissance or Reformation, at home and abroad, in sea, forest, plant, and mountains, will again light upon the travel-adventure of this ever-growing, ever-altered ego.—Thus self-knowledge becomes universal knowledge as regards the entire past, and, by another chain of observation, which can only be indicated here, self-direction and self-training in the freest and most farseeing spirits might become universal direction as regards all future humanity.

222 *

PASSION IN THE MIDDLE AGES. The Middle Ages are the period of great passions. Neither antiquity nor our period possesses this widening of the soul. Never was the capacity of the soul greater or measured by larger standards. The physical, primeval sensuality of the barbarian races and the oversoulful, overvigilant, overbrilliant eyes of Christian mystics, the most childish and youthful and the most overripe and world-weary, the savageness of the beast of prey and the effeminacy and excessive refinement of the late antique spirit—all these elements were then not seldom united in one and the same person. Thus, if a man was seized by a passion, the rapidity of the torrent must have been greater, the whirl more confused, the fall deeper than ever before.—We modern men may be content to feel that we have suffered a loss here.

* From *The Wanderer and His Shadow*.

292

THE VICTORY OF DEMOCRACY. All political powers nowadays attempt to exploit the fear of Socialism for their own strengthening. Yet in the long run democracy alone gains the advantage, for *all* parties are now compelled to flatter "the masses" and grant them facilities and liberties of all kinds, with the result that the masses finally become omnipotent. The masses are as far as possible removed from Socialism as a doctrine of altering the acquisition of property. If once they get the steering wheel into their hands, through great majorities in their parliaments, they will attack with progressive taxation the whole dominant system of capitalists, merchants, and financiers, and will in fact slowly create a middle class which may forget Socialism like a disease that has been overcome. The practical result of this increasing democratization will next be a European league of nations, in which each individual nation, delimited by the proper geographical frontiers, has the position of a canton with its separate rights. Small account will be taken of the historic memories of previously existing nations, because the pious affection for these memories will be gradually uprooted under the democratic regime, with all its craze for novelty and experiment. The corrections of frontiers that will prove necessary will be so carried out as to serve the interests of the great cantons and at the same time that of the whole federation, but not that of any venerable memories. To find the standpoints for these corrections will be the task of future diplomats, who will have to be at the same time students of civilization, agriculturists, and commercial experts, with no armies but motives and utilities at their back. Then only will foreign and home politics be inseparably connected, whereas today the latter follows its haughty dictator, and gleans in sorry baskets the stubble that is left over from the harvest of the former.

FROM THE DAWN OF DAY

176

THE CRITICISM OF OUR ANCESTORS. Why should we now endure the truth, even about the most recent past?

Because there is now always a new generation which feels itself in contradiction to the past and enjoys in this criticism the first fruits of its sense of power. In former times the new generation, on the contrary, wished to base itself on the old and began to feel conscious of its power, not only in accepting the opinions of its ancestors but, if possible, taking them even more seriously. To criticize ancestral authority was in former times a vice, but at the present time our idealists begin by making it their starting point.

FROM THE JOYFUL WISDOM

148

WHERE REFORMATIONS ORIGINATE. At the time of the great corruption of the church it was least of all corrupt in Germany: it was on that account that the Reformation originated *here*, as a sign that even the beginnings of corruption were felt to be unendurable. For, comparatively speaking, no people was ever more Christian than the Germans at the time of Luther; their Christian culture was just about to burst into bloom with a hundredfold splendor —one night only was still lacking, but that night brought the storm which put an end to all.

149

THE FAILURE OF REFORMATIONS. It testifies to the higher culture of the Greeks, even in rather early ages, that attempts to establish new Grecian religions frequently failed; it testifies that quite early there must have been a multitude of dissimilar individuals in Greece, whose dissimilar troubles were not cured by a single recipe of faith and hope. Pythagoras and Plato, perhaps also Empedocles, and already much earlier the Orphic enthusiasts, aimed at founding new religions; and the two first-named were so endowed with the qualifications for founding religions that one cannot be sufficiently astonished at their failure: they just reached the point of founding sects. Every time that the Reformation of an entire people fails and only sects raise their heads, one may conclude that the people already contains many types, and has begun to free itself from the gross herding instincts and the morality of custom—a momentous state of suspense, which one is accustomed to disparage as decay of morals and corruption, while it announces the maturing of the egg and the early rupture of the shell. That Luther's Reformation succeeded in the north is a sign that the north had remained backward in comparison with the south of Europe, and still had requirements tolerably uniform in color and kind; and there would have been no Christianizing of Europe at all if the culture of the old world of the south had not been gradually barbarized by an excessive admixture of the blood of German barbarians, and thus lost its ascendency. The more universally and unconditionally an individual, or the thought of an individual, can operate, so much more homogeneous and so much lower must be the mass that is there operated upon; while counterstrivings betray internal counterrequirements, which also want to gratify and realize themselves. Reversely, one may always conclude with regard to an actual elevation of culture, when powerful and ambitious natures only produce a limited and sectarian effect; this is true also for the separate arts, and for the provinces of knowledge. Where there is ruling there are masses: where there are masses there is need of slavery. Where there is slavery the individuals are but few, and have the instincts and conscience of the herd opposed to them.

337

FUTURE "HUMANITY." When I look at this age with the eye of a distant future, I find nothing so remarkable in the man of the present day as his peculiar virtue and sickness called "the historical sense." It is a tendency to something quite new and foreign in history: if this embryo were given several centuries and more, there might finally evolve out of it a marvelous plant, with a smell equally marvelous, on account of which our old earth might be more pleasant to live in than it has been hitherto. We moderns are just beginning to form the chain of a very powerful, future sentiment, link by link—we hardly know what we are doing. It almost seems to us as if it were not the question of a new sentiment, but of the decline of all old sentiments —the historical sense is still something so poor and cold, and many are attacked by it as by a frost, and are made poorer and colder by it. To others it appears as the indication of stealthily approaching age, and our planet is regarded by them as a melancholy invalid, who, in order to forget his present condition, writes the history of his youth. In fact, this is one aspect of the new sentiment. He who knows how to regard the history of man in its entirety as *his own history* feels in the immense generalization all the grief of the invalid who thinks of health, of the old man who thinks of the dream of his youth, of the lover who is robbed of his beloved, of the martyr whose ideal is destroyed, of the hero on the evening of the indecisive battle which has brought him wounds and the loss of a friend. But to bear this immense sum of grief of all kinds, to be able to bear it, and yet still be the hero who at the commencement of a second day of battle greets the dawn and his happiness, as one who has an horizon of centuries before and behind him, as the heir of all nobility, of all past intellect, and the obligatory heir (as the noblest) of all the old nobles; while at the same time the first of a new nobility, the equal of which has never been seen nor even dreamt of: to take all this upon his soul, the oldest, the newest, the losses, hopes, conquests, and victories of mankind: to have all this at last in one soul, and to comprise it in one feeling: this would necessarily furnish a happiness which man has not hitherto known—a God's happiness, full of power and love, full of tears and laughter, a happiness which, like the sun in the evening, continually gives of its inexhaustible riches and empties into the sea—and like the sun, too, feels itself richest when even the poorest fisherman rows with golden oars! This divine feeling might then be called—humanity!

362

MY BELIEF IN THE VIRILIZING OF EUROPE. We owe it to Napoleon (and not at all to the French Revolution, which had in view the "fraternity" of the nations, and the florid interchange of good graces among people generally) that several warlike centuries, which have not had their like in past history, may now follow one another—in short, that we have entered upon *the classical age of war*, war at the same time scientific and popular, on the grandest scale (as regards means, talents and discipline), to which all coming millenniums will look back with envy and awe as a work of perfection: for the national movement out of which this martial glory springs is only the counter-*choc* against Napoleon, and would not have existed without him. To him, consequently, one will one day be able to attribute the fact that *man* in Europe has again got the upper hand of the merchant and the Philistine; perhaps even of "woman" also, who has become pampered owing to Christianity and the extravagant spirit of the eighteenth century, and still more owing to "modern ideas." Napoleon, who saw in modern ideas, and accordingly in civilization, something like a personal enemy, has by this hostility proved himself one of the greatest continuators of the Renaissance: he has brought to the surface a whole block of the ancient character, the decisive block perhaps, the block of granite. And who knows but that this block of ancient character will in the end get the upper hand of the national movement, and will have to make itself in a *positive* sense the heir and continuator of Napoleon—who, as one knows, wanted *one* Europe, which was to be *mistress of the world*.

FROM BEYOND GOOD AND EVIL

224

The *historical sense* (or the capacity for divining quickly the order of rank of the valuations according to which a people, a community, or an individual has lived, the "divining instinct" for the relationships of these valuations, for the relation of the authority of the valuations to the authority of the operating forces)—this historical sense, which we Europeans claim as our specialty, has come to us in the train of the enchanting and mad *semibarbarity* into which Europe has been plunged by the democratic mingling of classes and races—it is only the nineteenth century that has recognized this faculty as its sixth sense. Owing to this mingling, the past of every form and mode of life, and of cultures which were formerly closely contiguous and superimposed on one another, flows forth into us "modern souls"; our instincts now run back in all directions, we ourselves are a kind of chaos: in the end, as we have said, the spirit perceives its advantage therein. By means of our semibarbarity in body and in desire, we have secret access everywhere, such as a noble age never had; we have access above all to the labyrinth of imperfect civilizations, and to every form of semibarbarity that has at any time existed on earth;

and insofar as the most considerable part of human civilization hitherto has just been semibarbarity, the "historical sense" implies almost the sense and instinct for everything, the taste and tongue for everything: whereby it immediately proves itself to be an *ignoble* sense. For instance, we enjoy Homer once more: it is perhaps our happiest acquisition that we know how to appreciate Homer, whom men of distinguished culture (as the French of the seventeenth century, like Saint-Évremond, who reproached him for his *esprit vaste* and even Voltaire, the last echo of the century) cannot and could not so easily appropriate—whom they scarcely permitted themselves to enjoy. The very decided Yea and Nay of their palate, their promptly ready disgust, their hesitating reluctance with regard to everything strange, their horror of the bad taste even of lively curiosity, and in general the averseness of every distinguished and self-sufficing culture to avow a new desire, a dissatisfaction with its own condition, or an admiration of what is strange: all this determines and disposes them unfavorably even toward the best things of the world which are not their property or *could not* become their prey—and no faculty is more unintelligible to such men than just this historical sense, with its truckling, plebeian curiosity. The case is not different with Shakespeare, that marvelous Spanish-Moorish-Saxon synthesis of taste, over whom an ancient Athenian of the circle of Aeschylus would have half-killed himself with laughter or irritation; but we—accept precisely this wild motleyness, this medley of the most delicate, the most coarse, and the most artificial, with a secret confidence and cordiality; we enjoy it as a refinement of art reserved expressly for us, and allow ourselves to be as little disturbed by the repulsive fumes and the proximity of the English populace in which Shakespeare's art and taste lives as perhaps on the Via Chiaia of Naples, where, with all our senses awake, we go our way, enchanted and voluntarily, in spite of the drain-odor of the lower quarters of the town. That as men of the "historical sense" we have our virtues is not to be disputed—we are unpretentious, unselfish, modest, brave, habituated to self-control and self-renunciation, very grateful, very patient, very complaisant—but with all this we are perhaps not very "tasteful." Let us finally confess it, that what is most difficult for us men of the "historical sense" to grasp, feel, taste, and love, what finds us fundamentally prejudiced and almost hostile, is precisely the perfection and ultimate maturity in every culture and art, the essentially noble in works and men, their moment of smooth sea and halcyon self-sufficiency, the goldenness and coldness which all things show that have perfected themselves. Perhaps our great virtue of the historical sense is in necessary contrast to *good* taste, at least to the very best taste; and we can only evoke in ourselves imperfectly, hesitatingly, and with compulsion the small, short, and happy godsends and glorifications of human life as they shine here and there: those moments and marvelous experiences, when a great power has voluntarily come to a halt before the boundless and infinite—when a superabundance of refined delight has been enjoyed by a sudden checking and petrifying, by standing firmly and planting oneself fixedly on still trembling ground. *Proportionateness* is strange to us, let us confess it to ourselves; our itching is really the itching for the infinite, the immeasurable. Like the rider on his forward panting horse, we let the reins fall before the infinite, we modern men, we semibarbarians—and are only in *our* highest bliss when we—*are in most danger.*

FROM THE TWILIGHT OF THE IDOLS

37

HAVE WE BECOME MORE MORAL? As might have been expected, the whole *ferocity* of moral stultification, which, as is well known, passes for morality itself in Germany, hurled itself against my concept "Beyond Good and Evil." I could tell you some nice tales about this. Above all, people tried to make me see the "incontestable superiority" of our age in regard to moral sentiment, and the *progress* we had made in these matters. Compared with us, a Caesar Borgia was by no means to be represented as "higher man," the sort of *Superman*, which I declared him to be. The editor of the Swiss paper the *Bund* went so far as not only to express his admiration for the courage displayed by my enterprise but also to pretend to "understand" that the intended purpose of my work was to abolish all decent feeling. Much obliged!—In reply, I venture to raise the following question: *have we really become more moral?* The fact that everybody believes that we have is already an objection to the belief. We modern men, so extremely delicate and susceptible, full of consideration one for the other, actually dare to suppose that the pampering fellow feeling which we all display, this unanimity which we have at last acquired in

sparing and helping and trusting one another marks a definite
step forward, and shows us to be far ahead of the man of
the Renaissance. But every age thinks the same, it is *bound*
to think the same. This at least is certain, that we should
not dare to stand amid the conditions which prevailed at
the Renaissance, we should not even dare to imagine ourselves in those conditions: our nerves could not endure that
reality, not to speak of our muscles. The inability to do
this, however, does not denote any progress; but simply the
different and more senile quality of our particular nature,
its greater weakness, delicateness, and susceptibility, out of
which a morality *more rich in consideration* was bound to
arise. If we imagine our delicateness and senility, our
physiological decrepitude as nonexistent, our morality of
"humanization" would immediately lose all value—no morality has any value per se—it would even fill us with scorn.
On the other hand, do not let us doubt that we moderns,
wrapped as we are in the thick cotton wool of our humani-
tarianism which would shrink even from grazing a stone,
would present a comedy to Caesar Borgia's contemporaries
which would literally make them die of laughter. We are indeed, without knowing it, exceedingly ridiculous with our
modern "virtues." . . . The decline of the instincts of hostility and of those instincts that arouse suspicion—for this if
anything is what constitutes our progress—is only one of the
results manifested by the general decline in *vitality:* it requires a hundred times more trouble and caution to live
such a dependent and senile existence. In such circumstances
everybody gives everybody else a helping hand, and, to a
certain extent, everybody is either an invalid or an invalid's
attendant. This is then called "virtue": among those men who
knew a different life—that is to say, a fuller, more prodigal,
more superabundant sort of life—it might have been called
by another name, possibly "cowardice," or "vileness," or
"old woman's morality." . . . Our mollification of morals
—this is my cry; this if you will is my *innovation*—is the
outcome of our decline; conversely hardness and terrible-
ness in morals may be the result of a surplus of life. When
the latter state prevails, much is dared, much is challenged,
and much is also *squandered*. That which formerly was simply
the salt of life would now be our *poison*. To be different—
even this is a form of strength—for that, likewise, we are
too senile, too decrepit; our morality of fellow feeling,
against which I was the first to raise a finger of warning,
that which might be called *moral impressionism*, is one
symptom the more of the excessive physiological irritability

which is peculiar to everything decadent. That movement which attempted to introduce itself in a scientific manner on the shoulders of Schopenhauer's morality of pity—a very sad attempt!—is in its essence the movement of decadence in morality, and as such it is intimately related to Christian morality. Strong ages and noble cultures see something contemptible in pity, in the "love of one's neighbor," and in a lack of egoism and of self-esteem. Ages should be measured according to their *positive forces;* valued by this standard that prodigal and fateful age of the Renaissance appears as the last *great* age, while we moderns with our anxious care of ourselves and love of our neighbors, with all our unassuming virtues of industry, equity, and scientific method —with our lust of collection, of economy, and of mechanism —represent a *weak* age. . . . Our virtues are necessarily determined, and are even stimulated, by our weakness. "Equality," a certain definite process of making everybody uniform, which only finds its expression in the theory of equal rights, is essentially bound up with a declining culture: the chasm between man and man, class and class, the multiplicity of types, the will to be one's self, and to distinguish one's self —that, in fact, which I call the *pathos of distance* is proper to all *strong* ages. The force of tension—nay, the tension itself—between extremes grows slighter every day—the extremes themselves are tending to become obliterated to the point of becoming identical. All our political theories and state constitutions, not by any means excepting "The German Empire," are the logical consequences, the necessary consequences of decline; the unconscious effect of *decadence* has begun to dominate even the ideals of the various sciences. My objection to the whole of English and French sociology still continues to be this, that it knows only the *decadent form* of society from experience, and with perfectly childlike innocence takes the instincts of decline as the *norm,* the standard, of sociological valuations. *Descending* life, the decay of all organizing power—that is to say, of all that power which separates, cleaves gulfs, and establishes rank above and below—formulated itself in modern sociology as *the* ideal. Our socialists are decadents: but Herbert Spencer was also a *decadent*—he saw something to be desired in the triumph of altruism! . . .

FROM THE ANTICHRIST*

4

Mankind does *not* represent a development toward a better, stronger, or higher type, in the sense in which this is supposed to occur today. "Progress" is merely a modern idea—that is to say, a false idea.† The modern European is still far below the European of the Renaissance in value. The process of evolution does not by any means imply elevation, enhancement, and increasing strength.

On the other hand, isolated and individual cases are continually succeeding in different places on earth, as the outcome of the most different cultures, and in these a *higher type* certainly manifests itself: something which by the side of mankind in general represents a kind of superman. Such lucky strokes of great success have always been possible and will perhaps always be possible. And even whole races, tribes, and nations may in certain circumstances represent such *lucky strokes.*

* From *The Twilight of the Idols.*

† Cf. Disraeli: "But enlightened Europe is not happy. Its existence is a fever which it calls progress. Progress to what?" (*Tancred*, Book III, Chap. vii).—TR.

VI. Music

FROM THE CASE OF WAGNER

1

YESTERDAY—would you believe it?—I heard Bizet's master-piece for the twentieth time. Once more I attended with the same gentle reverence; once again I did not run away. This triumph over my impatience surprises me. How such a work completes one! Through it one almost becomes a "masterpiece" oneself. And, as a matter of fact, each time I heard *Carmen* it seemed to me that I was more of a philosopher, a better philosopher than at other times: I became so forbearing, so happy, so Indian, so *settled*. . . . To sit for five hours: the first step to holiness!—May I be allowed to say that Bizet's orchestration is the only one that I can endure now? That other orchestration which is all the rage at present—the Wagnerian—is brutal, artificial, and "unsophisticated" withal, hence its appeal to all the three senses of the modern soul at once. How terribly Wagnerian orchestration affects me! I call it the sirocco. A disagreeable sweat breaks out all over me. All my fine weather vanishes.

Bizet's music seems to me perfect. It comes forward lightly, gracefully, stylishly. It is lovable, it does not sweat. "All that is good is easy, everything divine runs with light feet": this is the first principle of my aesthetics. This music is wicked, refined, fatalistic; and withal remains popular—it possesses the refinement of a race, not of an individual. It is rich. It is definite. It builds, organizes, completes; and in this sense it stands as a contrast to the polypus in music,

258

to "endless melody." Have more painful, more tragic accents ever been heard on the stage before? And how are they obtained? Without grimaces! Without counterfeiting of any kind! Free from the *lie* of the grand style!—In short: this music assumes that the listener is intelligent even as a musician—thereby it is the opposite of Wagner, who, apart from everything else, was in any case the most *ill-mannered* genius on earth (Wagner takes us as if . . ., he repeats a thing so often that we become desperate—that we ultimately believe it).

And once more: I become a better man when Bizet speaks to me. Also a better musician, a better *listener*. Is it in any way possible to listen better?—I even burrow behind this music with my ears. I hear its very cause. I seem to assist at its birth. I tremble before the dangers which this daring music runs, I am enraptured over those happy accidents for which even Bizet himself may not be responsible.—And, strange to say, at bottom I do not give it a thought, or am not aware how much thought I really do give it. For quite other ideas are running through my head the while. . . . Has anyone ever observed that music *emancipates* the spirit, gives wings to thought, and that the more one becomes a musician the more one is also a philosopher? The gray sky of abstraction seems thrilled by flashes of lightning; the light is strong enough to reveal all the details of things; to enable one to grapple with problems; and the world is surveyed as if from a mountaintop—With this I have defined philosophical pathos.—And unexpectedly *answers* drop into my lap, a small hailstorm of ice and wisdom, of problems *solved*. Where am I? Bizet makes me productive. Everything that is good makes me productive. I have gratitude for nothing else, nor have I any other touchstone for testing what is good.

2

Bizet's work also saves; Wagner is not the only "Saviour." With it one bids farewell to the *damp* north and to all the fog of the Wagnerian ideal. Even the action in itself delivers us from these things. From Merimée it has this logic even in passion, from him it has the direct line, *inexorable* necessity; but what it has above all else is that which belongs to subtropical zones—that dryness of atmosphere, that *limpidezza* of the air. Here in every respect the climate is altered. Here another kind of sensuality, another kind of sensitiveness, and another kind of cheerfulness make their appeal. This music is gay, but not in a French or German way. Its gaiety is African; fate hangs over it, its happiness is short, sudden, without reprieve. I envy Bizet for having had the courage of this sensitiveness, which hitherto in the cultured music of Europe has found no means of expression—of this southern, tawny, sunburnt sensitiveness. . . . What a joy the golden afternoon of its happiness is to us! When we look out, with this music in our minds, we wonder whether we have ever seen the sea so *calm*. And how soothing is this Moorish dancing! How, for once, even our insatiability gets sated by its lascivious melancholy!—And finally love, love translated back into *Nature!* Not the love of a "cultured girl!"—no Senta-sentimentality.* But love as fate, as a fatality, cynical, innocent, cruel—and precisely in this way *Nature!* The love whose means is war, whose very essence is the *mortal hatred* between the sexes!—I know no case in which the tragic irony, which constitutes the kernel of love, is expressed with such severity, or in so terrible a formula, as in the last cry of Don José with which the work ends:

> "Yes, it is I who have killed her,
> I—my adored Carmen!"

—Such a conception of love (the only one worthy of a philosopher) is rare: it distinguishes one work of art from among a thousand others. For, as a rule, artists are no better than the rest of the world, they are even worse—they *misunderstand* love. Even Wagner misunderstood it. They imagine that they are selfless in it because they appear to be seeking the advantage of another creature often to their own disadvantage. But in return they want to *possess* the other creature. . . . Even God is no exception to this rule, he is very far from thinking "What does it matter to thee whether I love thee or not?"—He becomes terrible if he is not loved in return. "*L'amour*—and with this principle one carries one's point against Gods and men—*est de tous les sentiments le plus égoïste, et par conséquent, lorsqu'il est blessé, le moins généreux*" (B. Constant).

3

Perhaps you are beginning to perceive how very much this

* Senta is the heroine in *The Flying Dutchman.—Tr.*

music *improves* me?—*Il faut méditerraniser la musique:* and I have my reasons for this principle (*Beyond Good and Evil*, pp. 216 *et seq.*). The return to Nature, health, good spirits, youth, *virtue!*—And yet I was one of the most corrupted Wagnerites. . . . I was able to take Wagner seriously. Oh, this old magician! what tricks has he not played upon us! The first thing his art places in our hands is a magnifying glass: we look through it, and we no longer trust our own eyes. Everything grows bigger, *even Wagner grows bigger.* . . . What a clever rattlesnake. Throughout his life he rattled "resignation," "loyalty," and "purity" about our ears, and he retired from the *corrupt* world with a song of praise to chastity!—And we believed it all. . . .

—But you will not listen to me? You *prefer* even the *problem* of Wagner to that of Bizet? But neither do I underrate it; it has its charm. The problem of salvation is even a venerable problem. Wagner pondered over nothing so deeply as over salvation: his opera is the opera of salvation. Someone always wants to be saved in his operas—now it is a youth; anon it is a maid—this is *his problem.*—And how lavishly he varies his leitmotiv! What rare and melancholy modulations! If it were not for Wagner, who would teach us that innocence has a preference for saving interesting sinners? (the case in *Tannhäuser*). Or that even the eternal Jew gets saved and *settled down* when he marries? (the case in *The Flying Dutchman*). Or that corrupted old females prefer to be saved by chaste young men? (the case of Kundry). Or that young hysterics like to be saved by their doctor? (the case in *Lohengrin*). Or that beautiful girls most love to be saved by a knight who also happens to be a Wagnerite? (the case in *Die Meistersinger*). Or that even married women also like to be saved by a knight? (the case of Isolde). Or that the venerable Almighty, after having compromised himself morally in all manner of ways, is at last delivered by a free spirit and an immoralist? (the case in the *Ring*). Admire more especially this last piece of wisdom! Do you understand it? I—take good care not to understand it. . . . That it is possible to draw yet other lessons from the works above mentioned, I am much more ready to prove than to dispute. That one may be driven by a Wagnerian ballet to desperation—*and* to virtue! (once again the case in *Tannhäuser*). That not going to bed at the right time may be followed by the worst consequences (once again the case of *Lohengrin*). That one can never be too sure of the spouse one actually marries (for the third time, the case of *Lohengrin.*) *Tristan and Isolde* glorifies the perfect husband who, in a certain case, can ask only one question: "But why have ye not told me this before? Nothing could be simpler than that!" Reply:

> "That I cannot tell thee.
> And what thou askest,
> That wilt thou never learn."

Lohengrin contains a solemn ban upon all investigation and questioning. In this way Wagner stood for the Christian concept, "Thou must and shalt *believe*." It is a crime against the highest and the holiest to be scientific. . . . *The Flying Dutchman* preaches the sublime doctrine that woman can moor the most erratic soul, or to put it into Wagnerian terms "save" him. Here we venture to ask a question. Supposing that this were actually true, would it therefore be desirable? What becomes of the "eternal Jew" whom a woman adores and *enchains?* He simply ceases from being eternal; he marries—that is to say, he concerns us no longer. Transferred into the realm of reality, the danger for the artist and for the genius—and these are of course the "eternal Jews"—resides in woman: *adoring* women are their ruin. Scarcely anyone has sufficient character not to be corrupted—"saved" when he finds himself treated as a God: he then immediately condescends to woman. Man is a coward in the face of all that is eternally feminine: and this the girls know. In many cases of woman's love, and perhaps precisely in the most famous ones, the love is no more than a refined form of parasitism, a making one's nest in another's soul and sometimes even in another's flesh—Ah! and how constantly at the cost of the host!

We know the fate of Goethe in old-maidish moralin-corroded Germany. He was always offensive to Germans, he found honest admirers only among Jewesses. Schiller, "noble" Schiller, who cried flowery words into their ears—he was a man after their own heart. What did they reproach Goethe with?—with the Mount of Venus, and with having composed certain Venetian epigrams. Even Klopstock preached him a moral sermon; there was a time when Herder was fond of using the word "Priapus" when he spoke of Goethe. Even *Wilhelm Meister* seemed to be only a symptom of decline, of a moral "going to the dogs." The "Menagerie of tame cattle," the worthlessness of the hero in this book, revolted Niebuhr, who finally bursts out in a plaint which Biterolf *

---

* A character in *Tannhäuser.*—TR.

might well have sung: "nothing so easily makes a painful impression as *when a great mind despoils itself of its wings and strives for virtuosity in something greatly inferior, while it renounces more lofty aims.*" But the most indignant of all was the cultured woman: all smaller courts in Germany, every kind of "Puritanism" made the sign of the cross at the sight of Goethe, at the thought of the "unclean spirit" in Goethe. This history was what Wagner set to music. He *saves* Goethe, that goes without saying; but he does so in such a clever way that he also takes the side of the cultured woman. Goethe gets saved: a prayer saves him, a cultured woman *draws him out of the mire.*

—As to what Goethe would have thought of Wagner?— Goethe once set himself the question, "What danger hangs over all romanticists: the fate of romanticists?" His answer was: "To choke over the rumination of moral and religious absurdities." In short: *Parsifal* . . . The philosopher writes thereto an epilogue. *Holiness*—the only remaining higher value still seen by the mob or by woman, the horizon of the ideal for all those who are naturally shortsighted. To philosophers, however, this horizon, like every other, is a mere misunderstanding, a sort of slamming of the door in the face of the real beginning of their world—their danger, their ideal, their desideratum. . . . In more polite language: *La philosophie ne suffit pas au grand nombre. Il lui faut la sainteté.* . . .

4

I shall once more relate the history of the *Ring*. This is its proper place. It is also the history of a salvation: except that in this case it is Wagner himself who is saved. —Half his lifetime Wagner believed in the *Revolution* as only a Frenchman could have believed in it. He sought it in the runic inscriptions of myths, he thought he had found a typical revolutionary in Siegfried.—"Whence arises all the evil in this world?" Wagner asked himself. From "old contracts": he replied, as all revolutionary ideologists have done. In plain English: from customs, laws, morals, institutions, from all those things upon which the ancient world and ancient society rests. "How can one get rid of the evil in this world? How can one get rid of ancient society?" Only by declaring war against "contracts" (traditions, morality). *This Siegfried does.* He starts early at the game, very early: his origin itself is already a declaration of war against morality

—he is the result of adultery, of incest. . . . Not the saga, but Wagner himself is the inventor of this radical feature; in this matter he *corrected* the saga. . . . Siegfried continues as he began: he follows only his first impulse, he flings all tradition, all respect, all *fear* to the winds. Whatever displeases him he strikes down. He tilts irreverently at old godheads. His principal undertaking, however, is to emancipate woman —"to deliver Brunnhilda." . . . Siegfried and Brunnhilda; the sacrament of free love; the dawn of the golden age; the twilight of the Gods of old morality—*evil is got rid of.* . . . For a long while Wagner's ship sailed happily along this course. There can be no doubt that along it Wagner sought his highest goal. What happened? A misfortune. The ship dashed on to a reef; Wagner had run aground. The reef was Schopenhauer's philosophy; Wagner had stuck fast on a *contrary* view of the world. What had he set to music? Optimism? Wagner was ashamed. It was moreover an optimism for which Schopenhauer had devised an evil expression— *unscrupulous* optimism. He was more than ever ashamed. He reflected for some time; his position seemed desperate. . . . At last a path of escape seemed gradually to open before him: what if the reef on which he had been wrecked could be interpreted as a goal, as the ulterior motive, as the actual purpose of his journey? To be wrecked here, this was also a goal. *Bene navigavi cum naufragium feci* . . . and he translated the *Ring* into Schopenhauerian language. Everything goes wrong, everything goes to wrack and ruin, the new world is just as bad as the old one: Nonentity, the Indian Circe beckons. . . . Brunnhilda, who according to the old plan had to retire with a song in honor of free love, consoling the world with the hope of a socialistic Utopia in which "all will be well," now gets something else to do. She must first study Schopenhauer. She must first versify the fourth book of *The World as Will and Idea.* *Wagner was saved.* . . . Joking apart, this *was* a salvation. The service which Wagner owes to Schopenhauer is incalculable. It was the *philosopher of decadence* who allowed the *artist of decadence* to find himself.

5

The *artist of decadence.* That is the word. And here I begin to be serious. I could not think of looking on approvingly while this *décadent* spoils our health—and music into the bargain. Is Wagner a man at all? Is he not rather a disease? Everything he touches he contaminates. *He has made music sick.*

A typical *décadent* who thinks himself necessary with his corrupted taste, who arrogates to himself a higher taste, who tries to establish his depravity as a law, as progress, as a fulfillment.

And no one guards against it. His powers of seduction attain monstrous proportions, holy incense hangs around him, the misunderstanding concerning him · is called the Gospel—and he has certainly not converted only the *poor in spirit* to his cause!

I should like to open the window a little. Air! More air!—

The fact that people in Germany deceive themselves concerning Wagner does not surprise me. The reverse would surprise me. The Germans have modeled a Wagner for themselves whom they can honor: never yet have they been psychologists; they are thankful that they misunderstand. But that people should also deceive themselves concerning Wagner in Paris! Where people are scarcely anything else than psychologists. And in Saint Petersburg! Where things are divined which even Paris has no idea of. How intimately related must Wagner be to the entire decadence of Europe for her not to have felt that he was decadent! He belongs to it: he is its protagonist, its greatest name. . . . We bring honor on ourselves by elevating him to the clouds. For the mere fact that no one guards against him is in itself already a sign of decadence. Instinct is weakened, what ought to be eschewed now attracts. People actually kiss that which plunges them more quickly into the abyss. Is there any need for an example? One has only to think of the regime which anemic, or gouty, or diabetic people prescribe for themselves. The definition of a vegetarian: a creature who has need of a corroborating diet. To recognize what is harmful as harmful, to be able to deny oneself what is harmful, is a sign of youth, of vitality. That which is harmful lures the exhausted: cabbage lures the vegetarian. Illness itself can be a stimulus to life: but one must be healthy enough for such a stimulus!—Wagner increases exhaustion: *therefore* he attracts the weak and exhausted to him. Oh, the rattlesnake joy of the old Master precisely because he always saw "the little children" coming unto him!

I place this point of view first and foremost: Wagner's art is diseased. The problems he sets on the stage are all concerned with hysteria; the convulsiveness of his emotions, his overexcited sensitiveness, his taste which demands ever sharper condimentation, his erraticness which he togged out to

look like principles, and, last but not least, his choice of
heroes and heroines, considered as physiological types (—a
hospital ward!—): the whole represents a morbid picture;
of this there can be no doubt. *Wagner est une névrose.*
Maybe, that nothing is better known today, or in any case
the subject of greater study, than the Protean character of
degeneration which has disguised itself here, both as an art
and as an artist. In Wagner our medical men and physiologists have a most interesting case, or at least a very complete one. Owing to the very fact that nothing is more modern than this thorough morbidness, this dilatoriness and
excessive irritability of the nervous machinery, Wagner is the
modern artist par excellence, the Cagliostro of modernity. All
that the world most needs today is combined in the most
seductive manner in his art—the three great stimulants of
exhausted people: *brutality, artificiality,* and *innocence*
(idiocy).

Wagner is a great corrupter of music. With it, he found
the means of stimulating tired nerves—and in this way he
made music ill. In the art of spurring exhausted creatures
back into activity, and of recalling half-corpses to life, the
inventiveness he shows is of no mean order. He is the master
of hypnotic trickery, and he fells the strongest like bullocks.
Wagner's *success*—his success with nerves, and therefore
with women—converted the whole world of ambitious musicians into disciples of his secret art. And not only the ambitious but also the *shrewd.* . . . Only with morbid music can
money be made today; our big theaters live on Wagner.

6

—Once more I will venture to indulge in a little levity. Let
us suppose that Wagner's *success* could become flesh and
blood and assume a human form; that, dressed up as a good-
natured musical savant, it could move among budding artists.
How do you think it would then be likely to express itself?

My friends, it would say, let us exchange a word or two in
private. It is easier to compose bad music than good music.
But what if apart from this it were also more profitable, more
effective, more convincing, more exalting, more secure, more
Wagnerian? . . . *Pulchrum est paucorum hominum.* Bad
enough in all conscience! We understand Latin, and perhaps we also understand which side our bread is buttered.
Beauty has its drawbacks: we know that. Wherefore beauty

then? Why not rather aim at size, at the sublime, the gigantic, that which moves the *masses?*—And to repeat: it is easier to be titanic than to be beautiful; we know that. . . .

We know the masses, we know the theater. The best of those who assemble there, German youths, horned Siegfrieds and other Wagnerites, require the sublime, the profound, and the overwhelming. This much still lies within our power. And as for the others who assemble there—the cultured cretins, the blasé pygmies, the eternally feminine, the gastrically happy, in short, the people—they also require the sublime, the profound, the overwhelming. All these people argue in the same way. "He who overthrows us is strong; he who elevates us is godly; he who makes us wonder vaguely is profound."—Let us make up our mind then, my friends in music: we do want to overthrow them, we do want to elevate them, we do want to make them wonder vaguely. This much still lies within our powers.

In regard to the process of making them wonder: it is here that our notion of "style" finds its starting-point. Above all, no thoughts! Nothing is more compromising than a thought! But the state of mind which *precedes* thought, the labor of the thought still unborn, the promise of future thought, the world as it was before God created it—a recrudescence of chaos. . . . Chaos makes people wonder. . .

In the words of the master: infinity but without melody.

In the second place, with regard to the overthrowing, this belongs at least in part to physiology. Let us, in the first place, examine the instruments. A few of them would convince even our intestines (—they *throw open* doors, as Handel would say), others becharm our very marrow. The *color of the melody is* all-important here; *the melody itself* is of no importance. Let us be precise about *this* point. To what other purpose should we spend our strength? Let us be characteristic in tone even to the point of foolishness! If by means of tones we allow plenty of scope for guessing, this will be put to the credit of our intellects. Let us irritate nerves, let us strike them dead: let us handle thunder and lightning—that is what overthrows. . . .

But what overthrows best is *passion*. We must try and be clear concerning this question of passion. Nothing is cheaper than passion! All the virtues of counterpoint may be dispensed with, there is no need to have learned anything, but passion is always within our reach! Beauty is difficult: let us beware of beauty! . . . And also of *melody!* However much in earnest we may otherwise be about the idea, let us slander, my friends, let us slander—let us slander melody! Nothing

is more dangerous than a beautiful melody! Nothing is more
certain to ruin taste! My friends, if people again set about
loving beautiful melodies, we are lost! . . .

First principle: melody is immoral. *Proof:* "Palestrina."
Application: Parsifal. The absence of melody is in itself
sanctifying. . . .

And this is the definition of passion. Passion—or the acrobatic feats of ugliness on the tightrope of enharmonic.—My
friends, let us dare to be ugly! Wagner dared it! Let us
heave the mud of the most repulsive harmonies undauntedly
before us. We must not even spare our hands! Only thus, shall
we become *natural.* . . .

And now a last word of advice. Perhaps it covers everything. *Let us be idealists!* If not the cleverest, it is at least
the wisest thing we can do. In order to elevate men we
ourselves must be exalted. Let us wander in the clouds, let us
harangue eternity, let us be careful to group great symbols
all around us! *Sursum! Bumbum!*—there is no better advice.
The "heaving breast" shall be our argument, "beautiful feelings" our advocates. Virtue still carries its point against counterpoint. "How could he who improves us help being better
than we?" man has ever thought thus. Let us therefore improve mankind!—in this way we shall become good (in this
way we shall even become "classics"—Schiller became a
"classic"). The straining after the base excitement of the
senses, after so-called beauty, shattered the nerves of the
Italians: let us remain German! Even Mozart's relation to
music—Wagner spoke this word of comfort to us—was at
bottom frivolous. . . . Never let us acknowledge that music
"may be a recreation," that it may "enliven," that it may
"give pleasure." *Never let us give pleasure!*—we shall be lost
if people once again think of music hedonistically. . . . That
belongs to the bad eighteenth century. . . . On the other hand,
nothing would be more advisable (between ourselves) than a
dose of—*cant, sit venia verbo.* This imparts dignity.—And
let us take care to select the precise moment when it would
be fitting to have black looks, to sigh openly, to sigh de-
voutly, to flaunt grand Christian sympathy before their eyes.
"Man is corrupt: who will save him? *what will save him?*"
Do not let us reply. We must be on our guard. We must
control our ambition, which would bid us found new religions. But no one must doubt that it is *we* who save him,
that in *our* music alone salvation is to be found. . . . (See
Wagner's essay, "Religion and Art.")

7

Enough! Enough! I fear that, beneath all my merry jests,
you are beginning to recognize the sinister truth only too
clearly—the picture of the decline of art, of the decline of
the artist. The latter, which is a decline of character, might
perhaps be defined provisonally in the following manner:
the musician is now becoming an actor, his art is developing
ever more and more into a talent for *telling lies*. In a certain
chapter of my principal work which bears the title "Concerning the Physiology of Art," * I shall have an opportunity
of showing more thoroughly how this transformation of art
as a whole into histrionics is just as much a sign of physiological degeneration (or more precisely a form of hysteria)
as any other individual corruption and infirmity peculiar to
the art which Wagner inaugurated: for instance the restlessness of its optics, which makes it necessary to change one's
attitude to it every second. They understand nothing of Wagner who see in him but a sport of nature, an arbitrary mood,
a chapter of accidents. He was not the "defective," "ill-
fated," "contradictory" genius that people have declared him
to be. Wagner was something *complete*, he was a typical
décadent, in whom every sign of "free will" was lacking, in
whom every feature was necessary. If there is anything at all
of interest in Wagner, it is the consistency with which a
critical physiological condition may convert itself, step by
step, conclusion after conclusion, into a method, a form of
procedure, a reform of all principles, a crisis in taste.

At this point I shall only stop to consider the question of
style. How is *decadence* in *literature* characterized? By the
fact that in it life no longer animates the whole. Words become predominant and leap right out of the sentence to which
they belong, the sentences themselves trespass beyond their
bounds, and obscure the sense of the whole page, and the
page in its turn gains in vigor at the cost of the whole—the
whole is no longer a whole. But this is the formula for every
decadent style: there is always anarchy among the atoms,
disaggregation of the will—in moral terms: "freedom of the
individual"—extended into a political theory: *"equal* rights
for all." Life, equal vitality, all the vibration and exuberance
of life, driven back into the smallest structure, and the remainder left almost lifeless. Everywhere paralysis, distress,

* See *The Will to Power*, Vol. II, authorized English edition.—*Tr.*

and numbness, or hostility and chaos: both striking one with ever increasing force the higher the forms of organization are into which one ascends. The whole no longer lives at all: it is composed, reckoned up, artificial, a fictitious thing.

In Wagner's case the first thing we notice is an hallucination, not of tones, but of attitudes. Only after he has the latter does he begin to seek the semeiotics of tone for them. If we wish to admire him, we should observe him at work here: how he separates and distinguishes, how he arrives at small unities, and how he galvanizes them, accentuates them, and brings them into pre-eminence. But in this way he exhausts his strength: the rest is worthless. How paltry, awkward, and amateurish is his manner of "developing," his attempt at combining incompatible parts. His manner in this respect reminds one of two people who even in other ways are not unlike him in style—the brothers Goncourt; one almost feels compassion for so much impotence. That Wagner disguised his inability to create organic forms, under the cloak of a principle, that he should have constructed a "dramatic style" out of what we should call the total inability to create any style whatsoever, is quite in keeping with that daring habit, which stuck to him throughout his life, of setting up a principle wherever capacity failed him. (In this respect he was very different from old Kant, who rejoiced in another form of daring, i.e., whenever a principle failed him, he endowed man with a "capacity" which took its place. . . .) Once more let it be said that Wagner is really only worthy of admiration and love by virtue of his inventiveness in small things, in his elaboration of details—here one is quite justified in proclaiming him a master of the first rank, as our greatest musical *miniaturist*, who compresses an infinity of meaning and sweetness into the smallest space. His wealth of color, of chiaroscuro, of the mystery of a dying light, so pampers our senses that afterward almost every other musician strikes us as being too robust. If people would believe me, they would not form the highest idea of Wagner from that which pleases them in him today. All that was only devised for convincing the masses, and people like ourselves recoil from it just as one would recoil from too garish a fresco. What concern have we with the irritating brutality of the overture to the *Tannhäuser*? Or with the Walkyrie Circus? Whatever has become popular in Wagner's art, including that which has become so outside the theater, is in bad taste and spoils taste. The *Tannhäuser* March seems to me to savor of the Philistine; the overture of *The Flying Dutchman* is much ado about nothing; the prelude to

Lohengrin was the first, only too insidious, only too successful example of how one can hypnotize with music (—I dislike all music which aspires to nothing higher than to convince the nerves). But apart from the Wagner who paints frescoes and practices magnetism, there is yet another Wagner who hoards small treasures: our greatest melancholic in music, full of side glances, loving speeches, and words of comfort, in which no one ever forestalled him—the tone master of melancholy and drowsy happiness. . . . A lexicon of Wagner's most intimate phrases—a host of short fragments of from five to fifteen bars each, of music which *nobody knows*. . . . Wagner had the virtue of *décadents*—pity. . . .

8

—"Very good! But how can this *décadent* spoil one's taste if perchance one is not a musician, if perchance one is not oneself a *décadent?*"—Conversely! How can one *help* it! *Just* you try it!—You know not what Wagner is: quite a great actor! Does a more profound, a more *ponderous* influence exist on the stage? Just look at these youthlets—all benumbed, pale, breathless! They are Wagnerites: they know nothing about music—and yet Wagner gets the mastery of them. Wagner's art presses with the weight of a hundred atmospheres: do but submit, there is nothing else to do. . . . Wagner the actor is a tyrant, his pathos flings all taste, all resistance, to the winds.—Who else has this persuasive power in his attitudes, who else sees attitudes so clearly before anything else! This holding-of-its-breath in Wagnerian pathos, this disinclination to have done with an intense feeling, this terrifying habit of dwelling on a situation in which every instant almost chokes one.——

Was Wagner a musician at all? In any case he was something else to *a much greater degree*—that is to say, an incomparable *histrio*, the greatest mime, the most astounding theatrical genius that the Germans have ever had, our *scenic artist par excellence*. He belongs to some other sphere than the history of music, with whose really great and genuine figure he must not be confounded. Wagner *and* Beethoven —this is blasphemy—and above all it does not do justice even to Wagner. . . . As a musician he was no more than what he was as a man: he *became* a musician, he *became* a poet, because the tyrant in him, his actor's genius, drove him to be both. Nothing is known concerning Wagner, so long as his dominating instinct has not been divined.

Wagner was *not* instinctively a musician. And this he proved by the way in which he abandoned all laws and rules, or, in more precise terms, all style in music, in order to make what he wanted with it, i.e., a rhetorical medium for the stage, a medium of expression, a means of accentuating an attitude, a vehicle of suggestion and of the psychologically picturesque. In this department Wagner may well stand as an inventor and an innovator of the first order —*he increased the powers of speech of music to an incalculable degree*—: he is the Victor Hugo of music as language, provided always we allow that under certain circumstances music may be something which is not music, but speech—instrument—*ancilla dramaturgica*. Wagner's music, *not* in the tender care of theatrical taste, which is very tolerant, is simply bad music, perhaps the worst that has ever been composed. When a musician can no longer count up to three, he becomes "dramatic," he becomes "Wagnerian." . . .

Wagner almost discovered the magic which can be wrought even now by means of music which is both incoherent and *elementary*. His consciousness of this attains to huge proportions, as does also his instinct to dispense entirely with higher law and *style*. The elementary factors—sound, movement, color, in short, the whole sensuousness of music—suffice. Wagner never calculates as a musician with a musician's conscience: all he strains after is effect, nothing more than effect. And he knows what he has to make an effect upon! In this he is as unhesitating as Schiller was, as any theatrical man must be; he has also the latter's contempt for the world which he brings to its knees before him. A man is an actor when he is ahead of mankind in his possession of this one view, that everything which has to strike people as true must not be true. This rule was formulated by Talma: it contains the whole psychology of the actor, it also contains —and this we need not doubt—all his morality. Wagner's music is never true.

—But it is supposed to be so: and thus everything is as it should be. As long as we are young, and Wagnerites into the bargain, we regard Wagner as rich, even as the model of a prodigal giver, even as a great landlord in the realm of sound. We admire him in very much the same way as young Frenchmen admire Victor Hugo—that is to say, for his "royal liberality." Later on we admire the one as well as the other for the opposite reason: as masters and paragons in economy, as *prudent* Amphitryons. Nobody can equal them in the art of providing a princely board with such a modest outlay.—The Wagnerite, with his credulous stomach, is even sated with the fare which his master conjures up before him. But we others who, in books as in music, desire above all to find *substance*, and who are scarcely satisfied with the mere representation of a banquet, are much worse off. In plain English, Wagner does not give us enough to masticate. His recitative—very little meat, more bones, and plenty of broth —I christened *"alla genovese"*: I had no intention of flattering the Genoese with this remark, but rather the *older recitativo*, the *recitativo secco*. And as to Wagnerian leitmotiv, I fear I lack the necessary culinary understanding for it. If hard pressed, I might say that I regard it perhaps as an ideal toothpick, as an opportunity of ridding one's self of what remains of one's meal. Wagner's "arias" are still left over. But now I shall hold my tongue.

9

Even in his general sketch of the action, Wagner is above all an actor. The first thing that occurs to him is a scene which is certain to produce a strong effect, a real *actio*,* with a basso-relievo of attitudes, an *overwhelming* scene, this he now proceeds to elaborate more deeply, and out of it he draws his characters. The whole of what remains to be done follows of itself, fully in keeping with a technical economy which has no reason to be subtle. It is not Corneille's public that Wagner has to consider, it is merely the nineteenth century. Concerning the "actual requirements of the stage" Wagner would have about the same opinion as any other actor of today: a series of powerful scenes, each stronger than the one that preceded it—and, in between, all kinds of *clever* nonsense. His first concern is to guarantee the effect of his work; he begins with the third act, he *approves* his work according to the quality of its final effect. Guided by this sort of understanding of the stage, there is not much danger of one's creating a drama unawares. Drama demands *inexorable*

---

* *Note.*—It was a real disaster for aesthetics when the word "drama" got to be translated by "action." Wagner is not the only culprit here; the whole world does the same—even the philologists who ought to know better. What ancient drama had in view was *grand pathetic scenes;* it even excluded action (or placed it *before* the piece or *behind* the scenes). The word "drama" is of Doric origin, and according to the usage of the Dorian language it meant "event," "history" —both words in a hieratic sense. The oldest drama represented local legends, "sacred history," upon which the foundation of the cult rested (—thus it was not "action," but fatality: δρᾶν in Doric has nothing to do with action).

logic: but what did Wagner care about logic? Again I say, it was not Corneille's public that he had to consider, but merely Germans! Everybody knows the technical difficulties before which the dramatist often has to summon all his strength and frequently to sweat his blood: the difficulty of making the *plot* seem necessary and the unravelment as well, so that both are conceivable only in a certain way, and so that each may give the impression of freedom (the principle of the smallest expenditure of energy). Now the very last thing that Wagner does is to sweat blood over the plot; and on this and the unravelment he certainly spends the smallest possible amount of energy. Let anybody put one of Wagner's "plots" under the microscope, and I wager that he will be forced to laugh. Nothing is more enlivening than the dilemma in *Tristan*, unless it be that in *Die Meistersinger*. Wagner is *no* dramatist; let nobody be deceived on this point. All he did was to love the word "drama"—he always loved fine words. Nevertheless, in his writings the word "drama" is merely a misunderstanding (—*and* a piece of shrewdness: Wagner always affected superiority in regard to the word "opera"—); just as the word "spirit" is a misunderstanding in the New Testament.—He was not enough of a psychologist for drama; he instinctively avoided a psychological plot— but how?—by always putting idiosyncrasy in its place . . . Very modern—eh? Very Parisian! very decadent! . . . Incidentally, the *plots* that Wagner knows how to unravel with the help of dramatic inventions are of quite another kind. For example, let us suppose that Wagner requires a female voice. A whole act without a woman's voice would be impossible! But in this particular instance not one of the heroines happens to be free. What does Wagner do? He emancipates the oldest woman on earth, Erda: "Step up, aged grandmamma! You have got to sing!" And Erda sings. Wagner's end has been achieved. Thereupon he immediately dismisses the old lady: "Why on earth did you come? Off with you! Kindly go to sleep again!" In short, a scene full of mythological awe, before which the Wagnerite *wonders* all kinds of things. . . .

—"But the substance of Wagner's texts! their mythical substance, their eternal substance!"—Question: how is this substance, this eternal substance tested? The chemical analyst replies: Translate Wagner into the real, into the modern— let us be even more cruel, and say: into the bourgeois! And what will then become of him?—Between ourselves, I have tried the experiment. Nothing is more entertaining, nothing more worthy of being recommended to a picnic-party, than to discuss Wagner dressed in a more modern garb: for instance Parsifal, as a candidate in divinity, with a public-school education (—the latter, quite indispensable *for pure* foolishness). What *surprises* await one! Would you believe it, that Wagner's heroines one and all, once they have been divested of the heroic husks, are almost indistinguishable from Mme. Bovary!—just as one can conceive conversely, of Flaubert's being *well able* to transform all his heroines into Scandinavian or Carthaginian women, and then to offer them to Wagner in this mythologized form as a libretto. Indeed, generally speaking, Wagner does not seem to have become interested in any other problems than those which engross the little Parisian decadents of today. Always five paces away from the hospital! All very modern problems, all problems which are at home *in big cities!* Do not doubt it! . . . Have you noticed (it is in keeping with this association of ideas) that Wagner's heroines never have any children?— They *cannot* have them. . . . The despair with which Wagner tackled the problem of arranging in some way for Siegfried's birth betrays how modern his feelings on this point actually were.—Siegfried "emancipated woman"—but not with any hope of offspring.—And now here is a fact which leaves us speechless: Parsifal is Lohengrin's father! However did he do it?—Ought one at this juncture to remember that "chastity works miracles"? . . .

Wagnerus dixit princeps in castitate auctoritas.

10

And now just a word *en passant* concerning Wagner's writings: they are among other things a school of *shrewdness*. The system of procedures of which Wagner disposes might be applied to a hundred other cases—he that hath ears to hear let him hear. Perhaps I may lay claim to some public acknowledgment, if I put three of the most valuable of these procedures into a precise form.

Everything that Wagner *cannot* do is bad.

Wagner could do much more than he does, but his strong principles prevent him.

Everything that Wagner *can* do, no one will ever be able to do after him, no one has ever done before him, and no one must ever do after him: Wagner is godly. . . .

These three propositions are the quintessence of Wagner's writings; the rest is merely—"literature."

—Not every kind of music hitherto has been in need of

literature; and it were well to try and discover the actual reason of this. Is it perhaps that Wagner's music is too difficult to understand? Or did he fear precisely the reverse—that it was too easy, that people might *not understand it with sufficient difficulty?*—As a matter of fact, his whole life long, he did nothing but repeat one proposition: that his music did not mean music alone! But something more! Something immeasurably more! . . . *Not music alone—no* musician would speak in this way. I repeat, Wagner could not create things as a whole; he had no choice, he was obliged to create things in bits; with "motives," attitudes, formulas, duplications, and hundreds of repetitions, he remained a rhetorician in music—and that is why he was at bottom *forced* to press "this means" into the foreground. "Music can never be anything else than a means": this was his theory; but above all it was the only *practice* that lay open to him. No musician, however, thinks in this way. Wagner was in need of literature in order to persuade the whole world to take his music seriously, profoundly, "because it *meant* an infinity of things"; all his life he was the commentator of the "Idea."—What does Elsa stand for? But without a doubt, Elsa is "the unconscious *mind of the people*" (—"when I realized this, I naturally became a thorough revolutionist"—).

Do not let us forget that, when Hegel and Schelling were misleading the minds of Germany, Wagner was still young: that he guessed, or rather fully grasped, that the only thing which Germans take seriously is—"the idea"—that is to say, something obscure, uncertain, wonderful; that among Germans lucidity is an objection, logic a refutation. Schopenhauer rigorously pointed out the dishonesty of Hegel's and Schelling's age—rigorously, but also unjustly; for he himself, the pessimistic old counterfeiter, was in no way more "honest" than his more famous contemporaries. But let us leave morality out of the question, Hegel is a *matter of taste.* . . . And not only of German but of European taste! . . . A taste which Wagner understood!—which he felt equal to! —which he has immortalized!—All he did was to apply it to music—he invented a style for himself, which might mean an "infinity of things"—he was *Hegel's* heir. . . . Music as "Idea."

And how well Wagner was understood!—The same kind of man who used to gush over Hegel now gushes over Wagner; in his school they even *write* Hegelian.* But he who

---

* Hegel and his school wrote notoriously obscure German.—*Tr.*

understood Wagner best was the German youthlet. The two
words "infinity" and "meaning" were sufficient for this: at
their sound the youthlet immediately began to feel exceptionally happy. Wagner did *not* conquer these boys with
music, but with the "idea": it is the enigmatical vagueness of
his art, its game of hide-and-seek amid a hundred symbols,
its polychromy in ideals, which leads and lures the lads. It is
Wagner's genius for forming clouds, his sweeps and swoops
through the air, his ubiquity and nullibicity—precisely the
same qualities with which Hegel led and lured in his time!
Moreover in the presence of Wagner's multifariousness,
plenitude and arbitrariness, they seem to themselves justified
—"saved." Tremulously they listen while the *great symbols*
in his art seem to make themselves heard from out the misty
distance, with a gentle roll of thunder, and they are not at
all displeased if at times it gets a little gray, gruesome, and
cold. Are they not one and all, like Wagner himself, on
quite intimate terms with bad weather, with German weather!
Wotan is their God: but Wotan is the God of bad weather.
. . . They are right, how could these German youths—in
their present condition—miss what we others, we *halcyonians*,
miss in Wagner? i.e., *la gaya scienza;* light feet, wit, fire,
grave, grand logic, stellar dancing, wanton intellectuality, the
vibrating light of the South, the calm sea—perfection. . . .

11

I have mentioned the sphere to which Wagner belongs
—certainly not to the history of music. What, however, does
he mean historically?—*The rise of the actor in music*: a
momentous event which not only leads me to think but also
to fear.

In a word: "Wagner and Liszt." Never yet have the "uprightness" and "genuineness" of musicians been put to such a
dangerous test. It is glaringly obvious: great success, mob
success is no longer the achievement of the genuine—in
order to get it a man must be an actor!—Victor Hugo and
Richard Wagner—they both prove one and the same thing:
that in declining civilizations, wherever the mob is allowed
to decide, genuineness becomes superfluous, prejudicial, unfavorable. The actor, alone, can still kindle *great* enthusiasm. And thus it is his *golden age* which is now dawning
—his and that of all those who are in any way related to
him. With drums and fifes, Wagner marches at the head of
all artists in declamation, in display and virtuosity. He began

by convincing the conductors of orchestras, the scene-shifters and stage-singers, not to forget the orchestra—he "delivered" them from monotony. . . . The movement that Wagner created has spread even to the land of knowledge: whole sciences pertaining to music are rising slowly, out of centuries of scholasticism. As an example of what I mean, let me point more particularly to *Riemann's* services to rhythmics; he was the first who called attention to the leading idea in punctuation—even for music (unfortunately he did so with a bad word; he called it "phrasing").—All these people, and I say it with gratitude, are the best, the most respectable among Wagner's admirers—they have a perfect right to honor Wagner. The same instinct unites them with one another; in him they recognize their highest type, and since he has inflamed them with his own ardor they feel themselves transformed into power, even into great power. In this quarter, if anywhere, Wagner's influence has really been *beneficent*. Never before has there been so much thinking, willing, and industry in this sphere. Wagner endowed all these artists with a new conscience: what they now exact and *obtain* from themselves, they had never exacted before Wagner's time— before then they had been too modest. Another spirit prevails on the stage since Wagner rules there: the most difficult things are expected, blame is severe, praise very scarce —the good and the excellent have become the rule. Taste is no longer necessary, nor even is a good voice. Wagner is sung only with ruined voices: this has a more "dramatic" effect. Even talent is out of the question. Expressiveness at all costs, which is what the Wagnerian ideal—the ideal of decadence—demands, is hardly compatible with talent. All that is required for this is virtue—that is to say, training, automatism, "self-denial." Neither taste, voices, nor gifts; Wagner's stage requires but one thing: *Germans!* . . . The definition of a German: an obedient man with long legs. . . . There is a deep significance in the fact that the rise of Wagner should have coincided with the rise of the "Empire": both phenomena are a proof of one and the same thing— obedience and long legs. Never have people been more obedient, never have they been so well ordered about. The conductors of Wagnerian orchestras, more particularly, are worthy of an age which posterity will one day call, with timid awe, the *classical age of war*. Wagner understood how to command; in this respect, too, he was a great teacher. He commanded as a man who had exercised an inexorable will over himself, as one who had practiced lifelong discipline; Wagner was, perhaps, the greatest example of self-violence in the whole of the history of art (even Alfieri, who in other respects is his next of kin, is outdone by him—the note of a Turinese).

12

This view, that our actors have become more worthy of respect than heretofore, does not imply that I believe them to have become less dangerous. . . . But who is in any doubt as to what I want—as to what the *three requisitions* are concerning which my wrath and my care and love of art have made me open my mouth on this occasion?

That the stage should not become master of the arts.

That the actor should not become the corrupter of the genuine.

That music should not become an art of lying.

FRIEDRICH NIETZSCHE.

Postscript

THE gravity of these last words allows me at this point to introduce a few sentences out of an unprinted essay which will at least leave no doubt as to my earnestness in regard to this question. The title of this essay is: "What Wagner has cost us."

One pays dearly for having been a follower of Wagner. Even today a vague feeling that this is so still prevails. Even Wagner's success, his triumph, did not uproot this feeling thoroughly. But formerly it was strong, it was terrible; it was a gloomy hate throughout almost three-quarters of Wagner's life. The resistance which he met with among us Germans cannot be too highly valued or too highly honored. People guarded themselves against him as against an illness, not with arguments—it is impossible to refute an illness—but with obstruction, with mistrust, with repugnance, with loathing, with somber earnestness, as though he were a great rampant danger. The aesthetes gave themselves away when out of three schools of German philosophy they waged an absurd war against Wagner's principles with "ifs" and "fors" —what did he care about principles, even his own! The

Germans themselves had enough instinctive good sense to dispense with every "if" and "for" in this matter. An instinct is weakened when it becomes conscious: for by becoming conscious it makes itself feeble. If there were any signs that in spite of the universal character of European decadence there was still a modicum of health, still an instinctive premonition of what is harmful and dangerous, residing in the German soul, then it would be precisely this blunt resistance to Wagner which I should least like to see underrated. It does us honor, it gives us some reason to hope: France no longer has such an amount of health at her disposal. The Germans, these *loiterers par excellence*, as history shows, are today the most backward among the civilized nations of Europe; this has its advantages, for they are thus relatively the youngest.

One pays dearly for having been a follower of Wagner. It is only quite recently that the Germans have overcome a sort of dread of him—the desire to be rid of him occurred to them again and again.* Does anybody remember a very curious occurrence in which, quite unexpectedly toward the end, this old feeling once more manifested itself? It happened at Wagner's funeral. The first Wagner Society, the one in Munich, laid a wreath on his grave with this inscription, which immediately became famous: "Salvation to the Saviour!" Everybody admired the lofty inspiration which had dictated this inscription, as also the taste which seemed to be the privilege of the followers of Wagner. Many also, however (it was singular enough), made this slight alteration in it: "Salvation *from* the Saviour."—People began to breath again.—

One pays dearly for having been a follower of Wagner. Let us try to estimate the influence of this worship upon culture. Whom did this movement press to the front? What did it make ever more and more pre-eminent?—In the first place the layman's arrogance, the arrogance of the art-maniac. Now these people are organizing societies, they wish

* Was Wagner a German at all? There are reasons enough for putting this question. It is difficult to find a single German trait in his character. Great learner that he was, he naturally imitated a great deal that was German—but that is all. His very soul contradicts everything which hitherto has been regarded as German; not to mention German musicians!—His father was an actor of the name of Geyer. . . . That which has been popularized hitherto as "Wagner's life" is *fable convenue* if not something worse. I confess my doubts on any point which is vouched for by Wagner alone. He was not proud enough to be able to suffer the truth about himself. Nobody had less pride than he. Like Victor Hugo he remained true to himself even in his biography—he remained an actor.

to make their taste prevail, they even wish to pose as judges *in rebus musicis et musicantibus*. Secondly: an ever increasing indifference toward severe, noble, and conscientious schooling in the service of art; and in its place the belief in genius, or in plain English, cheeky dilettantism (—the formula for this is to be found in *Die Meistersinger*). Thirdly, and this is the worst of all: *Theatrocracy*— the craziness of a belief in the pre-eminence of the theater, in the right of the theater to rule supreme over the arts, over Art in general. . . . But this should be shouted into the face of Wagnerites a hundred times over: that the theater is something lower than art, something secondary, something coarsened, above all something suitably distorted and falsified for the mob. In this respect Wagner altered nothing: Bayreuth is Grand Opera —and not even good opera. . . . The stage is a form of Demolatry in the realm of taste, the stage is an insurrection of the mob, a plebiscite against good taste. . . . The case of Wagner proves this fact: he captivated the masses—he depraved taste, he even perverted our taste for opera!

One pays dearly for having been a follower of Wagner. What has Wagner-worship made out of spirit? Does Wagner liberate the spirit? To him belong that ambiguity and equivocation and all other qualities which can convince the uncertain without making them conscious of why they have been convinced. In this sense Wagner is a seducer on a grand scale. There is nothing exhausted, nothing effete, nothing dangerous to life, nothing that slanders the world in the realm of spirit, which has not secretly found shelter in his art; he conceals the blackest obscurantism in the luminous orbs of the ideal. He flatters every nihilistic (Buddhistic) instinct and togs it out in music; he flatters every form of Christianity, every religious expression of decadence. He that hath ears to hear let him hear: everything that has ever grown out of the soil of impoverished life, the whole counterfeit coinage of the transcendental and of a Beyond found its most sublime advocate in Wagner's art, not in formulas (Wagner is too clever to use formulas), but in the persuasion of the senses which in their turn makes the spirit weary and morbid. Music in the form of Circe . . . in this respect his last work in his greatest masterpiece. In the art of seduction *Parsifal* will forever maintain its rank as a stroke of genius. . . . I admire this work. I would fain have composed it myself. Wagner was never better inspired than toward the end. The subtlety with which beauty and disease are united here reaches such a height that it casts, so to speak, a shadow upon all Wagner's earlier achievements: it seems too bright, too healthy. Do ye understand this? Health and brightness acting like a shadow? Almost like an objection? . . . To this extent are we already pure fools. . . . Never was there a greater Master in heavy hieratic perfumes —never on earth has there been such a connoisseur of paltry infinities, of all that thrills, of extravagant excesses, of all the feminism from out the vocabulary of happiness! My friends, do but drink the philters of this art! Nowhere will ye find a more pleasant method of enervating your spirit, of forgetting your manliness in the shade of a rosebush. . . . Ah, this old magician, mightiest of Klingsors; how he wages war against us with his art, against us free spirits! How he appeals to every form of cowardice of the modern soul with his charming girlish notes! There never was such a *mortal hatred* of knowledge! One must be a very cynic in order to resist seduction here. One must be able to bite in order to resist worshipping at this shrine. Very well, old seducer! The cynic cautions you—*cave canem*. . . .

One pays dearly for having been a follower of Wagner. I contemplate the youthlets who have long been exposed to his infection. The first relatively innocuous effect of it is the corruption of their taste. Wagner acts like chronic recourse to the bottle. He stultifies, he befouls the stomach. His specific effect: degeneration of the feeling for rhythm. What the Wagnerite calls rhythmical is what I call, to use a Greek metaphor, "stirring a swamp." Much more dangerous than all this, however, is the corruption of ideas. The youthlet becomes a mooncalf, an "idealist." He stands above science, and in this respect he has reached the master's heights. On the other hand, he assumes the airs of a philosopher; he writes for the *Bayreuth Journal;* he solves all problems in the name of the Father, the Son, and the Holy Master. But the most ghastly thing of all is the deterioration of the nerves. Let anyone wander through a large city at night, in all directions he will hear people doing violence to instruments with solemn rage and fury, a wild uproar breaks out at intervals. What is happening? It is the disciples of Wagner in the act of worshipping him. . . . Bayreuth is another word for a Hydro. A typical telegram from Bayreuth would read *bereits bereut* (I already repent). Wagner is bad for young men; he is fatal for women. What medically speaking is a female Wagnerite? It seems to me that a doctor could not be too serious in putting this alternative of conscience to young women: either one thing or the other. But they have already made their choice. You cannot serve two Masters when one of these is Wagner. Wagner redeemed woman; and in return woman built Bayreuth for him. Every sacrifice, every surrender: there was nothing that they were not prepared to give him. Woman impoverishes herself in favor of the Master, she becomes quite touching, she stands naked before him. The female Wagnerite, the most attractive equivocality that exists today: she is the incarnation of Wagner's cause: his cause triumphs with her as its symbol. . . . Ah, this old robber! He robs our young men; he even robs our women as well, and drags them to his cell. . . . Ah, this old Minotaur! What has he not already cost us? Every year processions of the finest young men and maidens are led into his labyrinth that he may swallow them up, every year the whole of Europe cries out "Away to Crete! Away to Crete!" . . .

Second Postscript

IT seems to me that my letter is open to some misunderstanding. On certain faces I see the expression of gratitude; I even hear modest but merry laughter. I prefer to be understood here as in other things. But since a certain animal, *the worm of* Empire, the famous *Rhinoxera*, has become lodged in the vineyards of the German spirit, nobody any longer understands a word I say. The *Kreuz-Zeitung* has brought this home to me, not to speak of the *Litterarisches Centralblatt*. I have given the Germans the deepest books that they have ever possessed—a sufficient reason for their not having understood a word of them. . . . If in this essay I declare war against Wagner—and incidentally against a certain form of German taste, if I seem to use strong language about the cretinism of Bayreuth, it must not be supposed that I am in the least anxious to glorify any other musician. Other musicians are not to be considered by the side of Wagner. Things are generally bad. Decay is universal. Disease lies at the very root of things. If Wagner's name represents the ruin of music, just as Bernini's stands for the ruin of sculpture, he is not on that account its cause. All he did was to accelerate the fall—though we are quite prepared to admit that he did it in a way which makes one recoil with horror from this almost instantaneous decline and fall to the depths. He possessed the ingenuousness of decadence; this constituted his superiority. He believed in it. He did not

halt before any of its logical consequences. The others hesi-
tated—that is their distinction. They have no other. What is
common to both Wagner and "the others" consists in this:
the decline of all organizing power; the abuse of traditional
means, without the capacity or the aim that would justify
this. The counterfeit imitation of grand forms, for which nobody nowadays is strong, proud, self-reliant, and healthy
enough; excessive vitality in small details; passion at all costs;
refinement as an expression of impoverished life, ever more
nerves in the place of muscle. I know only one musician
who today would be able to compose an overture as an
organic whole, and nobody else knows him.* . . . He who is
famous now does not write better music than Wagner, but
only less characteristic, less definite music—less definite, because half measures, even in decadence, cannot stand by the
side of completeness. But Wagner was complete; Wagner
represented thorough corruption; Wagner has had the courage, the will, and the conviction for corruption. What does
Johannes Brahms matter? . . . It was his good fortune to be
misunderstood by Germany; he was taken to be an antagonist
of Wagner—people required an antagonist! But he did not
write necessary music, above all he wrote too much music!
When one is not rich one should at least have enough pride
to be poor! . . . The sympathy which here and there was
meted out to Brahms, apart from party interests and party
misunderstandings, was for a long time a riddle to me until
one day through an accident, almost, I discovered that he
affected a particular type of man. He has the melancholy of
impotence. His creations are not the result of plenitude, he
thirsts after abundance. Apart from what he plagiarizes,
from what he borrows from ancient or exotically modern
styles—he is a master in the art of copying—there remains
as his most individual quality a *longing*. . . . And this is what
the dissatisfied of all kinds, and all those who yearn, divine
in him. He is much too little of a personality, too little of a
central figure. . . . The "impersonal," those who are not self-
centered, love him for this. He is especially the musician of a
species of dissatisfied women. Fifty steps further on, and we
find the female Wagnerite—just as we find Wagner himself
fifty paces ahead of Brahms. The female Wagnerite is a
more definite, a more interesting, and above all, a more attractive type. Brahms is touching so long as he dreams or
mourns over himself in private—in this respect he is modern;
he becomes cold, we no longer feel at one with him when he

* This undoubtedly refers to Nietzsche's only disciple and friend,
Peter Gast.—*Tr.*

poses as the child of the classics. . . . People like to call Brahms Beethoven's heir: I know of no more cautious euphemism. All that which today makes a claim to being the grand style in music is on precisely that account either false to us or false to itself. This alternative is suspicious enough; in itself it contains a casuistic question concerning the value of the two cases. The instinct of the majority protests against the alternative, "false to us"—they do not wish to be cheated —and I myself would certainly always prefer this type to the other ("false to itself"). This is *my* taste. Expressed more clearly for the sake of the "poor in spirit" it amounts to this: Brahms *or* Wagner. . . . Brahms is *not* an actor. A very great part of other musicians may be summed up in the concept Brahms. I do not wish to say anything about the clever apes of Wagner, as, for instance, Goldmark; when one has "The Queen of Sheba" to one's name, one belongs to a menagerie—one ought to put oneself on show. Nowadays all things that can be done well and even with a master hand are small. In this department alone is honesty still possible. Nothing, however, can cure music as a whole of its chief fault, of its fate, which is to be the expression of general physiological contradiction, which is, in fact, to be modern.

The best instruction, the most conscientious schooling, the most thorough familiarity, yea, and even isolation, with the Old Masters—all this only acts as a palliative, or, more strictly speaking, has but an illusory effect, because the first condition of the right thing is no longer in our bodies; whether this first condition be the strong race of a Handel or the overflowing animal spirits of a Rossini. Not everyone has the right to every teacher, and this holds good of whole epochs. In itself it is not impossible that there are still remains of stronger natures, typical unadapted men, somewhere in Europe; from this quarter the advent of a somewhat belated form of beauty and perfection, even in music, might still be hoped for. But the most that we can expect to see are exceptional cases. From the rule, that corruption is paramount, that corruption is a fatality—not even a God can save music.

Epilogue

AND now let us take breath and withdraw a moment from this narrow world which necessarily must be narrow, be-

cause we have to make enquiries relative to the value of
persons. A philosopher feels that he wants to wash his hands
after he has concerned himself so long with the "Case of
Wagner." I shall now give my notion of what is *modern.*
According to the measure of energy of every age, there is
also a standard that determines which virtues shall be allowed and which forbidden. The age either has the virtues of
ascending life, in which case it resists the virtues of degeneration with all its deepest instincts, or it is in itself an age of
degeneration, in which case it requires the virtues of declining life—in which case it hates everything that justifies
itself, solely as being the outcome of a plenitude, or a
superabundance of strength. Aesthetic is inextricably bound
up with these biological principles: there is decadent aesthetic
and *classical* aesthetic—"beauty in itself" is just as much
a chimera as any other kind of idealism. Within the narrow sphere of the so-called moral values, no greater antithesis could be found than that of *master-morality* and the
morality of *Christian* valuations: the latter having grown
out of a thoroughly morbid soil. The gospels present us with
the same physiological types, as do the novels of Dostoyevsky;
the master-morality ("Roman," "pagan," "classical," "Renaissance"), on the other hand, being the symbolic speech of
well-constitutedness, of *ascending* life, and of the Will to
Power as a vital principle. Master-morality *affirms* just as instinctively as Christian morality *denies* ("God," "Beyond,"
"self-denial"—all of them negations). The first reflects its
plenitude upon things—it transfigures, it embellishes, it *ra-
tionalizes* the world—the latter impoverishes, bleaches, mars
the value of things; it *suppresses* the world. "World" is a
Christian term of abuse. These antithetical forms in the
optics of values are *both* necessary; they are different points
of view which cannot be circumvented either with arguments
or counterarguments. One cannot refute Christianity; it is
impossible to refute a diseased eyesight. That people should
have combated pessimism as if it had been a philosophy,
was the very acme of learned stupidity. The concepts "true"
and "untrue" do not seem to me to have any sense in
optics. That, alone, which has to be guarded against is the
falsity, the instinctive duplicity which *would fain* regard this
antithesis as no antithesis at all: just as Wagner did—and
his mastery in this kind of falseness was of no mean
order. To cast sidelong glances at master-morality, at *noble*
morality (Icelandic saga is perhaps the greatest documentary
evidence of these values), and at the same time to have the
opposite teaching, the "gospel of the lowly," the doctrine of

the *need* of salvation, on one's lips! . . . Incidentally, I admire the modesty of Christians who go to Bayreuth. As for myself, I could *not* endure to hear the sound of certain words on Wagner's lips. There are some concepts which are too good for Bayreuth. . . . What? Christianity adjusted for female Wagnerites, perhaps *by* female Wagnerites—for, in his latter days Wagner was thoroughly *feminini generis*—? Again I say, the Christians of today are too modest for me. . . . If Wagner were a Christian, then Liszt was perhaps a Father of the Church! The need of *salvation*, the quintessence of all Christian needs, has nothing in common with such clowns; it is the most straightforward expression of decadence, it is the most convincing and most painful affirmation of decadence, in sublime symbols and practices. The Christian wishes *to be rid* of himself. *Le moi est toujours haïssable.* Noble morality, master-morality, on the other hand, is rooted in a triumphant saying of yea to *one's self*—it is the self-affirmation and self-glorification of life; it also requires sublime symbols and practices, but only "because its heart is too full." The whole of beautiful art and of great art belongs here: their common essence is gratitude. But we must allow it a certain instinctive repugnance *to décadents*, and a scorn and horror of the latter's symbolism; such things almost prove it. The noble Romans considered Christianity as a *foeda superstitio*; let me call to your minds the feelings which the last German of noble taste—Goethe—had in regard to the cross. It is idle to look for more valuable, more *necessary* contrasts.* . . .

But the kind of falsity which is characteristic of the Bayreuthians is not exceptional today. We all know the hybrid concept of the Christian gentleman. This *innocence* in contradiction, this "clean conscience" in falsehood, is rather modern par excellence, with it modernity is almost defined. Biologically, modern man represents a *contradiction of values*, he sits between two stools, he says yea and nay in one breath. No wonder that it is precisely in our age that falseness itself became flesh and blood, and even genius! No wonder *Wagner* dwelt amongst us! It was not without reason that I called Wagner the Cagliostro of modernity. . . .

---

* My *Genealogy of Morals* contains the best exposition of the antithesis "noble morality" and "Christian morality"; a more decisive turning point in the history of religious and moral science does not perhaps exist. This book, which is a touchstone by which I can discover who are my peers, rejoices in being accessible only to the most elevated and most severe minds: the others have not the ears to hear me. One must have one's passion in things, *wherein* no one has passion nowadays.

But all of us, though we do not have it, involuntarily have values, words, formulas, and morals in our bodies, which are quite *antagonistic* in their origin—regarded from a physiological standpoint, we are *false*. . . . How would a *diagnosis of the modern soul* begin? With a determined incision into this agglomeration of contradictory instincts, with the total suppression of its antagonistic values, with vivisection applied to its most *instructive* case. To philosophers the "Case of Wagner" is a *windfall*—this essay, as you observe, was inspired by gratitude.

FROM NIETZSCHE CONTRA WAGNER*

Wherein I Admire Wagner

I BELIEVE that artists very often do not know what they are best able to do. They are much too vain. Their minds are directed to something prouder than merely to appear like little plants, which, with freshness, rareness, and beauty, know how to sprout from their soil with real perfection. The ultimate goodness of their own garden and vineyard is superciliously underestimated by them, and their love and their insight are not of the same quality. Here is a musician who is a greater master than anyone else in the discovering of tones, peculiar to suffering, oppressed, and tormented souls, who can endow even dumb misery with speech. Nobody can approach him in the colors of late autumn, in the indescribably touching joy of a last, a very last, and all too short gladness; he knows of a chord which expresses those secret and weird midnight hours of the soul, when cause and effect seem to have fallen asunder, and at every moment something may spring out of nonentity. He is happiest of all when creating from out the nethermost depths of human happiness, and, so to speak, from out man's empty bumper, in which the bitterest and most repulsive drops have mingled with the sweetest for good or evil at last. He knows that weary shuffling along of the soul which is no longer able either to spring or to fly, nay, which is no longer able to walk; he has the modest glance of concealed suffering, of understanding without comfort, of leave-taking without word or sign; verily as the Orpheus of all secret misery he is

---

* From *The Case of Wagner*.

greater than anyone, and many a thing was introduced into art for the first time by him, which hitherto had not been given expression, had not even been thought worthy of art —the cynical revolts, for instance, of which only the greatest sufferer is capable, also many a small and quite microscopical feature of the soul, as it were the scales of its amphibious nature—yes indeed, he is the master of everything very small. But this he refuses to be! His tastes are much more in love with vast walls and with daring frescoes! . . . He does not see that his spirit has another desire and bent—a totally different outlook—that it prefers to squat peacefully in the corners of broken-down houses: concealed in this way, and hidden even from himself, he paints his really great masterpieces, all of which are very short, often only one bar in length—there, only, does he become quite good, great and perfect, perhaps there alone.—Wagner is one who has suffered much—and this elevates him above other musicians.— I admire Wagner wherever he sets *himself* to music.

Wherein I Raise Objections

WITH all this I do not wish to imply that I regard this music as healthy, and least of all in those places where it speaks of Wagner himself. My objections to Wagner's music are physiological objections. Why should I therefore begin by clothing them in aesthetic formulas? Aesthetic is indeed nothing more than applied physiology. The fact I bring forward, my *petit fait vrai*, is that I can no longer breathe with ease when this music begins to have its effect upon me; that my foot immediately begins to feel indignant at it and rebels; for what it needs is time, dance, march: even the young German Kaiser could not march to Wagner's Imperial March—what my foot demands in the first place from music is that ecstasy which lies in good walking, stepping, and dancing. But do not my stomach, my heart, my circulation also protest? Are not my intestines also troubled? And do I not become hoarse unawares? . . . in order to listen to Wagner I require Géraudel's Pastilles. . . . And then I ask myself, what is it that my whole body must have from music in general? for there is no such thing as a soul. . . . I believe it must have relief: as if all animal functions were accelerated by means of light, bold, unfettered, self-reliant rhythms; as if brazen and leaden life could lose its weight by means of delicate and smooth melodies. My melancholy would fain rest its head in the haunts and abysses of perfection: for this reason I need music. But Wagner makes one ill—What do I care about the theater? What do I care about the spasms of its moral ecstasies in which the mob—and who is not the mob today?—rejoices? What do I care about the whole pantomimic hocus-pocus of the actor? You are beginning to see that I am essentially antitheatrical at heart. For the stage, this mob art par excellence, my soul has that deepest scorn felt by every artist today. With a stage success a man sinks to such an extent in my esteem as to drop out of sight; failure in this quarter makes me prick my ears, makes me begin to pay attention. But this was not so with Wagner; next to the Wagner who created the most unique music that has ever existed there was the Wagner who was essentially a man of the stage, an actor, the most enthusiastic mimomaniac that has perhaps existed on earth, even as a musician. And let it be said *en passant* that if Wagner's theory was "drama is the object, music is only a means"—his practice was from beginning to end, "the attitude is the end, drama and even music can never be anything else than means." Music as the manner of accentuating, of strengthening, and deepening dramatic poses and all things which please the senses of the actor; and Wagnerian drama only an opportunity for a host of interesting attitudes!—Alongside of all other instincts he had the dictatorial instinct of a great actor in everything; and, as I have already said, as a musician also.—On one occasion, and not without trouble, I made this clear to a Wagnerite *pur sang*—clearness and a Wagnerite! I won't say another word. There were reasons for adding, "For heaven's sake, be a little more true unto yourself! We are not in Bayreuth now. In Bayreuth people are only upright in the mass; the individual lies, he even lies to himself. One leaves oneself at home when one goes to Bayreuth; one gives up all right to one's own tongue and choice, to one's own taste and even to one's own courage; one knows these things no longer as one is wont to have them and practice them before God and the world and between one's own four walls. In the theater no one brings the finest senses of his art with him, and least of all the artist who works for the theater—for here loneliness is lacking; everything perfect does not suffer a witness. . . . In the theater one becomes mob, herd, woman, Pharisee, electing cattle, patron, idiot—Wagnerite: there, the most personal conscience is bound to submit to the leveling charm of the great multitude, there the neighbor rules, there one *becomes* a neighbor."

Wagner as a Danger

1

The aim after which more modern music is striving, which is now given the strong but obscure name of "unending melody," can be clearly understood by comparing it to one's feelings on entering the sea. Gradually one loses one's footing and one ultimately abandons oneself to the mercy or fury of the elements: one has to swim. In the solemn, or fiery, swinging movement, first slow and then quick, of old music—one had to do something quite different; one had to dance. The measure which was required for this and the control of certain balanced degrees of time and energy, forced the soul of the listener to continual sobriety of thought. Upon the counterplay of the cooler currents of air which came from this sobriety, and from the warmer breath of enthusiasm, the charm of all good music rested—Richard Wagner wanted another kind of movement—he overthrew the physiological first principle of all music before his time. It was no longer a matter of walking or dancing—we must swim, we must hover. . . . This perhaps decides the whole matter. "Unending melody" really wants to break all the symmetry of time and strength; it actually scorns these things. Its wealth of invention resides precisely in what to an older ear sounds like rhythmic paradox and abuse. From the imitation or the prevalence of such a taste there would arise a danger for music—so great that we can imagine none greater—the complete degeneration of the feeling for rhythm, *chaos* in the place of rhythm. . . . The danger reaches its climax when such music cleaves ever more closely to naturalistic play-acting and pantomime, which governed by no laws of form aim at effect and nothing more. . . . Expressiveness at all costs and music a servant, a slave to attitudes—this is the end. . . .

2

What? Would it really be the first virtue of a performance (as performing musical artists now seem to believe) under all circumstances to attain to a *haut-relief* which cannot be surpassed? If this were applied to Mozart, for instance, would it not be a real sin against Mozart's spirit—Mozart's cheerful, enthusiastic, delightful, and loving spirit? He who fortunately was no German, and whose seriousness is a charming and golden seriousness and not by any means that of a German clodhopper. . . . Not to speak of the earnestness of the "marble statue." . . . But you seem to think that all music is the music of the "marble statue"—that all music should, so to speak, spring out of the wall and shake the listener to his very bowels? . . . Only thus could music have any effect! But on whom would the effect be made? Upon something on which a noble artist ought never to deign to act —upon the mob, upon the immature! upon the blasés! upon the diseased! upon idiots! upon *Wagnerites*! . . .

A Music Without a Future

Of all the arts which succeed in growing on the soil of a particular culture, music is the last plant to appear; maybe because it is the one most dependent upon our innermost feelings, and therefore the last to come to the surface—at a time when the culture to which it belongs is in its autumn season and beginning to fade. It was only in the art of the Dutch masters that the spirit of medieval Christianity found its expression—its architecture of sound is the youngest, but genuine and legitimate, sister of the Gothic. It was only in Handel's music that the best in Luther and in those like him found its voice, the Judaeo-heroic trait which gave the Reformation a touch of greatness—the Old Testament, *not* the New, become music. It was left to Mozart to pour out the epoch of Louis XIV, and of the art of Racine and Claude Lorrain, in *ringing* gold; only in Beethoven's and Rossini's music did the eighteenth century sing itself out—the century of enthusiasm, broken ideals, and *fleeting joy*. All real and original music is a swan song. Even our last form of music, despite its prevalence and its will to prevail, has perhaps only a short time to live, for it sprouted from a soil which was in the throes of a rapid subsidence—of a culture which will soon be *submerged*. A certain catholicism of feeling, and a predilection for some ancient indigenous (so-called national) ideals and eccentricities, was its first condition. Wagner's appropriation of old sagas and songs, in which scholarly prejudice taught us to see something German par excellence—now we laugh at it all, the resurrection of these Scandinavian monsters with a thirst for ecstatic sensuality and spiritualization— the whole of this taking and giving on Wagner's part, in the matter of subjects, characters, passions, and nerves, would also give unmistakable expression to the *spirit of his music* provided that this music, like any other, did not know how to speak about itself save ambiguously: for *musica is a woman.* . . . We must not let ourselves be misled concerning this state of things, by the fact that at this very moment we are living in a reaction, *in the heart itself* of a reaction. The age of international wars, of ultramontane martyrdom, in fact, the whole interlude-character which typifies the present condition of Europe may indeed help an art like Wagner's to sudden glory, without, however, in the least ensuring its *future prosperity*. The Germans themselves have no future. . . .

Where Wagner Is at Home

Even at the present day, France is still the refuge of the most intellectual and refined culture in Europe, it remains the high school of taste: but one must know where to find this France of taste. The *North-German Gazette,* for instance, or whoever expresses his sentiments in that paper, thinks that the French are "barbarians"—as for me, if I had to find the *blackest* spot on earth, where slaves still required to be liberated, I should turn in the direction of Northern Germany. . . . But those who form part of *that select* France take very good care to *conceal themselves*: they are a small body of men, and there may be some among them who do not stand on very firm legs—a few may be fatalists, hypochondriacs, invalids; others may be enervated, and artificial—such are those who would fain be artistic— but all the loftiness and delicacy which still remains to this world is in their possession. In this France of intellect, which is also the France of pessimism, Schopenhauer is already much more at home than he ever was in Germany; his principal work has already been translated twice, and the second time so excellently that now I prefer to read Schopenhauer in French (he was an *accident* among Germans, just as I am—the Germans have no fingers wherewith to grasp us; they haven't any fingers at all, but only claws). And I do not mention Heine—*l'adorable Heine*, as they say in Paris—who long since has passed into the flesh and blood of the more profound and more soulful of French lyricists. How could the horned cattle of Germany know how to deal with the *délicatesses* of such a nature! And as to Richard Wagner, it is obvious, it is even glaringly obvious, that Paris is the very *soil* for him: the more French music adapts itself to the needs of *l'âme moderne,* the more Wagnerian it will become—it is far enough advanced in this direction already. In this respect one should not allow one's self to be misled by Wagner himself—it was simply disgraceful on Wagner's part to scoff at Paris, as he did, in its agony in 1871. . . . In spite of it all, in Germany Wagner is only a misapprehension: who could be more incapable of understanding anything about Wagner than the Kaiser, for instance? To everybody familiar with the movement of European culture, this fact, however, is certain, that French romanticism and Richard Wagner are most intimately related. All dominated by literature, up to their very eyes and ears—the first European artists with a *universal literary* culture—most of them writers, poets, mediators, and minglers of the senses and the arts, all fanatics in *expression*, great discoverers in the realm of the sublime as also of the ugly and the gruesome, and still greater discoverers in passion, in working for effect, in the art of dressing their windows— all possessing talent far above their genius—virtuosos to their backbone, knowing of secret passages to all that seduces, lures, constrains, or overthrows; born enemies of logic and of straight lines, thirsting after the exotic, the strange and the monstrous, and all opiates for the senses and the understanding. On the whole, a daring daredevil, magnificently violent, soaring and high-springing crew of artists, who first had to teach their own century—it is the century of the mob —what the concept "artist" meant. But they were *ill.* . . .

Wagner as the Apostle of Chastity

1

Is this the German way?
Comes this low bleating forth from German hearts?
Should Teutons, sin repenting, lash themselves,
Or spread their palms with priestly unctuousness,
Exalt their feelings with the censer's fumes,
And cower and quake and bend the trembling knee,
And with a sickly sweetness plead a prayer?
Then ogle nuns, and ring the Ave bell,
And thus with morbid fervor outdo heaven?
Is this the German way?
Beware, yet are you free, yet your own Lords.
What yonder lures is Rome, Rome's faith sung without words.

2

There is no necessary contrast between sensuality and chastity; every good marriage, every genuine love affair is above this contrast; but in those cases where the contrast exists, it is very far from being necessarily a tragic one. This, at least, ought to hold good of all well-constituted and good-spirited mortals, who are not in the least inclined to reckon their unstable equilibrium between angel and *petite bête*, without further ado, among the objections to existence, the more refined and more intelligent like Hafis and Goethe, even regarded it as an additional attraction. It is precisely contradictions of this kind which lure us to life. . . . On the other hand, it must be obvious, that when Circe's unfortunate animals are induced to worship chastity, all they see and *worship* therein is their opposite—oh! and with what tragic groaning and fervor, may well be imagined—that same painful and thoroughly superfluous opposition which, toward the end of his life, Richard Wagner undoubtedly wished to set to music and to put on the stage. *And to what purpose?* we may reasonably ask.

3

And yet this other question can certainly not be circumvented: what business had he actually with that manly (alas!

so unmanly) "bucolic simplicity," that poor devil and son of nature—Parsifal, whom he ultimately makes a catholic by such insidious means—what?—was Wagner in earnest with Parsifal? For, that he was laughed at, I cannot deny, any more than Gottfried Keller can. . . . We should like to believe that *Parsifal* was meant as a piece of idle gaiety, as the closing act and satyric drama, with which Wagner the tragedian wished to take leave of us, of himself, and above all *of tragedy*, in a way which befitted him and his dignity, that is to say, with an extravagant, lofty, and most malicious parody of tragedy itself, of all the past and terrible earnestness and sorrow of this world, of the most *ridiculous* form of the unnaturalness of the ascetic ideal, at last overcome. For Parsifal is the subject par excellence for a comic opera. . . . Is Wagner's *Parsifal* his secret laugh of superiority at himself, the triumph of his last and most exalted state of artistic freedom, of artistic transcendence—is it Wagner able to *laugh* at himself? Once again we only wish it were so; for what could Parsifal be if he were *meant seriously?* Is it necessary in his case to say (as I have heard people say) that *Parsifal* is "the product of the mad hatred of knowledge, intellect, and sensuality"; a curse upon the senses and the mind in one breath and in one fit of hatred; an act of apostasy and a return to Christianly sick and obscurantist ideals? And finally even a denial of self, a deletion of self, on the part of an artist who theretofore had worked with all the power of his will in favor of the opposite cause, the spiritualization and sensualization of his art? And not only of his art, but also of his life? Let us remember how enthusiastically Wagner at one time walked in the footsteps of the philosopher Feuerbach. Feuerbach's words "healthy sensuality" struck Wagner in the thirties and forties very much as they struck many other Germans—they called themselves the young Germans—that is to say, as words of salvation. Did he ultimately *change his mind* on this point? It would seem that he had at least had the desire of *changing* his doctrine toward the end. . . . Had *the hatred of life* become dominant in him as in Flaubert? For *Parsifal* is a work of rancor, of revenge, of the most secret concoction of poisons with which to make an end of the first conditions of life; *it is a bad work.* The preaching of chastity remains an incitement to unnaturalness: I despise anybody who does not regard *Parsifal* as an outrage upon morality.

How I Got Rid of Wagner

1

Already in the summer of 1876, when the first festival at
Bayreuth was at its height, I took leave of Wagner in my
soul. I cannot endure anything double-faced. Since Wagner
had returned to Germany, he had condescended step by
step to everything that I despise—even to anti-Semitism. . . .
As a matter of fact, it was then high time to bid him farewell, but the proof of this came only too soon. Richard
Wagner, ostensibly the most triumphant creature alive—as a
matter of fact, though, a cranky and desperate *décadent*—
suddenly fell helpless and broken on his knees before the
Christian cross. . . . Was there no German at that time who
had the eyes to see, and the sympathy in his soul to feel, the
ghastly nature of this spectacle? Was I the only one who
suffered from it?—Enough, the unexpected event, like a
flash of lightning, made me see only too clearly what kind
of a place it was that I had just left—and it also made me
shudder as a man shudders who unawares has just escaped
a great danger. As I continued my journey alone, I trembled.
Not long after this I was ill, more than ill—I was *tired;*
tired of the continual disappointments over everything which
remained for us modern men to be enthusiastic about, of the
energy, industry, hope, youth, and love that are *squandered
everywhere;* tired out of loathing for the whole world of
idealistic lying and conscience-softening, which, once again,
in the case of Wagner, had scored a victory over a man who
was of the bravest; and last but not least, tired by the sadness of a ruthless suspicion—that I was now condemned
to be ever more and more suspicious, ever more and more
contemptuous, ever more and more *deeply* alone than I had
been theretofore. For I had no one save Richard Wagner. . . .
I was always *condemned* to the society of Germans. . . .

2

Henceforward alone and cruelly distrustful of myself, I
then took up sides—not without anger—*against myself* and
for all that which hurt me and fell hard upon me: and

thus I found the road to that courageous pessimism which is the opposite of all idealistic falsehood, and which, as it seems to me, is also the road to *me*—to *my mission*. . . . That hidden and dominating thing, for which for long ages we have had no name, until ultimately it comes forth as our mission—this tyrant in us wreaks a terrible revenge upon us for every attempt we make either to evade him or to escape him, for every one of our experiments in the way of befriending people to whom we do not belong, for every active occupation, however estimable, which may make us diverge from our principal object; aye, and even for every virtue which would fain protect us from the rigor of our most intimate sense of responsibility. Illness is always the answer, whenever we venture to doubt our right to *our* mission, whenever we begin to make things too easy for ourselves. Curious and terrible at the same time! It is for our relaxation that we have to pay most dearly! And should we wish after all to return to health, we then have no choice: we are compelled to burden ourselves *more* heavily than we had been burdened before. . . .

FROM HUMAN, ALL TOO HUMAN, VOL. I

215

MUSIC.—Music by and for itself is not so portentous for our inward nature, so deeply moving, that it ought to be looked upon as the *direct* language of the feelings; but its ancient union with poetry has infused so much symbolism into rhythmical movement, into loudness and softness of tone, that we now *imagine* it speaks directly *to* and comes *from* the inward nature. Dramatic music is only possible when the art of harmony has acquired an immense range of symbolical means, through song, opera, and a hundred attempts at description by sound. "Absolute music" is either form per se, in the rude condition of music, when playing in time and with various degrees of strength gives pleasure, or the symbolism of form which speaks to the understanding even without poetry, after the two arts were joined finally together after long development and the musical form had been woven about with threads of meaning and feeling. People who are backward in musical development can appreciate a piece of harmony merely as execution, while those who are advanced will comprehend it symbolically. No music is deep and full of meaning in itself, it does not speak of "will," of the "thing-in-itself"; that could be imagined by the intellect only in an age which had conquered for musical symbolism the entire range of inner life. It was the intellect itself that first *gave* this meaning to sound, just as it also gave meaning to the relation between lines and masses in architecture, but which in itself is quite foreign to mechanical laws.

219

THE RELIGIOUS SOURCE OF THE NEWER MUSIC. Soulful music arose out of the Catholicism re-established after the Council of Trent, through Palestrina, who endowed the newly awakened, earnest, and deeply moved spirit with sound; later on, in Bach, it appeared also in Protestantism, as far as this had been deepened by the Pietists and released from its originally dogmatic character. The supposition and necessary preparation for both origins is the familiarity with music which existed during and before the Renaissance, namely that learned occupation with music which was really scientific pleasure in the masterpieces of harmony and voice-training. On the other hand, the opera must have preceded it, wherein the layman made his protest against a music that had grown too· learned and cold, and endeavored to re-endow Polyhymnia with a soul. Without the change to that deeply religious sentiment, without the dying away of the inwardly moved temperament, music would have remained learned or operatic; the spirit of the counterreformation is the spirit of modern music (for that pietism in Bach's music is also a kind of counterreformation). So deeply are we indebted to the religious life. Music was the counterreformation in the field of art; to this belongs also the later painting of the Carracci and Caravaggi, perhaps also the baroque style, in *any* case more than the architecture of the Renaissance or of antiquity. And we might still ask: If our newer music could move stones, would it build them up into antique architecture? I very much doubt it. For that which predominates in this music, affections, pleasure in exalted, highly strained sentiments, the desire to be alive at any cost, the quick change of feeling, the strong relief-effects of light and shade, the combination of the ecstatic and the naïve—all this has already reigned in the plastic arts and created new laws of style: but it was neither in the time of antiquity nor of the Renaissance.

FROM HUMAN, ALL TOO HUMAN, VOL. II

134*

HOW THE SOUL SHOULD BE MOVED BY THE NEW MUSIC.—The artistic purpose followed by the new music, in what is now forcibly but none too lucidly termed "endless melody," can be understood by going into the sea, gradually losing one's firm tread on the bottom, and finally surrendering unconditionally to the fluid element. One has to *swim*. In the previous, older music one was forced, with delicate or stately or impassioned movement, to *dance*. The measure necessary for dancing, the observance of a distinct balance of time and force in the soul of the hearer, imposed a continual self-control. Through the counteraction of the cooler draught of air which came from this caution and the warmer breath of musical enthusiasm, that music exercised its spell.—Richard Wagner aimed at a different excitation of the soul, allied, as above said, to swimming and floating. This is perhaps the most essential of his innovations. His famous method, originating from this aim and adapted to it—the "endless melody"—strives to break and sometimes even to despise all mathematical equilibrium of time and force. He is only too rich in the invention of such effects, which sound to the old school like rhythmic paradoxes and blasphemies. He dreads petrifaction, crystallization, the development of music into the architectural. He accordingly sets up a three-time rhythm in opposition to the double-time, not infrequently introduces five-time and seven-time, immediately repeats a phrase, but with a prolation, so that its time is again doubled and trebled. From an easygoing imitation of such art may arise a great danger to music, for by the side of the superabundance of rhythmic emotion demoralization and decadence lurk in ambush. The danger will become very great if such music comes to associate itself more and more closely with a quite naturalistic

* From *Miscellaneous Maxims and Opinions*.

art of acting and pantomime, trained and dominated by no higher plastic models; an art that knows no measure in itself and can impart no measure to the kindred element, the all-too-womanish nature of music.

159

MUSIC AND DISEASE. The danger of the new music lies in the fact that it puts the cup of rapture and exaltation to the lips so invitingly, and with such a show of moral ecstasy, that even the noble and temperate man always drinks a drop too much. This minimum of intemperance, constantly repeated, can in the end bring about a deeper convulsion and destruction of mental health than any coarse excess could do. Hence nothing remains but some day to fly from the grotto of the nymph, and through perils and billowy seas to forge one's way to the smoke of Ithaca and the embraces of a simpler and more human spouse.

171

MUSIC AS A LATECOMER IN EVERY CULTURE. —Among all the arts that are accustomed to grow on a definite culture-soil and under definite social and political conditions, music is the last plant to come up, arising in the autumn and fading-season of the culture to which it belongs. At the same time, the first signs and harbingers of a new spring are usually already noticeable, and sometimes music, like the language of a forgotten age, rings out into a new, astonished world, and comes too late. In the art of the Dutch and Flemish musicians the soul of the Christian Middle Ages at last found its fullest tone: their sound-architecture is the posthumous but legitimate and equal sister of Gothic. Not until Handel's music was heard the note of the best in the soul of Luther and his kin, the great Judaeo-heroical impulse that created the whole Reformation movement. Mozart first expressed in golden melody the age of Louis XIV and the art of Racine and Claude Lorrain. The eighteenth century—that century of rhapsody, of broken ideals and transitory happiness—only sang itself out in the music of Beethoven and Rossini. A lover of sentimental similes might say that all really important music was a swan song. Music is, in fact, not a universal language for all time, as is so often said in its praise, but responds exactly to a particular period and warmth of emotion which involves a quite definite, individual culture, determined by time and place, as its inner law. The music of Palestrina would be quite unintelligible to a Greek; and again, what would the music of Rossini convey to Palestrina? It may be that our most modern German music, with all its pre-eminence and desire of pre-eminence, will soon be no longer understood. For this music sprang from a culture that is undergoing a rapid decay, from the soil of that epoch of reaction and restoration in which a certain Catholicism of feeling, as well as a delight in all indigenous, national, primitive manners, burst into bloom and scattered a blended perfume over Europe. These two emotional tendencies, adopted in their greatest strength and carried to their farthest limits, found final expression in the music of Wagner. Wagner's predilection for the old native sagas, his free idealization of their unfamiliar gods and heroes—who are really sovereign beasts of prey with occasional fits of thoughtfulness, magnanimity, and boredom—his reanimation of those figures, to which he gave in addition the medieval Christian thirst for ecstatic sensuality and spiritualization—all this Wagnerian give-and-take with regard to materials, souls, figures, and words—would clearly express the spirit of his music, if it could not, like all music, speak quite unambiguously of itself. This spirit wages the last campaign of reaction against the spirit of illumination which passed into this century from the last, and also against the supernatural ideas of French revolutionary romanticism and of English and American insipidity in the reconstruction of state and society. But is it not evident that the spheres of thought and emotion apparently suppressed by Wagner and his school have long since acquired fresh strength, and that his late musical protest against them generally rings into ears that prefer to hear different and opposite notes; so that one day that high and wonderful art will suddenly become unintelligible and will be covered by the spider's web of oblivion? In considering this state of affairs we must not let ourselves be led astray by those transitory fluctuations which arise like a reaction within a reaction, as a temporary sinking of the mountainous wave in the midst of the general upheaval. Thus, this decade of national war, ultramontane martyrdom, and socialistic unrest may, in its remoter aftereffect, even aid the Wagnerian art to acquire a sudden halo, without guaranteeing that it "has a future" or that it has *the* future. It is in the very nature of music that the fruits of its great culture-vintage should lose their taste and wither earlier than the fruits of the plastic arts or those that grow on the tree of knowledge. Among all the products of the human artistic sense ideas are the most solid and lasting.

167*

WHERE MUSIC IS AT HOME. Music reaches its high-water mark only among men who have not the ability or the right to argue. Accordingly, its chief promoters are princes, whose aim is that there should be not much criticism nor even much thought in their neighborhood. Next come societies which, under some pressure or other (political or religious), are forced to become habituated to silence, and so feel all the greater need of spells to charm away emotional ennui—these spells being generally eternal love-making and eternal music. Thirdly, we must reckon whole nations in which there is no "society," but all the greater number of individuals with a bent toward solitude, mystical thinking, and a reverence for all that is inexpressible; these are the genuine "musical souls." The Greeks, as a nation delighting in talking and argument, accordingly put up with music only as an hors d'oeuvre to those arts which really admit of discussion and dispute. About music one can hardly even *think* clearly. The Pythagoreans, who in so many respects were exceptional Greeks, are said to have been great musicians. This was the school that invented a five-years' silence,† but did not invent a dialectic.

168

SENTIMENTALITY IN MUSIC. We may be ever so much in sympathy with serious and profound music, yet nevertheless, or perhaps all the more for that reason, we shall at occasional moments be overpowered, entranced, and almost melted away by its opposite—I mean, by those simple Italian operatic airs which, in spite of all their monotony of rhythm and childishness of harmony, seem at times to sing to us like the very soul of music. Admit this or not as you please, you Pharisees of good taste, it is so, and it is my present task to propound the riddle that it is so, and to

* From *The Wanderer and His Shadow*.
† In the sixth century B.C. Pythagoras founded at Croton a "school" somewhat resembling a monastic order. Among the ordeals for novitiates was enforced silence for five years.—TR.

nibble a little myself at the solution.—In childhood's days
we tasted the honey of many things for the first time. Never
was honey so good as then; it seduced us to life, into
abundant life, in the guise of the first spring, the first flower,
the first butterfly, the first friendship. Then—perhaps in our
ninth year or so—we heard our first music, and this was
the first that we understood; thus the simplest and most
childish tunes, that were not much more than a sequel to
the nurse's lullaby and the strolling fiddler's tune, were our
first experience. (For even the most trifling "revelations" of
art need preparation and study; there is no "immediate"
effect of art, whatever charming fables the philosophers may
tell.) Our sensation on hearing these Italian airs is associated with those first musical raptures, the strongest of our
lives. The bliss of childhood and its flight, the feeling that
our most precious possession can never be brought back, all
this moves the chords of the soul more strongly than the
most serious and profound music can move them.—This
mingling of aesthetic pleasure with moral pain, which nowadays it is customary to call (rather too haughtily, I think)
"sentimentality"—it is the mood of Faust at the end of the
first scene—this "sentimentality" of the listener is all to the
advantage of Italian music. It is a feeling which the experienced connoisseurs in art, the pure "aesthetes," like to
ignore. Moreover, almost all music has a magical effect only
when we hear it speak the language of our own *past*. Accordingly, it seems to the layman that all the old music is
continually growing better, and that all the latest is of little
value. For the latter arouses no "sentimentality," that most
essential element of happiness, as aforesaid, for every man
who cannot approach this art with pure aesthetic enjoyment.

FROM THE DAWN OF DAY

216

EVIL PEOPLE AND MUSIC. Should the full bliss of
love, which consists in unlimited confidence, ever have fallen
to the lot of persons other than those who are profoundly
suspicious, evil, and bitter? For such people enjoy in this
bliss the gigantic, unlooked-for, and incredible *exception* of
their souls! One day they are seized with that infinite,
dreamy sensation which is entirely opposed to the remainder

of their private and public life, like a delicious enigma, full of golden splendor, and impossible to be described by mere words or similes. Implicit confidence makes them speechless—there is even a species of suffering and heaviness in this blissful silence; and this is why souls that are overcome with happiness generally feel more grateful to music than others and better ones do: for they see and hear through music, as through a colored mist, their love becoming, as it were, more distant, more touching, and less heavy. Music is the only means that such people have of observing their extraordinary condition and of becoming aware of its presence with a feeling of estrangement and relief. When the sound of music reaches the ears of every lover, he thinks: "It speaks of me, it speaks in my stead; it knows everything!"

239

A HINT TO MORALISTS. Our musicians have made a great discovery. They have found out that interesting ugliness is possible even in their art; this is why they throw themselves with such enthusiastic intoxication into this ocean of ugliness, and never before has it been so easy to make music. It is only now that we have got the general, dark-colored background, upon which every luminous ray of fine music, however faint, seems tinged with golden emerald luster; it is only now that we dare to inspire our audience with feelings of impetuosity and indignation, taking away their breath, so to speak, in order that we may afterward, in an interval of restful harmony, inspire them with a feeling of bliss which will be to the general advantage of a proper appreciation of music.

We have discovered the contrast: it is only now that the strongest effects are possible—and cheap. No one bothers any more about good music. But you must hurry up! When any art has once made this discovery, it has but a short space of time to live. Oh, if only our thinkers could probe into the depths of the souls of our musicians when listening to their music! How long we must wait until we again have an opportunity of surprising the inward man in the very act of his evil doing, and his innocence of this act! For our musicians have not the slightest suspicion that it is their own history, the history of the disfigurement of the soul, which they are transposing into music. In former times a good

musician was almost forced by the exigencies of his art
to become a good man—and now!

255

CONVERSATION ON MUSIC.

A. What do you say to that music?

B. It has overpowered me, I can say nothing about it.
Listen! there it is beginning again.

A. All the better! This time let us do our best to overpower it. Will you allow me to add a few words to this
music? And also to show you a drama which perhaps at
your first hearing you did not wish to observe?

B. Very well, I have two ears and even more if necessary; move up closer to me.

A. We have not yet heard what he wishes to say to us,
up to the present he has only promised to say something—
something as yet unheard, so he gives us to understand by
his gestures, for they are gestures. How he beckons! How he
raises himself up! How he gesticulates! And now the moment of supreme tension seems to have come to him: two
more fanfares, and he will present us with his superb and
splendidly adorned theme, rattling, as it were, with precious
stones.

Is it a handsome woman? Or a beautiful horse? Enough,
he looks about him as if enraptured, for he must assemble
looks of rapture. It is only now that his theme quite pleases
him; it is only now that he becomes inventive and risks new
and audacious features. How he forces out his theme! Ah,
take care!—he not only understands how to adorn, but also
how to gloss it over! Yes, he knows what the color of health
is, and he knows how to make it up—he is more subtle in
his self-consciousness than I thought. And now he is convinced that he has convinced his hearers; he sets off his
impromptus as if they were the most important things under
the sun: he points to his theme with an insolent finger as if
it were too good for this world.—Ah, how distrustful he is!
He is afraid we may get tired!—that is why he buries his
melody in sweet notes.—Now he even appeals to our coarser
senses that he may excite us and thus get us once again into
his power. Listen to him as he conjures up the elementary
force of tempestuous and thundering rhythms!

And now that he sees that these things have captivated
our attention, strangle us, and almost overwhelm us, he
once again ventures to introduce his theme amidst this play

of the elements in order to convince us, confused and agitated as we are, that our confusion and agitation are the effects of his miraculous theme. And from now onward his hearers believe in him: as soon as the theme is heard once more they are reminded of its thrilling elementary effects. The theme profits by this recollection—now it has become demoniacal! What a connoisseur of the soul he is! He gains command over us by all the artifices of the popular orator. But the music has stopped again.

B. And I am glad of it; for I could no longer bear listening to your observations! I should prefer ten times over to let myself be deceived than to knowing the truth once after your version.

A. That is just what I wished to hear from you. The best people now are just like you: you are quite content to let yourselves be deceived. You come here with coarse, lustful ears, and you do not bring with you your conscience of the art of listening. On the way here you have cast away your intellectual honesty, and thus you corrupt both art and artists. Whenever you applaud and cheer you have in your hands the conscience of the artists—and woe to art if they get to know that you cannot distinguish between innocent and guilty music! I do not indeed refer to "good" and "bad" music—we meet with both in the two kinds of music mentioned! But I call innocent music that which thinks only of itself and believes only in itself, and which on account of itself has forgotten the world at large—this spontaneous expression of the most profound solitude which speaks of itself and with itself, and has entirely forgotten that there are listeners, effects, misunderstandings, and failures in the world outside. In short, the music which we have just heard is precisely of this rare and noble type; and everything I said about it was a fable—pardon my little trick if you will!

B. Oh, then you like *this* music, too? In that case many sins shall be forgiven you!

FROM THE JOYFUL WISDOM

103

GERMAN MUSIC. German music, more than any other, has now become European music; because the changes which Europe experienced through the Revolution have therein alone found expression: it is only German music that knows how to express the agitation of popular masses, the tremendous artificial uproar, which does not even need to be very noisy —while Italian opera, for example, knows only the choruses of domestics or soldiers, but not "the people." There is the additional fact that in all German music a profound bourgeois jealousy of the noblesse can be traced, especially a jealousy of *esprit* and *élégance*, as the expressions of a courtly, chivalrous, ancient, and self-confident society. It is not music like that of Goethe's musician at the gate, which was pleasing also "in the hall," and to the king as well; it is not here said: "The knights looked on with martial air; with bashful eyes the ladies." Even the Graces are not allowed in German music without a touch of remorse; it is only with Pleasantness, the country sister of the Graces, that the German begins to feel morally at ease—and from this point up to his enthusiastic, learned, and often gruff "sublimity" (the Beethovenlike sublimity), he feels more and more so. If we want to imagine the man of *this* music—well, let us just imagine Beethoven as he appeared beside Goethe, say, at their meeting at Teplitz: as semibarbarism beside culture, as the masses beside the nobility, as the good-natured man beside the good and more than "good" man, as the visionary beside the artist, as the man needing comfort beside the comforted, as the man given to exaggeration and distrust beside the man of reason, as the crank and self-tormenter, as the foolish, enraptured, blessedly unfortunate, sincerely immoderate man, as the pretentious and awkward man—and altogether as the "untamed man": it was thus that Goethe conceived and characterized him, Goethe, the exceptional German, for whom a music of equal rank has not yet been found!—Finally, let us consider whether the present, continually extending contempt of melody and the stunting of the sense for melody among Germans should not be understood as a democratic impropriety and an aftereffect of the Revolution? For melody has such an obvious delight in conformity to law, and such an aversion to everything evolving, unformed, and arbitrary, that it sounds like a note out of the *ancient* European regime, and as a seduction and reduction back to it.

FROM BEYOND GOOD AND EVIL

245

The "good old" time is past, it sang itself out in Mozart—
how happy are *we* that his rococo still speaks to us, that
his "good company," his tender enthusiasm, his childish delight in the Chinese and in flourishes, his courtesy of
heart, his longing for the elegant, the amorous, the tripping,
the tearful, and his belief in the South, can still appeal to
something left in us! Ah, some time or other it will be over
with it!—but who can doubt that it will be over still sooner
with the intelligence and taste for Beethoven! For he was
only the last echo of a break and transition in style, and
not, like Mozart, the last echo of a great European taste
which had existed for centuries. Beethoven is the intermediate event between an old mellow soul that is constantly
breaking down, and a future overyoung soul that is always
coming; there is spread over his music the twilight of eternal
loss and eternal extravagant hope—the same light in which
Europe was bathed when it dreamed with Rousseau, when
it danced round the Tree of Liberty of the Revolution,
and finally almost fell down in adoration before Napoleon.
But how rapidly does *this* very sentiment now pale, how
difficult nowadays is even the *apprehension* of this sentiment, how strangely does the language of Rousseau, Schiller, Shelley, and Byron sound to our ear, in whom *collectively*
the same fate of Europe was able to *speak*, which knew how
to *sing* in Beethoven!—Whatever German music came afterward belongs to Romanticism, that is to say, to a movement
which, historically considered, was still shorter, more fleeting, and more superficial than that great interlude, the transition of Europe from Rousseau to Napoleon, and to the
rise of democracy. Weber—but what do *we* care nowadays
for *Freischütz* and *Oberon*! Or Marschner's *Hans Heiling*
and *Vampyr*! Or even Wagner's *Tannhäuser*! This is extinct,
although not yet forgotten music. This whole music of
romanticism, besides, was not noble enough, was not musical enough, to maintain its position anywhere but in the
theater and before the masses; from the beginning it was
second-rate music, which was little thought of by genuine
musicians. It was different with Felix Mendelssohn, that

halcyon master, who, on account of his lighter, purer, happier soul, quickly acquired admiration, and was equally quickly forgotten: as the beautiful *episode* of German music. But with regard to Robert Schumann, who took things seriously, and has been taken seriously from the first—he was the last that founded a school—do we not now regard it as a satisfaction, a relief, a deliverance, that this very romanticism of Schumann's has been surmounted? Schumann, fleeing into the "Saxon Switzerland" of his soul, with a half Wertherlike, half Jean-Paul-like nature (assuredly not like Beethoven! assuredly not like Byron!)—his *Manfred* music is a mistake and a misunderstanding to the extent of injustice; Schumann, with his taste, which was fundamentally a *petty* taste (that is to say, a dangerous propensity—doubly dangerous among Germans—for quiet lyricism and intoxication of the feelings), going constantly apart, timidly withdrawing and retiring, a noble weakling who reveled in nothing but anonymous joy and sorrow, from the beginning a sort of girl and *noli me tangere*—this Schumann was already merely a *German* event in music, and no longer a European event, as Beethoven had been, as in a still greater degree Mozart had been; with Schumann German music was threatened with its greatest danger, that of *losing the voice for the soul of Europe* and sinking into a merely national affair.

VII. Famous Men

FROM HUMAN, ALL TOO HUMAN, VOL. I

433

XANTIPPE.—Socrates found a wife such as he required—but he would not have sought her had he known her sufficiently well; even the heroism of his free spirit would not have gone so far. As a matter of fact, Xantippe forced him more and more into his peculiar profession, inasmuch as she made house and home doleful and dismal to him; she taught him to live in the streets and wherever gossiping and idling went on, and thereby made him the greatest Athenian street-dialectician, who had, at last, to compare himself to a gadfly which a god had set on the neck of the beautiful horse Athens to prevent it from resting.

FROM HUMAN, ALL TOO HUMAN, I

227*

GOETHE'S ERRORS.—Goethe is a signal exception among great artists in that he did not live within the limited confines of his real capacity, as if that must be the essential, the distinctive, the unconditional, and the last thing in him and for all the world. Twice he intended to possess something higher than he really possessed—and went astray in the second half of his life, where he seems quite convinced that he is one of the great scientific discoverers and illuminators. So too in the first half of his life he demanded of himself something higher than the poetic art seemed to

* From *Miscellaneous Maxims and Opinions*.

him—and here already he made a mistake. That nature wished to make him a plastic artist—*this* was his inwardly glowing and scorching secret, which finally drove him to Italy, that he might give vent to his mania in this direction and make to it every possible sacrifice. At last, shrewd as he was, and honestly averse to any mental perversion in himself, he discovered that a tricksy elf of desire had attracted him to the belief in this calling, and that he must free himself of the greatest passion of his heart and bid it farewell. The painful conviction, tearing and gnawing at his vitals, that it was necessary to bid farewell, finds full expression in the character of Tasso. Over Tasso, that Werther intensified, hovers the premonition of something worse than death, as when one says: "Now it is over, after this farewell: how shall I go on living without going mad?" These two fundamental errors of his life gave Goethe, in face of a purely literary attitude toward poetry (the only attitude then known to the world), such an unembarrassed and apparently almost arbitrary position. Not to speak of the period when Schiller (poor Schiller, who had no time himself and left no time to others) drove away his shy dread of poetry, his fear of all literary life and craftsmanship, Goethe appears like a Greek who now and then visits his beloved, doubting whether she be not a goddess to whom he can give no proper name. In all his poetry one notices the inspiring neighborhood of plastic art and Nature. The features of these figures that floated before him—and perhaps he always thought he was on the track of the metamorphoses of one goddess—became, without his will or knowledge, the features of all the children of his art. Without the extravagances of error he would not have been Goethe—that is, the only German artist in writing who has not yet become out of date—just because he desired as little to be a writer as a German by vocation.

86 *

SOCRATES.—If all goes well, the time will come when, in order to advance themselves on the path of moral reason, men will rather take up the *Memorabilia* of Socrates than

* From *The Wanderer and His Shadow*.

the Bible, and when Montaigne and Horace will be used as pioneers and guides for the understanding of Socrates, the simplest and most enduring of interpretative sages. In him converge the roads of the most different philosophic modes of life, which are in truth the modes of the different temperaments, crystallized by reason and habit and all ultimately directed toward the delight in life and in self. The apparent conclusion is that the most peculiar thing about Socrates was his share in all the temperaments. Socrates excels the founder of Christianity by virtue of his merry style of seriousness and by what wisdom of sheer roguish pranks which constitutes the best state of soul in a man. Moreover, he had a superior intelligence.

99

JEAN PAUL [Richter].—Jean Paul knew a great deal, but had no science; understood all manner of tricks of art, but had no art; found almost everything enjoyable, but had no taste; possessed feeling and seriousness, but in dispensing them poured over them a nauseous sauce of tears; had even wit, but, unfortunately for his ardent desire for it, far too little—whence he drives the reader to despair by his very lack of wit. In short, he was the bright, rank-smelling weed that shot up overnight in the fair pleasances of Schiller and Goethe. He was a good, comfortable man, and yet a destiny, a destiny in a dressing gown.*

103

LESSING.—Lessing had a genuine French talent, and, as writer, went most assiduously to the French school. He knows well how to arrange and display his wares in his shop window. Without this true art his thoughts, like the objects of them, would have remained rather in the dark, nor would the general loss be great. His art, however, has taught many (especially the last generation of German scholars) and has given enjoyment to a countless number. It is true his disciples had no need to learn from him, as they often did, his unpleasant tone with its mingling of petulance and candor. —Opinion is now unanimous on Lessing as "lyric poet," and will some day be unanimous on Lessing as "dramatic poet."

---

*It is interesting to compare this judgment with Carlyle's praise of Jean Paul. The dressing gown is an allusion to Jean Paul's favorite costume.—TR.

107

WIELAND.—Wieland wrote German better than anyone else, and had the genuine adequacies and inadequacies of the master. His translations of the letters of Cicero and Lucian are the best in the language. His ideas, however, add nothing to our store of thought. We can endure his cheerful moralities as little as his cheerful immoralities, for both are very closely connected. The men who enjoyed them were at bottom better men than we are, but also a good deal heavier. They *needed* an author of this sort. The Germans did not need Goethe, and therefore cannot make proper use of him. We have only to consider the best of our statesmen and artists in this light. None of them had or *could* have had Goethe as their teacher.

118

HERDER.—Herder fails to be all that he made people think he was and himself wished to think he was. He was no great thinker or discoverer, no newly fertile soil with the unexhausted strength of a virgin forest. But he possessed in the highest degree the power of scenting the future, he saw and picked the first fruits of the seasons earlier than all others, and they then believed that he had made them grow. Between darkness and light, youth and age, his mind was like a hunter on the watch, looking everywhere for transitions, depressions, convulsions, the outward and visible signs of internal growth. The unrest of spring drove him to and fro, but he was himself not the spring. At times, indeed, he had some inkling of this, and yet would fain not have believed it—he, the ambitious priest, who would have so gladly been the intellectual pope of his epoch! This is his despair. He seems to have lived long as a pretender to several kingdoms or even to a universal monarchy. He had his following which believed in him, among others the young Goethe. But whenever crowns were really distributed, he was passed over. Kant, Goethe, and then the first true German historians and scholars robbed him of what he thought he had reserved for himself (although in silence and secret he often thought the reverse). Just when he doubted in himself, he gladly clothed himself in dignity and enthusiasm: these were often in him mere garments, which had to hide a great deal and also to deceive and comfort him. He really had fire and enthusiasm, but his ambition was far greater! It blew impatiently at the fire, which flickered, crackled, and smoked—his *style* flickers, crackles, and smokes—but he yearned for the great flame which never broke out. He did not sit at the table of the genuine creators, and his ambition did not admit of his sitting modestly among those who simply enjoy. Thus he was a restless spirit, the taster of all intellectual dishes, which were collected by the Germans from every quarter and every age in the course of half a century. Never really happy and satisfied, Herder was also too often ill, and then at times envy sat by his bed, and hypocrisy paid her visit as well. He always had an air of being scarred and crippled, and he lacked simple, stalwart manliness more completely than any of the so-called "classical writers."

149

SEBASTIAN BACH.—Insofar as we do not hear Bach's music as perfect and experienced connoisseurs of counterpoint and all the varieties of the fugal style (and accordingly must dispense with real artistic enjoyment), we shall feel in listening to his music—in Goethe's magnificent phrase—as if "we were present at God's creation of the world." In other words, we feel here that something great is in the making but not yet made—our mighty modern music, which by conquering nationalities, the Church, and counterpoint has conquered the world. In Bach there is still too much crude Christianity, crude Germanism, crude scholasticism. He stands on the threshold of modern European music, but turns from thence to look at the Middle Ages.

150

HANDEL.—Handel, who in the invention of his music was bold, original, truthful, powerful, inclined to and akin to all the heroism of which a *nation* is capable, often proved stiff, cold, nay even weary of himself in composition. He applied a few well-tried methods of execution, wrote copiously and quickly, and was glad when he had finished—but that joy was not the joy of God and other creators in the eventide of their working day.

151

HAYDN.—So far as genius can exist in a man who is merely *good*, Haydn had genius. He went just as far as the limit which morality sets to intellect, and only wrote music that has "no past."

152

BEETHOVEN AND MOZART.—Beethoven's music often appears like a deeply emotional meditation on unexpectedly hearing once more a piece long thought to be forgotten, "Tonal Innocence": it is music about music. In the song of the beggar and child in the street, in the monotonous airs of vagrant Italians, in the dance of the village inn or in carnival nights he discovers his melodies. He stores them together like a bee, snatching here and there some notes or a short phrase. To him these are hallowed memories of "the better world," like the ideas of Plato.—Mozart stands in quite a different relation to his melodies. He finds his inspiration not in hearing music but in gazing at life, at the most stirring life of southern lands. He was always dreaming of Italy, when he was not there.

155

FRANZ SCHUBERT.—Franz Schubert, inferior as an artist to the other great musicians, had nevertheless the largest share of inherited musical wealth. He spent it with a free hand and a kind heart, so that for a few centuries musicians will continue to *nibble* at his ideas and inspirations. In his works we find a store of *unused* inventions; the greatness of others will lie in making use of those inventions. If Beethoven may be called the ideal listener for a troubadour, Schubert has a right to be called the ideal troubadour.

157

FELIX MENDELSSOHN.—Felix Mendelssohn's music is the music of the good taste that enjoys all the good things that have ever existed. It always points behind. How could it have much "in front," much of a future?—But did he want it to have a future? He possessed a virtue rare among artists, that of gratitude without *arrière-pensée*. This virtue, too, always points behind.

159

FREEDOM IN FETTERS—A PRINCELY FREEDOM. —Chopin, the last of the modern musicians, who gazed at and worshipped beauty, like Leopardi; Chopin, the Pole, the inimitable (none that came before or after him has a right to this name)—Chopin had the same princely punctilio in convention that Raphael shows in the use of the simplest traditional colors. The only difference is that Chopin applies them not to color but to melodic and rhythmic traditions. He admitted the validity of these traditions because he was born under the sway of etiquette. But in these fetters he plays and dances as the freest and daintiest of spirits, and, be it observed, he does not spurn the chain.

FROM THE DAWN OF DAY

88

LUTHER, THE GREAT BENEFACTOR.—Luther's most important result is the suspicion which he awakened against the saints and the entire Christian *vita contemplativa;* only since his day has an un-Christian *vita contemplativa* again become possible in Europe, only since then has contempt for laymen and worldly activity ceased. Luther continued to be an honest miner's son even after he had been shut up in a monastery, and there, for lack of other depths and "borings," he descended into himself, and bored terrifying and dark passages through his own depths—finally coming to recognize that an introspective and saintly life was impossible to him, and that his innate "activity" in body and soul would end by being his ruin. For a long time, too long, indeed, he endeavored to find the way to holiness through castigations; but at length he made up his mind, and said to himself: "There is no real *vita contemplativa!* We have been deceived. The saints were no better than the rest of us." This was truly a rustic way of gaining one's case; but for the Germans of that period it was the only proper way. How edified they felt when they could read in their Lutheran catechism: "Apart from the Ten Commandments there is no work which could find favor in the eyes of God —these much-boasted spiritual works of the saints are purely imaginary!"

163

AGAINST ROUSSEAU.—If it is true that there is something contemptible about our civilization, we have two alternatives: of concluding with Rousseau that, "This despicable civilization is to blame for our bad morality," or to infer, contrary to Rousseau's view, that "Our good morality is to blame for this contemptible civilization. Our social conceptions of good and evil, weak and effeminate as they are, and their enormous influence over both body and soul, have had the effect of weakening all bodies and souls and of crushing all unprejudiced, independent, and self-reliant men, the real pillars of a strong civilization: wherever we still find the evil morality today, we see the last crumbling ruins of these pillars." Thus let paradox be opposed by paradox! It is quite impossible for the truth to lie with both sides: and can we say, indeed, that it lies with either? Decide for yourself.

168

A MODEL.—What do I like about Thucydides, and how does it come that I esteem him more highly than Plato? He exhibits the most widespread and artless pleasure in everything typical in men and events, and finds that each type is possessed of a certain quantity of good sense: it is this good sense which he seeks to discover. He likewise exhibits a larger amount of practical justice than Plato; he never reviles or belittles those men whom he dislikes or who have in any way injured him in the course of his life. On the contrary: while seeing only types, he introduces something noble and additional into all things and persons; for what could posterity, to which he dedicates his work, do with things not typical! Thus this culture of the disinterested knowledge of the world attains in him, the poet-thinker, a final marvelous bloom— this culture which has its poet in Sophocles, its statesman in Pericles, its doctor in Hippocrates, and its natural philosopher in Democritus: this culture which deserves to be called by the name of its teachers, the Sophists, and which, unhappily, from the moment of its baptism at once begins to grow pale and incomprehensible to us—for henceforward we suspect that this culture, which was combated by Plato and all the Socratic schools, must have been very immoral! The truth of this matter is so complicated and entangled that we feel unwilling to unravel it: so let the old error (*error veritate simplicior*) run its old course.

496

THE EVIL PRINCIPLE. Plato has marvelously described how the philosophic thinker must necessarily be regarded as the essence of depravity in the midst of every existing society: for as the critic of all its morals he is naturally the antagonist of the moral man, and, unless he succeeds in becoming the legislator of new morals, he lives long in the memory of men as an instance of the "evil principle." From this we may judge to how great an extent the city of Athens, although fairly liberal and fond of innovations, abused the reputation of Plato during his lifetime. What wonder then that he—who, as he has himself recorded, had the "political instinct" in his body—made three different attempts in Sicily, where at that time a united Mediterranean Greek state appeared to be in process of formation?

It was in this state, and with its assistance, that Plato thought he could do for the Greeks what Mohammed did for the Arabs several centuries later; viz., establishing both minor and more important customs, and especially regulating the daily life of every man. His ideas were quite practicable just as certainly as those of Mohammed were practicable, for even much more incredible ideas, those of Christianity, proved themselves to be practicable! A few hazards less and a few hazards more—and then the world would have witnessed the Platonization of Southern Europe, and, if we suppose that this state of things had continued to our own days, we should probably be worshipping Plato now as the "good principle." But he was unsuccessful, and so his traditional character remains that of a dreamer and a Utopian—stronger epithets than these passed away with ancient Athens.

45

EPICURUS. Yes, I am proud of perceiving the character of Epicurus differently from anyone else perhaps, and of enjoying the happiness of the afternoon of antiquity in all that I hear and read of him: I see his eye gazing out on a broad whitish sea, over the shore rocks on which the sunshine rests, while great and small creatures play in its light, secure and calm like this light and that eye itself. Such happiness could only have been devised by a chronic sufferer, the happiness of an eye before which the sea of existence has become calm, and which can no longer tire of gazing at the surface and at the variegated, tender, tremulous skin of this sea. Never previously was there such a moderation of voluptuousness.

95

CHAMFORT. That such a judge of men and of the multitude as Chamfort should side with the multitude, instead of standing apart in philosophical resignation and defense—I am at a loss to explain, except as follows: There was an instinct in him stronger than his wisdom, and it had never been gratified: the hatred against all noblesse of blood; perhaps his mother's old and only too explicable hatred, which was consecrated in him by love of her—an instinct of revenge from his boyhood, which waited for the hour to avenge his mother. But then the course of his life, his genius, and alas! most of all, perhaps, the paternal blood in his veins, had seduced him to rank and consider himself equal to the noblesse—for many, many years! In the end, however, he could not endure the sight of himself, the "old man" under the old regime, any longer; he got into a violent, penitential passion, and *in this state* he put on the raiment of the populace as *his* special kind of hair shirt! His bad conscience was the neglect of revenge. If Chamfort had then been a little more of the philosopher, the Revolution would not have had its tragic wit and its sharpest sting; it would have been regarded as a much more stupid affair, and would have had no such seductive influence on men's minds. But Chamfort's hatred and revenge educated an entire generation, and the most illustrious men passed through his school. Let us but consider that Mirabeau looked up to Chamfort as to his higher and older self, from whom he expected (and endured) impulses, warnings, and condemnations—Mirabeau, who as a man belongs to an entirely different order of greatness, as the very foremost among the statesman-geniuses of yesterday and today.—Strange, that in spite of such a friend and advocate—we possess Mirabeau's letters to Chamfort—this wittiest of all moralists has remained unfamiliar to the French, quite the same as Stendhal, who has perhaps had the most penetrating eyes and ears of any Frenchman of *this* century. Is it because the latter had really too much of the German and the Englishman in his nature for the Parisians to endure him?—while Chamfort, a man with ample knowledge of the profundities and secret motives of the soul, gloomy, suffering, ardent—a thinker who found laughter necessary as the remedy of life, and who almost gave himself up as lost every day that he had not laughed—seems much more like an Italian, and related by blood to Dante and Leopardi, than like a Frenchman. One knows Chamfort's last words: *"Ah! mon ami,"* he said to Sieyès, *"je m'en vais enfin de ce monde, où il faut que le cœur se brise ou se bronze—."* These were certainly not the words of a dying Frenchman.

98

IN HONOR OF SHAKESPEARE. The best thing I could say in honor of Shakespeare, *the man,* is that he believed in Brutus and cast not a shadow of suspicion on the kind of virtue which Brutus represents! It is to him that Shakespeare consecrated his best tragedy—it is at present still called by a wrong name—to him and to the most terrible essence of lofty morality. Independence of soul!—that is the question at issue! No sacrifice can be too great there: one must be able to sacrifice to it even one's dearest friend, though he be also the grandest of men, the ornament of the world, the genius without peer—if one really loves freedom as the freedom of great souls, and if *this* freedom be threatened by him: it is thus that Shakespeare must have felt! The elevation in which he places Caesar is the most exquisite honor he could confer upon Brutus; it is thus only that he lifts into vastness the inner problem of his hero, and similarly the strength of soul which could cut *this knot!* And was it actually political freedom that impelled the poet to sympathy with Brutus—and made him the accomplice of Brutus? Or was political freedom merely a symbol for something inexpressible? Do we perhaps stand before some somber event or adventure of the poet's own soul, which has remained unknown, and of which he only cared to speak symbolically? What is all Hamlet-melancholy in comparison with the melancholy of Brutus!—and perhaps Shakespeare also knew this, as he knew the other, by experience! Perhaps he also had his dark hour and his bad angel, just as Brutus had them! But whatever similarities and secret relationships of that kind there may have been, Shakespeare cast himself on the ground and felt unworthy and alien in presence of the aspect and virtue of Brutus: he has inscribed the testimony thereof in the tragedy itself. He has twice brought in a poet in it, and twice heaped upon him such an impatient and extreme contempt that it sounds like a cry—like the cry of self-contempt. Brutus, even Brutus loses patience when the poet appears, self-important, pathetic, and obtrusive, as poets usually are —persons who seem to abound in the possibilities of greatness, even moral greatness, and nevertheless rarely attain even to ordinary uprightness in the philosophy of practice and of life. "He may know the times, *but I know his temper* —away with the jigging fool!"—shouts Brutus. We may translate this back into the soul of the poet that composed it.

101

VOLTAIRE. Wherever there has been a court, it has furnished the standard of good speaking, and with this also the standard of style for writers. The court language, however, is the language of the courtier who *has no profession,* and who even in conversations on scientific subjects avoids all convenient, technical expressions, because they smack of the profession; on that account the technical expression, and everything that betrays the specialist, is a *blemish of style* in countries which have a court culture. At present, when all courts have become caricatures of past and present times, one is astonished to find even Voltaire unspeakably reserved and scrupulous on this point (for example, in his judgments concerning such stylists as Fontenelle and Montesquieu we are now, all of us, emancipated from court taste, while Voltaire was its *perfecter!*

FROM THE TWILIGHT OF THE IDOLS

2

RENAN.—Theology, or the corruption of reason by original sin (Christianity). Proof of this—Renan, who, even in those rare cases where he ventures to say either Yes or No on a general question, invariably misses the point with painful regularity. For instance, he would fain associate science and nobility: but surely it must be obvious that science is democratic. He seems to be actuated by a strong desire to represent an aristocracy of intellect: but, at the same time he grovels on his knees, and not only on his knees, before the opposite doctrine, the gospel of the humble. What is the good of all free-spiritedness, modernity, mockery, and acrobatic suppleness, if in one's belly one is still a Christian, a Catholic, and even a priest! Renan's forte, precisely like that of a Jesuit and Father Confessor, lies in his seductiveness. His intellectuality is not devoid of that unctuous complacency of a parson—like all priests, he becomes dangerous only when he loves. He is second to none in the art of skillfully worshipping a dangerous thing. This intellect of Renan's, which in its action is enervating, is one calamity the more, for poor, sick France with her will power all going to pieces.

3

SAINTE-BEUVE.—There is naught of man in him; he is full of petty spite toward all virile spirits. He wanders erratically; he is subtle, inquisitive, a little bored, forever with his ear to keyholes—at bottom a woman, with all woman's revengefulness and sensuality. As a psychologist he is a genius of slander; inexhaustively rich in means to this end; no one understands better than he how to introduce a little poison into praise. In his fundamental instincts he is plebeian and next of kin to Rousseau's resentful spirit: consequently he is a romanticist—for beneath all romanticism Rousseau's instinct for revenge grunts and greeds. He is a revolutionary, but kept within bounds by "funk." He is embarrassed in the face of everything that is strong (public opinion, the Academy, the court, even Port Royal). He is embittered against

everything great in men and things, against everything that
believes in itself. Enough of a poet and of a female to be
able to feel greatness as power, he is always turning and
twisting, because, like the proverbial worm, he constantly
feels that he is being trodden upon. As a critic he has no
standard of judgment, no guiding principle, no backbone.
Although he possesses the tongue of the cosmopolitan liber-
tine which can chatter about a thousand things, he has not
the courage even to acknowledge his *libertinage*. As a historian he has no philosophy, and lacks the power of philosophical vision—hence his refusal to act the part of a judge,
and his adoption of the mask of "objectivity" in all important
matters. His attitude is better in regard to all those things in
which subtle and effete taste is the highest tribunal: in these
things he really does have the courage of his own personality
—he really does enjoy his own nature—he actually is a
master.—In some respects he is a prototype of Beaudelaire.

5

G. ELIOT.—They are rid of the Christian God and therefore think it all the more incumbent upon them to hold tight
to Christian morality: this is an English way of reasoning,
but let us not take it ill in moral females *à la* Eliot. In
England, every man who indulges in any trifling emancipation from theology must retrieve his honor in the most terrifying manner by becoming a moral fanatic. That is how
they do penance in that country. As for us, we act differently.
When we renounce the Christian faith, we abandon all right
to Christian morality. This is not by any means self-evident,
and in defiance of English shallowpates the point must be
made ever more and more plain. Christianity is a system, a
complete outlook upon the world, conceived as a whole. If
its leading concept, the belief in God, is wrenched from it,
the whole is destroyed; nothing vital remains in our grasp.
Christianity presupposes that man does not and cannot know
what is good or bad for him: the Christian believes in God
who, alone, can know these things. Christian morality is a
command, its origin is transcendental. It is beyond all criticism, all right to criticism; it is true only on condition that
God is truth—it stands or falls with the belief in God. If
the English really believe that they know intuitively, and of
their own accord, what is good and evil; if, therefore, they
assert that they no longer need Christianity as a guarantee of
morality, this in itself is simply the outcome of the dominion

of Christian valuations, and a proof of the strength and profundity of this dominion. It only shows that the origin of English morality has been forgotten and that its exceedingly relative right to exist is no longer felt. For Englishmen morality is not yet a problem.

12

I have been reading the life of Thomas Carlyle, that unconscious and involuntary farce, that heroic-moral interpretation of dyspeptic moods.—Carlyle, a man of strong words and attitudes, a rhetorician by necessity, who seems ever to be tormented by the desire of finding some kind of strong faith, and by his inability to do so (in this respect a typical romanticist!). To yearn for a strong faith is not the proof of a strong faith, but rather the reverse. If a man have a strong faith he can indulge in the luxury of scepticism; he is strong enough, firm enough, well-knit enough for such a luxury. Carlyle stupefies something in himself by means of the fortissimo of his reverence for men of a strong faith, and his rage over those who are less foolish: he is in sore need of noise. An attitude of constant and passionate dishonesty toward himself—this is his proprium; by virtue of this he is and remains interesting. Of course, in England he is admired precisely on account of his honesty. Well, that is English; and in view of the fact that the English are the nation of consummate cant, it is not only comprehensible but also very natural. At bottom, Carlyle is an English atheist who makes it a point of honor not to be so.

13

EMERSON.—He is much more enlightened, much broader, more versatile, and more subtle than Carlyle; but above all, he is happier. He is one who instinctively lives on ambrosia and who leaves the indigestible parts of things on his plate. Compared with Carlyle he is a man of taste. Carlyle, who was very fond of him, nevertheless declared that "he does not give us enough to chew." This is perfectly true but it is not unfavorable to Emerson. Emerson possesses that kindly intellectual cheerfulness which deprecates overmuch seriousness; he has absolutely no idea of how old he is already, and how young he will yet be—he could have said of himself, in Lope de Vega's words: *"yo me sucedo a mi mismo."* His mind is always finding reasons for being contented and even thankful; and at times he gets preciously near to that serene superiority of the worthy bourgeois who returning from an amorous rendezvous *tamquam re bene gesta* said gratefully *"Ut desint vires, tamen est laudanda voluptas."*

49

GOETHE.—No mere German, but a European event: a magnificent attempt to overcome the eighteenth century by means of a return to nature, by means of an ascent to the naturalness of the Renaissance, a kind of self-overcoming on the part of the century in question. He bore the strongest instincts of this century in his breast: its sentimentality, and idolatry of nature, its antihistoric, idealistic, unreal, and revolutionary spirit (the latter is only a form of the unreal). He enlisted history, natural science, antiquity, as well as Spinoza, and above all practical activity, in his service. He drew a host of very definite horizons around him; far from liberating himself from life, he plunged right into it; he did not give in; he took as much as he could on his own shoulders, and into his heart. That to which he aspired was *totality;* he was opposed to the sundering of reason, sensuality, feeling, and will (as preached with most repulsive scholasticism by Kant, the antipodes of Goethe); he disciplined himself into a harmonious whole, he *created* himself. Goethe in the midst of an age of unreal sentiment was a convinced realist: he said yea to everything that was like him in this regard—there was no greater event in his life than that *ens realissimum*, surnamed Napoleon. Goethe conceived a strong, highly cultured man, skillful in all bodily accomplishments, able to keep himself in check, having a feeling of reverence for himself, and so constituted as to be able to risk the full enjoyment of naturalness in all its rich profusion and be strong enough for this freedom; a man of tolerance, not out of weakness but out of strength, because he knows how to turn to his own profit that which would ruin the mediocre nature; a man unto whom nothing is any longer forbidden, unless it be weakness either as a vice or as a virtue. Such a spirit, *become free,* appears in the middle of the universe with a feeling of cheerful and confident fatalism; he believes that only individual things are bad, and that as a whole the universe justifies and affirms itself—*he no longer denies.* . . . But such a faith is the highest of all faiths: I christened it with the name of Dionysus.

VIII. The Spirit of Modernity

FROM THOUGHTS OUT OF SEASON, VOL. II

Schopenhauer As Educator

I

WHEN the traveler, who had seen many countries and nations and continents, was asked what common attribute he had found everywhere existing among men, he answered, "They have a tendency to sloth." Many may think that the fuller truth would have been, "They are all timid." They hide themselves behind "manners" and "opinions." At bottom every man knows well enough that he is a unique being, only once on this earth; and by no extraordinary chance will such a marvelously picturesque piece of diversity in unity as he is, ever be put together a second time. He knows this, but hides it like an evil conscience—and why? From fear of his neighbor, who looks for the latest conventionalities in him, and is wrapped up in them himself. But what is it that forces the man to fear his neighbor, to think and act with his herd, and not seek his own joy? Shyness perhaps, in a few rare cases, but in the majority it is idleness, the "taking things easily," in a word the "tendency to sloth," of which the traveler spoke. He was right; men are more slothful than timid, and their greatest fear is of the burdens that an uncompromising honesty and nakedness of speech and action would lay on them. It is only the artists who hate this lazy wandering in borrowed manners and ill-fitting opinions, and discover the secret of the evil conscience, the truth that each human being is a unique marvel. They show us, how in every little movement of his muscles the man is an individual

327

self, and further—as an analytical deduction from his individuality—a beautiful and interesting object, a new and incredible phenomenon (as is every work of nature), that can never become tedious. If the great thinker despises mankind, it is for their laziness; they seem mere indifferent bits of pottery, not worth any commerce or improvement. The man who will not belong to the general mass has only to stop "taking himself easily"; to follow his conscience, which cries out to him, "Be thyself! All that thou doest and thinkest and desirest is not—thyself!"

Every youthful soul hears this cry day and night, and quivers to hear it; for she divines the sum of happiness that has been from eternity destined for her, if she thinks of her true deliverance; and toward this happiness she can in no wise be helped, so long as she lies in the chains of Opinion and of Fear. And how comfortless and unmeaning may life become without this deliverance! There is no more desolate or Ishmaelitish creature in nature than the man who has broken away from his true genius, and does nothing but peer aimlessly about him. There is no reason to attack such a man at all, for he is a mere husk without a kernel, a painted cloth, tattered and sagging, a scarecrow ghost, that can rouse no fear, and certainly no pity. And though one be right in saying of a sluggard that he is "killing time," yet in respect of an age that rests its salvation on public opinion—that is, on private laziness—one must be quite determined that such a time shall be "killed," once and for all: I mean that it shall be blotted from life's true History of Liberty. Later generations will be greatly disgusted when they come to treat the movements of a period in which no living men ruled, but shadow-men on the screen of public opinion; and to some far posterity our age may well be the darkest chapter of history, the most unknown because the least human. I have walked through the new streets of our cities, and thought how of all the dreadful houses that these gentlemen with their public opinion have built for themselves, not a stone will remain in a hundred years, and that the opinions of these busy masons may well have fallen with them. But how full of hope should they all be who feel that they are no citizens of this age! If they were, they would have to help on the work of "killing their time," and of perishing with it —when they wish rather to quicken the time to life, and in that life themselves to *live*.

But even if the future leaves us nothing to hope for, the wonderful fact of our existing at this present moment of time gives us the greatest encouragement to live after our own rule and measure; so inexplicable is it, that we should be living just today, though there has been an infinity of time wherein we might have arisen, that we own nothing but a span's length of it, this "today," and must show in it wherefore and whereunto we have arisen. We have to answer for our existence to ourselves, and will therefore be our own true pilots, and not admit that our being resembles a blind fortuity. One must take a rather impudent and reckless way with the riddle, especially as the key is apt to be lost, however things turn out. Why cling to your bit of earth, or your little business, or listen to what your neighbor says? It is so provincial to bind oneself to views which are no longer binding a couple of hundred miles away. East and West are signs that somebody chalks up in front of us to fool such cowards as we are. "I will make the attempt to gain freedom," says the youthful soul, and will be hindered, just because two nations happen to hate each other and go to war, or because there is a sea between two parts of the earth, or a religion is taught in the vicinity which did not exist two hundred years ago. "And this is not—thyself," the soul says. "No one can build thee the bridge, over which thou must cross the river of life, save thyself alone. There are paths and bridges and demigods without number, that will gladly carry thee over, but only at the price of thine own self: thy self wouldst thou have to give in pawn, and then lose it. There is in the world one road whereon none may go, except thou: ask not whither it lead, but go forward. Who was it that spake that true word—'A man has never risen higher than when he knoweth not whither his road may yet lead him'?"

But how can we "find ourselves" again, and how can man "know himself"? He is a thing obscure and veiled; if the hare has seven skins, man can cast from him seventy times seven, and yet will not be able to say, "Here art thou in very truth; this is outer shell no more." Also this digging into one's self, this straight, violent descent into the pit of one's being, is a troublesome and dangerous business to start. A man may eaily take such hurt that no physician can heal him. And again, what is the use, since everything bears witness to our essence—our friendships and enmities, our looks and greetings, our memories and forgetfulnesses, our books and our writing! This is the most effective way: to let the youthful soul look back on life with the question, "What hast thou up to now truly loved, what has drawn thy soul upward, mastered it, and blessed it, too?" Set up these things that thou hast honored before thee, and, maybe, they will show thee, in their being and their order, a law which is the fundamental law of thine own self. Compare these objects, consider how one completes and broadens and transcends and explains another, how they form a ladder on which thou hast all the time been climbing to thy self: for thy true being lies not deeply hidden in thee, but an infinite height above thee, or at least above that which thou dost and commonly take to be thyself. The true educators and molders reveal to thee the real groundwork and import of thy being, something that in itself cannot be molded or educated: thy educators can be nothing but thy deliverers. And that is the secret of all culture: it does not give artificial limbs, wax noses, or spectacles for the eyes—a thing that could buy such gifts is but the base coin of education. But it is rather a liberation, a removal of all the weeds and rubbish and vermin that attack the delicate shoots, the streaming forth of light and warmth, the tender dropping of the night rain; it is the following and the adoring of Nature when she is pitifully-minded as a mother; her completion, when it bends before her fierce and ruthless blasts and turns them to good, and draws a veil over all expression of her tragic unreason—for she is a stepmother, too, sometimes.

There are other means of "finding ourselves," of coming to ourselves out of the confusion wherein we all wander as in a dreary cloud, but I know none better than to think on our educators. So I will today take as my theme the hard teacher Arthur Schopenhauer, and speak of others later.

II

In order to describe properly what an event my first look into Schopenhauer's writings was for me, I must dwell for a minute on an idea that recurred more constantly in my youth, and touched me more nearly, than any other. I wandered then as I pleased in a world of wishes, and thought that destiny would relieve me of the dreadful and wearisome duty of educating myself: some philosopher would come at the right moment to do it for me—some true philosopher, who could be obeyed without further question, as he would be trusted more than one's self. Then I said within me: "What would be the principles on which he might teach thee?" And I pondered in my mind what he would say to the two maxims of education that hold the field in our time. The first demands that the teacher should find out at once the strong point in his pupil, and then direct all his skill and will, all the moisture and all the sunshine, to bring the fruit of that single virtue to maturity. The second requires him to raise to a higher power all the qualities that already exist, cherish them, and bring them into a harmonious relation. But, we may ask, should one who has a decided talent for working in gold be made for that reason to learn music? And can we admit that Benvenuto Cellini's father was right in continually forcing him back to the "dear little horn"— the "cursed piping," as his son called it? We cannot think so in the case of such a strong and clearly marked talent as his, and it may well be that this maxim of harmonious development applies only to weaker natures, in which there is a whole swarm of desires and inclinations, though they may not amount to very much, singly or together. On the other hand, where do we find such a blending of harmonious voices —nay, the soul of harmony itself—as we see in natures like Cellini's, where everything—knowledge, desire, love and hate —tends toward a single point, the root of all, and a harmonious system, the resultant of the various forces, is built up through the irresistible domination of this vital center? And so perhaps the two maxims are not contrary at all: the one merely saying that man must have a center, the other, a circumference as well. The philosophic teacher of my dream would not only discover the central force, but would know how to prevent its being destructive of the other powers; his task, I thought, would be the welding of the whole man into a solar system with life and movement, and the discovery of its paraphysical laws.

In the meantime I could not find my philosopher, however I tried; I saw how badly we moderns compare with the Greeks and Romans, even in the serious study of educational problems. You can go through all Germany, and especially all the universities, with this need in your heart, and will not find what you seek; many humbler wishes than that are still unfulfilled there. For example, if a German seriously wishes to make himself an orator, or to enter a "school for authors," he will find neither master nor school; no one yet seems to have thought that speaking and writing are arts which cannot be learned without the most careful method and untiring application. But, to their shame, nothing shows more clearly the insolent self-satisfaction of our people than the lack of demand for educators; it comes partly from meanness, partly from want of thought. Anything will do as a so-called "family tutor," even among our most eminent and cultured people: and what a menagerie of crazy heads and moldy devices mostly go to make up the belauded gymnasium! And consider what we are satisfied with in our finishing schools—our universities. Look at our professors and their institutions! And compare the difficulty of the task of educating a man to be a man! Above all, the wonderful way in which the German savants fall to their dish of knowledge shows that they are thinking more of science than mankind, and they are trained to lead a forlorn hope in her service, in order to encourage ever new generations to the same sacrifice. If their traffic with knowledge be not limited and controlled by any more general principles of education, but allowed to run on indefinitely—"the more the better"—it is as harmful to learning as the economic theory of *laissez faire* to common morality. No one recognizes now that the education of the professors is an exceedingly difficult problem, if their humanity is not to be sacrificed or shriveled up; this difficulty can be actually seen in countless examples of natures warped and twisted by their reckless and premature devotion to science. There is a still more important testimony to the complete absence of higher education, pointing to a greater and more universal danger. It is clear at once why an orator or writer cannot now be educated—because there are no teachers—and why a savant must be a distorted and perverted thing—because he will have been trained by the inhuman abstraction, science. This being so, let a man ask himself: "Where are now the types of moral excellence and fame for all our generation—learned and unlearned, high and low—the visible abstract of constructive ethics for this age? Where has vanished all the reflection on moral questions that has occupied every great developed society at all epochs?" There is no fame for that now, and there are none to reflect; we are really drawing on the inherited moral capital which our predecessors accumulated for us, and which we do not know how to increase, but only to squander. Such things are either not mentioned in our society, or, if at all, with a naïve want of personal experience that makes one disgusted. It comes to this, that our schools and professors simply turn aside from any moral instruction or content themselves with formulas; virtue is a word and nothing more, on both sides, an old-fashioned word that they laugh at—and it is worse when they do not laugh, for then they are hypocrites.

An explanation of this faintheartedness and ebbing of all moral strength would be difficult and complex; but whoever is considering the influence of Christianity in its hour of victory on the morality of the medieval world must not forget that it reacts also in its defeat, which is apparently its position today. By its lofty ideal, Christianity has outbidden the ancient Systems of Ethics and their invariable naturalism, with which men came to feel a dull disgust, and afterward when they did reach the knowledge of what was better and higher, they found they had no longer the power, for all their desire, to return to its embodiment in the antique virtues. And so the life of the modern man is passed in seesawing between Christianity and paganism, between a furtive or hypocritical approach to Christian morality and an equally shy and spiritless dallying with the antique: and he does not thrive under it. His inherited fear of naturalism, and its more recent attraction for him, his desire to come to rest somewhere, while in the impotence of his intellect he swings backward and forward between the "good" and the "better" course—all this argues an instability in the modern mind that condemns it to be without joy or fruit. Never were moral teachers more necessary and never were they more unlikely to be found: physicians are most in danger themselves in times when they are most needed and many men are sick. For where are our modern physicians who are strong and sure-footed enough to hold up another or lead him by the hand? There lies a certain heavy gloom on the best men of our time, an eternal loathing for the battle that is fought in their hearts between honesty and lies, a wavering of trust in themselves, which makes them quite incapable of showing to others the way they must go.

So I was right in speaking of my "wandering in a world of wishes" when I dreamed of finding a true philosopher who could lift me from the slough of insufficiency, and teach me again simply and honestly to be in my thoughts and life, in the deepest sense of the word, "out of season"; simply and honestly—for men have now become such complicated machines that they must be dishonest, if they speak at all, or wish to act on their words.

With such needs and desires within me did I come to know Schopenhauer.

I belong to those readers of Schopenhauer who know perfectly well, after they have turned the first page, that they will read all the others, and listen to every word that he has spoken. My trust in him sprang to life at once, and has been the same for nine years. I understood him as though he had written for me (this is the most intelligible, though a rather foolish and conceited way of expressing it). Hence I never found a paradox in him, though occasionally some small errors: for paradoxes are only assertions that carry no conviction, because the author has made them himself without any conviction, wishing to appear brilliant, or to mislead, or, above all, to pose. Schopenhauer never poses; he writes for himself, and no one likes to be deceived—least of all a philosopher who has set this up as his law: "Deceive nobody, not even thyself," neither with the "white lies" of all social intercourse, which writers almost unconsciously imitate, still less with the more conscious deceits of the platform, and the artificial methods of rhetoric. Schopenhauer's speeches are to himself alone, or if you like to imagine an auditor, let it be a son whom the father is instructing. It is a rough, honest, good-humored talk to one who "hears and loves." Such writers are rare. His strength and sanity surround us at the first sound of his voice: it is like entering the heights of the forest, where we breathe deep and are well again. We feel a bracing air everywhere, a certain candor and naturalness of his own, that belongs to men who are at home with themselves, and masters of a very rich home indeed; he is quite different from the writers who are surprised at themselves if they have said something intelligent, and whose pronouncements for that reason have something nervous and unnatural about them. We are just as little reminded in Schopenhauer of the professor with his stiff joints worse for want of exercise, his narrow chest and scraggy figure, his slinking or strutting gait. And again his rough and rather grim soul leads us not so much to miss as to despise the suppleness and courtly grace of the excellent Frenchmen; and no one will find in him the gilded imitations of pseudogallicism that our German writers prize so highly. His style in places reminds me a little of Goethe, but is not otherwise on any German model. For he knows how to be profound with simplicity, striking without rhetoric, and severely logical without pedantry: and of what German could he have learnt that? He also keeps free from the hairsplitting, jerky, and (with all respect) rather un-German manner of Lessing: no small merit in him, for Lessing is the most tempting of all models for prose style. The highest praise I can give his manner of presentation is to apply his own phrase to himself: "A philosopher must be very honest to avail himself of no aid from poetry or rhetoric." That honesty is something, and even a virtue, is one of those private opinions which are forbidden in this age of public opinion; and so I shall not be praising Schopenhauer, but only giving him a distinguishing mark, when I repeat that he is honest, even as a writer; so few of them are that we are apt to mistrust everyone who writes at all. I only know a single author that I can rank with Schopenhauer, or even above him, in the matter of honesty, and that is Montaigne. The joy of living on this earth is increased by the existence of such a man. The effect on myself, at any rate, since my first acquaintance with that strong and masterful spirit, has been, that I can say of him as he of Plutarch—"As soon as I open him, I seem to grow a pair of wings." If I had the task of making myself at home on the earth, I would choose him as my companion.

Schopenhauer has a second characteristic in common with Montaigne, besides honesty; a joy that really makes others joyful. "Aliis laetus, sibi sapiens." There are two very different kinds of joyfulness. The true thinker always communicates joy and life, whether he is showing his serious or comic side, his human insight or his godlike forbearance: without surly looks or trembling hands or watery eyes, but simply and truly, with fearlessness and strength, a little cavalierly perhaps, and sternly, but always as a conqueror, and it is this that brings the deepest and intensest joy, to see the conquering god with all the monsters that he has fought. But the joyfulness one finds here and there in the mediocre writers and limited thinkers makes some of us miserable; I felt this, for example, with the "joyfulness" of David Strauss. We are generally ashamed of such a quality in our contemporaries, because they show the nakedness of our time, and of the men in it, to posterity. Such *fils de joie* do not see the sufferings and the monsters that they pretend, as philosophers, to see and fight, and so their joy deceives us, and we hate it; it tempts to the false belief that they have gained some victory. At bottom there is only joy where there is victory, and this applies to true philosophy as much as to any work of art. The contents may be forbidding and serious, as the problem of existence always is; the work will only prove tiresome and oppressive, if the slipshod thinker and the dilettante have spread the mist of their insufficiency over it: while nothing happier or better can come to man's lot than to be near one of those conquering spirits whose profound thought has made them love what is most vital, and whose wisdom has found its goal in beauty. They really speak; they are no stammerers or babblers; they live and move, and have no part in the *danse macabre* of the rest of humanity. And so in their company one feels a natural man again, and could cry out with Goethe—"What a wondrous and priceless thing is a living creature! How fitted to his surroundings, how true, and real!"

I have been describing nothing but the first, almost physiological, impression made upon me by Schopenhauer, the magical emanation of inner force from one plant of nature to another, that follows the slightest contact. Analyzing it, I find that this influence of Schopenhauer has three elements, his honesty, his joy, and his consistency. He is honest, as speaking and writing for himself alone; joyful, because his thought has conquered the greatest difficulties; consistent, because he cannot help being so. His strength rises like a flame in the calm air, straight up, without a tremor or deviation. He finds his way, without our noticing that he has been seeking it: so surely and cleverly and inevitably does he run his course, as if by some law of gravitation. If anyone has felt what it means to find, in our present world of Centaurs and Chimeras, a singlehearted and unaffected child of nature who moves unconstrained on his own road, he will understand my joy and surprise in discovering Schopenhauer: I knew in him the educator and philosopher I had so long desired. Only, however, in his writings: which was a great loss. All the more did I exert myself to see behind the book the living man whose testament it was, and who promised his inheritance to such as could, and would, be more than his readers —his pupils and his sons.

III

I get profit from a philosopher, just so far as he can be an example to me. There is no doubt that a man can draw whole nations after him by his example, as is shown by Indian history, which is practically the history of Indian philosophy. But this example must exist in his outward life, not merely in his books; it must follow the way of the Grecian philosophers, whose doctrine was in their dress and bearing and general manner of life rather than in their speech or writing. We have nothing yet of this "breathing testimony" in German philosophical life; the spirit has, apparently, long completed its emancipation, while the flesh has hardly begun; yet it is foolish to think that the spirit can be really free and independent when this victory over limitation—which is ultimately a formative limiting of one's self—is not embodied anew in every look and movement. Kant held to his university, submitted to its regulations, and belonged, as his colleagues and students thought, to a definite religious faith; and naturally his example has produced, above all, university professors of philosophy. Schopenhauer makes small account of the learned tribe, keeps himself exclusive, and cultivates an independence from state and society as his ideal, to escape the chains of circumstance here; that is his value to us. Many steps in the enfranchisement of the philosopher are unknown in Germany; they cannot always remain so.

Our artists live more bravely and honorably than our philosophers, and Richard Wagner, the best example of all, shows how genius need not fear a fight to the death with the established forms and ordinances, if we wish to bring the higher truth and order, that lives in him, to the light. The "truth," however, of which we hear so much from our professors, seems to be a far more modest being, and no kind of disturbance is to be feared from her; she is an easygoing and pleasant creature, who is continually assuring the powers that be that no one need fear any trouble from her quarter, for man is only "pure reason." And therefore I will say that philosophy in Germany has more and more to learn not to be "pure reason," and it may well take as its model "Schopenhauer the man."

It is no less than a marvel that he should have come to be this human kind of example, for he was beset, within and without, by the most frightful dangers, that would have crushed and broken a weaker nature. I think there was a strong likelihood of Schopenhauer the man going under, and leaving at best a residue of "pure reason": and only "at best"—it was more probable that neither man nor reason would survive.

A modern Englishman sketches the most usual danger to extraordinary men who live in a society that worships the ordinary, in this manner: "Such uncommon characters are first cowed, then become sick and melancholy, and then die. A Shelley could never have lived in England: a race of Shelleys would have been impossible." Our Hölderlins and Kleists were undone by their unconventionality, and were not strong enough for the climate of the so-called German culture; and only iron natures like Beethoven, Goethe, Schopenhauer, and Wagner could hold out against it. Even in them the effect of this weary toiling and moiling is seen in many lines and wrinkles; their breathing is harder and their voice is forced. The old diplomatist who had only just seen and spoken to Goethe, said to a friend—"Voilà un homme qui a eu de grands chagrins!" which Goethe translated to mean "That is a man who has taken great pains in his life." And he adds, "If the trace of the sorrow and activity we have gone through cannot be wiped from our features, it is no wonder that all that survives of us and our struggles should bear the same impress." And this is the Goethe to whom our cultured Philistines point as the happiest of Germans, that they may prove their thesis, that it must be possible to be happy among them—with the unexpressed corollary that no one can be pardoned for feeling unhappy and lonely among them. Hence they push their doctrine, in practice, to its merciless conclusion, that there is always a secret guilt in isolation. Poor Schopenhauer had this secret guilt, too, in his heart, the guilt of cherishing his philosophy more than his fellow men; and he was so unhappy as to have learned from Goethe that he must defend his philosophy at all costs from the neglect of his contemporaries, to save its very existence, for there is a kind of Grand Inquisitor's Censure in which the Germans, according to Goethe, are great adepts: it is called—inviolable silence. This much at least was accomplished by it—the greater part of the first edition of Schopenhauer's masterpiece had to be turned into wastepaper. The imminent risk that his great work would be undone, merely by neglect, bred in him a state of unrest—perilous and uncontrollable—for no single adherent of any note presented himself. It is tragic to watch his search for any evidence of recognition, and his piercing cry of triumph at last, that he would now really be read (*legor et legar*), touches us with a thrill of pain. All the traits in which we do not see the great philosopher show us the suffering man, anxious for his noblest possessions; he was tortured by the fear of losing his little property, and perhaps of no longer being able to maintain in its purity his truly antique attitude toward philosophy. He often chose falsely in his desire to find real trust and compassion in men, only to return with a heavy heart to his faithful dog again. He was absolutely alone, with no single friend of his own kind to comfort him, and between one and none there lies an infinity—as ever between something and nothing. No one who has true friends knows what real loneliness means, though he may have the whole world in antagonism round him. Ah, I see well ye do not know what isolation is! Whenever there are great societies with governments and religions and public opinions—where there is a tyranny, in short, there will the lonely philosopher be hated, for philosophy offers an asylum to mankind where no tyranny can penetrate, the inner sanctuary, the center of the heart's labyrinth, and the tyrants are galled at it. Here do the lonely men lie hid, but here, too, lurks their greatest danger. These men who have saved their inner freedom must also live and be seen in the outer world; they stand in countless human relations by their birth, position, education, and country, their own circumstances and the importunity of others, and so they are presumed to hold an immense number of opinions, simply because these happen to prevail: every look that is not a denial counts as an assent, every motion of the hand that does not destroy is regarded as an aid. These free and lonely men know that they perpetually seem other than they are. While they wish for nothing but truth and honesty, they are in a net of misunderstanding, and that ardent desire cannot prevent a mist of false opinions, of adaptations and wrong conclusions, of partial misapprehension and intentional reticence, from gathering round their actions. And there settles a cloud of melancholy on their brows, for such natures hate the necessity of pretense worse than death, and the continual bitterness gives them a threatening and volcanic character. They take revenge from time to time for their forced concealment and self-restraint; they issue from their dens with lowering looks; their words and deeds are explosive, and may lead to their own destruction. Schopenhauer lived amid dangers of this sort. Such lonely men need love, and friends, to whom they can be as open and sincere as to themselves, and in whose presence the deadening silence and hypocrisy may cease. Take their friends away, and there is left an increasing peril; Heinrich von Kleist was broken by the lack of love, and the most terrible weapon against unusual men is to drive them into themselves; and then their issuing forth again is a volcanic eruption. Yet there are always some demigods who can bear life under these fearful conditions and can be their conquerors, and if you would hear their lonely chant, listen to the music of Beethoven.

So the first danger in whose shadow Schopenhauer lived was—isolation. The second is called—doubting of the truth. To this every thinker is liable who sets out from the philosophy of Kant, provided he be strong and sincere in his sorrows and his desires, and not a mere tinkling thought-box or calculating machine. We all know the shameful state of things implied by this last reservation, and I believe it is only a very few men that Kant has so vitally affected as to change the current of their blood. To judge from what one reads, there must have been a revolution in every domain of thought since the work of this unobtrusive professor; I cannot believe it myself. For I see men, though darkly, as themselves needing to be revolutionized, before any "domains of thought" can be so. In fact, we find the first mark of any influence Kant may have had on the popular mind in a corrosive scepticism and relativity. But it is only in noble and active spirits who could never rest in doubt that the shattering despair of truth itself could take the place of doubt. This was, for example, the effect of the Kantian philosophy on Heinrich von Kleist. "It was only a short time ago," he writes in his poignant way, "that I became acquainted with the Kantian philosophy; and I will tell you my thought, though I cannot fear that it will rack you to your inmost soul, as it did me.—We cannot decide, whether what we call truth is really truth, or whether it only seems so to us. If the latter, the truth that we amass here does not exist after death, and all our struggle to gain a possession that may follow us even to the grave is in vain. If the blade of this thought do not cut your heart, yet laugh not at another who feels himself wounded by it in his Holy of Holies. My one highest aim has vanished, and I have no more." Yes, when will men feel again deeply as Kleist did, and learn to measure a philosophy by what it means to the "Holy of Holies"? And yet we must make this estimate of what Schopenhauer can mean to us, after Kant, as the first pioneer to bring us from the heights of sceptical disillusionment or "critical" renunciation, to the greater height of tragic contemplation, the nocturnal heaven with its endless crown of stars. His greatness is that he can stand opposite the picture of life, and interpret it to us as a whole, while all the clever people cannot escape the error of thinking one comes nearer to the interpretation by a laborious analysis of the colors and material of the picture, with the confession, probably, that the texture of the canvas is very complicated and the chemical composition of the colors undiscoverable. Schopenhauer knew that one must guess the painter in order to understand the picture. But now the whole learned fraternity is engaged on understanding the colors and canvas, and not the picture, and only he who has kept the universal panorama of life and being firmly before his eyes will use the individual sciences without harm to himself, for, without this general view as a norm, they are threads that lead nowhere and only confuse still more the maze of our existence. Here we see, as I said, the greatness of Schopenhauer, that he follows up every idea, as Hamlet follows the Ghost, without allowing himself to turn aside for a learned digression, or be drawn away by the scholastic abstractions of a rabid dialectic. The study of the minute philosophers is only interesting for the recognition that they have reached those stages in the great edifice of philosophy where learned disquisitions for and against, where hairsplitting objections and counterobjections are the rule; and for that reason they evade the demand of every great philosophy to speak *sub specie aeternitatis*—"This is the picture of the whole of life: learn thence the meaning of thine own life." And the converse: "Read thine own life, and understand thence the hieroglyphs of the universal life." In this way must Schopenhauer's philosophy always be interpreted: as an individualist philosophy, starting from the single man, in his own nature, to gain an insight into his personal miseries, and needs, and limitations, and find out the remedies that will console them, namely, the sacrifice of the ego, and its submission to the nobler ends, especially those of justice and mercy. He teaches us to distinguish between the true and the apparent furtherance of man's happiness: how neither the attainment of riches, nor honor, nor learning, can raise the individual from his deep despair at his unworthiness; and how the quest for these good things can only have meaning through a universal end that transcends and explains them—the gaining of power to aid our physical nature by them and, as far as may be, correct its folly and awkwardness. For one's self only, in the first instance, and finally, through one's self, for all. It is a task that leads to scepticism, for there is so much to be made better yet, in one and all!

Applying this to Schopenhauer himself, we come to the third and most intimate danger in which he lived, and which lay deep in the marrow of his being. Everyone is apt to discover a limitation in himself, in his gifts of intellect as well as his moral will, that fills him with yearning and melancholy, and as he strives after holiness through a consciousness of sin, so, as an intellectual being, he has a deep longing after the "genius" in himself. This is the root of all true culture, and if we say this means the aspiration of man to be "born again" as saint and genius, I know that one need not be a Buddhist to understand the myth. We feel a strong loathing when we find talent without such aspiration, in the circle of the learned, or among the so-called educated, for we see that such men, with all their cleverness, are no aid but a hindrance to the beginnings of culture and the blossoming of genius, the aim of all culture. There is a rigidity in them, parallel to the cold arrogance of conventional virtue, which also remains at the opposite pole to true holiness. Schopenhauer's nature contained an extraordinarily dangerous dualism. Few thinkers have felt as he did the complete and unmistakable certainty of genius within them, and his genius made him the highest of all promises—that there could be no deeper furrow than that which he was plowing in the ground of the modern world. He knew one half of his being to be fulfilled according to its strength, with no other need; and he followed with greatness and dignity his vocation of consolidating his victory. In the other half there was a gnawing aspiration, which we can understand when we hear that he turned away with a sad look from the picture of Rancé, the founder of the Trappists, with the words: "That is a matter of grace." For genius evermore yearns after holiness as it sees further and more clearly from its watchtower than other men, deep into the reconciliation of Thought and Being, the kingdom of peace and the denial of the will, and up to that other shore, of which the Indians speak. The wonder is, that Schopenhauer's nature should have been so inconceivably stable and unshakable that it could neither be destroyed nor petrified by this yearning. Everyone will understand this after the measure of his own character and greatness; none of us will understand it in the fullness of its meaning.

The more one considers these three dangers, the more extraordinary will appear his vigor in opposing them and his safety after the battle. True, he gained many scars and open wounds: and a cast of mind that may seem somewhat too bitter and pugnacious. But his single ideal transcends the highest humanity in him. Schopenhauer stands as a pattern to men, in spite of all those scars and scratches. We may even say, that what was imperfect and "all too human" in him brings us nearer to him as a man, for we see a sufferer and a kinsman to suffering, not merely a dweller on the unattainable heights of genius.

These three constitutional dangers that threatened Schopenhauer threaten us all. Each one of us bears a creative solitude within himself, and his consciousness of it forms an exotic aura of strangeness round him. Most men cannot endure it, because they are slothful, as I said, and because their solitude hangs round them a chain of troubles and burdens. No doubt, for the man with this heavy chain, life loses almost everything that one desires from it in youth,— joy, safety, honor; his fellow men pay him his due of— isolation! The wilderness and the cave are about him, wherever he may live. He must look to it that he be not enslaved and oppressed, and become melancholy thereby. And let him surround himself with the pictures of good and brave fighters such as Schopenhauer.

The second danger, too, is not rare. Here and there we find one dowered by nature with a keen vision; his thoughts dance gladly in the witches' Sabbath of dialectic; and if he uncautiously gives his talent therein, it is easy to lose all humanity and live a ghostly life in the realm of "pure reason"; or through the constant search for the "pros and cons" of things, he may go astray from the truth and live without courage or confidence, in doubt, denial, and discontent, and the slender hope that waits on disillusion: "No dog could live long thus!"

The third danger is a moral or intellectual hardening: man breaks the bond that united him to his ideal; he ceases to be fruitful and reproduce himself in this or that province, and becomes an enemy o. a parasite of culture. The solitude of his being has become an indivisible, unrelated atom, an icy stone. And one can perish of this solitude as well as of the fear of it, of one's self as well as one's self-sacrifice, of both aspiration and petrifaction; and to live is ever to be in danger.

Besides these dangers to which Schopenhauer would have been constitutionally liable, in whatever century he had lived, there were also some produced by his own time; and it is essential to distinguish between these two kinds, in order to grasp the typical and formative elements in his nature. The philosopher casts his eye over existence and wishes to give it a new standard value, for it has been the peculiar task of all great thinkers to be lawgivers for the weight and stamp in the mint of reality. And his task will be hindered if the men he sees near him be a weakly and worm-eaten growth. To be correct in his calculation of existence, the unworthiness of the present time must be a very small item in the addition. The study of ancient or foreign history is valuable, if at all, for a correct judgment on the whole destiny of man, which must be drawn not only from an average estimate but from a comparison of the highest destinies that can befall individuals or nations. The present is too much with us; it directs the vision even against the philosopher's will, and it will inevitably be reckoned too high in the final sum. And so he must put a low figure on his own time as against others, and suppress the present in his picture of life, as well as in himself; must put it into the background or paint it over, a difficult and almost impossible task. The judgment of the ancient Greek philosophers on the value of existence means so much more than our own, because they had the full bloom of life itself before them, and their vision was untroubled by any felt dualism between their wish for freedom and beauty on the grand scale and their search after truth, with its single question "What is the real *worth* of life?" Empedocles lived when Greek culture was full to overflowing with the joy of life, and all ages may take profit from his words; especially as no other great philosopher of that great time ventured to contradict them. Empedocles is only the clearest voice among them—they all say the same thing, if a man will but open his ears. A modern thinker

is always in the throes of an unfulfilled desire; he is looking for life—warm, red life—that he may pass judgment on
it; at any rate he will think it necessary to be a living man
himself before he can believe in his power of judging. And
this is the title of the modern philosophers to sit among
the great aiders of Life (or rather of the will to live), and
the reason why they can look from their own outwearied
time and aspire to a truer culture, and a clearer explanation.
Their yearning is, however, their danger; the reformer in
them struggles with the critical philosopher. And whichever
way the victory incline, it also implies a defeat. How was
Schopenhauer to escape this danger?

We like to consider the great man as the noble child of
his age, who feels its defects more strongly and intimately
than the smaller men, and therefore the struggle of the great
man *against* his age is apparently nothing but a mad fight
to the death with himself. Only apparently, however; he
only fights the elements in his time that hinder his own
greatness, in other words, his own freedom and sincerity.
And so, at bottom, he is only an enemy to that element
which is not truly himself, the irreconcilable antagonism of
the temporal and eternal in him. The supposed "child of his
age" proves to be but a stepchild. From boyhood Schopenhauer strove with his time, a false and unworthy mother to
him, and as soon as he had banished her, he could bring
back his being to its native health and purity. For this
very reason we can use his writings as mirrors of his time;
it is no fault of the mirror if everything contemporary appears in it stricken by a ravaging disease, pale and thin,
with tired looks and hollow eyes—the stepchild's sorrow
made visible. The yearning for natural strength, for a healthy
and simple humanity, was a yearning for himself; and as
soon as he had conquered his time within him, he was
face-to-face with his own genius. The secret of nature's being
and his own lay open, the stepmother's plot to conceal his
genius from him was foiled. And now he could turn a fearless eye toward the question, "What is the real worth of
life?" without having any more to weigh a bloodless and
chaotic age of doubt and hypocrisy. He knew that there
was something higher and purer to be won on this earth
than the life of his time, and a man does bitter wrong to
existence who only knows it and criticizes it in this hateful
form. Genius, itself the highest product of life, is now
summoned to justify life, if it can: the noble creative soul
must answer the question: "Dost thou in thy heart say 'Yea!'
unto this existence? Is it enough for thee? Wilt thou be its

advocate and its redeemer? One true 'Yea' from thy lips, and the sorely accused life shall go free." How shall he answer? In the words of Empedocles.

IV

The last hint may well remain obscure for a time; I have something more easy to explain, namely, how Schopenhauer can help us to educate ourselves *in opposition to* our age, since we have the advantage of really knowing our age, through him—if it be an advantage! It may be no longer possible in a couple of hundred years. I sometimes amuse myself with the idea that men may soon grow tired of books and their authors, and the savant of tomorrow come to leave directions in his will that his body be burned in the midst of his books, including, of course, his own writings. And in the gradual clearing of the forests, might not our libraries be very reasonably used for straw and brushwood? Most books are born from the smoke and vapor of the brain, and to vapor and smoke may they well return. For having no fire within themselves, they shall be visited with fire. And possibly to a later century our own may count as the "dark age," because our productions heated the furnace hotter and more continuously than ever before. We are anyhow happy that we can learn to know our time, and if there be any sense in busying ourselves with our time at all, we may as well do it as thoroughly as we can, so that no one may have any doubt about it. The possibility of this we owe to Schopenhauer.

Our happiness would, of course, be infinitely greater, if our inquiry showed that nothing so hopeful and splendid as our present epoch had ever existed. There are simple people in some corner of the earth today—perhaps in Germany—who are disposed to believe in all seriousness that the world was put right two years ago,* and that all stern and gloomy views of life are now contradicted by "facts." The foundation of the New German Empire is, to them, the decisive blow that annihilates all the "pessimistic" philosophizers—no doubt of it. To judge the philosopher's significance in our time, as an educator, we must oppose a widespread view like this, especially common in our universities. We must say, it is a shameful thing that such abominable flattery of the Time Fetish should be uttered by a herd of so-called reflective and honorable men; it is a proof that we no

---

* This was written in 1873.—Tʀ.

longer see how far the seriousness of philosophy is removed from that of a newspaper. Such men have lost the last remnant of feeling, not only for philosophy, but also for religion, and have put in its place a spirit not so much of optimism as of journalism, the evil spirit that broods over the day—and the daily paper. Every philosophy that believes the problem of existence to be shelved, or even solved, by a political event is a sham philosophy. There have been innumerable states founded since the beginning of the world; that is an old story. How should a political innovation manage once and for all to make a contented race of the dwellers on this earth? If anyone believes in his heart that this is possible, he should report himself to our authorities; he really deserves to be Professor of Philosophy in a German university, like Harms in Berlin, Jürgen Meyer in Bonn, and Carrière in Munich.

We are feeling the consequences of the doctrine, preached lately from all the housetops, that the state is the highest end of man and there is no higher duty than to serve it; I regard this not a relapse into paganism, but into stupidity. A man who thinks state service to be his highest duty very possibly knows no higher one; yet there are both men and duties in a region beyond, and one of these duties, that seems to me at least of higher value than state service, is to destroy stupidity in all its forms—and this particular stupidity among them. And I have to do with a class of men whose teleological conceptions extend further than the well-being of a state, I mean with philosophers—and only with them in their relation to the world of culture, which is again almost independent of the "good of the state." Of the many links that make up the twisted chain of humanity, some are of gold and others of pewter.

How does the philosopher of our time regard culture? Quite differently, I assure you, from the professors who are so content with their new state. He seems to see the symptoms of an absolute uprooting of culture in the increasing rush and hurry of life, and the decay of all reflection and simplicity. The waters of religion are ebbing, and leaving swamps or stagnant pools: the nations are drawing away in enmity again, and long to tear each other in pieces. The sciences, blindly driving along, on a *laissez faire* system, without a common standard, are splitting up, and losing hold of every firm principle. The educated classes are being swept along in the contemptible struggle for wealth. Never was the world more worldly, never poorer in goodness and love. Men of learning are no longer beacons or sanctuaries in the midst of this turmoil of worldliness; they themselves are daily becoming more restless, thoughtless, loveless. Everything bows before the coming barbarism, art and science included. The educated men have degenerated into the greatest foes of education, for they will deny the universal sickness and hinder the physician. They become peevish, these poor nerveless creatures, if one speaks of their weakness and combats the shameful spirit of lies in them. They would gladly make one believe that they have outstripped all the centuries, and they walk with a pretense of happiness which has something pathetic about it, because their happiness is so inconceivable. One would not even ask them, as Tannhäuser did Biterolf, "What hast thou, poor wretch, enjoyed!" For, alas! we know far better ourselves, in another way. There is a wintry sky over us, and we dwell on a high mountain, in danger and in need. Short-lived is all our joy, and the sun's rays strike palely on our white mountains. Music is heard; an old man grinds an organ, and the dancers whirl round, and the heart of the wanderer is shaken within him to see it: everything is so disordered, so drab, so hopeless. Even now there is a sound of joy, of clear thoughtless joy! But soon the mist of evening closes round, the note dies away, and the wanderer's footsteps are heard on the gravel; as far as his eye can reach there is nothing but the grim and desolate face of nature.

It may be one-sided to insist only on the blurred lines and the dull colors in the picture of modern life; yet the other side is no more encouraging, it is only more disturbing. There is certainly strength there, enormous strength, but it is wild, primitive, and merciless. One looks on with a chill expectancy, as though into the caldron of a witch's kitchen; every moment there may arise sparks and vapor to herald some fearful apparition. For a century we have been ready for a world-shaking convulsion, and though we have lately been trying to set the conservative strength of the so-called national state against the great modern tendency to volcanic destructiveness, it will only be, for a long time yet, an aggravation of the universal unrest that hangs over us. We need not be deceived by individuals behaving as if they knew nothing of all this anxiety: their own restlessness shows how well they know it. They think more exclusively of themselves than men ever thought before; they plant and build for their little day, and the chase for happiness is never greater than when the quarry must be caught today or tomorrow: the next day perhaps there is no more hunting. We live in the Atomic Age, or rather in the Atomic Chaos. The opposing forces were practically held together in medieval times by the Church, and in some measure assimilated by the strong pressure which she exerted. When the common tie broke and the pressure relaxed, they rose once more against each other. The Reformation taught that many things were "adiaphora"—departments that needed no guidance from religion: this was the price paid for its own existence. Christianity paid a similar one to guard itself against the far more religious antiquity: and laid the seeds of discord at once. Everything nowadays is directed by the fools and the knaves, the selfishness of the money-makers and the brute forces of militarism. The state in their hands makes a good show of reorganizing everything, and of becoming the bond that unites the warring elements; in other words, it wishes for the same idolatry from mankind as they showed to the Church.

And we shall yet feel the consequences. We are even now on the ice floes in the stream of the Middle Ages; they are thawing fast, and their movement is ominous; the banks are flooded, and giving way. The revolution, the atomistic revolution, is inevitable, but what *are* those smallest indivisible elements of human society?

There is surely far more danger to mankind in transitional periods like these than in the actual time of revolution and chaos; they are tortured by waiting, and snatch greedily at every moment, and this breeds all kinds of cowardice and selfishness in them; whereas the true feeling of a great and universal need ever inspires men, and makes them better. In the midst of such dangers, who will provide the guardians and champions for *Humanity*, for the holy and inviolate treasure that has been laid up in the temples, little by little, by countless generations? Who will set up again the *Image of Man*, when men in their selfishness and terror see nothing but the trail of the serpent or the cur in them, and have fallen from their high estate to that of the brute or the automaton?

There are three Images of Man fashioned by our modern time, which for a long while yet will urge mortal men to transfigure their own lives; they are the men of Rousseau, Goethe, and Schopenhauer. The first has the greatest fire, and is most calculated to impress the people; the second is only for the few, for those contemplative natures "in the grand style" who are misunderstood by the crowd. The third demands the highest activity in those who will follow it: only such men will look on that image without harm, for it breaks the spirit of that merely contemplative man, and the rabble shudder at it. From the first has come forth a strength that led and still leads to fearful revolution, for in all socialistic upheavals it is ever Rousseau's man who is the Typhoeus under the Etna. Oppressed and half crushed to death by the pride of caste and the pitilessness of wealth, spoiled by priests and bad education, a laughingstock even to himself, man cries in his need on "holy mother Nature," and feels suddenly that she is as far from him as any god of the Epicureans. His prayers do not reach her; so deeply sunk is he in the Chaos of the unnatural. He contemptuously throws aside all the finery that seemed his truest humanity a little while ago—all his arts and sciences, all the refinements of his life—he beats with his fists against the walls, in whose shadow he has degenerated, and goes forth to seek the light and the sun, the forest and the crag. And crying out, "Nature alone is good, the natural man alone is human," he despises himself and aspires beyond himself: a state wherein the soul is ready for a fearful resolve, but calls the noble and the rare as well from their utter depths.

Goethe's man is no such threatening force; in a certain sense he is a corrective and a sedative to those dangerous agitations of which Rousseau's man is a prey. Goethe himself in his youth followed the "gospel of kindly Nature" with all the ardor of his soul: his Faust was the highest and boldest picture of Rousseau's man, so far at any rate as his hunger for life, his discontent and yearning, his intercourse with the demons of the heart could be represented. But what comes from these congregated storm clouds? Not a single lightning flash! And here begins the new Image of Man—the man according to Goethe. One might have thought that Faust would have lived a continual life of suffering, as a revolutionary and a deliverer, as the negative force that proceeds from goodness, as the genius of ruin, alike religious and daemonic, in opposition to his utterly undaemonic companion; though of course he could not be free of this companion, and had at once to use and despise his evil and destructive scepticism—which is the tragic destiny of all revolutionary deliverers. One is wrong, however, to expect anything of the sort; Goethe's man here parts company with Rousseau's, for he hates all violence, all sudden transition—that is, all action; and the universal deliverer becomes merely the universal traveler. All the riches of life and nature, all antiquity—arts, mythologies, and sciences—pass before his eager eyes, his deepest desires are aroused and satisfied, Helen herself can hold him no more—and the moment must come for which his mocking companion is waiting. At a fair spot on the earth, his flight comes to an end: his pinions drop, and Mephistopheles is at his side. When the German ceases to be Faust, there is no danger greater than of becoming a Philistine and falling into the hands of the devil—heavenly powers alone can save him. Goethe's man is, as I said, the contemplative man in the grand style, who is only kept from dying of ennui by feeding on all the great and memorable things that have ever existed, and by living from desire to desire. He is not the active man, and when he does take a place among active men, as things are, you may be sure that no good will come of it (think, for example, of the zeal with which Goethe wrote for the stage!); and further, you may be sure that "things as they are" will suffer no change. Goethe's man is a conciliatory and conservative spirit, though in danger of degenerating into a Philistine, just as Rousseau's man may easily become a Catiline. All his virtues would be the better by the addition of a little brute force and elemental passion. Goethe appears to have seen where the weakness and danger of his creation lay, as is clear from Jarno's word to Wilhelm Meister: "You are bitter and ill-tempered—which is quite an excellent thing; if you could once become really angry, it would be still better."

To speak plainly, it is necessary to become really angry in order that things may be better. The picture of Schopenhauer's man can help us here. *Schopenhauer's man voluntarily takes upon himself the pain of telling the truth*: this pain serves to quench his individual will and make him ready for the complete transformation of his being, which it is the inner meaning of life to realize. This openness in him appears to other men to be an effect of malice, for they think the preservation of their shifts and pretenses to be the first duty of humanity, and anyone who destroys their playthings to be merely malicious. They are tempted to cry out to such a man, in Faust's words to Mephistopheles:

> "So to the active and eternal
> Creative force, in cold disdain
> You now oppose the fist infernal"—

and he who would live according to Schopenhauer would seem to be more like a Mephistopheles than a Faust—that is, to our weak modern eyes, which always discover signs of malice in any negation. But there is a kind of denial and destruction that is the effect of that strong aspiration after holiness and deliverance which Schopenhauer was the first philosopher to teach our profane and worldly generation. Everything that can be denied deserves to be denied, and real sincerity means the belief in a state of things which cannot be denied, or in which there is no lie. The sincere man feels that his activity has a metaphysical meaning. It can only be explained by the laws of a different and a higher life; it is in the deepest sense an affirmation, even if everything that he does seems utterly opposed to the laws of our present life. It must lead therefore to constant suffering, but he knows, as Meister Eckhard did, that "the quickest beast that will carry you to perfection is suffering." Everyone, I should think, who has such an ideal before him must feel a wider sympathy, and he will have a burning desire to become a "Schopenhauer man"; pure and wonderfully patient, on his intellectual side full of a devouring fire, and far removed from the cold and contemptuous "neutrality" of the so-called scientific man; so high above any warped and morose outlook on life as to offer himself as the first victim of the truth he has won, with a deep consciousness of the sufferings that must spring from his sincerity. His courage will destroy his happiness on earth; he must be an enemy to the men he loves and the institutions in which he grew up; he must spare neither person nor thing, however it may hurt him; he will be misunderstood and thought an ally of forces that he abhors; in his search for righteousness he will seem unrighteous by human standards; but he must comfort himself with the words that his teacher Schopenhauer once used: "A happy life is impossible, the highest thing that man can aspire to is a *heroic* life, such as a man lives who is always fighting against unequal odds for the good of others, and wins in the end without any thanks. After the battle is over, he stands like the Prince in the *re corvo* of Gozzi, with dignity and nobility in his eyes, but turned to stone. His memory remains, and will be reverenced as a hero's; his will, that has been mortified all his life by toiling and struggling, by evil payment and ingratitude, is absorbed into Nirvana." Such a heroic life, with its full "mortification"—corresponds very little to the paltry ideas of the people who talk most about it, and make festivals in memory of great men, in the belief that a great man is great in the sense that they are small, either through exercise of his gifts to please himself or by a blind mechanical obedience to this inner force; so that the man who does not possess the gift or feel the compulsion has the same right to be small as the other to be great. But "gift" and "compulsion" are contemptible words, mere means of escape from an inner voice, a slander on him who has listened to the voice—the great man; he least of all will allow himself to be given or compelled to anything, for he knows as well as any smaller man how easily life can be taken and how soft the bed whereon he might lie if he went the pleasant and conventional way with himself and his fellow creatures: all the regulations of mankind are turned to the end that the intense feeling of life may be lost in continual distractions. Now why will he so strongly choose the opposite and try to feel life, which is the same as to suffer from life? Because he sees that men will tempt him to betray himself, and that there is a kind of agreement to draw him from his den. He will prick up his ears and gather himself together and say, "I will remain mine own." He gradually comes to understand what a fearful decision it is. For he must go down into the depths of being, with a string of curious questions on his lips—"Why am I alive? What lesson have I to learn from life? How have I become what I am, and why do I suffer in this existence?" He is troubled, and sees that no one is troubled in the same way, but rather that the hands of his fellow men are passionately stretched out toward the fantastic drama of the political theater, or they themselves are treading the boards under many disguises, youths, men and graybeards, fathers, citizens, priests, merchants, and officials—busy with the comedy they are all playing, and never thinking of their own selves. To the question "To what end dost thou live?" they would all immediately answer, with pride, "To *become* a good citizen or professor or statesman"—and yet they *are* something which can never be changed, and why are they just—this? Ah, and why nothing better? The man who only regards his life as a moment in the evolution of a race or a state or a science, and will belong merely to a history of "becoming," has not understood the lesson of existence, and must learn it over again. This eternal "becoming something" is a lying puppet show, in which man has forgot himself; it is the force that scatters individuality to the four winds, the eternal childish game that the big baby time is playing in front of us—and with us. The heroism of sincerity lies in ceasing to be the plaything of time. Everything in the process of "becoming" is a hollow sham, contemptible and shallow: man can only find the solution of his riddle in "being" something definite and unchangeable. He begins to test how deep both "becoming" and "being" are rooted in him—and a fearful task is before his soul: to destroy the first, and bring all the falsity of things to the light. He wishes to know everything, not to feed a delicate taste, like Goethe's man, to take delight, from a safe place, in the multiplicity of existence: but he himself is the first sacrifice that he brings. The heroic man does not think of his happiness or misery, his virtues or his vices, or of his being the measure of things; he has no further hopes of himself and will accept the utter consequences of his hopelessness. His strength lies in his self-forgetfulness: if he have a thought for himself, it is only to measure the vast distance between himself and his aim, and to view what he has left behind him as so much dross. The old philosophers sought for happiness and truth with all their strength: and there is an evil principle in nature that not one shall find that which he cannot help seeking. But the man who looks for a lie in everything, and becomes a willing friend to unhappiness, shall have a marvelous disillusioning: there hovers near him something unutterable, of which truth and happiness are but idolatrous images born of the night; the earth loses her dragging weight, the events and powers of earth become as a dream, and a gradual clearness widens round him like a summer evening. It is as though the beholder of these things began to wake, and it had only been the clouds of a passing dream that had been weaving about him. They will at some time disappear: and then will it be day.

FROM HUMAN, ALL TOO HUMAN, I

23

THE AGE OF COMPARISON.—The less men are fettered by tradition, the greater becomes the inward activity of their motives; the greater, again, in proportion thereto, the outward restlessness, the confused flux of mankind, the polyphony of strivings. For whom is there still an absolute compulsion to bind himself and his descendants to one place? For whom is there still anything strictly compulsory? As all styles of arts are imitated simultaneously, so also are all grades and kinds of morality, of customs, of cultures. Such an age obtains its importance because in it the various views of the world, customs, and cultures can be compared and experienced simultaneously—which was formerly not possible with the always localized sway of every culture, corresponding to the rooting of all artistic styles in place and time. An increased aesthetic feeling will now at last decide amongst so many forms presenting themselves for comparison; it will allow the greater number, that is to say all those rejected by it, to die out. In the same way a selection amongst the forms and customs of the higher moralities is taking place, of which the aim can be nothing else than the downfall of the lower moralities. It is the age of comparison! That is its pride, but more justly also its grief. Let us not be afraid of this grief! Rather will we comprehend as adequately as possible the task our age sets us; posterity will bless us for doing so—a posterity which knows itself to be as much above the terminated original national cultures as above the culture of comparison, but which looks back with gratitude on both kinds of culture as upon antiquities worthy of veneration.

285

MODERN UNREST.—Modern restlessness increases toward the west, so that Americans look upon the inhabitants of Europe as altogether peace-loving and enjoying beings, whilst in reality they swarm about like wasps and bees. This restlessness is so great that the higher culture cannot mature its fruits, it is as if the seasons followed each other too quickly. For lack of rest our civilization is turning into a new barbarism. At no period have the active, that is, the restless, been of *more* importance. One of the necessary corrections, therefore, which must be undertaken in the character of humanity is to strengthen the contemplative element on a large scale. But every individual who is quiet and steady in heart and head already has the right to believe that he possesses not only a good temperament but also a generally useful virtue, and even fulfills a higher mission by the preservation of this virtue.

633

In essential respects we are still the same men as those of the time of the Reformation; how could it be otherwise? But the fact that we *no longer* allow ourselves certain means for promoting the triumph of our opinions distinguishes us from that age, and proves that we belong to a higher culture. He who still combats and overthrows opinions with calumnies and outbursts of rage, after the manner of the Reformation men, obviously betrays the fact that he would have burned his adversaries had he lived in other times, and that he would have resorted to all the methods of the Inquisition if he had been an opponent of the Reformation. The Inquisition was rational at that time, for it represented nothing else than the universal application of martial law, which had to be proclaimed throughout the entire domain of the Church, and which, like all martial law, gave a right to the extremest methods, under the presupposition, of course, (which we now no longer share with those people) that the Church *possessed* truth and had to preserve it at all costs, and at any sacrifice, for the salvation of mankind. Now, however, one does not so readily concede to anyone that he possesses the truth; strict methods of investigation have diffused enough of distrust and precaution, so that everyone who violently advocates opinions in word and deed is looked upon as an enemy of our modern culture, or, at least, as an atavist. As a matter of fact, the pathos that man possesses truth is now of very little consequence in comparison with the certainly milder and less noisy pathos of the search for truth, which is never weary of learning afresh and examining anew.

FROM THE DAWN OF DAY

9

CONCEPTION OF THE MORALITY OF CUSTOM.—In comparison with the mode of life which prevailed among men for thousands of years, we men of the present day are living in a very immoral age: the power of custom has been weakened to a remarkable degree, and the sense of morality is so refined and elevated that we might almost describe it as volatilized. That is why we latecomers experience such difficulty in obtaining a fundamental conception of the origin of morality: and even if we do obtain it, our words of explanation stick in our throats, so coarse would they sound if we uttered them! or to so great an extent would they seem to be a slander upon morality! Thus, for example, the fundamental clause: morality is nothing else (and, above all, nothing more) than obedience to customs, of whatsoever nature they may be. But customs are simply the traditional way of acting and valuing. Where there is no tradition there is no morality; and the less life is governed by tradition, the narrower the circle of morality. The free man is immoral, because it is his *will* to depend upon himself and not upon tradition: in all the primitive states of humanity "evil" is equivalent to "individual," "free," "arbitrary," "unaccustomed," "unforeseen," "incalculable." In such primitive conditions, always measured by this standard, any action performed—*not* because tradition commands it, but for other reasons (e.g., on account of its individual utility), even for the same reasons as had been formerly established by custom—is termed immoral, and is felt to be so even by the very man who performs it, for it has not been done out of obedience to the tradition.

What is tradition? A higher authority, which is obeyed, not because it commands what is useful to us, but merely because it commands. And in what way can this feeling for tradition be distinguished from a general feeling of fear? It is the fear of a higher intelligence which commands, the fear of an incomprehensible power, of something that is more than personal—there is *superstition* in this fear. In primitive times the domain of morality included education and hygienics, marriage, medicine, agriculture, war, speech, and silence, the relationship between man and man, and between man and the gods—morality required that a man should observe her prescriptions without thinking of *himself* as individual. Everything, therefore, was originally custom, and whoever wished to raise himself above it had first of all to make himself a kind of lawgiver and medicine man, a sort of demigod—in other words, he had to create customs, a dangerous and fearful thing to do! Who is the most moral man? On the one hand, he who most frequently obeys the law, e.g., he who, like the Brahmins, carries a consciousness of the law about with him wherever he may go, and introduces it into the smallest divisions of time, continually exercizing his mind in finding opportunities for obeying the law. On the other hand, he who obeys the law in the most difficult cases. The most moral man is he who makes the greatest *sacrifices* to morality, but what are the greatest sacrifices? In answering this question several different kinds of morality will be developed, but the distinction between the morality of the *most frequent obedience* and the morality of the *most difficult obedience* is of the greatest importance. Let us not be deceived as to the motives of that moral law which requires, as an indication of morality, obedience to custom in the most difficult cases! Self-conquest is required, not by reason of its useful consequences for the individual, but that custom and tradition may appear to be dominant, in spite of all individual counterdesires and advantages. The individual shall sacrifice himself—so demands the morality of custom.

On the other hand, those moralists who, like the followers of Socrates, recommend self-control and sobriety to the *individual* as his greatest possible advantage and the key to his greatest personal happiness are *exceptions*—and if we ourselves do not think so, this is simply due to our having been brought up under their influence. They all take a new path, and thereby bring down upon themselves the utmost disapproval of all the representatives of the morality of custom. They sever their connection with the community, as immoralists, and are, in the fullest sense of the word, evil ones. In the same way, every Christian who "sought, above all things, his *own* salvation" must have seemed evil to a virtuous Roman of the old school. Wherever a community exists, and consequently also a morality of custom, the feeling prevails that any punishment for the violation of a custom is inflicted, above all, on the community: this punishment is a supernatural punishment, the manifestations and limits of which are so difficult to understand, and are investigated with such superstitious fear. The community can compel any one member of it to make good, either to an individual or to the community itself, any ill consequences which may have followed upon such a member's action. It can also call down a sort of vengeance upon the head of the individual by endeavoring to show that, as the result of his action, a storm of divine anger has burst over the community—but, above all, it regards the guilt of the individual more particularly as *its own* guilt, and bears the punishment of the isolated individual as its own punishment—"Morals," they bewail in their innermost heart, "morals have grown lax, if such deeds as these are possible." And every individual action, every individual mode of thinking, causes dread. It is impossible to determine how much the more select, rare, and original minds must have suffered in the course of time by being considered as evil and dangerous, *yea, because they even looked upon themselves as such.* Under the dominating influence of the morality of custom, originality of every kind came to acquire a bad conscience, and even now the sky of the best minds seems to be more overcast by this thought than it need be.

179

AS LITTLE STATE AS POSSIBLE!—All political and
economic matters are not of such great value that they
ought to be dealt with by the most talented minds: such
a waste of intellect is at bottom worse than any state of
distress. These matters are, and ever will be, the province of
smaller minds, and others than the smaller minds should not
be at the service of this workshop: it would be better to
let the machinery work itself to pieces again! But as matters
stand at the present time, when not only do all people
believe that they must know all about it day by day, but
wish likewise to be always busy about it, and in so doing
neglect their own work, it is a great and ridiculous mistake. The price that has to be paid for the "public safety" is
far too high, and, what is maddest of all, we effect the
very opposite of "public safety," a fact which our own
dear century has undertaken to prove, as if this had never
been proved before! To make society secure against thieves
and fire, and to render it thoroughly fit for all kinds of
trade and traffic, and to transform the State in a good and
evil sense into a kind of Providence—these aims are low,
mediocre, and not by any means indispensable; and we
should not seek to attain them by the aid of the highest
means and instruments which exist—means which we should
reserve precisely for our highest and rarest aims! Our epoch,
however much it may babble about economy, is a spend-
thrift: it wastes intellect, the most precious thing of all.

429

THE NEW PASSION. Why do we fear and dread a possible return to barbarism? Is it because it would make people less happy than they are now? Certainly not! The barbarians of all ages possessed more happiness than we do—
let us not deceive ourselves on this point!—but our impulse toward knowledge is too widely developed to allow us
to value happiness without knowledge, or the happiness of
a strong and fixed delusion: it is painful to us even to imagine
such a state of things! Our restless pursuit of discoveries and
divinations has become for us as attractive and indispensable as hapless love to the lover, which on no account would
he exchange for indifference—nay, perhaps we, too, are

hapless lovers! Knowledge within us has developed into a passion, which does not shrink from any sacrifice, and at bottom fears nothing but its own extinction. We sincerely believe that all humanity, weighed down as it is by the burden of this passion, are bound to feel more exalted and comforted than formerly, when they had not yet overcome the longing for the coarser satisfaction which accompanies barbarism.

It may be that mankind may perish eventually from this passion for knowledge!—but even that does not daunt us. Did Christianity ever shrink from a similar thought? Are not love and death brother and sister? Yes, we detest barbarism —we all prefer that humanity should perish rather than that knowledge should enter into a stage of retrogression. And, finally, if mankind does not perish through some passion it will perish through some weakness: which would we prefer? This is the main question. Do we wish its end to be in fire and light, or in the sands?

FROM THE JOYFUL WISDOM

356

IN WHAT MANNER EUROPE WILL ALWAYS BE-COME "MORE ARTISTIC." Providing a living still enforces even in the present day (in our transition period when so much ceases to enforce) a definite role on almost all male Europeans, their so-called callings; some have the liberty, an apparent liberty, to choose this role themselves, but most have it chosen for them. The result is strange enough. Almost all Europeans confound themselves with their role when they advance in age; they themselves are the victims of their "good acting," they have forgotten how much chance, whim, and arbitariness swayed them when their "calling" was decided—and how many other roles they *could* perhaps have played: for it is now too late! Looked at more closely, we see that their characters have actually *evolved* out of their role, nature out of art. There were ages in which people believed with unshaken confidence, yea, with piety, in their predestination for this very business, for that very mode of livelihood, and would not at all acknowledge chance, or the fortuitous role, or arbitrariness therein. Ranks, guilds, and hereditary trade privileges succeeded, with

the help of this belief, in rearing those extraordinary broad
towers of society which distinguished the Middle Ages, and
of which all events one thing remains to their credit: capacity for duration (and duration is a value of the first rank
on earth!). But there are ages entirely the reverse, the properly democratic ages, in which people tend to become more
and more oblivious of this conviction, and a sort of impudent conviction and quite contrary mode of viewing things
comes to the front, the Athenian conviction which is first
observed in the epoch of Pericles, the American conviction
of the present day, which wants also more and more to become a European conviction, whereby the individual is
convinced that he can do almost anything, that he *can play
almost any role*, whereby everyone makes experiments with
himself, improvises, tries anew, tries with delight, whereby
all nature ceases and becomes art. . . . The Greeks, having
adopted this *role creed*—an artist creed, if you will—underwent step by step, as is well known, a curious transformation, not in every respect worthy of imitation: *they became
actual stage players;* and as such they enchanted, they conquered all the world, and at last even the conqueror of the
world (for the *Graeculus histrio* conquered Rome, and *not*
Greek culture, as the naïve are accustomed to say . . .).
What I fear, however, and what is at present obvious, if
we desire to perceive it, is that we modern men are quite
on the same road already; and whenever man begins to discover in what respect he plays a role, and to what extent he
can be a stage player, he *becomes* a stage player. . . . A
new flora and fauna of men thereupon springs up, which
cannot grow in more stable, more restricted eras—or is left
"at the bottom," under the ban and suspicion of infamy—
thereupon the most interesting and insane periods of history
always make their appearance, in which "stage players," *all*
kinds of stage players, are the real masters. Precisely thereby another species of man is always more and more injured,
and in the end made impossible: above all the great "architects"; the building power is now being paralyzed; the
courage that makes plans for the distant future is disheartened; there begins to be a lack of organizing geniuses.
Who is there who would now venture to undertake works for
the completion of which millenniums would have to be
reckoned upon? The fundamental belief is dying out, on the
basis of which one could calculate, promise, and anticipate
the future in one's plan, and offer it as a sacrifice thereto,
that in fact man has only value and significance insofar as
he is *a stone in a great building;* for which purpose he

has first of all to be *solid*, he has to be a "stone." . . .
Above all, not a—stage player! In short—alas! this fact will
be hushed up for some considerable time to come!—that
which from henceforth will no longer be built, and *can* no
longer be built, is—a society in the old sense of the term; to
build this structure everything is lacking, above all, the
material. *None of us are any longer material for a society:*
that is a truth which is seasonable at present! It seems to
me a matter of indifference that meanwhile the most shortsighted, perhaps the most honest, and at any rate the
noisiest species of men of the present day, our friends the
Socialists, believe, hope, dream, and above all scream and
scribble almost the opposite; in fact one already reads their
watchword of the future, "free society," on all tables and
walls. Free society? Indeed! Indeed! But you know, gentlemen, sure enough whereof one builds it? Out of wooden
iron! Out of the famous wooden iron! And not even out of
wooden . . .

FROM BEYOND GOOD AND EVIL

214

OUR virtues?—It is probable that we too have still our
virtues, although naturally they are not those sincere and
massive virtues on account of which we hold our grandfathers in esteem and also a little distance from us. We
Europeans of the day after tomorrow, we firstlings of the
twentieth century—with all our dangerous curiosity, our multifariousness and art of disguising, our mellow and seemingly sweetened cruelty in sense and spirit—we shall presumably, *if* we must have virtues, have those only which
have come to agreement with our most secret and heartfelt
inclinations, with our most ardent requirements: well, then,
let us look for them in our labyrinths!—where, as we know,
so many things lose themselves, so many things get quite
lost! And is there anything finer than to *search* for one's
own virtues? Is it not almost to *believe* in one's own virtues?
But this "believing in one's own virtues"—is it not practically
the same as what was formerly called one's "good conscience," that long, respectable pigtail of an idea, which our
grandfathers used to hang behind their heads, and often
enough also behind their understandings? It seems, there-

fore, that however little we may imagine ourselves to be old-fashioned and grandfatherly respectable in other respects, in one thing we are nevertheless the worthy grandchildren of our grandfathers, we last Europeans with good consciences: we also still wear their pigtail.—Ah! if you only knew how soon, so very soon—it will be different!

242

Whether we call it "civilization," or "humanizing," or "progress," which now distinguishes the European; whether we call it simply, without praise or blame, by the political formula: the *democratic* movement in Europe—behind all the moral and political foregrounds pointed to by such formulas, an immense *physiological* process goes on, which is ever extending: the process of the assimilation of Europeans; their increasing detachment from the conditions under which, climatically and hereditarily, united races originate; their increasing independence of every definite milieu, that for centuries would fain inscribe itself with equal demands on soul and body—that is to say, the slow emergence of an essentially *supernational* and nomadic species of man, who possesses, physiologically speaking, a maximum of the art and power of adaptation as his typical distinction. This process of the *evolving European*, which can be retarded in its *tempo* by great relapses, but will perhaps just gain and grow thereby in vehemence and depth—the still raging storm and stress of "national sentiment" pertains to it, and also the anarchism which is appearing at present—the process will probably arrive at results on which its naïve propagators and panegyrists, the apostles of "modern ideas," would least care to reckon. The same new conditions under which on an average a leveling and mediocrizing of man will take place—a useful, industrious, variously serviceable and clever, gregarious man—are in the highest degree suitable to give rise to exceptional men of the most dangerous and attractive qualities. For, while the capacity for adaptation, which is ever trying to change conditions, and begins a new work with every generation, almost with every decade, makes the *powerfulness* of the type impossible; while the collective impression of such future Europeans will probably be that of numerous, talkative, weak-willed, and very handy workmen who *require* a master, a commander, as they require their daily bread; while, therefore, the democratizing of Europe will tend to the production of a type prepared for *slavery* in the most subtle sense of the term: the *strong* man will necessarily in individual and exceptional cases become stronger and richer than he has perhaps ever been before—owing to the unprejudiceness of his schooling, owning to the immense variety of practice, art, and disguise. I meant to say that the democratizing of Europe is at the same time an involuntary arrangement for the rearing of *tyrants*—taking the word in all its meanings, even in its most spiritual sense.

FROM THE TWILIGHT OF THE IDOLS

39

A CRITICISM OF MODERNITY. Our institutions are no longer any good; on this point we are all agreed. But the fault does not lie with them, but with *us*. Now that we have lost all the instincts out of which institutions grow, the latter on their part are beginning to disappear from our midst because we are no longer fit for them. Democracy has always been the death agony of the power of organization: already in *Human, All Too Human*, Part I, Aph. 472, I pointed out that modern democracy, together with its half measures, of which the "German Empire" is an example, was a decaying form of the State. For institutions to be possible there must exist a sort of will, instinct, imperative, which cannot be otherwise than antiliberal to the point of wickedness: the will to tradition, to authority, to responsibility for centuries to come, to *solidarity* in long family lines forward and backward *in infinitum*. If this will is present, something is founded which resembles the *imperium Romanum:* or Russia, the *only* great nation today that has some lasting power and grit in her, that can bide her time, that can still promise something.—Russia the opposite of all wretched European petty-statism and neurasthenia, which the foundation of the German Empire has brought to a crisis. The whole of the Occident no longer possesses those instincts from which institutions spring, out of which a *future* grows: maybe nothing is more opposed to its "modern spirit" than these things. People live for the present, they live at top speed—they certainly live without any sense of responsibility; and this is precisely what they call "freedom." Everything in institutions which makes them institutions is scorned, loathed, and repudiated: everybody is in mortal fear of a new slavery, wherever the word "authority" is so much as whispered. The decadence of the valuing instinct, both in our politicians and in our political parties, goes so far that they instinctively prefer that which acts as a solvent, that which precipitates the final catastrophe. . . . As an example of this behold *modern* marriage. All reason has obviously been divorced from modern marriage, but this is no objection to matrimony itself but to modernity. The rational basis of marriage—it lay in the exclusive legal responsibility of the man: by this means some ballast was laid in the ship of matrimony, whereas nowadays it has a list, now on this side, now on that. The rational basis of marriage—it lay in its absolute indissolubleness: in this way it was given a gravity which knew how to make its influence felt, in the face of the accident of sentiment, passion, and momentary impulse: it lay also in the fact that the responsibility of choosing the parties to the contract lay with the families. By showing ever more and more favor to *love* marriages, the very foundation of matrimony, that which alone makes it an institution, has been undermined. No institution ever has been nor ever will be built upon an idiosyncrasy; as I say, marriage cannot be based upon "love." It can be based upon sexual desire; upon the instinct of property (wife and child as possessions); upon the instinct of dominion, which constantly organizes for itself the smallest form of dominion—the family which *requires* children and heirs in order to hold fast, also in the physiological sense, to a certain quantum of acquired power, influence, and wealth, so as to prepare for lasting tasks, and for solidarity in the instincts from one century to another. Marriage as an institution presupposes the affirmation of the greatest and most permanent form of organization; if society cannot as a whole *stand security* for itself into the remotest generations, marriage has no meaning whatsoever.—Modern marriage *has lost* its meaning; consequently it is being abolished.

IX. *Aristocratic Radicalism*

FROM HUMAN, ALL TOO HUMAN, VOL. I

27

A SUBSTITUTE FOR RELIGION. It is believed that
something good is said of philosophy when it is put forward
as a substitute for religion for the people. As a matter of
fact, in the spiritual economy there is need, at times, of an
intermediary order of thought: the transition from religion to
scientific contemplation is a violent, dangerous leap, which
is not to be recommended. To this extent the recommendation is justifiable. But one should eventually learn that the
needs which have been satisfied by religion and are now to
be satisfied by philosophy are not unchangeable; these themselves can be *weakened* and *eradicated*. Think, for instance,
of the Christian's distress of soul, his sighing over inward
corruption, his anxiety for salvation—all notions which
originate only in errors of reason and deserve not satisfaction
but destruction. A philosophy can serve either to *satisfy*
those needs or to *set them aside*; for they are acquired,
temporally limited needs, which are based upon suppositions
contradictory to those of science. Here, in order to make a
transition, *art* is far rather to be employed to relieve the
mind overburdened with emotions; for those notions receive
much less support from it than from a metaphysical phi-

losophy. It is easier, then, to pass over from art to a really liberating philosophical science.

31

THE ILLOGICAL NECESSARY. One of those things that may drive a thinker into despair is the recognition of the fact that the illogical is necessary for man, and that out of the illogical comes much that is good. It is so firmly rooted in the passions, in language, in art, in religion, and generally in everything that gives value to life, that it cannot be withdrawn without thereby hopelessly injuring these beautiful things. It is only the all-too-naïve people who can believe that the nature of man can be changed into a purely logical one; but if there were degrees of proximity to this goal, how many things would not have to be lost on this course! Even the most rational man has need of nature again from time to time, i.e., his *illogical fundamental attitude* toward all things.

32

INJUSTICE NECESSARY. All judgments on the value of life are illogically developed, and therefore unjust. The inexactitude of the judgment lies, firstly, in the manner in which the material is presented, namely, very imperfectly; secondly, in the manner in which the conclusion is formed out of it; and thirdly, in the fact that every separate element of the material is again the result of vitiated recognition, and this, too, of necessity. For instance, no experience of an individual, however near he may stand to us, can be perfect, so that we could have a logical right to make a complete estimate of him; all estimates are rash, and must be so. Finally, the standard by which we measure, our nature, is not of unalterable dimensions—we have moods and vacillations, and yet we should have to recognize ourselves as a fixed standard in order to estimate correctly the relation of anything whatever to ourselves. From this it will, perhaps, follow that we should make no judgments at all; if one could only live without making estimations, without having likes and dislikes! For all dislike is connected with an estimation, as well as all inclination. An impulse toward or away from anything without a feeling that something advantageous is desired, something injurious avoided, an impulse without any kind of conscious valuation of the worth of the aim does not exist in man. We are from the beginning illogical, and therefore unjust beings, *and can recognize this;* it is one of the greatest and most inexplicable discords of existence.

41

THE UNCHANGEABLE CHARACTER. That the character is unchangeable is not true in a strict sense; this favorite theory means, rather, that during the short lifetime of an individual the new influencing motives cannot penetrate deeply enough to destroy the ingrained marks of many thousands of years. But if one were to imagine a man of eighty thousand years, one would have in him an absolutely changeable character, so that a number of different individuals would gradually develop out of him. The shortness of human life misleads us into forming many erroneous ideas about the qualities of man.

101

JUDGE NOT. In considering earlier periods, care must be taken not to fall into unjust abuse. The injustice in slavery, the cruelty in the suppression of persons and nations, is not to be measured by our standard. For the instinct of justice was not then so far developed. Who dares to reproach the Genevese Calvin with the burning of the physician Servetus? It was an action following and resulting from his convictions, and in the same way the Inquisition had a good right; only the ruling views were false, and produced a result which seems hard to us because those views have now grown strange to us. Besides, what is the burning of a single individual compared with eternal pains of hell for almost all! And yet this idea was universal at that time, without essentially injuring by its dreadfulness the conception of a God. With us, too, political sectarians are hardly and cruelly treated, but because one is accustomed to believe in the necessity of the State, the cruelty is not so deeply felt here as it is where we repudiate the views. Cruelty to animals in children and Italians is due to ignorance, i.e., the animal, through the interests of Church teaching, has been placed too far behind man. Much that is dreadful and inhuman in history, much that one hardly likes to believe, is mitigated by the reflection that the one who commands and the one who carries out are different persons—the former does not behold the right and therefore does not experience the strong impression on the imagination; the latter obeys a superior and therefore feels no responsibility. Most princes and military heads, through lack of imagination, easily appear hard and cruel without really being so. *Egoism is not evil*, because the idea of the "neighbor"—the word is of Christian origin and does not represent the truth—is very weak in us; and we feel ourselves almost as free and irresponsible toward him as toward plants and stones. We have yet to *learn* that others suffer, and this can never be completely learned.

102

"MAN ALWAYS ACTS RIGHTLY." We do not complain of nature as immoral because it sends a thunderstorm and makes us wet—why do we call those who injure us immoral? Because in the latter case we take for granted a free will functioning voluntarily; in the former we see necessity. But this distinction is an error. Thus we do not call even intentional injury immoral in all circumstances; for instance, we kill a fly unhesitatingly and intentionally, only because its buzzing annoys us; we punish a criminal intentionally and hurt him in order to protect ourselves and society. In the first case it is the individual who, in order to preserve himself, or even to protect himself from worry, does intentional injury; in the second case it is the State. All morals allow intentional injury *in the case of necessity*, that is, when it is a matter of *self-preservation*! But these two points of view suffice to explain all evil actions committed by men against men, we are desirous of obtaining pleasure or avoiding pain; in any case it is always a question of self-preservation. Socrates and Plato are right: whatever man does he always does well, that is, he does that which seems to him good (useful) according to the degree of his intellect, the particular standard of his reasonableness.

106

AT THE WATERFALL. In looking at a waterfall we imagine that there is freedom of will and fancy in the countless turnings, twistings, and breakings of the waves; but everything is compulsory, every movement can be mathematically calculated. So it is also with human actions; one would have to be able to calculate every single action beforehand if one were all-knowing; equally so all progress of knowledge, every error, all malice. The one who acts certainly labors under the illusion of voluntariness; if the world's wheel were to stand still for a moment and an all-knowing, calculating reason were there to make use of this pause, it could foretell the future of every creature to the remotest times, and mark out every track upon which that wheel would continue to roll. The delusion of the acting agent about himself, the supposition of a free will, belongs to this mechanism which still remains to be calculated.

107

IRRESPONSIBILITY AND INNOCENCE. The complete irresponsibility of man for his actions and his nature is the bitterest drop which he who understands must swallow if he was accustomed to see the patent of nobility of his humanity in responsibility and duty. All his valuations, distinctions, disinclinations, are thereby deprived of value and become false—his deepest feeling for the sufferer and the hero was based on an error; he may no longer either praise or blame, for it is absurd to praise and blame nature and necessity. In the same way as he loves a fine work of art, but does not praise it, because it can do nothing for itself; in the same way as he regards plants, so must he regard his own actions and those of mankind. He can admire strength, beauty, abundance in themselves; but must find no merit therein —the chemical progress and the strife of the elements, the torments of the sick person who thirsts after recovery, are all equally as little merits as those struggles of the soul and states of distress in which we are torn hither and thither by different impulses until we finally decide for the strongest— as we say (but in reality it is the strongest motive which decides for us). All these motives, however, whatever fine names we may give them, have all grown out of the same root, in which we believe the evil poisons to be situated; between good and evil actions there is no difference of species, but at most of degree. Good actions are sublimated evil ones; evil actions are vulgarized and stupefied good ones. The single longing of the individual for self-gratification (together with the fear of losing it) satisfies itself in all circumstances: man may act as he can, that is as he must, be it in deeds of vanity, revenge, pleasure, usefulness, malice, cunning; be it in deeds of sacrifice, of pity, of knowledge. The degrees of the power of judgment determine whither anyone lets himself be drawn through this longing; to every society, to every individual, a scale of possessions is continually present, according to which he determines his actions and judges those of others. But this standard changes constantly; many actions are called evil and are only stupid, because the degree of intelligence which decided for them was very low. In a certain sense, even, *all* actions are still stupid; for the highest degree of human intelligence which can now be attained will assuredly be yet surpassed, and then, in a retrospect, all our actions and judgments will appear as limited and hasty as the actions and judgments of primitive wild peoples now appear limited and hasty to us. To recognize all this may be deeply painful, but consolation comes after: such pains are the pangs of birth. The butterfly wants to break through its chrysalis: it rends and tears it, and is then blinded and confused by the unaccustomed light, the kingdom of liberty. In such people as are *capable* of such sadness—and how few are!—the first experiment made is to see whether *mankind can change itself* from a *moral* into a *wise* mankind. The sun of a new gospel throws its rays upon the highest point in the soul of each single individual, then the mists gather thicker than ever, and the brightest light and the dreariest shadow lie side by side. Everything is necessity—so says the new knowledge, and this knowledge itself is necessity. Everything is innocence, and knowledge is the road to insight into this innocence. Are pleasure, egoism, vanity *necessary* for the production of the moral phenomena and their highest result, the sense for truth and justice in knowledge; were error and the confusion of the imagination the only means through which mankind could raise itself gradually to this degree of self-enlightenment and self-liberation—who would dare to undervalue these means? Who would dare to be sad if he perceived the goal to which those roads led? Everything in the domain of morality has evolved, is changeable, unstable, everything is dissolved, it is true; but *everything is also streaming toward one goal.* Even if the inherited habit of erroneous valuation, love and hatred, continue to reign in us, yet under the influence of growing knowledge it will become weaker; a new habit, that of comprehension, of not loving, not hating, of overlooking, is gradually implanting itself in us upon the same ground, and in thousands of years will perhaps be powerful enough to give humanity the strength to produce wise, innocent (consciously innocent) men, as it now produces unwise, guilt-conscious men—*that is the necessary preliminary step, not its opposite.*

283

THE CHIEF DEFICIENCY OF ACTIVE PEOPLE. Active people are usually deficient in the higher activity, I mean individual activity. They are active as officials, merchants, scholars, that is, as a species, but not as quite distinct separate and *single* individuals; in this respect they are idle. It is the misfortune of the active that their activity is almost always a little senseless. For instance, we must not ask the money-making banker the reason of his restless activity, it is foolish. The active roll as the stone rolls, according to the stupidity of mechanics. All mankind is divided, as it was at all times and is still, into slaves and freemen; for whoever has not two-thirds of his day for himself is a slave, be he otherwise whatever he likes, statesman, merchant, official, or scholar.

284

IN FAVOR OF THE IDLE. As a sign that the value of a contemplative life has decreased, scholars now vie with active people in a sort of hurried enjoyment, so that they appear to value this mode of enjoying more than that which really pertains to them, and which, as a matter of fact, is a far greater enjoyment. Scholars are ashamed of *otium*. But there is one noble thing about idleness and idlers. If idleness is really the *beginning* of all vice, it finds itself, therefore, at least in near neighborhood of all the virtues; the idle man is still a better man than the active. You do not suppose that in speaking of idleness and idlers I am alluding to you, you sluggards?

473

SOCIALISM, WITH REGARD TO ITS MEANS. Socialism is the fantastic younger brother of almost decrepit despotism, which it wants to succeed; its efforts are, therefore, in the deepest sense reactionary. For it desires such an amount of State power as only despotism has possessed—indeed, it outdoes all the past, in that it aims at the complete annihilation of the individual, whom it deems an unauthorized luxury of nature, which is to be improved by it into an appropriate *organ of the general community*. Owing to its relationship, it always appears in proximity to excessive developments of power, like the old typical socialist, Plato, at the court of the Sicilian tyrant; it desires (and under certain circumstances furthers) the Caesarian depotism of this century, because, as has been said, it would like to become its heir. But even this inheritance would not suffice for its objects, it requires the most submissive prostration of all citizens before the absolute State, such as has never yet been realized; and as it can no longer even count upon the old religious piety toward the State, but must rather strive involuntarily and continuously for the abolition thereof—because it strives for the abolition of all existing *States*—it can only hope for existence occasionally, here and there for short periods, by means of the extremest terrorism. It is therefore silently preparing itself for reigns of terror, and drives the word "justice" like a nail into the heads of the half-cultured masses in order to deprive them completely of their understanding (after they had already suffered seriously from the half-culture), and to provide them with a good conscience for the bad game they are to play. Socialism may serve to teach, very brutally and impressively, the danger of all accumulations of State power, and may serve so far to inspire distrust of the State itself. When its rough voice strikes up the war cry *"as much State as possible,"* the shout at first becomes louder than ever—but soon the opposition cry also breaks forth, with so much greater force: *"as little State as possible."*

477

WAR INDISPENSABLE. It is nothing but fantacism and beautiful soulism to expect very much (or even, much only) from humanity when it has forgotten how to wage war. For the present we know of no other means whereby the rough energy of the camp, the deep impersonal hatred, the cold-bloodedness of murder with a good conscience, the general ardor of the system in the destruction of the enemy, the proud indifference to great losses, to one's own existence and that of one's friends, the hollow, earthlike convulsion of the soul, can be as forcibly and certainly communicated to enervated nations as is done by every great war: owing to the brooks and streams that here break forth, which, certainly, sweep stones and rubbish of all sorts along with them and destroy the meadows of delicate cultures, the mechanism in the workshops of the mind is afterward, in favorable circumstances, rotated by new power. Culture can by no means dispense with passions, vices, and malignities. When the Romans, after having become Imperial, had grown rather tired of war, they attempted to gain new strength by beast-baitings, gladiatoral combats, and Christian persecutions. The English of today, who appear on the whole to have also renounced war, adopt other means in order to generate anew those vanishing forces; namely, the dangerous exploring expeditions, sea voyages, and mountaineerings, nominally undertaken for scientific purposes, but in reality to bring home surplus strength from adventures and dangers of all kinds. Many other such substitutes for war will be discovered, but perhaps precisely thereby it will become more and more obvious that such a highly cultivated and therefore necessarily enfeebled humanity as that of modern Europe not only needs wars, but the greatest and most terrible wars—consequently occasional relapses into barbarism—lest, by the means of culture, it should lose its culture and its very existence.

FROM HUMAN, ALL TOO HUMAN, II

88*

HOW ONE DIES IS INDIFFERENT. The whole way in which a man thinks of death during the prime of his life and strength is very expressive and significant for what we call his character. But the hour of death itself, his behavior on the deathbed, is almost indifferent. The exhaustion of waning life, especially when old people die, the irregular or insufficient nourishment of the brain during this last period, the occasionally violent pain, the novel and untried nature of the whole position, and only too often the ebb and flow of superstitious impressions and fears, as if dying were of much consequence and meant the crossing of bridges of the most terrible kind—all this forbids our using death as a testimony concerning the living. Nor is it true that the dying man is generally more honest than the living. On the contrary, through the solemn attitude of the by-standers, the repressed or flowing streams of tears and emo-

* From *Miscellaneous Maxims and Opinions.*

tions, everyone is inveigled into a comedy of vanity, now conscious, now unconscious. The serious way in which every dying man is treated must have been to many a poor despised devil the highest joy of his whole life and a sort of compensation and repayment for many privations.

74*

PRAYER. On two hypotheses alone is there any sense in prayer, that not quite extinct custom of olden times. It would have to be possible either to fix or alter the will of the godhead, and the devotee would have to know best himself what he needs and should really desire. Both hypotheses, axiomatic and traditional in all other religions, are denied by Christianity. If Christianity nevertheless maintained prayer side by side with its belief in the all-wise and all-provident divine reason (a belief that makes prayer really senseless and even blasphemous), it showed here once more its admirable "wisdom of the serpent." For an outspoken command, "Thou shalt not pray," would have led Christians by way of boredom to the denial of Christianity. In the Christian *ora et labora ora* plays the role of pleasure. Without *ora* what could those unlucky saints who renounced *labora* have done? But to have a chat with God, to ask him for all kinds of pleasant things, to feel a slight amusement at one's own folly in still having any wishes at all, in spite of so excellent a father—all that was an admirable invention for saints.

84

PRISONERS. One morning the prisoners entered the yard for work, but the warder was not there. Some, as their manner was, set to work at once; others stood idle and gazed defiantly around. Then one of them strode forward and cried, "Work as much as you will or do nothing, it all comes to the same. Your secret machinations have come to light; the warder has been keeping his eye on you of late, and will cause a terrible judgment to be passed upon you in a few days' time. You know him—he is of a cruel and resentful disposition. But now, listen: you have mistaken me hitherto. I am not what I seem, but far more—I am the son of the warder, and can get anything I like out of him. I can save

* From *The Wanderer and His Shadow*.

you—nay, I will save you. But remember this: I will only
save those of you who *believe* that I am the son of the
prison warder. The rest may reap the fruits of their unbelief." "Well," said an old prisoner after an interval of
silence, "what can it matter to you whether we believe you
or not? If you are really the son, and can do what you
say, then put in a good word for us all. That would be
a real kindness on your part. But have done with all talk
of belief and unbelief!" "What is more," cried a younger
man, "I don't believe him: he has only got a bee in his bonnet.
I'll wager that in a week's time we shall find ourselves in the
same place as we are today, and the warder will know
nothing." "And if the warder ever knew anything, he knows
it no longer," said the last of the prisoners, coming down into
the yard at that moment, "for he has just died suddenly."
"Ah ha!" cried several in confusion, "ah ha! Sir Son, Sir
Son, how stands it now with your title? Are we by any
chance *your* prisoners now?" "I told you," answered the
man gently, "I will set free all who believe in me, as surely
as my father still lives."—The prisoners did not laugh, but
shrugged their shoulders and left him to himself.

282

THE TEACHER A NECESSARY EVIL. Let us have
as few people as possible between the productive minds
and the hungry and recipient minds! The middlemen almost
unconsciously adulterate the food which they supply. For
their work as middlemen they want too high a fee for themselves, and this is drawn from the original, productive spirits
—namely, interest, admiration, leisure, money, and other
advantages.—Accordingly, we should always look upon the
teacher as a necessary evil, just like the merchant; as an evil
that we should make as small as possible.—Perhaps the prevailing distress in Germany has its main cause in the fact
that too many wish to live and live well by trade (in other
words, desiring as far as possible to diminish prices for
the producer and raise prices for the consumer, and thus
to profit by the greatest possible loss to both). In the same
way, we may certainly trace a main cause of the prevailing
intellectual poverty in the superabundance of teachers. It
is because of teachers that so little is learned, and that so
badly.

FROM THE DAWN OF DAY

13

TOWARD THE NEW EDUCATION OF MANKIND.
—Help us, all ye who are well-disposed and willing to
assist, lend your aid in the endeavor to do away with that
conception of punishment which has swept over the whole
world! No weed more harmful than this! It is not only to the
consequences of our actions that this conception has been
applied—and how horrible and senseless it is to confuse cause
and effect with cause and punishment!—but worse has
followed: the pure accidentality of events has been robbed
of its innocence by this execrable manner of interpreting
the conception of punishment. Yea, they have even pushed
their folly to such extremes that they would have us look
upon existence itself as a punishment—from which it would
appear that the education of mankind had hitherto been
confided to cranky jailers and hangmen.

14

THE SIGNIFICATION OF MADNESS IN THE HIS-
TORY OF MORALITY.—If, despite that formidable pressure of the "morality of custom," under which all human
communities lived—thousands of years before our own era,
and during our own era up to the present day (we ourselves
are dwelling in the small world of exceptions, and, as it were,
in an evil zone—if, I say, in spite of all this, new and divergent
ideas, valuations, and impulses have made their appearance
time after time, this state of things has been brought about
only with the assistance of a dreadful associate: it was insanity almost everywhere that paved the way for the new
thought and cast off the spell of an old custom and superstition. Do ye understand why this had to be done through
insanity? By something which is in both voice and appearance
as horrifying and incalculable as the demoniac whims of
wind and sea, and consequently calling for like dread
and respect? By something bearing upon it the signs of entire
lack of consciousness as clearly as the convulsions and foam
of the epileptic, which appeared to typify the insane person
as the mask and speaking trumpet of some divine being? By

something that inspired even the bearer of the new thought with awe and fear of himself, and that, suppressing all remorse, drove him on to become its prophet and martyr? —Well, in our own time, we continually hear the statement reiterated that genius is tinctured with madness instead of good sense. Men of earlier ages were far more inclined to believe that, wherever traces of insanity showed themselves, a certain proportion of genius and wisdom was likewise present —something "divine," as they whispered to one another. More than this, they expressed their opinions on the point with sufficient emphasis. "All the greatest benefits of Greece have sprung from madness," said Plato, setting on record the opinion of the entire ancient world. Let us take a step further: all those superior men, who felt themselves irresistibly urged on to throw off the yoke of some morality or other, had no other resource—*if they were not really mad* —than to feign madness, or actually to become insane. And this holds good for innovators in every department of life, and not only in religion and politics. Even the reformer of the poetic meter was forced to justify himself by means of madness. (Thus even down to gentler ages madness remained a kind of convention in poets, of which Solon, for instance, took advantage when urging the Athenians to reconquer Salamis.)—"How can one make one's self mad when one is not mad and dare not feign to be so?" Almost all the eminent men of antiquity have given themselves up to this dreadful mode of reasoning: a secret doctrine of artifices and dialectic jugglery grew up around this subject and was handed down from generation to generation, together with the feeling of the innocence, even sanctity, of such plans and meditations. The means of becoming a medicine man among the Indians, a saint among Christians of the Middle Ages, an angekok among Greenlanders, a Pagee among Brazilians, are the same in essence: senseless fasting, continual abstention from sexual intercourse, isolation in a wilderness, ascending a mountain or a pillar, "sitting on an aged willow that looks out upon a lake," and thinking of absolutely nothing but what may give rise to ecstasy or mental derangements.

Who would dare to glance at the desert of the bitterest and most superfluous agonies of spirit, in which probably the most productive men of all ages have pined away? Who could listen to the sighs of those lonely and troubled minds: "O ye heavenly powers, grant me madness! Madness, that I at length may believe in myself! Vouchsafe delirium and convulsions, sudden flashes of light and periods of darkness; frighten me with such shivering and feverishness as no mortal ever experienced before, with clanging noises and haunting specters; let me growl and whine and creep about like a beast, if only I can come to believe in myself! I am devoured by doubt. I have slain the law, and I now dread the law as a living person dreads a corpse. If I am not *above* the law, I am the most abandoned of wretches. Whence cometh this new spirit that dwelleth within me but from you? Prove to me, then, that I am one of you—nothing but madness will prove it to me." And only too often does such a fervor attain its object: at the very time when Christianity was giving the greatest proof of its fertility in the production of saints and martyrs, believing that it was thus proving itself, Jerusalem contained large lunatic asylums for shipwrecked saints, for those whose last spark of good sense had been quenched by the floods of insanity.

17

GOODNESS AND MALIGNITY. At first men imposed their own personalities on Nature: everywhere they saw themselves and their like, i.e. their own evil and capricious temperaments, hidden, as it were, behind clouds, thunderstorms, wild beasts, trees, and plants: it was then that they declared Nature was evil. Afterward there came a time, that of Rousseau, when they sought to distinguish themselves from Nature: they were so tired of each other that they wished to have separate little hiding-places where man and his misery could not penetrate: then they invented "nature is good."

18

THE MORALITY OF VOLUNTARY SUFFERING. What is the highest enjoyment for men living in a state of war in a small community, the existence of which is continually threatened, and the morality of which is the strictest possible, i.e., for souls which are vigorous, vindictive, malicious, full of suspicion, ready to face the direst events, hardened by privation and morality? The enjoyment of cruelty: just as, in such souls and in such circumstance, it would be regarded as a virtue to be ingenious and insatiable in cruelty. Such a community would find its delight in performing cruel deeds, casting aside, for once, the gloom of constant anxiety and precaution. Cruelty is one of the most ancient enjoyments at their festivities. As a consequence, it is believed that the gods likewise are pleased by the sight of cruelty and rejoice at it—and in this way the belief is spread that *voluntary suffering*, self-chosen martyrdom, has a high signification and value of its own. In the community custom gradually brings about a practice in conformity with this belief: henceforward people become more suspicious of all exuberant well-being, and more confident as they find themselves in a state of great pain; they think that the gods may be unfavorable to them on account of happiness, and favorable on account of pain—not compassionate! For compassion is looked upon with contempt, and unworthy of a strong and awe-inspiring soul—but agreeable to them, because the sight of human suffering put these gods into good humor and in the sensation of power. It was thus that the "most moral man" of the community was considered as such by virtue of his frequent suffering privation, laborious existence, and cruel mortification—not, to repeat it again and again, as a means of discipline or self-control or a desire for individual happiness—but as a virtue which renders the evil gods well-disposed toward the community, a virtue which continually wafts up to them the odor of an expiatory sacrifice. All those intellectual leaders of the nations who reached the point of being able to stir up the sluggish though prolific mire of their customs had to possess this factor of voluntary martyrdom as well as insanity in order to obtain belief—especially, and above all, as is always the case, belief in themselves! The more their minds followed new paths, and were consequently tormented by pricks of conscience, the more cruelly they battled against their own flesh, their own desires, and their own health—as if they were offering the gods a compensation in pleasure, lest these gods should wax wroth at the neglect of ancient customs and the setting up of new aims.

Let no one be too hasty in thinking that we have now entirely freed ourselves from such a logic of feeling! Let the most heroic souls among us question themselves on this very point. The least step forward in the domain of free thought and individual life has been achieved in all ages to the accompaniment of physical and intellectual tortures: and not only the mere step forward, no! But every form of movement and change has rendered necessary innumerable martyrs, throughout the entire course of thousands of years which sought their paths and laid down their foundation stones, years, however, which we do not think of when we speak about "world history," that ridiculously small division of mankind's existence. And even in this so-called world history, which in the main is merely a great deal of noise about the latest novelties, there is no more important theme than the old, old tragedy of the martyrs *who tried to move the mire.* Nothing has been more dearly brought than the minute portion of human reason and feeling of liberty upon which we now pride ourselves. But it is this very pride which makes it almost impossible for us today to be conscious of that enormous lapse of time, preceding the period of "world history" when "morality of custom" held the field, and to consider this lapse of time as *the real and decisive epoch that established the character of mankind:* an epoch when suffering was considered as a virtue, cruelty as a virtue, hypocrisy as a virtue, revenge as a virtue, and the denial of the reason as a virtue, whereas, on the other hand, well-being was regarded as a danger, longing for knowledge as a danger, peace as a danger, compassion as a danger: an epoch when being pitied was looked upon as an insult, work as an insult, madness as a divine attribute, and every kind of change as immoral and pregnant with ruin! You imagine that all this has changed, and that humanity must likewise have changed its character? Oh, ye poor psychologists, learn to know yourselves better!

28

STATE OF MIND AS ARGUMENT. Whence arises within us a cheerful readiness for action?—such is the question which has greatly occupied the attention of men. The most ancient answer, and one which we still hear, is: God is the cause; in this way He gives us to understand that He approves of our actions. When, in former ages, people consulted the oracles, they did so that they might return home strengthened by this cheerful readiness; and everyone answered the doubts which came to him, if alternative actions suggested themselves, by saying: "I shall do whatever brings about that feeling." They did not decide, in other words, for what was most reasonable, but upon some plan the conception of which imbued the soul with courage and hope. A cheerful outlook was placed in the scales as an argument and proved to be heavier than reasonableness; for the state of mind was interpreted in a superstitious manner as the action of a god who promises success; and who, by this argument, lets his reason speak as the highest reasonableness.

Now, let the consequences of such a prejudice be considered when shrewd men, thirsting for power, availed themselves of it—and still do so! "Bring about the right state of mind!" —in this way you can do without all arguments and overcome every objection!

30

REFINED CRUELTY AS VIRTUE. Here we have a morality which is based entirely upon our thirst for distinction—do not therefore entertain too high an opinion of it! Indeed, we may well ask what kind of an impulse it is, and what is its fundamental signification? It is sought, by our appearance, to grieve our neighbor, to arouse his envy, and to awaken his feelings of impotence and degradation; we endeavor to make him taste the bitterness of his fate by dropping a little of *our* honey on his tongue, and, while conferring this supposed benefit on him, looking sharply and triumphantly into his eyes.

Behold such a man, now become humble and perfect in his humility—and seek those for whom, through his humility, he has for a long time been preparing a torture; for you are sure to find them! Here is another man who shows mercy toward animals, and is admired for doing so —but there are certain people on whom he wishes to vent his cruelty by this very means. Look at that great artist: the pleasure he enjoyed beforehand in conceiving the envy of the rivals he had outstripped refused to let his powers lie dormant until he became a great man—how many bitter moments in the souls of other men has he asked for as payment for his own greatness! The nun's chastity: with what threatening eyes she looks into the faces of other women who live differently from her! What a vindictive joy shines in those eyes! The theme is short, and its variations, though they might well be innumerable, could not easily become tiresome—for it is still too paradoxical a novelty, and almost a painful one, to affirm that the morality of distinction is nothing, at bottom, but joy in refined cruelty. When I say "at bottom," I mean here, every time in the first generation. For, when the habit of some distinguished action becomes *hereditary*, its root, so to speak, is not transmitted, but only its fruits (for only feelings, and not thoughts, can become hereditary); and, if we presuppose that this root is not reintroduced by education, in the second generation the joy in the cruelty is no longer felt, but only pleasure in the habit as such. *This* joy, however, is the first degree of the "good."

31

PRIDE IN SPIRIT. The pride of man, which strives to oppose the theory of our own descent from animals and establishes a wide gulf between nature and man himself—this pride is founded upon a prejudice as to what the mind is; and this prejudice is relatively recent. In the long pre-historical period of humanity it was supposed that the mind was everywhere, and men did not look upon it as a particular characteristic of their own. Since, on the contrary, everything spiritual (including all impulses, maliciousness, and inclinations) was regarded as common property, and consequently accessible to everybody, primitive mankind was not ashamed of being descended from animals or trees (the noble races thought themselves honored by such legends), and saw in the spiritual that which unites us with nature, and not that which severs us from her. Thus man was brought up in modesty—and this likewise was the result of a prejudice.

48

"KNOW THYSELF" IS THE WHOLE OF SCIENCE. —Only when a man shall have acquired a knowledge of all things will he be able to know himself. For things are but the boundaries of man.

49

THE NEW FUNDAMENTAL FEELING: OUR FINAL CORRUPTIBILITY.—In former times people sought to show the feeling of man's greatness by pointing to his divine descent. This, however, has now become a forbidden path, for the ape stands at its entrance, and likewise other fearsome animals, showing their teeth in a knowing fashion, as if to say, No further this way! Hence people now try the opposite direction: the road along which humanity is proceeding shall stand as an indication of their greatness and their relationship to God. But alas! this, too, is useless! At the far end of this path stands the funeral urn of the last man and gravedigger (with the inscription, *Nihil humani a me alienum puto*). To whatever height mankind may have developed—and perhaps in the end it will not be so high as when they began!—there is as little prospect of their attaining to a higher order as there is for the ant and the earwig to enter into kinship with God and eternity at the end of their career on earth. What is to come will drag behind it that which has passed: why should any little star, or even any little species on that star, form an exception to that eternal drama? Away with such sentimentalities!

109

SELF-CONTROL AND MODERATION, AND THEIR FINAL MOTIVE.—I find not more than six essentially different methods for combating the vehemence of an impulse. First of all, we may avoid the occasion for satisfying the impulse, weakening and mortifying it by refraining from satisfying it for long and ever-lengthening periods. Secondly, we may impose a severe and regular order upon ourselves in regard to the satisfying of our appetites. By thus regulating the impulse and limiting its ebb and flow to fixed periods, we may obtain intervals in which it ceases to disturb us; and by beginning in this way we may perhaps be able to pass on to the first method. In the third place, we may deliberately give ourselves over to an unrestrained and unbounded gratification of the impulse in order that we may become disgusted with it, and to obtain by means of this very disgust a command over the impulse: provided, of course, that we do not imitate the rider who rides his horse to death and breaks his own neck in doing so. For this, unhappily, is generally the outcome of the application of this third method.

In the fourth place, there is an intellectual trick, which consists in associating the idea of the gratification so firmly with some painful thought, that after a little practice the thought of gratification is itself immediately felt as a very painful one. (For example, when the Christian accustoms himself to think of the presence and scorn of the devil in the course of sensual enjoyment, or everlasting punishment in hell for revenge by murder; or even merely of the contempt which he will meet with from those of his fellow men whom he most respects, if he steals a sum of money; or if a man has often checked an intense desire for suicide by thinking of the grief and self-reproaches of his relations and friends, and has thus succeeded in balancing himself upon the edge of life: for, after some practice, these ideas follow one another in his mind like cause and effect.) Among instances of this kind may be mentioned the cases of Lord Byron and Napoleon, in whom the pride of man revolted and took offense at the preponderance of one particular passion over the collective attitude and order of reason. From this arises the habit and joy of tyrannizing over the craving and making it, as it were, gnash its teeth. "I will not be a slave of any appetite," wrote Byron in his diary. In the fifth place, we may bring about a dislocation of our powers by imposing upon ourselves a particularly difficult and fatiguing task, or by deliberately submitting to some new charm and pleasure in order thus to turn our thoughts and physical powers into other channels. It comes to the same thing if we temporarily favor another impulse by affording it numerous opportunities of gratification, and thus rendering it the squanderer of the power which would otherwise be commandeered, so to speak, by the tyrannical impulse. A few, perhaps, will be able to restrain the particular passion which aspires to domination by granting their other known passions a temporary encouragement and license in order that they may devour the food which the tyrant wishes for himself alone.

In the sixth and last place, the man who can stand it, and thinks it reasonable to weaken and subdue his entire physical and psychical organization, likewise, of course, attains the goal of weakening a single violent instinct; as, for example, those who starve their sensuality and at the same time their vigor, and often destroy their reason into the bargain, such as the ascetics.—Hence, shunning the opportunities, regulating the impulse, bringing about satiety and disgust in the impulse, associating a painful idea (such as that of discredit, disgust, or offended pride), then the dislocation of one's forces, and finally general debility and exhaustion: these are the six methods. But the will to combat the violence of a craving is beyond our power, equally with the method we adopt and the success we may have in applying it. In all this process our intellect is rather merely the blind instrument of another rival craving, whether it be the impulse to repose, or the fear of disgrace and other evil consequences, or love. While "we" thus imagine that we are complaining of the violence of an impulse, it is at bottom merely one impulse which is complaining of another, i.e., the perception of the violent suffering which is being caused us presupposes that there is another equally or more violent impulse, and that a struggle is impending in which our intellect must take part.

173

THE FLATTERERS OF WORK. In the glorification of "work" and the never-ceasing talk about the "blessing of labor," I see the same secret *arrière-pensée* as I do in the praise bestowed on impersonal acts of a general interest, viz., a fear of everything individual. For at the sight of work—that is to say, severe toil from morning till night—we have the feeling that it is the best police, viz., that it holds everyone in check and effectively hinders the development of reason, of greed, and or desire for independence. For work uses up an extraordinary proportion of nervous force, withdrawing it from reflection, meditation, dreams, cares, love, and hatred; it dangles unimportant aims before the eyes of the worker and affords easy and regular gratification. Thus it happens that a society where work is continually being performed will enjoy greater security, and it is security which is now venerated as the supreme deity. —And now, horror of horrors! it is the "workman" himself who has become dangerous; the whole world is swarming with "dangerous individuals," and behind them follows the danger of dangers—*the* individuum!

206

THE IMPOSSIBLE CLASS.—Poverty, cheerfulness, and independence—it is possible to find those three qualities combined in one individual; poverty, cheerfulness, and slavery —this is likewise a possible combination: and I can say nothing better to the workmen who serve as factory slaves; presuming that it does not appear to them altogether to be a shameful thing to be utilized as they are, as the screws of a machine and the stopgaps, as it were, of the human spirit of invention. Fie on the thought that merely by means of higher wages the essential part of their misery, i.e., their impersonal enslavement, might be removed! Fie, that we should allow ourselves to be convinced that, by an increase of this impersonality within the mechanical working of a new society, the disgrace of slavery could be changed into a virtue! Fie, that there should be a regular price at which a man should cease to be a personality and become a screw instead!

Are you accomplices in the present madness of nations which desire above all to produce as much as possible, and to be as rich as possible? Would it not be your duty to present a counterclaim to them, and to show them what large sums of internal value are wasted in the pursuit of such an external object?

But where is your internal value when you no longer know what it is to breathe freely; when you have scarcely any command over your own selves, and often feel disgusted with yourselves as with some stale food; when you zealously study the newspapers and look enviously at your wealthy neighbor, made covetous by the rapid rise and fall of power, money, and opinions; when you no longer believe in a philosophy in rags, or in the freedom of spirit of a man who has few needs; when a voluntary and idyllic poverty without profession or marriage, such as should suit the more intellectual ones among you, has become for you an object of derision? On the other hand, the piping of the Socialistic rat-catchers who wish to inspire you with foolish hopes is continually sounding in your ears: they tell you to be ready and nothing further, ready from this day to the next, so that you wait and wait for something to come from outside, though living in all other respects as you lived before—until this waiting is at length changed into hunger and thirst and fever and madness, and the day of the *bestia triumphans* at last dawns in all its glory. Every one of you should on the contrary say to himself: "It would be better to emigrate and endeavor to become a master in new and savage countries, and especially to become master over myself, changing my place of abode whenever the least sign of slavery threatens me, endeavoring to avoid neither adventure nor war, and, if things come to the worst, holding myself ready to die: anything rather than continuing in this state of disgraceful thraldom, this bitterness, malice, and rebelliousness!" This would be the proper spirit: the workmen in Europe ought to make it clear that their position as a class has become a human impossibility, and not merely, as they at present maintain, the result of some hard and aimless arrangement of society. They should bring about an age of great swarming forth from the European beehive such as has never yet been seen, protesting by this voluntary and huge migration against machines and capital and the alternatives that now threaten them either of becoming slaves of the State or slaves of some revolutionary party.

May Europe be freed from one-fourth of her inhabitants! Both she and they will experience a sensation of relief. It is only far in the distance, in the undertaking of vast colonizations, that we shall be able to observe how much rationality, fairness, and healthy suspicion mother Europe has incorporated in her sons—these sons who could no longer endure life in the home of the dull old woman, always running the danger of becoming as bad-tempered, irritable, and pleasure-seeking as she herself. The European virtues will travel along with these workmen far beyond the boundaries of Europe; and those very qualities which on their native soil had begun to degenerate into a dangerous discontent and criminal inclinations will, when abroad, be transformed into a beautiful, savage naturalness and will be called heroism; so that at last a purer air would again be wafted over this old, over-populated, and brooding Europe of ours. What would it matter if there was a scarcity of "hands"? Perhaps people would then recollect that they had accustomed themselves to many wants merely because it was easy to gratify them—it would be sufficient to unlearn some of these wants! Perhaps also Chinamen would be called in, and these would bring with them their modes of living and thinking, which would be found very suitable for industrious ants. They would also perhaps help to imbue this fretful and restless Europe with some of their Asiatic calmness and contemplation, and—what is perhaps most needful of all—their Asiatic stability.

FROM THE JOYFUL WISDOM

124

IN THE HORIZON OF THE INFINITE.—We have left the land and have gone aboard ship! We have broken down the bridge behind us—nay, more, the land behind us! Well, little ship, look out! Beside thee is the ocean; it is true it does not always roar, and sometimes it spreads out like silk and gold and a gentle reverie. But times will come when thou wilt feel that it is infinite, and that there is nothing more frightful than infinity. Oh, the poor bird that felt itself free, and now strikes against the walls of this cage! Alas, if home-sickness for the land should attack thee, as if there had been more *freedom* there—and there is no "land" any longer!

125

THE MADMAN.—Have you ever heard of the madman who on a bright morning lighted a lantern and ran to the market place calling out unceasingly: "I seek God! I seek God!"—As there were many people standing about who did not believe in God, he caused a great deal of amusement. Why! is he lost? said one. Has he strayed away like a child? said another. Or does he keep himself hidden? Is he afraid of us? Has he taken a sea voyage? Has he emigrated?—the people cried out laughingly, all in a hubbub. The insane man jumped into their midst and transfixed them with his glances. "Where is God gone?" he called out. "I mean to tell you! *We have killed him*—you and I! We are all his murderers! But how have we done it? How were we able to drink up the sea? Who gave us the sponge to wipe away the whole horizon? What did we do when we loosened this earth from its sun? Whither does it now move? Whither do we move? Away from all suns? Do we not dash on unceasingly? Backward, sideways, forward, in all directions? Is there still an above and below? Do we not stray, as through infinite nothingness? Does not empty space breathe upon us? Has it not become colder? Does not night come on continually, darker and darker? Shall we not have to light lanterns in the morning? Do we not hear the noise of the gravediggers who are burying God? Do we not smell the divine putrefaction?— for even Gods putrefy! God is dead! God remains dead! And we have killed him! How shall we console ourselves, the most murderous of all murderers? The holiest and the mightiest that the world has hitherto possessed has bled to death under our knife—who will wipe the blood from us? With what water could we cleanse ourselves? What lustrums, what sacred games shall we have to devise? Is not the magnitude of this deed too great for us? Shall we not ourselves have to become Gods, merely to seem worthy of it? There never was a greater event, and on account of it, all who are born after us belong to a higher history than any history hitherto!"—Here the madman was silent and looked again at his hearers; they also were silent and looked at him in surprise. At last he threw his lantern on the ground, so that it broke in pieces and was extinguished. "I come too early," he then said, "I am not yet at the right time. This prodigious event is still on its way, and is traveling—it has not yet reached men's ears. Lightning and thunder need time, the light of the stars needs time, deeds need time, even after they are done, to be seen and heard. This deed is as yet further from them than the furthest star—*and yet they have done it!*"—It is further stated that the madman made his way into different churches on the same day, and there intoned his *Requiem aeternam deo.* When led out and called to account, he always gave the reply: "What are these churches now, if they are not the tombs and monuments of God?"

343

WHAT OUR CHEERFULNESS SIGNIFIES.—The most important of more recent events—that "God is dead," that the belief in the Christian God has become unworthy of belief—already begins to cast its first shadows over Europe. To the few at least whose eye, whose *suspecting* glance, is strong enough and subtle enough for this drama, some sun seems to have set, some old, profound confidence seems to have changed into doubt: our old world must seem to them daily more darksome, distrustful, strange, and "old." In the main, however, one may say that the event itself is far too great, too remote, too much beyond most people's power of apprehension, for one to suppose that so much as the report of it could have *reached* them; not to speak of many who already knew *what* had really taken place, and what must all collapse now that this belief had been undermined—because so much was built upon it, so much rested on it, and had become one with it: for example, our entire European morality. This lengthy, vast, and uninterrupted process of crumbling, destruction, ruin, and overthrow which is now imminent: who has realized it sufficiently today to have to stand up as the teacher and herald of such a tremendous logic of terror, as the prophet of a period of gloom and eclipse, the like of which has probably never taken place on earth before? . . . Even we, the born riddle-readers, who wait as it were on the mountains posted 'twixt today and tomorrow, and engirt by their contradiction, we, the firstlings and premature children of the coming century, into whose sight especially the shadows which must forthwith envelop Europe *should* already have come—how is it that even we, without genuine sympathy for this period of gloom, contemplate its advent without any *personal* solicitude or fear? Are we still, perhaps, too much under the *immediate effects* of the event—and are these effects, especially as regards *ourselves,* perhaps the reverse of what was to be expected—not at all sad and depressing, but rather like a new and indescribable variety of light, happiness, relief, enlivenment, encouragement, and dawning day? . . . In fact, we philosophers and "free spirits" feel ourselves irradiated as by a new dawn by the report that the "old God is dead"; our hearts overflow with gratitude, astonishment, presentiment, and expectation. At last the horizon seems open once more, granting even that it is not bright; our ships can at last put out to sea in face of every danger; every hazard is again permitted to the discerner; the sea, *our* sea, again lies open before us; perhaps never before did such an "open sea" exist.

344

TO WHAT EXTENT EVEN WE ARE STILL PIOUS.—
It is said with good reason that convictions have no civic rights in the domain of science: it is only when a conviction voluntarily condescends to the modesty of an hypothesis, a preliminary standpoint for experiment, or a regulative fiction, that its access to the realm of knowledge, and a certain value therein, can be conceded—always, however, with the restriction that it must remain under police supervision, under the police of our distrust. Regarded more accurately, however, does not this imply that only when a conviction *ceases* to be a conviction can it obtain admission into science? Does not the discipline of the scientific spirit just commence when one no longer harbors any conviction? . . . It is probably so: only, it remains to be asked whether, *in order that this discipline may commence*, it is not necessary that there should already be a conviction, and in fact one so imperative and absolute that it makes a sacrifice of all other convictions. One sees that science also rests on a belief: there is no science at all "without premises." The question whether *truth* is necessary must not merely be affirmed beforehand, but must be affirmed to such an extent that the principle, belief, or conviction finds expression, that "there is *nothing more necessary* than truth, and in comparison with it everything else has only a secondary value."—This absolute will to truth: what is it? Is it the will *not to allow ourselves to be deceived?* Is it the will *not to deceive?* For the will to truth could also be interpreted in this fashion, provided one includes under the generalization, "I will not deceive," the special case, "I will not deceive myself." But why not deceive? Why not allow oneself to be deceived?—Let it be noted that the reasons for the former eventuality belong to a category quite different from those for the latter: one does not

want to be deceived oneself, under the supposition that it is injurious, dangerous, or fatal to be deceived—in this sense science would be a prolonged process of caution, foresight, and utility; against which, however, one might reasonably make objections. What? is not-wishing-to-be-deceived really less injurious, less dangerous, less fatal? What do you know of the character of existence in all its phases to be able to decide whether the greater advantage is on the side of absolute distrust, or of absolute trustfulness? In case, however, of both being necessary, much trusting *and* much distrusting, whence then should science derive the absolute belief, the conviction on which it rests, that truth is more important than anything else, even than every other conviction? This conviction could not have arisen if truth *and* untruth had both continually proved themselves to be useful: as is the case. Thus—the belief in science, which now undeniably exists, cannot have had its origin in such a utilitarian calculation, but rather *in spite of* the fact of the inutility and dangerousness of the "will to truth," of "truth at all costs," being continually demonstrated. "At all costs": alas, we understand that sufficiently well, after having sacrificed and slaughtered one belief after another at this altar!—Consequently, "Will to truth" does *not* imply, "I will not allow myself to be deceived," but—there is no other alternative— "I will not deceive, not even myself": *and thus we have reached the realm of morality.* For, let one just ask oneself fairly: "Why wilt thou not deceive?" especially if it should seem—and it does seem—as if life were laid out with a view to appearance, I mean, with a view to error, deceit, dissimulation, delusion, self-delusion; and when on the other hand it is a matter of fact that the great type of life has always manifested itself on the side of the most unscrupulous πολύτροποι. Such an intention might perhaps, to express it mildly, be a piece of Quixotism, a little enthusiastic craziness; it might also, however, be something worse, namely, a destructive principle, hostile to life. . . . "Will to Truth," —that might be a concealed Will to Death. Thus the question, Why is there science? leads back to the moral problem: *What in general is the purpose of morality,* if life, nature, and history are "nonmoral"? There is no doubt that the conscientious man in the daring and extreme sense in which he is presupposed by the belief in science *affirms thereby a world other than* that of life, nature, and history; and insofar as he affirms this "other world," what? must he not just thereby—deny its counterpart, this world, *our* world? . . . But what I have in view will now be understood, namely, that it is always a *metaphysical belief* on which our belief in science rests—and that even we knowing ones of today, the godless and antimetaphysical, still take *our* fire from the conflagration kindled by a belief a millennium old, the Christian belief, which was also the belief of Plato, that God is truth, that the truth is divine. . . . But what if this itself always becomes more untrustworthy, what if nothing any longer proves itself divine, except it be error, blindness, and falsehood; what if God himself turns out to be our most persistent lie?

345

MORALITY AS A PROBLEM. A defect in personality revenges itself everywhere: an enfeebled, lank, obliterated, self-disavowing, and disowning personality is no longer fit for anything good—it is least of all fit for philosophy. "Selflessness" has no value either in heaven or on earth; the great problems all demand *great love,* and it is only the strong, well-rounded, secure spirits, those who have a solid basis, that are qualified for them. It makes the most material difference whether a thinker stands personally related to his problems, having his fate, his need, and even his highest happiness therein; or merely impersonally, that is to say, if he can only feel and grasp them with the tentacles of cold, prying thought. In the latter case I warrant that nothing comes of it, for the great problems, granting that they let themselves be grasped at all, do not let themselves be *held* by toads and weaklings: that has ever been their taste—a taste also which they share with all high-spirited women.— How is it that I have not yet met with anyone, not even in books, who seems to have stood to morality in this position, as one who knew morality as a problem, and this problem as *his own* personal need, affliction, pleasure, and passion? It is obvious that up to the present morality has not been a problem at all; it has rather been the very ground on which people have met, after all distrust, dissension, and contradiction, the hallowed place of peace, where thinkers could obtain rest even from themselves, could recover breath and revive. I see no one who has ventured to *criticize* the estimates of moral worth. I miss in this connection even the attempts of scientific curiosity, and the fastidious, groping imagination of psychologists and historians, which easily anticipates a problem and catches it on the wing, without rightly knowing what it catches. With difficulty I have discovered some scanty data for the purpose of furnishing a *history of the origin* of these feelings and estimates of value (which is something different from a criticism of them, and also something different from a history of ethical systems). In an individual case, I have done everything to encourage the inclination and talent for this kind of history—in vain, as it would seem to me at present. There is little to be learned from those historians of morality (especially Englishmen); they themselves are usually, quite unsuspiciously, under the influence of a definite morality, and act unwittingly as its armor-bearers and followers—perhaps still repeating sincerely the popular superstition of Christian Europe, that the characteristic of moral action consists in abnegation, self-denial, self-sacrifice, or in fellow feeling and fellow suffering. The usual error in their premises is their insistence on a certain *consensus* among human beings, at least among civilized human beings, with regard to certain propositions of morality, and from thence they conclude that these propositions are absolutely binding even upon you and me; or reversely, they come to the conclusion that *no* morality at all is binding, after the truth has dawned upon them that to different peoples moral valuations are *necessarily* different: both of which conclusions are equally childish follies. The error of the more subtle amongst them is that they discover and criticize the probably foolish opinions of a people about its own morality, or the opinions of mankind about human morality generally; they treat accordingly of its origin, its religious sanctions, the superstition of free will, and such matters; and they think that just by so doing they have criticized the morality itself. But the worth of a precept, "Thou shalt," is still fundamentally different from and independent of such opinions about it, and must be distinguished from the weeds of error with which it has perhaps been overgrown: just as the worth of a medicine to a sick person is altogether independent of the question whether he has a scientific opinion about medicine, or merely thinks about it as an old wife would do. A morality could even have grown *out of* an error, but with this knowledge the problem of its worth would not even be touched.—Thus, no one has hitherto tested the *value* of that most celebrated of all medicines, called morality: for which purpose it is first of all necessary for one—*to call it in question*. Well, that is just our work.

346

OUR NOTE OF INTERROGATION. But you don't understand it? As a matter of fact, an effort will be necessary
in order to understand us. We seek for words; we seek perhaps also for ears. Who are we after all? If we wanted simply
to call ourselves in older phraseology, atheists, unbelievers,
or even immoralists, we should still be far from thinking
ourselves designated thereby: we are all three in too late a
phase for people generally to conceive, for *you*, my inquisitive friends, to be able to conceive, what is our state of mind
under the circumstances. No! we have no longer the bitterness and passion of him who has broken loose, who has to
make for himself a belief, a goal, and even a martyrdom out
of his unbelief! We have become saturated with the conviction (and have grown cold and hard in it) that things are
not at all divinely ordered in this world, nor even according
to human standards do they go on rationally, mercifully, or
justly: we know the fact that the world in which we live is
ungodly, immoral, and "inhuman"—we have far too long interpreted it to ourselves falsely and mendaciously, according
to the wish and will of our veneration, that is to say, according to our *need*. For man is a venerating animal! But he is
also a distrustful animal: and that the world is *not* worth
what we have believed it to be worth is about the surest thing
our distrust has at last managed to grasp. So much distrust,
so much philosophy! We take good care not to say that the
world is of *less* value; it seems to us at present absolutely
ridiculous when man claims to devise values *to surpass* the
values of the actual world—it is precisely from that point
that we have retraced our steps; as from an extravagant error
of human conceit and irrationality, which for a long period
has not been recognized as such. This error had its last expression in modern Pessimism; an older and stronger manifestation in the teaching of Buddha; but Christianity also
contains it, more dubiously, to be sure, and more ambiguously, but none the less seductive on that account. The whole
attitude of "man *versus* the world," man as world-denying
principle, man as the standard of the value of things, as
judge of the world, who in the end puts existence itself on his
scales and finds it too light—the monstrous impertinence of
this attitude has dawned upon us as such, and has disgusted
us—we now laugh when we find, "Man *and* World" placed
beside one another, separated by the sublime presumption of

the little word "and"! But how is it? Have we not in our very laughing just made a further step in despising mankind? And consequently also in Pessimism, in despising the existence cognizable *by us?* Have we not just thereby become liable to a suspicion of an opposition between the world in which we have hitherto been at home with our venerations —for the sake of which we perhaps *endure* life—and another world *which we ourselves are:* an inexorable, radical, most profound suspicion concerning ourselves, which is continually getting us Europeans more annoyingly into its power, and could easily face the coming generation with the terrible alternative: Either do away with your venerations, or—*with yourselves!* The latter would be Nihilism—but would not the former also be Nihilism? This is *our* note of interrogation.

347

BELIEVERS AND THEIR NEED OF BELIEF. How much *faith* a person requires in order to flourish, how much "fixed opinion" he requires which he does not wish to have shaken, because he *holds* himself thereby—is a measure of his power (or more plainly speaking, of his weakness). Most people in old Europe, as it seems to me, still need Christianity at present, and on that account it still finds belief. For such is man: a theological dogma might be refuted to him a thousand times—provided, however, that he had need of it, he would again and again accept it as "true"—according to the famous "proof of power" of which the Bible speaks. Some have still need of metaphysics; but also the impatient *longing for certainty* which at present discharges itself in scientific, positivist fashion among large numbers of the people, the longing by all means to get at something stable (while on account of the warmth of the longing the establishing of the certainty is more leisurely and negligently undertaken): even this is still the longing for a hold, a support; in short, the *instinct of weakness,* which, while not actually creating religions, metaphysics, and convictions of all kinds, nevertheless—preserves them. In fact, around all these positivist systems there fume the vapors of a certain pessimistic gloom, something of weariness, fatalism, disillusionment, and fear of new disillusionment—or else manifest animosity, ill-humor, anarchic exasperation, and whatever there is of symptom or masquerade of the feeling of weakness. Even the readiness with which our cleverest contemporaries get lost in wretched corners and alleys, for example, in Vaterländerei (so I designate Jingoism, called *chauvinisme* in France, and *deutsch* in Germany), or in petty aesthetic creeds in the manner of Parisian *naturalisme* (which only brings into prominence and uncovers *that* aspect of nature which excites simultaneously disgust and astonishment—they like at present to call this aspect *la vérité vraie*), or in Nihilism in the St. Petersburg style (that is to say, in the *belief in unbelief,* even to martyrdom for it): this shows always and above all the need of belief, support, backbone, and buttress. . . . Belief is always most desired, most pressingly needed where there is a lack of will, for the will, as emotion of command, is the distinguishing characteristic of sovereignty and power. That is to say, the less a person knows how to command, the more urgent is his desire for one who commands, who commands sternly—a God, a prince, a caste, a physician, a confessor, a dogma, a party conscience. From whence perhaps it could be inferred that the two world religions, Buddhism and Christianity, might well have had the cause of their rise, and especially of their rapid extension, in an extraordinary *malady of the will.* And in truth it has been so: both religions lighted upon a longing, monstrously exaggerated by malady of the will, for an imperative, a "Thou shalt," a longing going the length of despair; both religions were teachers of fanaticism in times of slackness of will power, and thereby offered to innumerable persons a support, a new possibility of exercising will, an enjoyment in willing. For in fact fanaticism is the sole "volitional strength" to which the weak and irresolute can be excited, as a sort of hypnotizing of the entire sensory-intellectual system, in favor of the overabundant nutrition (hypertrophy) of a particular point of view and a particular sentiment, which then dominates—the Christian calls it his *faith.* When a man arrives at the fundamental conviction that he *requires* to be commanded, he becomes "a believer." Reversely, one could imagine a delight and a power of self-determining, and a *freedom* of will whereby a spirit could bid farewell to every belief, to every wish for certainty, accustomed as it would be to support itself on slender cords and possibilities, and to dance even on the verge of abysses. Such a spirit would be the *free spirit par excellence.*

352

WHY WE CAN HARDLY DISPENSE WITH MORALITY. The naked man is generally an ignominious spectacle

—I speak of us European males (and by no means of European females!). If the most joyous company at table suddenly found themselves stripped and divested of their garments through the trick of an enchanter, I believe that not only would the joyousness be gone and the strongest appetite lost—it seems that we Europeans cannot at all dispense with the masquerade that is called clothing. But should not the disguise of "moral men," the screening under moral formulas and notions of decency, the whole kindly concealment of our conduct under conceptions of duty, virtue, public sentiment, honorableness, and disinterestedness, have just as good reasons in support of it? Not that I mean hereby that human wickedness and baseness, in short, the evil wild beast in us, should be disguised; on the contrary, my idea is that it is precisely as *tame animals* that we are an ignominious spectacle and require moral disguising—that the "inner man" in Europe is far from having enough of intrinsic evil "to let himself be seen" with it (to be *beautiful* with it). The European disguises himself *in morality* because he has become a sick, sickly, crippled animal, who has good reasons for being "tame," because he is almost an abortion, an imperfect, weak, and clumsy thing. . . . It is not the fierceness of the beast of prey that finds moral disguise necessary, but the gregarious animal, with its profound mediocrity, anxiety, and ennui. *Morality dresses up the European*—let us acknowledge it!—in more distinguished, more important, more conspicuous guise—in "divine" guise.

372

WHY WE ARE NOT IDEALISTS. Formerly philosophers were afraid of the senses: have we, perhaps, been far too forgetful of this fear? We are at present all of us sensualists, we representatives of the present and of the future in philosophy—*not* according to theory, however, but in *praxis*, in practice. . . . Those former philosophers, on the contrary, thought that the senses lured them out of *their* world, the cold realm of "ideas," to a dangerous southern island, where they were afraid that their philosopher virtues would melt away like snow in the sun. "Wax in the ears," was then almost a condition of philosophizing; a genuine philosopher no longer listened to life, insofar as life is music, he *denied* the music of life—it is an old philosophical superstition that all music is Sirens' music. Now we should be inclined at the present day to judge precisely in the opposite manner (which in itself might be just as false), and to regard *ideas*, with their cold, anemic appearance, and not even in spite of this appearance, as worse seducers than the senses. They have always lived on the "blood" of the philosopher, they always consumed his senses, and indeed, if you will believe me, his "heart" as well. Those old philosophers were heartless: philosophizing was always a species of vampirism. At the sight of such figures even as Spinoza, do you not feel a profoundly enigmatical and disquieting sort of impression? Do you not see the drama which is here performed, the constantly *increasing pallor*, the spiritualization always more ideally displayed? Do you not imagine some long-concealed bloodsucker in the background, which makes its beginning with the senses, and in the end retains or leaves behind nothing but bones and their rattling?—I mean categories, formulas, and *words* (for you will pardon me in saying that what *remain*s of Spinoza, *amor intellectualis dei*, is rattling and nothing more! What is *amor*, what is *deus*, when they have lost every drop of blood? . . .) *In summa:* all philosophical idealism has hitherto been something like a disease, where it has not been, as in the case of Plato, the prudence of superabundant and dangerous healthfulness, the fear of *overpowerful* senses, and the wisdom of a wise Socratic. —Perhaps, is it the case that we moderns are merely not sufficiently sound *to require* Plato's idealism? And we do not fear the senses because——.

FROM BEYOND GOOD AND EVIL

4

The falseness of an opinion is not for us any objection to it: it is here, perhaps, that our new language sounds most strangely. The question is, how far an opinion is life-furthering, life-preserving, species-preserving, perhaps species-rearing; and we are fundamentally inclined to maintain that the falsest opinions (to which the synthetic judgments a priori belong) are the most indispensable to us; that without a recognition of logical fictions, without a comparison of reality with the purely *imagined* world of the absolute and immutable, without a constant counterfeiting of the world by means of numbers, man could not live—that the renunciation of false opinions would be a renunciation of life, a negation of life. *To recognize untruth as a condition of life:* that is certainly to impugn the traditional ideas of value in a dangerous manner, and a philosophy which ventures to do so has thereby alone placed itself beyond good and evil.

24

O SANCTA SIMPLICITAS! In what strange simplification and falsification man lives! One can never cease wondering when once one has got eyes for beholding this marvel! How we have made everything around us clear and free and easy and simple! How we have been able to give our senses a passport to everything superficial, our thoughts a godlike desire for wanton pranks and wrong inferences!—How from the beginning, we have contrived to retain our ignorance in order to enjoy an almost inconceivable freedom, thoughtlessness, imprudence, heartiness, and gaiety—in order to enjoy life! And only on this solidified, granitelike foundation of ignorance could knowledge rear itself hitherto, the will to knowledge on the foundation of a far more powerful will, the will to ignorance, to the uncertain, to the untrue! Not as its opposite, but—as its refinement! It is to be hoped, indeed, that *language,* here as elsewhere, will not get over its awkwardness, and that it will continue to talk of opposites where there are only degrees and many refinements of gradation; it is equally to be hoped that the incarnated Tartuffery of morals, which now belongs to our unconquerable "flesh and blood," will turn the words round in the mouths of us discerning ones. Here and there we understand it, and laugh at the way in which precisely the best knowledge seeks most to retain us in this *simplified,* thoroughly artificial, suitably imagined and suitably falsified world: at the way in which, whether it will or not, it loves error, because, as living itself, it loves life!

186

The moral sentiment in Europe at present is perhaps as subtle, belated, diverse, sensitive, and refined, as the "Science of Morals" belonging thereto is recent, initial, awkward, and coarse-fingered—an interesting contrast, which sometimes becomes incarnate and obvious in the very person of a moralist. Indeed, the expression, "Science of Morals," is, in respect to what is designated thereby, far too presumptuous and counter to *good* taste—which is always a foretaste of more modest expressions. One ought to avow with the utmost fairness *what* is still necessary here for a long time, *what* is alone proper for the present, namely, the collection of material, the comprehensive survey and classification of an immense domain of delicate sentiments of worth, and distinctions of worth, which live, grow, propagate, and perish—and perhaps attempts to give a clear idea of the recurring and more common forms of these living crystallizations—as preparation for a *theory of types* of morality. To be sure, people have not hitherto been so modest. All the philosophers, with a pedantic and ridiculous seriousness, demanded of themselves something very much higher, more pretentious, and ceremonious, when they concerned themselves with morality as a science: they wanted to *give a basis* to morality—and every philosopher hitherto has believed that he has given it a basis; morality itself, however, has been regarded as something "given." How far from their awkward pride was the seemingly insignificant problem—left in dust and decay—of a description of forms of morality, notwithstanding that the finest hands and senses could hardly be fine enough for it! It was precisely owing to moral philosophers knowing the moral facts imperfectly, in an arbitrary epitome, or an accidental abridgment—perhaps as the morality of their environment, their position, their church, their *Zeitgeist*, their climate and zone—it was precisely because they were badly instructed with regard to nations, eras, and past ages, and were by no means eager to know about these matters, that they did not even come in sight of the real problems of morals—problems which only disclose themselves by a comparison of *many* kinds of morality. In every "Science of Morals" hitherto, strange as it may sound, the problem of morality itself has been *omitted;* there has been no suspicion that there was anything problematic there! That which philosophers called "giving a basis to morality," and endeavored to realize, has, when seen in a right light, proved merely a learned form of good *faith* in prevailing morality, a new means of its *expression,* consequently just a matter-of-fact within the sphere of a definite morality, yea, in its ultimate motive, a sort of denial that it is *lawful* for this morality to be called in question—and in any case the reverse of the testing, analyzing, doubting, and vivisecting of this very faith. Hear, for instance, with what innocence—almost worthy of honor—Schopenhauer represents his own task, and draw your conclusions concerning the scientificalness of a "science" whose latest master still talks in the strain of children and old wives: "The principle," he says (page 136 of the *Grund-probleme der Ethik* *), "the axiom about the purport of which all moralists are *practically* agreed: *neminem laede, immo omnes quantum potes juva*—is *really* the proposition which all moral teachers strive to establish, . . . the *real* basis of ethics which has been sought, like the philosopher's stone, for centuries."—The difficulty of establishing the proposition referred to may indeed be great—it is well known that Schopenhauer also was unsuccessful in his efforts; and who-ever has thoroughly realized how absurdly false and senti-mental this proposition is, in a world whose essence is Will to Power, may be reminded that Schopenhauer, although a pessimist, *actually*—played the flute . . . daily after dinner: one may read about the matter in his biography. A question by the way: a pessimist, a repudiator of God and of the world, who *makes a halt* at morality—who assents to moral-ity, and plays the flute to *laede-neminem* morals, what? Is that really—a pessimist?

187

Apart from the value of such assertions as "there is a categorical imperative in us," one can always ask: What does such an assertion indicate about him who makes it? There are systems of morals which are meant to justify their author in the eyes of other people; other systems of morals are meant to tranquillize him, and make him self-satisfied; with other systems he wants to crucify and humble himself; with others he wishes to take revenge; with others to conceal himself; with others to glorify himself and gain superiority and distinction—this system of morals helps its author to forget, that system makes him, or something of him, for-gotten; many a moralist would like to exercise power and creative arbitrariness over mankind; many another, perhaps, Kant especially, gives us to understand by his morals that "what is estimable in me is that I know how to obey—and with you it *shall* not be otherwise than with me!" In short, systems of morals are only a *sign language of the emotions.*

188

In contrast to *laisser-aller*, every system of morals is a sort

* Pages 54–55 of Schopenhauer's *Basis of Morality,* translated by Arthur B. Bullock (1903).

of tyranny against "nature" and also against "reason"; that is, however, no objection, unless one should again decree by some system of morals, that all kinds of tyranny and unreasonableness are unlawful. What is essential and invaluable in every system of morals is that it is a long constraint. In order to understand Stoicism, or Port Royal, or Puritanism, one should remember the constraint under which every language has attained to strength and freedom—the metrical constraint, the tyranny of rhyme and rhythm. How much trouble have the poets and orators of every nation given themselves!—not excepting some of the prose writers of today, in whose ear dwells an inexorable conscientiousness —"for the sake of a folly," as utilitarian bunglers say, and thereby deem themselves wise—"from submission to arbitrary laws," as the anarchists say, and thereby fancy themselves "free," even free-spirited. The singular fact remains, however, that everything of the nature of freedom, elegance, boldness, dance, and masterly certainty, which exists or has existed, whether it be in thought itself, or in administration, or in speaking and persuading, in art just as in conduct, has only developed by means of the tyranny of such arbitrary law; and in all seriousness, it is not at all improbable that precisely this is "nature" and "natural" —and *not laisser-aller*! Every artist knows how different from the state of letting himself go is his "most natural" condition, the free arranging, locating, disposing, and constructing in the moments of "inspiration"—and how strictly and delicately he then obeys a thousand laws, which, by their very rigidness and precision, defy all formulation by means of ideas (even the most stable idea has, in comparison therewith, something floating, manifold, and ambiguous in it). The essential thing "in heaven and in earth" is, apparently (to repeat it once more), that there should be long *obedience* in the same direction; there thereby results, and has always resulted in the long run, something which has made life worth living; for instance, virtue, art, music, dancing, reason, spirituality—anything whatever that is transfiguring, refined, foolish, or divine. The long bondage of the spirit, the distrustful constraint in the communicability of ideas, the discipline which the thinker imposed on himself to think in accordance with the rules of a church or a court, or conformable to Aristotelian premises, the persistent spiritual will to interpret everything that happened according to a Christian scheme, and in every occurrence to rediscover and justify the Christian God—all this violence, arbitrariness, severity, dreadfulness, and unreasonableness has proved itself the disciplinary means whereby the European spirit has attained its strength, its remorseless curiosity and subtle mobility; granted also that much irrecoverable strength and spirit had to be stifled, suffocated, and spoiled in the process (for here, as everywhere, "nature" shows herself as she is, in all her extravagant and *indifferent* magnificence, which is shocking, but nevertheless noble). That for centuries European thinkers only thought in order to prove something—nowadays, on the contrary, we are suspicious of every thinker who "wishes to prove something"—that it was always settled beforehand what *was to be* the result of their strictest thinking, as it was perhaps in the Asiatic astrology of former times, or as it is still at the present day in the innocent, Christian-moral explanation of immediate personal events "for the glory of God," or "for the good of the soul": this tyranny, this arbitrariness, this severe and magnificent stupidity, has *educated* the spirit; slavery, both in the coarser and the finer sense, is apparently an indispensable means even of spiritual education and discipline. One may look at every system of morals in this light: it is "nature" therein which teaches to hate the *laisser-aller*, the too great freedom, and implants the need for limited horizons, for immediate duties—it teaches the *narrowing of perspectives*, and thus, in a certain sense, that stupidity is a condition of life and development. "Thou must obey someone, and for a long time; *otherwise* thou wilt come to grief, and lose all respect for thyself"—this seems to me to be the moral imperative of nature, which is certainly neither "categorical," as old Kant wished (consequently the "otherwise"), nor does it address itself to the individual (what does nature care for the individual!), but to nations, races, ages, and ranks, above all, however, to the animal "man" generally, to *mankind*.

202

Let us at once say again what we have already said a hundred times, for people's ears nowadays are unwilling to hear such truths—*our* truths. We know well enough how offensively it sounds when anyone plainly, and without metaphor, counts man among the animals; but it will be accounted to us almost a *crime*, that it is precisely in respect to men of "modern ideas" that we have constantly applied the terms "herd," "herd instincts," and such like expressions. What avail is it? We cannot do otherwise, for it is precisely here that our new insight is. We have found that in all the principal moral judgments Europe has become unanimous, including likewise the countries where European influence prevails; in Europe people evidently *know* what Socrates thought he did not know, and what the famous serpent of old once promised to teach—they "know" today what is good and evil. It must then sound hard and be distasteful to the ear, when we always insist that that which here thinks it knows, that which here glorifies itself with praise and blame, and calls itself good, is the instinct of the herding human animal: the instinct which has come and is ever coming more and more to the front, to preponderance and supremacy over other instincts, according to the increasing physiological approximation and resemblance of which it is the symptom. *Morality in Europe at present is herding-animal morality;* and therefore, as we understand the matter, only one kind of human morality, beside which, before which, and after which many other moralities, and above all *higher* moralities, are or should be possible. Against such a "possibility," against such a "should be," however, this morality defends itself with all its strength; it says obstinately and inexorably: "I am morality itself and nothing else is morality!" Indeed, with the help of a religion which has humored and flattered the sublimest desires of the herding-animal, things have reached such a point that we always find a more visible expression of this morality even in political and social arrangements: the *democratic* movement is the inheritance of the Christian movement. That its *tempo*, however, is much too slow and sleepy for the more impatient ones, for those who are sick and distracted by the herding instinct, is indicated by the increasingly furious howling, and always less disguised teeth-gnashing of the anarchist dogs, who are now roving through the highways of European culture. Apparently in opposition to the peacefully industrious democrats and Revolution-ideologues, and still more so to the awkward philosophasters and fraternity-visionaries who call themselves Socialists and want a "free society," those are really at one with them all in their thorough and instinctive hostility to every form of society other than that of the *autonomous* herd (to the extent even of repudiating the notions "master" and "servant"—*ni dieu ni maître*, says a socialist formula); at one in their tenacious opposition to every special claim, every special right and privilege (this means ultimately opposition to *every* right, for when all are equal, no one needs "rights" any longer); at one in their distrust of punitive justice (as though it were a violation of the weak, unfair to the *necessary* consequences of all former society); but equally at one in their religion of sympathy, in their compassion for all that feels, lives, and suffers (down to the very animals, up even to "God"—the extravagance of "sympathy for God" belongs to a democratic age); altogether at one in the cry and impatience of their sympathy, in their deadly hatred of suffering generally, in their almost feminine incapacity for witnessing it or *allowing* it; at one in their involuntary be-glooming and heart-softening, under the spell of which Europe seems to be threatened with a new Buddhism; at one in their belief in the morality of *mutual* sympathy, as though it were morality in itself, the climax, the *attained* climax of mankind, the sole hope of the future, the consolation of the present, the great discharge from all the obligations of the past; altogether at one in their belief in the community as the *deliverer*, in the herd, and therefore in "themselves."

228

I hope to be forgiven for discovering that all moral philosophy hitherto has been tedious and has belonged to the soporific appliances—and that "virtue," in my opinion, has been *more* injured by the *tediousness* of its advocates than by anything else; at the same time, however, I would not wish to overlook their general usefulness. It is desirable that as few people as possible should reflect upon morals, and consequently it is *very* desirable that morals should not some day become interesting! But let us not be afraid! Things still remain today as they have always been: I see no one in Europe who has (or *discloses*) an idea of the fact that philosophizing concerning morals might be conducted in a dangerous, captious, and ensnaring manner—that *calamity* might be involved therein. Observe, for example, the in-defatigable, inevitable English utilitarians: how ponderously and respectably they stalk on, stalk along (a Homeric meta-phor expresses it better) in the footsteps of Bentham, just as he had already stalked in the footsteps of the respectable Helvétius (no, he was not a dangerous man, Helvétius, *ce sénatuer Pococurante,* to use an expression of Galiani)! No new thought, nothing of the nature of a finer turning or better expression of an old thought, not even a proper history of what has been previously thought on the subject: an *impossible* literature, taking it all in all, unless one knows how to leaven it with some mischief. In effect, the old English vice called *cant,* which is *moral Tartuffism,* has insinuated itself also into these moralists (whom one must certainly read with an eye to their motives if one *must* read them), con-cealed this time under the new form of the scientific spirit;

moreover, there is not absent from them a secret struggle with the pangs of conscience, from which a race of former Puritans must naturally suffer, in all their scientific tinkering with morals. (Is not a moralist the opposite of a Puritan? That is to say, as a thinker who regards morality as questionable, as worthy of interrogation, in short, as a problem? Is moralizing not—immoral?) In the end, they all want *English* morality to be recognized as authoritative, inasmuch as mankind, or the "general utility," or "the happiness of the greatest number"—no! the happiness of *England*, will be best served thereby. They would like, by all means, to convince themselves that the striving after *English* happiness, I mean after *comfort* and *fashion* (and in the highest instance, a seat in Parliament), is at the same time the true path of virtue; in fact, that insofar as there has been virtue in the world hitherto, it has just consisted in such striving. Not one of those ponderous, conscience-striken herding animals (who undertake to advocate the cause of egoism as conducive to the general welfare) wants to have any knowledge or inkling of the fact that the "general welfare" is no ideal, no goal, no notion that can be at all grasped, but is only a nostrum—that what is fair to one *may not* at all be fair to another, that the requirement of one morality for all is really a detriment to higher men, in short, that there is a *distinction of rank* between man and man, and consequently between morality and morality. They are an unassuming and fundamentally mediocre species of men, these utilitarian Englishmen, and, as already remarked, insofar as they are tedious, one cannot think highly enough of their utility. One ought even to *encourage* them, as has been partially attempted in the following rhymes:

> Hail, ye worthies, barrow-wheeling,
> "Longer—better," aye revealing,
>   Stiffer aye in head and knee;
> Unenraptured, never jesting,
> Mediocre everlasting,
>   *Sans genie et sans esprit!*

229

In these later ages, which may be proud of their humanity, there still remains so much fear, so much *superstition* of the fear, of the "cruel wild beast," the mastering of which constitutes the very pride of these humaner ages—that even obvious truths, as if by the agreement of centuries, have long remained unuttered, because they have the appearance of helping the finally slain wild beast back to life again. I perhaps risk something when I allow such a truth to escape; let others capture it again and give it so much "milk of pious sentiment" * to drink, that it will lie down quiet and forgotten, in its old corner.—One ought to learn anew about cruelty, and open one's eyes; one ought at last to learn impatience, in order that such immodest gross errors—as, for instance, have been fostered by ancient and modern philosophers with regard to tragedy—may no longer wander about virtuously and boldly. Almost everything that we call "higher culture" is based upon the spiritualizing and intensifying of *cruelty*—this is my thesis; the "wild beast" has not been slain at all, it lives, it flourishes, it has only been—transfigured. That which constitutes the painful delight of tragedy is cruelty; that which operates agreeably in so-called tragic sympathy, and at the basis even of everything sublime, up to the highest and most delicate thrills of metaphysics, obtains its sweetness solely from the intermingled ingredient of cruelty. What the Roman enjoys in the arena, the Christian in the ecstasies of the cross, the Spaniard at the sight of the faggot and stake, and of the bullfight, the present-day Japanese who presses his way to the tragedy, the workman of the Parisian suburbs who has a homesickness for bloody revolutions, the Wagnerienne who, with unhinged will, "undergoes" the performance of *Tristan and Isolde*—what all these enjoy, and strive with mysterious ardor to drink in, is the philter of the great Circe "cruelty." Here, to be sure, we must put aside entirely the blundering psychology of former times, which could only teach with regard to cruelty that it originated at the sight of the suffering of *others:* there is an abundant, superabundant enjoyment even in one's own suffering, in causing one's own suffering—and wherever man has allowed himself to be persuaded to self-denial in the *religious* sense, or to self-mutilation, as among the Phoenicians and ascetics, or in general, to desensualization, decarnalization, and contrition, to Puritanical repentance-spasms, to vivisection of conscience and to Pascal-like *sacrifizio dell' intelleto*, he is secretly allured and impelled forward by his cruelty, by the dangerous thrill of cruelty *toward himself.*— Finally, let us consider that even the seeker of knowledge operates as an artist and glorifier of cruelty, in that he com-

* An expression from Schiller's *William Tell*, Act IV, Scene 3.

pels his spirit to perceive *against* its own inclination, and often enough against the wishes of his heart: he forces it to say Nay, where he would like to affirm, love, and adore; indeed, every instance of taking a thing profoundly and fundamentally is a violation, an intentional injuring of the fundamental will of the spirit, which instinctively aims at appearance and superficiality—even in every desire for knowledge there is a drop of cruelty.

230

Perhaps what I have here said about a "fundamental will of the spirit" may not be understood without further details; I may be allowed a word of explanation.—That imperious something which is popularly called "the spirit," wishes to be master internally and externally, and to feel itself master: it has the will of a multiplicity for simplicity, a binding, taming, imperious, and essentially ruling will. Its requirements and capacities here are the same as those assigned by physiologists to everything that lives, grows, and multiplies. The power of the spirit to appropriate foreign elements reveals itself in a strong tendency to assimilate the new to the old, to simplify the manifold, to overlook or repudiate the absolutely contradictory; just as it arbitrarily re-underlines, makes prominent, and falsifies for itself certain traits and lines in the foreign elements, in every portion of the "outside world." Its object thereby is the incorporation of new "experiences," the assortment of new things in the old arrangements—in short, growth; or more properly, the *feeling* of growth, the feeling of increased power—is its object. This same will has at its service an apparently opposed impulse of the spirit, a suddenly adopted preference of ignorance, of arbitrary shutting out, a closing of windows, an inner denial of this or that, a prohibition to approach, a sort of defensive attitude against much that is knowable, a contentment with obscurity, with the shutting-in horizon, an acceptance and approval of ignorance: as that which is all necessary according to the degree of its appropriating power, its "digestive power," to speak figuratively (and in fact "the spirit" resembles a stomach more than anything else). Here also belong an occasional propensity of the spirit to let itself be deceived (perhaps with a waggish suspicion that it is *not* so and so, but is only allowed to pass as such), a delight in uncertainty and ambiguity, an exulting enjoyment of arbitrary, out-of-the-way narrowness and mystery, of the too-near, of the foreground, of the magnified, the diminished, the misshapen, the beautified—an enjoyment of the arbitrariness of all these manifestations of power. Finally, in this connection, there is the not unscrupulous readiness of the spirit to deceive other spirits and dissemble before them—the constant pressing and straining of a creating, shaping, changeable power: the spirit enjoys therein its craftiness and its variety of disguises, it enjoys also its feeling of security therein—it is precisely by its Protean arts that it is best protected and concealed!— *Counter to this* propensity for appearance, for simplification, for a disguise, for a cloak, in short, for an outside—for every outside is a cloak—there operates the sublime tendency of the man of knowledge, which takes, and *insists* on taking things profoundly, variously, and thoroughly; as a kind of cruelty of the intellectual conscience and taste, which every courageous thinker will acknowledge in himself, provided, as it ought to be, that he has sharpened and hardened his eye sufficiently long for introspection, and is accustomed to severe discipline and even severe words. He will say: "There is something cruel in the tendency of my spirits": let the virtuous and amiable try to convince him that it is not so! In fact, it would sound nicer, if, instead of our cruelty, perhaps our "extravagant honesty" were talked about, whispered about, and glorified—we free, *very* free spirits—and some day perhaps *such* will actually be our—posthumous glory! Meanwhile—for there is plenty of time until then—we should be least inclined to deck ourselves out in such florid and fringed moral verbiage; our whole former work has just made us sick of this taste and its sprightly exuberance. They are beautiful, glistening, jingling, festive words: honesty, love of truth, love of wisdom, sacrifice for knowledge, heroism of the truthful—there is something in them that makes one's heart swell with pride. But we anchorites and marmots have long ago persuaded ourselves in all the secrecy of an anchorite's conscience, that this worthy parade of verbiage also belongs to the old false adornment, frippery, and gold dust of unconscious human vanity, and that even under such flattering color and repainting, the terrible original text *homo natura* must again be recognized. In effect, to translate man back again into nature; to master the many vain and visionary interpretations and subordinate meanings which have hitherto been scratched and daubed over the eternal original text, *homo natura*; to bring it about that man shall henceforth stand before man as he now, hardened by the discipline of science, stands before the *other* forms of nature, with fearless Oedipus-eyes, and stopped Ulysses-ears, deaf to the enticements of old metaphysical birdcatchers, who have piped to him far too long: "Thou art more! Thou art higher! Thou hast a different origin!"—this may be a strange and foolish task, but that it is a *task*, who can deny! Why did we choose it, this foolish task? Or, to put the question differently: "Why knowledge at all?" Everyone will ask us about this. And thus pressed, we, who have asked ourselves the question a hundred times, have not found, and cannot find any better answer. . . .

FROM THE GENEALOGY OF MORALS

10

The revolt of the slaves in morals begins in the very principle of *resentment* becoming creative and giving birth to values—a resentment experienced by creatures who, deprived as they are of the proper outlet of action, are forced to find their compensation in an imaginary revenge. While every aristocratic morality springs from a triumphant affirmation of its own demands, the slave morality says "no" from the very outset to what is "outside itself," "different from itself," and "not itself": and this "no" is its creative deed. This *volte-face* of the valuing standpoint—this *inevitable gravitation to the objective instead of back to the subjective*— is typical of "resentment": the slave morality requires as the condition of its existence an external and objective world, to employ physiological terminology, it requires objective stimuli to be capable of action at all—its action is fundamentally a reaction. The contrary is the case when we come to the aristocrat's system of values: it acts and grows spontaneously, it merely seeks its antithesis in order to pronounce a more grateful and exultant "yes" to its own self; its negative conception, "low," "vulgar," "bad," is merely a pale late-born foil in comparison with its positive and fundamental conception (saturated as it is with life and passion) of "we aristocrats, we good ones, we beautiful ones, we happy ones."

When the aristocratic morality goes astray and commits sacrilege on reality, this is limited to that particular sphere with which it is *not* sufficiently acquainted—a sphere with which it disdainfully defends itself. It misjudges, in some cases, the sphere which it despises, the sphere of the common vulgar man and the low people: on the other hand, due weight should be given to the consideration that in any case the mood of contempt, or disdain, or superciliousness, even on the supposition that it *falsely* portrays the object of its contempt, will always be far removed from that degree of falsity which will always characterize the attacks—in effigy, of course—of the vindictive hatred and revengefulness of the weak in onslaughts on their enemies. In point of fact, there is in contempt too strong an admixture of nonchalance, of casualness, of boredom, of impatience, even of personal exultation, for it to be capable of distorting its victim into a real caricature or a real monstrosity. Attention again should be paid to the almost benevolent *nuances* which, for instance, the Greek nobility imports into all the words by which it distinguishes the common people from itself; note how continuously a kind of pity, care, and consideration imparts its honeyed *flavor*, until at last almost all the words which are applied to the vulgar man survive finally as expressions for "unhappy," "worthy of pity" (compare δειλός, δείλαιος, πονηρός, μοχθηρός; the latter two names really denoting the vulgar man as labor-slave and beast of burden)—and how, conversely, "bad," "low," "unhappy" have never ceased to ring in the Greek ear with a tone in which "unhappy" is the predominant note: this is a heritage of the old noble aristrocratic morality, which remains true to itself even in contempt (let philologists remember the sense in which ὀιζυρός, ἄνολβος, τλήμων, δυστυχεῖν, ξυμφορά used to be employed). The "well-born" simply *felt* themselves the "happy"; they did not have to manufacture their happiness artifically through looking at their enemies, or in cases to talk and *lie themselves into* happiness (as is the custom with all resentful men); and similarly, complete men as they were, exuberant with strength, and consequently *necessarily* energetic, they were too wise to dissociate happiness from action—activity becomes in their minds necessarily counted as happiness (that is the etymology of εὖ πράττειν) — all in sharp contrast to the "happiness" of the weak and the oppressed, with their festering venom and malignity, among whom happiness appears esentially as a narcotic, a deadening, a quietude, a peace, a "Sabbath," an enervation of the mind and relaxation of the limbs—in short, a purely *passive* phenomenon. While the aristocratic man lived in confidence and openness with himself (γενναῖος, "noble-born," emphasizes the nuance "sincere," and perhaps also "naïve"), the resentful man, on the other hand, is neither sincere nor naïve, nor honest and candid with himself. His soul *squints*: his mind loves hidden crannies, tortorous paths, and back doors, everything secret appeals to

him as *his* world, *his* safety, *his* balm; he is past master in
silence, in not forgetting, in waiting, in provisional self-
depreciation and self-abasement. A race of such *resentful*
men will of necessity eventually prove more *prudent* than any
aristocratic race, it will honor prudence on quite a distinct
scale, as, in fact, a paramount condition of existence, while
prudence among aristocratic men is apt to be tinged with a
delicate flavor of luxury and refinement; so among them it
plays nothing like so integral a part as that complete
certainty of function of the governing *unconscious* instincts,
or as indeed a certain lack of prudence, such as a vehement
and valiant charge, whether against danger or the enemy, or
as those ecstatic bursts of rage, love, reverence, gratitude,
by which at all times noble souls have recognized each other.
When the resentment of the aristocratic man manifests itself,
it fulfills and exhausts itself in an immediate reaction, and
consequently instills no *venom*: on the other hand, it never
manifests itself at all in countless instances, when in the case
of the feeble and weak it would be inevitable. An inability
to take seriously for any length of time their enemies, their
disasters, their *misdeeds*—that is the sign of the full strong
natures who possess a superfluity of molding plastic force,
that heals completely and produces forgetfulness: a good
example of this in the modern world is Mirabeau, who had
no memory for any insult and meannesses which were practiced on him, and who was only incapable of forgiving
because he forgot. Such a man indeed shakes off with a
shrug many a worm which would have buried itself in
another; it is only in characters like these that we see the
possibility (supposing, of course, that there is such a possibility in the world) of the real *"love* of one's enemies."
What respect for his enemies is found, forsooth, in an aristocratic man—and such a reverence is already a bridge to
love! He insists on having his enemy to himself as his distinction. He tolerates no other enemy but a man in whose
character there is nothing to despise and *much* to honor! On
the other hand, imagine the "enemy" as the resentful man
conceives him—and it is here exactly that we see his work,
his creativeness; he has conceived "the evil enemy," the
"evil one," and indeed that is the root idea from which he
now evolves as a contrasting and corresponding figure a
"good one," himself—his very self!

11

The method of this man is quite contrary to that of
the aristocratic man, who conceives the root idea "good"

spontaneously and straightaway, that is to say, out of himself, and from that material then creates for himself a concept of "bad"! This "bad" of aristocratic origin and that
"evil" out of the cauldron of unsatisfied hatred—the former
an imitation, an "extra," an additional nuance; the latter,
on the other hand, the original, the beginning, the essential act in the conception of the slave morality—these two
words "bad" and "evil," how great a difference do they mark,
in spite of the fact that they have an identical contrary in
the idea "good." But the idea "good" is *not* the same: much
rather let the question be asked, "Who is really evil according to the meaning of the morality of resentment?"
In all sternness let it be answered thus: *just* the good man of
the other morality, just the aristocrat, the powerful one, the
one who rules, but who is distorted by the venomous eye
of resentfulness, into a new color, a new signification, a
new appearance. This particular point we would be the last
to deny: the man who learned to know those "good" ones only
as enemies learned at the same time not to know them
only as *"evil enemies,"* rigorously in bounds through convention, respect, custom, and gratitude, though much more
through mutual vigilance and jealousy *inter pares*, these men
who in their relations with each other find so many new
ways of manifesting consideration, self-control, delicacy,
loyalty, pride and friendship, these men are in reference to
what is outside their circle (where the foreign element, a
foreign country, begins), not much better than beasts of
prey, which have been let loose. They enjoy there freedom
from all social control, they feel that in the wilderness they
can give vent with impunity to that tension which is produced by enclosure and imprisonment in the peace of society, they *revert* to the innocence of the beast-of-prey conscience, like jubilant monsters, who perhaps come from a
ghastly bout of murder, arson, rape, and torture, with bravado
and a moral equanimity as though merely some wild student's prank had been played, perfectly convinced that the
poets have now an ample theme to sing and celebrate. It
is impossible not to recognize at the core of all these aristocratic races the beast of prey; the magnificent *blonde brute*,
avidly rampant for spoil and victory; this hidden core
needed an outlet from time to time, the beast must get loose
again, must return into the wilderness—the Roman, Arabic,
German, and Japanese nobility, the Homeric heroes, the
Scandinavian Vikings, are all alike in this need. It is the
aristocratic races who have left the idea "Barbarian" on all
the tracks in which they have marched; nay, a conscious-

ness of this very barbarianism, and even a pride in it, manifests itself even in their highest civilization (for example, when Pericles says to his Athenians in that celebrated funeral oration, "Our audacity has forced a way over every land and sea, rearing everywhere imperishable memorials of itself for good and for evil"). This audacity of aristocratic races, mad, absurd, and spasmodic as may be its expression; the incalculable and fantastic nature of their enterprises Pericles sets in special relief and glory the ῥαθυμία of the Athenians, their nonchalance and contempt for safety, body, life, and comfort, their awful joy and intense delight in all destruction, in all the ecstasies of victory and cruelty— all these features become crystallized for those who suffered thereby in the picture of the "barbarian," of the "evil enemy," perhaps of the "Goth" and of the "Vandal." The profound, icy mistrust which the German provokes, as soon as he arrives at power—even at the present time—is always still an aftermath of that inextinguishable horror with which for whole centuries Europe has regarded the wrath of the blonde Teuton beast (although between the old German and ourselves there exists scarcely a psychological, let alone a physical, relationship). I have once called attention to the embarrassment of Hesiod, when he conceived the series of social ages, and endeavored to express them in gold, silver, and bronze. He could only dispose of the contradiction, with which he was confronted, by the Homeric world, an age magnificent indeed, but at the same time so awful and so violent, by making two ages out of one, which he henceforth placed one behind each other —first, the age of the heroes and demigods, as that world had remained in the memories of the aristocratic families, who found therein their own ancestors; secondly, the bronze age, as that corresponding age appeared to the descendants of the oppressed, spoiled, ill-treated, exiled, enslaved; namely, as an age of bronze, as I have said, hard, cold, terrible, without feelings and without conscience, crushing everything, and bespattering everything with blood. Granted the truth of the theory now believed to be true, that the very *essence of all civilization* is to *train* out of man, the beast of prey, a tame and civilized animal, a domesticated animal, it follows indubitably that we must regard as the real *tools of civilization* all those instincts of reaction and resentment, by the help of which the aristocratic races, together with their ideals, were finally degraded and overpowered; though that has not yet come to be synonymous with saying that the bearers of those tools also *represented* the civilization. It is rather the contrary that is not only probable—nay, it is *palpable* today; these bearers of vindictive instincts that have to be bottled up, these descendants of all European and non-European slavery, especially of the pre-Aryan population—these people, I say, represent the *decline* of humanity! These "tools of civilization" are a disgrace to humanity, and constitute in reality more of an argument against civilization, more of a reason why civilization should be suspected. One may be perfectly justified in being always afraid of the blonde beast that lies at the core of all aristocratic races, and in being on one's guard: but who would not a hundred times prefer to be afraid, when one at the same time admires, than to be immune from fear, at the cost of being perpetually obsessed with the loathsome spectacle of the distorted, the dwarfed, the stunted, the envenomed? And is that not our fate? What produces today our repulsion toward "man"? —for we *suffer* from "man," there is no doubt about it. It is not fear; it is rather that we have nothing more to fear from men; it is that the worm "man" is in the foreground and pullulates; it is that the "tame man," the wretched mediocre and unedifying creature, has learned to consider himself a goal and a pinnacle, an inner meaning, an historic principle, a "higher man"; yes, it is that he has a certain right so to consider himself, insofar as he feels that in contrast to that excess of deformity, disease, exhaustion, and effeteness whose odor is beginning to pollute present-day Europe, he at any rate has achieved a relative success, he at any rate still says "yes" to life.

FROM THE TWILIGHT OF THE IDOLS

Morality as the Enemy of Nature

1

THERE is a time when all passions are simply fatal in their action, when they wreck their victims with the weight of their folly—and there is a later period, a very much later period, when they marry with the spirit, when they "spiritualize" themselves. Formerly, owing to the stupidity inherent in passion, men waged war against passion itself: men pledged themselves to annihilate it—all ancient moralmongers were unanimous on this point, *"il faut tuer les passions.*" The most famous formula for this stands in the New Testament, in that Sermon on the Mount, where, let it be said incidentally, things are by no means regarded *from a height*. It is said there, for instance, with an application to sexuality; "if thy eye offend thee, pluck it out"; fortunately no Christian acts in obedience to this precept. To annihilate the passions and desires, simply on account of their stupidity, and to obviate the unpleasant consequences of their stupidity, seems to us today merely an aggravated form of stupidity. We no longer admire those dentists who extract teeth simply in order that they may not ache again. On the other hand, it will be admitted with some reason, that on the soil from which Christianity grew, the idea of the "spiritualization of passion" could not possibly have been conceived. The early Church, as everyone knows, certainly did wage war against the "intelligent," in favor of the "poor in spirit." In these circumstances how could the passions be combated intelligently? The Church combats passion by means of excision of all kinds: its practice, its "remedy," is *castration*. It never inquires "how can a desire be spiritualized, beautified, deified?"—In all ages it has laid the weight of discipline in the process of extirpation (the extirpation of sensuality, pride, lust of dominion, lust of property, and revenge).—But to attack the passions at their roots means attacking life itself at its source: the method of the Church is hostile to life.

5

Admitting that you have understood the villainy of such a mutiny against life as that which has become almost sacrosanct in Christian morality, you have fortunately understood something besides; and that is the futility, the fictitiousness, the absurdity and the falseness of such a mutiny. For the condemnation of life by a living creature is after all but the symptom of a definite kind of life: the question as to whether the condemnation is justified or the reverse is not even raised. In order even to approach the problem of the value of life, a man would need to be placed outside life, and moreover know it as well as one, as many, as all in fact, who have lived it. These are reasons enough to prove to us that this problem is an inaccessible one to us. When we speak of values, we speak under the inspiration, and through the optics of life: life itself urges us to determine values: life itself values through us when we determine values. From which it follows that even that morality which is antagonistic to life, and which conceives God as the opposite and the condemnation of life, is only a valuation of life—of what life? of what kind of life? But I have already answered this question: it is the valuation of declining, of enfeebled, of exhausted, and of condemned life. Morality, as it has been understood hitherto—as it was finally formulated by Schopenhauer in the words "the Denial of the Will to Life"—is the instinct of degeneration itself, which converts itself into an imperative: it says: "Perish!" It is the death sentence of men who are already doomed.

6

Let us at last consider how exceedingly simple it is on our part to say: "Man should be thus and thus!" Reality shows us a marvelous wealth of types, and a luxuriant variety of forms and changes: and yet the first wretch of a moral loafer that comes along cries "No! Man should be different!" He even knows what man should be like, does this sanctimonious prig: he draws his own face on the wall and declares: "*ecce homo!*" But even when the moralist addresses himself only to the individual and says "thus and thus shouldst thou be!" he still makes an ass of himself. The individual in his past and future is a piece of fate, one law the more, one necessity the more for all that is to come and is to be. To say to him "change thyself," is tantamount to saying that everything should change, even backward as well. Truly these have been consistent moralists, they wished man to be different, i.e., virtuous; they wished him to be after their own image—that is to say sanctimonious humbugs. And to this end they denied the world! No slight form of insanity! No modest form of immodesty! Morality, insofar as it condemns per se, and *not* out of any aim, consideration, or motive of life, is a specific error, for which no one should feel any mercy, a degenerate idiosyncrasy, that has done an unutterable amount of harm. We others, we immoralists, on the contrary, have opened our hearts wide to all kinds of comprehension, understanding, and approbation. * We do not deny readily, we glory in saying yea to things. Our eyes have opened ever wider

* Cf. Spinoza, who says in the *Tractatus politicus* (1677), Chap. I, § 4: "*Sedulo curavi, humanas actiones non ridere, non lugere, neque detestari, sed intelligere*" ("I have carefully endeavored not to deride, or deplore, or detest human actions, but to understand them").—Tr.

and wider to that economy which still employs and knows how to use to its own advantage all that which the sacred craziness of priests and the morbid reason in priests rejects; to that economy in the law of life which draws its own advantage even out of the repulsive race of bigots, the priests and the virtuous—what advantage?—But we ourselves, we immoralists, are the reply to this question.

The Four Great Errors

1

THE ERROR OF THE CONFUSION OF CAUSE AND EFFECT. There is no more dangerous error than to confound the effect with the cause: I call this error the intrinsic perversion of reason. Nevertheless this error is one of the most ancient and most recent habits of mankind. In one part of the world it has even been canonized, and it bears the name of "Religion" and "Morality." Every postulate formulated by religion and morality contains it. Priests and the promulgators of moral laws are the promoters of this perversion of reason. Let me give you an example. Everybody knows the book of the famous Cornaro, in which he recommends his slender diet as the recipe for a long, happy, and also virtuous life. Few books have been so widely read, and to this day many thousand copies of it are still printed annually in England. I do not doubt that there is scarcely a single book (the Bible of course excepted) that has worked more mischief, shortened more lives, than this well-meant curiosity. The reason for this is the confusion of effect and cause. This worthy Italian saw the cause of his long life in his diet: whereas the prerequisites of long life, which are exceptional slowness of molecular change, and a low rate of expenditure in energy, were the cause of his meager diet. He was not at liberty to eat a small or a great amount. His frugality was not the result of free choice, he would have been ill had he eaten more. He who does not happen to be a carp, however, is not only wise to eat well, but is also compelled to do so. A scholar of the present day, with his rapid consumption of nervous energy, would soon go to the dogs on Cornaro's diet. *Crede experto.*

2

The most general principle lying at the root of every religion and morality is this: "Do this and that and avoid this and that—and thou wilt be happy. Otherwise—." Every morality and every religion is this Imperative—I call it the great original sin of reason, *immortal unreason*. In my mouth this principle is converted into its opposite—first example of my "Transvaluation of all Values": a well-constituted man, a man who is one of "Nature's lucky strokes," *must* perform certain actions and instinctively fear other actions; he introduces the element of order, of which he is the physiological manifestation, into his relations with men and things. In a formula: his virtue is the consequence of his good constitution. Longevity and plentiful offspring are not the reward of virtue, virtue itself is on the contrary that retardation of the metabolic process which, among other things, results in a long life and in plentiful offspring, in short, in *Cornarism*. The Church and morality say: "A race, a people perish through vice and luxury." My reinstated reason says: when a people are going to the dogs, when they are degenerating physiologically, vice and luxury (that is to say, the need of ever stronger and more frequent stimuli such as all exhausted natures are acquainted with) are bound to result. Such and such a young man grows pale and withered prematurely. His friends say this or that illness is the cause of it. I say: the fact that he became ill, the fact that he did not resist illness, was in itself already the outcome of impoverished life, of hereditary exhaustion. The newspaper reader says: such and such a party by committing such an error will meet its death. My superior politics say: a party that can make such mistakes is in its last agony —it no longer possesses any certainty of instinct. Every mistake is in every sense the sequel to degeneration of the instincts, to disintegration of the will. This is almost the definition of evil. Everything valuable is instinct—and consequently easy, necessary, free. Exertion is an objection, the god is characteristically different from the hero (in my language: light feet are the first attribute of divinity).

3

THE ERROR OF FALSE CAUSALITY. In all ages men

have believed that they knew what a cause was, but whence did we derive this knowledge, or more accurately, this faith in the fact that we know? Out of the realm of the famous "inner facts of consciousness," not one of which has yet proved itself to be a fact. We believed ourselves to be causes even in the action of the will; we thought that in this matter at least we caught causality red-handed. No one doubted that all the *antecedentia* of an action were to be sought in consciousness, and could be discovered there—as "motive"—if only they were sought. Otherwise we should not have been free to perform them, we should not have been responsible for them. Finally who would have questioned that a thought is caused, that the ego causes the thought? Of these three "facts of inner consciousness" by means of which causality seemed to be guaranteed, the first and most convincing is that of the will as cause; the conception of consciousness ("spirit") as a cause, and subsequently that of the ego (the "subject") as a cause, were merely born afterward, once the causality of the will stood established as "given," as a fact of experience. Meanwhile we have come to our senses. Today we no longer believe a word of all this. The "inner world" is full of phantoms and will-o'-the-wisps: the will is one of these. The will no longer actuates, consequently it no longer explains anything—all it does is to accompany processes; it may even be absent. The so-called "motive" is another error. It is merely a ripple on the surface of consciousness, a side issue of the action, which is much more likely to conceal than to reveal the *antecedentia* of the latter. And as for the ego! It has become legendary, fictional, a play upon words: it has ceased utterly and completely from thinking, feeling, and willing! What is the result of it all? There are no such things as spiritual causes. The whole of popular experience on this subject went to the devil! That is the result of it all. For we had blissfully abused that experience, we had built the world upon it as a world of causes, as a world of will, as a world of spirit. The most antiquated and most traditional psychology has been at work here, it has done nothing else: all phenomena were deeds in the light of this psychology, and all deeds were the result of will; according to it the world was a complex mechanism of agents, an agent (a "subject") lay at the root of all things. Man projected his three "inner facts of consciousness," the will, the spirit, and the ego in which he believed most firmly, outside himself. He first deduced the concept Being out of the concept Ego, he supposed "things" to exist as he did himself, according to his notion of the ego as cause. Was it to be wondered at that later on he always found in things only that which he had laid in them?—The thing itself, I repeat, the concept thing was merely a reflex of the belief in the ego as cause. And even your atom, my dear good Mechanists and Physicists, what an amount of error, of rudimentary psychology still adheres to it!—Not to speak of the "thing-in-itself," of the *horrendum pudendum* of the metaphysicians! The error of spirit regarded as a cause, confounded with reailty! And made the measure of reality! And called *God!*

4

THE ERROR OF IMAGINARY CAUSES. Starting out from dreamland, we find that to any definite sensation, like that produced by a distant cannon shot for instance, we are wont to ascribe a cause after the fact (very often quite a little romance in which the dreamer himself is, of course, the hero). Meanwhile the sensation becomes protracted like a sort of continuous echo, until, as it were, the instinct of causality allows it to come to the front rank, no longer, however, as a chance occurrence, but as a thing which has some meaning. The cannon shot presents itself in a *causal* manner, by means of an apparent reversal in the order of time. That which occurs last, the motivation, is experienced first, often with a hundred details which scramble past like lightning, and the shot is the *result*. What has happened? The ideas suggested by a particular state of our senses are misinterpreted as the cause of that state. As a matter of fact we proceed in precisely the same manner when we are awake. The greater number of our general sensations—every kind of obstacle, pressure, tension, explosion in the interplay of the organs, and more particularly the condition of the *nervus sympathicus*—stimulate our instinct of causality: we will have a reason which will account for our feeling thus or thus—for feeling ill or well. We are never satisfied by merely ascertaining the fact that we feel thus or thus: we admit this fact—we become conscious of it—only when we have attributed it to some kind of motivation. Memory, which, in such circumstances unconsciously becomes active, adduces former conditions of a like kind, together with the causal interpretations with which they are associated—but not their real cause. The belief that the ideas, the accompanying processes of consciousness, have been the causes, is certainly produced by the agency of memory. And in this way we become *accustomed* to a particular interpretation of causes which, truth to tell, actually hinders and even utterly prevents the investigation of the proper cause.

5

THE PSYCHOLOGICAL EXPLANATION OF THE ABOVE FACT. To trace something unfamiliar back to something familiar is at once a relief, a comfort, and a satisfaction, while it also produces a feeling of power. The unfamiliar involves danger, anxiety, and care—the fundamental instinct is to get rid of these painful circumstances. First principle: any explanation is better than none at all. Since, at bottom, it is only a question of shaking one's self free from certain oppressive ideas, the means employed to this end are not selected with overmuch punctiliousness: the first idea by means of which the unfamiliar is revealed as familiar produces a feeling of such comfort that it is "held to be true." The proof of happiness ("of power") as the criterion of truth. The instinct of causality is therefore conditioned and stimulated by the feeling of fear. Whenever possible, the question "why?" should not only educe the cause as cause, but rather a certain kind of cause—a comforting, liberating, and reassuring cause. The first result of this need is that something known or already experienced, and recorded in the memory, is posited as the cause. The new factor, that which has not been experienced and which is unfamiliar, is excluded from the sphere of causes. Not only do we try to find a certain kind of explanation as the cause, but those kinds of explanations are selected and preferred which dissipate most rapidly the sensation of strangeness, novelty and unfamiliarity—in fact the most ordinary explanations. And the result is that a certain manner of postulating causes tends to predominate ever more and more, becomes concentrated into a system, and finally reigns supreme, to the complete exclusion of all other causes and explanations. The banker thinks immediately of business, the Christian of "sin," and the girl of her love affair.

6

THE WHOLE DOMAIN OF MORALITY AND RELIGION MAY BE CLASSIFIED UNDER THE RUBRIC "IMAGINARY CAUSES." The "explanation" of general unpleasant sensations. These sensations are dependent upon certain creatures who are hostile to us (evil spirits: the most famous example of this—the mistaking of hysterical women for witches). These sensations are dependent upon actions which are reprehensible (the feeling of "sin," "sinfulness" is a manner of accounting for a certain physiological disorder —people always find reasons for being dissatisfied with themselves). These sensations depend upon punishment, upon the paying off of something which we ought not to have done, which we ought not to have been (this idea was generalized in a more impudent form by Schopenhauer, into that principle in which morality appears in its real colors, that is to say, as a veritable poisoner and slanderer of life: "All great suffering, whether mental or physical, reveals what we deserve: for it could not visit us if we did not deserve it,"—*The World as Will and Idea*, Vol. 2, p. 666). These sensations are the outcome of ill-considered actions, having evil consequences—the passions, the senses, postulated as causes, as guilty. By means of other calamities distressing physiological conditions are interpreted as "merited."—The "explanation" of pleasant sensations. These sensations are dependent upon a trust in God. They may depend upon our consciousness of having done one or two good actions (a so-called "good conscience" is a physiological condition, which may be the outcome of good digestion). They may depend upon the happy issue of certain undertakings (an ingenuous mistake: the happy issue of an undertaking certainly does not give a hypochondriac or a Pascal any general sensation of pleasure). They may depend upon faith, love and hope—the Christian virtues. As a matter of fact all these pretended explanations are but the results of certain states, and, as it were, translations of feelings of pleasure and pain into a false dialect: a man is in a condition of hopefulness because the dominant physiological sensation of his being is again one of strength and wealth; he trusts in God because the feeling of abundance and power gives him a peaceful state of mind. Morality and religion are completely and utterly parts of the psychology of error: in every particular case cause and effect are confounded; as truth is confounded with the effect of that which is believed to be true; or a certain state of consciousness is confounded with the chain of causes which brought it about.

7

THE ERROR OF FREE WILL. At present we no longer have any mercy upon the concept "free will": we

know only too well what it is—the most egregious theological
trick that has ever existed for the purpose of making mankind "responsible" in a theological manner, that is to say,
to make mankind dependent upon theologians. I will now
explain to you only the psychology of the whole process of
inculcating the sense of responsibility. Wherever men try to
trace responsibility home to anyone, it is the instinct of
punishment and of the desire to judge which is active. Becoming is robbed of its innocence when any particular condition of things is traced to a will, to intentions and to responsible actions. The doctrine of the will was invented
principally for the purpose of punishment, that is to say, with
the intention of tracing guilt. The whole of ancient psychology, or the psychology of the will, is the outcome of the
fact that its originators, who were the priests at the head of
ancient communities, wanted to create for themselves a
right to administer punishments—or the right for God to do
so. Men were thought of as "free" in order that they might
be judged and punished—in order that they might be held
guilty: consequently every action had to be regarded as volu-
tary, and the origin of every action had to be imagined as
lying in consciousness (in this way the most fundamentally
fraudulent character of psychology was established as the
very principle of psychology itself). Now that we have entered upon the opposite movement, now that we immoralists are trying with all our power to eliminate the concepts
of guilt and punishment from the world once more, and to
cleanse psychology, history, nature, and all social institutions
and customs of all signs of those two concepts, we recognize no more radical opponents than the theologians,
who with their notion of "a moral order of things" still
continue to pollute the innocence of Becoming with punishment and guilt. Christianity is the metaphysics of the hangman.

8

What then, alone, can our teaching be?—That no one
gives man his qualities, neither God, society, his parents,
his ancestors, nor himself (this nonsensical idea, which is
at last refuted here, was taught as "intelligible freedom"
by Kant, and perhaps even as early as Plato himself). No
one is responsible for the fact that he exists at all, that he
is constituted as he is, and that he happens to be in certain
circumstances and in a particular environment. The fatality

of his being cannot be divorced from the fatality of all that
which has been and will be. This is not the result of an
individual attention, of a will, of an aim, there is no attempt at attaining to any "ideal man," or "ideal happiness"
or "ideal morality" with him—it is absurd to wish him to
be careering toward some sort of purpose. *We* invented the
concept "purpose"; in reality purpose is altogether lacking.
One is necessary, one is a piece of fate, one belongs to the
whole, one is in the whole—there is nothing that could
judge, measure, compare, and condemn our existence, for
that would mean judging, measuring, comparing and condemning the whole. *But there is nothing outside the whole!* The
fact that no one shall any longer be made responsible, that
the nature of existence may not be traced to a *causa prima,*
that the world is an entity neither as a sensorium nor as a
spirit—*this alone is the great deliverance*—thus alone is the
innocence of Becoming restored. . . . The concept "God" has
been the greatest objection to existence hitherto. . . . We
deny God, we deny responsibility in God: thus alone do we
save the world.

36

A MORAL FOR DOCTORS. The sick man is a parasite of society. In certain cases it is indecent to go on
living. To continue to vegetate in a state of cowardly dependence upon doctors and special treatments, once the meaning
of life, the right to life, has been lost ought to be regarded
with the greatest contempt by society. The doctors, for their
part, should be the agents for imparting this contempt—they
should no longer prepare prescriptions, but should every day
administer a fresh dose of *disgust* to their patients. A new
responsibility should be created, that of the doctor—the
responsibility of ruthlessly suppressing and eliminating *degenerate* life, in all cases in which the highest interests of life
itself, of ascending life, demand such a course—for instance in favor of the right of procreation, in favor of the
right of being born, in favor of the right to live. One should
die proudly when it is no longer possible to live proudly.
Death should be chosen freely—death at the right time,
faced clearly and joyfully and embraced while one is surrounded by one's children and other witnesses. It should be
effected in such a way that a proper farewell is still possible, that he who is about to take leave of us is still *himself,* and really capable not only of valuing what he has

achieved and willed in life but also of *summing up* the value of life itself. Everything precisely the opposite of the ghastly comedy which Christianity has made of the hour of death. We should never forgive Christianity for having so abused the weakness of the dying man as to do violence to his conscience, or for having used his manner of dying as a means of valuing both man and his past!—In spite of all cowardly prejudices, it is our duty, in this respect, above all to reinstate the proper—that is to say, the physiological, aspect of so-called *natural* death, which after all is perfectly "unnatural" and nothing else than suicide. One never perishes through anybody's fault but one's own. The only thing is that the death which takes place in the most contemptible circumstances, the death that is not free, the death which occurs at the wrong time, is the death of a coward. Out of the very love one bears to life, one should wish death to be different from this—that is to say, free, deliberate, and neither a matter of chance nor of surprise. Finally let me whisper a word of advice to our friends the pessimists and all other decadents. We have not the power to prevent ourselves from being born, but this error—for sometimes it is an error—can be rectified if we choose. The man who does away with himself performs the most estimable of deeds; he almost deserves to live for having done so. Society—nay, life itself—derives more profit from such a deed than from any sort of life spent in renunciation, anemia, and other virtues—at least the suicide frees others from the sight of him, at least he removes one objection against life. Pessimism *pur et vert* can *be proved only* by the self-refutation of the pessimists themselves: one should go a step further in one's consistency; one should not merely deny life with "The World as Will and Idea," as Schopenhauer did; one should in the first place *deny Schopenhauer*. . . . Incidentally, pessimism, however infectious it may be, does not increase the morbidness of an age as of a whole species; it is rather the expression of that morbidness. One falls a victim to it in the same way as one falls a victim to cholera; one must already be predisposed to the disease. Pessimism in itself does not increase the number of the world's *decadents* by a single unit. Let me remind you of the statistical fact that in those years in which cholera rages, the total number of deaths does not exceed that of other years.

FROM THE ANTICHRIST*

2

What is good?—All that enhances the feeling of power, the Will to Power, and power itself in man. What is bad? —All that proceeds from weakness. What is happiness? —The feeling that power is *increasing*—that resistance has been overcome.

Not contentment, but more power; not peace at any price, but war; not virtue, but efficiency† (virtue in the Renaissance sense, *virtù*, free from all moralic acid). The weak and the botched shall perish: first principle of our humanity. And they ought even to be helped to perish.

What is more harmful than any vice?—Practical sympathy with all the botched and the weak—Christianity.

6

A painful and ghastly spectacle has just risen before my eyes. I tore down the curtain which concealed mankind's *corruption*. This word in my mouth is at least secure from the suspicion that it contains a moral charge against mankind. It is—I would fain emphasize this again—free from moralic acid: to such an extent is this so, that I am most thoroughly conscious of the corruption in question precisely in those quarters in which hitherto people have aspired with most determination to "virtue" and to "godliness." As you have already surmised, I understand corruption in the sense of *decadence*. What I maintain is this, that all the values upon which mankind builds its highest hopes and desires are *decadent* values.

I call an animal, a species, an individual corrupt when it loses its instincts, when it selects and *prefers* that which is detrimental to it. A history of the "higher feelings," of "human ideals"—and it is not impossible that I shall have to write it—would almost explain why man is so corrupt.

---

* From *The Twilight of the Idols*.

† The German *Tüchtigkeit* has a nobler ring than our word "efficiency."—Tr.

Life itself, to my mind, is nothing more nor less than the instinct of growth, of permanence, of accumulating forces, of power: where the will to power is lacking, degeneration sets in. My contention is that all the highest values of mankind *lack* this will—that the values of decline and of *nihilism* are exercising the sovereign power under the cover of the holiest names.

13

Do not let us undervalue the fact that we *ourselves,* we free spirits, are already a "transvaluation of all values," an incarnate declaration of war against all the old concepts "true" and "untrue" and of a triumph over them. The most valuable standpoints are always the last to be found, but the most valuable standpoints are the methods. All the methods and the first principles of our modern scientific procedure had for years to encounter the profoundest contempt: association with them meant exclusion from the society of decent people—one was regarded as an "enemy of God," as a scoffer at truth, and as "one possessed." With one's scientific nature, one belonged to the chandala. We have had the whole pathos of mankind against us; hitherto their notion of that which ought to be truth, of that which ought to serve the purpose of truth, every "thou shalt," has been directed against us. . . . Our objects, our practices, our calm, cautious distrustful manner—everything about us seemed to them absolutely despicable and beneath contempt. After all, it might be asked with some justice, whether the thing which kept mankind blindfolded so long, were not an aesthetic taste: what they demanded of truth was a *picturesque* effect, and from the man of science what they expected was that he should make a forcible appeal to their senses. It was our *modesty* which ran counter to their taste so long. . . And oh! how well they guessed this, did these divine turkey cocks!

14

We have altered our standpoint. In every respect we have become more modest. We no longer derive man from the "spirit," and from the "godhead"; we have thrust him back among the beasts. We regard him as the strongest animal because he is the craftiest: one of the results thereof is his intellectuality. On the other hand we guard against the vain pretension, which even here would fain assert itself, that man is the great *arrière pensée* of organic evolution! He is by no means the crown of creation, beside him, every other creature stands at the same stage of perfection. . . . And even in asserting this we go a little too far; for, relatively speaking, man is the most botched and diseased of animals, and he has wandered furthest from his instincts. Be all this as it may, he is certainly the most *interesting*! As regards animals, Descartes was the first, with really admirable daring, to venture the thought that the beast was *machina,* and the whole of our physiology is endeavoring to prove this proposition. Moreover, logically we do not set man apart, as Descartes did: the extent to which man is understood today goes only so far as he has been understood mechanistically. Formerly man was given "free will," as his dowry from a higher sphere; nowadays we have robbed him even of will, in view of the fact that no such faculty is any longer known. The only purpose served by the old word "will" is to designate a result, a sort of individual reaction which necessarily follows upon a host of partly discordant and partly harmonious stimuli: the will no longer "effects" or "moves" anything. . . . Formerly people thought that man's consciousness, his "spirit," was a proof of his lofty origin, of his divinity. With the idea of perfecting man, he was conjured to draw his senses inside himself, after the manner of the tortoise, to cut off all relations with terrestrial things, and to divest himself of his mortal shell. Then the most important thing about him, the "pure spirit," would remain over. Even concerning these things we have improved our standpoint. Consciousness, "spirit," now seem to us rather a symptom of relative imperfection in the organism, as an experiment, a groping, a misapprehension, an affliction which absorbs an unnecessary quantity of nervous energy. We deny that anything can be done perfectly so long as it is done consciously. "Pure spirit" is a piece of "pure stupidity": if we discount the nervous system, the senses, and the "mortal shell," we have miscalculated—that it is all! . . .

FROM THUS SPAKE ZARATHUSTRA

Zarathustra's Prologue

1

When Zarathustra was thirty years old, he left his home and the lake of his home, and went into the mountains. There he enjoyed his spirit and his solitude, and for ten years did not weary of it. But at last his heart changed, and rising one morning with the rosy dawn, he went before the sun, and spake thus unto it:

Thou great star! What would be thy happiness if thou hadst not those for whom thou shinest!

For ten years hast thou climbed hither unto my cave: thou wouldst have wearied of thy light and of the journey, had it not been for me, mine eagle, and my serpent.

But we awaited thee every morning, took from thee thine overflow, and blessed thee for it.

Lo! I am weary of my wisdom, like the bee that hath gathered too much honey; I need hands outstretched to take it.

I would fain bestow and distribute, until the wise have once more become joyous in their folly, and the poor happy in their riches.

Therefore must I descend into the deep: as thou doest in the evening, when thou goest behind the sea, and givest light also to the nether world, thou exuberant star!

Like thee must I *go down,* as men say, to whom I shall descend.

Bless me, then, thou tranquil eye, that canst behold even the greatest happiness without envy!

Bless the cup that is about to overflow, that the water may flow golden out of it, and carry everywhere the reflection of thy bliss!

Lo! This cup is again going to empty itself, and Zarathustra is again going to be a man.

Thus began Zarathustra's downgoing.

2

Zarathustra went down the mountain alone, no one meeting him. When he entered the forest, however, there suddenly stood before him an old man, who had left his holy cot to seek roots. And thus spake the old man to Zarathustra:

"No stranger to me is this wanderer: many years ago passed he by. Zarathustra he was called; but he hath altered.

Then thou carriedst thine ashes into the mountains: wilt thou now carry thy fire into the valleys? Fearest thou not the incendiary's doom?

Yea, I recognize Zarathustra. Pure is his eye, and no loathing lurketh about his mouth. Goeth he not along like a dancer?

Altered is Zarathustra; a child hath Zarathustra become; an awakened one is Zarathustra: what wilt thou do in the land of the sleepers?

As in the sea hast thou lived in solitude, and it hath borne thee up. Alas, wilt thou now go ashore? Alas, wilt thou again drag thy body thyself?"

Zarathustra answered: "I love mankind."

"Why," said the saint, "Did I go into the forest and the desert? Was it not because I loved men far too well?

Now I love God: men, I do not love. Man is a thing too imperfect for me. Love to man would be fatal to me."

Zarathustra answered: "What spake I of love! I am bringing gifts unto men."

"Give them nothing," said the saint. "Take rather part of their load, and carry it along with them—that will be most agreeable unto them: if only it be agreeable unto thee!

If, however, thou wilt give unto them, give them no more than an alms, and let them also beg for it!"

"No," replied Zarathustra, "I give no alms. I am not poor enough for that."

The saint laughed at Zarathustra, and spake thus: "Then see to it that they accept thy treasures! They are distrustful of anchorites, and do not believe that we come with gifts.

The fall of our footsteps ringeth too hollow through their streets. And just as at night, when they are in bed and hear a man abroad long before sunrise, so they ask themselves concerning us: Where goeth the thief?

Go not to men, but stay in the forest! Go rather to the animals! Why not be like me—a bear amongst bears, a bird amongst birds?"

"And what doeth the saint in the forest?" asked Zarathustra.

The saint answered: "I make hymns and sing them; and in making hymns I laugh and weep and mumble: thus do I praise God.

With singing, weeping, laughing, and mumbling do I praise the God who is my God. But what dost thou bring us as a gift?"

When Zarathustra had heard these words, he bowed to the saint and said: "What should I have to give thee! Let me rather hurry hence lest I take aught away from thee!"—And thus they parted from one another, the old man and Zarathustra, laughing like schoolboys.

When Zarathustra was alone, however, he said to his heart: "Could it be possible! This old saint in the forest hath not yet heard of it, that *God is dead!*"

3

When Zarathustra arrived at the nearest town which adjoineth the forest, he found many people assembled in the market place; for it had been announced that a ropedancer would give a performance. And Zarathustra spake thus unto the people:

I teach you the Superman. Man is something that is to be surpassed. What have ye done to surpass man?

All beings hitherto have created something beyond themselves: and ye want to be the ebb of that great tide, and would rather go back to the beast than surpass man?

What is the ape to man? A laughingstock, a thing of shame. And just the same shall man be to the Superman: a laughingstock, a thing of shame.

Ye have made your way from the worm to man, and much within you is still worm. Once were ye apes, and even yet man is more of an ape than any of the apes.

Even the wisest among you is only a disharmony and hybrid of plant and phantom. But do I bid you become phantoms or plants?

Lo! I teach you the Superman!

The Superman is the meaning of the earth. Let your will say: The Superman *shall be* the meaning of the earth!

I conjure you, my brethren, *remain true to the earth,* and believe not those who speak unto you of superearthly hopes! Poisoners are they, whether they know it or not.

Despisers of life are they, decaying ones and poisoned ones themselves, of whom the earth is weary: so away with them!

Once blasphemy against God was the greatest blasphemy, but God died, and therewith also those blasphemers. To blaspheme the earth is now the dreadfulest sin, and to rate the heart of the unknowable higher than the meaning of the earth!

Once the soul looked contemptuously on the body, and then that contempt was the supreme thing: the soul wished the body meager, ghastly, and famished. Thus it thought to escape from the body and the earth.

Oh, that soul was itself meager, ghastly and famished; and cruelty was the delight of that soul!

But ye, also, my brethren, tell me: What doth your body say about your soul? Is your soul not poverty and pollution and wretched self-complacency?

Verily, a polluted stream is man. One must be a sea to receive a polluted stream without becoming impure.

Lo, I teach you the Superman: he is that sea; in him can your great contempt be submerged.

What is the greatest thing ye can experience? It is the hour of great contempt. The hour in which even your happiness becometh loathsome unto you, and so also your reason and virtue.

The hour when ye say: "What good is my happiness! It is poverty and pollution and wretched self-complacency. But my happiness should justify existence itself!"

The hour when ye say: "What good is my reason! Doth it long for knowledge as the lion for his food? It is poverty and pollution and wretched self-complacency!"

The hour when ye say: "What good is my virtue! As yet it hath not made me passionate. How weary I am of my good and my bad! It is all poverty and pollution and wretched self-complacency!"

The hour when ye say: "What good is my pity! Is not see that I am fervor and fuel. The just, however, are fervor and fuel!"

The hour when we say: "What good is my pity! Is not pity the cross on which he is nailed who loveth man? But my pity is not a crucifixion."

Have ye ever spoken thus? Have ye ever cried thus? Ah! would that I had heard you crying thus!

It is not your sin—it is your self-satisfaction that crieth unto heaven; your very sparingness in sin crieth unto heaven!

Where is the lightning to lick you with its tongue? Where is the frenzy with which ye should be inoculated?

Lo, I teach you the Superman: he is that lightning, he is that frenzy!—

When Zarathustra had thus spoken, one of the people called out: "We have now heard enough of the ropedancer; it is time now for us to see him!" And all the people laughed at Zarathustra. But the ropedancer, who thought the words applied to him, began his performance.

4

Zarathustra, however, looked at the people and wondered. Then he spake thus:

Man is a rope stretched between the animal and the Superman—a rope over an abyss.

A dangerous crossing, a dangerous wayfaring, a dangerous looking-back, a dangerous trembling and halting.

What is great in man is that he is a bridge and not a goal: what is lovable in man is that he is an *overgoing* and a *downgoing*.

I love those that know not how to live except as downgoers, for they are the overgoers.

I love the great despisers, because they are the great adorers, and arrows of longing for the other shore.

I love those who do not first seek a reason beyond the stars for going down and being sacrifices, but sacrifice themselves to the earth, that the earth of the Superman may hereafter arrive.

I love him who liveth in order to know, and seeketh to know in order that the Superman may hereafter live. Thus seeketh he his own downgoing.

I love him who laboreth and inventeth, that he may build the house for the Superman, and prepare for him earth, animal, and plant: for thus seeketh he his own downgoing.

I love him who loveth his virtue: for virtue is the will to downgoing, and an arrow of longing.

I love him who reserveth no share of spirit for himself, but wanteth to be wholly the spirit of his virtue: thus walketh he as spirit over the bridge.

I love him who maketh his virtue his inclination and destiny: thus, for the sake of his virtue, he is willing to live on, or live no more.

I love him who desireth not too many virtues. One virtue is more of a virtue than two, because it is more of a knot for one's destiny to cling to.

I love him whose soul is lavish, who wanteth no thanks and doth not give back: for he always bestoweth, and desireth not to keep for himself.

I love him who is ashamed when the dice fall in his favor, and who then asketh: "Am I a dishonest player?"— for he is willing to succumb.

I love him who scattereth golden words in advance of his deeds, and always doeth more than he promiseth: for he seeketh his own downgoing.

I love him who justifieth the future ones, and redeemeth the past ones: for he is willing to succumb through the present ones.

I love him who chasteneth his God, because he loveth his God: for he must succumb through the wrath of his God.

I love him whose soul is deep even in the wounding, and may succumb through a small matter: thus goeth he willingly over the bridge.

I love him whose soul is so overfull that he forgetteth himself, and all things are in him: thus all things become his downgoing.

I love him who is of a free spirit and a free heart: thus is his head only the bowels of his heart; his heart, however, causeth his downgoing.

I love all who are like heavy drops falling one by one out of the dark cloud that lowereth over man: they herald the coming of the lightning, and succumb as heralds.

Lo, I am a herald of the lightning, and a heavy drop out of the cloud: the lightning, however, is the *Superman*.

5

When Zarathustra had spoken these words, he again looked at the people, and was silent. "There they stand," said he to his heart; "there they laugh: they understand me not; I am not the mouth for these ears.

Must one first batter their ears, that they may learn to hear with their eyes? Must one clatter like kettledrums and penitential preachers? Or do they only believe the stammerer?

They have something whereof they are proud. What do they call it, that which maketh them proud? Culture, they call it; it distinguisheth them from the goatherds.

They dislike, therefore, to hear of 'contempt' of themselves. So I will appeal to their pride.

I will speak unto them of the most contemptible thing: that, however, is *the last man!*"

And thus spake Zarathustra unto the people:

It is time for man to fix his goal. It is time for man to plant the germ of his highest hope.

Still is his soil rich enough for it. But that soil will one day be poor and exhausted, and no lofty tree will any longer be able to grow thereon.

Alas! There cometh the time when man will no longer launch the arrow of his longing beyond man—and the string of his bow will have unlearned to whizz!

I tell you: one must still have chaos in one, to give birth to a dancing star. I tell you: ye have still chaos in you.

Alas! There cometh the time when man will no longer give birth to any star. Alas! There cometh the time of the most despicable man, who can no longer despise himself.

Lo! I show you *the last man.*

"What is love? What is creation? What is longing? What is a star?"—so asketh the last man and blinketh.

The earth hath then become small, and on it there hoppeth the last man who maketh everything small. His species is ineradicable like that of the ground flea; the last man liveth longest.

"We have discovered happiness"—say the last men, and blink thereby.

They have left the regions where it is hard to live; for they need warmth. One still loveth one's neighbor and rubbeth against him; for one needeth warmth.

Turning ill and being distrustful, they consider sinful: they walk warily. He is a fool who still stumbleth over stones or men!

A little poison now and then: that maketh pleasant dreams. And much poison at last for a pleasant death.

One still worketh, for work is a pastime. But one is careful lest the pastime should hurt one.

One no longer becometh poor or rich; both are too burdensome. Who still wanteth to rule? Who still wanteth to obey? Both are too burdensome.

No shepherd, and one herd! Everyone wanteth the same; everyone is equal: he who hath other sentiments goeth voluntarily into the madhouse.

"Formerly all the world was insane"—say the subtlest of them, and blink thereby.

They are clever and know all that hath happened, so there is no end to their raillery. People still fall out, but are soon reconciled—otherwise it spoileth their stomachs.

They have their little pleasures for the day, and their little pleasures for the night, but they have a regard for health.

"We have discovered happiness"—say the last men, and blink thereby.

And here ended the first discourse of Zarathustra, which is also called "The Prologue"; for at this point the shouting and mirth of the multitude interrupted him. "Give us this

last man, O Zarathustra,"—they called out—"make us into
these last men! Then will we make thee a present of the
Superman!" And all the people exulted and smacked their
lips. Zarathustra, however, turned sad, and said to his heart:

"They understand me not: I am not the mouth for these
ears.

Too long, perhaps, have I lived in the mountains; too much
have I hearkened unto the brooks and trees: now do I
speak unto them as unto the goatherds.

Calm is my soul, and clear, like the mountains in the
morning. But they think me cold, and a mocker with terrible
jests.

And now do they look at me and laugh, and while they
laugh they hate me, too. There is ice in their laughter."

6

Then, however, something happened which made every
mouth mute and every eye fixed. In the meantime, of course,
the ropedancer had commenced his performance: he had
come out at a little door, and was going along the rope
which was stretched between two towers, so that it hung
above the market place and the people. When he was just
midway across, the little door opened once more, and a
gaudily dressed fellow like a buffoon sprang out, and went
rapidly after the first one. "Go on, halt-foot," cried his frightful voice, "go on, lazybones, interloper, sallow-face!—lest
I tickle thee with my heel! What dost thou here between
the towers? In the tower is the place for thee, thou shouldst
be locked up; to one better than thyself thou blockest
the way!"—And with every word he came nearer and nearer
the first one. When, however, he was but a step behind, there
happened the frightful thing which made every mouth mute
and every eye fixed: he uttered a yell like a devil, and jumped
over the other who was in his way. The latter, however,
when he thus saw his rival triumph, lost at the same time
his head and his footing on the rope; he threw his pole
away, and shot downward faster than it, like an eddy of
arms and legs, into the depth. The market place and the
people were like the sea when the storm cometh on: they
all flew apart and in disorder, especially where the body
was about to fall.

Zarathustra, however, remained standing, and just beside
him fell the body, badly injured and disfigured, but not
yet dead. After a while consciousness returned to the shat-

tered man, and he saw Zarathustra kneeling beside him. "What art thou doing there?" said he at last. "I knew long ago that the devil would trip me up. Now he draggeth me to hell: wilt thou prevent him?"

"On mine honor, my friend," answered Zarathustra, "there is nothing of all that whereof thou speakest: there is no devil and no hell. Thy soul will be dead even sooner than thy body: fear, therefore, nothing any more!"

The man looked up distrustfully. "If thou speakest the truth," said he, "I lose nothing when I lose my life. I am not much more than an animal which hath been taught to dance by blows and scanty fare."

"Not at all," said Zarathustra, "thou hast made danger thy calling; therein there is nothing contemptible. Now thou perishest by thy calling: therefore will I bury thee with mine own hands."

When Zarathustra had said this the dying one did not reply further, but he moved his hand as if he sought the hand of Zarathustra in gratitude.

7

Meanwhile the evening came on, and the market place veiled itself in gloom. Then the people dispersed, for even curiosity and terror become fatigued. Zarathustra, however, still sat beside the dead man on the ground, absorbed in thought: so he forgot the time. But at last it became night, and a cold wind blew upon the lonely one. Then arose Zarathustra and said to his heart:

Verily, a fine catch of fish hath Zarathustra made today! It is not a man he hath caught, but a corpse.

Somber is human life, and as yet without meaning: a buffoon may be fateful to it.

I want to teach men the sense of their existence, which is the Superman, the lightning out of the dark cloud—man.

But still am I far from them, and my sense speaketh not unto their sense. To men I am still something between a fool and a corpse.

Gloomy is the night, gloomy are the ways of Zarathustra. Come, thou cold and stiff companion! I carry thee to the place where I shall bury thee with mine own hands.

8

When Zarathustra had said this to his heart, he put the corpse upon his shoulders and set out on his way. Yet had he not gone a hundred steps, when there stole a man up to him and whispered in his ear—and lo! he that spake was the buffoon from the tower. "Leave this town, O Zarathustra," said he, "there are too many here who hate thee. The good and just hate thee, and call thee their enemy and despiser; the believers in the orthodox belief hate thee, and call thee a danger to the multitude. It was thy good fortune to be laughed at: and verily thou spakest like a buffoon. It was thy good fortune to associate with the dead dog; by so humiliating thyself thou hast saved thy life today. Depart, however, from this town—or tomorrow I shall jump over thee, a living man over a dead one." And when he had said this, the buffoon vanished; Zarathustra, however, went on through the dark streets.

At the gate of the town the gravediggers met him: they shone their torch on his face, and recognizing Zarathustra, they sorely derided him. "Zarathustra is carrying away the dead dog: a fine thing that Zarathustra hath turned a gravedigger! For our hands are too cleanly for that roast. Will Zarathustra steal the bite from the devil? Well then, good luck to the repast! If only the devil is not a better thief than Zarathustra!—he will steal them both, he will eat them both!" And they laughed among themselves, and put their heads together.

Zarathustra made no answer thereto, but went on his way. When he had gone on for two hours, past forests and swamps, he had heard too much of the hungry howling of the wolves, and he himself became hungry. So he halted at a lonely house in which a light was burning.

"Hunger attacketh me," said Zarathustra, "like a robber. Among forests and swamps my hunger attacketh me, and late in the night.

"Strange humors hath my hunger. Often it cometh to me only after a repast, and all day it hath failed to come: where hath it been?"

And thereupon Zarathustra knocked at the door of the house. An old man appeared, who carried a light, and asked: "Who cometh unto me and my bad sleep?"

"A living man and a dead one," said Zarathustra. "Give me something to eat and drink, I forgot it during the day.

He that feedeth the hungry refresheth his own soul, saith wisdom."

The old man withdrew, but came back immediately and offered Zarathustra bread and wine. "A bad country for the hungry," said he; "that is why I live here. Animal and man come unto me, the anchorite. But bid thy companion eat and drink also, he is wearier than thou." Zarathustra answered: "My companion is dead; I shall hardly be able to persuade him to eat." "That doth not concern me," said the old man sullenly; "he that knocketh at my door must take what I offer him. Eat, and fare ye well!"—

Thereafter Zarathustra again went on for two hours, trusting to the path and the light of the stars: for he was an experienced nightwalker, and liked to look into the face of all that slept. When the morning dawned, however, Zarathustra found himself in a thick forest, and no path was any longer visible. He then put the dead man in a hollow tree at his head—for he wanted to protect him from the wolves—and laid himself down on the ground and moss. And immediately he fell asleep, tired in body, but with a tranquil soul.

9

Long slept Zarathustra; and not only the rosy dawn passed over his head but also the morning. At last, however, his eyes opened, and amazedly he gazed into the forest and the stillness, amazedly he gazed into himself. Then he arose quickly, like a seafarer who all at once seeth the land; and he shouted for joy: for he saw a new truth. And he spake thus to his heart:

A light hath dawned upon me: I need companions—living ones; not dead companions and corpses, which I carry with me where I will.

But I need living companions, who will follow me because they want to follow themselves—and to the place where I will.

A light hath dawned upon me. Not to the people is Zarathustra to speak, but to companions! Zarathustra shall not be the herd's herdsman and hound!

To allure many from the herd—for that purpose have I come. The people and the herd must be angry with me: a robber shall Zarathustra be called by the herdsmen.

Herdsmen, I say, but they call themselves the good and just. Herdsmen, I say, but they call themselves the believers in the orthodox belief.

Behold the good and just! Whom do they hate most? Him who breaketh up their tables of values, the breaker, the lawbreaker: he, however, is the creator.

Behold the believers of all beliefs! Whom do they hate most? Him who breaketh up their tables of values, the breaker, the lawbreaker: he, however, is the creator.

Companions, the creator seeketh, not corpses—and not herds or believers either. Fellow creators the creator seeketh —those who grave new values on new tables.

Companions, the creator seeketh, and fellow reapers: for everything is ripe for the harvest with him. But he lacketh the hundred sickles: so he plucketh the ears of corn and is vexed.

Companions, the creator seeketh, and such as know how to whet their sickles. Destroyers, will they be called, and de-spisers of good and evil. But they are the reapers and re-joicers.

Fellow creators, Zarathustra seeketh; fellow reapers and fellow rejoicers, Zarathustra seeketh: what hath he to do with herds and herdsmen and corpses!

And thou, my first companion, rest in peace! Well have I buried thee in thy hollow tree; well have I hid thee from the wolves.

But I part from thee; the time hath arrived. 'Twixt rosy dawn and rosy dawn there came unto me a new truth.

I am not to be a herdsman, I am not to be a gravedigger. Not any more will I discourse unto the people; for the last time have I spoken unto the dead.

With the creators, the reapers, and the rejoicers will I associate: the rainbow will I show them, and all the stairs to the Superman.

To the lone-dwellers will I sing my song, and to the twain-dwellers; and unto him who hath still ears for the unheard will I make the heart heavy with my happiness.

I make for my goal, I follow my course; over the loitering and tardy will I leap. Thus let my ongoing be their down-going!

10

This had Zarathustra said to his heart when the sun stood at noontide. Then he looked inquiringly aloft—for he heard above him the sharp call of a bird. And behold! An eagle swept through the air in wide circles, and on it hung a serpent, not like a prey, but like a friend: for it kept itself coiled round the eagle's neck.

"They are mine animals," said Zarathustra, and rejoiced in his heart.

"The proudest animal under the sun, and the wisest animal under the sun—they have come out to reconnoiter.

They want to know whether Zarathustra still liveth. Verily, do I still live?

More dangerous have I found it among men than among animals; in dangerous paths goeth Zarathustra. Let mine animals lead me!"

When Zarathustra had said this, he remembered the words of the saint in the forest. Then he sighed and spake thus to his heart:

"Would that I were wiser! Would that I were wise from the very heart, like my serpent!

But I am asking the impossible. Therefore do I ask my pride to go always with my wisdom!

And if my wisdom should some day forsake me—alas! it loveth to fly away!—may my pride then fly with my folly!"

Thus began Zarathustra's downgoing.

First Part

The Three Metamorphoses

Three metamorphoses of the spirit do I designate to you: how the spirit becometh a camel, the camel a lion, and the lion at last a child.

Many heavy things are there for the spirit, the strong load-bearing spirit in which reverence dwelleth: for the heavy and the heaviest longeth for its strength.

What is heavy? so asketh the load-bearing spirit; then kneeleth it down like the camel, and wanteth to be well laden.

What is the heaviest thing, ye heroes? asketh the load-bearing spirit, that I may take it upon me and rejoice in my strength.

Is it not this: To humiliate oneself in order to mortify one's pride? To exhibit one's folly in order to mock at one's wisdom?

Or is it this: To desert our cause when it celebrateth its triumph? To ascend high mountains to tempt the tempter?

Or is it this: To feed on the acorns and grass of knowledge, and for the sake of truth to suffer hunger of soul?

Or is it this: To be sick and dismiss comforters, and make friends of the deaf, who never hear thy requests?

Or is it this: To go into foul water when it is the water of truth, and not disclaim cold frogs and hot toads?

Or is it this: To love those who despise us, and give one's hand to the phantom when it is going to frighten us?

All these heaviest things the load-bearing spirit taketh upon itself: and like the camel, which, when laden, hasteneth into the wilderness, so hasteneth the spirit into its wilderness.

But in the loneliest wilderness happeneth the second metamorphosis: here the spirit becometh a lion; freedom will it capture, and lordship in its own wilderness.

Its last Lord it here seeketh: hostile will it be to him, and to its last God; for victory will it struggle with the great dragon.

What is the great dragon which the spirit is no longer inclined to call Lord and God? "Thou-shalt," is the great dragon called. But the spirit of the lion saith, "I will."

"Thou-shalt," lieth in its path, sparkling with gold—a scale-covered beast; and on every scale glittereth golden, "Thou shalt!"

The values of a thousand years glitter on those scales, and thus speaketh the mightiest of all dragons: "All the values of things—glitter on me.

All values have already been created, and all created values —do I represent. Verily, there shall be no 'I will' any more." Thus speaketh the dragon.

My brethren, wherefore is there need of the lion in the spirit? Why sufficeth not the beast of burden, which renounceth and is reverent?

To create new values—that, even the lion cannot yet accomplish: but to create itself freedom for new creating— that can the might of the lion do.

To create itself freedom, and give a holy Nay even unto duty: for that, my brethren, there is need of the lion.

To assume the right to new values—that is the most formidable assumption for a load-bearing and reverent spirit. Verily, unto such a spirit it is preying, and the work of a beast of prey.

As its holiest, it once loved "Thou-shalt": now is it forced to find illusion and arbitrariness even in the holiest things, that it may capture freedom from its love: the lion is needed for this capture.

But tell me, my brethren, what the child can do, which even the lion could not do? Why hath the preying lion still to become a child?

Innocence is the child, and forgetfulness, a new beginning, a game, a self-rolling wheel, a first movement, a holy Yea.

Aye, for the game of creating, my brethren, there is needed a holy Yea unto life: *its own* will, willeth now the spirit; *his own* world winneth the world's outcast.

Three metamorphoses of the spirit have I designated to you: how the spirit became a camel, the camel a lion, and the lion at last a child.—

XVII.—*The Way of the Creating One*

Thus spake Zarathustra. And at that time he abode in the town which is called The Pied Cow.

Wouldst thou go into isolation, my brother? Wouldst thou seek the way unto thyself? Tarry yet a little and hearken unto me.

"He who seeketh may easily get lost himself. All isolation is wrong": so say the herd. And long didst thou belong to the herd.

The voice of the herd will still echo in thee. And when thou sayest, "I have no longer a conscience in common with you," then will it be a plaint and a pain.

Lo, that pain itself did the same conscience produce; and the last gleam of that conscience still gloweth on thine affliction.

But thou wouldst go the way of thine affliction, which is the way unto thyself? Then show me thine authority and thy strength to do so!

Art thou a new strength and a new authority? A first motion? A self-rolling wheel? Canst thou also compel stars to revolve around thee?

Alas! there is so much lusting for loftiness! There are so many convulsions of the ambitions! Show me that thou art not a lusting and ambitious one!

Alas! there are so many great thoughts that do nothing more than the bellows: they inflate, and make emptier than ever.

Free, dost thou call thyself? Thy ruling thought would I hear of, and not that thou hast escaped from a yoke.

Art thou one *entitled* to escape from a yoke? Many a one hath cast away his final worth when he hath cast away his servitude.

Free from what? What doth that matter to Zarathustra! Clearly, however, shall thine eye show unto me: free *for what?*

Canst thou give unto thyself thy bad and thy good, and set up thy will as a law over thee? Canst thou be judge for thyself, and avenger of thy law?

Terrible is aloneness with the judge and avenger of one's own law. Thus is a star projected into desert space, and into the icy breath of aloneness.

Today sufferest thou still from the multitude, thou individual; today hast thou still thy courage unabated, and thy hopes.

But one day will the solitude weary thee; one day will thy pride yield, and thy courage quail. Thou wilt one day cry: "I am alone!"

One day wilt thou see no longer thy loftiness, and see too closely thy lowliness; thy sublimity itself will frighten thee as a phantom. Thou wilt one day cry: "All is false!"

There are feelings which seek to slay the lonesome one; if they do not succeed, then must they themselves die! But art thou capable of it—to be a murderer?

Hast thou ever known, my brother, the word "disdain"? And the anguish of thy justice in being just to those that disdain thee?

Thou forcest many to think differently about thee; that, charge they heavily to thine account. Thou camest nigh unto them, and yet wentest past: for that they never forgive thee.

Thou goest beyond them: but the higher thou risest, the smaller doth the eye of envy see thee. Most of all, however, is the flying one hated.

"How could ye be just unto me!"—must thou say—"I choose your injustice as my allotted portion."

Injustice and filth cast they at the lonesome one: but, my brother, if thou wouldst be a star, thou must shine for them none the less on that account!

And be on thy guard against the good and just! They would fain crucify those who devise their own virtue—they hate the lonesome ones.

Be on thy guard, also, against holy simplicity! All is unholy to it that is not simple; fain, likewise, would it play with the fire—of the fagot and stake.

And be on thy guard, also, against the assaults of thy love! Too readily doth the recluse reach his hand to anyone who meeteth him.

To many a one mayest thou not give thy hand, but only thy paw; and I wish thy paw also to have claws.

But the worst enemy thou canst meet, wilt thou thyself always be; thou waylayest thyself in caverns and forests.

Thou lonesome one, thou goest the way to thyself! And past thyself and thy seven devils leadeth thy way!

A heretic wilt thou be to thyself, and a wizard and a soothsayer, and a fool, and a doubter, and a reprobate, and a villain.

Ready must thou be to burn thyself in thine own flame; how couldst thou become new if thou have not first become ashes!

Thou lonesome one, thou goest the way of the creating one: a God wilt thou create for thyself out of thy seven devils!

Thou lonesome one, thou goest the way of the loving one: thou lovest thyself, and on that account despisest thou thyself, as only the loving ones despise.

To create, desireth the loving one, because he despiseth! What knoweth he of love who hath not been obliged to despise just what he loved!

With thy love, go into thine isolation, my brother, and with thy creating; and late only will justice limp after thee.

With my tears, go into thine isolation, my brother. I love him who seeketh to create beyond himself, and thus succumbeth.—

Thus spake Zarathustra.

XXII.—The Bestowing Virtue

1

When Zarathustra had taken leave of the town to which his heart was attached, the name of which is "The Pied Cow," there followed him many people who called themselves his disciples, and kept him company. Thus came they to a crossroad. Then Zarathustra told them that he now wanted to go alone, for he was fond of going alone. His disciples, however, presented him at his departure with a staff, on the golden handle of which a serpent twined round the sun. Zarathustra rejoiced on account of the staff, and supported himself thereon; then spake he thus to his disciples:

Tell me, pray: how came gold to the highest value? Because it is uncommon, and unprofiting, and beaming, and soft in luster; it always bestoweth itself.

Only as image of the highest virtue came gold to the highest value. Goldlike, beameth the glance of the bestower. Gold-luster maketh peace between moon and sun.

Uncommon is the highest virtue, and unprofiting, beaming is it, and soft of luster: a bestowing virtue is the highest virtue.

Verily, I divine you well, my disciples: ye strive like me for the bestowing virtue. What should ye have in common with cats and wolves?

It is your thirst to become sacrifices and gifts yourselves: and therefore have ye the thirst to accumulate all riches in your soul.

Insatiably striveth your soul for treasures and jewels, because your virtue is insatiable in desiring to bestow.

Ye constrain all things to flow toward you and into you, so that they shall flow back again out of your fountain as the gifts of your love.

Verily, an appropriator of all values must such bestowing love become; but healthy and holy, call I this selfishness.

Another selfishness is there, an all-too-poor and hungry kind, which would always steal—the selfishness of the sick, the sickly selfishness.

With the eye of the thief it looketh upon all that is lustrous; with the craving of hunger it measureth him who hath abundance; and ever doth it prowl round the tables of bestowers.

Sickness speaketh in such craving, and invisible degeneration; of a sickly body, speaketh the larcenous craving of this selfishness.

Tell me, my brother, what do we think bad, and worst of all? Is it not *degeneration?*—And we always suspect degeneration when the bestowing soul is lacking.

Upward goeth our course from genera on to super-genera. But a horror to us is the degenerating sense, which saith: "All for myself."

Upward soareth our sense: thus is it a simile of our body, a simile of an elevation. Such similes of elevations are the names of the virtues.

Thus goeth the body through history, a becomer and fighter. And the spirit—what is it to the body? Its fights' and victories' herald, its companion and echo.

Similes are all names of good and evil; they do not speak out, they only hint. A fool who seeketh knowledge from them!

Give heed, my brethren, to every hour when your spirit would speak in similes: there is the origin of your virtue.

Elevated is then your body, and raised up; with its delight, enraptureth it the spirit; so that it becometh creator, and valuer, and lover, and everything's benefactor.

When your heart overfloweth broad and full like the river, a blessing and a danger to the lowlanders: there is the origin of your virtue.

When ye are exalted above praise and blame, and your will would command all things, as a loving one's will: there is the origin of your virtue.

When ye despise pleasant things, and the effeminate couch, and cannot couch far enough from the effeminate: there is the origin of your virtue.

When ye are willers of one will, and when that change of every need is needful to you: there is the origin of your virtue.

Verily, a new good and evil is it! Verily, a new deep murmuring, and the voice of a new fountain!

Power is it, this new virtue; a ruling thought is it, and around it a subtle soul: a golden sun, with the serpent of knowledge around it.

2

Here paused Zarathustra awhile, and looked lovingly on his disciples. Then he continued to speak thus—and his voice had changed:

Remain true to the earth, my brethren, with the power of your virtue! Let your bestowing love and your knowledge be devoted to be the meaning of the earth! Thus do I pray and conjure you.

Let it not fly away from the earthly and beat against eternal walls with its wings! Ah, there hath always been so much flown-away virtue!

Lead, like me, the flown-away virtue back to the earth—yea, back to body and life: that it may give to the earth its meaning, a human meaning!

A hundred times hitherto hath spirit as well as virtue

flown away and blundered. Alas! in our body dwelleth still all this delusion and blundering: body and will hath it there become.

A hundred times hitherto hath spirit as well as virtue attempted and erred. Yea, an attempt hath man been. Alas, much ignorance and error hath become embodied in us!

Not only the rationality of millenniums—also their madness, breaketh out in us. Dangerous is it to be an heir.

Still fight we step by step with the giant Chance, and over all mankind hath hitherto ruled nonsense, the lack-of-sense.

Let your spirit and your virtue be devoted to the sense of the earth, my brethren: let the value of everything be determined anew by you! Therefore shall ye be fighters! Therefore shall ye be creators!

Intelligently doth the body purify itself; attempting with intelligence it exalteth itself; to the discerners all impulses sanctify themselves; to the exalted the soul becometh joyful.

Physician, heal thyself: then wilt thou also heal thy patient. Let it be his best cure to see with his eyes him who maketh himself whole.

A thousand paths are there which have never yet been trodden; a thousand salubrities and hidden islands of life. Unexhausted and undiscovered is still man and man's world.

Awake and hearken, ye lonesome ones! From the future come winds with stealthy pinions, and to fine ears good tidings are proclaimed.

Ye lonesome ones of today, ye seceding ones, ye shall one day be a people: out of you who have chosen yourselves shall a chosen people arise—and out of it the Superman.

Verily, a place of healing shall the earth become! And already is a new odor diffused around it, a salvation-bringing odor—and a new hope!

3

When Zarathustra had spoken these words, he paused, like one who had not said his last word; and long did he balance the staff doubtfully in his hand. At last he spake thus —and his voice had changed:

I now go alone, my disciples! Ye also now go away, and alone! So will I have it.

Verily, I advise you: depart from me, and guard yourselves against Zarathustra! And better still: be ashamed of him! Perhaps he hath deceived you.

The man of knowledge must be able not only to love his enemies, but also to hate his friends.

One requiteth a teacher badly if one remain merely a scholar. And why will ye not pluck at my wreath?

Ye venerate me, but what if your veneration should some-day collapse? Take heed lest a statue crush you!

Ye say, ye believe in Zarathustra? But of what account is Zarathustra! Ye are my believers: but of what account are all believers!

Ye had not yet sought yourselves: then did ye find me. So do all believers; therefore all belief is of so little account.

Now do I bid you lose me and find yourselves; and only when ye have all denied me will I return unto you.

Verily, with other eyes, my brethren, shall I then seek my lost ones; with another love shall I then love you.

And once again shall ye have become friends unto me, and children of one hope: then will I be with you for the third time, to celebrate the great noontide with you.

And it is the great noontide, when man is in the middle of his course between animal and Superman, and celebrateth his advance to the evening as his highest hope: for it is the advance to a new morning.

At such time will the downgoer bless himself, that he should be an overgoer; and the sun of his knowledge will be at noontide.

"Dead are all the Gods: now do we desire the Superman to live."—Let this be our final will at the great noontide!—

Thus spake Zarathustra.

LVI.—*Old and New Tables*

1

Here do I sit and wait, old broken tables around me and also new half-written tables. When cometh mine hour?

—The hour of my descent, of my downgoing: for once more will I go unto men.

For that hour do I now wait: for first must the signs come unto me that it is *mine* hour—namely, the laughing lion with the flock of doves.

Meanwhile do I talk to myself as one who hath time. No one telleth me anything new, so I tell myself mine own story.

2

When I came unto men, then found I them resting on an old infatuation: all of them thought they had long known what was good and bad for men.

An old wearisome business seemed to them all discourse about virtue, and he who wished to sleep well spake of "good" and "bad" ere retiring to rest.

This somnolence did I disturb when I taught that *no one yet knoweth* what is good and bad—unless it be the creating one!

—It is he, however, who createth man's goal, and giveth to the earth its meaning and its future: he only *effecteth* it *that* aught is good or bad.

And I bade them upset their old academic chairs, and wherever that old infatuation had sat; I bade them laugh at their great moralists, their saints, their poets, and their Saviours.

At their gloomy sages did I bid them laugh, and whoever had sat admonishing as a black scarecrow on the tree of life.

On their great grave-highway did I seat myself, and even beside the carrion and vultures—and I laughed at all their bygone and its mellow decaying glory.

Verily, like penitential preachers and fools did I cry wrath and shame on all their greatness and smallness. Oh, that their best is so very small! Oh, that their worst is so very small! Thus did I laugh.

Thus did my wise longing, born in the mountains, cry and laugh in me; a wild wisdom, verily!—my great pinion-rustling longing.

And oft did it carry me off and up and away and in the midst of laughter; then flew I quivering like an arrow with sun-intoxicated rapture:

—Out into distant futures, which no dream hath yet seen, into warmer souths than ever sculptor conceived, where gods in their dancing are ashamed of all clothes:

(That I may speak in parables and halt and stammer like the poets: and verily I am ashamed that I have still to be a poet!)

Where all becoming seemed to me dancing of Gods, and wantoning of Gods, and the world unloosed and unbridled and fleeing back to itself:—

—As an eternal self-fleeing and re-seeking of one another

of many Gods, as the blessed self-contradicting, recommuning, and refraternizing with one another of many Gods:—

Where all time seemed to me a blessed mockery of moments, where necessity was freedom itself, which played happily with the goad of freedom:—

Where I also found again mine old devil and archenemy, the spirit of gravity, and all that it created: constraint, law, necessity and consequence and purpose and will and good and evil:—

For must there not be that which is danced *over*, danced beyond? Must there not, for the sake of the nimble, the nimblest, be moles and clumsy dwarfs?

3

There was it also where I picked up from the path the word "Superman," and that man is something that must be surpassed.

—That man is a bridge and not a goal—rejoicing over his noontides and evenings, as advances to new rosy dawns:

—The Zarathustra word of the great noontide, and whatever else I have hung up over men like purple evening-afterglows.

Verily, also new stars did I make them see, along with new nights; and over cloud and day and night, did I spread out laughter like a gay-colored canopy.

I taught them all *my* poetization and aspiration: to compose and collect into unity what is fragment in man, and riddle and fearful chance;—

—As composer, riddle-reader, and redeemer of chance, did I teach them to create the future, and all that *hath been*—to redeem by creating.

The past of man to redeem, and every "It was" to transform, until the Will saith: "But so did I will it! So shall I will it—"

—This did I call redemption; this alone taught I them to call redemption.——

Now do I await *my* redemption—that I may go unto them for the last time.

For once more will I go unto men: *amongst* them will my sun set; in dying will I give them my choicest gift!

From the sun did I learn this, when it goeth down, the exuberant one: gold doth it then pour into the sea, out of inexhaustible riches,—

—So that the poorest fisherman roweth even with *golden*

oars! For this did I once see, and did not tire of weeping in beholding it.——

Like the sun will also Zarathustra go down: now sitteth he here and waiteth, old broken tables around him, and also new tables—half-written.

4

Behold, here is a new table; but where are my brethren who will carry it with me to the valley and into hearts of flesh?—

Thus demandeth my great love to the remotest ones: *be not considerate of thy neighbor!* Man is something that must be surpassed.

There are many divers ways and modes of surpassing: see *thou* thereto! But only a buffoon thinketh: "Man can also be *overleapt*."

Surpass thyself even in thy neighbor: and a right which thou canst seize upon shalt thou not allow to be given thee!

What thou doest can no one do to thee again. Lo, there is no requital.

He who cannot command himself shall obey. And many a one *can* command himself, but still sorely lacketh self-obedience!

5

Thus wisheth the type of noble souls: they desire to have nothing *gratuitously,* least of all, life.

He who is of the populace wisheth to live gratuitously; we others, however, to whom life hath given itself—we are ever considering *what* we can best give *in return!*

And verily it is a noble dictum which saith: "What life promiseth *us,* that promise will *we* keep—to life!"

One should not wish to enjoy where one doth not contribute to the enjoyment. And one should not *wish* to enjoy!

For enjoyment and innocence are the most bashful things. Neither like to be sought for. One should *have* them—but one should rather *seek* for guilt and pain!

O my brethren, he who is a firstling is ever sacrificed. Now, however, are we firstlings!

We all bleed on secret sacrificial altars, we all burn and broil in honor of ancient idols.

Our best is still young: this exciteth old palates. Our
flesh is tender, our skin is only lambs' skin:—how could
we not excite old idol-priests!

In ourselves dwelleth he still, the old idol-priest, who
broileth our best for his banquet. Ah, my brethren, how could
firstlings fail to be sacrifices!

But so wisheth our type; and I love those who do not
wish to preserve themselves, the downgoing ones do I love
with mine entire love: for they go beyond.

7

To be true—that *can* few be! And he who can, will
not! Least of all, however, can the good be true.

Oh, those good ones! *Good men never speak the truth.*
For the spirit, thus to be good, is a malady.

They yield, those good ones, they submit themselves;
their heart repeateth, their soul obeyeth: *he,* however, who
obeyeth *doth not listen to himself!*

All that is called evil by the good must come together in
order that one truth may be born. O my brethren, are ye
also evil enough for *this* truth?

The daring venture, the prolonged distrust, the cruel Nay,
the tedium, the cutting-into-the-quick—how seldom do *these*
come together! Out of such seed, however—is truth produced!

Beside the bad conscience hath hitherto grown all *knowledge!* Break up, break up, ye discerning ones, the old tables!

8

When the water hath planks, when gangways and railings o'erspan the stream, verily he is not believed who then
saith: "All is in flux."

But even the simpletons contradict him. "What?" say the
simpletons, "all in flux? Planks and railings are still *over*
the stream!"

"*Over* the stream all is stable, all the values of things,
the bridges and bearings, all 'good' and 'evil': these are all
stable!"—

Cometh, however, the hard winter, the stream-tamer, then
learn even the wittiest distrust, and verily not only the
simpletons then say: "Should not everything—*stand still?*"

"Fundamentally standeth everything still"—that is an appropriate winter doctrine, good cheer for an unproductive period, a great comfort for winter-sleepers and fireside-loungers.

"Fundamentally standeth everything still"—: but *contrary* thereto, preacheth the thawing wind!

The thawing wind, a bullock, which is no plowing bullock—a furious bullock, a destroyer, which with angry horns breaketh the ice! The ice however——*breaketh gangways!*

O my brethren, is not everything *at present in flux?* Have not all railings and gangways fallen into the water? Who would still *hold on* to "good" and "evil"?

"Woe to us! Hail to us! The thawing wind bloweth!"— Thus preach, my brethren, through all the streets!

9

There is an old illusion—it is called good and evil. Around soothsayers and astrologers hath hitherto revolved the orbit of this illusion.

Once did one *believe* in soothsayers and astrologers; and *therefore* did one believe, "Everything is fate: thou shalt, for thou must!"

Then again did one distrust all soothsayers and astrologers; and *therefore* did one believe, "Everything is freedom: thou canst, for thou willest!"

O my brethren, concerning the stars and the future there hath hitherto been only illusion, and not knowledge; and *therefore* concerning good and evil there hath hitherto been only illusion and not knowledge!

10

"Thou shalt not rob! Thou shalt not slay!"—such precepts were once called holy; before them did one bow the knee and the head, and took off one's shoes.

But I ask you: Where have there ever been better robbers and slayers in the world than such holy precepts?

Is there not even in all life—robbing and slaying? And for such precepts to be called holy, was not *truth* itself thereby—slain?

—Or was it a sermon of death that called holy what contradicted and dissuaded from life?—O my brethren, break up, break up for me the old tables!

11

It is my sympathy with all the past that I see it is abandoned,—

—Abandoned to the favor, the spirit, and the madness of every generation that cometh, and reinterpreteth all that hath been as its bridge!

A great potentate might arise, an artful prodigy, who with approval and disapproval could strain and constrain all the past, until it became for him a bridge, a harbinger, a herald, and a cock-crowing.

This, however, is the other danger, and mine other sympathy: he who is of the populace, his thoughts go back to his grandfather—with his grandfather, however, doth time cease.

Thus is all the past abandoned: for it might someday happen for the populace to become master, and drown all time in shallow waters.

Therefore, O my brethren, a *new nobility* is needed, which shall be the adversary of all populace and potentate rule, and shall inscribe anew the word "noble" on new tables. For many noble ones are needed, and many kinds of noble ones, *for a new nobility!* Or, as I once said in parable: "That is just divinity, that there are Gods, but no God!"

12

O my brethren, I consecrate you and point you to a new nobility: ye shall become procreators and cultivators and sowers of the future;—

—Verily, not to a nobility which ye could purchase like traders with traders' gold; for little worth is all that hath its price.

Let it not be your honor henceforth whence ye come, but whither ye go! Your Will and your feet which seek to surpass you—let these be your new honor!

Verily, not that ye have served a prince—of what account are princes now!— nor that ye have become a bulwark to that which standeth, that it may stand more firmly.

Not that your family have become courtly at courts, and that ye have learned—gay-colored, like the flamingo—to stand long hours in shallow pools:

(For *ability*-to-stand is a merit in courtiers, and all

courtiers believe that unto blessedness after death pertaineth
—*permission*-to-sit!)

Nor even that a Spirit called Holy led your forefathers
into promised lands, which I do not praise: for where the
worst of all trees grew—the cross—in that land there is
nothing to praise!—

—And verily, wherever this "Holy Spirit" led its knights,
always in such campaigns did—goats and geese, and wry-heads
and guy-heads run *foremost!*—

O my brethren, not backward shall your nobility gaze, but
outward! Exiles shall ye be from all fatherlands and fore-
fatherlands!

Your *children's land* shall ye love: let this love be your
new nobility—the undiscovered in the remotest seas! For
it do I bid your sails search and search!

Unto your children shall ye *make amends* for being the
children of your fathers: all the past shall ye *thus* redeem!
This new table do I place over you!

13

"Why should one live? All is vain! To live—that is to
thrash straw; to live—that is to burn oneself and yet not
get warm."—

Such ancient babbling still passeth for "wisdom"; because it is old, however, and smelleth mustily, *therefore*
is it the more honored. Even mold ennobleth.—

Children might thus speak: they *shun* the fire because it
hath burnt them! There is much childishness in the old books
of wisdom.

And he who ever "thrasheth straw," why should he be
allowed to rail at thrashing! Such a fool one would have
to muzzle!

Such persons sit down to the table and bring nothing
with them, not even good hunger—and then do they rail:
"All is vain!"

But to eat and drink well, my brethren, is verily no vain
art! Break up, break up for me the tables of the never-
joyous ones!

14

"To the clean are all things clean"—thus say the people.

I, however, say unto you: To the swine all things become swinish!

Therefore preach the visionaries and bowed-heads (whose hearts are also bowed down): "The world itself is a filthy monster."

For these are all unclean spirits; especially those, however, who have no peace or rest, unless they see the world *from the backside*—the backworldsmen!

To those do I say it to the face, although it sound unpleasantly: the world resembleth man, in that it hath a backside—*so much* is true!

There is in the world much filth; *so much* is true! But the world itself is not therefore a filthy monster!

There is wisdom in the fact that much in the world smelleth badly: loathing itself createth wings, and fountain-divining powers!

In the best there is still something to loathe; and the best is still something that must be surpassed!—

O my brethren, there is much wisdom in the fact that much filth is in the world!

15

Such sayings did I hear pious backworldsmen speak to their consciences, and verily without wickedness or guile—although there is nothing more guileful in the world, or more wicked.

"Let the world be as it is! Raise not a finger against it!"

"Let whoever will choke and stab and skin and scrape the people: raise not a finger against it! Thereby will they learn to renounce the world."

"And thine own reason—this shalt thou thyself stifle and choke; for it is a reason of this world—thereby wilt thou learn thyself to renounce the world."—

—Shatter, shatter, O my brethren, those old tables of the pious! Tatter the maxims of the world-maligners!

16

"He who learneth much unlearneth all violent cravings"—that do people now whisper to one another in all the dark lanes.

"Wisdom wearieth, nothing is worth while; thou shalt not

crave!"—this new table found I hanging even in the public markets.

Break up for me, O my brethren, break up also that *new* table! The weary-o'-the-world put it up, and the preachers of death and the jailer: for lo, it is also a sermon for slavery:—

Because they learned badly and not the best, and everything too early and everything too fast; because they *ate* badly: from thence hath resulted their ruined stomach;—

—For a ruined stomach is their spirit: *it* persuadeth to death! For verily, my brethren, the spirit *is* a stomach!

Life is a well of delight, but to him in whom the ruined stomach speaketh, the father of affliction, all fountains are poisoned.

To discern: that is *delight* to the lion-willed! But he who hath become weary, is himself merely "willed"; with him play all the waves.

And such is always the nature of weak men: they lose themselves on their way. And at last asketh their weariness: "Why did we ever go on the way? All is indifferent!"

To them soundeth it pleasant to have preached in their ears: "Nothing is worth while! Ye shall not will!" That, however, is a sermon for slavery.

O my brethren, a fresh blustering wind cometh Zarathustra unto all way-weary ones; many noses will he yet make sneeze!

Even through walls bloweth my free breath, and in into prisons and imprisoned spirits!

Willing emancipateth: for willing is creating: so do I teach. And *only* for creating shall ye learn!

And also the learning shall ye *learn* only from me, the learning well!—He who hath ears let him hear!

17

There standeth the boat—thither goeth it over, perhaps into vast nothingness—but who willeth to enter into this "Perhaps"?

None of you want to enter into the death-boat! How should ye then be *world-weary* ones!

World-weary ones! And have not even withdrawn from the earth! Eager did I ever find you for the earth, amorous still of your own earth-weariness!

Not in vain doth your lip hang down: a small worldly wish still sitteth thereon! And in your eye—floateth there not a cloudlet of unforgotten earthly bliss?

There are on the earth many good inventions, some useful, some pleasant: for their sake is the earth to be loved.

And many such good inventions are there, that they are like woman's breasts: useful at the same time, and pleasant.

Ye world-weary ones, however! Ye earth-idlers! You, shall one beat with stripes! With stripes shall one again make you sprightly limbs.

For if ye be not invalids, or decrepit creatures, of whom the earth is weary, then are ye sly sloths, or dainty, sneaking pleasure-cats. And if ye will not again *run* gaily, then shall ye—pass away!

To the incurable shall one not seek to be a physician: thus teacheth Zarathustra: so shall ye pass away!

But more *courage* is needed to make an end than to make a new verse: that do all physicians and poets know well.

18

O my brethren, there are tables which weariness framed, and tables which slothfulness framed, corrupt slothfulness: although they speak similarly, they want to be heard differently.—

See this languishing one! Only a span-breadth is he from his goal; but from weariness hath he lain down obstinately in the dust, this brave one!

From weariness yawneth he at the path, at the earth, at the goal, and at himself: not a step further will he go—this brave one!

Now gloweth the sun upon him, and the dogs lick at his sweat: but he lieth there in his obstinacy and preferreth to languish:—

—A span-breadth from his goal, to languish! Verily, ye will have to drag him into his heaven by the hair of his head—this hero!

Better still that ye let him lie where he hath lain down, that sleep may come unto him, the comforter, with cooling patter-rain.

Let him lie, until of his own accord he awakeneth—until of his own accord he repudiateth all weariness, and what weariness hath taught through him!

Only, my brethren, see that ye scare the dogs away from him, the idle skulkers, and all the swarming vermin:—

—All the swarming vermin of the "cultured," that—feast on the sweat of every hero!

19

I form circles around me and holy boundaries; ever fewer ascend with me ever higher mountains: I build a mountain range out of ever holier mountains.—

But wherever ye would ascend with me, O my brethren, take care lest a *parasite* ascend with you!

A parasite: that is a reptile, a creeping, cringing reptile, that trieth to fatten on your infirm and sore places.

And *this* is its art: it divineth where ascending souls are weary, in your trouble and dejection, in your sensitive modesty, doth it build its loathsome nest.

Where the strong are weak, where the noble are all-too-gentle—there buildeth it its loathsome nest; the parasite liveth where the great have small sore places.

What is the highest of all species of being, and what is the lowest? The parasite is the lowest species; he, however, who is of the highest species feedeth most parasites.

For the soul which hath the longest ladder, and can go deepest down: how could there fail to be most parasites upon it?—

—The most comprehensive soul, which can run and stray and rove furthest in itself; the most necessary soul, which out of joy flingeth itself into chance:—

—The soul in Being, which plungeth into Becoming; the possessing soul, which *seeketh* to attain desire and longing:—

—The soul fleeing from itself, which overtaketh itself in the widest circuit; the wisest soul, unto which folly speaketh most sweetly:—

—The soul most self-loving, in which all things have their current and countercurrent, their ebb and their flow:—oh, how could *the loftiest soul* fail to have the worst parasites?

20

O my brethren, am I then cruel? But I say: What falleth, that shall one also push!

Everything of today—it falleth, it decayeth; who would preserve it! But I—I wish also to push it!

Know ye the delight which rolleth stones into precipitous depths?—Those men of today, see just how they roll into my depths!

A prelude am I to better players, O my brethren! An example! *Do* according to mine example!

And him whom ye do not teach to fly, teach I pray you —*to fall faster!*

21

I love the brave: but it is not enough to be a swordsman —one must also know *whereon* to use swordsmanship!

And often is it greater bravery to keep quiet and pass by, that *thereby* one may reserve oneself for a worthier foe!

Ye shall only have foes to be hated; but not foes to be despised: ye must be proud of your foes. Thus have I already taught.

For the worthier foe, O my brethren, shall ye reserve yourselves: therefore must ye pass by many a one,—

—Especially many of the rabble, who din your ears with noise about people and peoples.

Keep your eye clear of their For and Against! There is there much right, much wrong: he who looketh on becometh wroth.

Therein viewing, therein hewing—they are the same thing: therefore depart into the forests and lay your sword to sleep!

Go *your* ways! and let the people and peoples go theirs! —gloomy ways, verily, on which not a single hope glinteth any more!

Let there the trader rule, where all that still glittereth is— traders' gold. It is the time of kings no longer: that which now calleth itself the people is unworthy of kings.

See how these peoples themselves now do just like the traders: they pick up the smallest advantage out of all kinds of rubbish!

They lay lures for one another, they lure things out of one another—that they call "good neighborliness." O blessed remote period when a people said to itself: "I will be—*master* over peoples!"

For, my brethren, the best shall rule, the best also *willeth* to rule! And where the teaching is different, there—the best *is lacking*.

22

If *they* had—bread for nothing, alas! for what would

they cry! Their maintainment—that is their true entertainment; and they shall have it hard!

Beasts of prey are they: in their "working"—there is even plundering, in their "earning"—there is even overreaching! Therefore shall they have it hard!

Better beasts of prey shall they thus become, subtler, cleverer, *more manlike:* for man is the best beast of prey.

All the animals hath man already robbed of their virtues: that is why of all animals it hath been hardest for man.

Only the birds are still beyond him. And if man should yet learn to fly, alas! *to what height*—would his rapacity fly!

23

Thus would I have man and woman: fit for war, the one; fit for maternity, the other; both, however, fit for dancing with head and legs.

And lost be the day to us in which a measure hath not been danced. And false be every truth which hath not had laughter along with it!

24

Your marriage arranging: see that it be not a bad *arranging!* Ye have arranged too hastily: so there *followeth* therefrom—marriage breaking!

And better marriage breaking than marriage bending, marriage lying!—Thus spake a woman unto me: "Indeed, I broke the marriage, but first did the marriage break—me!"

The badly paired found I ever the most revengeful: they make everyone suffer for it that they no longer run singly.

On that account want I the honest ones to say to one another: "We love each other: let us *see to it* that we maintain our love! Or shall our pledging be blundering?"

—"Give us a set term and a small marriage, that we may see if we are fit for the great marriage! It is a great matter always to be twain."

Thus do I counsel all honest ones; and what would be my love to the Superman, and to all that is to come, if I should counsel and speak otherwise!

Not only to propagate yourselves onward but *upward*—thereto, O my brethren, may the garden of marriage help you!

25

He who hath grown wise concerning old origins, lo, he will at last seek after the fountains of the future and new origins.—

O my brethren, not long will it be until *new peoples* shall arise and new fountains shall rush down into new depths.

For the earthquake—it choketh up many wells, it causeth much languishing: but it bringeth also to light inner powers and secrets.

The earthquake discloseth new fountains. In the earthquake of old peoples new fountains burst forth.

And whoever calleth out: "Lo, here is a well for many thirsty ones, one heart for many longing ones, one will for many instruments":—around him collecteth a *people*, that is to say, many attempting ones.

Who can command, who must obey—*that is there attempted!* Ah, with what long seeking and solving and failing and learning and reattempting!

Human society: it is an attempt—so I teach—a long seeking: it seeketh, however, the ruler!—

—An attempt, my brethren! And *no* "contract"! Destroy, I pray you, destroy that word of the softhearted and half-and-half!

26

O my brethren! With whom lieth the greatest danger to the whole human future? Is it not with the good and just?—

—As those who say and feel in their hearts: "We already know what is good and just, we possess it also; woe to those who still seek thereafter!"

And whatever harm the wicked may do, the harm of the good is the harmfulest harm!

And whatever harm the world-maligners may do, the harm of the good is the harmfulest harm!

O my brethren, into the hearts of the good and just looked someone once on a time who said: "They are the Pharisees." But people did not understand him.

The good and just themselves were not free to understand him; their spirit was imprisoned in their good conscience. The stupidity of the good is unfathomably wise.

It is the truth, however, that the good *must* be Pharisees—they have no choice!

The good *must* crucify him who deviseth his own virtue! That *is* the truth!

The second one, however, who discovered their country—the country, heart, and soil of the good and just—it was he who asked: "Whom do they hate most?"

The *creator,* hate they most, him who breaketh the tables and old values, the breaker—him they call the lawbreaker.

For the good—they *cannot* create; they are always the beginning of the end:—

—They crucify him who writeth new values on new tables, they sacrifice *unto themselves* the future—they crucify the whole human future!

The good—they have always been the beginning of the end.

27

O my brethren, have ye also understood this word? And what I once said of the "last man"?——

With whom lieth the greatest danger to the whole human future? Is it not with the good and just?

Break up, break up, I pray you, the good and just!—O my brethren, have ye understood also this word?

28

Ye flee from me? Ye are frightened? Ye tremble at this word?

O my brethren, when I enjoined on you to break up the good, and the tables of the good, then only did I embark man on his high seas.

And now only cometh unto him the great terror, the great outlook, the great sickness, the great nausea, the great sea-sickness.

False shores and false securities did the good teach you; in the lies of the good were ye born and bred. Everything hath been radically contorted and distorted by the good.

But he who discovered the country of "man" discovered also the country of "man's future." Now shall ye be sailors for me, brave, patient!

Keep yourselves up betimes, my brethren, learn to keep yourselves up! The sea stormeth: many seek to raise yourselves again by you.

The sea stormeth: all is in the sea. Well! Cheer up! Ye old seaman-hearts!

What of fatherland! *Thither* striveth our helm where our *children's land* is! Thitherward, stormier than the sea, stormeth our great longing!

29

"Why so hard!"—said to the diamond one day the charcoal. "Are we then not near relatives?"—

Why so soft? O my brethren; thus do *I* ask you: are ye then not—my brethren?

Why so soft, so submissive and yielding? Why is there so much negation and abnegation in your hearts? Why is there so little fate in your looks?

And if ye will not be fates and inexorable ones, how can ye one day—conquer with me?

And if your hardness will not glance and cut and chip to pieces, how can ye one day—create with me?

For the creators are hard. And blessedness must it seem to you to press your hand upon millenniums as upon wax,—

—Blessedness to write upon the will of millenniums as upon brass—harder than brass, nobler than brass. Entirely hard is only the noblest.

This new table, O my brethren, put I up over you: *Become hard!*

30

O thou, my Will! Thou change of every need, *my* needfulness! Preserve me from all small victories!

Thou fatedness of my soul, which I call fate! Thou In-me! Over-me! Preserve and spare me for one great fate!

And thy last greatness, my Will, spare it for thy last—that thou mayest be inexorable *in* thy victory! Ah, who hath not succumbed to his victory!

Ah, whose eye hath not bedimmed in this intoxicated twilight! Ah, whose foot hath not faltered and forgotten in victory—how to stand!—

—That I may one day be ready and ripe in the great noontide: ready and ripe like the glowing ore, the lightning-bearing cloud, and the swelling milk-udder:—

—Ready for myself and for my most hidden Will: a bow eager for its arrow, an arrow eager for its star:—

—A star, ready and ripe in its noontide, glowing, pierced, blessed, by annihilating sun-arrows:—

—A sun itself, and an inexorable sun-will, ready for annihilation in victory!

O Will, thou change of every need, *my* needfulness! Spare me for one great victory!——

Thus spake Zarathustra.

LVII.—The Convalescent

1

One morning, not long after his return to his cave, Zarathustra sprang up from his couch like a madman, crying with a frightful voice, and acting as if someone still lay on the couch who did not wish to rise. Zarathustra's voice also resounded in such a manner that his animals came to him frightened, and out of all the neighboring caves and lurking-places all the creatures slipped away—flying, fluttering, creeping, or leaping, according to their variety of foot or wing. Zarathustra, however, spake these words:

Up, abysmal thought out of my depth! I am thy cock and morning dawn, thou overslept reptile: Up! Up! My voice shall soon crow thee awake!

Unbind the fetters of thine ears: listen! For I wish to hear thee! Up! Up! There is thunder enough to make the very graves listen!

And rub the sleep and all the dimness and blindness out of thine eyes! Hear me also with thine eyes: my voice is a medicine even for those born blind.

And once thou art awake, then shalt thou ever remain awake. It is not *my* custom to awake great-grandmothers out of their sleep that I may bid them—sleep on!

Thou stirrest, stretchest thyself, wheezest? Up! Up! Not wheeze, shalt thou—but speak unto me! Zarathustra called thee, Zarathustra the godless!

I, Zarathustra, the advocate of living, the advocate of suffering, the advocate of the circuit—thee do I call, my most abysmal thought!

Joy to me! Thou comest—I hear thee! Mine abyss *speaketh*, my lowest depth have I turned over into the light!

Joy to me! Come hither! Give me thy hand—ha! let be!
aha!—Disgust, disgust, disgust——alas to me!

2

Hardly, however, had Zarathustra spoken these words,
when he fell down as one dead, and remained long as one
dead. When, however, he again came to himself, then was he
pale and trembling, and remained lying; and for long he
would neither eat nor drink. This condition continued for
seven days; his animals, however, did not leave him day nor
night, except that the eagle flew forth to fetch food. And
what it fetched and foraged, it laid on Zarathustra's couch: so
that Zarathustra at last lay among yellow and red berries,
grapes, rosy apples, sweet-smelling herbage, and pine cones.
At his feet, however, two lambs were stretched, which the
eagle had with difficulty carried off from their shepherds.

At last, after seven days, Zarathustra raised himself upon
his couch, took a rosy apple in his hand, smelled it and
found its smell pleasant. Then did his animals think the time
had come to speak unto him.

"O Zarathustra," said they, "now hast thou lain thus for
seven days with heavy eyes: wilt thou not set thyself again
upon thy feet?

Step out of thy cave: the world waiteth for thee as a
garden. The wind playeth with heavy fragrance which seeketh
for thee; and all brooks would like to run after thee.

All things long for thee, since thou hast remained alone for
seven days—step forth out of thy cave! All things want to
be thy physicians!

Did perhaps a new knowledge come to thee, a bitter,
grievous knowledge? Like leavened dough layest thou, thy
soul arose and swelled beyond all its bounds.—"

—"O mine animals," answered Zarathustra, "talk on thus
and let me listen! It refresheth me so to hear your talk:
where there is talk, there is the world as a garden unto me.

How charming it is that there are words and tones; are not
words and tones rainbows and seeming bridges 'twixt the
eternally separated?

To each soul belongeth another world; to each soul is every
other soul a back-world.

Among the most alike doth semblance deceive most delightfully: for the smallest gap is most difficult to bridge over.

For me—how could there be an outside-of-me? There is no

outside! But this we forget on hearing tones; how delightful
it is that we forget!

Have not names and tones been given unto things that
man may refresh himself with them? It is a beautiful folly,
speaking; therewith danceth man over everything.

How lovely is all speech and all falsehoods of tones! With
tones danceth our love on variegated rainbows.—"

—"O Zarathustra," said then his animals, "to those who
think like us, things all dance themselves: they come and
hold out the hand and laugh and flee—and return.

Everything goeth, everything returneth; eternally rolleth
the wheel of existence. Everything dieth, everything blos-
someth forth again; eternally runneth on the year of existence.

Everything breaketh, everything is integrated anew; eternally
buildeth itself in the same house of existence. All things
separate, all things again greet one another; eternally true to
itself remaineth the ring of existence.

Every moment beginneth existence, around every 'Here'
rolleth the ball 'There.' The middle is everywhere. Crooked is
the path of eternity."—

—"O ye wags and barrel organs!" answered Zarathustra,
and smiled once more, "how well do ye know what had to
be fulfilled in seven days:—

—And how that monster crept into my throat and choked
me! But I bit off its head and spat it away from me.

And ye—ye have made a lyre-lay out of it? Now, however,
do I lie here, still exhausted with that biting and spitting-
away, still sick with mine own salvation.

And ye looked on at it all? O mine animals, are ye also
cruel? Did ye like to look at my great pain as men do? For
man is the cruelest animal.

At tragedies, bullfights, and crucifixions hath he hitherto
been happiest on earth; and when he invented his hell, behold, that was his heaven on earth.

When the great man crieth—: immediately runneth the
little man thither, and his tongue hangeth out of his mouth
for very lusting. He, however, called it his 'pity.'

The little man, especially the poet—how passionately doth
he accuse life in words! Hearken to him, but do not fail to
hear the delight which is in all accusation!

Such accusers of life—them life overcometh with a glance
of the eye. 'Thou lovest me?' saith the insolent one. 'Wait a
little, as yet have I no time for thee.'

Toward himself man is the cruelest animal; and in all who
call themselves 'sinners' and 'bearers of the cross' and 'peni-

tents,' do not overlook the voluptuousness in their plaints and accusations!

And I myself—do I thereby want to be man's accuser? Ah, mine animals, this only have I learned hitherto, that for man his baddest is necessary for his best,—

—That all that is baddest is the best *power*, and the hardest stone for the highest creator; and that man must become better *and* badder:—

Not to *this* torture-stake was I tied, that I know man is bad, but I cried, as no one hath yet cried:

'Ah, that his baddest is so very small! Ah, that his best is so very small!'

The great disgust at man—*it* strangled me and had crept into my throat: and what the soothsayer had presaged: 'All is alike, nothing is worth while, knowledge strangleth.'

A long twilight limped on before me, a fatally weary, fatally intoxicated sadness, which spake with yawning mouth.

'Eternally he returneth, the man of whom thou art weary, the small man'—so yawned my sadness, and dragged its foot and could not go to sleep.

A cavern became the human earth to me; its breast caved in; everything living became to me human dust and bones and moldering past.

My sighing sat on all human graves, and could no longer arise: my sighing and questioning croaked and choked, and gnawed and nagged day and night:

—'Ah, man returneth eternally! The small man returneth eternally!'

Naked had I once seen both of them, the greatest man and the smallest man: all too like one another—all too human, even the greatest man!

All too small, even the greatest man!—that was my disgust at man! And the eternal return also of the smallest man! —that was my disgust at all existence!

Ah, Disgust! Disgust! Disgust!"——Thus spake Zarathustra, and sighed and shuddered; for he remembered his sickness. Then did his animals prevent him from speaking further.

"Do not speak further, thou convalescent!"—so answered his animals, "but go out where the world waiteth for thee like a garden.

Go out unto the roses, the bees, and the flocks of doves! Especially, however, unto the singing birds, to learn *singing* from them!

For singing is for the convalescent; the sound ones may

talk. And when the sound also want songs, then want they other songs than the convalescent."

—"O ye wags and barrel organs, do be silent!" answered Zarathustra, and smiled at his animals. "How well ye know what consolation I devised for myself in seven days!

That I have to sing once more—*that* consolation did I devise for myself, and *this* convalesence: would ye also make another lyre-lay thereof?"

—"Do not talk further," answered his animals once more; "rather, thou convalescent, prepare for thyself first a lyre, a new lyre!

For behold, O Zarathustra! For thy new lays there are needed new lyres.

Sing and bubble over, O Zarathustra, heal thy soul with new lays: that thou mayest bear thy great fate, which hath not yet been anyone's fate!

For thine animals know it well, O Zarathustra, who thou are and must become: behold, *thou art the teacher of the eternal return*—that is now *thy* fate!

That thou must be the first to teach this teaching—how could this great fate not be thy greatest danger and infirmity!

Behold, we know what thou teachest: that all things eternally return, and ourselves with them, and that we have already existed times without number, and all things with us.

Thou teachest that there is a great year of Becoming, a prodigy of a great year; it must, like a sandglass, ever turn up anew, that it may anew run down and run out:—

—So that all those years are like one another in the greatest and also in the smallest, so that we ourselves, in every great year, are like ourselves in the greatest and also in the smallest.

And if thou wouldst now die, O Zarathustra, behold, we know also how thou wouldst then speak to thyself:—but thine animals beseech thee not to die yet!

Thou wouldst speak, and without trembling, buoyant rather with bliss, for a great weight and worry would be taken from thee, thou patientest one!—

'Now do I die and disappear,' wouldst thou say, 'and in a moment I am nothing. Souls are as mortal as bodies.

But the plexus of causes returneth in which I am intertwined—it will again create me! I myself pertain to the causes of the eternal return.

I come again with this sun, with this earth, with this

eagle, with this serpent—*not* to a new life, or a better life, or a similar life:

—I come again eternally to this identical and selfsame life, in its greatest and its smallest, to teach again the eternal return of all things,—

—To speak again the word of the great noontide of earth and man, to announce again to man the Superman.

I have spoken my word. I break down by my word: so willeth mine eternal fate—as announcer do I succumb!

The hour hath now come for the downgoer to bless himself. Thus—*endeth* Zarathustra's downgoing.'"——

When the animals had spoken these words they were silent and waited, so that Zarathustra might say something to them: but Zarathustra did not hear that they were silent. On the contrary, he lay quietly with closed eyes like a person sleeping, although he did not sleep; for he communed just then with his soul. The serpent, however, and the eagle, when they found him silent in such wise, respected the great stillness around him, and prudently retired.

LVIII.—The Great Longing

O my soul, I have taught thee to say "today" as "once on a time" and "formerly," and to dance thy measure over every Here and There and Yonder.

O my soul, I delivered thee from all by-places, I brushed down from thee dust and spiders and twilight.

O my soul, I washed the petty shame and the by-place virtue from thee, and persuaded thee to stand naked before the eyes of the sun.

With the storm that is called "spirit" did I blow over thy surging sea; all clouds did I blow away from it; I strangled even the strangler called "sin."

O my soul, I gave thee the right to say Nay like the storm, and to say Yea as the open heaven saith Yea: calm as the light remainest thou, and now walkest through denying storms.

O my soul, I restored to thee liberty over the created and the uncreated; and who knoweth, as thou knowest, the voluptuousness of the future?

O my soul, I taught thee the contempt which doth not

come like worm-eating, the great, the loving contempt, which loveth most where it contemneth most.

O my soul, I taught thee so to persuade that thou persuadest even the grounds themselves to thee: like the sun, which persuadeth even the sea to its height.

O my soul, I have taken from thee all obeying and knee-bending and homage-paying; I have myself given thee the names, "Change of need" and "Fate."

O my soul, I have given thee new names and gay-colored playthings, I have called thee "Fate" and "the Circuit of circuits" and "the Navel-string of time" and "the Azure bell."

O my soul, to thy domain gave I all wisdom to drink, all new wines, and also all immemorially old strong wines of wisdom.

O my soul, every sun shed I upon thee, and every night and every silence and every longing—then grewest thou up for me as a vine.

O my soul, exuberant and heavy dost thou now stand forth, a vine with swelling udders and full clusters of brown golden grapes:—

—Filled and weighted by thy happiness, waiting from superabundance, and yet ashamed of thy waiting.

O my soul, there is nowhere a soul which could be more loving and more comprehensive and more extensive! Where could future and past be closer together than with thee?

O my soul, I have given thee everything, and all my hands have become empty by thee—and now! Now sayest thou to me, smiling and full of melancholy: "Which of us oweth thanks?—

—Doth the giver not owe thanks because the receiver received? Is bestowing not a necessity? Is receiving not—pitying?"—

O my soul, I understand the smiling of thy melancholy: thine overabundance itself now stretcheth out longing hands!

Thy fullness looketh forth over raging seas, and seeketh and waiteth: the longing of overfullness looketh forth from the smiling heaven of thine eyes!

And verily, O my soul! Who could see thy smiling and not melt into tears? The angels themselves melt into tears through the overgraciousness of thy smiling.

Thy graciousness and overgraciousness, is it which will not complain and weep: and yet, O my soul, longeth thy smiling for tears, and thy trembling mouth for sobs.

"Is not all weeping complaining? And all complaining, accusing?" Thus speakest thou to thyself; and therefore, O my soul, wilt thou rather smile than pour forth thy grief—

—Than in gushing tears pour forth all thy grief concerning the craving of the vine for the vintager and the vintage-knife!

But wilt thou not weep, wilt thou not weep forth thy purple melancholy, then wilt thou have to *sing*, O my soul!—Behold, I smile myself, who foretell thee this:

—Thou wilt have to sing with passionate song, until all seas turn calm to hearken unto thy longing,—

—Until over calm longing seas the bark glideth, the golden marvel, around the gold of which all good, bad, and marvelous things frisk:—

—Also many large and small animals, and everything that hath light marvelous feet, so that it can run on violet-blue paths,—

—Toward the golden marvel, the spontaneous bark, and its master: he, however, is the vintager who waiteth with the diamond vintage-knife,—

—Thy great deliverer, O my soul, the nameless one——for whom future songs only will find names! And verily already hath thy breath the fragrance of future songs,—

—Already glowest thou and dreamest, already drinkest thou thirstily at all deep echoing wells of consolation, already reposeth thy melancholy in the bliss of future songs!——

O my soul, now have I given thee all, and even my last possession, and all my hands have become empty by thee:—*that I bade thee sing*, behold, that was my last thing to give!

That I bade thee sing,—say now, say: *which* of us now—oweth thanks?—Better still, however: sing unto me, sing, O my soul! And let me thank thee!—

Thus spake Zarathustra.

LIX.—The Second Dance Song

1

"Into thine eyes gazed I lately, O Life: gold saw I gleam in thy night-eyes—my heart stood still with delight:

—A golden bark saw I gleam on darkened waters, a sinking, drinking, reblinking, golden swing-bark!

At my dance-frantic foot, dost thou cast a glance, a laughing, questioning, melting, thrown glance:

Twice only movedst thou thy rattle with thy little hands—
then did my feet swing with dance fury.—

My heels reared aloft, my toes they hearkened—thee they
would know: hath not the dancer his ear—in his toe!

Unto thee did I spring: then fledst thou back from my
bound; and toward me waved thy fleeing, flying tresses
round!

Away from thee did I spring, and from thy snaky tresses:
then stoodst thou there half-turned, and in thine eyes caresses.

With crooked glances—dost thou teach me crooked
courses; on crooked courses learn my feet—crafty fancies!

I fear thee near, I love thee far; thy flight allureth me,
thy seeking secureth me:—I suffer, but for thee, what would
I not gladly bear!

For thee, whose coldness inflameth, whose hatred mis-
leadeth, whose flight enchaineth, whose mockery—pleadeth:

—Who would not hate thee, thou great bindress, inwind-
ress, temptress, seekress, findress! Who would not love thee,
thou innocent, impatient, wind-swift, child-eyed sinner!

Whither pullest thou me now, thou paragon and tomboy?
And now foolest thou me fleeing; thou sweep romp dost
annoy!

I dance after thee, I follow even faint traces lonely. Where
art thou? Give me thy hand! Or thy finger only!

Here are caves and thickets: we shall go astray!—Halt!
Stand still! Seest thou not owls and bats in fluttering fray?

Thou bat! Thou owl! Thou wouldst play me foul? Where
are we? From the dogs hast thou learned thus to bark and
howl.

Thou gnashest on me sweetly with little white teeth; thine
evil eyes shoot out upon me, thy curly little mane from underneath!

This is a dance over stock and stone: I am the hunter—
wilt thou be my hound, or my chamois anon?

Now beside me! And quickly, wickedly springing! Now up!
And over!—Alas! I have fallen myself overswinging!

Oh, see me lying, thou arrogant one, and imploring grace!
Gladly would I walk with thee—in some lovelier place!

—In the paths of love, thou bushes variegated, quiet, trim!
Or there along the lake, where goldfishes dance and swim!

Thou are now aweary? There above are sheep and sunset
stripes: is it not sweet to sleep—the shepherd pipes?

Thou are so very weary? I carry thee thither; let just thine
arm sink! And art thou thirsty—I should have something;
but thy mouth would not like it to drink!—

—Oh, that cursed, nimble, supple serpent and lurking-witch! Where art thou gone? But in my face do I feel through thy hand, two spots and red blotches itch!

I am verily weary of it, ever thy sheepish shepherd to be. Thou witch, if I have hitherto sung unto thee, now shalt *thou*—cry unto me!

To the rhythm of my whip shalt thou dance and cry! I forget not my whip?—Not I!"

2

Then did Life answer me thus, and kept thereby her fine ears closed:

"O Zarathustra! Crack not so terribly with thy whip! Thou knowest surely that noise killeth thought—and just now there came to me such delicate thoughts.

We are both of us genuine ne'er-do-wells and ne'er-do-ills. Beyond good and evil found we our island and our green meadow—we two alone! Therefore must we be friendly to each other!

And even should we not love each other from the bottom of our hearts—must we then have a grudge against each other if we do not love each other perfectly?

And that I am friendly to thee, and often too friendly, that knowest thou: and the reason is that I am envious of thy Wisdom. Ah, this mad old fool, Wisdom!

If thy Wisdom should one day run away from thee, ah! then would also my love run away from thee quickly."

Thereupon did Life look thoughtfully behind and around, and said softly: "O Zarathustra, thou art not faithful enough to me!

Thou lovest me not nearly so much as thou sayest; I know thou thinkest of soon leaving me.

There is an old heavy, heavy, booming-clock: it boometh by night up to thy cave:—

—When thou hearest this clock strike the hours at midnight, then thinkest thou between one and twelve thereon—

—Thou thinkest thereon, O Zarathustra, I know it—of soon leaving me!"

"Yea," answered I, hesitatingly, "but thou knowest it also."—And I said something into her ear, in amongst her confused, yellow, foolish tresses.

"Thou *knowest* that, O Zarathustra? That knoweth no one——."

And we gazed at each other, and looked at the green meadow o'er which the cool evening was just passing, and we wept together.—Then, however, was Life dearer unto me than all my Wisdom had ever been.—

Thus spake Zarathustra.

3

One!

O man! Take heed!

Two!

What saith deep midnight's voice indeed?

Three!

"I slept my sleep—

Four!

"From deepest dream I've woke and plead:—

Five!

"The world is deep,

Six!

"And deeper than the day could read.

Seven!

"Deep is its woe—

Eight!

"Joy—deeper still than grief can be:

Nine!

"Woe saith: Hence! Go!

Ten!

"But joys all want eternity—

Eleven!

"Want deep profound eternity!"

Twelve!

LX.—*The Seven Seals*

(Or the Yea and Amen Lay)

1

If I be a diviner and full of the divining spirit which wandereth on high mountain ridges, 'twixt two seas,—

Wandereth 'twixt the past and the future as a heavy cloud—hostile to sultry plains, and to all that is weary and can neither die nor live:

Ready for lightning in its dark bosom, and for the redeeming flash of light, charged with lightnings which say Yea! which laugh Yea! ready for divining flashes of lightning:—

—Blessed, however, is he who is thus charged! And verily long must he hang like a heavy tempest on the mountain, who shall one day kindle the light of the future!—

Oh, how could I not be ardent for Eternity and for the marriage ring of rings—the ring of the return?

Never yet have I found the woman by whom I should like to have children, unless it be this woman whom I love: for I love thee, O Eternity!

For I love thee, O Eternity!

2

If ever my wrath hath burst graves, shifted landmarks, or rolled old shattered tables into precipitous depths:

If ever my scorn hath scattered moldered words to the winds, and if I have come like a besom to cross spiders, and as a cleansing wind to old charnel houses:

If ever I have sat rejoicing where old Gods lie buried, world-blessing, world-loving, beside the monuments of old world-maligners:—

—For even churches and Gods'-graves do I love, if only heaven looketh through their ruined roofs with pure eyes;

gladly do I sit like grass and red poppies on ruined churches—
Oh, how could I not be ardent for Eternity, and for the
marriage ring of rings—the ring of the return?
Never yet have I found the woman by whom I should like
to have children, unless it be this woman whom I love: for
I love thee, O Eternity!

For I love thee, O Eternity!

3

If ever a breath hath come to me of the creative breath,
and of the heavenly necessity which compelleth even chances
to dance star-dances:
If ever I have laughed with the laughter of the creative
lightning, to which the long thunder of the deed followeth,
grumblingly, but obediently:
If ever I have played dice with the Gods at the divine
table of the earth, so that the earth quaked and ruptured,
and snorted forth fire streams:—
—For a divine table is the earth, and trembling with new
creative dictums and dice casts of the Gods:
Oh, how could I not be ardent for Eternity, and for the
marriage ring of rings—the ring of the return?
Never yet have I found the woman by whom I should like
to have children, unless it be this woman whom I love: for
I love thee, O Eternity!

For I love thee, O Eternity!

4

If ever I have drunk a full draught of the foaming
spice and confection bowl in which all things are well mixed:
If ever my hand hath mingled the furthest with the nearest,
fire with spirit, joy with sorrow, and the harshest with the
kindest:
If I myself am a grain of the saving salt which maketh
everything in the confection bowl mix well:—
—For there is a salt which uniteth good with evil; and
even the evilest is worthy, as spicing and as final overfoam-
ing:—
Oh, how could I not be ardent for Eternity, and for the
marriage ring of rings—the ring of the return?
Never yet have I found the woman by whom I should like
to have children, unless it be this woman whom I love: for
I love thee, O Eternity!

For I love thee, O Eternity!

5

If I be fond of the sea, and all that is sealike, and fondest of it when it angrily contradicteth me:

If the exploring delight be in me, which impelleth sails to the undiscovered, if the seafarer's delight be in my delight:

If ever my rejoicing hath called out: "The shore hath vanished—now hath fallen from me the last chain—

The boundless roareth around me, far away sparkle for me space and time—well! cheer up! old heart!"—

Oh, how could I not be ardent for Eternity, and for the marriage ring of rings—the ring of the return?

Never yet have I found the woman by whom I should like to have children, unless it be this woman whom I love: for I love thee, O Eternity!

For I love thee, O Eternity!

6

If my virtue be a dancer's virtue, and if I have often sprung with both feet into golden-emerald rapture:

If my wickedness be a laughing wickedness, at home among rose banks and hedges of lilies:

—For in laughter is all evil present, but it is sanctified and absolved by its own bliss:—

And if it be my Alpha and Omega that everything heavy shall become light, everybody a dancer, and every spirit a bird: and verily that is my Alpha and Omega!—

Oh, how could I not be ardent for Eternity, and for the marriage ring of rings—the ring of the return?

Never yet have I found the woman by whom I should like to have children, unless it be this woman whom I love: for I love thee, O Eternity!

For I love thee, O Eternity!

7

If ever I have spread out a tranquil heaven above me, and have flown into mine own heaven with mine own pinions:

If I have swum playfully in profound luminous distances, and if my freedom's avian wisdom hath come to me:—

—Thus, however, speaketh avian wisdom:—"Lo, there is

no above and no below! Throw thyself about—outward, backward, thou light one! Sing! speak no more!

—Are not all words made for the heavy? Do not all words lie to the light ones? Sing! speak no more!"—

Oh, how could I not be ardent for Eternity, and for the marriage ring of rings—the ring of the return?

Never yet have I found the woman by whom I should like to have children, unless it be this woman whom I love: for I love thee, O Eternity!

For I love thee, O Eternity!

Fourth and Last Part

Ah, where in the world have there been greater follies than with the pitiful? And what in the world hath caused more suffering than the follies of the pitiful?

Woe unto all loving ones who have not an elevation which is above their pity!

Thus spake the devil unto me, once on a time: "Even God hath his hell: it is his love for man."

And lately did I hear him say these words: "God is dead: of his pity for man hath God died."

—ZARATHUSTRA, II, "The Pitiful" (pp. 104–5).

LXVI.—Out of Service

Not long, however, after Zarathustra had freed himself from the magician, he again saw a person sitting beside the path which he followed, namely, a tall, black man, with a haggard, pale countenance: *this man* grieved him exceedingly. "Alas," said he to his heart, "there sitteth disguised affliction; methinketh he is of the type of the priests: what do *they* want in my domain?

What! Hardly have I escaped from that magician, and must another necromancer again run across my path,—

—Some sorcerer with laying-on-of-hands, some somber wonder-worker by the grace of God, some anointed world maligner, whom, may the devil take!

But the devil is never at the place which would be his right place: he always cometh too late, that cursed dwarf and clubfoot!"—

Thus cursed Zarathustra impatiently in his heart, and considered how with averted look he might slip past the black man. But behold, it came about otherwise. For at the same moment had the sitting one already perceived him; and not unlike one whom an unexpected happiness overtaketh, he sprang to his feet, and went straight toward Zarathustra.

"Whoever thou art, thou traveler," said he, "help a strayed one, a seeker, an old man, who may here easily come to grief!

The world here is strange to me, and remote; wild beasts also did I hear howling; and he who could have given me protection—he is himself no more.

I was seeking the last pious man, a saint and an anchorite, who, alone in his forest, had not yet heard of what all the world knoweth at present."

"*What* doth all the world know at present?" asked Zarathustra. "Perhaps that the old God no longer liveth, in whom all the world once believed?"

"Thou sayest it," answered the old man sorrowfully. "And I served that old God until his last hour.

Now, however, am I out of service, without master, and yet not free; likewise am I no longer merry even for an hour, except it be in recollections.

Therefore did I ascend into these mountains, that I might finally have a festival for myself once more, as becometh an old pope and church father: for know it, that I am the last pope!—a festival of pious recollections and divine services.

Now, however, is he himself dead, the most pious of men, the saint in the forest, who praised his God constantly with singing and mumbling.

He himself found I no longer when I found his cot—but two wolves found I therein, which howled on account of his death—for all animals loved him. Then did I haste away.

Had I thus come in vain into these forests and mountains? Then did my heart determine that I should seek an-

other, the most pious of all those who believe not in God—
my heart determined that I should seek Zarathustra!"

Thus spake the hoary man, and gazed with keen eyes at
him who stood before him. Zarathustra, however, seized the
hand of the old pope and regarded it a long while with admiration.

"Lo! thou venerable one," said he then, "what a fine and
long hand! That is the hand of one who hath ever dispensed blessings. Now, however, doth it hold fast him whom
thou seekest, me, Zarathustra.

It is I, the ungodly Zarathustra, who saith: 'Who is un-
godlier than I, that I may enjoy his teaching?' "—

Thus spake Zarathustra, and penetrated with his glances
the thoughts and arrear-thoughts of the old pope. At last the
latter began:

"He who most loved and possessed him hath now also lost
him most—:

—Lo, I myself am surely the most godless of us at
present? But who could rejoice at that!"—

—"Thou servedst him to the last?" asked Zarathustra
thoughtfully, after a deep silence. "Thou knowest *how* he
died? Is it true what they say, that sympathy choked him;

—That he saw how *man* hung on the cross, and could not
endure it;—that his love to man became his hell, and at last
his death?"——

The old pope, however, did not answer, but looked aside
timidly, with a painful and gloomy expression.

"Let him go," said Zarathustra, after prolonged meditation,
still looking the old man straight in the eye.

"Let him go, he is gone. And though it honoreth thee that
thou speakest only in praise of this dead one, yet thou
knowest as well as I *who* he was, and that he went curious
ways."

"To speak before three eyes," said the old pope cheerfully
(he was blind of one eye), "in divine matters I am more enlightened than Zarathustra himself—and may well be so.

My love served him long years, my will followed all his
will. A good servant, however, knoweth everything, and
many a thing even which a master hideth from himself.

He was a hidden God, full of secrecy. Verily, he did not
come by his son otherwise than by secret ways. At the door
of his faith standeth adultery.

Whoever extolleth him as a God of love doth not think
highly enough of love itself. Did not that God want also to
be judge? But the loving one loveth irrespective of reward
and requital.

When he was young, that God out of the Orient, then was he harsh and revengeful, and built himself a hell for the delight of his favorites.

At last, however, he became old and soft and mellow and pitiful, more like a grandfather than a father, but most like a tottering old grandmother.

There did he sit shriveled in his chimney-corner, fretting on account of his weak legs, world-weary, will-weary, and one day he suffocated of his all-too-great pity."——

"Thou old pope," said here Zarathustra interposing, "hast thou seen *that* with thine eyes? It could well have happened in that way: in that way, *and* also otherwise. When Gods die, they always die many kinds of death.

Well! At all events, one way or other—he is gone! He was counter to the taste of mine ears and eyes; worse than that I should not like to say against him.

I love everything that looketh bright and speaketh honestly. But he—thou knowest it, forsooth, thou old priest, there was something of thy type in him, the priest type—he was equivocal.

He was also indistinct. How he raged at us, this wrath-snorter, because we understood him badly! But why did he not speak more clearly?

And if the fault lay in our ears, why did he give us ears that heard him badly? If there was dirt in our ears, well! who put it in them?

Too much miscarried with him, this potter who had not learned thoroughly! That he took revenge on his pots and creations, however, because they turned out badly—that was a sin against *good taste*.

There is also good taste in piety: *this* at last said: 'Away with *such* a God! Better to have no God, better to set up destiny on one's own account, better to be a fool, better to be God oneself!' "

—"What do I hear!" said then the old pope, with intent ears; "O Zarathustra, thou art more pious than thou believest, with such an unbelief! Some God in thee hath converted thee to thine ungodliness.

Is it not thy piety itself which no longer letteth thee believe in a God? And thine overgreat honesty will yet lead thee even beyond good and evil!

Behold, what hath been reserved for thee? Thou hast eyes and hands and mouth, which have been predestined for blessing from eternity. One doth not bless with the hand alone.

Nigh unto thee, though thou professest to be the ungodliest one, I feel a hale and holy odor of long benedictions: I feel glad and grieved thereby.

Let me be thy guest, O Zarathustra, for a single night! Nowhere on earth shall I now feel better than with thee!"—

"Amen! So shall it be!" said Zarathustra with great astonishment; "up thither leadeth the way, there lieth the cave of Zarathustra.

Gladly, forsooth, would I conduct thee thither myself, thou venerable one; for I love all pious men. But now a cry of distress calleth me hastily away from thee.

In my domain shall no one come to grief; my cave is a good haven. And best of all would I like to put every sorrowful one again on firm land and firm legs.

Who, however, could take *thy* melancholy off thy shoulders? For that I am too weak. Long verily should we have to wait until someone reawoke thy God for thee.

For that old God liveth no more: he is indeed dead."—

Thus spake Zarathustra.

LXVII.—The Ugliest Man

—And again did Zarathustra's feet run through mountains and forests, and his eyes sought and sought, but nowhere was he to be seen whom they wanted to see—the sorely distressed sufferer and crier. On the whole way, however, he rejoiced in his heart and was full of gratitude. "What good things," said he, "hath this day given me, as amends for its bad beginning! What strange interlocutors have I found!

At their words will I now chew a long while as at good corn; small shall my teeth grind and crush them, until they flow like milk into my soul!"—

When, however, the path again curved round a rock, all at once the landscape changed, and Zarathustra entered into a realm of death. Here bristled aloft black and red cliffs, without any grass, tree, or bird's voice. For it was a valley which all animals avoided, even the beasts of prey, except that a species of ugly, thick, green serpent came here to die when they became old. Therefore the shepherds called this valley: "Serpent-death."

Zarathustra, however, became absorbed in dark recollections, for it seemed to him as if he had once before stood in this valley. And much heaviness settled on his mind, so that he walked slowly and always more slowly, and at last stood still. Then, however, when he opened his eyes, he saw something sitting by the wayside shaped like a man, and hardly like a man, something nondescript. And all at once there came over Zarathustra a great shame, because he had gazed on such a thing. Blushing up to the very roots of his white hair, he turned aside his glance, and raised his foot that he might leave this ill-starred place. Then, however, became the dead wilderness vocal: for from the ground a noise welled up, gurgling and rattling, as water gurgleth and rattleth at night through stopped-up water pipes; and at last it turned into human voice and human speech: it sounded thus:

"Zarathustra! Zarathustra! Read my riddle! Say, say! *What is the revenge on the witness?*

I entice thee back; here is smooth ice! See to it, see to it, that thy pride do not here break its legs!

Thou thinkest thyself wise, thou proud Zarathustra! Read then the riddle, thou hard nutcracker—the riddle that I am! Say then: who am *I!*"

—When, however, Zarathustra had heard these words, what think ye then took place in his soul? *Pity overcame him;* and he sank down all at once, like an oak that hath long withstood many tree-fellers—heavily, suddenly, to the terror even of those who meant to fell it. But immediately he got up again from the ground, and his countenance became stern.

"I know thee well," said he, with a brazen voice, "*thou art the murderer of God!* Let me go.

Thou couldst not *endure* him who beheld *thee*—who ever beheld thee through and through, thou ugliest man. Thou tookest revenge on this witness!"

Thus spake Zarathustra and was about to go; but the nondescript grasped at a corner of his garment and began anew to gurgle and seek for words. "Stay," said he at last—

—"Stay! Do not pass by! I have divined what ax it was that struck thee to the ground: hail to thee, O Zarathustra, that thou art again upon thy feet!

Thou hast divined, I know it well, how the man feeleth who killed him—the murderer of God. Stay! Sit down here beside me; it is not to no purpose.

To whom would I go but unto thee? Stay, sit down! Do not, however, look at me! Honor thus—mine ugliness!

They persecute me: now art *thou* my last refuge. *Not*

with their hatred, *not* with their bailiffs; oh, such persecution would I mock at, and be proud and cheerful!

Hath not all success hitherto been with the well-persecuted ones? And he who persecuteth well learneth readily to be *obsequent*—when once he is—put behind! But it is their *pity*—

—Their pity is it from which I flee away and flee to thee. O Zarathustra, protect me, thou, my last refuge, thou sole one who divinedst me:

—Thou hast divined how the man feeleth who killed *him*. Stay! And if thou wilt go, thou impatient one, go not the way that I came. *That* way is bad.

Art thou angry with me because I have already racked language too long? Because I have already counseled thee? But know that it is I, the ugliest man,—

—Who have also the largest, heaviest feet. Where *I* have gone, the way is bad. I tread all paths to death and destruction.

But that thou passedst me by in silence, that thou blushedst —I saw it well: thereby did I know thee as Zarathustra.

Everyone else would have thrown to me his alms, his pity, in look and speech. But for that—I am not beggar enough: that didst thou divine.

For that I am too *rich*, rich in what is great, frightful, ugliest, most unutterable! Thy shame, O Zarathustra, *honored* me!

With difficulty did I get out of the crowd of the pitiful— that I might find the only one who at present teacheth that 'pity is obtrusive'—thyself, O Zarathustra!

—Whether it be the pity of a God, or whether it be human pity, it is offensive to modesty. And unwillingness to help may be nobler than the virtue that rushed to do so.

That, however—namely, pity—is called virtue itself at present by all petty people: they have no reverence for great misfortune, great ugliness, great failure.

Beyond all these do I look, as a dog looketh over the backs of thronging flocks of sheep. They are petty, good-wooled, good-willed, gray people.

As the heron looketh contemptuously at shallow pools, with backward-bent head, so do I look at the throng of gray little waves and wills and souls.

Too long have we acknowledged them to be right, those petty people: *so* we have at last given them power as well; and now do they teach that 'good is only what petty people call good.'

And 'truth' is at present what the preacher spake who

himself sprang from them, that singular saint and advocate of the petty people, who testified of himself: 'I—am the truth.'

That immodest one hath long made the petty people greatly puffed up—he who taught no small error when he taught: 'I—am the truth.'

Hath an immodest one ever been answered more courteously?—Thou, however, O Zarathustra, passedst him by, and saidst: 'Nay! Nay! Three times Nay!'

Thou warnedst against his error; thou warnedst—the first to do so—against pity:—not everyone, not none, but thyself and thy type.

Thou art ashamed of the shame of the great sufferer; and verily when thou sayest: 'From pity there cometh a heavy cloud; take heed ye men!'

—When thou teachest: 'All creators are hard, all great love is beyond their pity': O Zarathustra, how well versed dost thou seem to me in weather signs!

Thou thyself, however, warn thyself also against *thy* pity! For many are on their way to thee, many suffering, doubting, despairing, drowning, freezing ones—

I warn thee also against myself. Thou hast read my best, my worst riddle, myself, and what I have done. I know the ax that felleth thee.

But he—*had to* die: he looked with eyes which beheld *everything*—he beheld men's depths and dregs, all his hidden ignominy and ugliness.

His pity knew no modesty: he crept into my dirtiest corners. This most prying, overintrusive, overpitiful one had to die.

He ever beheld *me:* on such a witness I would have revenge—or not live myself.

The God who beheld everything, *and also man:* that God had to die! Man cannot *endure* it that such a witness should live."

Thus spake the ugliest man. Zarathustra however got up, and prepared to go on: for he felt frozen to the very bowels.

"Thou nondescript," said he, "thou warnedst me against thy path. As thanks for it I praise mine to thee. Behold, up thither is the cave of Zarathustra.

My cave is large and deep and hath many corners; there findeth he that is most hidden his hiding-place. And close beside it, there are a hundred lurking-places and by-places for creeping, fluttering, and hopping creatures.

Thou outcast, who hast cast thyself out, thou wilt not live

amongst men and men's pity? Well then, do like me! Thus wilt thou learn also from me; only the door learneth.

And talk first and foremost to mine animals! The proudest animal and the wisest animal—they might well be the right counselors for us both!"——

Thus spake Zarathustra and went his way, more thoughtfully and slowly even than before: for he asked himself many things, and hardly knew what to answer.

"How poor indeed is man," thought he in his heart, "how ugly, how wheezy, how full of hidden shame!

They tell me that man loveth himself. Ah, how great must that self-love be! How much contempt is opposed to it!

Even this man hath loved himself, as he hath despised himself—a great lover methinketh he is, and a great despiser.

No one have I yet found who more thoroughly despised himself: even *that* is elevation. Alas, was *this* perhaps the higher man whose cry I heard?

I love the great despisers. Man is something that hath to be surpassed."——

LXXIII.—The Higher Man

1

When I came unto men for the first time, then did I commit the anchorite folly, the great folly: I appeared on the market place.

And when I spake unto all, I spake unto none. In the evening, however, ropedancers were my companions, and corpses; and I myself almost a corpse.

With the new morning, however, there came unto me a new truth: then did I learn to say: "Of what account to me are market place and populace and populace-noise and long populace-cars!"

Ye higher men, learn *this* from me: On the market place no one believeth in higher men. But if ye will speak there, very well! The populace, however, blinketh: "We are all equal."

"Ye higher men,"—so blinketh the populace—"there are no higher men, we are all equal; man is man, before God —we are all equal!"

Before God!—Now, however, this God hath died. Before

the populace, however, we will not be equal. Ye higher men, away from the market place!

2

Before God!—Now however this God hath died! Ye higher men, this God was your greatest danger.

Only since he lay in the grave have ye again arisen. Now only cometh the great noontide, now only doth the higher man become—master!

Have ye understood this word, O my brethren? Ye are frightened: do your hearts turn giddy? Doth the abyss here yawn for you? Doth the hellhound here yelp at you?

Well! Take heart! ye higher men! Now only travaileth the mountain of the human future. God hath died: now do *we* desire—the Superman to live.

3

The most careful ask today: "How is man to be maintained?" Zarathustra, however, asketh, as the first and only one: "How is man to be *surpassed?*"

The Superman, I have at heart; *that* is the first and only thing to me—and *not* man: not the neighbor, not the poorest, not the sorriest, not the best.—

O my brethren, what I can love in man is that he is an overgoing and a downgoing. And also in you there is much that maketh me love and hope.

In that ye have despised, ye higher men, that maketh me hope. For the great despisers are the great reverers.

In that ye have despaired, there is much to honor. For ye have not learned to submit yourselves, ye have not learned petty policy.

For today have the petty people become master: they all preach submission and humility and policy and diligence and consideration and the long et cetera of petty virtues.

Whatever is of the effeminate type, whatever originateth from the servile type, and especially the populace-mishmash —*that* wisheth now to be master of all human destiny—O disgust! Disgust! Disgust!

That asketh and asketh and never tireth: "How is man to maintain himself best, longest, most pleasantly?" Thereby— are they the masters of today.

These masters of today—surpass them, O my brethren—

these petty people: *they* are the Superman's greatest danger!

Surpass, ye higher men, the petty virtues, the petty policy, the sand-grain considerateness, the ant-hill trumpery, the pitiable comfortableness, the "happiness of the greatest number"—!

And rather despair than submit yourselves. And verily I love you, because ye know not today how to live, ye higher men! For thus do *ye* live—best!

4

Have ye courage, O my brethren? Are ye stouthearted? *Not* the courage before witnesses, but anchorite and eagle courage, which not even a God any longer beholdeth?

Cold souls, mules, the blind and the drunken, I do not call stouthearted. He hath heart who knoweth fear, but *vanquisheth* it; who seeth the abyss, but with *pride*.

He who seeth the abyss, but with eagle's eyes, he who with eagle's talons *graspeth* the abyss: he hath courage.

5

"Man is evil"—so said to me for consolation, all the wisest ones. Ah, if only it be still true today! For the evil is man's best force.

"Man must become better and eviler"—so do *I* teach. The evilest is necessary for the Superman's best.

It may have been well for the preacher of the petty people to suffer and be burdened by men's sin. I, however, rejoice in great sin as my great *consolation*.—

Such things, however, are not said for long ears. Every word, also, is not suited for every mouth. These are fine, faraway things: at them sheep's claws shall not grasp!

6

Ye higher men, think ye that I am here to put right what ye have put wrong?

Or that I wished henceforth to make snugger couches for you sufferers? Or show you restless, miswandering, misclimbing ones, new and easier footpaths?

Nay! Nay! Three times Nay! Always more, always better ones of your type shall succumb—for ye shall always have it worst and harder. Thus only—

—Thus only groweth man aloft to the height where the lightning striketh and shattereth him: high enough for the lightning!

Toward the few, the long, the remote go forth my soul and my seeking: of what account to me are your many little, short miseries!

Ye do not yet suffer enough for me! For ye suffer from yourselves, ye have not yet suffered *from man*. Ye would lie if ye spake otherwise! None of you suffereth from what *I* have suffered.

7

It is not enough for me that the lightning no longer doeth harm. I do not wish to conduct it away: it shall learn—to work for *me*.—

My wisdom hath accumulated long like a cloud, it becometh stiller and darker. So doeth all wisdom which shall one day bear *lightnings.*—

Unto these men of today will I not be *light*, nor be called light. *Them*—will I blind: lightning of my wisdom! put out their eyes!

8

Do not will anything beyond your power: there is a bad falseness in those who will beyond their power.

Especially when they will great things! For they awaken distrust in great things, these subtle false coiners and stage players:—

—Until at last they are false toward themselves, squint-eyed, whited cankers, glossed over with strong words, parade virtues, and brilliant false deeds.

Take good care there, ye higher men! For nothing is more precious to me, and rarer, than honesty.

Is this today not that of the populace? The populace, however, knoweth not what is great and what is small, what is straight and what is honest: it is innocently crooked, it ever lieth.

9

Have a good distrust today, ye higher men, ye enheartened

ones! Ye open-hearted ones! And keep your reasons secret! For this today is that of the populace.

What the populace once learned to believe without reasons, who could—refute it to them by means of reasons?

And on the market place one convinceth with gestures. But reasons make the populace distrustful.

And when truth hath once triumphed there, then ask yourselves with good distrust: "What strong error hath fought for it?"

Be on your guard also against the learned! They hate you, because they are unproductive! They have cold, withered eyes before which every bird is unplumed.

Such persons vaunt about not lying: but inability to lie is still far from being love to truth. Be on your guard!

Freedom from fever is still far from being knowledge! Refrigerated spirits I do not believe in. He who cannot lie doth not know what truth is.

10

If ye would go up high, then use your own legs! Do not get yourselves *carried* aloft: do not seat yourselves on other people's backs and heads!

Thou hast mounted, however, on horseback? Thou now ridest briskly up to thy goal? Well, my friend! But thy lame foot is also with thee on horseback!

When thou reachest thy goal, when thou alightest from thy horse: precisely on thy *height*, thou higher man, then wilt thou stumble!

11

Ye creating ones, ye higher men! One is only pregnant with one's own child.

Do not let yourselves be imposed upon or put upon! Who then is *your* neighbor? Even if ye act "for your neighbor" —ye still do not create for him!

Unlearn, I pray you, this "for," ye creating ones: your very virtue wisheth you to have naught to do with "for" and "on account of" and "because." Against these false little words shall ye stop your ears.

"For one's neighbor" is the virtue only of the petty people: there it is said "like and like," and "hand washeth hand":—

they have neither the right nor the power for *your* self-seeking!

In your self-seeking, ye creating ones, there is the foresight and foreseeing of the pregnant! What no one's eye hath yet seen, namely, the fruit—this sheltereth and saveth and nourisheth your entire love.

Where your entire love is, namely, with your child, there is also your entire virtue! Your work, your will is *your* "neighbor": let no false values impose upon you!

12

Ye creating ones, ye higher men! Whoever hath to give birth is sick; whoever hath given birth, however, is unclean.

Ask women: one giveth birth not because it giveth pleasure. The pain maketh hens and poets cackle.

Ye creating ones, in you there is much uncleanness. That is because ye have had to be mothers.

A new child: oh, how much new filth hath also come into the world! Go apart! He who hath given birth shall wash his soul!

13

Be not virtuous beyond your powers! And seek nothing from yourselves opposed to probability!

Walk in the footsteps in which your fathers' virtue hath already walked! How would ye rise high, if your fathers' will should not rise with you?

He, however, who would be a firstling, let him take care lest he also become a lastling! And where the vices of your fathers are there should ye not set up as saints!

He whose fathers were inclined for women, and for strong wine and flesh of wild boar swine, what would it be if he demanded chastity of himself?

A folly would it be! Much verily doth it seem to me for such a one, if he should be the husband of one or of two or of three women.

And if he founded monasteries, and inscribed over their portals: "The way to holiness,"—I should still say: What good is it! It is a new folly!

He hath founded for himself a penance house and refuge house: much good may it do! But I do not believe in it.

In solitude there groweth what anyone bringeth into it—

also the brute in one's nature. Thus is solitude inadvisable unto many.

Hath there ever been anything filthier on earth than the saints of the wilderness? *Around them* was not only the devil loose—but also the swine.

14

Shy, ashamed, awkward, like the tiger whose spring hath failed—thus, ye higher men, have I often seen you slink aside. A *cast* which ye made had failed.

But what doth it matter, ye dice players! Ye had not learned to play and mock, as one must play and mock! Do we not ever sit at a great table of mocking and playing?

And if great things have been a failure with you, have ye yourselves therefore—been a failure? And if ye yourselves have been a failure, hath man therefore—been a failure? If man, however, hath been a failure: well then! never mind!

15

The higher its type, always the seldomer doth a thing succeed. Ye higher men here, have ye not all—been failures?

Be of good cheer; what doth it matter? How much is still possible! Learn to laugh at yourselves, as ye ought to laugh!

What wonder even that ye have failed and only half succeeded, ye half-shattered ones! Doth not—man's *future* strive and struggle in you?

Man's furthest, profoundest, star-highest issues, his prodigious powers—do not all these foam through one another in your vessel?

What wonder that many a vessel shattereth! Learn to laugh at yourselves, as ye ought to laugh! Ye higher men, oh, how much is still possible!

And verily, how much hath already succeeded! How rich is this earth in small, good, perfect things, in well-constituted things!

Set around you small, good, perfect things, ye higher men. Their golden maturity healeth the heart. The perfect teacheth one to hope.

16

What hath hitherto been the greatest sin here on earth?

Was it not the word of him who said: "Woe unto them that laugh now!"

Did he himself find no cause for laughter on the earth? Then he sought badly. A child even findeth cause for it.

He—did not love sufficiently: otherwise would he also have loved us, the laughing ones! But he hated and hooted us; wailing and teeth gnashing did he promise us.

Must one then curse immediately, when one doth not love? That—seemeth to me bad taste. Thus did he, however, this absolute one. He sprang from the populace.

And he himself just did not love sufficiently; otherwise would he have raged less because people did not love him. All great love doth not *seek* love: it seeketh more.

Go out of the way of all such absolute ones! They are a poor sickly type, a populace type: they look at this life with ill will, they have an evil eye for this earth.

Go out of the way of all such absolute ones! They have heavy feet and sultry hearts: they do not know how to dance. How could the earth be light to such ones!

17

Tortuously do all good things come nigh to their goal. Like cats they curve their backs, they purr inwardly with their approaching happiness—all good things laugh.

His step betrayeth whether a person already walketh on *his own* path: just see me walk! He, however, who cometh nigh to his goal danceth.

And verily, a statue have I not become, not yet do I stand there stiff, stupid, and stony, like a pillar; I love fast racing.

And though there be on earth fens and dense afflictions, he who hath light feet runneth even across the mud, and danceth, as upon well-swept ice.

Lift up your hearts, my brethren, high, higher! And do not forget your legs! Lift up also your legs, ye good dancers, and better still, if ye stand upon your heads!

18

This crown of the laugher, this rose-garland crown: I myself have put on this crown, I myself have consecrated my laughter. No one else have I found today potent enough for this.

Zarathustra the dancer, Zarathustra the light one, who

beckoneth with his pinions, one ready for flight, beckoning
unto all birds, ready and prepared, a blissfully light-spirited
one:—

Zarathustra the soothsayer, Zarathustra the soothlaugher,
no impatient one, no absolute one, one who loveth leaps
and side leaps; I myself have put on this crown!

19

Lift up your hearts, my brethren, high, higher! And do
not forget your legs! Lift up also your legs, ye good dancers,
and better still if ye stand upon your heads!

There are also heavy animals in a state of happiness, there
are clubfooted ones from the beginning. Curiously do they
exert themselves, like an elephant which endeavoreth to stand
upon its head.

Better, however, to be foolish with happiness than foolish
with misfortune, better to dance awkwardly than walk lame-
ly. So learn, I pray you, my wisdom, ye higher men: even
the worst thing hath two good reverse sides.—

—Even the worst thing hath good dancing legs: so learn,
I pray you, ye higher men, to put yourselves on your proper
legs!

So unlearn, I pray you, the sorrow-sighing, and all the
populace-sadness! Oh, how sad the buffoons of the populace
seem to me today! This today, however, is that of the
populace.

X. Truth and Illusion

FROM HUMAN, ALL TOO HUMAN, VOL. I

28

ILL-FAMED WORDS. Away with those wearisomely hackneyed terms Optimism and Pessimism! For the occasion for using them becomes less and less from day to day; only the chatterboxes still find them so absolutely necessary. For why in all the world should anyone wish to be an optimist unless he had a God to defend who *must* have created the best of worlds if he himself be goodness and perfection—what thinker, however, still needs the hypothesis of a God? But every occasion for a pessimistic confession of faith is also lacking when one has no interest in being annoyed at the advocates of God (the theologians, or the theologizing philosophers), and in energetically defending the opposite view, that evil reigns, that pain is greater than pleasure, that the world is a bungled piece of work, the manifestation of an ill will to life. But who still bothers about the theologians now—except the theologians? Apart from all theology and its contentions, it is quite clear that the world is not good and not bad (to say nothing of its being the best or the worst), and that the terms "good" and "bad" have only significance with respect to man, and indeed, perhaps, they are not justified even here in the way they are usually employed; in any case we must get rid of both the calumniating and the glorifying conception of the world.

33

ERROR ABOUT LIFE NECESSARY FOR LIFE. Every belief in the value and worthiness of life is based on vitiated thought; it is only possible through the fact that sympathy for the general life and suffering of mankind is very weakly developed in the individual. Even the rarer people who think outside themselves do not contemplate this general life, but only a limited part of it. If one understands how to direct one's attention chiefly to the exceptions—I mean to the highly gifted and the rich souls—if one regards the production of these as the aim of the whole world-development and rejoices in its operation, then one may believe in the value of life, because one thereby *overlooks* the other men—one consequently thinks fallaciously. So, too, when one directs one's attention to all mankind, but only considers *one* species of impulses in them, the less egoistical ones, and excuses them with regard to the other instincts, one may then again entertain hopes of mankind in general and believe so far in the value of life, consequently in this case also through fallaciousness of thought. Let one, however, behave in this or that manner: with such behavior one is an *exception* amongst men. Now, most people bear life without any considerable grumbling, and consequently *believe* in the value of existence, but precisely because each one is solely self-seeking and self-affirming, and does not step out of himself like those exceptions, everything extrapersonal is imperceptible to them, or at most seems only a faint shadow. Therefore on this alone is based the value of life for the ordinary everyday man, that he regards himself as more important than the world. The great lack of imagination from which he suffers is the reason why he cannot enter into the feelings of other beings, and therefore sympathizes as little as possible with their fate and suffering. He, on the other hand, who really *could* sympathize therewith would have to despair of the value of life; were he to succeed in comprehending and feeling in himself the general consciousness of mankind, he would collapse with a curse on existence; for mankind as a whole has *no* goals, consequently man, in considering his whole course, cannot find in it his comfort and support, but his despair. If, in all that he does, he considers the final aimlessness of man, his own activity assumes in his eyes the character of wastefulness. But to feel one's self just as much wasted as humanity (and not only as an individual) as we see the single blossom of nature wasted, is a feeling above all other feelings. But who is capable of it? Assuredly only a poet, and poets always know how to console themselves.

51

HOW APPEARANCE BECOMES ACTUALITY. The actor finally reaches such a point that even in the deepest sorrow he cannot cease from thinking about the impression made by his own person and the general scenic effect; for instance, even at the funeral of his child, he will weep over his own sorrow and its expression like one of his own audience. The hypocrite, who always plays one and the same part, ceases at last to be a hypocrite; for instance, priests, who as young men are generally conscious or unconscious hypocrites, become at last natural, and are then really without any affectation, just priests; or if the father does not succeed so far, perhaps the son does, who makes use of his father's progress and inherits his habits. If anyone long and obstinately desires to *appear* something, he finds it difficult at last to *be* anything else. The profession of almost every individual, even of the artist, begins with hypocrisy, with an imitating from without, with a copying of the effective. He who always wears the mask of a friendly expression must eventually obtain a power over well-meaning dispositions without which the expression of friendliness is not to be compelled—and finally, these, again, obtain a power over him, he *is* well-meaning.

53

THE NOMINAL DEGREES OF TRUTH. One of the commonest mistakes is this: because someone is truthful and honest toward us, he must speak the truth. Thus the child believes in its parents' judgment, the Christian in the assertions of the Founder of the Church. In the same way men refuse to admit that all those things which men defended in former ages with the sacrifice of life and happiness were nothing but errors; it is even said, perhaps, that they were degrees of the truth. But what is really meant is that when a man has honestly believed in something, and has fought and died for his faith, it would really be too *unjust* if he had only been inspired by an error. Such a thing seems a contradiction of eternal justice; therefore the heart of sensitive man ever enunciates against his head the axiom: between moral action and intellectual insight there must absolutely be a necessary connection. It is unfortunately otherwise, for there is no eternal justice.

146

THE ARTIST'S SENSE OF TRUTH. With regard to recognition of truths, the artist has a weaker morality than the thinker; he will on no account let himself be deprived of brilliant and profound interpretations of life, and defends himself against temperate and simple methods and results. He is apparently fighting for the higher worthiness and meaning of mankind; in reality he will not renounce the *most effective* suppositions for his art, the fantastical, mythical, uncertain, extreme, the sense of the symbolical, the overvaluation of personality, the belief that genius is something miraculous—he considers, therefore, the continuance of his art of creation as more important than the scientific devotion to truth in every shape, however simple this may appear.

483

THE ENEMIES OF TRUTH. Convictions are more dangerous enemies of truth than lies.

506

THE CHAMPIONS OF TRUTH. Truth does not find fewest champions when it is dangerous to speak it, but when it is dull.

516

TRUTH. Nobody dies nowadays of fatal truths, there are too many antidotes to them.

517

A FUNDAMENTAL INSIGHT. There is no pre-established harmony between the promotion of truth and the welfare of mankind.

519

TRUTH AS CIRCE. Error has made animals into men; is truth perhaps capable of making man into an animal again?

43

THE CONSCIENTIOUS. It is more convenient to follow one's conscience than one's intelligence, for at every failure conscience finds an excuse and an encouragement in itself. That is why there are so many conscientious and so few intelligent people.

FROM THE DAWN OF DAY

93

WHAT IS TRUTH? Who will not be pleased with the conclusions which the faithful take such delight in coming

to?—"Science cannot be true; for it denies God. Hence it does not come from God; and consequently it cannot be true—for God is truth." It is not the deduction but the premise which is fallacious. What if God were not exactly truth, and if this were proved? And if he were instead the vanity, the desire for power, the ambitions, the fear, and the enraptured and terrified folly of mankind?

424

FOR WHOM THE TRUTH EXISTS. Up to the present time errors have been the power most fruitful in consolations: we now expect the same effects from accepted truths, and we have been waiting rather too long for them. What if these truths could not give us this consolation we are looking for? Would that be an argument against them? What have these truths in common with the sick condition of suffering and degenerate men that they should be useful to them? It is, of course, no proof against the truth of a plant when it is clearly established that it does not contribute in any way to the recovery of sick people. Formerly, however, people were so convinced that man was the ultimate end of nature that they believed that knowledge could reveal nothing that was not beneficial and useful to man—nay, there could not, should not be, any other things in existence.

Perhaps all this leads to the conclusion that truth as an entity and a coherent whole exists only for those natures who, like Aristotle, are at once powerful and harmless, joyous and peaceful: just as none but these would be in a position to seek such truths, for the others seek remedies for themselves—however proud they may be of their intellect and its freedom, they do not seek truth. Hence it comes about that these others take no real joy in science, but reproach it for its coldness, dryness, and inhumanity. This is the judgment of sick people about the games of the healthy.—Even the Greek gods were unable to administer consolation; and when at length the entire Greek world fell ill, this was a reason for the destruction of such gods.

507

AGAINST THE TYRANNY OF TRUTH. Even if we were mad enough to consider all our opinions as truth, we should nevertheless not wish them alone to exist. I cannot see why we should ask for an autocracy and omnipotence of truth: it is sufficient for me to know that it is a great power. Truth, however, must meet with opposition and be able to fight, and we must be able to rest from it at times in falsehood—otherwise truth will grow tiresome, powerless, and insipid, and will render us equally so.

TRUTH AND FALSITY IN AN ULTRAMORAL SENSE

IN some remote corner of the universe, effused into innumerable solar systems, there was once a star upon which clever animals invented cognition. It was the haughtiest, most mendacious moment in the history of this world, but yet only a moment. After Nature had taken breath awhile, the star congealed and the clever animals had to die.—Someone might write a fable after this style, and yet he would not have illustrated sufficiently, how wretched, shadowlike, transitory, purposeless, and fanciful the human intellect appears in Nature. There were eternities during which this intellect did not exist, and when it has once more passed away, there will be nothing to show that it has existed. For this intellect is not concerned with any further mission transcending the sphere of human life. No, it is purely human and none but its owner and procreator regards it so pathetically as to suppose that the world revolves around it. If, however, we and the gnat could understand each other, we should learn that even the gnat swims through the air with the same pathos, and feels within itself the flying center of the world. Nothing in Nature is so bad or so insignificant that it will not, at the smallest puff of that force cognition, immediately swell up like a balloon, and just as a mere porter wants to have his admirer, so the very proudest man, the philosopher, imagines he sees from all sides the eyes of the universe telescopically directed upon his actions and thoughts.

It is remarkable that this is accomplished by the intellect, which after all has been given to the most unfortunate, the most delicate, the most transient beings only as an expedient, in order to detain them for a moment in existence, from which without that extra gift they would have every cause to flee as swiftly as Lessing's son.* That haughtiness connected with cognition and sensation, spreading blinding fogs before the eyes and over the senses of men, deceives itself therefore as to the value of existence owing to the fact that it bears within itself the most flattering evaluation of cognition. Its most general effect is deception, but even its most particular effects have something of deception in their nature.

---

* The German poet, Lessing, had been married for just a little over one year to Eva König. A son was born and died the same day, and the mother's life was despaired of. In a letter to his friend Eschenburg the poet wrote: ". . . and I lost him so unwillingly, this son! For he had so much understanding! so much understanding! Do not suppose that the few hours of fatherhood have made me an ape of a father! I know what I say. Was it not understanding, that they had to drag him into the world with a pair of forceps? that he so soon suspected the evil of this world? Was it not understanding, that he seized the first opportunity to get away from it? . . ."
Eva König died a week later.—TR.

The intellect, as a means for the preservation of the individual, develops its chief power in dissimulation; for it is by dissimulation that the feebler and less robust individuals preserve themselves, since it has been denied them to fight the battle of existence with horns or the sharp teeth of beasts of prey. In man this art of dissimulation reaches its acme of perfection: in him deception, flattery, falsehood and fraud, slander, display, pretentiousness, disguise, cloaking convention, and acting to others and to himself, in short, the continual fluttering to and fro around the *one* flame—Vanity: all these things are so much the rule, and the law, that few things are more incomprehensible than the way in which an honest and pure impulse to truth could have arisen among men. They are deeply immersed in illusions and dream fancies; their eyes glance only over the surface of things and see "forms"; their sensation nowhere leads to truth, but contents itself with receiving stimuli and, so to say, with playing hide-and-seek on the back of things. In addition to that, at night man allows his dreams to lie to him a whole lifetime long, without his moral sense ever trying to prevent them; whereas men are said to exist who by the exercise of a strong will have overcome the habit of snoring. What indeed *does* man know about himself? Oh! that he could but once see himself complete, placed as it were in an illuminated glass case! Does not nature keep secret from him most things, even about his body, e.g., the convolutions of the intestines, the quick flow of the blood currents, the intricate vibrations of the fibers, so as to banish and lock him up in proud, delusive knowledge? Nature threw away the key; and woe to the fateful curiosity which might be able for a moment to look out and down through a crevice in the chamber of consciousness and discover that man, indifferent to his own ignorance, is resting on the pitiless, the greedy, the insatiable, the murderous, and, as it were, hanging in dreams on the back of a tiger. Whence, in the wide world, with this state of affairs, arises the impulse to truth?

As far as the individual tries to preserve himself against other individuals, in the natural state of things he uses the intellect in most cases only for dissimulation; since, however, man both from necessity and boredom wants to exist socially and gregariously, he must needs make peace and at least endeavor to cause the greatest *bellum omnium contra omnes* to disappear from his world. This first conclusion of peace brings with it a something which looks like the first step toward the attainment of that enigmatical bent for truth. For that which henceforth is to be "truth" is now fixed;

that is to say, a uniformly valid and binding designation of things is invented and the legislature of language also gives the first laws of truth: since here, for the first time, originates the contrast between truth and falsity. The liar uses the valid designations, the words, in order to make the unreal appear as real, e.g., he says, "I am rich," whereas the right designation for his state would be "poor." He abuses the fixed conventions by convenient substitution or even inversion of terms. If he does this in a selfish and moreover harmful fashion, society will no longer trust him but will even exclude him. In this way men avoid not so much being defrauded, but being injured by fraud. At bottom, at this juncture, too, they hate not deception, but the evil, hostile consequences of certain species of deception. And it is in a similarly limited sense only that man desires truth: he covets the agreeable, life-preserving consequences of truth; he is indifferent toward pure, ineffective knowledge; he is even inimical toward truths which possibly might prove harmful or destroying. And, moreover, what after all are those conventions of language? Are they possibly products of knowledge, of the love of truth; do the designations and the things coincide? Is language the adequate expression of all realities?

Only by means of forgetfulness can man ever arrive at imagining that he possesses "truth" in that degree just indicated. If he does not mean to content himself with truth in the shape of tautology, that is, with empty husks, he will always obtain illusions instead of truth. What is a word? The expression of a nerve stimulus in sounds. But to infer a cause outside us from the nerve stimulus is already the result of a wrong and unjustifiable application of the proposition of causality. How should we dare, if truth with the genesis of language, if the point of view of certainty with the designations had alone been decisive; how indeed should we dare to say: the stone is hard; as if "hard" was known to us otherwise, and not merely as an entirely subjective stimulus! We divide things according to genders; we designate the tree as masculine,* the plant as feminine: † what arbitrary metaphors! How far-flown beyond the canon of certainty! We speak of a "serpent"; ‡ the designation fits nothing but the sinuosity, and could therefore also appertain to the worm. What arbitrary demarcations! What one-sided preferences given sometimes to this, sometimes to that quality

---

* In German the tree—der Baum—is masculine.—TR.

† In German the plant—die Pflanze—is feminine.—TR.

‡ Cf. the German die Schlange and schlingen, the English serpent from the Latin serpere.—TR.

of a thing! The different languages placed side by side show
that with words truth or adequate expression matters little:
for otherwise there would not be so many languages. The
"Thing-in-itself" (it is just this which would be the pure
ineffective truth) is also quite incomprehensible to the creator
of language and not worth making any great endeavor to obtain. He designates only the relations of things to men and
for their expression he calls to his help the most daring
metaphors. A nerve stimulus, first transformed into a percept! First metaphor! The percept again copied into a sound!
Second metaphor! And each time he leaps completely out of
one sphere right into the midst of an entirely different one.
One can imagine a man who is quite deaf and has never
had a sensation of tone and of music; just as this man will
possibly marvel at Chladni's sound figures in the sand, will
discover their cause in the vibrations of the string, and will
then proclaim that now he knows what man calls "tone";
even so does it happen to us all with language. When we
talk about trees, colors, snow, and flowers, we believe we
know something about the things themselves, and yet we
only possess metaphors of the things, and these metaphors
do not in the least correspond to the original essentials. Just
as the sound shows itself as a sad figure, in the same way
the enigmatical x of the Thing-in-itself is seen first as nerve
stimulus, then as percept, and finally as sound. At any rate
the genesis of language did not therefore proceed on logical
lines, and the whole material in which and with which the
man of truth, the investigator, the philosopher works and
builds, originates, if not from Nephelococcygia, cloudland,
at any rate not from the essence of things.

Let us especially think about the formation of ideas.
Every word becomes at once an idea not by having, as one
might presume, to serve as a reminder for the original experience happening but once and absolutely ididividualized,
to which experience such word owes its origin, no, but by
having simultaneously to fit innumerable, more or less similar
(which really means never equal, therefore altogether unequal) cases. Every idea originates through equating the unequal. As certainly as no one leaf is exactly similar to any
other, so certain is it that the idea "leaf" has been formed
through an arbitrary omission of these individual differences,
through a forgetting of the differentiating qualities, and this
idea now awakens the notion that in nature there is, besides the leaves, a something called *the* "leaf," perhaps a
primal form according to which all leaves were woven, drawn,
accurately measured, colored, crinkled, painted, but by un-

skilled hands, so that no copy had turned out correct and
trustworthy as a true copy of the primal form. We call a
man "honest"; we ask, why has he acted so honestly today?
Our customary answer runs, "On account of his honesty."
The Honesty! That means again: the "leaf" is the cause of
the leaves. We really and truly do not know anything at all
about an essential quality which might be called *the* honesty,
but we do know about numerous individualized, and therefore unequal actions, which we equate by omission of the
unequal, and now designate as honest actions; finally out of
them we formulate a *qualitas occulta* with the name "Honesty." The disregarding of the individual and real furnishes
us with the idea, as it likewise also gives us the form;
whereas nature knows of no forms and ideas, and therefore
knows no species but only an *x*, to us inaccessible and indefinable. For our antithesis of individual and species is
anthropomorphic too and does not come from the essence of
things, although on the other hand we do not dare to say
that it does not correspond to it; for that would be a dogmatic
assertion and as such just as undemonstrable as its contrary.

What therefore is truth? A mobile army of metaphors,
metonymies, anthropomorphisms: in short a sum of human
relations which became poetically and rhetorically intensified,
metamorphosed, adorned, and after long usage seems to a
nation fixed, canonic, and binding; truths are illusions of
which one has forgotten that they *are* illusions; worn-out
metaphors which have become powerless to affect the senses;
coins which have their obverse effaced and now are no longer
of account as coins but merely as metal.

Still we do not yet know whence the impulse to truth
comes, for up to now we have heard only about the obligation which society imposes in order to exist: to be truthful,
that is, to use the usual metaphors, therefore expressed morally: we have heard only about the obligation to lie according
to a fixed convention, to lie gregariously in a style binding
for all. Now man, of course, forgets that matters are going
thus with him; he therefore lies in that fashion pointed out
unconsciously and according to habits of centuries' standing
—and by *this very unconsciousness*, by this very forgetting,
he arrives at a sense for truth. Through this feeling of being
obliged to designate one thing as "red," another as "cold,"
a third one as "dumb," awakes a moral emotion relating
to truth. Out of the antithesis "liar" whom nobody trusts,
whom all exclude, man demonstrates to himself the venerable-
ness, reliability, usefulness of truth. Now as a *"rational"*
being he submits his actions to the sway of abstractions; he

no longer suffers himself to be carried away by sudden impressions, by sensations, he first generalizes all these impressions into paler, cooler ideas, in order to attach to them the ship of his life and actions. Everything which makes man stand out in bold relief against the animal depends on this faculty of volatilizing the concrete metaphors into a schema, and therefore resolving a perception into an idea. For within the range of those schemata a something becomes possible that never could succeed under the first perceptual impressions: to build up a pyramidal order with castes and grades, to create a new world of laws, privileges, suborders, delimitations, which now stands opposite the other perceptual world of first impressions and assumes the appearance of being the more fixed, general, known, human of the two and therefore the regulating and imperative one. Whereas every metaphor of perception is individual and without its equal and therefore knows how to escape all attempts to classify it, the great edifice of ideas shows the rigid regularity of a Roman columbarium and in logic breathes forth the sternness and coolness which we find in mathematics. He who has been breathed upon by this coolness will scarcely believe that the idea, too, bony and hexahedral and permutable as a die, remains, however, only as the *residuum of a metaphor*, and that the illusion of the artistic metamorphosis of a nerve stimulus into percepts is, if not the mother, then the grandmother of every idea. Now in this game of dice, "Truth" means to use every die as it is designated, to count its points carefully, to form exact classifications, and never to violate the order of castes and the sequences of rank. Just as the Romans and Etruscans for their benefit cut up the sky by means of strong mathematical lines and banned a god as it were into a *templum*, into a space limited in this fashion, so every nation has above its head such a sky of ideas divided up mathematically, and it understands the demand for truth to mean that every conceptual god is to be looked for only in *his* own sphere. One may here well admire man, who succeeded in piling up an infinitely complex dome of ideas on a movable foundation and as it were on running water, as a powerful genius of architecture. Of course in order to obtain hold on such a foundation it must be as an edifice piled up out of cobwebs, so fragile as to be carried away by the waves, so firm as not to be blown asunder by every wind. In this way man as an architectural genius rises high above the bee; she builds with wax, which she brings together out of nature; he with the much more delicate material of ideas, which he must first manu-

facture within himself. He is very much to be admired here
—but not on account of his impulse for truth, his bent for
pure cognition of things. If somebody hides a thing behind
a bush, seeks it again and finds it in the selfsame place,
then there is not much to boast of, respecting this seeking
and finding; thus, however, matters stand with the seeking
and finding of "truth" within the realm of reason. If I make
the definition of the mammal and then declare after inspect-
ing a camel, "Behold a mammal," then no doubt a truth is
brought to light thereby, but it is of very limited value, I
mean it is anthropomorphic through and through, and does
not contain one single point which is "true-in-itself," real,
and universally valid, apart from man. The seeker after such
truths seeks at the bottom only the metamorphosis of the
world in man; he strives for an understanding of the world
as a humanlike thing and by his battling gains at best the
feeling of an assimilation. Similarly, as the astrologer contemplated the stars in the service of men and in connection
with their happiness and unhappiness, such a seeker contemplates the whole world as related to man, as the infinitely
protracted echo of an original sound: man; as the multiplied
copy of the one archtype: man. His procedure is to apply
man as the measure of all things, whereby he starts from
the error of believing that he has these things immediately
before him as pure objects. He therefore forgets that the
original metaphors of perception *are* metaphors, and takes
them for the things themselves.

Only by forgetting that primitive world of metaphors, only
by the congelation and coagulation of an original mass of
similes and percepts pouring forth as a fiery liquid out of
the primal faculty of human fancy, only by the invincible
faith, that *this* sun, *this* window, *this* table is a truth in
itself: in short only by the fact that man forgets himself as
subject, and what is more as an *artistically creating* subject,
only by all this does he live with some repose, safety, and
consequence. If he were able to get out of the prison walls
of this faith, even for an instant only, his "self-consciousness" would be destroyed at once. Already it costs him some
trouble to admit to himself that the insect and the bird
perceive a world different from his own, and that the question, which of the two world-perceptions is more accurate,
is quite a senseless one, since to decide this question it
would be necessary to apply the standard of *right perception*,
i.e., to apply a standard which *does not exist*. On the whole
it seems to me that the "right perception"—which would
mean the adequate expression of an object in the subject—

is a nonentity full of contradictions: for between two utterly different spheres, as between subject and object, there is no causality, no accuracy, no expression, but at the utmost an *aesthetical* relation, I mean a suggestive metamorphosis, a stammering translation into quite a distinct foreign language, for which purpose, however, there is needed at any rate an intermediate sphere, an intermediate force, freely composing and freely inventing. The word "phenomenon" contains many seductions, and on that account I avoid it as much as possible, for it is not true that the essence of things appears in the empiric world. A painter who had no hands and wanted to express the picture distinctly present to his mind by the agency of song would still reveal much more with this permutation of spheres than the empiric world reveals about the essence of things. The very relation of a nerve stimulus to the produced percept is in itself no necessary one; but if the same percept has been reproduced millions of times and has been the inheritance of many successive generations of man, and in the end appears each time to all mankind as the result of the same cause, then it attains finally for man the same importance as if it were *the* unique, necessary percept and as if that relation between the original nerve stimulus and the percept produced were a close relation of causality: just as a dream eternally repeated would be perceived and judged as though real. But the congelation and coagulation of a metaphor does not at all guarantee the necessity and exclusive justification of that metaphor.

Surely every human being who is at home with such contemplations has felt a deep distrust against any idealism of that kind, as often as he has distinctly convinced himself of the eternal rigidity, omnipresence, and infallibility of nature's laws: he has arrived at the conclusion that as far as we can penetrate the heights of the telescopic and the depths of the microscopic world, everything is quite secure, complete, infinite, determined, and continuous. Science will have to dig in these shafts eternally and successfully and all things found are sure to have to harmonize and not to contradict one another. How little does this resemble a product of fancy, for if it were one it would necessarily betray somewhere its nature of appearance and unreality. Against this it may be objected in the first place that if each of us had for himself a different sensibility, if we ourselves were only able to perceive sometimes as a bird, sometimes as a worm, sometimes as a plant, or if one of us saw the same stimulus as red, another as blue, if a third person even perceived it as a tone, then nobody would talk of such an orderliness of nature, but would conceive of her only as an extremely subjective structure. Secondly, what is, for us in general, a law of nature? It is not known in itself but only in its effects, that is to say, in its relations to other laws of nature, which again are known to us only as sums of relations. Therefore all these relations refer only one to another and are absolutely incomprehensible to us in their essence; only that which we add: time, space, i.e., relations of sequence and numbers, are really known to us in them. Everything wonderful, however, that we marvel at in the laws of nature, everything that demands an explanation and might seduce us into distrusting idealism, lies really and solely in the mathematical rigor and inviolability of the conceptions of time and space. These, however, we produce within ourselves and throw them forth with that necessity with which the spider spins; since we are compelled to conceive all things under these forms only, then it is no longer wonderful that in all things we actually conceive none but these forms: for they all must bear within themselves the laws of number, and this very idea of number is the most marvelous in all things. All obedience to law which impresses us so forcibly in the orbits of stars and in chemical processes coincides at the bottom with those qualities which we ourselves attach to those things, so that it is we who thereby make the impression upon ourselves. Whence it clearly follows that that artistic formation of metaphors with which every sensation in us begins already presupposes those forms, and is therefore only consummated within them; only out of the persistency of these primal forms the possibility explains itself, how afterward out of the metaphors themselves a structure of ideas could again be compiled. For the latter is an imitation of the relations of time, space, and number in the realm of metaphors.

2

As we saw, it is *language* which has worked originally at the construction of ideas; in later times it is *science*. Just as the bee works at the same time at the cells and fills them with honey, thus science works irresistibly at that great columbarium of ideas, the cemetery of perceptions; builds ever newer and higher storeys; supports, purifies, renews the old cells; and endeavors above all to fill that gigantic framework and to arrange within it the whole of the empiric world, i.e., the anthropomorphic world. And as the man of action binds his life to reason and its ideas, in order to avoid being swept away and losing himself, so the seeker after truth builds his hut close to the towering edifice of science in order to collaborate with it and to find protection. And he needs protection. For there are awful powers which continually press upon him, and which hold out against the "truth" of science "truths" fashioned in quite another way, bearing devices of the most heterogeneous character.

That impulse toward the formation of metaphors, that fundamental impulse of man, which we cannot reason away for one moment—for thereby we should reason away man himself—is in truth not defeated nor even subdued by the fact that out of its evaporated products, the ideas, a regular and rigid new world has been built as a stronghold for it. This impulse seeks for itself a new realm of action and another river-bed, and finds it in *Mythos* and more generally in *Art*. This impulse constantly confuses the rubrics and cells of the ideas by putting up new figures of speech, metaphors, metonymies; it constantly shows its passionate longing for shaping the existing world of waking man as motley, irregular, inconsequentially incoherent, attractive, and eternally new as the world of dreams is. For indeed, waking man per se is only clear about his being awake through the rigid and orderly woof of ideas, and it is for this very reason that he sometimes comes to believe that he was dreaming when that woof of ideas has for a moment been torn by Art. Pascal is quite right when he asserts that if the same dream came to us every night, we should be just as much occupied by it as by the things which we see every day; to quote his words, "If an artisan were certain that he would dream every night for fully twelve hours that he was a king, I believe that he would be just as happy as a king who dreams every night for twelve hours that he is an artisan." The wide-awake day of a people mystically excitable, let us say of the earlier Greeks, is in fact through the continually working wonder, which the mythos presupposes, more akin to the dream than to the day of the thinker sobered by silence. If every tree may at some time talk as a nymph, or a god under the disguise of a bull carry away virgins, if the goddess Athena herself be suddenly seen as, with a beautiful team, she drives, accompanied by Pisistratus, through the markets of Athens—and every honest Athenian did believe this—at any moment, as in a dream, everything is possible; and all nature swarms around man as if she were nothing but the masquerade of the gods, who found it a huge joke to deceive man by assuming all possible forms.

Man himself, however, has an invincible tendency to let himself be deceived, and he is like one enchanted with happiness when the rhapsodist narrates to him epic romances in such a way that they appear real or when the actor on the stage makes the king appear more kingly than reality shows him. Intellect, that master of dissimulation, is free and dismissed from his service as slave, so long as It is able to deceive without *injuring*, and then It celebrates Its Saturnalia. Never is It richer, prouder, more luxuriant, more skillful and daring; with a creator's delight It throws metaphors into confusion, shifts the boundary stones of the abstractions, so that, for instance, It designates the stream as the mobile way which carries man to that place whither he would otherwise go. Now It has thrown off Its shoulders the emblem of servitude. Usually with gloomy officiousness It endeavors to point out the way to a poor individual coveting existence, and It fares forth for plunder and booty like a servant for his master, but now It Itself has become a master and may wipe from Its countenance the expression of indigence. Whatever It now does, compared with Its former doings, bears within itself dissimulation, just as Its former doings bore the character of distortion. It copies human life, but takes it for a good thing and seems to rest quite satisfied with it. That enormous framework and hoarding of ideas, by clinging to which needy man saves himself through life, is to the freed intellect only a scaffolding and a toy for Its most daring feats, and when It smashes it to pieces, throws it into confusion, and then puts it together ironically, pairing the strangest, separating the nearest items, then It manifests that It has no use for those makeshifts of misery, and that It is now no longer led by ideas but by intuitions. From these intuitions no regular road leads into the land of the spectral schemata, the abstractions; for them the word is not made, when man sees them he is dumb, or speaks in forbidden metaphors and in unheard-of combinations of ideas, in order to correspond creatively with the impression of the powerful present intuition at least by destroying and jeering at the old barriers of ideas.

There are ages, when the rational and the intuitive man stand side by side, the one full of fear of the intuition, the other full of scorn for the abstraction; the latter just as irrational as the former is inartistic. Both desire to rule over life; the one by knowing how to meet the most important needs with foresight, prudence, regularity; the other as an "overjoyous" hero by ignoring those needs and taking that life only as real which simulates appearance and beauty.

Whenever intuitive man, as for instance in the earlier history of Greece, brandishes his weapons more powerfully and victoriously than his opponent, there under favorable conditions, a culture can develop and art can establish her rule over life. That dissembling, that denying of neediness, that splendor of metaphorical notions and especially that directness of dissimulation accompany all utterances of such a life. Neither the house of man, nor his way of walking, nor his clothing, nor his earthen jug suggest that necessity invented them; it seems as if they all were intended as the expressions of a sublime happiness, an olympic cloudlessness, and, as it were, a playing at seriousness. Whereas the man guided by ideas and abstractions only wards off misfortune by means of them, without even enforcing for himself happiness out of the abstractions; whereas he strives after the greatest possible freedom from pains, the intuitive man dwelling in the midst of culture has from his intuitions a harvest: besides the warding off of evil, he attains a continuous inpouring of enlightenment, enlivenment, and redemption. Of course when he *does* suffer, he suffers more: and he even suffers more frequently since he cannot learn from experience, but again and again falls into the same ditch into which he has fallen before. In suffering he is just as irrational as in happiness; he cries aloud and finds no consolation. How different matters are in the same misfortune with the Stoic, taught by experience and ruling himself by ideas! He who otherwise only looks for uprightness, truth, freedom from deceptions and shelter from ensnaring and sudden attack, in his misfortune performs the masterpiece of dissimulation, just as the other did in his happiness; he shows no twitching mobile human face but, as it were, a mask with dignified, harmonious features; he does not cry out and does not even alter his voice; when a heavy thundercloud bursts upon him, he wraps himself up in his cloak and with slow and measured step walks away from beneath it.

XI. Art and Beauty

FROM HUMAN, ALL TOO HUMAN, VOL. I

149

THE SLOW ARROW OF BEAUTY. The noblest kind of beauty is that which does not transport us suddenly, which does not make stormy and intoxicating impressions (such a kind easily arouses disgust), but that which slowly filters into our minds, which we take away with us almost unnoticed, and which we encounter again in our dreams; but which, however, after having long lain modestly on our hearts, takes entire possession of us, fills our eyes with tears and our hearts with longing. What is it that we long for at the sight of beauty? We long to be beautiful, we fancy it must bring much happiness with it. But that is a mistake.

150

THE ANIMATION OF ART. Art raises its head where creeds relax. It takes over many feelings and moods engendered by religion, lays them to its heart, and itself becomes deeper, more full of soul, so that it is capable of transmitting exultation and enthusiasm, which it previously was not able to do. The abundance of religious feelings which have grown into a stream are always breaking forth again and desire to conquer new kingdoms, but the growing enlightenment has shaken the dogmas of religion and inspired a deep mistrust—thus the feeling, thrust by enlightenment out of the religious sphere, throws itself upon art, in a few cases into political life, even straight into science. Everywhere where human endeavor wears a loftier, gloomier aspect, it may be assumed that the fear of spirits, incense, and church-shadows have remained attached to it.

152

THE ART OF THE UGLY SOUL. Art is confined within too narrow limits if it be required that only the orderly, respectable, well-behaved soul should be allowed to express itself therein. As in the plastic arts, so also in music and poetry: there is an art of the ugly soul side by side with the art of the beautiful soul; and the mightiest effects of art, the crushing of souls, moving of stones, and humanizing of beasts, have perhaps been best achieved precisely by that art.

157

THE SUFFERING OF GENIUS AND ITS VALUE. The artistic genius desires to give pleasure, but if his mind is on a very high plane he does not easily find anyone to share his pleasure; he offers entertainment but nobody accepts it. This gives him, in certain circumstances, a comically touching pathos; for he has really no right to force pleasure on men. He pipes, but none will dance: can that be tragic? Perhaps.—As compensation for this deprivation, however, he finds more pleasure in creating than the rest of mankind experiences in all other species of activity. His sufferings are considered as exaggerated, because the sound of his complaints is louder and his tongue more eloquent; and yet *sometimes* his sufferings are really very great; but only because his ambition and his envy are so great. The learned genius, like Kepler and Spinoza, is usually not so covetous and does not make such an exhibition of his really greater sufferings and deprivations. He can reckon with greater certainty on future fame and can afford to do without the present, whilst an artist who does this always plays a desperate game that makes his heart ache. In very rare cases, when in one and the same individual are combined the genius of power and of knowledge and the moral genius, there is added to the above-mentioned pains that species of pain which must be regarded as the most curious exception in the world; those extra- and superpersonal sensations which are experienced on behalf of a nation, of humanity, of all civilization, all suffering existence, which acquire their value through the connection with particularly difficult and remote perceptions (pity in itself is worth but little). But what standard, what proof is there for its genuineness? Is it not almost imperative to be mistrustful of all who *talk* of feeling sensations of this kind?

161

THE OVERVALUATION OF SELF IN THE BELIEF IN ARTISTS AND PHILOSOPHERS. We are all prone to think that the excellence of a work of art or of an artist is proved when it moves and touches us. But there *our own excellence* in judgment and sensibility must have been proved first, which is not the case. In all plastic art, who had greater power to effect a charm than Bernini, who made a greater effect than the orator that appeared after Demosthenes introduced the Asiatic style and gave it a predominance which lasted throughout two centuries? This predominance during whole centuries is not a proof of the excellence and enduring validity of a style; therefore we must not be too certain in our good opinion of any artist—this is not only belief in the truthfulness of our sensations but also in the infallibility of our judgment, whereas judgment or sensation, or even both, may be too coarse or too fine, exaggerated or crude. Neither are the blessings and blissfulness of a philosophy or of a religion proofs of its truth; just as little as the happiness which an insane person derives from his fixed idea is a proof of the reasonableness of this idea.

164

THE DANGER AND THE GAIN IN THE CULT OF GENIUS. The belief in great, superior, fertile minds is not necessarily, but still very frequently, connected with that wholly or partly religious superstition that those spirits are of superhuman origin and possess certain marvelous faculties, by means of which they obtained their knowledge in ways quite different from the rest of mankind. They are credited with having an immediate insight into the nature of the world, through a peephole in the mantle of the phenomenon as it were, and it is believed that, without the trouble and severity of science, by virtue of this marvelous prophetic sight, they could impart something final and decisive about mankind and the world. So long as there are still believers in miracles in the world of knowledge it may perhaps be admitted that the believers themselves derive a benefit therefrom, inasmuch as by their absolute subjection to great minds they obtain the best discipline and schooling for their own minds during the period of development. On the other hand, it may at least be questioned whether the superstition of genius, of its privileges and special faculties, is useful for a genius himself when it implants itself in him. In any case it is a dangerous sign when man shudders at his own self, be it that famous Caesarean shudder or the shudder of genius which applies to this case, when the incense of sacrifice, which by rights is offered to a God alone, penetrates into the brain of the genius, so that he begins to waver and to look upon himself as something superhuman. The slow consequences are: the feeling of irresponsibility, the exceptional rights, the belief that mere intercourse with him confers a favor, and frantic rage at any attempt to compare him with others or even to place him below them and to bring into prominence whatever is unsuccessful in his work. Through the fact that he ceases to criticize himself one opinion after another falls out of his plumage—that superstition undermines the foundation of his strength and even makes him a hypocrite after his power has failed him. For great minds it is, therefore, perhaps better when they come to an understanding about their strength and its source, when they comprehend what purely human qualities are mingled in them, what a combination they are of fortunate conditions: thus once it was continual energy, a decided application to individual aims, great personal courage, and then the good fortune of an education, which at an early period provided the best teachers, examples, and methods. Assuredly, if its aim is to make the greatest possible *effect,* abstruseness has always done much for itself and that gift of partial insanity; for at all times that power has been admired and envied by means of which men were deprived of will and imbued with the fancy that they were preceded by supernatural leaders. Truly, men are exalted and inspired by the belief that someone among them is endowed with supernatural powers, and in this respect insanity, as Plato says, has brought the greatest blessings to mankind. In a few rare cases this form of insanity may also have been the means by which an all-round exuberant nature was kept within bounds; in individual life the imaginings of frenzy frequently exert the virtue of remedies which are poisons in themselves; but in every "genius" that believes in his own divinity the poison shows itself at last in the same proportion as the "genius" grows old; we need but recollect the example of Napoleon, for it was most assuredly through his faith in himself and his star, and through his scorn of mankind, that he grew to that mighty unity which distinguished him from all modern men, until at last, however, this faith developed into an almost insane fatalism, robbed him of his quickness of comprehension and penetration, and was the cause of his downfall.

169

THE SOURCE OF THE COMIC ELEMENT. If we consider that for many thousands of years man was an animal that was susceptible in the highest degree to fear, and that everything sudden and unexpected had to find him ready for battle, perhaps even ready for death; that even later, in social relations, all security was based on the expected, on custom in thought and action, we need not be surprised that at everything sudden and unexpected in word and deed, if it occurs without danger or injury, man becomes exuberant and passes over into the very opposite of fear—the terrified, trembling, crouching being shoots upward, stretches itself: man laughs. This transition from momentary fear into short-lived exhilaration is called the *comic*. On the other hand, in the tragic phenomenon, man passes quickly from great enduring exuberance into great fear; but as amongst mortals great and lasting exuberance is much rarer than the cause for fear, there is far more comedy than tragedy in the world; we laugh much oftener than we are agitated.

171

WHAT IS NEEDFUL TO A WORK OF ART. Those who talk so much about the needful factors of a work of art exaggerate; if they are artists they do so *in majorem artis gloriam,* if they are laymen, from ignorance. The form of a work of art, which gives speech to their thoughts and is, therefore, their mode of talking, is always somewhat uncer-

tain, like all kinds of speech. The sculptor can add or omit
many little traits, as can also the exponent, be he an actor
or, in music, performer or conductor. These many little
traits and finishing touches afford him pleasure one day and
none the next; they exist more for the sake of the artist
than the art, for he also has occasionally need of sweet-
meats and playthings to prevent him from becoming morose
with the severity and self-restraint which the representation
of the dominant idea demands from him.

212

OLD DOUBTS ABOUT THE EFFECT OF ART. Should
pity and fear really be unburdened through tragedy, as
Aristotle would have it, so that the hearers return home
colder and quieter? Should ghost stories really make us
less fearful and superstitious? In the case of certain physical processes, in the satisfaction of love, for instance, it is
true that with the fulfillment of a need there follows an al-
leviation and temporary decrease in the impulse. But fear and
pity are not in this sense the needs of particular organs
which require to be relieved. And in time every instinct is
even *strengthened* by practice in its satisfaction, in spite of
that periodical mitigation. It might be possible that in each
single case pity and fear should be soothed and relieved by
tragedy; nevertheless, they might, on the whole, be increased by tragic influences, and Plato would be right in saying that tragedy makes us altogether more timid and susceptible. The tragic poet himself would then of necessity
acquire a gloomy and fearful view of the world, and a
yielding, irritable, tearful soul; it would also agree with
Plato's view if the tragic poets, and likewise the entire part
of the community that derived particular pleasure from
them, degenerated into ever greater licentiousness and intemperance. But what right, indeed, has our age to give an
answer to that great question of Plato's as to the moral influence of art? If we ever had art, where have we an influence, *any kind* of an art-influence?

213

PLEASURE IN NONSENSE. How can we take pleasure
in nonsense? But wherever there is laughter in the world
this is the case: it may even be said that almost everywhere

where there is happiness, there is found pleasure in nonsense. The transformation of experience into its opposite, of the suitable into the unsuitable, the obligatory into the optional (but in such a manner that this process produces no injury and is only imagined in jest), is a pleasure; for it temporarily liberates us from the yoke of the obligatory, suitable, and experienced, in which we usually find our pitiless masters; we play and laugh when the expected (which generally causes fear and expectancy) happens without bringing any injury. It is the pleasure felt by slaves in the Saturnalian feasts.

217

THE SPIRITUALIZING OF HIGHER ART. By virtue of extraordinary intellectual exercise through the art-development of the new music, our ears have been growing more intellectual. For this reason we can now endure a much greater volume of sound, much more "noise," because we are far better practiced in listening for the *sense* in it than were our ancestors. As a matter of fact, all our senses have been somewhat blunted, because they immediately look for the sense, that is, they ask what "it means" and not what "it is"—such a blunting betrays itself, for instance, in the absolute dominion of the temperature of sounds; for ears which still make the finer distinctions, between *cis* and *des,* for instance, are now amongst the exceptions. In this respect our ear has grown coarser. And then the ugly side of the world, the one originally hostile to the senses, has been conquered for music; its power has been immensely widened, especially in the expression of the noble, the terrible, and the mysterious: our music now gives utterance to things which had formerly no tongue. In the same way certain painters have rendered the eye more intellectual, and have gone far beyond that which was formerly called pleasure in color and form. Here, too, that side of the world originally considered as ugly has been conquered by the artistic intellect. What results from all this? The more capable of thought that eye and ear become, the more they approach the limit where they become senseless, the seat of pleasure is moved into the brain, the organs of the senses themselves become dulled and weak, the symbolical takes more and more the place of the actual—and thus we arrive at barbarism in this way as surely as in any other. In the meantime we may say the world is uglier than ever, but it *represents* a more beautiful world than has ever existed. But the more the amber-scent of meaning is dispersed and evaporated, the rarer become those who perceive it, and the remainder halt at what is ugly and endeavor to enjoy it direct, an aim, however, which they never succeed in attaining. Thus, in Germany there is a twofold direction of musical development, here a throng of ten thousand with even higher, finer demands, ever listening more and more for the "it means," and there the immense countless mass which yearly grows more incapable of understanding what is important even in the form of sensual ugliness, and which therefore turns ever more willingly to what in music is ugly and foul in itself, that is, to the basely sensual.

218

A STONE IS MORE OF A STONE THAN FORMERLY. As a general rule we no longer understand architecture, at least by no means in the same way as we understand music. We have outgrown the symbolism of lines and figures, just as we are no longer accustomed to the sound effects of rhetoric, and have not absorbed this kind of mother's milk of culture since our first moment of life. Everything in a Greek or Christian building originally had a meaning, and referred to a higher order of things; this feeling of inexhaustible meaning enveloped the edifice like a mystic veil. Beauty was only a secondary consideration in the system, without in any way materially injuring the fundamental sentiment of the mysteriously exalted, the divinely and magically consecrated; at the most, beauty *tempered horror*—but this horror was everywhere presupposed. What is the beauty of a building now? The same thing as the beautiful face of a stupid woman, a kind of mask.

220

THE BEYOND IN ART. It is not without deep pain that we acknowledge the fact that in their loftiest soarings, artists of all ages have exalted and divinely transfigured precisely those ideas which we now recognize as false; they are the glorifiers of humanity's religious and philosophical errors, and they could not have been this without belief in the absolute truth of these errors. But if the belief in such truth diminishes at all, if the rainbow colors at the farthest ends of human knowledge and imagination fade, then this kind of art can never reflourish, for, like the *Divina Commedia*, Raphael's paintings, Michelangelo's frescoes, and Gothic cathedrals, they indicate not only a cosmic but also a metaphysical meaning in the work of art. Out of all this will grow a touching legend that such an art and such an artistic faith once existed.

223

THE AFTERGLOW OF ART. Just as in old age we remember our youth and celebrate festivals of memory, so in a short time mankind will stand toward art: its relation will be that of a *touching memory* of the joys of youth. Never, perhaps, in former ages was art dealt with so seriously and thoughtfully as now when it appears to be surrounded by the magic influence of death. We call to mind that Greek city in southern Italy, which once a year still celebrates its Greek feasts, amidst tears and mourning, that foreign barbarism triumphs ever more and more over the customs its people brought with them into the land; and never has Hellenism been so much appreciated, nowhere has this golden nectar been drunk with so great delight, as amongst these fast disappearing Hellenes. The artist will soon come to be regarded as a splendid relic, and to him, as to a wonderful stranger on whose power and beauty depended the happiness of former ages, there will be paid such honor as is not often enjoyed by one of our race. The best in us is perhaps inherited from the sentiments of former times, to which it is hardly possible for us now to return by direct ways; the sun has already disappeared, but the heavens of our life are still glowing and illumined by it, although we can behold it no longer.

372

IRONY. Irony is only permissible as a pedagogic expedient, on the part of a teacher when dealing with his pupils; its purpose is to humble and to shame, but in the wholesome way that causes good resolutions to spring up and teaches people to show honor and gratitude, as they would to a doctor, to him who has so treated them. The ironical man pretends to be ignorant, and does it so well that the pupils conversing with him are deceived, and in their firm belief in their own superior knowledge they grow bold and expose all their weak points; they lose their cautiousness and reveal themselves as they are—until all of a sudden the light which they have held up to the teacher's face casts its rays back very humiliatingly upon themselves. Where such a relation, as that between teacher and pupil, does not exist, irony is a rudeness and a vulgar conceit. All ironical writers count on the silly species of human beings, who like to feel themselves superior to all others in common with the author himself, whom they look upon as the mouthpiece of their arrogance. Moreover, the habit of irony, like that of sarcasm, spoils the character; it gradually fosters the quality of a malicious superiority; one finally grows like a snappy dog, that has learned to laugh as well as to bite.

FROM HUMAN, ALL TOO HUMAN, II

99 *

THE POET AS GUIDE TO THE FUTURE. All the surplus poetical force that still exists in modern humanity, but is not used under our conditions of life, should (without any deduction) be devoted to a definite goal—not to depicting the present nor to reviving and summarizing the past, but to pointing the way to the future. Nor should this be so done as if the poet, like an imaginative political economist, had to anticipate a more favorable national and social state of things and picture their realization. Rather will he, just as the earlier poets portrayed the images of the Gods, portray the fair images of men. He will divine those cases where, in the midst of our modern world and reality (which will not be shirked or repudiated in the usual poetic fashion), a great, noble soul is still possible, where it may be embodied in harmonious, equable conditions, where it may become permanent, visible, and representative of a type, and so, by the stimulus to imitation and envy, help to create the future. The poems of such a poet would be distinguished by appearing secluded and protected from the heated atmosphere of the passions. The irremediable failure, the shattering of all the strings of the human instrument, the scornful laughter and gnashing of teeth, and all tragedy and

* From *Miscellaneous Maxims and Opinions.*

comedy in the usual old sense, would appear by the side of this new art as mere archaic lumber, a blurring of the outlines of the world-picture. Strength, kindness, gentleness, purity, and an unsought, innate moderation in the personalities and their action: a leveled soil, giving rest and pleasure to the foot: a shining heaven mirrored in faces and events: science and art welded into a new unity: the mind living together with her sister, the soul, without arrogance or jealousy, and enticing from contrasts the grace of seriousness, not the impatience of discord—all this would be the general environment, the background on which the delicate differences of the embodied ideals would make the real picture, that of ever-growing human majesty. Many roads to this poetry of the future start from Goethe, but the quest needs good pathfinders and above all a far greater strength than is possessed by modern poets, who unscrupulously represent the half-animal and the immaturity and intemperance that are mistaken by them for power and naturalness.

105

SPEECH AND EMOTION. That speech is not given to us to communicate our emotions may be seen from the fact that all simple men are ashamed to seek for words to express their deeper feelings. These feelings are expressed only in actions, and even here such men blush if others seem to divine their motives. After all, among poets, to whom God generally denies this shame, the more noble are more monosyllabic in the language of emotion, and evince a certain constraint: whereas the real poets of emotion are for the most part shameless in practical life.

109

LIVING WITHOUT ART AND WINE. It is with works of art as with wine—it is better if one can do without both and keep to water, and if from the inner fire and inner sweetness of the soul the water spontaneously changes again into wine.

115

DEGENERATE SPECIES OF ART. Side by side with

the genuine species of art, those of great repose and great movement, there are degenerate species—weary, blasé art and excited art. Both would have their weakness taken for strength and wish to be confounded with the genuine species.

119

ORIGINS OF TASTE IN WORKS OF ART. If we consider the primary germs of the artistic sense, and ask ourselves what are the various kinds of joy produced by the firstlings of art—as, for example, among savage tribes—we find first of all the joy of understanding what another means. Art in this case is a sort of conundrum, which causes its solver pleasure in his own quick and keen perceptions.— Then the roughest works of art remind us of the pleasant things we have actually experienced, and so give joy—as, for example, when the artist alludes to a chase, a victory, a wedding.—Again, the representation may cause us to feel excited, touched, inflamed, as for instance in the glorification of revenge and danger. Here the enjoyment lies in the excitement itself, in the victory over tedium.—The memory, too, of unpleasant things, so far as they have been overcome or make us appear interesting to the listener as subjects for art (as when the singer describes the mishaps of a daring seaman), can inspire great joy, the credit for which is given to art.—A more subtle variety is the joy that arises at the sight of all that is regular and symmetrical in lines, points, and rhythms. For by a certain analogy is awakened the feeling for all that is orderly and regular in life, which one has to thank alone for all well-being. So in the cult of symmetry we unconsciously do homage to rule and proportion as the source of our previous happiness, and the joy in this case is a kind of hymn of thanksgiving. Only when a certain satiety of the last-mentioned joy arises does a more subtle feeling step in, that enjoyment might even lie in a violation of the symmetrical and regular. This feeling, for example, impels us to seek reason in apparent unreason, and the sort of aesthetic riddle-guessing that results is in a way the higher species of the first-named artistic joy.—He who pursues this speculation still further will know what kind of hypotheses for the explanation of aesthetic phenomena are hereby fundamentally rejected.

126

THE OLDER ART AND THE SOUL OF THE PRES-
ENT. Since every art becomes more and more adapted to
the expression of spiritual states, of the more lively, delicate,
energetic, and passionate states, the later masters, spoiled by
these means of expression, do not feel at their ease in the
presence of the old-time works of art. They feel as if the
ancients had merely been lacking in the means of making
their souls speak clearly, also perhaps in some necessary
technical preliminaries. They think that they must render
some assistance in this quarter, for they believe in the similarity or even unity of all souls. In truth, however, measure,
symmetry, a contempt for graciousness and charm, an unconscious severity and morning chilliness, an evasion of passion, as if passion meant the death of art—such are the
constituents of sentiment and morality in all old masters, who
selected and arranged their means of expression not at random but in a necessary connection with their morality.
Knowing this, are we to deny those that come after the right
to animate the older works with their soul? No, for these
works can only survive through our giving them our soul,
and our blood alone enables them to speak to *us*. The real
"historic" discourse would talk ghostly speech to ghosts. We
honor the great artists less by that barren timidity that allows every word, every note to remain intact than by energetic endeavors to aid them continually to a new life.—
True, if Beethoven were suddenly to come to life and hear
one of his works performed with that modern animation
and nervous refinement that bring glory to our masters of
execution, he would probably be silent for a long while, uncertain whether he should raise his hand to curse or to bless,
but perhaps say at last: "Well, well! That is neither I nor
not-I, but a third thing—it seems to me, too, something right,
if not just *the* right thing. But you must know yourselves
what to do, as in any case it is you who have to listen. As
our Schiller says, 'the living man is right.' So have it your
own way, and let me go down again."

131

THE EXCITING ELEMENT IN THE HISTORY OF
ART. We fall into a state of terrible tension when we fol-

low the history of an art—as, for example, that of Greek oratory—and, passing from master to master, observe their increasing precautions to obey the old and the new laws and all these self-imposed limitations. We see that the bow *must* snap, and that the so-called "loose" composition, with the wonderful means of expression smothered and concealed (in this particular case the florid style of Asianism), was once necessary and almost *beneficial*.

144

*LE STYLE BAROQUE.** He who as thinker and writer is not born or trained to dialectic and the consecutive arrangement of ideas will unconsciously turn to the rhetoric and dramatic forms. For, after all, his object is to make himself understood and to carry the day by force, and he is indifferent whether, as shepherd, he honestly guides to himself the hearts of his fellow men, or, as robber, he captures them by surprise. This is true of the plastic arts as of music: where the feeling of insufficient dialectic or a deficiency in expression or narration, together with an urgent, overpowerful impulse to form, gives birth to that species of style known as "baroque." Only the ill-educated and the arrogant will at once find a depreciatory force in this word. The baroque style always arises at the time of decay of a great art, when the demands of art in classical expression have become too great. It is a natural phenomenon which will be observed with melancholy—for it is a forerunner of the night—but at the same time with admiration for its peculiar compensatory arts of expression and narration. To this style belongs already a choice of material and subjects of the highest dramatic tension, at which the heart trembles even when there is no art, because heaven and hell are all too near the emotions: then, the oratory of strong passion and gestures, of ugly sublimity, of great masses, in fact of absolute quantity per se (as is shown in Michelangelo, the father or grandfather of the Italian baroque stylists): the lights of dusk, illumination, and conflagration playing upon those strongly molded forms: ever-new ventures in means and aims, strongly underscored by artists for artists, while the layman must fancy he sees an unconscious overflowing of all the horns of plenty of an original nature-art: all these

---

* In German *Barockstil,* i.e., the degenerate post-Renaissance style in art and literature, which spread from Italy in the seventeenth century.—Tʀ.

characteristics that constitute the greatness of that style are neither possible nor permitted in the earlier anteclassical and classical periods of a branch of art. Such luxuries hang long on the tree like forbidden fruit. Just now, when music is passing into this last phase, we may learn to know the phenomenon of the baroque style in peculiar splendor, and, by comparison, find much that is instructive for earlier ages. For from Greek times onward there has often been a baroque style, in poetry, oratory, prose writing, sculpture, and, as is well known, in architecture. This style, though wanting in the highest nobility—the nobility of an innocent, unconscious, triumphant perfection—has nevertheless given pleasure to many of the best and most serious minds of their time. Hence, as aforesaid, it is presumptuous to depreciate it without reserve, however happy we may feel because our taste for it has not made us insensible to the purer and greater style.

150

BEYOND HIS LIMITS. When an artist wants to be more than an artist—for example, the moral awakener of his people—he at last falls in love, as a punishment, with a monster of moral substance. The Muse laughs, for, though a kind-hearted Goddess, she can also be malignant from jealousy. Milton and Klopstock are cases in point.

177

WHAT ALL ART WANTS TO DO AND CANNOT. The last and hardest task of the artist is the presentment of what remains the same, reposes in itself, is lofty and simple and free from the bizarre. Hence the noblest forms of moral perfection are rejected as inartistic by weaker artists, because the sight of these fruits is too painful for their ambition. The fruit gleams at them from the topmost branches of art, but they lack the ladder, the courage, the grip to venture so high. In himself a Phidias is quite possible as a poet, but, if modern strength be taken into consideration, almost solely in the sense that to God nothing is impossible. The desire for a poetical Claude Lorrain is already an immodesty at present, however earnestly one man's heart may yearn for such a consummation.—The presentment of the highest man, the most simple and at the same time the most complete, has hitherto been beyond the scope of all artists. Perhaps, however, the Greeks, in the ideal of Athena, saw farther than any men did before or after their time.

206

WHY SAVANTS ARE NOBLER THAN ARTISTS. Science requires nobler natures than does poetry; natures that are more simple, less ambitious, more restrained, calmer, that think less of posthumous fame and can bury themselves in studies which, in the eye of the many, scarcely seem worthy of such a sacrifice of personality. There is another loss of which they are conscious. The nature of their occupation, its continual exaction of the greatest sobriety, weakens their will; the fire is not kept up so vigorously as on the hearths of poetic minds. As such, they often lose their strength and prime earlier than artists do—and, as has been said, they are aware of their danger. Under all circumstances they seem less gifted because they shine less, and thus they will always be rated below their value.

128 *

GLOOMY AND SERIOUS AUTHORS. He who commits his sufferings to paper becomes a gloomy author, but he becomes a serious one if he tells us what he *has* suffered and why he is now enjoying a pleasurable repose.

214

EUROPEAN BOOKS. In reading Montaigne, La Rochefoucauld, La Bruyère, Fontenelle (especially the *Dialogues des Morts*), Vauvenargues, and Chamfort we are nearer to antiquity than in any group of six authors of other nations. Through these six the spirit of the last centuries before Christ has once more come into being, and they collectively form an important link in the great and still continuous chain of the Renaissance. Their books are raised above all changes of national taste and philosophical nuances from which as a rule every book takes and must take its hue in order to become famous. They contain more real ideas than all the books of German philosophers put together: ideas of the sort that breed ideas——I am at a loss how to define

* From *The Wanderer and His Shadow.*

to the end: enough to say that they appear to me writers who wrote neither for children nor for visionaries, neither for virgins nor for Christians, neither for Germans nor for——I am again at a loss how to finish my list. To praise them in plain terms, I may say that had they been written in Greek, they would have been understood by Greeks. How much, on the other hand, would even a Plato have understood of the writings of our best German thinkers—Goethe and Schopenhauer, for instance—to say nothing of the repugnance that he would have felt to their style, particularly to its obscure, exaggerated, and occasionally dry-as-dust elements? And these are defects from which these two among German thinkers suffer least and yet far too much (Goethe as thinker was fonder than he should have been of embracing the cloud, and Schopenhauer almost constantly wanders, not with impunity, among symbols of objects rather than among the objects themselves).—On the other hand, what clearness and graceful precision there is in these Frenchmen! The Greeks, whose ears were most refined, could not but have approved of this art, and one quality they would even have admired and reverenced—the French verbal wit: they were extremely fond of this quality, without being particularly strong in it themselves.

217

CLASSIC AND ROMANTIC. Both classically and romantically minded spirits—two species that always exist—cherish a vision of the future; but the former derive their vision from the strength of their time, the latter from its weakness.

FROM THE DAWN OF DAY

240

THE MORALITY OF THE STAGE. The man who imagines that the effect of Shakespeare's plays is a moral one, and that the sight of Macbeth irresistibly induces us to shun the evil of ambition, is mistaken, and he is mistaken once more if he believes that Shakespeare himself thought so. He who is truly obsessed by an ardent ambition takes delight in beholding this picture of himself; and when the hero is driven to destruction by his passion, this is the most pungent spice in the hot drink of this delight. Did the poet feel this in another way? How royally and with how little of the knave in him does his ambitious hero run his course from the moment of his great crime! It is only from this moment that he becomes "demoniacally" attractive, and that he encourages similar natures to imitate him.—There is something demoniacal here: something which is in revolt against advantage and life, in favor of a thought and an impulse. Do you think that Tristan and Isolde are warnings against adultery, merely because adultery has resulted in the death of both of them? This would be turning poets upside down, these poets who, especially Shakespeare, are in love with the passions in themselves, and not less so with the readiness for death which they give rise to: this mood in which the heart no more clings to life than a drop of water does to the glass. It is not the guilt and its pernicious consequences which interests these poets—Shakespeare as little as Sophocles (in the *Ajax, Philoctetes, Oepidus*)—however easy it might have been in the cases just mentioned to make the guilt the lever of the play, it was carefully avoided by the poets.

In the same way the tragic poet by his images of life does not wish to set us against life. On the contrary, he exclaims: "It is the charm of charms, this exciting, changing, and dangerous existence of ours, so often gloomy and so often bathed in sun! Life is an adventure—whichever side you may take in life it will always retain this character!"—Thus speaks the poet of a restless and vigorous age, an age which is almost intoxicated and stupefied by its superabundance of blood and energy, in an age more evil than our own: and this is why it is necessary for us to adapt and accommodate ourselves first to the purpose of a Shakespearean play, that is, by misunderstanding it.

324

THE PSYCHOLOGY OF THE ACTOR. It is the blissful illusion of all great actors to imagine that the historical personages whom they are representing were really in the same state of mind as they themselves are when interpreting them—but in this they are very much mistaken. Their powers of imitation and divination, which they would fain exhibit as a clairvoyant faculty, penetrate only far enough to explain gestures, accent, and looks, and in general anything exterior: that is, they can grasp the shadow of the soul of a great hero, statesman, or warrior, or of an ambitious, jealous, or desperate person—they penetrate fairly near to the soul, but they never reach the inmost spirit of the man they are imitating.

It would, indeed, be a fine thing to discover that instead of thinkers, psychologists, or experts we required nothing but clairvoyant actors to throw light upon the essence of any condition. Let us never forget, whenever such pretensions are heard, that the actor is nothing but an ideal ape—so much of an ape is he, indeed, that he is not capable of believing in the "essence" or in the "essential": everything becomes for him merely performance, intonation, attitude, stage, scenery, and public.

FROM THE JOYFUL WISDOM

57

TO THE REALISTS. Ye sober beings, who feel yourselves armed against passion and fantasy, and would gladly make a pride and an ornament out of your emptiness, ye call yourselves realists and give to understand that the world is actually constituted as it appears to you; before you alone reality stands unveiled, and ye yourselves would perhaps be the best part of it—oh, ye dear images of Sais! But are not ye also in your unveiled condition still extremely passionate and dusky beings compared with the fish, and still all too like an enamored artist? *—and what is "reality" to an enamored artist! Ye still carry about with you the valuations of things which had their origin in the passions and infatuations of earlier centuries! There is still a secret and ineffaceable drunkenness embodied in your sobriety! Your love of "reality," for example—oh, that is an old, primitive "love"! In every feeling, in every sense impression, there is a portion of this old love: and similarly also some kind of fantasy, prejudice, irrationality, ignorance, fear, and whatever else has become mingled and woven into it. There is that mountain! There is that cloud! What is "real" in them?

---

* Schiller's poem, "The Veiled Image of Sais," is again referred to here.—TR.

Remove the phantasm and the whole human *element* therefrom, ye sober ones! Yes, if ye could do *that!* If ye could
forget your origin, your past, your preparatory schooling—
your whole history as man and beast! There is no "reality"
for us—nor for you either, ye sober ones—we are far from
being so alien to one another as ye suppose, and perhaps
our good will to get beyond drunkenness is just as respectable
as your belief that ye are altogether *incapable* of drunkenness.

107

OUR ULTIMATE GRATITUDE TO ART. If we had
not approved of the Arts and invented this sort of cult of
the untrue, the insight into the general untruth and falsity
of things now given us by science—an insight into delusion
and error as conditions of intelligent and sentient existence
—would be quite unendurable. *Honesty* would have disgust
and suicide in its train. Now, however, our honesty has a
counterpoise which helps us to escape such consequences,
namely, Art, as the *good will* to illusion. We do not always
restrain our eyes from rounding off and perfecting in imagination: and then it is no longer the eternal imperfection that
we carry over the river of Becoming—for we think we carry
a *goddess*, and are proud and artless in rendering this service. As an aesthetic phenomenon existence is still *endurable*
to us; and by Art, eye and hand and above all the good
conscience are given to us, *to be able* to make such a
phenomenon out of ourselves. We must rest from ourselves
occasionally by contemplating and looking down upon ourselves, and by laughing or weeping *over* ourselves from an
artistic remoteness: we must discover the *hero*, and likewise
the *fool*, that is hidden in our passion for knowledge; we
must now and then be joyful in our folly, that we may continue to be joyful in our wisdom! And just because we
are heavy and serious men in our ultimate depth, and are
rather weights than men, there is nothing that does us so
much good as the *fool's cap and bells:* we need them in
presence of ourselves—we need all arrogant, soaring, dancing, mocking, childish, and blessed Art, in order not to lose
the *free dominion over things* which our ideal demands of
us. It would be *backsliding* for us, with our susceptible integrity, to lapse entirely into morality, and actually become
virtuous monsters and scarecrows, on account of the over-
strict requirements which we here lay down for ourselves.

We ought also to *be able* to stand *above* morality, and not only stand with the painful stiffness of one who every moment fears to slip and fall, but we should also be able to soar and play above it! How could we dispense with Art for that purpose, how could we dispense with the fool?—And as long as you are still *ashamed* of yourselves in any way, you still do not belong to us!

299

WHAT ONE SHOULD LEARN FROM ARTISTS. What means have we for making things beautiful, attractive, and desirable, when they are not so?—and I suppose they are never so in themselves! We have here something to learn from physicians, when, for example, they dilute what is bitter, or put wine and sugar into their mixing bowl; but we have still more to learn from artists, who, in fact, are continually concerned in devising such inventions and artifices. To withdraw from things until one no longer sees much of them, until one has even to see things into them, *in order to see them at all*—or to view them from the side, and as in a frame—or to look at them through colored glasses, or in the light of the sunset—or to furnish them with a surface or skin which is not fully transparent: we should learn all that from artists, and moreover be wiser than they. For this fine power of theirs usually ceases with them where art ceases and life begins; *we*, however, want to be the poets of our life, and first of all in the smallest and most commonplace matters.

370

WHAT IS ROMANTICISM? It will be remembered perhaps, at least among my friends, that at first I assailed the modern world with some gross errors and exaggerations, but at any rate with *hope* in my heart. I recognized—who knows from what personal experiences?—the philosophical pessimism of the nineteenth century as the symptom of a higher power of thought, a more daring courage and a more triumphant *plenitude* of life than had been characteristic of the eighteenth century, the age of Hume, Kant, Condillac, and the sensualists: so that the tragic view of things seemed to me the peculiar *luxury* of our culture, its most precious, noble, and dangerous mode of prodigality; but neverthe-

less, in view of its overflowing wealth, a *justifiable* luxury.
In the same way I interpreted for myself German music as the
expression of a Dionysian power in the German soul: I
thought I heard in it the earthquake by means of which a
primeval force that had been imprisoned for ages was finally
finding vent—indifferent as to whether all that usually calls
itself culture was thereby made to totter. It is obvious that I
then misunderstood what constitutes the veritable character
both of philosophical pessimism and of German music, namely, their *romanticism*. What is romanticism? Every art and
every philosophy may be regarded as a healing and helping
appliance in the service of growing, struggling life: they always
presuppose suffering and sufferers. But there are two kinds of
sufferers: on the one hand those that suffer from *overflowing vitality*, who need Dionysian art, and require a
tragic view and insight into life; and on the other hand those
who suffer from *reduced vitality*, who seek repose, quietness,
calm seas, and deliverance from themselves through art or
knowledge, or else intoxication, spasm, bewilderment, and
madness. All romanticism in art and knowledge responds to
the twofold craving of the *latter;* to them Schopenhauer as
well as Wagner responded (and responds) to name those
most celebrated and decided romanticists who were then
misunderstood by me (*not* however to their disadvantage, as
may be reasonably conceded to me). The being richest in
overflowing vitality, the Dionysian God and man, may not
only allow himself the spectacle of the horrible and questionable, but even the fearful deed itself, and all the luxury
of destruction, disorganization, and negation. With him evil,
senselessness, and ugliness seem, as it were, licensed, in consequence of the overflowing plentitude of procreative, fructi-
fying power, which can convert every desert into a luxuriant
orchard. Conversely, the greatest sufferer, the man poorest
in vitality, would have most need of mildness, peace, and
kindliness in thought and action: he would need, if possible,
a God who is specially the God of the sick, a "Saviour";
similarly he would have need of logic, the abstract intelligibility of existence—for logic soothes and gives confidence;
in short he would need a certain warm, fear-dispelling narrowness and imprisonment within optimistic horizons. In
this manner I gradually began to understand Epicurus, the
opposite of a Dionysian pessimist; in a similar manner also
the "Christian," who in fact is only a type of Epicurean,
and like him essentially a romanticist: and my vision has
always become keener in tracing that most difficult and

insidious of all forms of *retrospective inference*, in which
most mistakes have been made—the inference from the work
to its author from the deed to its doer, from the ideal to
him who *needs* it, from every mode of thinking and valuing
to the imperative *want* behind it.—In regard to all aesthetic
values I now avail myself of this radical distinction: I ask in
every single case, "Has hunger or superfluity become creative
here?" At the outset another distinction might seem to recommend itself more—it is far more conspicuous—namely, to
have in view whether the desire for rigidity, for perpetuation, for *being* is the cause of the creating, or the desire for
destruction, for change, for the new, for the future—for
becoming. But when looked at more carefully, both these
kinds of desire prove themselves ambiguous, and are explicable precisely according to the before-mentioned and, as
it seems to me, rightly preferred scheme. The desire for
destruction, change, and becoming may be the expression of
overflowing power, pregnant with futurity (my *terminus* for
this is of course the word "*Dionysian*"); but it may also
be the hatred of the ill-constituted, destitute, and unfortunate,
which destroys, and *must* destroy, because the enduring,
yea, all that endures, in fact all being, excites and provokes
it. To understand this emotion we have but to look closely at
our anarchists. The will to *perpetuation* requires equally a
double interpretation. It may on the one hand proceed
from gratitude and love: art of this origin will always be an
art of apotheosis, perhaps dithyrambic, as with Rubens, mocking divinely, as with Hafiz, or clear and kindhearted, as
with Goethe, and spreading a Homeric brightness and glory
over everything (in this case I speak of *Apollonian* art). It
may also, however, be the tyrannical will of a sorely-suffer-
ing, struggling, or tortured being, who would like to stamp
his most personal, individual, and narrow characteristics,
the very idiosyncrasy of his suffering, as an obligatory law
and constraint on others; who, as it were, takes revenge on
all things, in that he imprints, enforces, and brands *his*
image, the image of *his* torture, upon them. The latter is
romantic pessimism in its most extreme form, whether it be
as Schopenhauerian will-philosophy, or as Wagnerian music:
romantic pessimism, the last *great* event in the destiny of
our civilization. (That there *may be* quite a different kind of
pessimism, a classical pessimism—this presentiment and vision belongs to me, as something inseparable from me, as
my *proprium* and *ipsissimum;* only that the word "classical" is repugnant to my ears, it has become far too worn,

too indefinite and indistinguishable. I call that pessimism of the future—for it is coming! I see it coming!—*Dionysian* pessimism.)

FROM THE TWILIGHT OF THE IDOLS

8

CONCERNING THE PSYCHOLOGY OF THE ART-IST. For art to be possible at all—that is to say in order that an aesthetic mode of action and of observation may exist, a certain preliminary physiological state is indispensable: *ecstasy.** This state of ecstasy must first have intensified the susceptibility of the whole machine: otherwise, no art is possible. All kinds of ecstasy, however differently produced, have this power to create art, and above all the state dependent upon sexual excitement—this most venerable and primitive form of ecstasy. The same applies to that ecstasy which is the outcome of all great desires, all strong passions: the ecstasy of the feast, of the arena, of the act of bravery, of victory, of all extreme action; the ecstasy of cruelty; the ecstasy of destruction; the ecstasy following upon certain meteorological influences, as for instance that of springtime, or upon the use of narcotics; and finally the ecstasy of will, that ecstasy which results from accumulated and surging will power.—The essential feature of ecstasy is the feeling of increased strength and abundance. Actuated by this feeling a man gives of himself to things, he *forces* them to partake of his riches, he does violence to them—this proceeding is called *idealizing*. Let us rid ourselves of a prejudice here: idealizing does not consist, as is generally believed, in a suppression or an elimination of detail or of unessential features. A stupendous *accentuation* of the principal characteristic is by far the most decisive factor at work, and in consequence the minor characteristics vanish.

9

In this state a man enriches everything from out his own

* The German word *Rausch* as used by Nietzsche here suggests a blend of our two English words "intoxication" and "elation."—Tr.

abundance: what he sees, what he wills, he sees distended, compressed, strong, overladen with power. He transfigures things until they reflect his power—until they are stamped with his perfection. This compulsion to transfigure into the beautiful is—Art. Everything—even that which he is not—is nevertheless to such a man a means of rejoicing over himself; in Art man rejoices over himself as perfection.—It is possible to imagine a contrary state, a specifically antiartistic state of the instincts—a state in which a man impoverishes, attenuates, and draws the blood from everything. And, truth to tell, history is full of such antiartists, of such creatures of low vitality who have no choice but to appropriate everything they see and to suck its blood and make it thinner. This is the case with the genuine Christian, Pascal, for instance. There is no such thing as a Christian who is also an artist. . . . Let no one be so childish as to suggest Raphael or any homeopathic Christian of the nineteenth century as an objection to this statement: Raphael said Yea, Raphael *did* Yea—consequently Raphael was no Christian.

19

BEAUTIFUL AND UGLY. Nothing is more relative, let us say, more restricted, than our sense of the beautiful. He who would try to divorce it from the delight man finds in his fellows would immediately lose his footing. "Beauty in itself" is simply a word, it is not even a concept. In the beautiful, man postulates himself as the standard of perfection; in exceptional cases he worships himself as that standard. A species has no other alternative than to say "yea" to itself alone, in this way. Its lowest instinct, the instinct of self-preservation and self-expansion, still radiates in such sublimities. Man imagines the world itself to be overflowing with beauty—he forgets that he is the cause of it all. He alone has endowed it with beauty. Alas! and only with human all-too-human beauty! Truth to tell man reflects himself in things, he thinks everything beautiful that throws his own image back at him. The judgment "beautiful" is the "vanity of his species." . . . A little demon of suspicion may well whisper into the sceptic's ear: is the world really beautified simply because man thinks it beautiful? He has only humanized it—that is all. But nothing, absolutely nothing proves to us that it is precisely man who is the proper model of beauty. Who knows what sort of figure he would cut in the eyes of a higher judge of taste? He might seem a little *outré*? Perhaps even somewhat amusing? Perhaps a trifle arbitrary? "O Dionysus, thou divine one, why dost thou pull mine ears?" Ariadne asks on one occasion of her philosophic lover, during one of those famous conversations on the island of Naxos. "I find a sort of humor in thine ears, Ariadne: why are they not a little longer?"

20

Nothing is beautiful; man alone is beautiful: all aesthetic rests on this piece of ingenuousness, it is the first axiom of this science. And now let us straightway add the second to it: nothing is ugly save the degenerate man—within these two first principles the realm of aesthetic judgments is confined. From the physiological standpoint, everything ugly weakens and depresses man. It reminds him of decay, danger, impotence; he literally loses strength in its presence. The effect of ugliness may be gauged by the dynamometer. Whenever man's spirits are downcast, it is a sign that he scents the proximity of something "ugly." His feeling of power, his will to power, his courage and his pride—these things collapse at the sight of what is ugly, and rise at the sight of what is beautiful. In both cases an inference is drawn; the premises to which are stored with extraordinary abundance in the instincts. Ugliness is understood to signify a hint and a symptom of degeneration: that which reminds us however remotely of degeneracy impels us to the judgment "ugly." Every sign of exhaustion, of gravity, of age, of fatigue; every kind of constraint, such as cramp, or paralysis; and above all the smells, colors and forms associated with decomposition and putrefaction, however much they may have been attenuated into symbols—all these things provoke the same reaction, which is the judgment "ugly." A certain hatred expresses itself here: who is it that man hates? Without a doubt it is the *decline of his type*. In this regard his hatred springs from the deepest instincts of the race: there is horror, caution, profundity, and far-reaching vision in this hatred—it is the most profound hatred that exists. On its account alone Art is profound.

24

L'ART POUR L'ART. The struggle against a purpose in art is always a struggle against the moral tendency in art, against its subordination to morality. *L'art pour l'art* means, "let morality go to the devil!"—But even this hostility betrays the preponderating power of the moral prejudice. If art is deprived of the purpose of preaching morality and of improving mankind, it does not by any means follow that art is absolutely pointless, purposeless, senseless, in short *l'art pour l'art*—a snake which bites its own tail. "No purpose at all is better than a moral purpose!"—thus does pure passion speak. A psychologist, on the other hand, puts the question: what does all art do? does it not praise? does it not glorify? does it not select? does it not bring things into prominence? In all this it strengthens or weakens certain valuations. Is this only a secondary matter? An accident? Something in which the artist's instinct has no share? Or is it not rather the very prerequisite which enables the artist to accomplish something? . . . Is his most fundamental instinct concerned with art? Is it not rather concerned with the purpose of art, with life? With a certain desirable kind of life? Art is the great stimulus to life: how can it be regarded as purposeless, as pointless, as *l'art pour l'art?*—There still remains one question to be answered: Art also reveals much that is ugly, hard, and questionable in life—does it not thus seem to make life intolerable?—And, as a matter of fact, there have been philosophers who have ascribed this function to art. According to Schopenhauer's doctrine, the general object of art was to "free one from the Will"; and what he honored as the great utility of tragedy was that it "made people more resigned."—But this, as I have already shown, is a pessimistic standpoint; it is the "evil eye": the artist himself must be appealed to. What is it that the soul of the tragic artist communicates to others? Is it not precisely his fearless attitude toward that which is terrible and questionable? This attitude is in itself a highly desirable one; he who has once experienced it honors it above everything else. He communicates it. He must communicate, provided he is an artist and a genius in the art of communication. A courageous and free spirit, in the presence of a mighty foe, in the presence of a sublime misfortune, and face to face with a problem that inspires horror—this is the triumphant attitude which the tragic artist selects and which he glorifies. The martial elements in our soul celebrate their Saturnalia in tragedy; he who is used to suffering, he who looks out for suffering, the heroic man, extols his existence by means of tragedy—to him alone does the tragic artist offer this cup of sweetest cruelty.

XII. *Philosophy and Philosophers*

FROM HUMAN, ALL TOO HUMAN, VOL. I

68

MORALITY AND CONSEQUENCES. It is not only the spectators of a deed who frequently judge of its morality or immorality according to its consequences, but the doer of the deed himself does so. For the motives and intentions are seldom sufficiently clear and simple, and sometimes memory itself seems clouded by the consequences of the deed, so that one ascribes the deed to false motives or looks upon unessential motives as essential. Success often gives an action the whole honest glamour of a good conscience; failure casts the shadow of remorse over the most estimable deed. Hence arises the well-known practice of the politician, who thinks, "Only grant me success, with that I bring all honest souls over to my side and make myself honest in my own eyes." In the same way success must replace a better argument. Many educated people still believe that the triumph of Christianity over Greek philosophy is a proof of the greater truthfulness of the former—although in this case it is only the coarser and more powerful that has triumphed over the more spiritual and delicate. Which possesses the greater truth may be seen from the fact that the awakening sciences have agreed with Epicurus' philosophy on point after point, but on point after point have rejected Christianity.

56

VICTORY OF KNOWLEDGE OVER RADICAL EVIL.
It is of great advantage to him who desires to be wise to
have witnessed for a time the spectacle of a thoroughly evil
and degenerate man; it is false, like the contrary spectacle,
but for whole long periods it held the mastery, and its
roots have even extended and ramified themselves to us and
our world. In order to understand *ourselves* we must understand *it*; but then, in order to mount higher we must rise
above it. We recognize, then, that there exist no sins in the
metaphysical sense; but, in the same sense, also no virtues;
we recognize that the entire domain of ethical ideas is
perpetually tottering, that there are higher and deeper conceptions of good and evil, of moral and immoral. He who
does not desire much more from things than a knowledge of
them easily makes peace with his soul, and will make a
mistake (or commit a sin, as the world calls it) at the most
from ignorance, but hardly from covetousness. He will no
longer wish to excommunicate and exterminate desires; but
his only, his wholly dominating ambition, to *know* as well
as possible at all times, will make him cool and will soften
all the savageness in his disposition. Moreover, he has been
freed from a number of tormenting conceptions, he has no
more feeling at the mention of the words "punishments of
hell," "sinfulness," "incapacity for good," he recognizes in
them only the vanishing shadow-pictures of false views of
the world and of life.

39

THE FABLE OF INTELLIGIBLE FREEDOM. The
history of the sentiments by means of which we make a
person responsible consists of the following principal phases.
First, all single actions are called good or bad without any
regard to their motives, but only on account of the useful or
injurious consequences which result for the community.
But soon the origin of these distinctions is forgotten, and it
is deemed that the qualities "good" or "bad" are contained in
the action itself without regard to its consequences, by the
same error according to which language describes the stone
as hard, the tree as green—with which, in short, the result
is regarded as the cause. Then the goodness or badness is

implanted in the motive, and the action in itself is looked upon as morally ambiguous. Mankind even goes further, and applies the predicate good or bad no longer to single motives, but to the whole nature of an individual, out of whom the motive grows as the plant grows out of the earth. Thus, in turn, man is made responsible for his operations, then for his actions, then for his motives, and finally for his nature. Eventually it is discovered that even this nature cannot be responsible, inasmuch as it is an absolutely necessary consequence concreted out of the elements and influences of past and present things—that man, therefore, cannot be made responsible for anything, neither for his nature, nor his motives, nor his actions, nor his effects. It has therewith come to be recognized that the history of moral valuations is at the same time the history of an error, the error of responsibility, which is based upon the error of the freedom of will. Schopenhauer thus decided against it: because certain actions bring ill-humor ("consciousness of guilt") in their train, there must be a responsibility; for there would be *no reason* for this ill-humor if not only all human actions were not done of necessity—which is actually the case and also the belief of this philosopher—but man himself from the same necessity is precisely the *being* that he is—which Schopenhauer denies. From the fact of that ill-humor Schopenhauer thinks he can prove a liberty which man must somehow have had, not with regard to actions, but with regard to nature; liberty, therefore, to *be* thus or otherwise, not to *act* thus or otherwise. From the *esse*, the sphere of freedom and responsibility, there results, in his opinion, the *operari*, the sphere of strict causality, necessity, and irresponsibility. This ill-humor is apparently directed to the *operari*—in so far it is erroneous —but in reality it is directed to the *esse*, which is the deed of a free will, the fundamental cause of the existence of an individual, man becomes that which he *wishes* to be, his will is anterior to his existence. Here the mistaken conclusion is drawn that from the fact of the ill-humor, the justification, the reasonable *admissibleness* of this ill-humor is presupposed; and starting from this mistaken conclusion, Schopenhauer arrives at his fantastic sequence of the so-called intelligible freedom. But the ill-humor after the deed is not necessarily reasonable, indeed it is assuredly not reasonable, for it is based upon the erroneous presumption that the action need *not* have inevitably followed. Therefore, it is only because man *believes* himself to be free, not because he is free, that he experiences remorse and pricks of conscience. Moreover, this ill-humor is a habit that can be broken off;

in many people it is entirely absent in connection with actions where others experience it. It is a very changeable thing, and one which is connected with the development of customs and culture, and probably only existing during a comparatively short period of the world's history. Nobody is responsible for his actions, nobody for his nature; to judge is identical with being unjust. This also applies when an individual judges himself. The theory is as clear as sunlight, and yet everyone prefers to go back into the shadow and the untruth, for fear of the consequences.

15

NO INTERNAL AND EXTERNAL IN THE WORLD. As Democritus transferred the concepts "above" and "below" to endless space where they have no sense, so philosophers in general have transferred the concepts "Internal" and "External" to the essence and appearance of the world; they think that with deep feelings one can penetrate deeply into the internal and approach the heart of Nature. But these feelings are only deep insofar as along with them, barely noticeable, certain complicated groups of thoughts, which we call deep, are regularly excited; a feeling is deep because we think that the accompanying thought is deep. But the "deep" thought can nevertheless be very far from the truth, as, for instance, every metaphysical one; if one takes away from the deep feeling the commingled elements of thought, then the *strong* feeling remains, and this guarantees nothing for knowledge but itself, just as strong faith proves only its strength and not the truth of what is believed in.

9

THE METAPHYSICAL WORLD. It is true that there *might* be a metaphysical world; the absolute possibility of it is hardly to be disputed. We look at everything through the human head and cannot cut this head off; while the question remains, What would be left of the world if it had been cut off? This is a purely scientific problem, and one not very likely to trouble mankind; but everything which has hitherto made metaphysical suppositions *valuable, terrible, delightful* for man, what has produced them, is passion, error, and self-deception; the very worst methods of knowledge, not the best, have taught belief therein. When these methods have been discovered as the foundation of all existing religions and metaphysics, they have been refuted. Then there still always remains that possibility; but there is nothing to be done with it, much less is it possible to let happiness, salvation, and life depend on the spider-thread of such a possibility. For nothing could be said of the metaphysical world but that it would be a different condition, a condition inaccessible and incomprehensible to us; it would be a thing of negative qualities. Were the existence of such a world ever so well proved, the fact would nevertheless remain that it would be precisely the most irrelevant of all forms of knowledge: more irrelevant than the knowledge of the chemical analysis of water to the sailor in danger in a storm.

6

THE SCIENTIFIC SPIRIT PARTIALLY BUT NOT WHOLLY POWERFUL. The *smallest* subdivisions of science taken separately are dealt with purely in relation to themselves—the general, great sciences, on the contrary, regarded as a whole, call up the question—certainly a very non-objective one—"Wherefore? To what end?" It is this utilitarian consideration which causes them to be dealt with less impersonally when taken as a whole than when considered in their various parts. In philosophy, above all, as the apex of the entire pyramid of science, the question as to the utility of knowledge is involuntarily brought forward, and every philosophy has the unconscious intention of ascribing to it the *greatest* usefulness. For this reason there is so much highflying metaphysics in all philosophies and such a shyness of the apparently unimportant solutions of physics; for the importance of knowledge for life *must* appear as great as possible. Here is the antagonism between the separate provinces of science and philosophy. The latter desires, what art does, to give the greatest possible depth and meaning to life and actions; in the former one seeks knowledge and nothing further, whatever may emerge thereby. So far there has been no philosopher in whose hands philosophy has not grown into an apology for knowledge; on this point, at least, everyone is an optimist, that the greatest usefulness must be ascribed to knowledge. They are all tyrannized over by logic, and this is optimism—in its essence.

7

THE KILL-JOY IN SCIENCE. Philosophy separated from science when it asked the question, "Which is the knowledge of the world and of life which enables man to live most happily?" This happened in the Socratic schools; the veins of scientific investigation were bound up by the point of view of *happiness*—and are so still.

1

CHEMISTRY OF IDEAS AND SENSATIONS. Philosophical problems adopt in almost all matters the same form of question as they did two thousand years ago; how can anything spring from its opposite? For instance, reason out of unreason, the sentient out of the dead, logic out of unlogic, disinterested contemplation out of covetous willing, life for others out of egoism, truth out of error? Metaphysical philosophy has helped itself over those difficulties hitherto by denying the origin of one thing in another, and assuming a miraculous origin for more highly valued things, immediately out of the kernel and essence of the "thing in itself." Historical philosophy, on the contrary, which is no longer to be thought of as separate from physical science, the youngest of all philosophical methods, has ascertained in single cases (and presumably this will happen in everything) that there are no opposites except in the usual exaggeration of the popular or metaphysical point of view, and that an error of reason lies at the bottom of the opposition: according to this explanation, strictly understood, there is neither an unegoistical action nor an entirely disinterested point of view; they are both only sublimations in which the fundamental element appears almost evaporated, and is only to be discovered by the closest observation. All that we require, and which can only be given us by the present advance of the single sciences, is a *chemistry* of the moral, religious, aesthetic ideas and sentiments, as also of those emotions which we experience in ourselves both in the great and in the small phases of social and intellectual intercourse, and even in solitude; but what if this chemistry should result in the fact that also in this case the most beautiful colors have been obtained from base, even despised materials? Would many be inclined to pursue such examinations? Humanity likes to put all questions as to origin and beginning out of its mind; must one not be almost dehumanized to feel a contrary tendency in one's self?

2

INHERITED FAULTS OF PHILOSOPHERS. All philosophers have the common fault that they start from man in his present state and hope to attain their end by an analysis of him. Unconsciously they look upon "man" as an *aeterna veritas*, as a thing unchangeable in all commotion, as a sure standard of things. But everything that the philosopher says about man is really nothing more than testimony about the man of a *very limited* space of time. A lack of the historical sense is the hereditary fault of all philosophers; many, indeed, unconsciously mistake the very latest variety of man, such as has arisen under the influence of certain religions, certain political events, for the permanent form from which one must set out. They will not learn that man has developed, that his faculty of knowledge has developed also; whilst for some of them the entire world is spun out of this faculty of knowledge. Now everything *essential* in human development happened in prehistoric times, long before those four thousand years which we know something of; man may not have changed much during this time. But the philosopher sees "instincts" in the present man and takes it for granted that this is one of the unalterable facts of mankind, and, consequently, can furnish a key to the understanding of the world; the entire teleology is so constructed that man of the last four thousand years is spoken of as an *eternal* being, toward which all things in the world have from the beginning a natural direction. But everything has evolved; there are *no eternal facts*, as there are likewise no absolute truths. Therefore, *historical philosophizing* is henceforth necessary, and with it the virtue of diffidence.

275

CYNICS AND EPICUREANS. The cynic recognizes the connection between the multiplied and stronger pains of the more highly cultivated man and the abundance of requirements; he comprehends, therefore, that the multitude of opinions about what is beautiful, suitable, seemly, and pleasing must also produce very rich sources of enjoyment, but also of displeasure. In accordance with this view he educates himself backward by giving up many of these opinions and withdrawing from certain demands of culture; he thereby gains a feeling of freedom and strength; and gradually, when habit has made his manner of life endurable, his sensations of displeasure are, as a matter of fact, rarer and weaker than those of cultivated people, and approach those of the domestic animal; moreover, he experiences everything with the charm of contrast, and—he can also scold to his heart's content; so that thereby he again rises high above the sensation range of the animal. The Epicurean has the same point of view as the cynic; there is usually only a difference of temperament between them. Then the Epicurean makes use of his higher culture to render himself independent of prevailing opinions, he raises himself above them, whilst the cynic only remains negative. He walks, as it were, in wind-protected, well-sheltered, half-dark paths, whilst over him, in the wind, the tops of the trees rustle and show him how violently agitated is the world out there. The cynic, on the contrary, goes, as it were, naked into the rushing of the wind and hardens himself to the point of insensibility.

608

CONFUSION OF CAUSE AND EFFECT. Unconsciously we seek the principles and opinions which are suited to our temperament, so that at last it seems as if these principles and opinions had formed our character and given it support and stability, whereas exactly the contrary has taken place. Our thoughts and judgments are, apparently, to be taken subsequently as the causes of our nature, but as a matter of fact *our* nature is the cause of our so thinking and judging. And what induces us to play this almost unconscious comedy? Inertness and convenience, and to a large extent also the vain desire to be regarded as thoroughly consistent and homogeneous in nature and thought; for this wins respect and gives confidence and power.

638

THE WANDERER. He who has attained intellectual emancipation to any extent cannot, for a long time, regard himself otherwise than as a wanderer on the face of the earth—and not even as a traveler *toward* a final goal, for there is no such thing. But he certainly wants to observe and keep his eyes open to whatever actually happens in the world; therefore he cannot attach his heart too firmly to anything individual; he must have in himself something wandering that takes pleasure in change and transitoriness. To be sure such a man will have bad nights, when he is weary and finds the gates of the town that should offer him rest closed; perhaps he may also find that, as in the East, the desert reaches to the gates, that wild beasts howl far and near, that a strong wind arises, and that robbers take away his beasts of burden. Then the dreadful night closes over him like a second desert upon the desert, and his heart grows weary of wandering. Then when the morning sun rises upon him, glowing like a Deity of anger, when the town is opened, he sees perhaps in the faces of the dwellers therein still more desert, uncleanliness, deceit, and insecurity than outside the gates—and the day is almost worse than the night. Thus it may occasionally happen to the wanderer; but then there come as compensation the delightful mornings of other lands and days, when already in the gray of the dawn he sees the throng of muses dancing by, close to him, in the mist of the mountain; when afterward, in the symmetry of his antemeridian soul, he strolls silently under the trees, out of whose crests and leafy hiding places all manner of good and bright things are flung to him, the gifts of all the free spirits who are at home in mountains, forests, and solitudes, and who, like himself, alternately merry and thoughtful, are wanderers and philosophers. Born of the secrets of the early dawn, they ponder the question how the day, between the hours of ten and twelve, can have such a pure, transparent, and gloriously cheerful countenance: they seek the *antemeridian* philosophy.

FROM HUMAN, ALL TOO HUMAN, II

201 *

ERROR OF PHILOSOPHERS. The philosopher believes that the value of his philosophy lies in the whole, in the structure. Posterity finds it in the stone with which he built

* From *Miscellaneous Maxims and Opinions*.

and with which, from that time forth, men will build oftener and better—in other words, in the fact that the structure may be destroyed and yet have value as material.

271

EVERY PHILOSOPHY IS THE PHILOSOPHY OF A PERIOD OF LIFE. The period of life in which a philosopher finds his teaching is manifested by his teaching; he cannot avoid that, however elevated above time and hour he may feel himself. Thus, Schopenhauer's philosophy remains a mirror of his hot and melancholy youth—it is no mode of thought for older men. Plato's philosophy reminds one of the middle thirties, when a warm and a cold current generally rush together, so that spray and delicate clouds and, under favorable circumstances and glimpses of sunshine, enchanting rainbow-pictures result.

31

IN THE DESERT OF SCIENCE. As the man of science proceeds on his modest and toilsome wanderings, which must often enough be journeys in the desert, he is confronted with those brilliant mirages known as "philosophic systems." With magic powers of deception they show him that the solution of all riddles and the most refreshing draught of true water of life are close at hand. His weary heart rejoices, and he well-nigh touches with his lips the goal of all scientific endurance and hardship, so that almost unconsciously he presses forward. Other natures stand still, as if spellbound by the beautiful illusion: the desert swallows them up, they become lost to science. Other natures, again, that have often experienced these subjective consolations, become very disheartened and curse the salty taste which these mirages leave behind in the mouth and from which springs a raging thirst—without one's having come one step nearer to any sort of a spring.

32

THE SO-CALLED "REAL REALITY." When the poet depicts the various callings—such as those of the warrior, the silk-weaver, the sailor—he feigns to know all these things thoroughly, to be an expert. Even in the exposition of human actions and destinies he behaves as if he had been present at the spinning of the whole web of existence. In so far he is an impostor. He practices his frauds on pure ignoramuses, and that is why he succeeds. They praise him for his deep, genuine knowledge, and lead him finally into the delusion that he really knows as much as the individual experts and creators, yes, even as the great world-spinners themselves. In the end, the impostor becomes honest, and actually believes in his own sincerity. Emotional people say to his very face that he has the "higher" truth and sincerity—for they are weary of reality for the time being, and accept the poetic dream as a pleasant relaxation and a night's rest for head and heart. The visions of the dream now appear to them of more value, because, as has been said, they find them more beneficial, and mankind has always held that what is apparently of more value is more true, more real. All that is generally called reality, the poets, conscious of this power, proceed with intention to disparage and to distort into the uncertain, the illusory, the spurious, the impure, the sinful, sorrowful, and deceitful. They make use of all doubts about the limits of knowledge, of all sceptical excesses, in order to spread over everything the rumpled veil of uncertainty. For they desire that when this darkening process is complete their wizardry and soul-magic may be accepted without hesitation as the path to "true truth" and "real reality."

9*

ORIGIN OF THE DOCTRINE OF FREE WILL. Necessity sways one man in the shape of his passions, another as a habit of hearing and obeying, a third as a logical conscience, a fourth as a caprice and a mischievous delight in evasions. These four, however, seek the freedom of their will at the very point where they are most securely fettered. It is as if the silkworm sought freedom of will in spinning. What is the reason? Clearly this, that everyone thinks himself most free where his vitality is strongest; hence, as I have said, now in passion, now in duty, now in knowledge, now in caprice. A man unconsciously imagines that where he is strong, where he feels most thoroughly alive, the element of his freedom must lie. He thinks of dependence and apathy, independence and vivacity as forming inevitable pairs.—Thus

* From *The Wanderer and His Shadow.*

an experience that a man has undergone in the social and political sphere is wrongly transferred to the ultimate metaphysical sphere. There the strong man is also the free man, there the vivid feeling of joy and sorrow, the high hopes, the keen desires, the powerful hates are the attributes of the ruling, independent natures, while the thrall and the slave live in a state of dazed oppression.—The doctrine of free will is an invention of the ruling classes.

16

WHERE INDIFFERENCE IS NECESSARY. Nothing would be more perverse than to wait for the truths that science will finally establish concerning the first and last things, and until then to think (and especially to believe) in the traditional way, as one is so often advised to do. The impulse that bids us seek nothing but *certainties* in this domain is a religious offshoot, nothing better—a hidden and only apparently sceptical variety of the "metaphysical needs," the underlying idea being that for a long time no view of these ultimate certainties will be obtainable, and that until then the "believer" has the right not to trouble himself about the whole subject. We have no need of these certainties about the farthermost horizons in order to live a full and efficient human life, any more than the ant needs them in order to be a good ant. Rather must we ascertain the origin of that troublesome significance that we have attached to these things for so long. For this we require the history of ethical and religious sentiments, since it is only under the influence of such sentiments that these most acute problems of knowledge have become so weighty and terrifying. Into the outermost regions to which the mental eye can penetrate (without ever penetrating *into* them), we have smuggled such concepts as guilt and punishment (everlasting punishment, too!). The darker those regions, the more careless we have been. For ages men have let their imaginations run riot where they could establish nothing, and have induced posterity to accept these fantasies as something serious and true, with this abominable lie as their final trump card: that faith is worth more than knowledge. What we need now in regard to these ultimate things is not knowledge as against faith, but indifference as against faith and pretended knowledge in these matters!—Everything must lie nearer to us than what has hitherto been preached to us as the most important thing, I mean the questions: "What end does man serve?" "What is his fate after death?" "How does he make his peace with God?" and all the rest of that bag of tricks. The problems of the dogmatic philosophers, be they idealists, materialists, or realists, concern us as little as do these religious questions. They all have the same object in view— to force us to a decision in matters where neither faith nor knowledge is needed. It is better even for the most ardent lover of knowledge that the territory open to investigation and to reason should be encircled by a belt of fog-laden, treacherous marshland, a strip of ever watery, impenetrable, and indeterminable country. It is just by the comparison with the realm of darkness on the edge of the world of knowledge that the bright, accessible region of that world rises in value.—We must once more become good friends of the "everyday matters," and not, as hitherto, despise them and look beyond them at clouds and monsters of the night. In forests and caverns, in marshy tracts and under dull skies, on the lowest rungs of the ladder of culture, man has lived for aeons, and lived in poverty. There he has learned to despise the present, his neighbors, his life, and himself, and we, the inhabitants of the brighter fields of Nature and mind, still inherit in our blood some taint of this contempt for everyday matters.

17

PROFOUND INTERPRETATIONS. He who has interpreted a passage in an author "more profoundly" than was intended has not interpreted the author but has obscured him. Our metaphysicians are in the same relation, or even in a worse relation, to the text of Nature. For, to apply their profound interpretations, they often alter the text to suit their purpose—or, in other words, corrupt the text. A curious example of the corruption and obscuration of an author's text is furnished by the ideas of Schopenhauer on the pregnancy of women. "The sign of a continuous will to life in time," he says, "is copulation; the sign of the light of knowledge which is associated anew with this will and holds the possibility of a deliverance, and that too in the highest degree of clearness, is the renewed incarnation of the will to life. This incarnation is betokened by pregnancy, which is therefore frank and open, and even proud, whereas copulation hides itself like a criminal." He declares that every woman, if surprised in the sexual act, would be likely to die of shame, but "displays her pregnancy without a trace of shame, nay even with a sort of pride." Now, firstly, this condition cannot easily be displayed more aggressively than it displays itself, and when Schopenhauer gives prominence only to the intentional character of the display, he is fashioning his text to suit the interpretation. Moreover, his statement of the universality of the phenomenon is not true. He speaks of "every woman." Many women, especially the younger, often appear painfully ashamed of their condition, even in the presence of their nearest kinsfolk. And when women of riper years, especially in the humbler classes, do actually appear proud of their condition, it is because they would give us to understand that they are still desirable to their husbands. That a neighbor on seeing them or a passing stranger should say or think "Can it be possible?" —that is an alms always acceptable to the vanity of women of low mental capacity. In the reverse instance, to conclude from Schopenhauer's proposition, the cleverest and most intelligent women would tend more than any to exult openly in their condition. For they have the best prospect of giving birth to an intellectual prodigy, in whom "the will" can once more "negative" itself for the universal good. Stupid women, on the other hand, would have every reason to hide their pregnancy more modestly than anything they hide.—It cannot be said that this view corresponds to reality. Granted, however, that Schopenhauer was right on the general principle that women show more self-satisfaction when pregnant than at any other time, a better explanation than this lies to hand. One might imagine the clucking of a hen even before she lays an egg, saying, "Look! look! I shall lay an egg! I shall lay an egg!"

19

IMMORALISTS. Moralists must now put up with being rated as immoralists, because they dissect morals. He, however, who would dissect must kill, but only in order that we may know more, judge better, live better, not in order that all the world may dissect. Unfortunately, men still think that every moralist in his every action must be a pattern for others to imitate. They confound him with the preacher of morality. The older moralists did not dissect enough and preached too often, whence that confusion and the unpleasant consequences for our latter-day moralists are derived.

20

A CAUTION AGAINST CONFUSION. There are moralists who treat the strong, noble, self-denying attitude of such beings as the heroes of Plutarch, or the pure, enlightened, warmth-giving state of soul peculiar to truly good men and women, as difficult scientific problems. They investigate the origin of such phenomena, indicating the complex element in the apparent simplicity, and directing their gaze to the tangled skein of motives, the delicate web of conceptual illusions, and the sentiments of individuals or of groups, that are a legacy of ancient days gradually increased. Such moralists are very different from those with whom they are most commonly confounded, from those petty minds that do not believe at all in these modes of thought and states of soul, and imagine their own poverty to be hidden somewhere behind the glamour of greatness and purity. The moralists say, "Here are problems," and these pitiable creatures say, "Here are impostors and deceptions." Thus the latter deny the existence of the very things which the former are at pains to explain.

FROM THE DAWN OF DAY

41

TO DETERMINE THE VALUE OF THE *VITA CONTEMPLATIVA.* Let us not forget, as men leading a contemplative life, what kind of evil and misfortunes have overtaken the men of the *vita activa* as the result of contemplation—in short, what sort of contra-account the *vita activa* has to offer *us*, if we exhibit too much boastfulness before it with respect to our good deeds. It would show us, in the first place, those so-called religious natures, who predominate among the lovers of contemplation and consequently represent their commonest type. They have at all times acted in such a manner as to render life difficult to practical men, and tried to make them disgusted with it, if possible: to darken the sky, to obliterate the sun, to cast suspicion upon joy, to depreciate hope, to paralyze the active hand—all this they knew how to do, just as, for miserable times and feelings, they had their consolations, alms, blessings, and benedictions. In the second place, it can show us the artists, a species of men leading the *vita contemplativa*, rarer than the religious element, but still often to be met with. As beings, these people are usually intolerable, capricious, jealous, violent, quarrelsome: this, however, must be deduced from the joyous and exalting effects of their works.

Thirdly, we have the philosophers, men who unite religious and artistic qualities, combined, however, with a third element, namely, dialectics and the love of controversy. They are the authors of evil in the same sense as the religious men and artists, in addition to which they have wearied many of their fellow men with their passion for dialectics, though their number has always been very small. Fourthly, the thinkers and scientific workers. They but rarely strove after effects, and contented themselves with silently sticking to their own groove. Thus they brought about little envy and discomfort, and often, as objects of mockery and derision, they served, without wishing to do so, to make life easier for the men of the *vita activa*. Lastly, science ended by becoming of much advantage to all; and if, *on account of this utility*, many of the men who were destined for the *vita activa* are now slowly making their way along the road to science in the sweat of their brow, and not without brain-racking and maledictions, this is not the fault of the crowd of thinkers and scientific workers: it is "self-wrought pain." *

544

HOW PHILOSOPHY IS NOW PRACTICED. I can see quite well that our philosophizing youths, women, and artists require from philosophy exactly the opposite of what the Greeks derived from it. What does he who does not hear the continual exultation that resounds through every speech and counterargument in a Platonic dialogue, this exultation over the new invention of rational thinking, know about Plato or about ancient philosophy? At that time souls were filled with enthusiasm when they gave themselves up to the severe and sober sport of ideas, generalizations, refutations—that enthusiasm which perhaps those old, great, severe, and prudent

* M. Henri Albert points out that this refers to a line of Paul Gerhardt's well-known song: "Befiel du deine Wege." Tr.

contrapuntists in music have also known. At that time the Greek palate still possessed that older and formerly omnipotent taste: and by the side of this taste their new taste appeared to be enveloped in so much charm that the divine art of dialectic was sung by hesitating voices as if its followers were intoxicated with the frenzy of love. That old form of thinking, however, was thought within the bounds of morality, and for it nothing existed but fixed judgments and established facts, and it had no reasons but those of authority. Thinking, therefore, was simply a matter of repetition, and all the enjoyment of speech and dialogue could only lie in their form.

Wherever the substance of a thing is looked upon as eternal and universally approved, there is only one great charm, the charm of variable forms, that is, of fashion. Even in the poets ever since the time of Homer, and later on in the case of the sculptors, the Greeks did not enjoy originality, but its contrary. It was Socrates who discovered another charm, that of cause and effect, of reason and sequence, and we moderns have become so used to it, and have been brought up to the necessity of logic that we look upon it as the normal taste, and as such it cannot but be repugnant to ardent and presumptuous people. Such people are pleased by whatever stands out boldly from the normal: their more subtle ambition leads them to believe only too readily that they are exceptional souls, not dialectic and rational beings, but, let us say, "intuitive" beings gifted with an "inner sense," or with a certain "intellectual perception." Above all, however, they wish to be "artistic natures" with a genius in their heads, and a demon in their bodies, and consequently with special rights in this world and in the world to come—especially the divine privilege of being incomprehensible.

And people like these are "going in for" philosophy nowadays! I fear they will discover one day that they have made a mistake—what they are looking for is religion!

FROM THE JOYFUL WISDOM

7

SOMETHING FOR THE LABORIOUS. He who at present wants to make moral questions a subject of study has an immense field of labor before him. All kinds of passions must be thought about singly, and followed singly throughout periods, peoples, great and insignificant individuals; all their rationality, all their valuations and elucidations of things, ought to come to light! Hitherto all that has given color to existence has lacked a history: where would one find a history of love, of avarice, of envy, of conscience, of piety, of cruelty? Even a comparative history of law, as also of punishment, has hitherto been completely lacking. Have the different divisions of the day, the consequences of a regular appointment of the times for labor, feast, and repose, ever been made the object of investigation? Do we know the moral effects of the alimentary substances? Is there a philosophy of nutrition? (The ever-recurring outcry for and against vegetarianism proves that as yet there is no such philosophy!) Have the experiences with regard to communal living, for example, in monasteries, been collected? Has the dialectic of marriage and friendship been set forth? The customs of the learned, of tradespeople, of artists, and of mechanics—have they already found their thinkers? There is so much to think of thereon! All that up till now has been considered as the "conditions of existence," of human beings, and all reason, passion, and superstition in this consideration—have they been investigated to the end? The observation alone of the different degrees of development which the human impulses have attained, and could yet attain, according to the different moral climates, would furnish too much work for the most laborious; whole generations, and regular co-operating generations of the learned, would be needed in order to exhaust the points of view and the material here furnished. The same is true of the determining of the reasons for the differences of the moral climates ("*on what account* does this sun of a fundamental moral judgment and standard of highest value shine here —and that sun there?"). And there is again a new labor which points out the erroneousness of all these reasons, and determines the entire essence of the moral judgments hitherto made. Supposing all these labors to be accomplished, the most critical of all questions would then come into the foreground: whether science is in a position to *furnish* goals for human action, after it has proved that it can take them away and annihilate them—and then would be the time for a process of experimenting in which every kind of heroism could satisfy itself, an experimenting for centuries, which would put into the shade all the great labors and sacrifices of previous history. Science has not hitherto built its Cyclopic structures; for that also the time will come.

110

ORIGIN OF KNOWLEDGE. Throughout immense stretches of time the intellect has produced nothing but errors; some of them proved to be useful and preservative of the species: he who fell in with them, or inherited them, waged the battle for himself and his offspring with better success. Those erroneous articles of faith which were successively transmitted by inheritance, and have finally become almost the property and stock of the human species, are, for example, the following: that there are enduring things, that there are equal things, that there are things, substances, and bodies, that a thing is what it appears, that our will is free, that what is good for me is also good absolutely. It was only very late that the deniers and doubters of such propositions came forward—it was only very late that truth made its appearance as the most impotent form of knowledge. It seemed as if it were impossible to get along with truth, our organism was adapted for the very opposite; all its higher functions, the perceptions of the senses, and in general every kind of sensation co-operated with those primevally embodied, fundamental errors. Moreover, those propositions became the very standards of knowledge according to which the "true" and the "false" were determined—throughout the whole domain of pure logic. The *strength* of conceptions does not, therefore, depend on their degree of truth, but on their antiquity, their embodiment, their character as conditions of life. Where life and knowledge seemed to conflict, there has never been serious contention; denial and doubt have there been regarded as madness. The exceptional thinkers like the Eleatics, who, in spite of this, advanced and maintained the antitheses of the natural errors, believed that it was possible also *to live* these counterparts: it was they who devised the sage as the man of immutability, impersonality, and universality of intuition, as one and all at the same time, with a special faculty for that reverse kind of knowledge; they were of the belief that their knowledge was at the same time the principle of *life*. To be able to affirm all this, however, they had to *deceive* themselves concerning their own condition: they had to attribute to themselves impersonality and unchanging permanence, they had to mistake the nature of the philosophic individual, deny the force of the impulses in cognition, and conceive of reason generally as an entirely free and self-originating activity; they kept their eyes shut to the fact that they also had reached their doctrines in contradiction to valid methods, or through their longing for repose or for exclusive possession or for domination. The subtler development of sincerity and of scepticism finally made these men impossible; their life also and their judgments turned out to be dependent on the primeval impulses and fundamental errors of all sentient being.—The subtler sincerity and scepticism arose whenever two antithetical maxims appeared to be *applicable* to life, because both of them were compatible with the fundamental errors; where, therefore, there could be contention concerning a higher or lower degree of *utility* for life; and likewise where new maxims proved to be, not in fact useful, but at least not injurious, as expressions of an intellectual impulse to play a game that was, like all games, innocent and happy. The human brain was gradually filled with such judgments and convictions; and in this tangled skein there arose ferment, strife, and lust for power. Not only utility and delight, but every kind of impulse took part in the struggle for "truths": the intellectual struggle became a business, an attraction, a calling, a duty, an honor: cognizing and striving for the true finally arranged themselves as needs among other needs. From that moment, not only belief and conviction, but also examination, denial, distrust, and contradiction became *forces;* and "evil" instincts were subordinated to knowledge, were placed in its service, and acquired the prestige of the permitted, the honored, the useful, and finally the appearance and innocence of the *good.* Knowledge thus became a portion of life itself, and as life it became a continually growing power: until finally the cognitions and those primeval, fundamental errors clashed with each other, both as life, both as power, both in the same man. The thinker is now the being in whom the impulse to truth and those life-preserving errors wage their first conflict, now that the impulse to truth has also *proved* itself to be a life-preserving power. In comparison with the importance of this conflict everything else is indifferent; the final question concerning the conditions of life is here raised, and the first attempt is here made to answer it by experiment. How far is truth susceptible of embodiment?—that is the question, that is the experiment.

III

ORIGIN OF THE LOGICAL. Where has logic originated in men's heads? Undoubtedly out of the illogical, the domain of which must originally have been immense. But numberless beings who reasoned otherwise than we do at present perished; albeit that they may have come nearer to truth than we! Whoever, for example, could not discern the "like" often enough with regard to food, and with regard to animals dangerous to him, whoever, therefore, deduced too slowly, or was too circumspect in his deductions, had smaller probability of survival than he who in all similar things immediately divined the equality. The preponderating inclination, however, to deal with the similar as the equal—an illogical inclination, for there is nothing equal in itself—first created the whole basis of logic. It was just so (in order that the conception of substance might originate, this being indispensable to logic, although in the strictest sense nothing actual corresponds to it) that for a long period the changing process in things had to be overlooked, and remain unperceived; the beings not seeing correctly had an advantage over those who saw everything "in flux." In itself every high degree of circumspection in conclusions, every sceptical inclination, is a great danger to life. No living being would have been preserved unless the contrary inclination—to affirm rather than suspend judgment, to mistake and fabricate rather than wait, to assent rather than deny, to decide rather than be in the right—had been cultivated with extraordinary assiduity.—The course of logical thought and reasoning in our modern brain corresponds to a process and struggle of impulses, which singly and in themselves are all very illogical and unjust; we experience usually only the result of the struggle, so rapidly and secretly does this primitive mechanism now operate in us.

301

ILLUSION OF THE CONTEMPLATIVE. Higher men are distinguished from lower, by seeing and hearing immensely more, and in a thoughtful manner—and it is precisely this that distinguishes man from the animal, and the higher animal from the lower. The world always becomes fuller for him who grows up into the full stature of humanity; there are always more interesting fishing hooks thrown out to him; the number of his stimuli is continually on the increase, and similarly the varieties of his pleasure and pain—the higher man becomes always at the same time happier and unhappier. An *illusion,* however, is his constant accompaniment all along: he thinks he is placed as a *spectator* and *auditor* before the great pantomime and concert of life; he calls his nature a *contemplative nature,* and thereby overlooks the fact that he himself is also a real creator, and continuous poet of life—that he no doubt differs greatly from the *actor* in this drama, the so-called practical man, but differs still more from a mere onlooker or spectator *before* the stage. There is certainly *vis contemplativa,* and re-examination of his work peculiar to him as poet, but at the same time, and first and foremost, he has the *vis creativa,* which the practical man or doer *lacks,* whatever appearance and current belief may say to the contrary. It is we, we who think and feel, that actually and unceasingly *make* something which does not yet exist: the whole eternally increasing world of valuations, colors, weights, perspectives, gradations, affirmations, and negations. This composition of ours is continually learned, practiced, and translated into flesh and actuality, and even into the commonplace, by the so-called practical men (our actors, as we have said). Whatever has *value* in the present world has it not in itself, by its nature—nature is always worthless— but a value was once given to it, bestowed upon it, and it was *we* who gave and bestowed! We only have created the world *which is of any account to man!*—But it is precisely this knowledge that we lack, and when we get hold of it for a moment we have forgotten it the next: we misunderstand our highest power, we contemplative men, and estimate ourselves at too low a rate—we are neither as *proud nor as happy* as we might be.

355

THE ORIGIN OF OUR CONCEPTION OF "KNOWLEDGE." I take this explanation from the street. I heard one of the people saying that "he knew me," so I asked myself: What do the people really understand by knowledge? What do they want when they seek "knowledge"? Nothing more than that what is strange is to be traced back to something *known.* And we philosophers—have we really understood *anything more* by knowledge? The known, that is to say, what we are accustomed to, so that we no longer marvel at it, the commonplace, any kind of rule to which we are habituated, all and everything in which we know ourselves to be at home—what? is our need of knowing not just this need of the known? the will to discover in everything strange, unusual, or questionable, something which no longer disquiets us? Is it not possible that it should be the *instinct of fear* which enjoins upon us to know? Is it not possible that the rejoicing of the discerner should be just his rejoicing in the regained feeling of security? . . . One philosopher imagined the world "known" when he had traced it back to the "idea": alas, was it not because the idea was so known, so familiar to him? because he had so much less fear of the "idea"—oh, this moderation of the discerners! Let us but look at their principles, and at their solutions of the riddle of the world in this connection! When they again find aught in things, among things, or behind things, that is unfortunately very well known to us, for example, our multiplication table, or our logic, or our willing and desiring, how happy they immediately are! For "what is known is understood": they are unanimous as to that. Even the most circumspect among them think that the known is at least *more easily understood* than the strange; that, for example, it is methodically ordered to proceed outward from the "inner world," from "the facts of consciousness," because it is the world which is *better known to us!* Error of errors! The known is the accustomed, and the accustomed is the most difficult of all to "understand," that is to say, to perceive as a problem, to perceive as strange, distant, "outside of us." . . . The great certainty of the natural sciences in comparison with psychology and the criticism of the elements of consciousness—*unnatural* sciences as one might almost be entitled to call them—rests precisely on the fact that they take *what is strange* as their object: while it is almost like something contradictory and absurd *to wish* to take generally what is not strange as an object. . . .

FROM BEYOND GOOD AND EVIL

6

It has gradually become clear to me what every great philosophy up till now has consisted of—namely, the confession of its originator, and a species of involuntary and unconscious autobiography; and moreover that the moral (or immoral) purpose in every philosophy has constituted the true vital germ out of which the entire plant has always grown. Indeed, to understand how the abstrusest metaphysical assertions of a philosopher have been arrived at, it is always well (and wise) to first ask oneself: "What morality do they (or does he) aim at?" Accordingly, I do not believe that an "impulse to knowledge" is the father of philosophy; but that another impulse, here as elsewhere, has only made use of knowledge (and mistaken knowledge!) as an instrument. But whoever considers the fundamental impulses of man with a view to determining how far they may have here acted as *inspiring* genii (or as demons and kobolds) will find that they have all practiced philosophy at one time or another, and that each one of them would have been only too glad to look upon itself as the ultimate end of existence and the legitimate *lord* over all the other impulses. For every impulse is imperious, and as *such,* attempts to philosophize. To be sure, in the case of scholars, in the case of really scientific men, it may be otherwise—"better," if you will; there there may really be such a thing as an "impulse to knowledge," some kind of small, independent clockwork, which, when well wound up, works away industriously to that end, *without* the rest of the scholarly impulses taking any material part therein. The actual "interests" of the scholar, therefore, are generally in quite another direction—in the family, perhaps, or in money-making, or in politics; it is, in fact, almost indifferent at what point of research his little machine is placed, and whether the hopeful young worker becomes a good philologist, a mushroom specialist, or a chemist; he is not *characterized* by becoming this or that. In the philosopher, on the contrary, there is absolutely nothing impersonal; and above all, his morality furnishes a decided and decisive testimony as to *who he is,* that is to say, in what order the deepest impulses of his nature stand to each other.

7

How malicious philosophers can be! I know of nothing more stinging than the joke Epicurus took the liberty of making on Plato and the Platonists: he called them *Dionysiokolakes.* In its original sense, and on the face of it, the word signifies "Flatterers of Dionysius"—consequently, tyrants' accessories and lickspittles; besides this, however, it is as much as to say, "They are all *actors,* there is nothing

genuine about them" (for *Dionysiokolax* was a popular name
for an actor). And the latter is really the malignant reproach
that Epicurus cast upon Plato: he was annoyed by the
grandiose manner, the *mise en scène* style of which Plato
and his scholars were masters—of which Epicurus was not a
master! He, the old schoolteacher of Samos, who sat concealed in his little garden at Athens and wrote three hundred books, perhaps out of rage and ambitious envy of Plato,
who knows! Greece took a hundred years to find out who
the garden-god Epicurus really was. Did she ever find out?

8

There is a point in every philosophy at which the "conviction" of the philosopher appears on the scene; or, to put
it in the words of an ancient mystery:

Adventavit asinus,
Pulcher et fortissimus.

9

You desire to *live* "according to Nature"? Oh, you noble
Stoics, what fraud of words! Imagine to yourselves a being
like Nature, boundlessly extravagant, boundlessly indifferent,
without purpose or consideration, without pity or justice, at
once fruitful and barren and uncertain: imagine to yourselves *indifference* as a power—how *could* you live in accordance with such indifference? To live—is not that just
endeavoring to be otherwise than this Nature? Is not living
valuing, preferring, being unjust, being limited, endeavoring
to be different? And granted that your imperative, "living
according to Nature," means actually the same as "living
according to life"—how could you do *differently?* Why
should you make a principle out of what you yourselves
are, and must be? In reality, however, it is quite otherwise
with you: while you pretend to read with rapture the canon
of your law in Nature, you want something quite the contrary, you extraordinary stage players and self-deluders!
In your pride you wish to dictate your morals and ideals
to Nature, to Nature herself, and to incorporate them therein;
you insist that it shall be Nature "according to the Stoa,"
and would like everything to be made after your own image,
as a vast, eternal glorification and generalization of Stoi-

cism! With all your love for truth, you have forced yourselves so long, so persistently, and with such hypnotic rigidity to see Nature *falsely*, that is to say, Stoically, that you are no longer able to see it otherwise—and to crown all, some unfathomable superciliousness gives you the Bedlamite hope that *because* you are able to tyrannize over yourselves —Stoicism is self-tyranny—Nature will also allow herself to be tyrannized over: is not the Stoic a *part* of Nature? . . . But this is an old and everlasting story: what happened in old times with the Stoics still happens today, as soon as ever a philosophy begins to believe in itself. It always creates the world in its own image; it cannot do otherwise; philosophy is this tyrannical impulse itself, the most spiritual Will to Power, the will to "creation of the world," the will to the *causa prima*.

42

A new order of philosophers is appearing; I shall venture to baptize them by a name not without danger. As far as I understand them, as far as they allow themselves to be understood—for it is their nature to *wish* to remain something of a puzzle—these philosophers of the future might rightly, perhaps also wrongly, claim to be designated as *"tempters."* This name itself is after all only an attempt, or, if it be preferred, a temptation.

43

Will they be new friends of "truth," these coming philosophers? Very probably, for all philosophers hitherto have loved their truths. But assuredly they will not be dogmatists. It must be contrary to their pride, and also contrary to their taste, that their truth should still be truth for everyone— that which has hitherto been the secret wish and ultimate purpose of all dogmatic efforts. "My opinion is *my* opinion: another person has not easily a right to it"—such a philosopher of the future will say, perhaps. One must renounce the bad taste of wishing to agree with many people. "Good" is no longer good when one's neighbor takes it into his mouth. And how could there be a "common good"! The expression contradicts itself; that which can be common is always of small value. In the end things must be as they are and have always been—the great things remain for the great, the abysses for the profound, the delicacies and thrills for the refined, and, to sum up shortly, everything rare for the rare.

54

What does all modern philosophy mainly do? Since Descartes—and indeed more in defiance of him than on the basis of his procedure—an *attentat* has been made on the part of all philosophers on the old conception of the soul, under the guise of a criticism of the subject and predicate conception—that is to say, an *attentat* on the fundamental presupposition of Christian doctrine. Modern philosophy, as epistemological scepticism, is secretly or openly *anti-Christian*, although (for keener ears, be it said) by no means antireligious. Formerly, in effect, one believed in "the soul" as one believed in grammar and the grammatical subject: one said, "I" is the condition, "think" is the predicate and is conditioned—to think is an activity for which one *must* suppose a subject as cause. The attempt was then made, with marvelous tenacity and subtlety, to see if one could not get out of this net—to see if the opposite was not perhaps true: "think" the condition, and "I" the conditioned; "I," therefore, only a synthesis which has been *made* by thinking itself. *Kant* really wished to prove that, starting from the subject, the subject could not be proved—nor the object either: the possibility of an *apparent existence* of the subject, and therefore of "the soul," may not always have been strange to him—the thought which once had an immense power on earth as the Vedanta philosophy.

204

At the risk that moralizing may also reveal itself here as that which it has always been—namely, resolutely *montrer ses plaies*, according to Balzac—I would venture to protest against an improper and injurious alteration of rank, which quite unnoticed, and as if with the best conscience, threatens nowadays to establish itself in the relations of science and philosophy. I mean to say that one must have the right out of one's own *experience*—experience, as it seems to me, always implies unfortunate experience—to treat of such an important question of rank, so as not to speak of color like the blind, or *against* science like women and artists ("Ah!

this dreadful science!" sigh their instinct and their shame, "it always *finds things out!*"). The declaration of independence of the scientific man, his emancipation from philosophy, is one of the subtler aftereffects of democratic organization and disorganization: the self-glorification and self-conceitedness of the learned man is now everywhere in full bloom, and in its best springtime—which does not mean to imply that in this case self-praise smells sweetly. Here also the instinct of the populace cries, "Freedom from all masters!" and after science has, with the happiest results, resisted theology, whose "handmaid" it had been too long, it now proposes in its wantonness and indiscretion to lay down laws for philosophy, and in its turn to play the "master"—what am I saying! to play the *philosopher* on its own account. My memory—the memory of a scientific man, if you please! —teems with the naïvetés of insolence which I have heard about philosophy and philosophers from young naturalists and old physicians (not to mention the most cultured and most conceited of all learned men, the philologists and schoolmasters, who are both the one and the other by profession). On one occasion it was the specialist and the Jack Horner who instinctively stood on the defensive against all synthetic tasks and capabilities; at another time it was the industrious worker who had got a scent of *otium* and refined luxuriousness in the internal economy of the philosopher, and felt himself aggrieved and belittled thereby. On another occasion it was the color blindness of the utilitarian, who sees nothing in philosophy but a series of *refuted* systems, and an extravagant expenditure which "does nobody any good." At another time the fear of disguised mysticism and of the boundary adjustment of knowledge became conspicuous, at another time the disregard of individual philosophers, which had involuntarily extended to disregard of philosophy generally. In fine, I found most frequently, behind the proud disdain of philosophy in young scholars, the evil aftereffect of some particular philosopher, to whom on the whole obedience had been foresworn, without, however, the spell of his scornful estimates of other philosophers having been got rid of—the result being a general ill will to all philosophy. (Such seems to me, for instance, the aftereffect of Schopenhauer on the most modern Germany: by his unintelligent rage against Hegel, he has succeeded in severing the whole of the last generation of Germans from its connection with German culture, which culture, all things considered, has been an elevation and a divining refinement of the *historical sense;* but precisely at this point Schopen-

hauer himself was poor, irreceptive, and un-German to the
extent of ingeniousness.) On the whole, speaking generally, it
may just have been the humanness, all-too-humanness of the
modern philosophers themselves, in short, their contemptible-
ness, which has injured most radically the reverence for
philosophy and opened the doors to the instinct of the populace. Let it but be acknowledged to what an extent our
modern world diverges from the whole style of the world of
Heraclites, Plato, Empedocles, and whatever else all the
royal and magnificent anchorites of the spirit were called;
and with what justice an honest man of science *may* feel
himself of a better family and origin, in view of such representatives of philosophy, who, owing to the fashion of the
present day, are just as much aloft as they are down below
—in Germany, for instance, the two lions of Berlin, the
anarchist Eugen Dühring and the amalgamist Eduard von
Hartmann. It is especially the sight of those hotchpotch philosophers, who call themselves "realists," or "positivists,"
which is calculated to implant a dangerous distrust in the
soul of a young and ambitious scholar: those philosophers,
at the best, are themselves but scholars and specialists, that
is very evident! All of them are persons who have been
vanquished and *brought back again* under the dominion of
science, who at one time or another claimed more from
themselves, without having a right to the "more" and its
responsibility—and who now, creditably, rancorously, and
vindictively, represent in word and deed *disbelief* in the
master-task and supremacy of philosophy. After all, how
could it be otherwise? Science flourishes nowadays and has
the good conscience clearly visible on its countenance; while
that to which the entire modern philosophy has gradually
sunk, the remnant of philosophy of the present day, excites
distrust and displeasure, if not scorn and pity. Philosophy
reduced to a "theory of knowledge," no more in fact than a
diffident science of epochs and doctrine of forbearance: a
philosophy that never even gets beyond the threshold, and
rigorously *denies* itself the right to enter—that is philosophy
in its last throes, an end, an agony, something that awakens
pity. How could such a philosophy—*rule!*

205

The dangers that beset the evolution of the philosopher
are, in fact, so manifold nowadays, that one might doubt
whether this fruit could still come to maturity. The extent

and towering structure of the sciences have increased enormously, and therewith also the probability that the philosopher will grow tired even as a learner, or will attach himself somewhere and "specialize": so that he will no longer attain to his elevation, that is to say, to his superspection, his circumspection, and his *despection*. Or he gets aloft too late, when the best of his maturity and strength is past; or when he is impaired, coarsened, and deteriorated, so that his view, his general estimate of things, is no longer of much importance. It is perhaps just the refinement of his intellectual conscience that makes him hesitate and linger on the way; he dreads the temptation to become a dilettante, a millepede, a milleantenna; he knows too well that as a discerner, one who has lost his self-respect no longer commands, no longer *leads;* unless he should aspire to become a great play actor, a philosophical Cagliostro and spiritual ratcatcher—in short, a misleader. This is in the last instance a question of taste, if it has not really been a question of conscience. To double once more the philosopher's difficulties, there is also the fact that he demands from himself a verdict, a Yea or Nay, not concerning science, but concerning life and the worth of life—he learns unwillingly to believe that it is his right and even his duty to obtain this verdict, and he has to seek his way to the right and the belief only through the most extensive (perhaps disturbing and destroying) experiences, often hesitating, doubting, and dumbfounded. In fact, the philosopher has long been mistaken and confused by the multitude, either with the scientific man and ideal scholar, or with the religiously elevated, desensualized, desecularized visionary and God-intoxicated man; and even yet when one hears anybody praised, because he lives "wisely," or "as a philosopher," it hardly means anything more than "prudently and apart." Wisdom: that seems to the populace to be a kind of flight, a means and artifice for withdrawing successfully from a bad game; but the *genuine* philosopher—does it not seem so to *us*, my friends? —lives "unphilosophically" and "unwisely," above all, *imprudently*, and feels the obligation and burden of a hundred attempts and temptations of life—he risks *himself* constantly, he plays *this* bad game.

206

In relation to the genius, that is to say, a being who either *engenders* or *produces*—both words understood in their fullest sense—the man of learning, the scientific average man, has always something of the old maid about him; for, like her, he is not conversant with the two principal functions of man. To both, of course, to the scholar and to the old maid, one concedes respectability, as if by way of indemnification —in these cases one emphasizes the respectability—and yet, in the compulsion of this concession, one has the same admixture of vexation. Let us examine more closely: what is the scientific man? Firstly, a commonplace type of man, with commonplace virtues: that is to say, a nonruling, nonauthoritative, and nonself-sufficient type of man; he possesses industry, patient adaptableness to rank and file, equability and moderation in capacity and requirement; he has the instinct for people like himself, and for that which they require—for instance: the portion of independence and green meadow without which there is no rest from labor, the claim to honor and consideration (which first and foremost presupposes recognition and recognizability), the sunshine of a good name, the perpetual ratification of his value and usefulness, with which the inward *distrust* which lies at the bottom of the heart of all dependent men and gregarious animals has again and again to be overcome. The learned man, as is appropriate, has also maladies and faults of an ignoble kind: he is full of petty envy, and has a lynx-eye for the weak points in those natures to whose elevations he cannot attain. He is confiding, yet only as one who lets himself go, but does not *flow;* and precisely before the man of the great current he stands all the colder and more reserved—his eye is then like a smooth and irresponsive lake, which is no longer moved by rapture or sympathy. The worst and most dangerous thing of which a scholar is capable results from the instinct of mediocrity of his type, from the Jesuitism of mediocrity, which labors instinctively for the destruction of the exceptional man, and endeavors to break—or still better, to relax—every bent bow. To relax, of course, with consideration, and naturally with an indulgent hand—to *relax* with confiding sympathy: that is the real art of Jesuitism, which has always understood how to introduce itself as the religion of sympathy.

207

However gratefully one may welcome the *objective* spirit —and who has not been sick to death of all subjectivity and its confounded *ipsissimosity!*—in the end, however, one must learn caution even with regard to one's gratitude, and put a stop to the exaggeration with which the unselfing and de-personalizing of the spirit has recently been celebrated, as if it were the goal in itself, as if it were salvation and glorification—as is especially accustomed to happen in the pessimist school, which has also in its turn good reasons for paying the highest honors to "disinterested knowledge." The objective man, who no longer curses and scolds like the pes-simist, the *ideal* man of learning in whom the scientific in-stinct blossoms forth fully after a thousand complete and partial failures, is assuredly one of the most costly instru-ments that exist, but his place is in the hand of one who is more powerful. He is only an instrument; we may say, he is a *mirror*—he is no "purpose in himself." The objective man is in truth a mirror: accustomed to prostration before every-thing that wants to be known, with such desires only as knowing or "reflecting" imply—he waits until something comes, and then expands himself sensitively, so that even the light footsteps and gliding past of spiritual beings may not be lost on his surface and film. Whatever "personality" he still possesses seems to him accidental, arbitrary, or still oftener, disturbing; so much has he come to regard himself as the passage and reflection of outside forms and events. He calls up the recollection of "himself" with an effort, and not infrequently wrongly; he readily confounds himself with other persons, he makes mistakes with regard to his own needs, and here only is he unrefined and negligent. Perhaps he is troubled about the health, or the pettiness and confined atmosphere of wife and friend, or the lack of companions and society—indeed, he sets himself to reflect on his suffer-ing, but in vain! His thoughts already rove away to the *more general* case, and tomorrow he knows as little as he knew yesterday how to help himself. He does not now take himself seriously and devote time to himself: he is serene, *not* from lack of trouble, but from lack of capacity for grasping and dealing with *his* trouble. The habitual complaisance with respect to all objects and experiences, the radiant and im-partial hospitality with which he receives everything that comes his way, his habit of inconsiderate good nature, of dangerous indifference as to Yea and Nay: alas! there are enough of cases in which he has to atone for these virtues of his!—and as man generally, he becomes far too easily the *caput mortuum* of such virtues. Should one wish love or hatred from him—I mean love and hatred as God, woman, and animal understand them—he will do what he can, and furnish what he can. But one must not be surprised if it should not be much—if he should show himself just at this point to be false, fragile, questionable, and deteriorated. His love is constrained, his hatred is artificial, and rather *un tour de force*, a slight ostentation and exaggeration. He is only genuine so far as he can be objective; only in his serene totality is he still "nature" and "natural." His mirroring and eternally self-polishing soul no longer knows how to affirm, no longer how to deny; he does not command; neither does he destroy. *"Je ne méprise presque rien"*—he says, with Leibnitz: let us not overlook nor undervalue the *presque!* Neither is he a model man; he does not go in advance of anyone, nor after either; he places himself generally too far off to have any reason for espousing the cause of either good or evil. If he has been so long confounded with the *philosopher*, with the Caesarean trainer and dictator of civilization, he has had far too much honor, and what is most essential in him has been overlooked—he is an instrument, something of a slave, though certainly the sublimest sort of slave, but nothing in himself—*presque rien!* The objective man is an instrument, a costly, easily injured, easily tarnished, measuring instrument and mirroring apparatus, which is to be taken care of and respected; but he is no goal, no outgoing nor upgoing, no complementary man in whom the *rest* of existence justifies itself, no termination—and still less a commencement, an engendering, or primary cause, nothing hardy, powerful, self-centered, that wants to be master; but rather only a soft, inflated, delicate, movable potter's-form, that must wait for some kind of content and frame to "shape" itself thereto—for the most part a man without frame and content, a "selfless" man. Consequently, also, nothing for women, *in parenthesi.*

208

When a philosopher nowadays makes known that he is not a sceptic—I hope that has been gathered from the foregoing description of the objective spirit?—people all hear it impatiently; they regard him on that account with some apprehension, they would like to ask so many, many questions . . . indeed among timid hearers, of whom there are now so many, he is henceforth said to be dangerous. With his repudiation of scepticism, it seems to them as if they heard some evil-threatening sound in the distance, as if a new kind of explosive were being tried somewhere, a dynamite of the spirit, perhaps a newly discovered Russian *nihiline*, a pessimism *bonae voluntatis*, that not only denies, means denial, but—dreadful thought! *practices* denial. Against this kind of "good will"—a will to the veritable, actual negation of life—there is, as is generally acknowledged nowadays, no better soporific and sedative than scepticism, the mild, pleasing, lulling poppy of scepticism; and Hamlet himself is now prescribed by the doctors of the day as an antidote to the "spirit," and its underground noises. "Are not our ears already full of bad sounds?" say the sceptics, as lovers of repose, and almost as a kind of safety police, "This subterranean Nay is terrible! Be still, ye pessimistic moles!" The sceptic, in effect, that delicate creature, is far too easily frightened; his conscience is schooled so as to start at every Nay, and even at every sharp, decided Yea, and feels something like a bite thereby. Yea! and Nay!—they seem to him opposed to morality; he loves, on the contrary, to make a festival to his virtue by a noble aloofness, while perhaps he says with Montaigne: "What do I know?" Or with Socrates: "I know that I know nothing." Or: "Here I do not trust myself, no door is open to me." Or: "Even if the door were open why should I enter immediately?" Or: "What is the use of any hasty hypotheses? It might quite well be in good taste to make no hypotheses at all. Are you absolutely obliged to straighten at once what is crooked? to stuff every hole with some kind of oakum? Is there not time enough for that? Has not the time leisure? Oh, ye demons, can ye not at all *wait?* The uncertain also has its charms, the Sphinx, too, is a Circe, and Circe, too, was a philosopher."—Thus does a sceptic console himself; and in truth he needs some consolation. For scepticism is the most spiritual expression of a certain many-sided physiological temperament, which in ordinary language is called nervous debility and sickliness; it arises whenever races or classes which have been long separated, decisively and suddenly blend with one another. In the new generation, which has inherited, as it were, different standards and valuations in its blood, everything is disquiet, derangement, doubt, and tentative; the best powers operate restrictively, the very virtues prevent each other growing and becoming strong, equilibrium, ballast, and perpendicular stability are lacking in body and soul. That, however, which is most diseased and degenerated in such nondescripts is the *will;* they are no longer familiar with independence of decision, or the courageous feeling of pleasure in willing— they are doubtful of the "freedom of the will" even in their dreams. Our present-day Europe, the scene of a senseless, precipitate attempt at a radical blending of classes, and *consequently* of races, is therefore sceptical in all its heights and depths, sometimes exhibiting the mobile scepticism which springs impatiently and wantonly from branch to branch, sometimes with gloomy aspect, like a cloud overcharged with interrogative signs—and often sick unto death of its will! Paralysis of will; where do we not find this cripple sitting nowadays! And yet how bedecked oftentimes! How seductively ornamented! There are the finest gala dresses and disguises for this disease; and that, for instance, most of what places itself nowadays in the showcases as "objectiveness," "the scientific spirit," "*l'art pour l'art*," and "pure voluntary knowledge," is only decked-out scepticism and paralysis of will—I am ready to answer for this diagnosis of the European disease.—The disease of the will is diffused unequally over Europe; it is worst and most varied where civilization has longest prevailed; it decreases according as "the barbarian" still—or again—asserts his claims under the loose drapery of Western culture. It is therefore in the France of today, as can be readily disclosed and comprehended, that the will is most infirm; and France, which has always had a masterly aptitude for converting even the portentous crises of its spirit into something charming and seductive, now manifests emphatically its intellectual ascendency over Europe, by being the school and exhibition of all the charms of scepticism. The power to will and to persist, moreover, in a resolution, is already somewhat stronger in Germany, and again in the North of Germany it is stronger than in Central Germany; it is considerably stronger in England, Spain, and Corsica, associated with phlegm in the former and with hard skulls in the latter—not to mention Italy, which is too young yet to know what it wants, and must first show whether it can exercise will; but it is strongest and most surprising of all in that immense middle empire where Europe, as it were, flows back to Asia—namely, in Russia. There the power to will has been long stored up and accumulated, there the will—uncertain whether to be negative or affirmative—waits threateningly to be discharged (to borrow their pet phrase from our physicists). Perhaps not only Indian wars and complications in Asia would be necessary to free Europe from its greatest danger, but also internal subversion, the shattering of the empire into small states, and above all the introduction of parliamentary imbecility, together with the obligation of everyone to read his newspaper at breakfast. I do not say this as one who desires it; in my heart I should rather prefer the contrary—I mean such an increase in the threatening attitude of Russia, that Europe would have to make up its mind to become equally threatening—namely, *to acquire one will*, by means of a new caste to rule over the Continent, a persistent, dreadful will of its own, that can set its aims thousands of years ahead; so that the long spun-out comedy of its petty-statism, and its dynastic as well as its democratic many-willedness, might finally be brought to a close. The time for petty politics is past; the next century will bring the struggle for the dominion of the world— the *compulsion* to great politics.

209

As to how far the new warlike age on which we Europeans have evidently entered may perhaps favor the growth of another and stronger kind of scepticism, I should like to express myself preliminarily merely by a parable, which the lovers of German history will already understand. That unscrupulous enthusiast for big, handsome grenadiers (who, as King of Prussia, brought into being a military and sceptical genius—and therewith, in reality, the new and now triumphantly emerged type of German), the problematic, crazy father of Frederick the Great, had on one point the very knack and lucky grasp of the genius: he knew what was then lacking in Germany, the want of which was a hundred times more alarming and serious than any lack of culture and social form—his ill will to the young Frederick resulted from the anxiety of a profound instinct. *Men were lacking;* and he suspected, to his bitterest regret, that his own son was not man enough. There, however, he deceived himself; but who would not have deceived himself in his place? He saw his son lapsed to atheism, to the *esprit*, to the pleasant frivolity of clever Frenchmen—he saw in the background the great bloodsucker, the spider scepticism; he suspected the incurable wretchedness of a heart no longer hard enough either for evil or good, and of a broken will that no longer commands, is no longer *able* to command. Meanwhile, however, there grew up in his son that new kind of harder and more dangerous scepticism—who knows *to what extent* it was encouraged just by his father's hatred and the icy melancholy of a will condemned to solitude?—the scepticism of daring manliness, which is closely related to the genius for war and conquest, and made its first entrance into Germany in the person of the great Frederick. This scepticism despises and nevertheless grasps; it undermines and takes pos-

session; it does not believe, but it does not thereby lose itself; it gives the spirit a dangerous liberty, but it keeps strict
guard over the heart. It is the *German* form of scepticism,
which, as a continued Fredericianism, risen to the highest
spirituality, has kept Europe for a considerable time under
the dominion of the German spirit and its critical and historical distrust. Owing to the insuperably strong and tough
masculine character of the great German philologists and
historical critics (who, rightly estimated, were also all of
them artists of destruction and dissolution), a *new* conception of the German spirit gradually established itself—in
spite of all romanticism in music and philosophy—in which
the leaning toward masculine scepticism was decidedly prominent: whether, for instance, as fearlessness of gaze, as courage and sternness of the dissecting hand, or as resolute will
to dangerous voyages of discovery, to spiritualized North
Pole expeditions under barren and dangerous skies. There
may be good grounds for it when warm-blooded and superficial humanitarians cross themselves before this spirit, *cet
esprit fataliste, ironique, méphistophélique*, as Michelet
calls it, not without a shudder. But if one would realize how
characteristic is this fear of the "man" in the German spirit
which awakened Europe out of its "dogmatic slumber," let
us call to mind the former conception which had to be overcome by this new one—and that it is not so very long ago
that a masculinized woman could dare, with unbridled presumption, to recommend the Germans to the interest of Europe as gentle, goodhearted, weak-willed, and poetical fools.
Finally, let us only understand profoundly enough Napoleon's astonishment when he saw Goethe: it reveals what had
been regarded for centuries as the "German spirit." *"Voilà
un homme!"*—that was as much as to say: "But this is a
man! And I only expected to see a German!"

210

Supposing, then, that in the picture of the philosophers of
the future, some trait suggests the question whether they
must not perhaps be sceptics in the last-mentioned sense,
something in them would only be designated thereby—and
not they themselves. With equal right they might call themselves critics; and assuredly they will be men of experiments.
By the name with which I ventured to baptize them, I have
already expressly emphasized their attempting and their love
of attempting: is this because, as critics in body and soul,

they will love to make use of experiments in a new, and perhaps wider and more dangerous sense? In their passion for knowledge, will they have to go further in daring and painful attempts than the sensitive and pampered taste of a democratic century can approve of?—There is no doubt: these coming ones will be least able to dispense with the serious and not unscrupulous qualities which distinguish the critic from the sceptic: I mean the certainty as to standards of worth, the conscious employment of a unity of method, the wary courage, the standing alone, and the capacity for self-responsibility; indeed, they will avow among themselves a *delight* in denial and dissection, and a certain considerate cruelty, which knows how to handle the knife surely and deftly, even when the heart bleeds. They will be *sterner* (and perhaps not always toward themselves only) than humane people may desire, they will not deal with the "truth" in order that it may "please" them, or "elevate" and "inspire" them—they will rather have little faith in *"truth"* bringing with it such revels for the feelings. They will smile, those rigorous spirits, when anyone says in their presence: "That thought elevates me, why should it not be true?" or: "That work enchants me, why should it not be beautiful?" or: "That artist enlarges me, why should he not be great?" Perhaps they will not only have a smile, but a genuine disgust for all that is thus rapturous, idealistic, feminine, and hermaphroditic; and if anyone could look into their inmost heart, he would not easily find therein the intention to reconcile "Christian sentiments" with "antique taste," or even with "modern parliamentarism" (the kind of reconciliation necessarily found even amongst philosophers in our very uncertain and consequently very conciliatory century). Critical discipline, and every habit that conduces to purity and rigor in intellectual matters, will not only be demanded from themselves by these philosophers of the future; they may even make a display thereof as their special adornment —nevertheless they will not want to be called critics on that account. It will seem to them no small indignity to philosophy to have it decreed, as is so welcome nowadays, that "philosophy itself is criticism and critical science—and nothing else whatever!" Though this estimate of philosophy may enjoy the approval of all the Positivists of France and Germany (and possibly it even flattered the heart and taste of Kant: let us call to mind the titles of his principal works), our new philosophers will say, notwithstanding, that critics are instruments of the philosopher, and just on that account, as instruments, they are far from being philosophers them-

selves! Even the great Chinaman of Königsberg was only
a great critic.

211

I insist upon it that people finally cease confounding philosophical workers, and in general scientific men, with philosophers—that precisely here one should strictly give "each
his own," and not give those far too much, these far too little. It may be necessary for the education of the real philosopher that he himself should have once stood upon all those
steps upon which his servants, the scientific workers of philosophy, remain standing, and *must* remain standing: he himself must perhaps have been critic, and dogmatist, and historian, and besides, poet, and collector, and traveler, and riddle reader, and moralist, and seer, and "free spirit," and
almost everything, in order to traverse the whole range of
human values and estimations, and that he may *be able* with
a variety of eyes and consciences to look from a height to
any distance, from a depth up to any height, from a nook
into any expanse. But all these are only preliminary conditions for his task; this task itself demands something else—
it requires him *to create values*. The philosophical workers,
after the excellent pattern of Kant and Hegel, have to fix
and formalize some great existing body of valuations—that
is to say, former *determinations of value,* creations of value,
which have become prevalent, and are for a time called
"truths"—whether in the domain of the *logical,* the *political*
(moral), or the *artistic.* It is for these investigators to make
whatever has happened and been esteemed hitherto, conspicuous, conceivable, intelligible, and manageable, to
shorten everything long, even "time" itself, and to *subjugate*
the entire past: an immense and wonderful task, in the carrying out of which all refined pride, all tenacious will, can
surely find satisfaction. *The real philosophers, however, are
commanders and lawgivers;* they say: "Thus *shall* it be!" They
determine first the Whither and the Why of mankind, and
thereby set aside the previous labor of all philosophical workers, and all subjugators of the past—they grasp at the future
with a creative hand, and whatever is and was becomes for
them thereby a means, an instrument, and a hammer. Their
"knowing" is *creating,* their creating is a lawgiving, their
will to truth is—*Will to Power.*—Are there at present such
philosophers? Have there ever been such philosophers? *Must*
there not be such philosophers some day? . . .

It is always more obvious to me that the philosopher, as a man *indispensable* for the morrow and the day after the morrow, has ever found himself, and *has been obliged* to find himself, in contradiction to the day in which he lives; his enemy has always been the ideal of his day. Hitherto all those extraordinary furtherers of humanity whom one calls philosophers—who rarely regarded themselves as lovers of wisdom, but rather as disagreeable fools and dangerous interrogators—have found their mission, their hard, involuntary, imperative mission (in the end, however, the greatness of their mission), in being the bad conscience of their age. In putting the vivisector's knife to the breast of the very *virtues of their age*, they have betrayed their own secret; it has been for the sake of a *new* greatness of man, a new untrodden path to his aggrandizement. They have always disclosed how much hypocrisy, indolence, self-indulgence, and self-neglect, how much falsehood was concealed under the most venerated types of contemporary morality, how much virtue was *outlived;* they have always said: "We must remove hence to where *you* are least at home." In face of a world of "modern ideas," which would like to confine everyone in a corner, in a "specialty," a philosopher, if there could be philosophers nowadays, would be compelled to place the greatness of man, the conception of "greatness," precisely in his comprehensiveness and multifariousness, in his all-roundness; he would even determine worth and rank according to the amount and variety of that which a man could bear and take upon himself, according to the *extent* to which a man could stretch his responsibility. Nowadays the taste and virtue of the age weaken and attenuate the will; nothing is so adapted to the spirit of the age as weakness of will: consequently, in the ideal of the philosopher, strength of will, sternness and capacity for prolonged resolution, must specially be included in the conception of "greatness"; with as good a right as the opposite doctrine, with its ideal of a silly, renouncing, humble, selfless humanity, was suited to an opposite age—such as the sixteenth century, which suffered from its accumulated energy of will, and from the wildest torrents and floods of selfishness. In the time of Socrates, among men only of worn-out instincts, old conservative Athenians who let themselves go—"for the sake of happiness," as they said; for the sake of pleasure, as their conduct indicated—and who had continually on their lips the old pompous words to which they had long forfeited the right by the life they led, *irony* was perhaps necessary for greatness of soul, the wicked Socratic assurance of the old physician and plebeian, who cut ruthlessly into his own flesh, as into the flesh and heart of the "noble," with a look that said plainly enough: "Do not dissemble before me! here —we are equal!" At present, on the contrary, when through-out Europe the herding animal alone attains to honors, and dispenses honors, when "equality of right" can too readily be transformed into equality in wrong: I mean to say into general war against everything rare, strange, and privileged, against the higher man, the higher soul, the higher duty, the higher responsibility, the creative plenipotence and lord-liness—at present it belongs to the conception of "greatness" to be noble, to wish to be apart, to be capable of being different, to stand alone, to have to live by personal initiative; and the philosopher will betray something of his own ideal when he asserts: "He shall be the greatest who can be the most solitary, the most concealed, the most divergent, the man beyond good and evil, the master of his virtues, and of superabundance of will; precisely this shall be called *greatness:* as diversified as can be entire, as ample as can be full." And to ask once more the question: Is greatness *possible* —nowadays?

292

A philosopher: that is a man who constantly experiences, sees, hears, suspects, hopes, and dreams extraordinary things; who is struck by his own thoughts as if they came from the outside, from above and below, as a species of events and lightning flashes *peculiar to him;* who is perhaps himself a storm pregnant with new lightnings; a portentous man, around whom there is always rumbling and mumbling and gaping and something uncanny going on. A philosopher: alas, a being who often runs away from himself, is often afraid of himself—but whose curiosity always makes him "come to himself" again.

FROM THE GENEALOGY OF MORALS

1

THOSE English psychologists, who up to the present are the only philosophers who are to be thanked for any endeavor to get as far as a history of the origin of morality—these men, I say, offer us in their own personalities no paltry problem; they even have, if I am to be quite frank about it, in their capacity of living riddles, an advantage over their books—*they themselves are interesting!* These English psychologists—what do they really mean? We always find them voluntarily or involuntarily at the same task of pushing to the front the *partie honteuse* of our inner world, and looking for the efficient, governing, and decisive principle in that precise quarter where the intellectual self-respect of the race would be the most reluctant to find it (for example, in the *vis inertiae* of habit, or in forgetfulness, or in a blind and fortuitous mechanism and association of ideas, or in some factor that is purely passive, reflex, molecular, or fundamentally stupid)—what is the real motive power which always impels these psychologists in precisely *this* direction? Is it an instinct for human disparagement somewhat sinister, vulgar, and malignant, or perhaps incomprehensible even to itself? Or perhaps a touch of pessimistic jealousy, the mistrust of disillusioned idealists who have become gloomy, poisoned, and bitter? Or a petty subconscious enmity and rancor against Christianity (and Plato) that has conceivably never crossed the threshold of consciousness? Or just a vicious taste for those elements of life which are bizarre, painfully paradoxical, mystical, and illogical? Or, as a final alternative, a dash of each of these motives—a little vulgarity, a little gloominess, a little anti-Christianity, a little craving for the necessary piquancy?

But I am told that it is simply a case of old frigid and tedious frogs crawling and hopping around men and inside men, as if they were as thoroughly at home there, as they would be in a *swamp*.

I am opposed to this statement, nay, I do not believe it; and if, in the impossibility of knowledge, one is permitted to wish, so do I wish from my heart that just the converse metaphor should apply, and that these analysts with their psychological microscopes should be, at bottom, brave, proud, and magnanimous animals who know how to bridle both their hearts and their smarts, and have specifically trained themselves to sacrifice what is desirable to what is true, *any* truth in fact, even the simple, bitter, ugly, repulsive, unchristian, and immoral truths—for there are truths of that description.

2

All honor, then, to the noble spirits who would fain dominate these historians of morality. But it is certainly a pity that they lack the *historical sense* itself, that they themselves are quite deserted by all the beneficent spirits of history. The whole train of their thought runs, as was always the way of old-fashioned philosophers, on *thoroughly* unhistorical lines: there is no doubt on this point. The crass ineptitude of their genealogy of morals is immediately apparent when the question arises of ascertaining the origin of the idea and judgment of "good." "Man had originally," so speaks their decree, "praised and called 'good' altruistic acts from the standpoint of those on whom they were conferred, that is, those to whom they were *useful;* subsequently the origin of this praise was *forgotten,* and altruistic acts, simply because, as a sheer matter of habit, they were praised as good, came also to be felt as good—as though they contained in themselves some intrinsic goodness." The thing is obvious: this initial derivation contains already all the typical and idiosyncratic traits of the English psychologists—we have "utility," "forgetting," "habit," and finally "error," the whole assemblage forming the basis of a system of values, on which the higher man has up to the present prided himself as though it were a kind of privilege of man in general. This pride *must* be brought low, this system of values *must* lose its values: is that attained?

Now the first argument that comes ready to my hand is that the real homestead of the concept "good" is sought and located in the wrong place: the judgment "good" did *not* originate among those to whom goodness was shown. Much rather has it been the good themselves, that is, the aristocratic, the powerful, the high-stationed, the high-minded who have felt that they themselves were good, and that their actions were good, that is to say of the first order, in contradistinction to all the low, the low-minded, the vulgar, and the plebeian. It was out of this pathos of distance that they first arrogated the right to create values for their own profit, and to coin the names of such values: what had they to do with utility? The standpoint of utility is as alien and as inapplicable as it could possibly be, when we have to deal with so volcanic an effervescence of supreme values, creating and demarcating as they do a hierarchy within themselves: it is at this juncture that one arrives at an appreciation of the contrast to that tepid temperature, which is the presupposition on which every combination of worldly wisdom and every calculation of practical expediency is always based—and not for one occasional, not for one exceptional instance, but chronically. The pathos of nobility and distance, as I have said, the chronic and despotic *esprit de corps* and fundamental instinct of a higher dominant race coming into association with a meaner race, an "under race," this is the origin of the antithesis of good and bad.

(The masters' right of giving names goes so far that it is permissible to look upon language itself as the expression of the power of the masters: they say "this *is* that, and that," they seal finally every object and every event with a sound, and thereby at the same time take possession of it.) It is because of this origin that the word "good" is far from having any necessary connection with altruistic acts, in accordance with the superstitious belief of these moral philosophers. On the contrary, it is on the occasion of the *decay* of aristocratic values, that the antithesis between "egoistic" and "altruistic" presses more and more heavily on the human conscience—it is, to use my own language, the *herd instinct* which finds in this antithesis an expression in many ways. And even then it takes a considerable time for this instinct to become sufficiently dominant, for the valuation to be inextricably dependent on this antithesis (as is the case in contemporary Europe); for today that prejudice is predominant which, acting even now with all the intensity of an obsession and brain disease, holds that "moral," "altruistic," and *"désintéressé"* are concepts of equal value.

FROM THE TWILIGHT OF THE IDOLS

"Reason" in Philosophy

1

You ask me what all idiosyncrasy is in philosophers? . . . For instance their lack of the historical sense, their hatred even of the idea of Becoming, their Egyptianism. They imagine that they do honor to a thing by divorcing it from history *sub specie aeterni*—when they make a mummy of it. All the ideas that philosophers have treated for thousands of years have been mummied concepts; nothing real has ever come out of their hands alive. These idolators of concepts merely kill, and stuff things when they worship—they threaten the life of everything they adore. Death, change, age, as well as procreation and growth, are in their opinion objections— even refutations. That which is cannot evolve; that which evolves *is* not. Now all of them believe, and even with desperation, in Being. But, as they cannot lay hold of it, they try to discover reasons why this privilege is withheld from them. "Some merely apparent quality, some deception must be the cause of our not being able to ascertain the nature of Being: where is the deceiver?" "We have him," they cry rejoicing, "it is sensuality!" These senses, *which in other things are so immoral,* cheat us concerning the true world. Moral: we must get rid of the deception of the senses, of Becoming, of history, of falsehood.—History is nothing more than the belief in the senses, the belief in falsehood. Moral: we must say "no" to everything in which the senses believe: to all the rest of mankind: all that belongs to the "people." Let us be philosophers, mummies, monotono-theists, gravediggers! —And above all, away with the *body,* this wretched *idée fixe* of the senses, affected with all the faults of logic that exist, refuted, even impossible, although it be impudent enough to pose as if it were real!

2

With a feeling of great reverence I except the name of *Heraclitus.* If the rest of the philosophic gang rejected the evidences of the senses, because the latter revealed a state of multifariousness and change, he rejected the same evidence because it revealed things as if they possessed permanence and unity. Even Heraclitus did an injustice to the senses. The latter lie neither as the Eleatics believed them to lie, nor as he believed them to lie—they do not lie at all. The interpretations we give to their evidence is what first introduces falsehood into it; for instance the lie of unity, the lie of matter, of substance and of permanence. Reason is the cause of our falsifying the evidence of the senses. Insofar as the senses show us a state of Becoming, of transiency, and of change, they do not lie. But in declaring that Being was an empty illusion, Heraclitus will remain eternally right. The "apparent" world is the only world: the "true world" is no more than a false adjunct thereto.

3

And what delicate instruments of observation we have
in our senses! This human nose, for instance, of which no
philosopher has yet spoken with reverence and gratitude, is,
for the present, the most finely adjusted instrument at our
disposal: it is able to register even such slight changes of
movement as the spectroscope would be unable to record.
Our scientific triumphs at the present day extend precisely
so far as we have accepted the evidence of our senses—as
we have sharpened and armed them, and learned to follow
them up to the end. What remains is abortive and not yet
science—that is to say, metaphysics, theology, psychology,
epistemology, or formal science, or a doctrine of symbols,
like logic and its applied form mathematics. In all these
things reality does not come into consideration at all, even
as a problem; just as little as does the question concerning
the general value of such a convention of symbols as logic.

4

The other idiosyncrasy of philosophers is no less dangerous; it consists in confusing the last and the first things.
They place that which makes its appearance last—unfortunately! for it ought not to appear at all!—the "highest concept," that is to say, the most general, the emptiest, the last
cloudy streak of evaporating reality, at the beginning as the
beginning. This again is only their manner of expressing
their veneration: the highest thing must not have grown out
of the lowest, it must not have grown at all. . . . Moral:
every being of the first rank must be *causa sui*. To have been
derived from something else is as good as an objection, it sets
the value of a thing in question. All superior values are of the
first rank, all the highest concepts—that of Being, of the
Absolute, of Goodness, of Truth, and of Perfection; all these
things cannot have been evolved, they must therefore be
causa sui. All these things cannot, however, be unlike one
another, they cannot be opposed to one another. Thus they
attain to their stupendous concept "God." The last, most
attenuated, and emptiest thing is postulated as the first thing,
as the absolute cause, as *ens realissimum*. Fancy humanity
having to take the brain diseases of morbid cobweb-spinners
seriously!—And it has paid dearly for having done so.

5

—Against this let us set the different manner in which we (you observe that I am courteous enough to say "we") conceive the problem of the error and deceptiveness of things. Formerly people regarded change and evolution in general as the proof of appearance, as a sign of the fact that something must be there that leads us astray. Today, on the other hand, we realize that precisely as far as the rational bias forces us to postulate unity, identity, permanence, substance, cause, materiality, and being, we are in a measure involved in error, driven necessarily to error; however certain we may feel, as the result of a strict examination of the matter, that the error lies here. It is just the same here as with the motion of the sun: In its case it was our eyes that were wrong; in the matter of the concepts above mentioned it is our language itself that pleads most constantly in their favor. In its origin language belongs to an age of the most rudimentary forms of psychology: if we try to conceive of the first conditions of the metaphysics of language, i.e., in plain English, of reason, we immediately find ourselves in the midst of a system of fetishism. For here, the doer and his deed are seen in all circumstances, will is believed in as a cause in general; the ego is taken for granted, the ego as Being, and as substance, and the faith in the ego as substance is projected into all things—in this way, alone, the concept "thing" is created. Being is thought into and insinuated into everything as cause; from the concept "ego," alone, can the concept "Being" proceed. At the beginning stands the tremendously fatal error of supposing the will to be something that actuates—a faculty. Now we know that it is only a word.* Very much later, in a world a thousand times more enlightened, the assurance, the subjective certitude, in the handling of the categories of reason came into the minds of philosophers as a surprise. They concluded that these categories could not be derived from experience—on the contrary, the whole of experience rather contradicts them. *Whence do they come therefore?* In India, as in Greece, the same mistake was made: "We must already once have lived in a higher world (instead of in a much lower one, which would have been the truth!), we must have been divine, for

---

* Nietzsche here refers to the concept "free will" of the Christians; this does not mean that there is no such thing as will—that is to say a powerful determining force from within.—TR.

we possess reason!" . . . Nothing indeed has exercised a more simple power of persuasion hitherto than the error of Being, as it was formulated by the Eleatics for instance: in its favor are every word and every sentence that we utter! —Even the opponents of the Eleatics succumbed to the seductive powers of their concept of Being. Among others there was Democritus in his discovery of the atom. "Reason" in language!—oh what a deceptive old witch it has been! I fear we shall never be rid of God, so long as we still believe in grammar.

6

People will feel grateful to me if I condense a point of view, which is at once so important and so new, into four theses: by this means I shall facilitate comprehension, and shall likewise challenge contradiction.

Proposition One. The reasons upon which the apparent nature of "this" world have been based rather tend to prove its reality—any other kind of reality defies demonstration.

Proposition Two. The characteristics with which man has endowed the "true Being" of things are the characteristics of non-Being, of *nonentity*. The "true world" has been erected upon a contradiction of the real world; and it is indeed an apparent world, seeing that it is merely a *moralo-optical* delusion.

Proposition Three. There is no sense in spinning yarns about another world, provided, of course, that we do not possess a mighty instinct which urges us to slander, belittle, and cast suspicion upon this life: in this case we should be avenging ourselves on this life with the phantasmagoria of "another," of a "better" life.

Proposition Four. To divide the world into a "true" and an "apparent" world, whether after the manner of Christianity or of Kant (after all a Christian in disguise) is only a sign of decadence—a symptom of *degenerating* life. The fact that the artist esteems the appearance of a thing higher than reality is no objection to this statement. For "appearance" signifies once more reality here, but in a selected, strengthened, and corrected form. The tragic artist is no pessimist—he says *Yea* to everything questionable and terrible, he is Dionysian.

FROM THE ANTICHRIST*

10

Among Germans I am immediately understood when I say that philosophy is ruined by the blood of theologians. The Protestant minister is the grandfather of German philosophy, Protestantism itself is the latter's *peccatum originale*. Definition of Protestantism: the partial paralysis of Christianity—and of reason. . . . One needs only to pronounce the words "Tübingen Seminary" in order to understand what German philosophy really is at bottom, i.e., theology *in disguise*. . . . The Swabians are the best liars in Germany, they lie innocently. . . . Whence came all the rejoicing with which the appearance of Kant was greeted by the scholastic world of Germany, three-quarters of which consists of clergymen's and schoolmasters' sons? Whence came the German conviction, which finds an echo even now, that Kant inaugurated a change for the *better?* The theologian's instinct in the German scholar divined what had once again been made possible. . . . A back-staircase leading into the old ideal was discovered, the concept "true world," the concept morality as the *essence* of the world (those two most vicious errors that have ever existed!), were, thanks to a subtle and wily scepticism once again, if not demonstrable, at least no longer *refutable*. . . . Reason, the *prerogative* of reason, does not extend so far. . . . Out of reality they had made "appearance," and an absolutely false world—that of being—had been declared to be reality. Kant's success is merely a theologian's success. Like Luther, and like Leibniz, Kant was one brake the more upon the already squeaky wheel of German uprightness.

11

One word more against Kant as a *moralist*. A virtue *must* be *our* invention, our most personal defense and need: in every other sense it is merely a danger. That which does not constitute a condition of our life is merely harmful to it:

* From *The Twilight of the Idols*.

to possess a virtue merely because one happens to respect the concept "virtue," as Kant would have us do, is pernicious. "Virtue," "Duty," "Goodness in itself," goodness stamped with the character of impersonality and universal validity—these things are mere mental hallucinations, in which decline the final devitalization of life and Koenigsbergian Chinadom find expression. The most fundamental laws of preservation and growth demand precisely the reverse, namely, that each should discover *his* own virtue, his own Categorical Imperative. A nation goes to the dogs when it confounds its concept of duty with the general concept of duty. Nothing is more profoundly, more thoroughly pernicious, than every impersonal feeling of duty, than every sacrifice to the Moloch of abstraction.—Fancy no one's having thought Kant's Categorical Imperative *dangerous to life!* . . . The instinct of the theologist alone took it under its wing!—An action stimulated by the instinct of life is proved to be a proper action by the happiness that accompanies it: and that nihilist with the bowels of a Christian dogmatist regarded happiness as an *objection.* . . . What is there that destroys a man more speedily than to work, think, feel, as an automaton of "duty," without internal promptings, without a profound personal predilection, without joy? This is the recipe par excellence of decadence and even of idiocy. . . . Kant became an idiot.—And he was the contemporary of Goethe! This fatal spider was regarded as *the* German philosopher—is still regarded as such! . . . I refrain from saying what I think of the Germans. . . . Did Kant not see in the French Revolution the transition of the State from the inorganic to the *organic* form? Did he not ask himself whether there was a single event on record which could be explained otherwise than as a moral faculty of mankind; so that by means of it, "mankind's tendency toward good" might be *proved* once and for all? Kant's reply: "That is the Revolution." Instinct at fault in anything and everything, hostility to nature as an instinct, German decadence made into philosophy—*that is Kant!*

XIII. Psychology

FROM HUMAN, ALL TOO HUMAN, VOL. I

13

THE LOGIC OF DREAMS. In sleep our nervous system is perpetually excited by numerous inner occurrences; nearly all the organs are disjointed and in a state of activity, the blood runs its turbulent course, the position of the sleeper causes pressure on certain limbs, his coverings influence his sensations in various ways, the stomach digests and by its movements it disturbs other organs, the intestines writhe, the position of the head occasions unaccustomed play of muscles, the feet, unshod, not pressing upon the floor with the soles, occasion the feeling of the unaccustomed just as does the different clothing of the whole body: all this, according to its daily change and extent, excites by its extraordinariness the entire system to the very functions of the brain, and thus there are a hundred occasions for the spirit to be surprised and to seek for the *reasons* of this excitation; the dream, however, is *the seeking and representing of the causes* of those excited sensations, that is, of the supposed causes. A person who, for instance, binds his feet with two straps will perhaps dream that two serpents are coiling round his feet; this is first hypothesis, then a belief, with an accompanying *mental* picture and interpretation— "These serpents must be the *causa* of those sensations which I, the sleeper, experience,"—so decides the mind of the sleeper. The immediate past, so disclosed, becomes to him the present through his excited imagination. Thus everyone knows from experience how quickly the dreamer weaves into his dream a loud sound that he hears, such as the ringing of bells or the firing of cannon, that is to say, explains it from *afterward* so that he first *thinks* he experiences the producing circumstances and then that sound. But how does it happen that the mind of the dreamer is always so mistaken, while the same mind when awake is accustomed to be so temperate, careful, and sceptical with regard to its hypotheses? So that the first random hypothesis for the explanation of a feeling suffices for him to believe immediately in its truth? (For in dreaming we believe in the dream as if it were a reality, i.e., we think our hypothesis completely proved.) I hold, that as man now still reasons in dreams, so men reasoned also *when awake* through thousands of years; the first *causa* which occurred to the mind to explain anything that required an explanation was sufficient and stood for truth. (Thus, according to travelers' tales, savages still do to this very day.) This ancient element in human nature still manifests itself in our dreams, for it is the foundation upon which the higher reason has developed and still develops in every individual; the dream carries us back into remote conditions of human culture, and provides a ready means of understanding them better. Dream-thinking is now so easy to us because during immense periods of human development we have been so well drilled in this form of fantastic and cheap explanation, by means of the first agreeable notions. In so far, dreaming is a recreation for the brain, which by day has to satisfy the stern demands of thought, as they are laid down by the higher culture. We can at once discern an allied process even in our awakened state, as the door and anteroom of the dream. If we shut our eyes, the brain produces a number of impressions of light and color, probably as a kind of afterplay and echo of all those effects of light which crowd in upon it by day. Now, however, the understanding, together with the imagination, instantly works up this play of color, shapeless in itself, into definite figures, forms, landscapes, and animated groups. The actual accompanying process thereby is again a kind of conclusion from the effect to the cause: since the mind asks, "Whence come these impressions of light and color?" it supposes those figures and forms as causes; it takes them for the origin of those colors and lights, because in the daytime, with open eyes, it is accustomed to find a producing cause for every color, every effect of light. Here, therefore, the imagination constantly places pictures before the mind, since it supports itself on the visual impressions of the day in their production, and the dream-imagination does just the same thing, that is, the supposed cause is deduced from the effect and represented after the effect; all this happens with extraordinary rapidity, so that here, as with the conjuror, a confusion of judgment may arise and a sequence may look like something simultaneous, or even like a reversed sequence. From these circumstances we may gather *how lately* the more acute logical thinking, the strict discrimination of cause and effect has been developed, when our reasoning and understanding faculties *still* involuntarily hark back to those primitive forms of deduction, and when we pass about half our life in this condition. The poet, too, and the artist assign causes for their moods and conditions which are by no means the true ones; in this they recall an older humanity and can assist us to the understanding of it.

35

ADVANTAGES OF PSYCHOLOGICAL OBSERVATION. That reflection on the human, all-too-human—or, according to the learned expression, psychological observation—is one of the means by which one may lighten the burden of life, that exercise in this art produces presence of mind in difficult circumstances, in the midst of tiresome surroundings, even that from the most thorny and unpleasant periods of one's own life one may gather maxims and thereby feel a little better: all this was believed, was known in former centuries. Why was it forgotten by our century, when in Germany at least, even in all Europe, the poverty of psychological observation betrays itself by many signs? Not exactly in novels, tales, and philosophical treatises—they are the work of exceptional individuals—rather in the judgments on public events and personalities; but above all there is a lack of the art of psychological analysis and summing up in every rank of society, in which a great deal is talked about men, but nothing about *man*. Why do we allow the richest and most harmless subject of conversation to escape us? Why are not the great masters of psychological maxims more read? For, without any exaggeration, the educated man in Europe who has read La Rochefoucauld and his kindred in mind and art is rarely found, and still more rare is he who knows them and does not blame them. It is probable, however, that even this exceptional reader will find much less pleasure in them than the form of this artist should afford him; for even the clearest head is not capable of rightly estimating the art of shaping and polishing maxims unless he has really been brought up to it and has competed in it. Without this practical teaching one deems this shaping and polishing to be easier than it is; one has not a sufficient perception of fitness and charm. For this reason the present readers of maxims find in them a comparatively small pleasure, hardly a mouthful of pleasantness, so that they resemble the people who generally look at cameos, who praise because they cannot love, and are very ready to admire, but still more ready to run away.

36

OBJECTION. Or should there be a counterreckoning to that theory that places psychological observation amongst the means of charming, curing, and relieving existence? Should one have sufficiently convinced one's self of the unpleasant consequences of this art to divert from it designedly the attention of him who is educating himself in it? As a matter of fact, a certain blind belief in the goodness of human nature, an innate aversion to the analysis of human actions, a kind of shamefacedness with respect to the nakedness of the soul may really be more desirable for the general well-being of a man than that quality, useful in isolated cases, of psychological sharp-sightedness; and perhaps the belief in goodness, in virtuous men and deeds, in an abundance of impersonal good will in the world, has made men better inasmuch as it has made them less distrustful. When one imitates Plutarch's heroes with enthusiasm, and turns with disgust from a suspicious examination of the motives for their actions, it is not truth which benefits thereby, but the welfare of human society; the psychological mistake and, generally speaking, the insensibility on this matter helps humanity forward, while the recognition of truth gains more through the stimulating power of hypothesis than La Rochefoucauld has said in his preface to the first edition of his *"Sentences et maximes morales."* . . . *"Ce que le monde nomme vertu n'est d'ordinaire qu'un fantôme formé par nos passions, à qui on donne un nom honnête pour faire impunément ce qu'on veut."* La Rochefoucauld and those other French masters of soul-examination (who have lately been joined by a German, the author of *Psychological Observations* *) resemble good marksmen who again and again

* Dr. Paul Rée.

hit the bull's-eye; but it is the bull's-eye of human nature. Their art arouses astonishment; but in the end a spectator who is not led by the spirit of science, but by humane intentions, will probably execrate an art which appears to implant in the soul the sense of the disparagement and suspicion of mankind.

37

NEVERTHELESS. However it may be with reckoning and counterreckoning, in the present condition of philosophy the awakening of moral observation is necessary. Humanity can no longer be spared the cruel sight of the psychological dissecting-table with its knives and forceps. For here rules that science which inquires into the origin and history of the so-called moral sentiments, and which, in its progress, has to draw up and solve complicated sociological problems: the older philosophy knows the latter one not at all, and has always avoided the examination of the origin and history of moral sentiments on any feeble pretext. With what consequences it is now very easy to see, after it has been shown by many examples how the mistakes of the greatest philosophers generally have their starting-point in a wrong explanation of certain human actions and sensations, just as on the ground of an erroneous analysis—for instance, that of the so-called unselfish actions—a false ethic is built up; then, to harmonize with this again, religion and mythological confusion are brought in to assist, and finally the shades of these dismal spirits fall also over physics and the general mode of regarding the world. If it is certain, however, that superficiality in psychological observation has laid, and still lays, the most dangerous snares for human judgments and conclusions, then there is need now of that endurance of work which does not grow weary of piling stone upon stone, pebble on pebble; there is need of courage not to be ashamed of such humble work and to turn a deaf ear to scorn. And this is also true—numberless single observations on the human and all-too-human have first been discovered, and given utterance to, in circles of society which were accustomed to offer sacrifice therewith to a clever desire to please, and not to scientific knowledge—and the odor of that old home of the moral maxim, a very seductive odor, has attached itself almost inseparably to the whole species, so that on its account the scientific man involuntarily betrays a certain distrust of this species and its earnestness. But it is sufficient to point to the consequences, for already it begins to be seen what results of a serious kind spring from the ground of psychological observation. What, after all, is the principal axiom to which the boldest and coldest thinker, the author of the book *On the Origin of Moral Sensations*,* has attained by means of his incisive and decisive analyses of human actions? "The moral man," he says, "is no nearer to the intelligible (metaphysical) world than is the physical man." This theory, hardened and sharpened under the hammer blow of historical knowledge, may some time or other, perhaps in some future period, serve as the ax which is applied to the root of the "metaphysical need" of man—whether *more* as a blessing than a curse to the general welfare it is not easy to say, but in any case as a theory with the most important consequences, at once fruitful and terrible, and looking into the world with that Janus-face which all great knowledge possesses.

38

HOW FAR USEFUL. It must remain forever undecided whether psychological observation is advantageous or disadvantageous to man; but it is certain that it is necessary, because science cannot do without it. Science, however, has no consideration for ultimate purposes, any more than Nature has, but just as the latter occasionally achieves things of the greatest suitableness without intending to do so, so also true science, as the *imitator of nature in ideas*, will occasionally and in many ways further the usefulness and welfare of man—*but also without intending to do so.*

But whoever feels too chilled by the breath of such a reflection has perhaps too little fire in himself; let him look around him meanwhile and he will become aware of illnesses which have need of ice-poultices, and of men who are so "kneaded together" of heat and spirit that they can hardly find an atmosphere that is cold and biting enough. Moreover, as individuals and nations that are too serious have need of frivolities, as others too mobile and excitable have need occasionally of heavily oppressing burdens for the sake of their health, should not we, the more *intellectual* people of this age, that grows visibly more and more inflamed, seize

* Dr. Paul Rée.

all quenching and cooling means that exist, in order that we
may at least remain as constant, harmless, and moderate
as we still are, and thus, perhaps, serve some time or other as
mirror and self-contemplation for this age?

44

GRATITUDE AND REVENGE. The reason why the
powerful man is grateful is this: his benefactor, through the
benefit he confers, has mistaken and intruded into the sphere
of the powerful man—now the latter, in return, penetrates
into the sphere of the benefactor by the act of gratitude.
It is a milder form of revenge. Without the satisfaction of
gratitude, the powerful man would have shown himself powerless, and would have been reckoned as such ever after.
Therefore every society of the good, which originally meant
the powerful, places gratitude amongst the first duties.
—Swift propounded the maxim that men were grateful in
the same proportion as they were revengeful.

47

HYPOCHONDRIA. There are people who become hypo-
chondriacal through their sympathy and concern for another
person; the kind of sympathy which results therefrom is
nothing but a disease. Thus there is also a Christian hypochondria, which afflicts those solitary, religiously-minded people who keep constantly before their eyes the sufferings and
death of Christ.

49

GOOD WILL. Amongst the small, but countlessly frequent and therefore very effective, things to which science
should pay more attention than to the great, rare things, is
to be reckoned good will; I mean that exhibition of a friendly
disposition in intercourse, that smiling eye, that clasp of the
hand, that cheerfulness with which almost all human actions
are usually accompanied. Every teacher, every official, adds
this to whatever is his duty; it is the perpetual occupation of
humanity, and at the same time the waves of its light, in
which everything grows; in the narrowest circle, namely,
within the family, life blooms and flourishes only through

that good will. Kindliness, friendliness, the courtesy of the heart, are ever-flowing streams of unegoistic impulses, and have given far more powerful assistance to culture than even those much more famous demonstrations which are called pity, mercy, and self-sacrifice. But they are thought little of, and, as a matter of fact, there is not much that is unegoistic in them. The *sum* of these small doses is nevertheless mighty, their united force is amongst the strongest forces. Thus one finds much more happiness in the world than sad eyes see, if one only reckons rightly, and does not forget all those moments of comfort in which every day is rich, even in the most harried of human lives.

61

THE POWER OF WAITING. Waiting is so difficult that even great poets have not disdained to take incapability of waiting as the motive for their works. Thus Shakespeare in Othello or Sophocles in Ajax, to whom suicide, had he been able to let his feelings cool down for one day, would no longer have seemed necessary, as the oracle intimated; he would probably have snapped his fingers at the terrible whisperings of wounded vanity, and said to himself, "Who has not already, in my circumstances, mistaken a fool for a hero? Is it something so very extraordinary?" On the contrary, it is something very commonly human; Ajax might allow himself that consolation. Passion will not wait; the tragedy in the lives of great men frequently lies *not* in their conflict with the times and the baseness of their fellow men, but in their incapacity of postponing their work for a year or two; they cannot wait. In all duels advising friends have one thing to decide, namely, whether the parties concerned can still wait awhile; if this is not the case, then a duel is advisable, inasmuch as each of the two says, "Either I continue to live and that other man must die immediately, or vice versa." In such case waiting would mean a prolonged suffering of the terrible martyrdom of wounded honor in the face of the insulter, and this may entail more suffering than life is worth.

65

WHITHER HONESTY CAN LEAD. Somebody had the bad habit of occasionally talking quite frankly about the

motives of his actions, which were as good and as bad as
the motives of most men. He first gave offense, then aroused
suspicion, was then gradually excluded from society and declared a social outlaw, until at last justice remembered such
an abandoned creature, on occasions when it would otherwise have had no eyes, or would have closed them. The
lack of power to hold his tongue concerning the common
secret, and the irresponsible tendency to see what no one
wishes to see—himself—brought him to a prison and an
early death.

100

SHAME. Shame exists everywhere where there is a "mystery"; this, however, is a religious idea, which was widely
extended in the older times of human civilization. Everywhere were found bounded domains to which access was forbidden by divine right, except under certain conditions; at
first locally, as, for example, certain spots that ought not
to be trodden by the feet of the uninitiated, in the neighborhood of which these latter experienced horror and fear.
This feeling was a good deal carried over into other relations, for instance, the sex relations, which, as a privilege
and ἄδυτον of riper years, had to be withheld from the
knowledge of the young for their advantage, relations for
the protection and sanctification of which many gods were
invented and were set up as guardians in the nuptial chamber. (In Turkish this room is on this account called harem,
"sanctuary," and is distinguished with the same name, therefore, that is used for the entrance courts of the mosques.)
Thus the kingdom is as a center from which radiate power
and glory, to the subjects a mystery full of secrecy and
shame, of which many aftereffects may still be felt among
nations which otherwise do not by any means belong to
the bashful type. Similarly, the whole world of inner conditions, the so-called "soul," is still a mystery for all who are
not philosophers, after it has been looked upon for endless
ages as of divine origin and as worthy of divine intercourse; according to this it is an ἄδυτον and arouses shame.

81

ERRORS OF THE SUFFERER AND THE DOER.
When a rich man deprives a poor man of a possession (for

instance, a prince taking the sweetheart of a plebeian), an error arises in the mind of the poor man; he thinks that the rich man must be utterly infamous to take away from him the little that he has. But the rich man does not estimate so highly the value of a *single* possession, because he is accustomed to have many; hence he cannot imagine himself in the poor man's place, and does not commit nearly so great a wrong as the latter supposes. They each have a mistaken idea of the other. The injustice of the powerful, which, more than anything else, rouses indignation in history, is by no means so great as it appears. Alone the mere inherited consciousness of being a higher creation, with higher claims produces a cold temperament, and leaves the conscience quiet; we all of us feel no injustice when the difference is very great between ourselves and another creature, and kill a fly, for instance, without any pricks of conscience. Therefore it was no sign of badness in Xerxes (whom even all Greeks describe as superlatively noble) when he took a son away from his father and had him cut in pieces, because he had expressed a nervous, ominous distrust of the whole campaign; in this case the individual is put out of the way like an unpleasant insect; he is too lowly to be allowed any longer to cause annoyance to a ruler of the world. Yes, every cruel man is not so cruel as the ill-treated one imagines; the idea of pain is not the same as its endurance. It is the same thing in the case of unjust judges, of the journalist who leads public opinion astray by small dishonesties. In all these cases cause and effect are surrounded by entirely different groups of feelings and thoughts; yet one unconsciously takes it for granted that doer and sufferer think and feel alike, and according to this supposition we measure the guilt of the one by the pain of the other.

333

DANGER IN THE VOICE. In conversation we are sometimes confused by the tone of our own voice, and misled to make assertions that do not at all correspond to our opinions.

335

FEAR OF OUR NEIGHBOR. We are afraid of the

animosity of our neighbor, because we are apprehensive that he may thereby discover our secrets.

345

A COMEDY SCENE IN REAL LIFE. Someone conceives an ingenious idea on a theme in order to express it in society. Now in a comedy we should hear and see how he sets all sail for that point, and tries to land the company at the place where he can make his remark, how he continuously pushes the conversation toward the one goal, sometimes losing the way, finding it again, and finally then one of the company takes the remark itself out of his mouth! What will he do? Oppose his own opinion?

346

UNINTENTIONALLY DISCOURTEOUS. When a person treats another with unintentional discourtesy—for instance, not greeting him because not recognizing him—he is vexed by it, although he cannot reproach his own sentiments; he is hurt by the bad opinion which he has produced in the other person, or fears the consequences of his bad humor, or is pained by the thought of having injured him—vanity, fear, or pity may therefore be aroused; perhaps all three together.

348

TO INJURE AND TO BE INJURED. It is far pleasanter to injure and afterward beg for forgiveness than to be injured and grant forgiveness. He who does the former gives evidence of power and afterward of kindness of character. The person injured, however, if he does not wish to be considered inhuman, *must* forgive; his enjoyment of the other's humiliation is insignificant on account of this constraint.

351

PRICKS OF CONSCIENCE AFTER SOCIAL GATHERINGS. Why does our conscience prick us after ordinary social gatherings? Because we have treated serious things light-

ly, because in talking of persons we have not spoken quite
justly or have been silent when we should have spoken, because, sometimes, we have not jumped up and run away—
in short, because we have behaved in society as if we belonged to it.

352

WE ARE MISJUDGED. He who always listens to hear
how he is judged is always vexed. For we are misjudged
even by those who are nearest to us ("who know us best").
Even good friends sometimes vent their ill-humor in a spiteful word; and would they be our friends if they knew us
rightly? The judgments of the indifferent wound us deeply,
because they sound so impartial, so objective almost. But
when we see that someone hostile to us knows us in a concealed point as well as we know ourselves, how great is then
our vexation!

355

MISUNDERSTOOD HONESTY. When anyone quotes
himself in conversation ("I then said," "I am accustomed to
say"), it gives the impression of presumption; whereas it often
proceeds from quite an opposite source; or at least from
honesty, which does not wish to deck and adorn the present
moment with wit which belongs to an earlier moment.

359

BAIT. "Every man has his price"—that is not true. But
perhaps everyone can be found a bait of one kind or other
at which he will snap. Thus, in order to gain some supporters
for a cause, it is only necessary to give it the glamour of
being philanthropic, noble, charitable, and self-denying—and
to what cause could this glamour not be given! It is the
sweetmeat and dainty of *their* soul; others have different
ones.

535

IMAGINATION IN ANGUISH. When one is afraid of

anything, one's imagination plays the part of that evil spirit which springs on one's back just when one has the heaviest load to bear.

549

CONTEMPT. Man is more sensitive to the contempt of others than to self-contempt.

562

BEING A TARGET. The bad things others say about us are often not really aimed at us, but are the manifestations of spite or ill-humor occasioned by quite different causes.

588

MODESTY. There is true modesty (that is the knowledge that we are not the works we create); and it is especially becoming in a great mind, because such a mind can well grasp the thought of absolute irresponsibility (even for the good it creates). People do not hate a great man's presumptuousness insofar as he feels his strength, but because he wishes to prove it by injuring others, by dominating them, and seeing how long they will stand it. This, as a rule, is even a proof of the absence of a secure sense of power, and makes people doubt his greatness. We must therefore beware of presumption from the standpoint of wisdom.

606

DESIRE FOR SORE AFFLICTION. When passion is over it leaves behind an obscure longing for it, and even in disappearing it casts a seductive glance at us. It must have afforded a kind of pleasure to have been beaten with this scourge. Compared with it, the more moderate sensations appear insipid; we still prefer, apparently, the more violent displeasure to languid delight.

595

PLEASING BY DISPLEASING. People who prefer to attract attention, and thereby to displease, desire the same thing as those who neither wish to please nor to attract attention, only they seek it more ardently and indirectly by means of a step by which they apparently move away from their goal. They desire influence and power, and therefore show their superiority, even to such an extent that it becomes disagreeable; for they know that he who has finally attained power pleases in almost all he says and does, and that even when he displeases he still seems to please. The free spirit also, and in like manner the believer, desire power, in order someday to please thereby; when, on account of their doctrine, evil fate, persecution, dungeon, or execution threaten them, they rejoice in the thought that their teaching will thus be engraved and branded on the heart of mankind; though its effect is remote they accept their fate as a painful but powerful means of still attaining to power.

611

ENNUI AND PLAY. Necessity compels us to work, with the product of which the necessity is appeased; the ever new awakening of necessity, however, accustoms us to work. But in the intervals in which necessity is appeased and asleep, as it were, we are attacked by ennui. What is this? In a word it is the habituation to work, which now makes itself felt as a new and additional necessity; it will be all the stronger the more a person has been accustomed to work, perhaps, even, the more a person has suffered from necessities. In order to escape ennui, a man either works beyond the extent of his former necessities, or he invents play, that is to say, work that is only intended to appease the general necessity for work. He who has become satiated with play, and has no new necessities impelling him to work, is sometimes attacked by the longing for a third state, which is related to play as gliding is to dancing, as dancing is to walking, a blessed, tranquil movement; it is the artists' and philosophers' vision of happiness.

FROM HUMAN, ALL TOO HUMAN, II

25 *

COURAGE FOR TEDIUM. He who has not the courage
to allow himself and his work to be considered tedious is
certainly no intellect of the first rank, whether in the arts or
in the sciences.—A scoffer, who happened for once in a
way to be a thinker, might add, with a glance at the world
and at history: "God did not possess this courage, for he
wanted to make and he made all things so interesting."

FROM HUMAN, ALL TOO HUMAN, I

625

LONELY PEOPLE. Some people are so much accustomed to being alone in self-communion that they do not
at all compare themselves with others, but spin out their
soliloquizing life in a quiet, happy mood, conversing pleasantly, and even hilariously, with themselves. If, however,
they are brought to the point of comparing themselves with
others, they are inclined to a brooding underestimation of
their own worth, so that they have first to be compelled by
others *to form* once more a good and just opinion of themselves, and even from this acquired opinion they will always
want to subtract and abate something. We must not, therefore, grudge certain persons their loneliness or foolishly com-
miserate them on that account, as is so often done.

FROM HUMAN, ALL TOO HUMAN, II

56 *

HONEST TOWARD HONESTY. One who is openly honest toward himself ends by being rather conceited about

* From *Miscellaneous Maxims and Opinions.*

this honesty. He knows only too well why he is honest—for the same reason that another man prefers outward show and hypocrisy.

348

FROM CANNIBAL COUNTRY. In solitude the lonely man is eaten up by himself, among crowds by the many. Choose which you prefer.

369

ENNUI. There is an ennui of the most subtle and cultured brains, to which the best that the world can offer has become stale. Accustomed to eat ever more and more recherché fare and to feel disgust at coarser diet, they are in danger of dying of hunger. For the very best exists but in small quantities, and has sometimes become inaccessible or hard as stone, so that even good teeth can no longer bite it.

370

THE DANGER IN ADMIRATION. The admiration of a quality or of an art may be so strong as to deter us from aspiring to possess that quality or art.

377

PITY. In the gilded sheath of pity is sometimes hidden the dagger of envy.

29 *

ENVY AND HER NOBLER SISTER. Where equality is really recognized and permanently established, we see the rise of that propensity that is generally considered immoral, and would scarcely be conceivable in a state of nature—envy. The envious man is susceptible to every sign of individual superiority to the common herd, and wishes to de-

* From *The Wanderer and His Shadow*.

press everyone once more to the level—or raise himself to the superior plane. Hence arise two different modes of action, which Hesiod designated good and bad Eris. In the same way, in a condition of equality there arises indignation if A is prosperous above and B unfortunate beneath their deserts and equality. These latter, however, are emotions of nobler natures. They feel the want of justice and equity in things that are independent of the arbitrary choice of men—or, in other words, they desire the equality recognized by man to be recognized as well by Nature and chance. They are angry that men of equal merits should not have equal fortune.

27

EXPLANATION OF MALICIOUS JOY. Malicious joy arises when a man consciously finds himself in evil plight and feels anxiety or remorse or pain. The misfortune that overtakes B makes him equal to A, and A is reconciled and no longer envious.—If A is prosperous, he still hoards up in his memory B's misfortune as a capital, so as to throw it in the scale as a counterweight when he himself suffers adversity. In this case, too, he feels "malicious joy" (*Schadenfreude*). The sentiment of equality thus applies its standard to the domain of luck and chance. Malicious joy is the commonest expression of victory and restoration of equality, even in a higher state of civilization. This emotion has only been in existence since the time when man learned to look upon another as his equal—in other words, since the foundation of society.

33

ELEMENTS OF REVENGE. The word "revenge" is spoken so quickly that it almost seems as if it could not contain more than one conceptual and emotional root. Hence we are still at pains to find this root. Our economists, in the same way, have never wearied of scenting a similar unity in the word "value," and of hunting after the primitive root idea of value. As if all words were not pockets, into which this or that or several things have been stuffed at once! So "revenge" is now one thing, now another, and sometimes more composite. Let us first distinguish that defensive counterblow, which we strike, almost unconsciously, even at in-

animate objects (such as machinery in motion) that have
hurt us. The notion is to set a check to the object that has
hurt us, by bringing the machine to a stop. Sometimes the
force of this counterblow, in order to attain its object, will
have to be strong enough to shatter the machine. If the
machine be too strong to be disorganized by one man, the
latter will all the same strike the most violent blow he can
—as a sort of last attempt. We behave similarly toward persons who hurt us, at the immediate sensation of the hurt. If
we like to call this an act of revenge, well and good: but we
must remember that here self-preservation alone has set its
cogwheels of reason in motion, and that after all we do not
think of the doer of the injury but only of ourselves. We act
without any idea of doing injury in return, only with a view
to getting away safe and sound.—It needs time to pass in
thought from oneself to one's adversary and ask oneself at
what point he is most vulnerable. This is done in the second
variety of revenge, the preliminary idea of which is to consider the vulnerability and susceptibility of the other. The
intention then is to give pain. On the other hand, the idea
of securing himself against further injury is in this case so
entirely outside the avenger's horizon that he almost regularly brings about his own further injury and often foresees
it in cold blood. If in the first sort of revenge it was the fear
of a second blow that made the counterblow as strong as possible, in this case there is an almost complete indifference to
what one's adversary will do: the strength of the counterblow is only determined by what he has *already* done to us.
Then what has he done? What profit is it to us if he is now
suffering, after we have suffered through him? This is a case
of readjustment, whereas the first act of revenge only serves
the purpose of self-preservation. It may be that through our
adversary we have lost property, rank, friends, children—
these losses are not recovered by revenge, the readjustment
only concerns a subsidiary loss which is added to all the
other losses. The revenge of readjustment does not preserve
one from further injury, it does not make good the injury already suffered—except in one case. If our honor has suffered
through our adversary, revenge can restore it. But in any
case honor *has* suffered an injury if intentional harm has
been done us, because our adversary proved thereby that he
was not afraid of us. By revenge we prove that we are not
afraid of him either, and herein lies the settlement, the
readjustment. (The intention of showing their complete lack
of fear goes so far in some people that the dangers of revenge—loss of health or life or other losses—are in their

eyes an indispensable condition of every vengeful act. Hence they practice the duel, although the law also offers them aid in obtaining satisfaction for what they have suffered. They are not satisfied with a safe means of recovering their honor, because this would not prove their fearlessness.)—In the first-named variety of revenge it is just fear that strikes the counterblow; in the second case it is the absence of fear, which, as has been said, wishes to manifest itself in the counterblow.—Thus nothing appears more different than the motives of the two courses of action which are designated by the one word "revenge." Yet it often happens that the avenger is not precisely certain as to what really prompted his deed: perhaps he struck the counterblow from fear and the instinct of self-preservation, but in the background, when he has time to reflect upon the standpoint of wounded honor, he imagines that he has avenged himself for the sake of his honor—this motive is in any case more *reputable* than the other. An essential point is whether he sees his honor injured in the eyes of others (the world) or only in the eyes of his offenders: in the latter case he will prefer secret, in the former open revenge. Accordingly, as he enters strongly or feebly into the soul of the doer and the spectator, his revenge will be more bitter or more tame. If he is entirely lacking in this sort of imagination, he will not think at all of revenge, as the feeling of "honor" is not present in him, and accordingly cannot be wounded. In the same way, he will not think of revenge if he despises the offender and the spectator; because as objects of his contempt they cannot give him honor, and accordingly cannot rob him of honor. Finally, he will forego revenge in the not uncommon case of his loving the offender. It is true that he then suffers loss of honor in the other's eyes, and will perhaps become less worthy of having his love returned. But even to renounce all requital of love is a sacrifice that love is ready to make when its only object is to avoid hurting the beloved object: this would mean hurting oneself more than one is hurt by the sacrifice.—Accordingly, everyone will avenge himself, unless he be bereft of honor or inspired by contempt or by love for the offender. Even if he turns to the law courts, he desires revenge as a private individual; but also, as a thoughtful, prudent man of society, he desires the revenge of society upon one who does not respect it. Thus by legal punishment private honor as well as that of society is restored—that is to say, punishment is revenge. Punishment undoubtedly contains the first-mentioned element of revenge, in as far as by its means society helps to preserve itself, and strikes a counterblow in self-defense. Punishment desires to prevent further injury, to scare other offenders. In this way the two elements of revenge, different as they are, are united in punishment, and this may perhaps tend most of all to maintain the above-mentioned confusion of ideas, thanks to which the individual avenger generally does not know what he really wants.

60

THE WORD "VANITY." It is annoying that certain words, with which we moralists positively cannot dispense, involve in themselves a kind of censorship of morals, dating from the times when the most ordinary and natural impulses were denounced. Thus that fundamental conviction that on the waves of society we either find navigable waters or suffer shipwreck far more through what we appear than through what we are (a conviction that must act as guiding principle of all action in relation to society) is branded with the general word "vanity." In other words, one of the most weighty and significant of qualities is branded with an expression which denotes it as essentially empty and negative: a great thing is designated by a diminutive, ay, even slandered by the strokes of caricature. There is no help for it; we must use such words, but then we must shut our ears to the insinuations of ancient habits.

FROM THE DAWN OF DAY

63

HATRED OF ONE'S NEIGHBOR. Supposing that we felt toward our neighbor as he does himself—Schopenhauer calls this compassion, though it would be more correct to call it autopassion, fellow feeling—we should be compelled to hate him, if, like Pascal, he thought himself hateful. And this was probably the general feeling of Pascal regarding mankind, and also that of ancient Christianity, which, under Nero, was "convicted" of *odium generis humani*, as Tacitus has recorded.

113

STRIVING FOR DISTINCTION. When we strive after distinction we must ceaselessly keep our eyes fixed on our neighbor and endeavor to ascertain what his feelings are; but the sympathy and knowledge which are necessary to satisfy this desire are far from being inspired by harmlessness, compassion, or kindness. On the contrary, we wish to perceive or find out in what way our neighbor suffers from us, either internally or externally, how he loses control over himself, and yields to the impression which our hand or even our mere appearance makes on him. Even when he who aspires to distinction makes or wishes to make a joyful, elevating, or cheerful impression, he does not enjoy this success in that he rejoices, exalts, or cheers his neighbor, but in that he leaves his impress on the latter's soul, changing its form and dominating it according to his will. The desire for distinction is the desire to subject one's neighbor, even if it be merely in an indirect fashion, one only felt or even only dreamed of. There is a long series of stages in this secretly desired will to subdue, and a very complete record of them would perhaps almost be like an excellent history of culture from the early distortions of barbarism down to the caricatures of modern overrefinement and sickly idealism.

This desire for distinction entails upon our neighbor—to indicate only a few rungs of the long ladder—torture first of all, followed by blows, then terror, anxious surprise, wonder, envy, admiration, elevation, pleasure, joy, laughter, derision, mockery, sneers, scourging and self-inflicted torture. There at the very top of the ladder stands the ascetic and martyr, who himself experiences the utmost satisfaction, because he inflicts on himself, as a result of his desire for distinction, that pain which his opposite, the barbarian on the first rung of the ladder, inflicts upon those others, upon whom and before whom he wishes to distinguish himself. The triumph of the ascetic over himself, his introspective glance, which beholds a man split up into a sufferer and a spectator, and which henceforth never looks at the outside world but to gather from it, as it were, wood for his own funeral pyre: this final tragedy of the desire for distinction which shows us only one person who, so to speak, is consumed internally—that is an end worthy of the beginning: in both cases there is an inexpressible happiness at the sight of torture; indeed, happiness considered as a feeling of power developed to the utmost has perhaps never reached a higher pitch of perfection on earth than in the souls of superstitious ascetics. This is expressed by the Brahmins in the story of King Visvamitra, who obtained so much strength by thousands of years of penance that he undertook to construct a new heaven. I believe that in the entire category of inward experiences the people of our time are mere novices and clumsy guessers who "try to have a shot at it": four thousand years ago much more was known about these execrable refinements of self-enjoyment. Perhaps at that time the creation of the world was imagined by some Hindu dreamer to have been an ascetic operation which a god took upon himself! Perhaps this god may have wished to join himself to a mobile nature as an instrument of torture in order thus to feel his happiness and power doubled! And even supposing him to have been a god of love: what a delight it would have been for him to create a suffering mankind in order that he himself might suffer divinely and superhumanly from the sight of the continual torture of his creatures, and thus to tyrannize over himself! And, again, supposing him to have been not only a god of love but also a god of holiness, we can scarcely conceive the ecstasies of this divine ascetic while creating sins and sinners and eternal punishment, and an immense place of eternal torture below his throne where there is a continual weeping and wailing and gnashing of teeth!

It is not by any means impossible that the soul of a St. Paul, a Dante, or a Calvin, and people like them, may once have penetrated into the terrifying secrets of such voluptuousness of power, and in view of such souls we may well ask whether the circle of this desire for distinction has come to a close with the ascetic. Might it not be possible for the course of this circle to be traversed a second time, by uniting the fundamental idea of the ascetic, and at the same time that of a compassionate Deity? In other words, pain would be given to others in order that pain might be given to one's self, so that in this way one could triumph over one's self and one's pity to enjoy the extreme voluptuousness of power. —Forgive me these digressions, which come to my mind when I think of all the possibilities in the vast domain of psychical debaucheries to which one may be led by the desire for power!

114

ON THE KNOWLEDGE OF THE SUFFERER. The state of sick men who have suffered long and terribly from the torture inflicted upon them by their illness, and whose reason has nevertheless not been in any way affected, is not without a certain amount of value in our search for knowledge—quite apart from the intellectual benefits which follow upon every profound solitude and every sudden and justified liberation from duties and habits. The man who suffers severely looks forth with terrible calmness from his state of suffering upon outside things: all those little lying enchantments, by which things are usually surrounded when seen through the eye of a healthy person, have vanished from the sufferer; his own life even lies there before him, stripped of all bloom and color. If by chance it has happened that up to then he has lived in some kind of dangerous fantasy, this extreme disenchantment through pain is the means, and possibly the only means, of extricating him from it. (It is possible that this is what happened to the Founder of Christianity when suspended from the Cross; for the bitterest words ever pronounced, "My God, My God, why hast Thou forsaken Me?" if understood in their deepest sense, as they ought to be understood, contain the evidence of a complete disillusionment and enlightenment in regard to the deceptions of life: in that moment of supreme suffering Christ obtained a clear insight into Himself, just as in the poet's narrative did the poor dying Don Quixote.)

The formidable tension of the intellect that wishes to hold its own against pain shows everything that one now looks upon in a new light, and the inexpressible charm of this new light is often powerful enough to withstand all the seductiveness of suicide and to make the continuation of life seem very desirable to the sufferer. His mind scornfully turns to the warm and comfortable dream world in which the healthy man moves about thoughtlessly, and he thinks with contempt of the noblest and most cherished illusions in which he formerly indulged. He experiences delight in conjuring up this contempt as if from the depths of hell, and thus inflicting the bitterest sufferings upon his soul: it is by this counterpoise that he bears up against physical suffering—he feels that such a counterpoise is now essential! In one terrible moment of clear-sightedness he says to himself, "Be for once thine own accuser and hangman; for once regard thy suffering as a punishment which thou hast inflicted on thyself! Enjoy thy superiority as a judge: better still, enjoy thine own will and pleasure, thy tyrannical arbitrariness! Raise thyself above thy life as above thy suffering, and look down into the depth of reason and unreason!"

Our pride revolts as it never did before, it experiences an

incomparable charm in defending life against such a tyrant as suffering and against all the insinuations of this tyrant, who would fain urge us to give evidence against life—we are taking the part of life in the face of this tyrant. In this state of mind we take up a bitter stand against all pessimism in order that it may not appear to be a consequence of our condition, and thus humiliate us as conquered ones. The charm of being just in our judgments was also never greater than now; for now this justice is a triumph over ourselves and over so irritated a state of mind that unfairness of judgment might be excused—but we will not be excused, it is now, if ever, that we wish to show that we need no excuse. We pass through downright orgies of pride.

And now appears the first ray of relief, of recovery, and one of its first effects is that we turn against the preponderance of our pride: we call ourselves foolish and vain, as if we had undergone some unique experience. We humiliate ungratefully this all-powerful pride, the aid of which enabled us to endure the pain we suffered, and we call vehemently for some antidote for this pride: we wish to become strangers to ourselves and to be freed from our own person after pain has forcibly made us personal too long. "Away with this pride," we cry, "it was only another illness and convulsion!" Once more we look longingly at men and nature and recollect with a sorrowful smile that now since the veil has fallen we regard many things concerning them in a new and different light—but we are refreshed by once more seeing the softened lights of life, and emerge from that fearfully dispassionate daylight in which we as sufferers saw things and through things. We do not get angry when we see the charms of health resume their play, and we contemplate the sight as if transformed, gently and still fatigued. In this state we cannot listen to music without weeping.

116

THE UNKNOWN WORLD OF THE "SUBJECT." What men have found it so difficult to understand from the most ancient times down to the present day is their ignorance in regard to themselves, not merely with respect to good and evil, but something even more essential. The oldest of illusions lives on, namely, that we know, and know precisely in each case, how human action is originated. Not only "God who looks into the heart," not only the man who acts and reflects upon his action, but everybody does not doubt

that he understands the phenomena of action in everyone else. "I know what I want and what I have done, I am
free and responsible for my act, and I make others responsible for their acts; I can mention by its name every
moral possibility and every internal movement which precedes an act—ye may act as ye will, I understand myself
and I understand you all!" Such was what everyone thought
once upon a time, and almost everyone thinks so even now.
Socrates and Plato, who in this matter were great sceptics
and admirable innovators, were nevertheless intensely credulous in regard to that fatal prejudice, that profound error,
which holds that "The right knowledge must necessarily be
followed by the right action." In holding this principle they
were still the heirs of the universal folly and presumption
that knowledge exists concerning the essence of an action.

"It would indeed be dreadful if the comprehension of the
essence of a right action were not followed by that right
action itself"—this was the only manner in which these great
men thought it necessary to demonstrate this idea, the contrary seemed to them to be inconceivable and mad; and nevertheless this contrary corresponds to the naked reality which
has been demonstrated daily and hourly from time immemorial. Is it not a "dreadful" truth that all that we know
about an act is never sufficient to accomplish it, that the
bridge connecting the knowledge of the act with the act
itself has never yet been built? Acts are never what they
appear to us to be. We have taken great pains to learn that
external things are not as they appear to us.—Well! It is
the same with internal phenomena. All moral acts are in
reality "something different"—we cannot say anything more
about them, and all acts are essentially unknown to us. The
general belief, however, has been and still is quite the contrary: the most ancient realism is against us: up to the present
humanity has thought, "An action is what it appears to be."
(In rereading these words a very expressive passage from
Schopenhauer occurs to me, and I will quote it as a proof
that he, too, without the slightest scruple, continued to adhere to this moral realism: "Each one of us is in reality
a competent and perfect moral judge, knowing exactly good
and evil, made holy by loving good and despising evil—such
is everyone of us insofar as the acts of others and not his
own are under consideration, and when he has merely to
approve or disapprove, whilst the burden of the performance
of the acts is borne by other shoulders. Everyone is therefore justified in occupying as confessor the place of God.")

137

WHY DOUBLE THE "EGO"? To view our own experiences in the same light as we are in the habit of looking at those of others is very comforting and an advisable medicine. On the other hand, to look upon the experiences of others and adopt them as if they were our own—which is called for by the philosophy of pity—would ruin us in a very short time: let us only make the experiment without trying to imagine it any longer! The first maxim is, in addition, undoubtedly more in accordance with reason and good will toward reason; for we estimate more objectively the value and significance of an event when it happens to others —the value, for instance, of a death, loss of money, or slander. But pity, taking as its principle of action the injunction, "Suffer the misfortune of another as much as he himself," would lead the point of view of the ego with all its exaggerations and deviations to become the point of view of the other person, the sympathizer: so that we should have to suffer at the same time from our own ego and the other's ego. In this way we would voluntarily overload ourselves with a double irrationality, instead of making the burden of our own as light as possible.

138

BECOMING MORE TENDER. Whenever we love someone and venerate and admire him, and afterward come to perceive that he is suffering—which always causes us the utmost astonishment, since we cannot but feel that the happiness we derive from him must flow from a superabundant source of personal happiness—our feelings of love, veneration, and admiration are essentially changed: they become more tender; that is, the gap that separates us seems to be bridged over and there appears to be an approach to equality. It now seems possible to give him something in return, whilst we had previously imagined him as being altogether above our gratitude. Our ability to requite him for what we have received from him arouses in us feelings of much joy and pleasure. We endeavor to ascertain what can best calm the grief of our friend, and we give it to him; if he wishes for kind words, looks, attentions, services, or presents, we give them; but, above all, if he would like to see us suffering from the sight of his suffering, we pretend to suffer, for all this secures for us the enjoyment of active gratitude, which is equivalent in a way to good-natured revenge. If he wants none of these things, and refuses to accept them from us, we depart from him chilled and sad, almost mortified; it appears to us as if our gratitude had been declined, and on this point of honor even the best of men is still somewhat touchy. It results from all this that even in the best case there is something humiliating in suffering, and something elevating and superior in sympathy—a fact which will keep the two feelings apart forever and ever.

142

SYMPATHY. In order to understand our neighbor, that is, in order to reproduce his sentiments in ourselves, we often, no doubt, plumb the cause of his feelings, as, for example, by asking ourselves, Why is he sad? in order that we may become sad ourselves for the same reason. But we much more frequently neglect to act thus, and we produce these feelings in ourselves in accordance with the *effects* which they exhibit in the person we are studying—by imitating in our own body the expression of his eyes, his voice, his gait, his attitude (or, at any rate, the likeness of these things in words, pictures, and music), or we may at least endeavor to mimic the action of his muscles and nervous system. A like feeling will then spring up in us as the result of an old association of movements and sentiments which has been trained to run backward and forward. We have developed to a very high pitch this knack of sounding the feelings of others, and when we are in the presence of anyone else we bring this faculty of ours into play almost involuntarily— let the inquirer observe the animation of a woman's countenance and notice how it vibrates and quivers with animation as the result of the continual imitation and reflection of what is going on around her.

It is music, however, more than anything else that shows us what past masters we are in the rapid and subtle divination of feelings and sympathy; for even if music is only the imitation of an imitation of feelings, nevertheless, despite its distance and vagueness, it often enables us to participate in those feelings, so that we become sad without any reason for feeling so, like the fools that we are, merely because we hear certain sounds and rhythms that somehow or other remind us of the intonation and the movements, or perhaps even only of the behavior, of sorrowful people. It is related of a certain Danish king that he was wrought up to such a pitch of warlike enthusiasm by the song of a minstrel that he sprang to his feet and killed five persons of his assembled court: there was neither war nor enemy; there was rather the exact opposite; yet the power of the retrospective inference from a feeling to the cause of it was sufficiently strong in this king to overpower both his observation and his reason. Such, however, is almost invariably the effect of music (provided that it thrills us), and we have no need of such paradoxical instances to recognize this—the state of feeling into which music transports us is almost always in contradiction to the appearance of our actual state, and of our reasoning power which recognizes this actual state and its causes.

If we inquire how it happened that this imitation of the feelings of others has become so common, there will be no doubt as to the answer: man being the most timid of all beings because of his subtle and delicate nature has been made familiar through his timidity with this sympathy for, and rapid comprehension of, the feelings of others, even of animals. For century after century he saw danger in everything that was unfamiliar to him, in anything that happened to be alive, and whenever the spectacle of such things and creatures came before his eyes he imitated their features and attitude, drawing at the same time his own conclusion as to the nature of the evil intentions they concealed. This interpretation of all movements and all facial characteristics in the sense of intentions, man has even brought to bear on things inanimate—urged on as he was by the illusion that there was nothing inanimate. I believe that this is the origin of everything that we now call a feeling for nature, that sensation of joy which men experience at the sight of the sky, the fields, the rocks, the forests, the storms, the stars, the landscapes, and spring: without our old habits of fear which forced us to suspect behind everything a kind of second and more recondite sense, we should now experience no delight in nature, in the same way as men and animals do not cause us to rejoice if we have not first been deterred by that source of all understanding, namely, fear. For joy and agreeable surprise, and finally the feeling of ridicule, are the younger children of sympathy, and the much younger brothers and sisters of fear. The faculty of rapid perception, which is based on the faculty of rapid dissimulation, decreases in proud and autocratic men and nations, as they are less timid; but, on the other hand, every category of understanding and dissimulation is well known to timid peoples, and among them is to be found the real home of imitative arts and superior intelligence.

When, proceeding from the theory of sympathy such as I have just outlined, I turn my attention to the theory, now so popular and almost sacrosanct, of a mystical process by means of which pity blends two beings into one, and thus permits them immediately to understand one another, when I recollect that even so clear a brain as Schopenhauer's delighted in such fantastic nonsense, and that he in his turn transplanted this delight into other lucid and semilucid brains, I feel unlimited astonishment and compassion. How great must be the pleasure we experience in this senseless tomfoolery! How near must even a sane man be to insanity as soon as he listens to his own secret intellectual desires!— Why did Schopenhauer really feel so grateful, so profoundly indebted to Kant? He revealed on one occasion the undoubted answer to this question. Someone had spoken of the way in which the *qualitas occulta* of Kant's Categorical Imperative might be got rid of, so that the theory itself might be rendered intelligible. Whereupon Schopenhauer gave utterance to the following outburst: "An intelligible Categorical Imperative! Preposterous idea! Stygian darkness! God forbid that it should ever become intelligible! The fact that there is actually something unintelligible, that this misery of the understanding and its conceptions is limited, conditional, final, and deceptive—this is beyond question Kant's great gift." Let anyone consider whether a man can be in possession of a desire to gain an insight into moral things when he feels himself comforted from the start by a belief in the inconceivableness of these things! One who still honestly believes in illuminations from above, in magic, in ghostly appearances, and in the metaphysical ugliness of the toad!

FROM THE JOYFUL WISDOM

14

WHAT IS CALLED LOVE. The lust of property and love: what different associations each of these ideas evoke!— and yet it might be the same impulse twice named: on the one occasion disparaged from the standpoint of those already possessing (in whom the impulse has attained something of repose, and who are now apprehensive for the safety of their "possession"); on the other occasion viewed from the standpoint of the unsatisfied and thirsty, and therefore glorified as "good." Our love of our neighbor—is it not a striving after new *property?* And similarly our love of knowledge, of truth; and in general all the striving after novelties? We gradually become satiated with the old, the securely possessed, and again stretch out our hands; even the finest landscape in which we live for three months is no longer certain of our love, and any kind of more distant coast excites our covetousness: the possession for the most part becomes smaller through possessing. Our pleasure in ourselves seeks to maintain itself, by always transforming something new *into ourselves*—that is just possessing. To become satiated with a possession, that is to become satiated with ourselves. (One can also suffer from excess—even the desire to cast away, to share out, can assume the honorable name of "love.") When we see anyone suffering, we willingly utilize the opportunity then afforded to take possession of him; the beneficent and sympathetic man, for example, does this; he also calls the desire for new possession awakened in him, by the name of "love," and has enjoyment in it, as in a new acquisition suggesting itself to him. The love of the sexes, however, betrays itself most plainly as the striving after possession: the lover wants the unconditioned, sole possession of the person longed for by him; he wants just as absolute power over her soul as over her body; he wants to be loved solely, and to dwell and rule in the other soul as what is highest and most to be desired. When one considers that this means precisely to *exclude* all the world from a precious possession, a happiness, and an enjoyment; when one considers that the lover has in view the impoverishment and privation of all other rivals, and would like to become the dragon of his golden hoard, as the most inconsiderate and selfish of all "conquerors" and exploiters; when one considers finally that to the lover himself, the whole world besides appears indifferent, colorless, and worthless, and that he is ready to make every sacrifice, disturb every arrangement, and put every other interest behind his own— one is verily surprised that this ferocious lust of property and injustice of sexual love should have been glorified and deified to such an extent at all times; yea, that out of this love the conception of love as the antithesis of egoism should have been derived, when it is perhaps precisely the most unqualified expression of egoism. Here, evidently, the nonpossessors and desirers have determined the usage of language—there were, of course, always too many of them. Those who have been favored with much possession

and satiety have, to be sure, dropped a word now and then
about the "raging demon," as, for instance, the most lovable
and most beloved of all the Athenians—Sophocles; but Eros
always laughed at such revilers—they were always his greatest favorites.—There is, of course, here and there on this
terrestrial sphere a kind of sequel to love, in which that
covetous longing of two persons for one another has yielded
to a new desire and covetousness, to a *common*, higher
thirst for a superior ideal standing above them: but who
knows this love? Who has experienced it? Its right name is
friendship.

FROM THE TWILIGHT OF THE IDOLS

7

A MORAL FOR PSYCHOLOGISTS. Do not go in for
any notebook psychology! Never observe for the sake of observing! Such things lead to a false point of view, to a squint,
to something forced and exaggerated. To experience things
on purpose—this is not a bit of good. In the midst of an
experience a man should not turn his eyes upon himself;
in such cases any eye becomes the "evil eye." A born psychologist instinctively avoids seeing for the sake of seeing.
And the same holds good of the born painter. Such a man
never works "from nature"—he leaves it to his instinct, to
his camera obscura to sift and to define the "fact," "nature,"
the "experience." The general idea, the conclusion, the result, is the only thing that reaches his consciousness. He
knows nothing of that willful process of deducing from particular cases. What is the result when a man sets about this
matter differently?—when, for instance, after the manner of
Parisian novelists, he goes in for notebook psychology on a
large and small scale? Such a man is constantly spying on
reality, and every evening he bears home a handful of fresh
curios. . . . But look at the result!—a mass of daubs, at
best a piece of mosaic, in any case something heaped together, restless and garish. The Goncourts are the greatest
sinners in this respect: they cannot put three sentences together which are not absolutely painful to the eye—the eye
of the psychologist. From an artistic standpoint, nature is
no model. It exaggerates, distorts, and leaves gaps. Nature
is the *accident*. To study "from nature" seems to me a
bad sign: it betrays submission, weakness, fatalism—this lying

in the dust before trivial facts is unworthy of a thorough artist. To see *what is*—is the function of another order of intellects, the *antiartistic*, the matter-of-fact. One must know *who* one is.

18

CONCERNING "THE CONSCIENCE OF THE INTEL-LECT." Nothing seems to me more uncommon today than genuine hypocrisy. I strongly suspect that this growth is unable to flourish in the mild climate of our culture. Hypocrisy belongs to an age of strong faith—one in which one does not lose one's own faith in spite of the fact that one has to make an outward show of holding another faith. Nowadays a man gives it up; or, what is still more common, he acquires a second faith—in any case, however, he remains honest. Without a doubt it is possible to have a much larger number of convictions at present, than it was formerly: *possible*—that is to say, allowable—that is to say, *harmless*. From this there arises an attitude of toleration toward one's self. Toleration toward one's self allows of a greater number of convictions: the latter live comfortably side by side, and they take jolly good care, as all the world does today, not to compromise themselves. How does a man compromise himself today? When he is consistent; when he pursues a straight course; when he has anything less than five faces; when he is genuine. . . . I very greatly fear that modern man is much too fond of comfort for certain vices; and the consequence is the latter are dying out. Everything evil which is the outcome of strength of will—and maybe there is nothing evil without strength of will—degenerates, in our muggy atmosphere, into virtue. The few hypocrites I have known only imitated hypocrisy: like almost every tenth man today, they were actors.

FROM THE ANTICHRIST*

54

Do not allow yourselves to be deceived: great minds are sceptical. Zarathustra is a sceptic. Strength and the *freedom*

* From *The Twilight of the Idols.*

which proceeds from the power and excessive power of the mind *manifests* itself through scepticism. Men of conviction are of no account whatever in regard to all principles of value or of nonvalue. Convictions are prisons. They never see far enough, they do not look down from a sufficient height: but in order to have any say in questions of value and nonvalue, a man must see five hundred convictions *beneath* him—*behind* him. . . . A spirit who desires great things, and who also desires the means thereto, is necessarily a sceptic. Freedom from every kind of conviction *belongs* to strength, to the *ability* to open one's eyes freely. . . . The great passion of a sceptic, the basis and power of his being, which is more enlightened and more despotic than he is himself, enlists all his intellect into its service; it makes him unscrupulous; it even gives him the courage to employ unholy means; in certain circumstances it even allows him convictions. Conviction as a *means:* much is achieved merely by means of a conviction. Great passion makes use of and consumes convictions, it does not submit to them—it knows that it is a sovereign power. Conversely; the need of faith, of anything either absolutely affirmative or negative, Carlylism (if I may be allowed this expression), is the need of *weakness*. The man of beliefs, the "believer" of every sort and condition, is necessarily a dependent man; he is one who cannot regard *himself* as an aim, who cannot postulate aims from the promptings of his own heart. The "believer" does not belong to himself, he can be only a means, he must be *used up*, he is in need of someone who uses him up. His instinct accords the highest honor to a morality of self-abnegation: everything in him, his prudence, his experience, his vanity, persuade him to adopt this morality. Every sort of belief is in itself an expression of self-denial, of self-estrangement. . . . If one considers how necessary a regulating code of conduct is to the majority of people, a code of conduct which constrains them and fixes them from outside; and how control, or in a higher sense, *slavery*, is the only and ultimate condition under which the weak-willed man, and especially woman, flourish; one also understands conviction, "faith." The man of conviction finds in the latter his *backbone*. To be *blind* to many things, to be impartial about nothing, to belong always to a particular side, to hold a strict and necessary point of view in all matters of values—these are the only conditions under which such a man can survive at all. But all this is the reverse of, the *antagonist* of, the truthful man—of truth. . . . The believer is not at liberty to have a conscience for the question "true" and "untrue": to be upright on *this* point would mean his immediate downfall. The pathological limitations of his standpoint convert the convinced man into the fanatic —Savonarola, Luther, Rousseau, Robespierre, Saint-Simon— these are the reverse type of the strong spirit that has become *free.* But the grandiose poses of these *morbid* spirits, of these epileptics of ideas, exercise an influence over the masses—fanatics are picturesque, mankind prefers to look at poses than to listen to reason.

55

One step further in the psychology of conviction of "faith." It is already some time since I first thought of considering whether convictions were not perhaps more dangerous enemies of truth than lies (*Human, All Too Human,* Part I, Aphs. 54 and 483). Now I would fain put the decisive question: is there any difference at all between a lie and a conviction?—All the world believes that there is, but what in Heaven's name does not all the world believe! Every conviction has its history, its preliminary stages, its period of groping and of mistakes: it becomes a conviction only after it has *not* been one for a long time, only after it has *scarcely* been one for a long time. What? might not falsehood be the embryonic form of conviction?—At times all that is required is a change of personality: very often what was a lie in the father becomes a conviction in the son.—I call a lie, to refuse to see something that one sees, to refuse to see it exactly *as* one sees it: whether a lie is perpetrated before witnesses or not is beside the point.—The most common sort of lie is the one uttered to one's self; to lie to others is relatively exceptional. Now this refusal to see what one sees, this refusal to see a thing exactly as one sees it, is almost the first condition for all those who belong to a *party* in any sense whatsoever: the man who belongs to a party perforce becomes a liar. German historians, for instance, are convinced that Rome stood for despotism, whereas the Teutons introduced the spirit of freedom into the world: what difference is there between this conviction and a lie? After this is it to be wondered at, that all parties including German historians, instinctively adopt the grandiloquent phraseology of morality—that morality almost owes its *survival* to the fact that the man who belongs to a party, no matter what it may be, is in need of morality every moment?—"This is our conviction: we confess it to the whole

world, we live and die for it—let us respect everything that
has a conviction!"—I have actually heard anti-Semites speak
in this way. On the contrary, my dear sirs! An anti-Semite
does not become the least bit more respectable because he
lies on principle. . . . Priests, who in such matters are more
subtle, and who perfectly understand the objection to which
the idea of a conviction lies open, that is to say, of a falsehood which is perpetrated on principle *because* it serves a
purpose, borrowed from the Jews the prudent measure of
setting the concept "God," "Will of God," "Revelation of
God," at this place. Kant, too, with his categorical imperative, was on the same road: this was his *practical* reason.—
There are some questions in which it is *not* given to man
to decide between true and false; all the principal questions, all the principal problems of value, stand beyond
human reason. . . . To comprehend the limits of reason—
this alone is genuine philosophy. For what purpose did God
give man revelation? Would. God have done anything
superfluous? Man cannot of his own accord know what is
good and what is evil, that is why God taught man his
will. . . . Moral: the priest does *not* lie; such questions as
"truth" or "falseness" have nothing to do with the things
concerning which the priest speaks; such things do not allow
of lying. For, in order to lie, it would be necessary to know
what is true in this respect. But that is precisely what man
cannot know: hence the priest is only the mouthpiece of
God.—This sort of sacerdotal syllogism is by no means exclusively Judaic or Christian; the right to lie and the
prudent measure of "revelation" belong to the priestly type,
whether of decadent periods or of Pagan times (Pagans are
all those who say yea to life, and to whom "God" is the
word for the great yea to all things). The "law," the "will
of God," the "holy book," and inspiration.—All these things
are merely words for the conditions under which the priest
attains to power, and with which he maintains his power—
these concepts are to be found at the base of all sacerdotal
organizations, of all priestly or philosophical and ecclesiastical governments. The "holy lie," which is common to Con-
fucius, to the lawbook of Manu, to Mohammed, and to the
Christian church, is not even absent in Plato. "Truth is
here"; this phrase means, wherever it is uttered: *the priest
lies.* . . .

56

After all, the question is, to what *end* are falsehoods

perpetrated? The fact that, in Christianity, "holy" ends are entirely absent, constitutes *my* objection to the means it employs. Its ends are only *bad* ends: the poisoning, the calumniation and the denial of life, the contempt of the body, the degradation and self-pollution of man by virtue of the concept sin—consequently its means are bad as well.—My feelings are quite the reverse when I read the lawbook of *Manu*, an incomparably intellectual and superior work, which it would be a sin against the *spirit* even to *mention* in the same breath with the Bible. You will guess immediately why: it has a genuine philosophy behind it, *in* it, not merely an evil-smelling Jewish distillation of Rabbinism and superstition—it gives something to chew even to the most fastidious psychologist. And, *not* to forget the most important point of all, it is fundamentally different from every kind of Bible: by means of it the *noble classes*, the philosophers, and the warriors guard and guide the masses; it is replete with noble values, it is filled with a feeling of perfection, with a saying of yea to life, and a triumphant sense of well-being in regard to itself and to life—the sun shines upon the whole book.—All those things which Christianity smothers with its bottomless vulgarity: procreation, woman, marriage, are here treated with earnestness, with reverence, with love and confidence. How can one possibly place in the hands of children and women, a book that contains those vile words: "to avoid fornication, let every man have his own wife, and let every woman have her own husband . . . it is better to marry than to burn."* And is it decent to be a Christian so long as the very origin of man is Christianized—that is to say, befouled, by the idea of the *immaculata conceptio?* . . . I know of no book in which so many delicate and kindly things are said to woman, as in the Lawbook of Manu; these old graybeards and saints have a manner of being gallant to women which, perhaps, cannot be surpassed. "The mouth of a woman," says Manu on one occasion, "the breast of a maiden, the prayer of a child, and the smoke of the sacrifice, are always pure." Elsewhere he says: "There is nothing purer than the light of the sun, the shadow cast by a cow, air, water, fire, and the breath of a maiden." And finally—perhaps this is also a holy lie: "All the openings of the body above the navel are pure, all those below the navel are impure. Only in a maiden is the whole body pure."

* I Corinthians vii. 2, 9.—Tr.

XIV. Random Reflections

FROM HUMAN, ALL TOO HUMAN, VOL. I

243

THE FUTURE OF THE PHYSICIAN. There is now no profession which would admit of such an enhancement as that of the physician; that is, after the spiritual physicians, the so-called pastors, are no longer allowed to practice their conjuring tricks to public applause, and a cultured person gets out of their way. The highest mental development of a physician has not yet been reached, even if he understands the best and newest methods, is practiced in them, and knows how to draw those rapid conclusions from effects to causes for which the diagnostics are celebrated; besides this, he must possess a gift of eloquence that adapts itself to every individual and draws his heart out of his body; a manliness, the sight of which alone drives away all despondency (the canker of all sick people); the tact and suppleness of a diplomatist in negotiations between such as have need of joy for their recovery and such as, for reasons of health, must (and can) give joy; the acuteness of a detective and an attorney to divine the secrets of a soul without betraying them—in short, a good physician now has need of all the artifices and artistic privileges of every other professional class. Thus equipped, he is then ready to be a benefactor of the whole of society, by increasing good works, mental joys, and fertility, by preventing evil thoughts, projects, and villainies (the evil source of which is so often the belly), by the restoration of a mental and physical aristocracy (as a maker and hinderer of marriages), by judiciously checking all so-called soul-torments and pricks of conscience. Thus from a "medicine man" he becomes a saviour, and yet need work no miracle, neither is he obliged to let himself be crucified.

244

IN THE NEIGHBORHOOD OF INSANITY. The sum of sensations, knowledge, and experiences, the whole burden of culture, therefore, has become so great that an overstraining of nerves and powers of thought is a common danger, indeed, the cultivated classes of European countries are throughout neurotic, and almost every one of their great families is on the verge of insanity in one of their branches. True, health is now sought in every possible way; but in the main a diminution of that tension of feeling, of that oppressive burden of culture, is needful, which, even though it might be bought at a heavy sacrifice, would at least give us room for the great hope of a *new Renaissance*. To Christianity, to the philosophers, poets, and musicians we owe an abundance of deeply emotional sensations; in order that these may not get beyond our control we must invoke the spirit of science, which on the whole makes us somewhat colder and more sceptical, and in particular cools the faith in final and absolute truths; it is chiefly through Christianity that it has grown so wild.

251

THE FUTURE OF SCIENCE. To him who works and seeks in her, Science gives much pleasure—to him who *learns* her facts, very little. But as all important truths of science must gradually become commonplace and everyday matters, even this small amount of pleasure ceases, just as we have long ceased to take pleasure in learning the admirable multiplication table. Now if Science goes on giving less pleasure in herself, and always takes more pleasure in throwing suspicion on the consolations of metaphysics, religion and art, that greatest of all sources of pleasure, to which mankind owes almost its whole humanity, become impoverished. Therefore a higher culture must give man a double brain, two brain-chambers, so to speak, one to feel science and the other to feel nonscience, which can lie side by side, without confusion, divisible, exclusive; this is a necessity of health. In one part lies the source of strength, in the other lies the regulator; it must be heated with illusions, onesidednesses, passions; and the malicious and dangerous consequences of overheating must be averted by the help of conscious Science. If this necessity of the higher culture is not satisfied, the further course of human development can almost certainly be foretold: the interest in what is true ceases as it guarantees less pleasure; illusion, error, and imagination reconquer step by step the ancient territory, because they are united to pleasure; the ruin of science, the relapse into barbarism, is the next result; mankind must begin to weave its web afresh after having, like Penelope, destroyed it during the night. But who will assure us that it will always find the necessary strength for this?

368

THE TALENT FOR FRIENDSHIP. Two types are distinguished amongst people who have a special faculty for friendship. The one is ever on the ascent, and for every phase of his development he finds a friend exactly suited to him. The series of friends which he thus acquires is seldom a consistent one, and is sometimes at variance and in contradiction, entirely in accordance with the fact that the later phases of his development neutralize or prejudice the earlier phases. Such a man may jestingly be called a *ladder*. The other type is represented by him who exercises an attractive influence on very different characters and endowments, so that he wins a whole circle of friends; these, however, are thereby brought voluntarily into friendly relations with one another in spite of all differences. Such a man may be called a *circle*, for this homogeneousness of such different temperaments and natures must somehow be typified in him. Furthermore, the faculty for having good friends is greater in many people than the faculty for being a good friend.

373

ARROGANCE. There is nothing one should so guard against as the growth of the weed called arrogance, which spoils all one's good harvest; for there is arrogance in cordiality, in showing honor, in kindly familiarity, in caressing, in friendly counsel, in acknowledgment of faults, in sympathy for others—and all these fine things arouse aversion when the weed in question grows up among them. The arrogant man—that is to say, he who desires to appear more than he is *or passes for*—always miscalculates. It is true that he obtains a momentary success, inasmuch as those with whom he is arrogant generally give him the amount of honor that he demands, owing to fear or for the sake of convenience; but they take a bad revenge for it, inasmuch as they subtract from the value which they hitherto attached to him just as much as he demands above that amount. There is nothing for which men ask to be paid dearer than for humiliation. The arrogant man can make his really great merit so suspicious and small in the eyes of others that they tread on it with dusty feet. If at all, we should only allow ourselves a *proud* manner where we are quite sure of not being misunderstood and considered as arrogant; as, for instance, with friends and wives. For in social intercourse there is no greater folly than to acquire a reputation for arrogance; it is still worse than not having learned to deceive politely.

374

TÊTE À TÊTE. Private conversation is the perfect conversation, because everything the one person says receives its particular coloring, its tone, and its accompanying gestures *out of strict consideration for the other person* engaged in the conversation; it therefore corresponds to what takes place in intercourse by letter, viz., that one and the same person exhibits ten kinds of psychical expression, according as he writes now to this individual and now to that one. In duologue there is only a single refraction of thought; the person conversed with produces it, as the mirror in whom we want to behold our thoughts anew in their finest form. But how is it when there are two or three, or even more persons conversing with one? Conversation then necessarily loses something of its individualizing subtlety, different considerations thwart and neutralize each other; the style which pleases one does not suit the taste of another. In intercourse with several individuals a person is therefore to withdraw within himself and represent facts as they are; but he has also to remove from the subjects the pulsating ether of humanity which makes conversation one of the pleasantest things in the world. Listen only to the tone in which those who mingle with whole groups of men are in the habit of speaking; it is as if the fundamental base of all speech were, "It is *my-*

self; I say this, so make what you will of it!" That is the reason why clever ladies usually leave a singular, painful, and forbidding impression on those who have met them in society; it is the talking to many people, before many people, that robs them of all intellectual amiability and shows only their conscious dependence on themselves, their tactics, and their intention of gaining a public victory in full light; whilst in a private conversation the same ladies become womanly again, and recover their intellectual grace and charm.

484

A TOPSY-TURVY WORLD. We criticize a thinker more severely when he puts an unpleasant statement before us; and yet it would be more reasonable to do so when we find his statement pleasant.

485

508

DECIDED CHARACTER. A man far oftener appears to have a decided character from persistently following his temperament than from persistently following his principles.

508

FREE NATURE. We are so fond of being out among Nature, because it has no opinions about us.

510

CONSOLATORY ARGUMENTS. In the case of a death we mostly use consolatory arguments not so much to alleviate the grief as to make excuses for feeling so easily consoled.

513

"THE LIFE" AS THE PROCEEDS OF LIFE. A man may stretch himself out ever so far with his knowledge; he may seem to himself ever so objective, but eventually he realizes nothing therefrom but his own biography.

FROM HUMAN, ALL TOO HUMAN, II

193*

THE SADDEST DESTINY OF A PROPHET. He has worked twenty years to convince his contemporaries, and succeeds at last, but in the meantime his adversaries have also succeeded—he is no longer convinced of himself.

FROM HUMAN, ALL TOO HUMAN, I

579

UNSUITABLE FOR A PARTY MAN. Whoever thinks much is unsuitable for a party man, his thinking leads him too quickly beyond the party.

580

A BAD MEMORY. The advantage of a bad memory is that one enjoys several times the same good things for the *first* time.

581

SELF-AFFLICTION. Want of consideration is often the sign of a discordant inner nature, which craves for stupefaction.

526

FORGETTING EXPERIENCES. Whoever thinks much and to good purpose easily forgets his own experiences, but not the thoughts which these experiences have called forth.

* From *Miscellaneous Maxims and Opinions*.

FROM HUMAN, ALL TOO HUMAN, II

253*

IMPOLITENESS. Impoliteness is often the sign of a clumsy modesty, which when taken by surprise loses its head and would fain hide the fact by means of rudeness.

124†

THE FAUST-IDEA. A little sempstress is seduced and plunged into despair: a great scholar of all the four Faculties is the evildoer. That cannot have happened in the ordinary course, surely? No, certainly not! Without the aid of the devil incarnate, the great scholar would never have achieved the deed.—Is this really destined to be the greatest German "tragic idea," as one hears it said among Germans?—But for Goethe even this idea was too terrible. His kind heart could not avoid placing the little sempstress, "the good soul that forgot itself but once," near to the saints, after her involuntary death. Even the great scholar, "the good man" with "the dark impulse," is brought into haven in the nick of time, by a trick which is played upon the devil at the decisive moment. In heaven the lovers find themselves again. Goethe once said that his nature was too conciliatory for really tragic subjects.

261

LETTERS. A letter is an unannounced visit, and the postman is the intermediary of impolite surprises. Every week we ought to have one hour for receiving letters, and then go and take a bath.

262

PREJUDICED. Someone said: I have been prejudiced

---

* From *Miscellaneous Maxims and Opinions*.
† From *The Wanderer and His Shadow*.

against myself from childhood upward, and hence I find some truth in every censure and some absurdity in every eulogy. Praise I generally value too low and blame too high.

286

THE VALUE OF LABOR. If we try to determine the value of labor by the amount of time, industry, good or bad will, constraint, inventiveness or laziness, honesty or make-believe bestowed upon it, the valuation can never be a just one. For the whole personality would have to be thrown into the scale, and this is impossible. Here the motto is, "Judge not!" But after all the cry for justice is the cry we now hear from those who are dissatisfied with the present valuation of labor. If we reflect further we find every person nonresponsible for his product, the labor; hence merit can never be derived therefrom, and every labor is as good or as bad as it must be through this or that necessary concatenation of forces and weaknesses, abilities and desires. The worker is not at liberty to say whether he shall work or not, or to decide how he shall work. Only the standpoints of usefulness, wider and narrower, have created the valuation of labor. What we at present call justice does very well in this sphere as a highly refined utility, which does not only consider the moment and exploit the immediate opportunity, but looks to the permanence of all conditions, and thus also keeps in view the well-being of the worker, his physical and spiritual contentment: in order that he and his posterity may work well for our posterity and become trustworthy for longer periods than the individual span of human life. The *exploitation* of the worker was, as we now understand, a piece of folly, a robbery at the expense of the future, a jeopardization of society. We almost have the war now, and in any case the expense of maintaining peace, of concluding treaties and winning confidence, will henceforth be very great, because the folly of the exploiters was very great and long-lasting.

FROM HUMAN, ALL TOO HUMAN, II

497

UNINTENTIONALLY NOBLE. A person behaves with

unintentional nobleness when he has accustomed himself to seek naught from others and always to give to them.

499

FRIENDS. Fellowship in joy, and not sympathy in sorrow, makes people friends.

FROM BEYOND GOOD AND EVIL

156

Insanity in individuals is something rare—but in groups, parties, nations, and epochs it is the rule.

157

The thought of suicide is a great consolation: by means of it one gets successfully through many a bad night.

162

"Our fellow creature is not our neighbor, but our neighbor's neighbor": so thinks every nation.

248

There are two kinds of geniuses: one which above all engenders and seeks to engender, and another which willingly lets itself be fructified and brings forth. And similarly, among the gifted nations, there are those on whom the woman's problem of pregnancy has devolved, and the secret task of forming, maturing, and perfecting—the Greeks, for instance, were a nation of this kind, and so are the French; and others which have to fructify and become the cause of new modes of life—like the Jews, the Romans, and, in all modesty be it asked: like the Germans?—nations tortured and enraptured by unknown fevers and irresistibly forced out of themselves, amorous and longing for foreign races (for such as "let themselves be fructified"), and withal imperious, like everything conscious of being full of generative force, and consequently empowered "by the grace of God." These two kinds of geniuses seek each other like man and woman; but they also misunderstand each other—like man and woman.

FROM THE TWILIGHT OF THE IDOLS

37

Thou runnest *ahead?*—Dost thou do so as a shepherd or as an exception? A third alternative would be the fugitive. . . . First question of conscience.

38

Art thou genuine or art thou only an actor? Art thou a representative or the thing represented, itself? Finally, art thou perhaps simply a copy of an actor? . . . Second question of conscience.

39

The disappointed man speaks:—I sought for great men, but all I found were the apes of their ideal.

40

Art thou one who looks on, or one who put his own shoulder to the wheel?—Or art thou one who looks away, or who turns aside? . . . Third question of conscience.

41

Wilt thou go in company, or lead, or go by thyself? . . . A man should know what he desires, and that he desires something.—Fourth question of conscience.

FROM THE JOYFUL WISDOM

278

THE THOUGHT OF DEATH.—It gives me a melancholy happiness to live in the midst of this confusion of streets, of necessities, of voices: how much enjoyment, impatience, and desire, how much thirsty life and drunkenness of life comes to light here every moment! And yet it will soon be so still for all these shouting, lively, life-loving people! How everyone's shadow, his gloomy traveling companion stands behind him! It is always as in the last moment before the departure of an emigrant-ship: people have more than ever to say to one another, the hour presses, the ocean with its lonely silence waits impatiently behind all the noise—so greedy, so certain of its prey! And all, all, suppose that the past has been nothing, or a small matter, that the near future is everything: hence this haste, this crying, this self-deafening and self-overreaching! Everyone wants to be foremost in this future—and yet death and the stillness of death are the only things certain and common to all in this future! How strange that this sole thing that is certain and common to all exercises almost no influence on men, and that they are the *furthest* from regarding themselves as the brotherhood of death! It makes me happy to see that men do not want to think at all of the idea of death! I would fain do something to make the idea of life even a hundred times *more worthy of their attention.*